![Haynes logo]

Vauxhall/Opel Corsa
Owners Workshop Manual

John S. Mead

(6335 - 320)

Models covered

Hatchback & Van

Petrol: 1.0 litre (998cc) 3-cylinder, 1.2 litre (1229cc) & 1.4 litre (1398cc) 4-cylinder

Turbo-diesel: 1.3 litre (1248cc) CDTi

Does NOT cover models with 1.4 litre turbo or 1.6 litre petrol engines, or 1.7 litre diesel models
Does NOT cover new Corsa range introduced January 2015

© J H Haynes & Co. Ltd. 2016

ABCDE
FGHIJ
KLMN

A book in the **Haynes Owners Workshop Manual Series**

ISBN **978 1 78521 335 9**

British Library Cataloguing in Publication Data
A catalogue record for this book is available from the British Library.

Printed in India

J H Haynes & Co. Ltd.
Sparkford, Yeovil, Somerset BA22 7JJ, England

Haynes North America, Inc
859 Lawrence Drive, Newbury Park, California 91320, USA

Contents

The Vauxhall/Opel Corsa-D model was initially introduced in the UK in 2006 as a replacement for the previous Corsa, the 'C' model. This manual covers the revised and facelifted version of the Corsa-D, introduced in October 2010. The models covered are available in 3- and 5-door Hatchback, and 3-door Van versions with 1.0 litre, 1.2 litre and 1.4 litre (normally aspirated) petrol engines, and a 1.3 litre diesel engine. The engines are of the four-cylinder double overhead camshaft (DOHC) configuration, in-line type, with the exception of the 1.0 litre petrol engine which is a three-cylinder unit. The engines all have fuel injection and are fitted with a range of emission control systems. 1.6 litre petrol and 1.7 litre diesel engines are also available, but are not covered in this manual.

According to engine type, the manual gearbox is of the five- or six-speed all synchromesh type, with a four-speed electronically-controlled automatic transmission optionally available on 1.4 litre petrol engine models. An 'Easytronic' manual/automatic transmission is also available on 1.2 litre petrol engine models.

All models have front-wheel-drive with fully-independent front suspension, and semi-independent rear suspension with a torsion beam and trailing arms.

A wide range of standard and optional equipment is available within the Corsa range to suit most tastes, including electric power steering, air conditioning, remote central locking, electric windows, electric sunroof, anti-lock braking system, electronic alarm system and supplemental restraint systems.

For the home mechanic, the Corsa is a relatively straightforward vehicle to maintain, and most of the items requiring frequent attention are easily accessible.

Your Vauxhall/Opel Corsa manual

The aim of this manual is to help you get the best value from your vehicle. It can do so in several ways. It can help you decide what work must be done (even should you choose to get it done by a garage), provide information on routine maintenance and servicing, and give a logical course of action and diagnosis when random faults occur. However, it is hoped that you will use the manual by tackling the work yourself. On simpler jobs, it may even be quicker than booking the car into a garage and going there twice, to leave and collect it. Perhaps most important, a lot of money can be saved by avoiding the costs a garage must charge to cover its labour and overheads.

The manual has drawings and descriptions to show the function of the various components, so that their layout can be understood. Then the tasks are described and photographed in a clear step-by-step sequence.

References to the 'left' or 'right' are in the sense of a person in the driver's seat, facing forward.

Project vehicles

The main vehicle used in the preparation of this manual, and which appears in many of the photographic sequences, was a Vauxhall Corsa Hatchback with a 1.3 litre diesel engine. Additional work was carried out on a Corsa Hatchback with a 1.4 litre petrol engine.

Acknowledgements

Certain illustrations are the copyright of Vauxhall Motors Limited, and are used with their permission. Thanks are also due to Draper Tools Limited, who provided some of the workshop tools, and to all those people at Sparkford who helped in the production of this manual.

We take great pride in the accuracy of information given in this manual, but vehicle manufacturers make alterations and design changes during the production run of a particular vehicle of which they do not inform us. No liability can be accepted by the authors or publishers for loss, damage or injury caused by any errors in, or omissions from, the information given.

Contents

Working on your car can be dangerous. This page shows just some of the potential risks and hazards, with the aim of creating a safety-conscious attitude.

General hazards

Scalding

• Don't remove the radiator or expansion tank cap while the engine is hot.
• Engine oil, transmission fluid or power steering fluid may also be dangerously hot if the engine has recently been running.

Burning

• Beware of burns from the exhaust system and from any part of the engine. Brake discs and drums can also be extremely hot immediately after use.

Crushing

• When working under or near a raised vehicle, always supplement the jack with axle stands, or use drive-on ramps. *Never venture under a car which is only supported by a jack*.
• Take care if loosening or tightening high-torque nuts when the vehicle is on stands. Initial loosening and final tightening should be done with the wheels on the ground.

Fire

• Fuel is highly flammable; fuel vapour is explosive.
• Don't let fuel spill onto a hot engine.
• Do not smoke or allow naked lights (including pilot lights) anywhere near a vehicle being worked on. Also beware of creating sparks (electrically or by use of tools).
• Fuel vapour is heavier than air, so don't work on the fuel system with the vehicle over an inspection pit.
• Another cause of fire is an electrical overload or short-circuit. Take care when repairing or modifying the vehicle wiring.
• Keep a fire extinguisher handy, of a type suitable for use on fuel and electrical fires.

Electric shock

• Ignition HT and Xenon headlight voltages can be dangerous, especially to people with heart problems or a pacemaker. Don't work on or near these systems with the engine running or the ignition switched on.

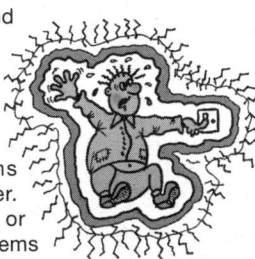

• Mains voltage is also dangerous. Make sure that any mains-operated equipment is correctly earthed. Mains power points should be protected by a residual current device (RCD) circuit breaker.

Fume or gas intoxication

• Exhaust fumes are poisonous; they can contain carbon monoxide, which is rapidly fatal if inhaled. Never run the engine in a confined space such as a garage with the doors shut.
• Fuel vapour is also poisonous, as are the vapours from some cleaning solvents and paint thinners.

Poisonous or irritant substances

• Avoid skin contact with battery acid and with any fuel, fluid or lubricant, especially antifreeze, brake hydraulic fluid and Diesel fuel. Don't syphon them by mouth. If such a substance is swallowed or gets into the eyes, seek medical advice.
• Prolonged contact with used engine oil can cause skin cancer. Wear gloves or use a barrier cream if necessary. Change out of oil-soaked clothes and do not keep oily rags in your pocket.
• Air conditioning refrigerant forms a poisonous gas if exposed to a naked flame (including a cigarette). It can also cause skin burns on contact.

Asbestos

• Asbestos dust can cause cancer if inhaled or swallowed. Asbestos may be found in gaskets and in brake and clutch linings. When dealing with such components it is safest to assume that they contain asbestos.

Special hazards

Hydrofluoric acid

• This extremely corrosive acid is formed when certain types of synthetic rubber, found in some O-rings, oil seals, fuel hoses etc, are exposed to temperatures above 400ºC. The rubber changes into a charred or sticky substance containing the acid. *Once formed, the acid remains dangerous for years. If it gets onto the skin, it may be necessary to amputate the limb concerned.*
• When dealing with a vehicle which has suffered a fire, or with components salvaged from such a vehicle, wear protective gloves and discard them after use.

The battery

• Batteries contain sulphuric acid, which attacks clothing, eyes and skin. Take care when topping-up or carrying the battery.
• The hydrogen gas given off by the battery is highly explosive. Never cause a spark or allow a naked light nearby. Be careful when connecting and disconnecting battery chargers or jump leads.

Air bags

• Air bags can cause injury if they go off accidentally. Take care when removing the steering wheel and trim panels. Special storage instructions may apply.

Diesel injection equipment

• Diesel injection pumps supply fuel at very high pressure. Take care when working on the fuel injectors and fuel pipes.

⚠ *Warning: Never expose the hands, face or any other part of the body to injector spray; the fuel can penetrate the skin with potentially fatal results.*

Remember...

DO

• Do use eye protection when using power tools, and when working under the vehicle.
• Do wear gloves or use barrier cream to protect your hands when necessary.
• Do get someone to check periodically that all is well when working alone on the vehicle.
• Do keep loose clothing and long hair well out of the way of moving mechanical parts.
• Do remove rings, wristwatch etc, before working on the vehicle – especially the electrical system.
• Do ensure that any lifting or jacking equipment has a safe working load rating adequate for the job.

DON'T

• Don't attempt to lift a heavy component which may be beyond your capability – get assistance.
• Don't rush to finish a job, or take unverified short cuts.
• Don't use ill-fitting tools which may slip and cause injury.
• Don't leave tools or parts lying around where someone can trip over them. Mop up oil and fuel spills at once.
• Don't allow children or pets to play in or near a vehicle being worked on.

The following pages are intended to help in dealing with common roadside emergencies and breakdowns. You will find more detailed fault finding information at the back of the manual, and repair information in the main chapters.

If your car won't start and the starter motor doesn't turn

☐ If it's a model with automatic transmission, make sure the selector is in P or N.
☐ Open the bonnet and make sure that the battery terminals are clean and tight.
☐ Switch on the headlights and try to start the engine. If the headlights go very dim when you're trying to start, the battery is probably flat. Get out of trouble by jump starting (see next page) using a friend's car.

If your car won't start even though the starter motor turns as normal

☐ Is there fuel in the tank?
☐ Is there moisture on electrical components under the bonnet? Switch off the ignition, then wipe off any obvious dampness with a dry cloth. Spray a water-repellent aerosol product (WD-40 or equivalent) on ignition and fuel system electrical connectors like those shown in the photos. Pay special attention to the ignition coil wiring connector and HT leads.

A On petrol engines, check that the wiring to the ignition module is connected firmly.

B Check that the airflow meter or air temperature sensor wiring is connected securely.

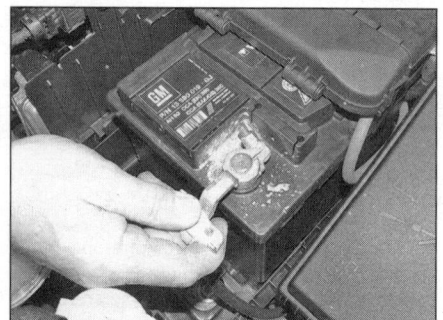

C Check the security and condition of the battery connections.

Check that electrical connections are secure (with the ignition switched off) and spray with water dispersant if you suspect a problem due to damp.

D Check all multiplugs and wiring connectors for security.

E Check that all fuses are still in good condition and none have blown.

Jump starting

When jump-starting a car using a booster battery, observe the following precautions:

✔ Before connecting the booster battery, make sure that the ignition is switched off.

Caution: Remove the key in case the central locking engages when the jump leads are connected

✔ Ensure that all electrical equipment (lights, heater, wipers, etc) is switched off.

✔ Take note of any special precautions printed on the battery case.

✔ Make sure that the booster battery is the same voltage as the discharged one in the vehicle.

✔ If the battery is being jump-started from the battery in another vehicle, the two vehicles MUST NOT TOUCH each other.

✔ Make sure that the transmission is in neutral (or PARK, in the case of automatic transmission).

HAYNES HiNT

Jump starting will get you out of trouble, but you must correct whatever made the battery go flat in the first place. There are three possibilities:

1 *The battery has been drained by repeated attempts to start, or by leaving the lights on.*

2 *The charging system is not working properly (alternator drivebelt slack or broken, alternator wiring fault or alternator itself faulty).*

3 *The battery itself is at fault (electrolyte low, or battery worn out).*

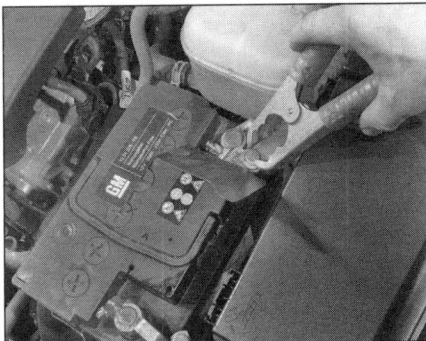

1 Connect one end of the red jump lead to the positive (+) terminal of the flat battery

2 Connect the other end of the red lead to the positive (+) terminal of the booster battery.

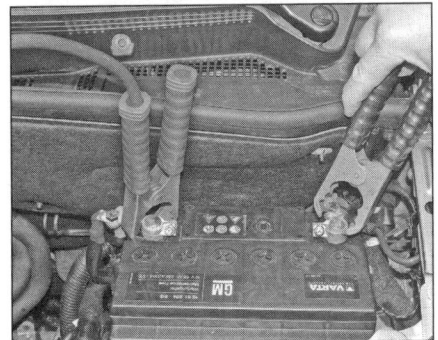

3 Connect one end of the black jump lead to the negative (-) terminal of the booster battery

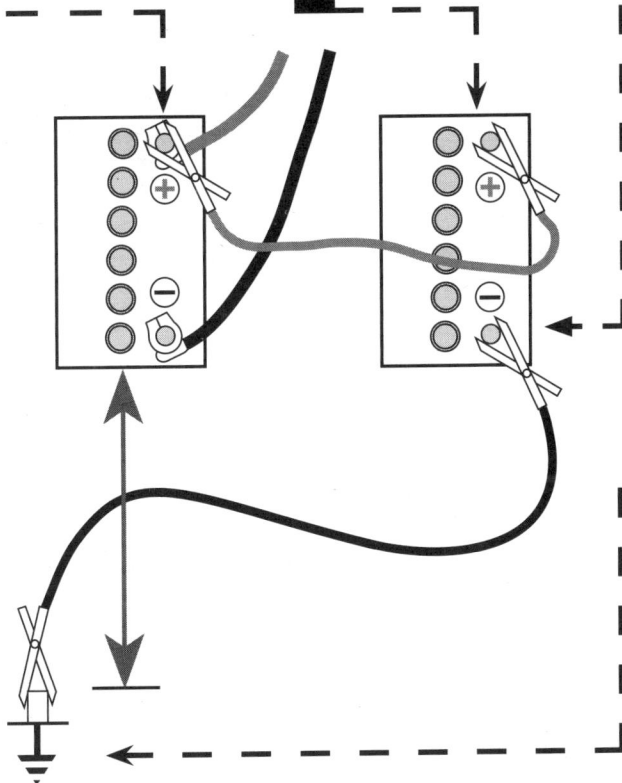

4 Connect the other end of the black jump lead to a bolt or bracket on the engine block, well away from the battery, on the vehicle to be started.

5 Make sure that the jump leads will not come into contact with the fan, drive-belts or other moving parts of the engine.

6 Start the engine using the booster battery and run it at idle speed. Switch on the lights, rear window demister and heater blower motor, then disconnect the jump leads in the reverse order of connection. Turn off the lights etc.

Wheel changing

Note: *Certain Corsa models are equipped with a puncture repair kit and do not have a spare wheel and jack. If your car has a puncture repair kit, refer to the information contained on the next page.*

⚠ **Warning: Do not change a wheel in a situation where you risk being hit by other traffic. On busy roads, try to stop in a lay-by or a gateway. Be wary of passing traffic while changing the wheel – it is easy to become distracted by the job in hand.**

Preparation

☐ When a puncture occurs, stop as soon as it is safe to do so.
☐ Park on firm level ground, if possible, and well out of the way of other traffic.
☐ Use hazard warning lights if necessary.

☐ If you have one, use a warning triangle to alert other drivers of your presence.
☐ Apply the handbrake and engage first or reverse gear (or Park on models with automatic transmission).

☐ Chock the wheel diagonally opposite the one being removed – a couple of large stones will do for this.
☐ If the ground is soft, use a flat piece of wood to spread the load under the jack.

Changing the wheel

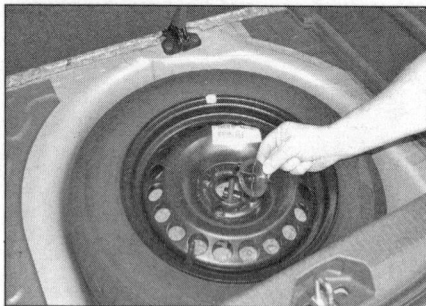

1 Lift the floor covering and unscrew the spare wheel clamp nut. Lift out the spare wheel.

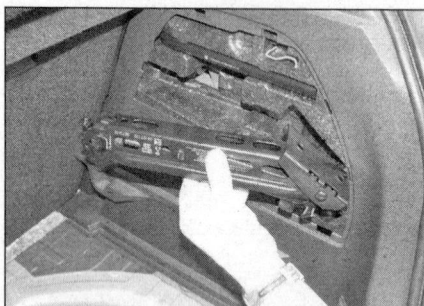

2 The jack and tools are located in the storage compartment on the right-hand side of the luggage compartment. Open the cover and lift out the tools.

3 Use the special tool or screwdriver provided to pull the wheel trim from the wheel or wheel bolts, then slacken each wheel bolt by half a turn.

4 Locate the jack head below the jacking point nearest the wheel to be changed; the jacking point is indicated by an arrow in the sill. Turn the handle until the base of the jack touches the ground ensuring that the jack is vertical. Raise the vehicle until the wheel is clear of the ground. If the tyre is flat make sure that the vehicle is raised sufficiently to allow the spare wheel to be fitted.

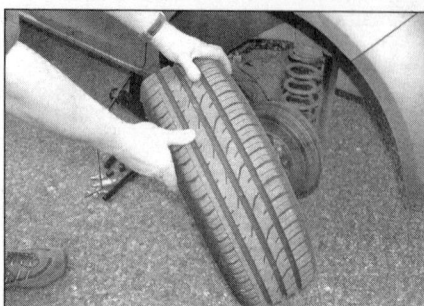

5 Remove the bolts and lift the wheel from the vehicle. Place it beneath the sill as a precaution against the jack failing.

6 Fit the spare wheel and tighten the bolts moderately with the wheel brace.

7 Lower the vehicle to the ground, then finally tighten the wheel bolts in a diagonal sequence. Refit the wheel trim. Note that the wheel bolts should be tightened to the specified torque at the earliest opportunity.

Finally . . .

☐ Remove the wheel chocks.
☐ Stow the jack and tools in the correct locations in the car.
☐ Check the tyre pressure on the wheel just fitted. If it is low, or if you don't have a pressure gauge with you, drive slowly to the next garage and inflate the tyre to the correct pressure.
☐ Have the damaged tyre or wheel repaired as soon as possible, or another puncture will leave you stranded.

Using the puncture repair kit

⚠️ *Warning: Do not attempt to repair a punctured tyre in a situation where you risk being hit by other traffic. On busy roads, try to stop in a lay-by or a gateway. Be wary of passing traffic while using the kit – it is easy to become distracted by the job in hand.*

Preparation

☐ When a puncture occurs, stop as soon as it is safe to do so.

☐ Park on firm level ground, if possible, and well out of the way of other traffic.

☐ Use hazard warning lights if necessary.

☐ If you have one, use a warning triangle to alert other drivers of your presence.

☐ Apply the handbrake and engage first or reverse gear (or Park on models with automatic transmission).

Repairing the puncture

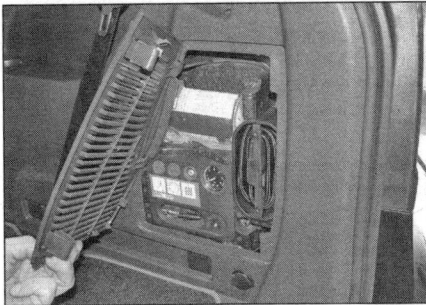

1 Open the storage compartment cover on the right-hand side of the luggage compartment. Take out the sealant bottle and bracket together with the air hose.

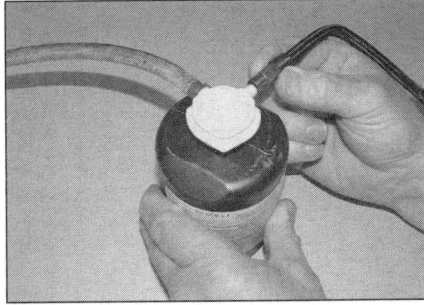

2 Detach the air hose from the bracket and screw it onto the sealant bottle connection.

3 Slide the sealant bottle onto the bracket making sure it is fully located and will not fall over.

4 Unscrew the dust cap from the punctured tyre, and screw the sealant bottle short air hose onto the tyre valve.

5 Take the long air hose into the car and screw it onto the connection on the electric pump. To avoid discharging the battery when the electric pump is running, it is advisable to start the engine.

6 Plug the electrical cable into the accessory socket or cigarette lighter socket then press the '+' button on the electric pump to start the pump. The pump will initially pump the sealant into the tyre which will take approximately 30 seconds, and then start to inflate the tyre. During the initial 30 second period the pressure gauge on the pump will indicate up to 6 bar (87 psi) and then drop. The correct tyre pressure (see Lubricants, fluids and tyre pressures) should be obtained within 10 minutes. The electric pump can then be switched off by pressing the '+' button again.

Important notes

☐ If the correct tyre pressure is not obtained within 10 minutes, it is likely that the tyre is too badly damaged to be repaired with the kit.

☐ If it is necessary to release the pressure in the tyre, press the '–' button on the electric pump.

☐ The maximum speed sticker attached to the sealant bottle should be placed in the driver's field of view. Do not exceed the permitted maximum speed until an undamaged wheel and tyre have been fitted.

☐ On completion, disconnect the sealant bottle, tyre repair kit and long air hose, and connect the end of the short air hose to the free connection on the sealant bottle. This will prevent any remaining sealant from leaking out.

☐ Continue driving immediately so that the sealant is evenly distributed around the inside of the tyre.

☐ After driving approximately 6 miles (but no more than 10 minutes) stop and check the tyre pressure by connecting the long air hose directly to the tyre valve. As long as the pressure indicated on the gauge is more than 1.3 bar (19 psi) it may be adjusted to the correct value using the electric pump. If the pressure has fallen below 1.3 bar (19 psi) the repair has not been successful and the car should not be driven. It will therefore be necessary to seek roadside assistance.

Identifying leaks

Puddles on the garage floor or drive, or obvious wetness under the bonnet or underneath the car, suggest a leak that needs investigating. It can sometimes be difficult to decide where the leak is coming from, especially if an engine undershield is fitted. Leaking oil or fluid can also be blown rearwards by the passage of air under the car, giving a false impression of where the problem lies.

⚠️ **Warning: Most automotive oils and fluids are poisonous. Wash them off skin, and change out of contaminated clothing, without delay.**

HAYNES HiNT *The smell of a fluid leaking from the car may provide a clue to what's leaking. Some fluids are distinctively coloured. It may help to remove the engine undershield, clean the car carefully and to park it over some clean paper overnight as an aid to locating the source of the leak. Remember that some leaks may only occur while the engine is running.*

Sump oil

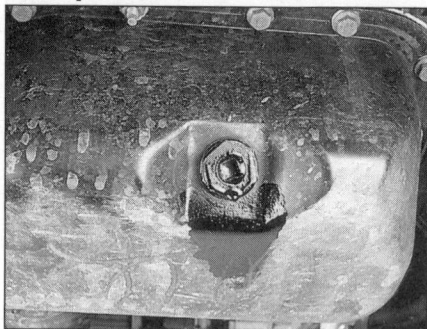

Engine oil may leak from the drain plug...

Oil from filter

...or from the base of the oil filter.

Gearbox oil

Gearbox oil can leak from the seals at the inboard ends of the driveshafts.

Antifreeze

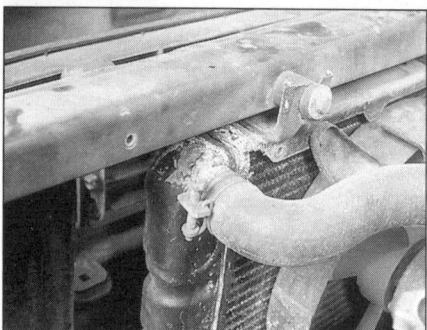

Leaking antifreeze often leaves a crystalline deposit like this.

Brake fluid

A leak occurring at a wheel is almost certainly brake fluid.

Power steering fluid

Power steering fluid may leak from the pipe connectors on the steering rack.

Towing

When all else fails, you may find yourself having to get a tow home – or of course you may be helping somebody else. Long-distance recovery should only be done by a garage or breakdown service. For shorter distances, DIY towing using another car is easy enough, but observe the following points:

☐ Use a proper tow-rope – they are not expensive. The vehicle being towed must display an ON TOW sign in its rear window.

☐ Always turn the ignition key to the 'On' position when the vehicle is being towed, so that the steering lock is released, and the direction indicator and brake lights work.

☐ A towing eye is provided with the tool kit in the luggage compartment. Only attach the tow-rope to the towing eye.

☐ To fit the towing eye, remove the circular cover from the front or rear bumper, as required, then screw in the towing eye anti-clockwise as far as it will go using the handle of the wheel brace to turn the eye. **Note that the towing eye has a left-hand thread.**

☐ Before being towed, release the handbrake and select neutral on the transmission. On models with automatic transmission, special precautions apply. If in doubt, do not tow, or transmission damage may result.

☐ Note that greater-than-usual pedal pressure will be required to operate the brakes, since the vacuum servo unit is only operational with the engine running.

☐ Greater-than-usual steering effort will also be required.

☐ The driver of the car being towed must keep the tow-rope taut at all times to avoid snatching.

☐ Make sure that both drivers know the route before setting off.

☐ Only drive at moderate speeds and keep the distance towed to a minimum. Drive smoothly and allow plenty of time for slowing down at junctions.

Introduction

There are some very simple checks which need only take a few minutes to carry out, but which could save you a lot of inconvenience and expense.

These *Weekly checks* require no great skill or special tools, and the small amount of time they take to perform could prove to be very well spent, for example:

☐ Keeping an eye on tyre condition and pressures, will not only help to stop them wearing out prematurely, but could also save your life.

☐ Many breakdowns are caused by electrical problems. Battery-related faults are particularly common, and a quick check on a regular basis will often prevent the majority of these.

☐ If your car develops a brake fluid leak, the first time you might know about it is when your brakes don't work properly. Checking the level regularly will give advance warning of this kind of problem.

☐ If the oil or coolant levels run low, the cost of repairing any engine damage will be far greater than fixing the leak, for example.

Underbonnet check points

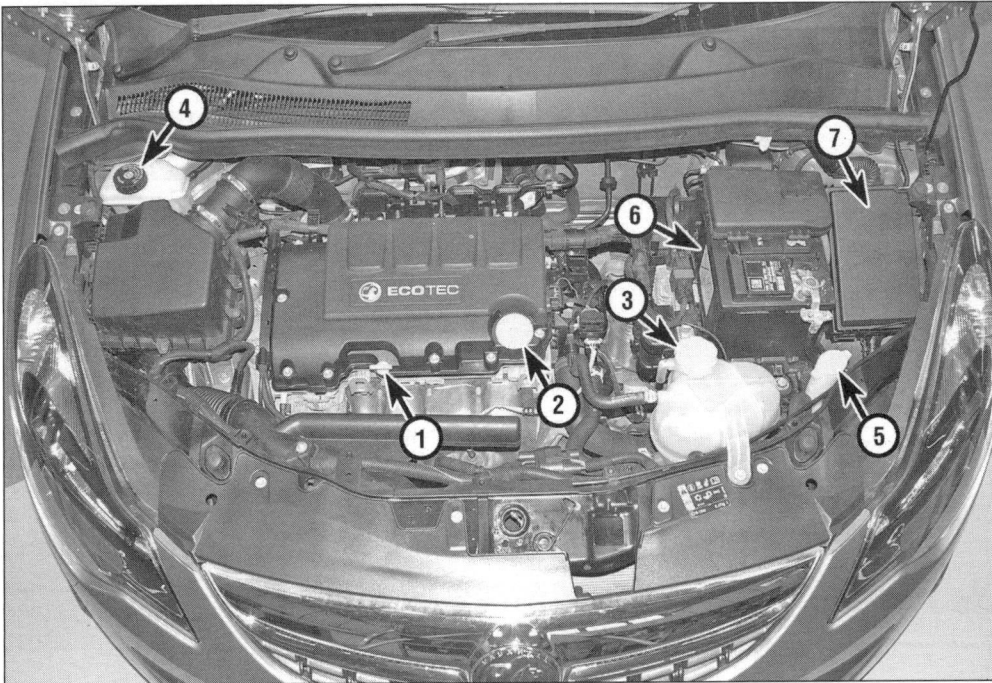

◄ Petrol engine models

1 Engine oil level dipstick
2 Engine oil filler cap
3 Coolant reservoir (expansion tank)
4 Brake and clutch fluid reservoir
5 Washer fluid reservoir
6 Battery
7 Fuse/relay box

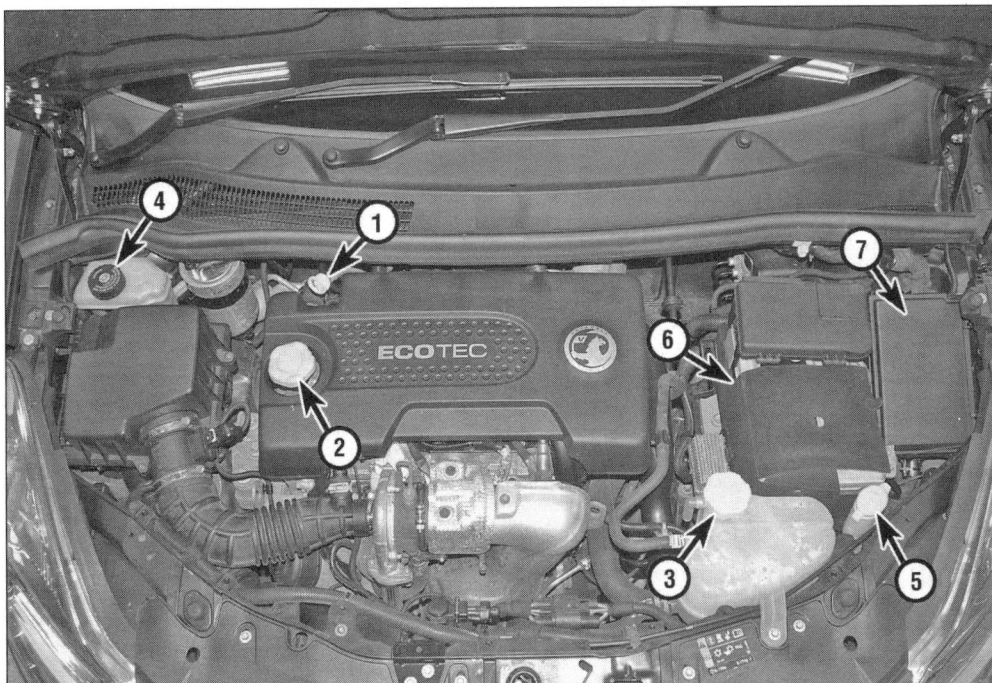

◄ Diesel engine models

1 Engine oil level dipstick
2 Engine oil filler cap
3 Coolant reservoir (expansion tank
4 Brake and clutch fluid reservoir
5 Washer fluid reservoir
6 Battery
7 Fuse/relay box

Engine oil level

Before you start
✔ Make sure that the car is on level ground.
✔ The oil level must be checked with the engine at normal operating temperature, however, wait at least 5 minutes after the engine has been switched off.

HAYNES HINT *If the oil is checked immediately after driving the vehicle, some of the oil will remain in the upper engine components, resulting in an inaccurate reading on the dipstick.*

The correct oil
Modern engines place great demands on their oil. It is very important that the correct oil for your car is used (see *Lubricants and fluids*).

Car care
● If you have to add oil frequently, you should check whether you have any oil leaks. Place some clean paper under the car overnight, and check for stains in the morning. If there are no leaks, then the engine may be burning oil.
● Always maintain the level between the upper and lower dipstick marks (see photo 3). If the level is too low, severe engine damage may occur. Oil seal failure may result if the engine is overfilled by adding too much oil.

1 The dipstick is brightly coloured for easy identification (see *Underbonnet check points* for exact location). Withdraw the dipstick.

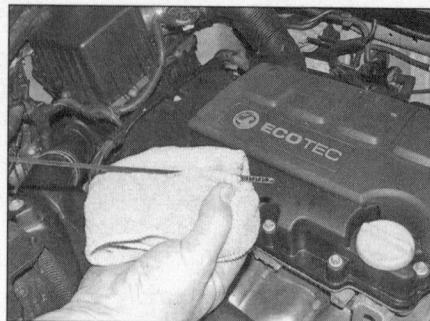

2 Using a clean rag or paper towel remove all oil from the dipstick. Insert the clean dipstick into the tube as far as it will go, then withdraw it again.

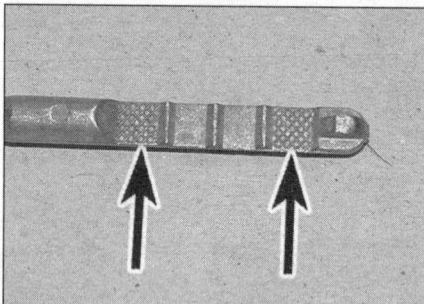

3 Note the level on the end of the dipstick, which should be between the upper (MAX) mark and lower (MIN) mark. Approximately 1.0 litre of oil will raise the level from the lower mark to the upper mark.

4 Oil is added through the filler cap. Unscrew the cap and top-up the level. A funnel may help to reduce spillage. Add the oil slowly, checking the level on the dipstick frequently. Avoid overfilling (see *Car care*).

Coolant level

⚠️ **Warning: Do not attempt to remove the expansion tank pressure cap when the engine is hot, as there is a very great risk of scalding. Do not leave open containers of coolant about, as it is poisonous.**

Car care
● Adding coolant should not be necessary on a regular basis. If frequent topping-up is required, it is likely there is a leak. Check the radiator, all hoses and joint faces for signs of staining or wetness, and rectify as necessary.
● It is important that antifreeze is used in the cooling system all year round, not just during the winter months. Don't top-up with water alone, as the antifreeze will become too diluted.
● The coolant level varies with the temperature of the engine. When the engine is cold, the coolant level should be slightly above the KALT/COLD mark on the side of the tank. When the engine is hot, the level will rise.

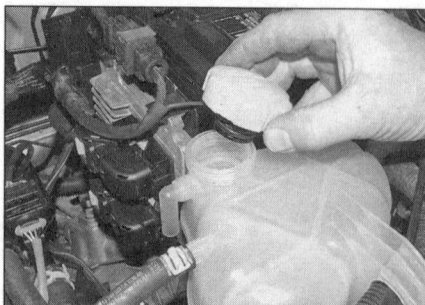

1 If topping-up is necessary, **wait until the engine is cold**. Slowly unscrew the expansion tank cap, to release any pressure present in the cooling system, and remove it.

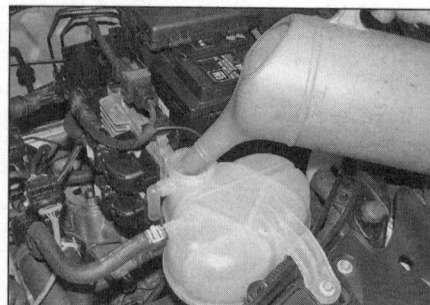

2 Add a mixture of water and antifreeze to the expansion tank until the coolant is up to the KALT/COLD level mark. Refit the cap and tighten it securely.

Brake and clutch fluid level

⚠️ **Warning:**
• **Brake fluid can harm your eyes and damage painted surfaces, so use extreme caution when handling and pouring it.**
• **Do not use fluid that has been standing open for some time, as it absorbs moisture from the air, which can cause a dangerous loss of braking effectiveness.**

Safety first!

● If the reservoir requires repeated topping-up this is an indication of a fluid leak somewhere in the system, which should be investigated immediately.

● If a leak is suspected, the car should not be driven until the braking system has been checked. Never take any risks where brakes are concerned.

HAYNES HiNT
• *Make sure that your car is on level ground.*
• *The fluid level in the reservoir will drop slightly as the brake pads and shoes wear down, but the fluid level must never be allowed to drop below the MIN mark.*

1 The MAX and MIN marks are indicated on the side of the reservoir. The fluid level must be kept between the marks at all times.

2 If topping-up is necessary, first wipe clean the area around the filler cap to prevent dirt entering the hydraulic system. Unscrew the reservoir cap.

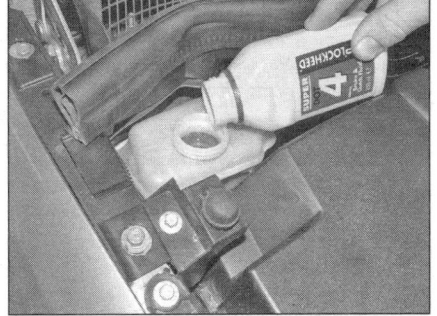

3 Carefully add fluid, taking care not to spill it onto the surrounding components. Use only the specified fluid; mixing different types can cause damage to the system. After topping-up to the correct level, securely refit the cap and wipe off any spilt fluid.

Screen washer fluid level

● Screenwash additives not only keep the windscreen clean during bad weather, they also prevent the washer system freezing in cold weather – which is when you are likely to need it most. Don't top-up using plain water, as the screenwash will become diluted, and will freeze in cold weather.

⚠️ **Warning: On no account use engine coolant antifreeze in the screen washer system – this may damage the paintwork.**

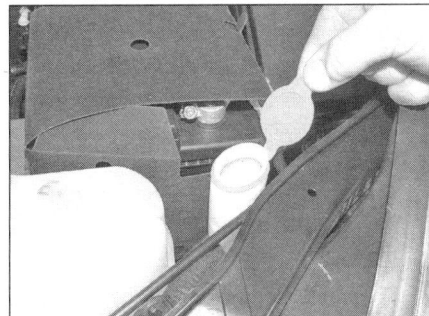

1 The reservoir for the windscreen, rear window and headlight (where applicable) washer systems is located on the front left-hand side of the engine compartment. If topping-up is necessary, open the filler cap.

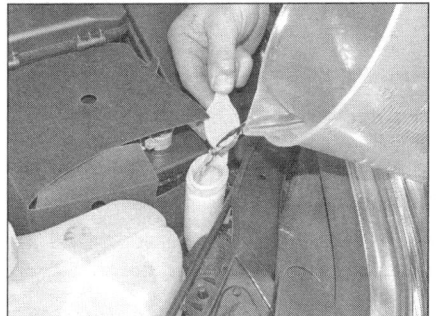

2 When topping-up the reservoir a screen wash additive should be added in the quantities recommended on the bottle.

Tyre condition and pressure

It is very important that tyres are in good condition, and at the correct pressure - having a tyre failure at any speed is highly dangerous. Tyre wear is influenced by driving style - harsh braking and acceleration, or fast cornering, will all produce more rapid tyre wear. As a general rule, the front tyres wear out faster than the rears. Interchanging the tyres from front to rear ("rotating" the tyres) may result in more even wear. However, if this is completely effective, you may have the expense of replacing all four tyres at once!

Remove any nails or stones embedded in the tread before they penetrate the tyre to cause deflation. If removal of a nail does reveal that the tyre has been punctured, refit the nail so that its point of penetration is marked. Then immediately change the wheel, and have the tyre repaired by a tyre dealer.

Regularly check the tyres for damage in the form of cuts or bulges, especially in the sidewalls. Periodically remove the wheels, and clean any dirt or mud from the inside and outside surfaces. Examine the wheel rims for signs of rusting, corrosion or other damage. Light alloy wheels are easily damaged by "kerbing" whilst parking; steel wheels may also become dented or buckled. A new wheel is very often the only way to overcome severe damage.

New tyres should be balanced when they are fitted, but it may become necessary to re-balance them as they wear, or if the balance weights fitted to the wheel rim should fall off. Unbalanced tyres will wear more quickly, as will the steering and suspension components. Wheel imbalance is normally signified by vibration, particularly at a certain speed (typically around 50 mph). If this vibration is felt only through the steering, then it is likely that just the front wheels need balancing. If, however, the vibration is felt through the whole car, the rear wheels could be out of balance. Wheel balancing should be carried out by a tyre dealer or garage.

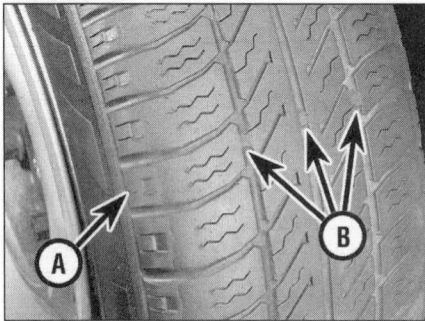

1 *Tread Depth - visual check*
The original tyres have tread wear safety bands (B), which will appear when the tread depth reaches approximately 1.6 mm. The band positions are indicated by a triangular mark on the tyre sidewall (A).

2 *Tread Depth - manual check*
Alternatively, tread wear can be monitored with a simple, inexpensive device known as a tread depth indicator gauge.

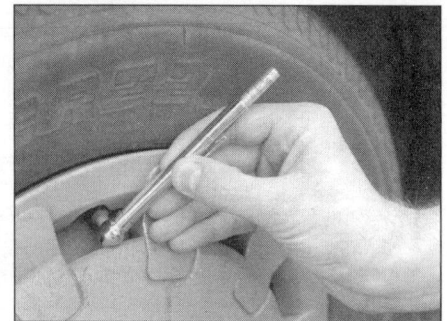

3 *Tyre Pressure Check*
Check the tyre pressures regularly with the tyres cold. Do not adjust the tyre pressures immediately after the vehicle has been used, or an inaccurate setting will result.

Tyre tread wear patterns

Shoulder Wear

Underinflation (wear on both sides)
Under-inflation will cause overheating of the tyre, because the tyre will flex too much, and the tread will not sit correctly on the road surface. This will cause a loss of grip and excessive wear, not to mention the danger of sudden tyre failure due to heat build-up.
Check and adjust pressures
Incorrect wheel camber (wear on one side)
Repair or renew suspension parts
Hard cornering
Reduce speed!

Centre Wear

Overinflation
Over-inflation will cause rapid wear of the centre part of the tyre tread, coupled with reduced grip, harsher ride, and the danger of shock damage occurring in the tyre casing.
Check and adjust pressures

If you sometimes have to inflate your car's tyres to the higher pressures specified for maximum load or sustained high speed, don't forget to reduce the pressures to normal afterwards.

Uneven Wear

Front tyres may wear unevenly as a result of wheel misalignment. Most tyre dealers and garages can check and adjust the wheel alignment (or "tracking") for a modest charge.
Incorrect camber or castor
Repair or renew suspension parts
Malfunctioning suspension
Repair or renew suspension parts
Unbalanced wheel
Balance tyres
Incorrect toe setting
Adjust front wheel alignment
Note: *The feathered edge of the tread which typifies toe wear is best checked by feel.*

Wiper blades

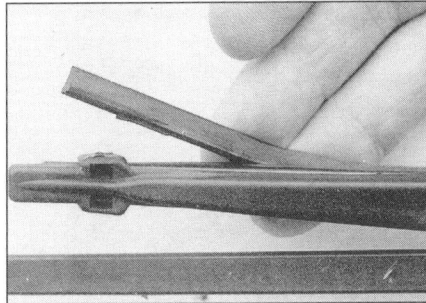

1 Check the condition of the wiper blades; if they are cracked or show any signs of deterioration, or if the glass swept area is smeared, renew them. Wiper blades should be renewed annually.

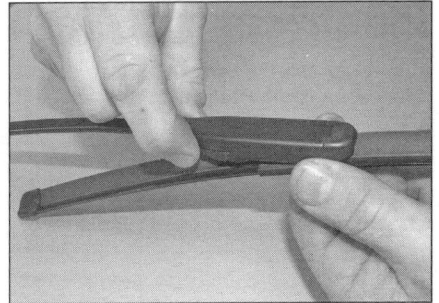

2 To remove a windscreen wiper blade, pull the arm fully away from the screen until it locks. Depress the tabs on the side of the blade.

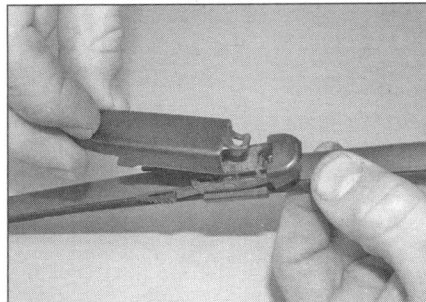

3 Disengage the end of the blade from the arm and lift away the blade.

4 Don't forget to check the tailgate wiper blade as well which is removed by simply disengaging the blade from the pivot pin in the arm.

Battery

Caution: Before carrying out any work on the vehicle battery, read the precautions given in 'Safety first!' at the start of this manual. If the battery is to be disconnected, refer to 'Disconnecting the battery' in the Reference Chapter, before proceeding.

✔ Make sure that the battery tray is in good condition, and that the clamp is tight. Corrosion on the tray, retaining clamp and the battery itself can be removed with a solution of water and baking soda, after removing the affected components from the car (see Chapter 5A). Thoroughly rinse all cleaned areas with water. Any metal parts damaged by corrosion should be covered with a zinc-based primer, then painted.

✔ Periodically (approximately every three months), check the charge condition of the battery as described in Chapter 5A.

✔ If the battery is flat, and you need to jump start your vehicle, see *Roadside Repairs*.

HAYNES HiNT *Battery corrosion can be kept to a minimum by applying a layer of petroleum jelly to the clamps and terminals after they are reconnected.*

1 The battery is located at the front, left-hand side of the engine compartment. Where fitted, open the insulation jacket around the battery, then check the tightness of battery clamps to ensure good electrical connections. You should not be able to move them. Also check each cable for cracks and frayed conductors.

2 If corrosion (white, fluffy deposits) is evident, remove the cables from the battery terminals, clean them with a small wire brush, then refit them. Automotive stores sell a tool for cleaning the battery post . . .

3 . . . as well as the battery cable clamps

Electrical systems

✔ Check all external lights and the horn. Refer to the appropriate Sections of Chapter 12 for details if any of the circuits are found to be inoperative.

✔ Visually check all accessible wiring connectors, harnesses and retaining clips for security, and for signs of chafing or damage.

HAYNES HiNT *If you need to check your brake lights and indicators unaided, back up to a wall or garage door and operate the lights. The reflected light should show if they are working properly.*

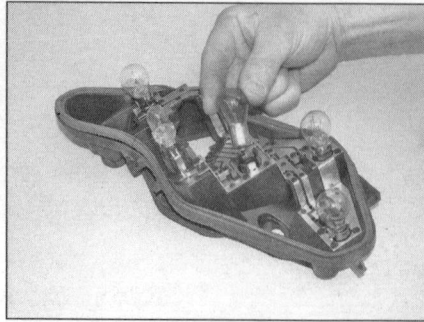

1 If a single indicator light, stop-light or headlight has failed, it is likely that a bulb has blown and will need to be renewed. Refer to Chapter 12 for details. If both stop-lights have failed, it is possible that the switch has failed (see Chapter 9).

2 If more than one indicator light or headlight has failed, it is likely that either a fuse has blown or that there is a fault in the circuit (see Chapter 12). The main fuses are located in the fuse/relay box on the left-hand side of the engine compartment.

3 Additional fuses and relays are located behind a cover in the glove compartment. Open the glove compartment and remove the cover for access to the fuses. On certain models, further fuses are located behind the trim panel on the left-hand side of the luggage compartment. Refer to the wiring diagrams at the end of Chapter 12 for details of the fuse locations and circuits protected.

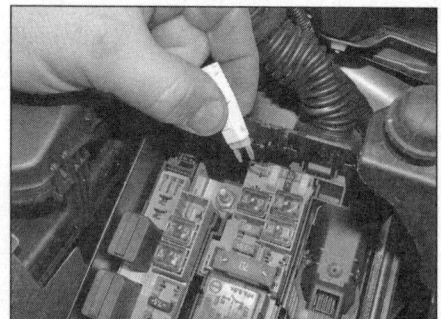

4 To renew a blown fuse, remove it, where applicable, using the plastic tool provided. Fit a new fuse of the same rating, available from car accessory shops. It is important that you find the reason that the fuse blew (see *Electrical fault finding* in Chapter 12).

Lubricants and fluids

Engine (petrol and diesel) . . . . Multigrade engine oil, viscosity SAE 5W/30 to General Motors dexos 2™ specification

Manual and Easytronic transmissions . . . . Vauxhall/Opel gear oil (09 120 541)

Automatic transmission . . . . Vauxhall/Opel automatic transmission fluid (91 17 946)

Cooling system . . . . Vauxhall/Opel silicate-free coolant (09 194 431/19 40 650)

Brake/clutch fluid reservoir . . . . Hydraulic fluid to DOT 4

Tyre pressures

Details of the tyre pressures applicable to your vehicle are given on a sticker attached to the inside of the fuel filler flap or to the front door pillar on the right-hand side.

Chapter 1 Part A
Routine maintenance and servicing – petrol models

Contents

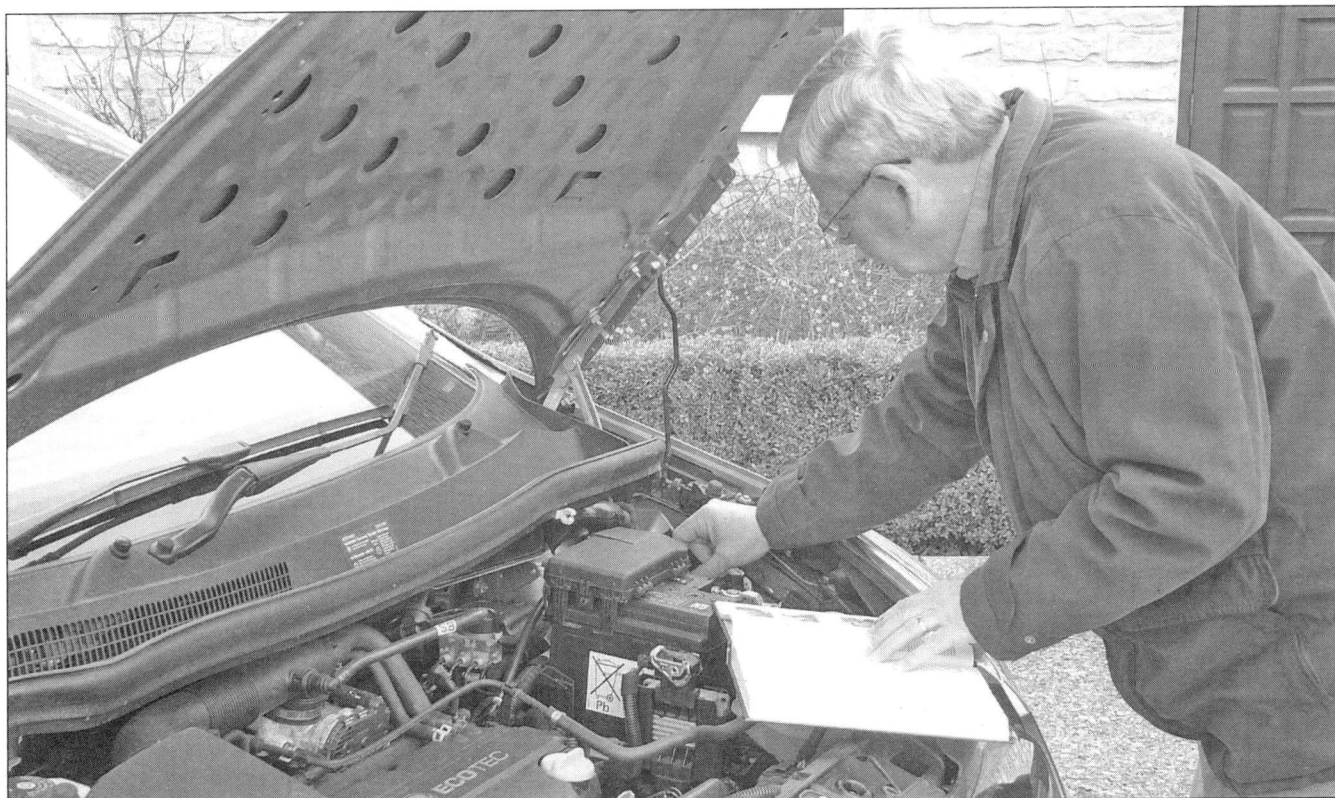

Degrees of difficulty

| **Easy,** suitable for novice with little experience | **Fairly easy,** suitable for beginner with some experience | **Fairly difficult,** suitable for competent DIY mechanic | **Difficult,** suitable for experienced DIY mechanic | **Very difficult,** suitable for expert DIY or professional |

Specifications

Lubricants and fluids.................................... Refer to *Lubricants, fluids and tyre pressures* on page 0•17

Capacities

Engine oil (including oil filter)
1.0 litre engines .... 3.0 litres
1.2 litre engines .... 4.0 litres
1.4 litre engines .... 4.0 litres
Difference between MIN and MAX dipstick marks................ 1.0 litre

Cooling system
1.0 litre engines .... 4.6 litres
1.2 litre engines .... 6.0 litres
1.4 litre engines .... 6.0 litres

Transmission
Manual transmission:
   5-speed transmission................................... 1.6 litres
   6-speed transmission................................... 1.8 litres
Automatic transmission (at fluid change)..................... 3.3 litres (approximately)
Easytronic transmission .... 1.2 litres

Washer fluid reservoir
All models.. 2.2 litres

Fuel tank
All models.. 45 litres

Cooling system
Antifreeze mixture:
   50% antifreeze .... Protection down to -40°C

Ignition system
Spark plugs:
   Type .... Bosch FQR 8 LEU2
   Electrode gap .... 0.9 mm

Brakes
Friction material minimum thickness:
   Front brake pads .... 2.0 mm
   Rear brake shoes .... 2.0 mm

Torque wrench settings

	Nm	lbf ft
Oil filter housing cap-to-filter housing	25	18
Roadwheel bolts	110	81
Spark plugs	25	18
Sump drain plug	10	7

1 Maintenance schedule

1 The maintenance intervals in this manual are provided with the assumption that you, not the dealer, will be carrying out the work. These are the minimum maintenance intervals based on the standard service schedule recommended by the manufacturer for vehicles driven daily. If you wish to keep your vehicle in peak condition at all times, you may wish to perform some of these procedures more often. We encourage frequent maintenance, because it enhances the efficiency, performance and resale value of your vehicle.
2 If the vehicle is driven in dusty areas, used to tow a trailer, or driven frequently at slow speeds (idling in traffic) or on short journeys, more frequent maintenance intervals are recommended.
3 When the vehicle is new, it should be serviced by a dealer service department (or other workshop recognised by the vehicle manufacturer as providing the same standard of service) in order to preserve the warranty. The vehicle manufacturer may reject warranty claims if you are unable to prove that servicing has been carried out as and when specified, using only original equipment parts or parts certified to be of equivalent quality.

Every 250 miles or weekly
☐ Refer to *Weekly checks*

Every 10 000 miles or 6 months – whichever comes first
☐ Renew the engine oil and filter (Section 5)
Note: *Vauxhall/Opel recommend that the engine oil and filter are changed every 20 000 miles or 12 months if the vehicle is being operated under the standard service schedule. However, oil and filter changes are good for the engine and we recommend that the oil and filter are renewed more frequently, especially if the vehicle is used on a lot of short journeys.*

Every 20 000 miles or 12 months – whichever comes first
☐ Check all underbonnet and underbody components, pipes and hoses for leaks (Section 6)
☐ Check the Easytronic clutch hydraulic fluid level (Section 7)
☐ Check the condition of the front brake pads, the calipers and discs (Section 8)
☐ Check the condition of the rear brake shoes (Section 9)
☐ Check the condition of all brake fluid pipes and hoses (Section 10)
☐ Check the condition of the front suspension and steering components, particularly the rubber gaiters and seals (Section 11)
☐ Check the condition of the driveshaft joint gaiters, and the driveshaft joints (Section 12)
☐ Check the condition of the exhaust system components (Section 13)
☐ Check the condition of the rear suspension components (Section 14)
☐ Check the bodywork and underbody for damage and corrosion, and check the condition of the underbody corrosion protection (Section 15)
☐ Check the tightness of the roadwheel bolts (Section 16)
☐ Lubricate all door, bonnet and tailgate hinges and locks (Section 17)
☐ Check the operation of the horn, all lights, and the wipers and washers (Section 18)
☐ Carry out a road test (Section 19)
☐ Reset the service interval indicator (Section 20)

Every 40 000 miles or 2 years – whichever comes first
☐ Renew the pollen filter (Section 21)
☐ Check the auxiliary drivebelt and tensioner (Section 22)
☐ Check the operation of the handbrake and adjust if necessary (Section 23)
☐ Check the headlight beam alignment (Section 24)

Every 2 years, regardless of mileage
☐ Renew the battery for the remote control handset (Section 25)
☐ Renew the brake and clutch fluid (Section 26)
☐ Renew the coolant (Section 27)
☐ Exhaust emission test (Section 28)
Note: *Vehicles using Vauxhall/Opel silicate-free coolant do not need the coolant renewed on a regular basis.*

Every 40 000 miles or 4 years – whichever comes first
☐ Renew the air cleaner filter element (Section 29)
☐ Renew the spark plugs (Section 30)
☐ Renew the automatic transmission fluid (Section 31)

Every 100 000 miles or 6 years – whichever comes first
☐ Renew the auxiliary drivebelt (Section 32)

2 Component location

Underbonnet view of a 1.2 litre model

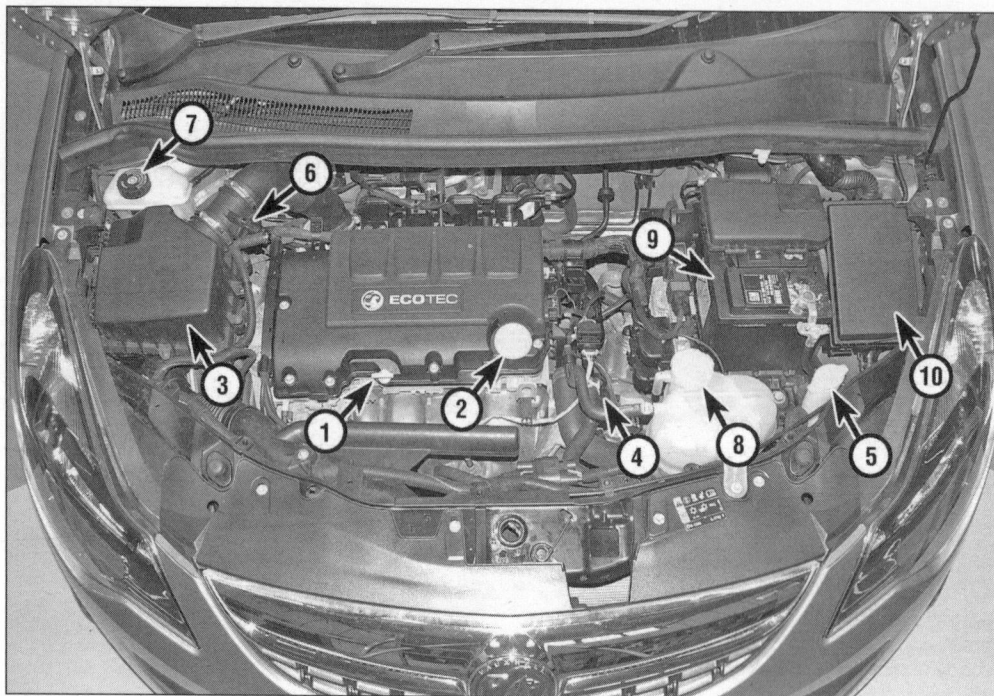

1 Engine oil level dipstick
2 Engine oil filler cap
3 Air cleaner assembly
4 Oil filter
5 Screen washer fluid reservoir
6 Inlet air temperature sensor
7 Brake (and clutch) fluid reservoir
8 Coolant expansion tank
9 Battery
10 Fuse/relay box

Front underbody view

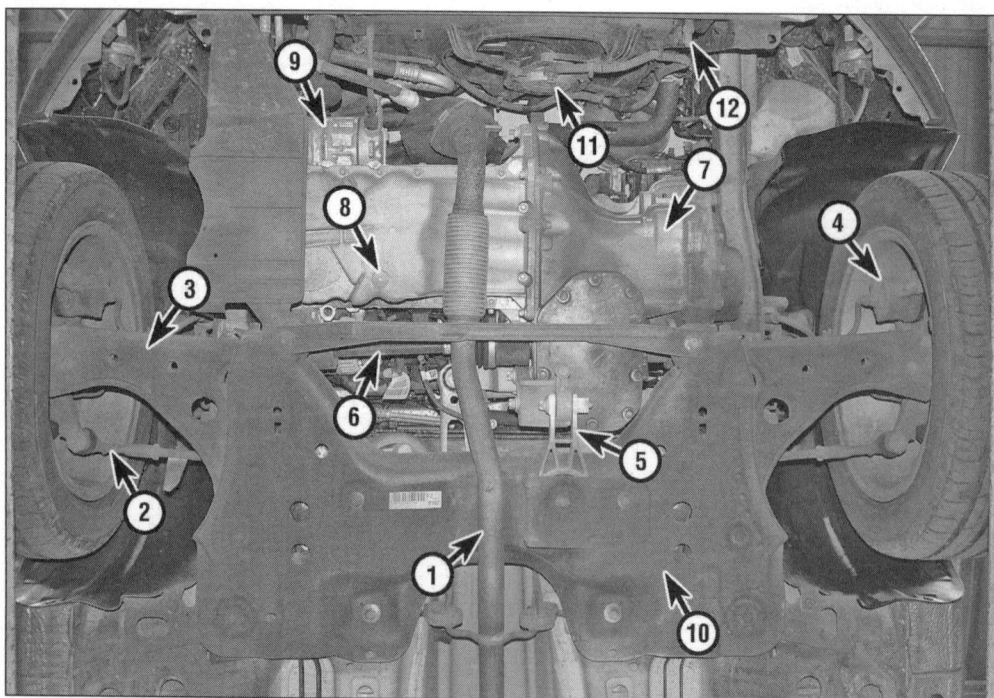

1 Exhaust front pipe
2 Steering track rod
3 Front suspension lower arm
4 Front brake caliper
5 Engine mounting rear torque link
6 Right-hand driveshaft
7 Manual transmission
8 Engine oil drain plug
9 Air conditioning compressor
10 Front subframe
11 Radiator cooling fan
12 Coolant drain plug

Rear underbody view

1 Exhaust tailpipe and
   silencer
2 Rear suspension torsion
   beam and trailing arms
3 Fuel tank
4 Handbrake cables
5 Spare wheel well
6 Rear coil springs
7 Rear shock absorber
   lower mountings
8 Fuel tank heat shield

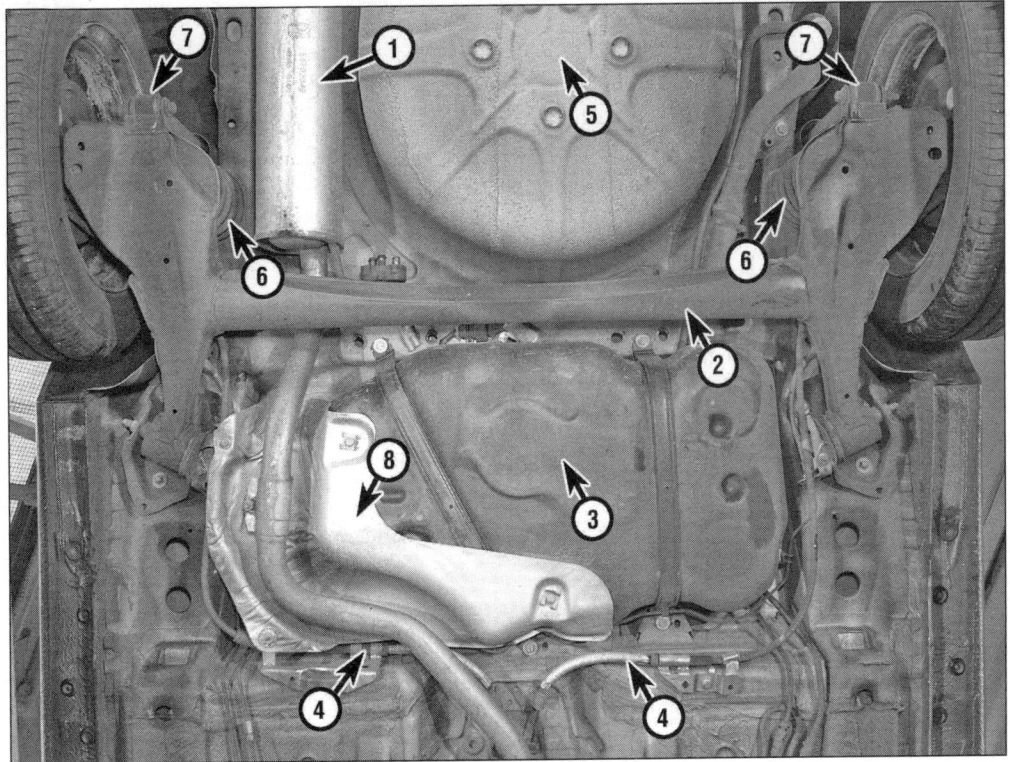

3 General Information

1 This Chapter is designed to help the home mechanic maintain his/her vehicle for safety, economy, long life and peak performance.
2 The Chapter contains a master maintenance schedule, followed by Sections dealing specifically with each task in the schedule. Visual checks, adjustments, component renewal and other helpful items are included. Refer to the accompanying illustrations of the engine compartment and the underside of the vehicle for the locations of the various components.
3 Servicing your vehicle in accordance with the mileage/time maintenance schedule and the following Sections will provide a planned maintenance programme, which should result in a long and reliable service life. This is a comprehensive plan, so maintaining some items but not others at the specified service intervals, will not produce the same results.
4 As you service your vehicle, you will discover that many of the procedures can – and should – be grouped together, because of the particular procedure being performed, or because of the proximity of two otherwise-unrelated components to one another. For example, if the vehicle is raised for any reason, the exhaust can be inspected at the same time as the suspension and steering components.

5 The first step in this maintenance programme is to prepare yourself before the actual work begins. Read through all the Sections relevant to the work to be carried out, then make a list and gather all the parts and tools required. If a problem is encountered, seek advice from a parts specialist, or a dealer service department.

4 Regular maintenance

1 If, from the time the vehicle is new, the routine maintenance schedule is followed closely, and frequent checks are made of fluid levels and high-wear items, as suggested throughout this manual, the engine will be kept in relatively good running condition, and the need for additional work will be minimised.
2 It is possible that there will be times when the engine is running poorly due to the lack of regular maintenance. This is even more likely if a used vehicle, which has not received regular and frequent maintenance checks, is purchased. In such cases, additional work may need to be carried out, outside of the regular maintenance intervals.
3 If engine wear is suspected, a compression test will provide valuable information regarding the overall performance of the main internal components. Such a test can be used as a basis to decide on the extent of the work to be carried out. If, for example, a compression

test indicates serious internal engine wear, conventional maintenance as described in this Chapter will not greatly improve the performance of the engine, and may prove a waste of time and money, unless extensive overhaul work is carried out first.
4 The following series of operations are those most often required to improve the performance of a generally poor-running engine:

Primary operations

a) Clean, inspect and test the battery (refer to Weekly checks).
b) Check all the engine-related fluids (refer to Weekly checks).
c) Check the condition and tension of the auxiliary drivebelt (Section 22).
d) Renew the spark plugs (Section 30).
e) Check the condition of the air cleaner element, and renew if necessary (Section 29).
f) Check the condition of all hoses, and check for fluid leaks (Section 6).
5 If the above operations do not prove fully effective, carry out the following secondary operations:

Secondary operations

6 All items listed under Primary operations, plus the following:
a) Check the ignition system (Chapter 5B).
b) Check the charging system (Chapter 5A).
c) Check the fuel, exhaust and emission control systems (refer to Chapter 4A or Chapter 4C).

5.11a Fit a new sealing O-ring to the oil filter housing cap...

5.11b...then clip the new oil filter element to the cap

As the drain plug threads release, move it sharply away so the stream of oil issuing from the sump runs into the container, not up your sleeve.

Every 10 000 miles or 6 months

5 Engine oil and filter renewal

HAYNES HiNT
Frequent oil and filter changes are the most important preventative maintenance procedures which can be undertaken by the DIY owner. As engine oil ages, it becomes diluted and contaminated, which leads to premature engine wear.

1 Before starting this procedure, gather together all the necessary tools and materials. Also make sure that you have plenty of clean rags and newspapers handy, to mop-up any spills. Ideally, the engine oil should be warm, as it will drain more easily, and more built-up sludge will be removed with it. Take care not to touch the exhaust or any other hot parts of the engine when working under the vehicle. To avoid any possibility of scalding, and to protect yourself from possible skin irritants and other harmful contaminants in used engine oils, it is advisable to wear gloves when carrying out this work.
2 Access to the underside of the vehicle will be greatly improved if it can be raised on a lift, driven onto ramps, or jacked up and supported on axle stands (see *Jacking and vehicle support*). Whichever method is chosen, make sure that the vehicle remains level, or if it is at an angle, that the drain plug is at the lowest point.
3 Remove the oil filler cap from the camshaft cover (twist it through a quarter-turn anti-clockwise and withdraw it).
4 Using a spanner, or preferably a suitable socket and bar, slacken the drain plug about half a turn. Position the draining container under the drain plug, then remove the plug completely **(see Haynes Hint)**.
5 Allow some time for the oil to drain, noting that it may be necessary to reposition the container as the oil flow slows to a trickle.
6 Position another container under the oil filter, located on the front left-hand side of the cylinder block.
7 Unscrew the oil filter housing cap and withdraw the cap, together with the filter, from the oil filter housing.
8 Withdraw the filter from the oil filter housing cap.
9 Use clean rags to remove all remaining oil, dirt and sludge from the oil filter housing.
10 Remove the sealing O-ring from the oil filter housing cap.
11 Fit a new sealing O-ring to the oil filter housing cap then clip the new oil filter element to the cap **(see illustrations)**.
12 Fit the cap and filter element assembly to the oil filter housing and screw the cap into position. Finally, tighten the cap to the specified torque.
13 After all the oil has drained, wipe the drain plug and the sealing washer/O-ring with a clean rag. Examine the condition of the sealing washer/O-ring, and renew it if it shows signs of damage which may prevent an oil-tight seal. Clean the area around the drain plug opening, and refit the plug complete with the washer/O-ring. Tighten the plug to the specified torque, using a torque wrench.
14 Remove the old oil and all tools from under the vehicle then lower the vehicle to the ground.
15 Fill the engine through the filler hole in the camshaft cover, using the correct grade and type of oil (refer to *Weekly checks* for details of topping-up). Pour in half the specified quantity of oil first, then wait a few minutes for the oil to drain into the sump. Continue to add oil, a small quantity at a time, until the level is up to the lower mark on the dipstick. Adding approximately a further 1.0 litre will bring the level up to the upper mark on the dipstick.
16 Start the engine and run it until it reaches normal operating temperature. While the engine is warming-up, check for leaks around the oil filter and the sump drain plug.
17 Stop the engine, and wait at least five minutes for the oil to settle in the sump once more. With the new oil circulated and the filter now completely full, recheck the level on the dipstick, and add more oil as necessary.
18 Dispose of the used engine oil and filter safely, with reference to *General repair procedures*. Do not discard the old filter with domestic household waste. The facility for waste oil disposal provided by many local council refuse tips and/or recycling centres generally has a filter receptacle alongside.

Every 20 000 miles or 12 months

6 Hose and fluid leak check

Note: *Also refer to Section 10.*
1 Visually inspect the engine joint faces, gaskets and seals for any signs of water or oil leaks. Pay particular attention to the areas around the camshaft cover, cylinder head, oil filter and sump joint faces. Similarly, check the transmission and (where applicable) the air conditioning compressor for oil leakage. Bear in mind that, over a period of time, some very slight seepage from these areas is to be expected; what you are really looking for is any indication of a serious leak. Should a leak be found, renew the offending gasket or oil seal by referring to the appropriate Chapters in this manual.
2 Also check the security and condition of all the engine-related pipes and hoses. Ensure that all cable ties or securing clips are in place, and in good condition. Clips which are broken or missing can lead to chafing of the hoses pipes or wiring, which could cause more serious problems in the future.
3 Carefully check the radiator hoses and heater hoses along their entire length.

A leak in the cooling system will usually show up as white- or antifreeze coloured deposits on the area adjoining the leak.

Renew any hose which is cracked, swollen or deteriorated. Cracks will show up better if the hose is squeezed. Pay close attention to the hose clips that secure the hoses to the cooling system components. Hose clips can pinch and puncture hoses, resulting in cooling system leaks. If wire-type hose clips are used, it may be a good idea to update them with screw-type clips.

4 Inspect all the cooling system components (hoses, joint faces, etc) for leaks. Where any problems of this nature are found on system components, renew the component or gasket with reference to Chapter 3 **(see Haynes Hint)**.

5 Where applicable, inspect the automatic transmission fluid cooler hoses for leaks or deterioration.

6 With the vehicle raised, inspect the fuel tank and filler neck for punctures, cracks and other damage. The connection between the filler neck and tank is especially critical. Sometimes, a rubber filler neck or connecting hose will leak due to loose retaining clamps or deteriorated rubber.

7 Carefully check all rubber hoses and

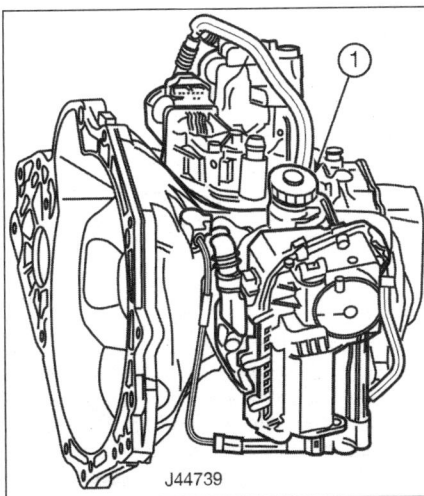

7.2 Clutch fluid reservoir (1) on Easytronic models

metal or plastic fuel lines leading away from the fuel tank. Check for loose connections, deteriorated hoses, crimped lines and other damage. Pay particular attention to the vent pipes and hoses, which often loop up around the filler neck and can become blocked or crimped. Follow the lines to the front of the vehicle, carefully inspecting them all the way. Renew damaged sections as necessary. Similarly, whilst the vehicle is raised, take the opportunity to inspect all underbody brake fluid pipes and hoses.

8 From within the engine compartment, check the security of all fuel hose attachments and pipe unions, and inspect the fuel hoses and vacuum hoses for kinks, chafing and deterioration.

7 Clutch hydraulic fluid level check – Easytronic models

1 The clutch hydraulic fluid level markings are on the side of the fluid reservoir located on the front of the transmission. The use of a mirror will be helpful.

2 Check that the level of the fluid is at or near the MAX marking on the side of the reservoir **(see illustration)**.

3 If topping-up is required, unscrew the filler cap and pour in fresh fluid until the level is at the MAX marking. Retighten the cap on completion.

8 Front brake pad and disc check

1 Firmly apply the handbrake, then jack up the front of the vehicle and support it securely on axle stands (see *Jacking and vehicle support*). Remove the front roadwheels.

2 For a quick check, the pad thickness can be carried out via the inspection hole on the caliper **(see Haynes Hint)**. Using a steel rule, measure the thickness of the pad friction linings. This must not be less than that indicated in the Specifications.

3 The view through the caliper inspection hole gives a rough indication of the state of the brake pads. For a comprehensive check, the brake pads should be removed and cleaned. The operation of the caliper can then also be checked, and the condition of the brake disc itself can be fully examined on both sides. Chapter 9, Section 6 contains a detailed description of how the brake disc should be checked for wear and/or damage.

4 If any pad's friction material is worn to the specified thickness or less, all four pads must be renewed as a set. Refer to Chapter 9, Section 4 for details.

5 On completion, refit the roadwheels and lower the vehicle to the ground.

For a quick check, the thickness of friction material remaining on the inner brake pad can be measured through the aperture in the caliper body.

9 Rear brake shoe check

1 Chock the front wheels, then jack up the rear of the vehicle, and support it securely on axle stands (see *Jacking and vehicle support*).

2 For a quick check, the thickness of friction material remaining on one of the brake shoes can be observed through the hole in the brake backplate which is exposed by prising out the sealing grommet **(see illustration)**. If a rod of the same diameter as the specified minimum friction material thickness is placed against the shoe friction material, the amount of wear can be assessed. An electric torch or inspection light will probably be required. If the friction material on any shoe is worn down to the specified minimum thickness or less, all four shoes must be renewed as a set.

3 For a comprehensive check, the brake drum should be removed and cleaned. This will allow the wheel cylinders to be checked, and the condition of the brake drum itself to be fully examined (see Chapter 9, Section 7).

10 Brake fluid pipe and hose check

1 The brake hydraulic system includes a

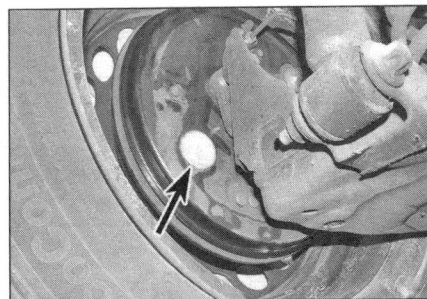

9.2 The rear brake shoe friction material thickness can be observed by prising out the backplate sealing grommet

11.4 Check for wear in the hub bearings by grasping the wheel and trying to rock it

number of metal pipes, which run from the master cylinder to the hydraulic modulator of the anti-lock braking system (ABS) and then to the front and rear brake assemblies. Flexible hoses are fitted between the pipes and the front and rear brake assemblies, to allow for steering and suspension movement.

2 When checking the system, first look for signs of leakage at the pipe or hose unions, then examine the flexible hoses for signs of cracking, chafing or deterioration of the rubber. Bend the hoses sharply between the fingers (but do not actually bend them double, or the casing may be damaged) and check that this does not reveal previously-hidden cracks, cuts or splits. Check that the pipes and hoses are securely fastened in their clips.

3 Carefully working along the length of the metal pipes, look for dents, kinks, damage of any sort, or corrosion. Light corrosion can be polished off, but if the depth of pitting is significant, the pipe must be renewed.

11 Front suspension and steering check

1 Firmly apply the handbrake, then jack up the front of the vehicle and support it securely on axle stands (see *Jacking and vehicle support*).

2 Inspect the balljoint dust covers and the steering gear gaiters for splits, chafing or deterioration.

3 Any wear of these components will cause loss of lubricant, and may allow water to

12.2 Check the condition of the driveshaft gaiters (1) and retaining clips (2)

enter the components, resulting in rapid deterioration of the balljoints or steering gear.

4 Grasp each roadwheel at the 12 o'clock and 6 o'clock positions, and try to rock it **(see illustration)**. Very slight free play may be felt, but if the movement is appreciable, further investigation is necessary to determine the source. Continue rocking the wheel while an assistant depresses the footbrake. If the movement is now eliminated or significantly reduced, it is likely that the hub bearings are at fault. If the free play is still evident with the footbrake depressed, then there is wear in the suspension joints or mountings.

5 Now grasp each wheel at the 9 o'clock and 3 o'clock positions, and try to rock it as before. Any movement felt now may again be caused by wear in the hub bearings or the steering track rod end balljoints. If the track rod end balljoint is worn, the visual movement will be obvious.

6 Using a large screwdriver or flat bar, check for wear in the suspension mounting bushes by levering between the relevant suspension component and its attachment point. Some movement is to be expected, as the mountings are made of rubber, but excessive wear should be obvious. Also check the condition of any visible rubber bushes, looking for splits, cracks or contamination of the rubber.

7 Check for any signs of fluid leakage around the suspension struts, or from the rubber gaiters around the piston rods. Should any fluid be noticed, the suspension strut is defective internally, and should be renewed. **Note:** *Suspension struts should always be renewed in pairs on the same axle.*

8 With the vehicle standing on its wheels, have an assistant turn the steering wheel back-and-forth about an eighth of a turn each way. There should be very little, if any, lost movement between the steering wheel and roadwheels. If this is not the case, closely observe the joints and mountings previously described. In addition, check the steering column universal joints for wear, and also check the rack-and-pinion steering gear itself.

9 The efficiency of each suspension strut may be checked by bouncing the vehicle at each front corner. Generally speaking, the body will return to its normal position and stop after

13.3 Exhaust mountings

being depressed. If it rises and returns on a rebound, the suspension strut is probably suspect. Also examine the suspension strut upper mountings for any signs of wear.

12 Driveshaft check

1 Firmly apply the handbrake, then jack up the front of the vehicle and support it securely on axle stands (see *Jacking and vehicle support*).

2 Turn the steering onto full lock then slowly rotate the roadwheel. Inspect the condition of the outer constant velocity (CV) joint rubber gaiters while squeezing the gaiters to open out the folds **(see illustration)**. Check for signs of cracking, splits or deterioration of the rubber which may allow the grease to escape and lead to water and grit entry into the joint. Also check the security and condition of the retaining clips. Repeat these checks on the inner CV joints. If any damage or deterioration is found, the gaiters should be renewed as described in Chapter 8, Section 3.

3 At the same time, check the general condition of the CV joints themselves by first holding the driveshaft and attempting to rotate the wheel. Repeat this check by holding the inner joint and attempting to rotate the driveshaft. Any appreciable movement indicates wear in the joints, wear in the driveshaft splines or loose driveshaft retaining nut.

13 Exhaust system check

1 With the engine cold (at least an hour after the vehicle has been driven), check the complete exhaust system from the engine to the end of the tailpipe. The exhaust system is most easily checked with the vehicle raised on a hoist, or suitably-supported on axle stands, so that the exhaust components are readily visible and accessible (see *Jacking and vehicle support*).

2 Check the exhaust pipes and connections for evidence of leaks, severe corrosion and damage. Make sure that all brackets and mountings are in good condition, and that all relevant nuts and bolts are tight. Leakage at any of the joints or in other parts of the system will usually show up as a black sooty stain in the vicinity of the leak.

3 Rattles and other noises can often be traced to the exhaust system, especially the brackets and mountings **(see illustration)**. Try to move the pipes and silencers. If the components are able to come into contact with the body or suspension parts, secure the system with new mountings. Otherwise separate the joints (if possible) and twist the pipes as necessary to provide additional clearance.

14 Rear suspension check

1 Chock the front wheels, then jack up the rear of the vehicle and support securely on axle stands (see *Jacking and vehicle support*).
2 Inspect the rear suspension components for any signs of obvious wear or damage. Pay particular attention to the rubber mounting bushes, and renew if necessary (see Chapter 10).
3 Grasp each roadwheel at the 12 o'clock and 6 o'clock positions **(see illustration 11.4)**, and try to rock it. Any excess movement indicates wear in the wheel bearings. Wear may also be accompanied by a rumbling sound when the wheel is spun, or a noticeable roughness if the wheel is turned slowly. The wheel bearing can be renewed as described in Chapter 10.
4 Check for any signs of fluid leakage around the shock absorber bodies. Should any fluid be noticed, the shock absorber is defective internally, and should be renewed.
Note: *Shock absorbers should always be renewed in pairs on the same axle.*
5 With the vehicle standing on its wheels, the efficiency of each shock absorber may be checked by bouncing the vehicle at each rear corner. Generally speaking, the body will return to its normal position and stop after being depressed. If it rises and returns on a rebound, the shock absorber is probably suspect.

15 Bodywork and underbody condition check

Note: *This work should be carried out by a Vauxhall/Opel dealer in order to validate the vehicle warranty. The work includes a thorough inspection of the vehicle paintwork and underbody for damage and corrosion.*

Bodywork damage and corrosion check

1 Once the car has been washed, and all tar spots and other surface blemishes have been cleaned off, carefully check all paintwork, looking closely for chips or scratches. Pay particular attention to vulnerable areas such as the front panels (bonnet and spoiler), and around the wheel arches. Any damage to the paintwork must be rectified as soon as possible, to comply with the terms of the manufacturer's anti-corrosion warranties; check with a Vauxhall/Opel dealer for details.
2 If a chip or light scratch is found which is recent and still free from rust, it can be touched-up using the appropriate touch-up stick which can be obtained from Vauxhall/Opel dealers. Any more serious damage, or rusted stone chips, can be repaired as described in Chapter 11, Section 4, but if damage or corrosion is so severe that a panel

must be renewed, seek professional advice as soon as possible.
3 Always check that the door and ventilation opening drain holes and pipes are completely clear, so that water can drain out.

Corrosion protection check

4 The wax-based underbody protective coating should be inspected annually, preferably just prior to Winter, when the underbody should be washed down as thoroughly as possible without disturbing the protective coating. Any damage to the coating should be repaired using a suitable wax-based sealer. If any of the body panels are disturbed for repair or renewal, do not forget to re-apply the coating. Wax should be injected into door cavities, sills and box sections, to maintain the level of protection provided by the vehicle manufacturer – seek the advice of a Vauxhall/Opel dealer.

16 Roadwheel bolt tightness check

1 Where applicable, remove the wheel trims from the wheels.
2 Using a torque wrench on each wheel bolt in turn, ensure that the bolts are tightened to the specified torque.
3 Where applicable, refit the wheel trims on completion, making sure they are fitted correctly.

17 Hinge and lock lubrication

1 Work around the vehicle and lubricate the hinges of the bonnet, doors and tailgate with a light machine oil.
2 Lightly lubricate the bonnet release mechanism and exposed section of inner cable with a smear of grease.
3 Check the security and operation of all hinges, latches and locks, adjusting them where required. Check the operation of the central locking system.
4 Check the condition and operation of the bonnet and tailgate support struts, renewing them both if either is leaking or no longer able to support the bonnet/tailgate securely when raised.

18 Electrical systems check

1 Check the operation of all the electrical equipment, ie, lights, direction indicators, horn, etc. Refer to the appropriate sections of Chapter 12 for details if any of the circuits are found to be inoperative.
2 Note that the stop-light switch is described in Chapter 9.

3 Check all accessible wiring connectors, harnesses and retaining clips for security, and for signs of chafing or damage. Rectify any faults found.

19 Road test

Instruments and electrical equipment

1 Check the operation of all instruments, warning lights and electrical equipment.
2 Make sure that all instruments read correctly, and switch on all electrical equipment in turn, to check that it functions properly.

Steering and suspension

3 Check for any abnormalities in the steering, suspension, handling or road 'feel'.
4 Drive the vehicle, and check that there are no unusual vibrations or noises.
5 Check that the steering feels positive, with no excessive 'sloppiness', or roughness, and check for any suspension noises when cornering and driving over bumps.

Drivetrain

6 Check the performance of the engine, clutch, transmission and driveshafts.
7 Listen for any unusual noises from the engine, clutch and transmission.
8 Make sure that the engine runs smoothly when idling, and that there is no hesitation when accelerating.
9 Check that, where applicable, the clutch action is smooth and progressive, that the drive is taken up smoothly, and that the pedal travel is not excessive. Also listen for any noises when the clutch pedal is depressed.
10 Check that all gears can be engaged smoothly without noise, and that the gear lever action is smooth and not abnormally vague or 'notchy'.
11 On automatic transmission models, make sure that all gearchanges occur smoothly, without snatching, and without an increase in engine speed between changes. Check that all of the gear positions can be selected with the vehicle at rest. If any problems are found, they should be referred to a Vauxhall/Opel dealer.
12 Listen for a metallic clicking sound from the front of the vehicle, as the vehicle is driven slowly in a circle with the steering on full-lock. Carry out this check in both directions. If a clicking noise is heard, this indicates wear in a driveshaft joint (see Chapter 8).

Braking system

13 Make sure that the vehicle does not pull to one side when braking.
14 Check that there is no vibration through the steering when braking.
Note: *Under heavy braking on models equipped with ABS, vibration may be felt through the brake pedal. This is a normal*

feature of ABS operation, and does not constitute a fault.

15 Check that the handbrake operates correctly, without excessive movement of the lever, and that it holds the vehicle stationary on a slope.

16 Test the operation of the brake servo unit as follows. Depress the footbrake four or five times to exhaust the vacuum, then start the engine. As the engine starts, there should be a noticeable 'give' in the brake pedal as vacuum builds-up. Allow the engine to run for at least two minutes, and then switch it off. If the brake pedal is now depressed again, it should be possible to detect a hiss from the servo as the pedal is depressed. After about four or five applications, no further hissing should be heard, and the pedal should feel considerably harder.

20 Service interval indicator reset

1 With the ignition switched off, depress and hold the trip odometer reset button located on the instrument panel. After approximately 3 seconds, the message 'InSP 0' will appear. Keep the reset button depressed and also depress the brake pedal.

2 Switch on the ignition, with the reset button and brake pedal still depressed, and 'InSP – – – -' will appear, flashing, in the display. Keep the reset button and brake pedal depressed until the display changes.

3 After approximately 10 seconds the display will change to show the maximum mileage before the next required service. Release the reset button and the brake pedal, then switch off the ignition. When the button and brake pedal are released, the odometer will appear again.

Every 40 000 miles or 2 years

21 Pollen filter renewal

1 Remove the glovebox (see Chapter 11, Section 26).

2 Release the plastic expanding rivet and remove the passenger's side footwell air duct **(see illustration)**.

3 Unclip the pollen filter access cover from the side of the heater/ventilation air distribution housing **(see illustration)**.

4 Withdraw the pollen filter from the housing **(see illustration)**.

5 Fit the new filter using a reversal of the removal procedure; make sure that the filter is fitted the correct way up as indicated on the edge of the filter.

22 Auxiliary drivebelt condition check

Note: *The manufacturers recommend that the tensioner roller is checked and if necessary renewed at the same time as the drivebelt.*

Checking

1 Due to their function and material make-up, drivebelts are prone to failure after a long period of time and should therefore be inspected regularly.

2 Apply the handbrake, then jack up the front of the vehicle and support it on axle stands (see *Jacking and vehicle support*). Remove the right-hand front roadwheel and the wheel arch liner cover for access to the right-hand side of the engine.

3 With the engine stopped, inspect the full length of the drivebelt for cracks and separation of the belt plies. It will be necessary to turn the engine (using a spanner or socket and bar on the crankshaft pulley bolt) so that the belt can be inspected thoroughly. Twist the belt between the pulleys so that both sides can be viewed. Also check for fraying, and glazing which gives the belt a shiny appearance. Check the pulleys for nicks, cracks, distortion and corrosion. If the belt shows signs of wear or damage, it should be renewed as a precaution against breakage in service.

Renewal

4 If not already done, apply the handbrake, then jack up the front of the vehicle and support it on axle stands (see *Jacking and vehicle support*). Remove the right-hand front roadwheel and the wheel arch liner cover for access to the right-hand side of the engine.

5 For additional working clearance, remove the air cleaner assembly as described in Chapter 4A, Section 2.

6 If the drivebelt is to be re-used, mark it to indicate its normal running direction.

7 Support the engine and remove the right- hand engine mounting with reference to Chapter 2A, Section 15 or Chapter 2B, Section 16.

Note: *On these engines, the engine mounting locates within the auxiliary drivebelt.*

8 Note the routing of the drivebelt, then, using a Torx key on the pulley centre bolt, turn the tensioner clockwise against the

21.2 Release the expanding rivet and remove the passenger's side footwell air duct

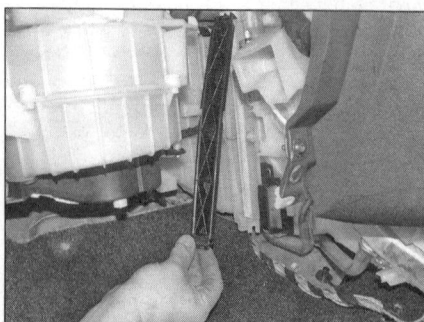

21.3 Unclip the pollen filter access cover from the side of the air distribution housing

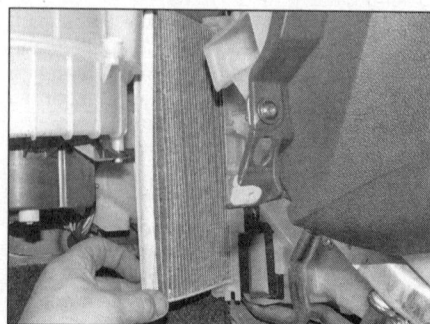

21.4 Withdraw the pollen filter from the housing

spring tension. Hold the tensioner in this position by inserting a suitable locking pin/bolt through the special hole provided **(see illustration)**.

9 Slip the auxiliary drivebelt off of the pulleys.

10 Locate the auxiliary drivebelt onto the pulleys in the correct routing. If the drivebelt is being re-used, make sure it is fitted the correct way around.

11 Turn back the tensioner and remove the locking bolt, then release it, making sure that the drivebelt ribs locate correctly on each of the pulley grooves.

12 Refit the right-hand engine mounting with reference to Chapter 2A, Section 15 or Chapter 2B, Section 16.

13 Refit the air cleaner assembly, then refit the wheel arch liner and roadwheel, and lower the vehicle to the ground.

23 Handbrake operation and adjustment check

1 With the vehicle on a slight slope, apply the handbrake lever by up to 3 clicks of the ratchet, and check that it holds the vehicle stationary, then release the lever and check that there is no resistance to movement of the vehicle.

2 If necessary, adjust the handbrake as follows.

3 Chock the front wheels then jack up the rear of the car and securely support it on axle stands (see *Jacking and vehicle support*).

4 Fully depress, then release the brake pedal at least five times. Similarly, fully apply, then release the handbrake at least five times.

5 Unclip the handbrake lever gaiter from the centre console and fold it up the handbrake lever **(see illustration)**. The handbrake cable adjuster nut is situated by the handbrake lever inside the vehicle.

6 Move the handbrake lever to the fully released position, then turn the cable adjuster nut anti-clockwise to remove all tension from the cables **(see illustration)**.

7 With the handbrake lever set on the second notch of the ratchet mechanism, rotate the adjuster nut clockwise until a reasonable amount of force is required to turn each wheel.

Note: *The force required should be equal for each wheel.*

8 Now pull the handbrake lever up to the third notch of the ratchet mechanism and check that both rear wheels are locked. Once this is so, fully release the handbrake lever and check that the wheels rotate freely. Check the adjustment by applying the handbrake fully whilst counting the clicks emitted from the handbrake ratchet and, if necessary, re-adjust.

9 On completion of adjustment, refit the handbrake lever gaiter, then lower the vehicle to the ground.

24 Headlight beam alignment check

1 Accurate adjustment of the headlight beam is only possible using optical beam-setting equipment, and this work should therefore be carried out by a Vauxhall/Opel dealer or service station with the necessary facilities. Refer to Chapter 12, Section 8 for further information.

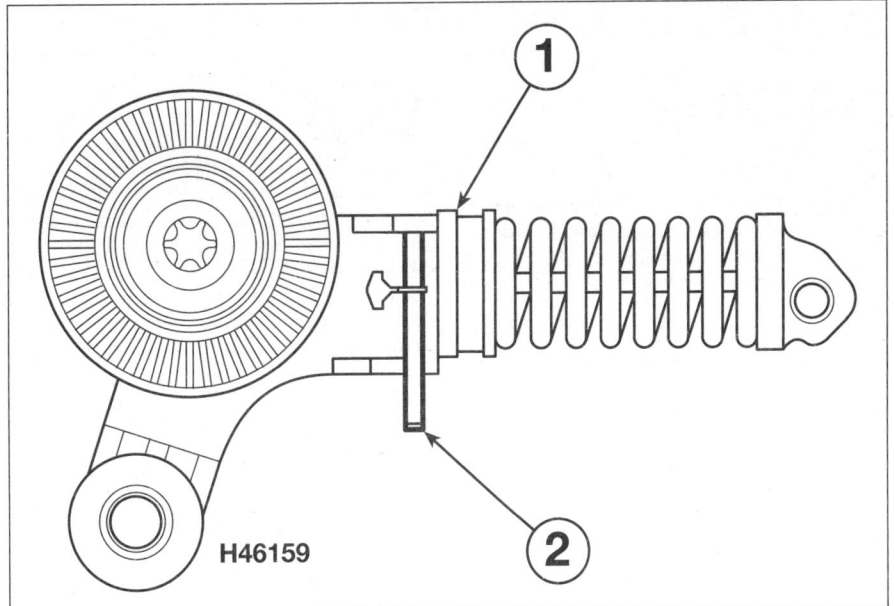
22.8 Auxiliary drivebelt tensioner
1 Tensioner body   2 Locking pin/bolt

23.5 Unclip the handbrake lever gaiter from the centre console...

23.6...for access to the handbrake cable adjuster nut

Every 2 years, regardless of mileage

25 Remote control battery renewal

1 Using a screwdriver, prise the battery cover from the ignition key fob **(see illustration)**.
2 Note how the circular battery is fitted, then carefully remove it from the contacts **(see illustration)**.
3 Fit the new battery (type CR 2032) and refit the cover making sure that it clips fully onto the base.
4 After changing the battery, lock and unlock the driver's door with the key in the lock, then switch on the ignition to synchronise the remote control unit.

26 Hydraulic fluid renewal

Note: *It is not possible for the home mechanic to bleed the clutch hydraulic system on Easytronic models. Refer to Chapter 7C for additional information.*

⚠️ *Warning: Hydraulic fluid can harm your eyes and damage painted surfaces, so use extreme caution when handling and pouring it. Do not use fluid that has been standing open for some time, as it absorbs moisture from the air. Excess moisture can cause a dangerous loss of braking effectiveness.*

1 The procedure is similar to that for the bleeding of the hydraulic system as described in Chapter 9, Section 2 (brake) and Chapter 6, Section 2 (clutch).
2 Working as described in Chapter 9, Section 2, open the first bleed screw in the sequence, and pump the brake pedal gently until nearly all the old fluid has been emptied from the master cylinder reservoir. Top-up to the MAX level with new fluid, and continue pumping until only the new fluid remains in the reservoir, and new fluid can be seen emerging from the bleed screw. Tighten the screw, and top the reservoir level up to the MAX level line.

25.1 Prise the battery cover from the ignition key fob

HAYNES HINT *Old hydraulic fluid is invariably much darker in colour than the new, making it easy to distinguish the two.*

3 Work through all the remaining bleed screws in the sequence until new fluid can be seen at all of them. Be careful to keep the master cylinder reservoir topped-up to above the MIN level at all times, or air may enter the system and greatly increase the length of the task.
4 Bleed the fluid from the clutch hydraulic system as described in Chapter 6, Section 2.
5 When the operation is complete, check that all bleed screws are securely tightened, and that their dust caps are refitted. Wash off all traces of spilt fluid, and recheck the master cylinder reservoir fluid level.
6 Check the operation of the brakes and clutch before taking the car on the road.

27 Coolant renewal

Note: *Vauxhall/Opel do not specify renewal intervals for the antifreeze mixture, as the mixture used to fill the system when the vehicle is new is designed to last the lifetime of the vehicle. However, it is strongly recommended that the coolant is renewed at the intervals specified in the Maintenance schedule as a precaution against possible engine corrosion problems. This is particularly advisable if the coolant has been renewed using an antifreeze other than that specified by Vauxhall/Opel. With many antifreeze types, the corrosion inhibitors become progressively less effective with age. It is up to the individual owner whether or not to follow this advice.*

⚠️ *Warning: Wait until the engine is cold before starting this procedure. Do not allow antifreeze to come in contact with your skin, or with the painted surfaces of the vehicle. Rinse off spills immediately with plenty of water. Never leave antifreeze lying around*

25.2 Carefully remove the battery from the contacts

in an open container, or in a puddle in the driveway or on the garage floor. Children and pets are attracted by its sweet smell, but antifreeze can be fatal if ingested.

Cooling system draining

1 To drain the cooling system, first cover the expansion tank cap with a wad of rag, and slowly turn the cap anti-clockwise to relieve the pressure in the cooling system (a hissing sound will normally be heard). Wait until any pressure remaining in the system is released, then continue to turn the cap until it can be removed.
2 Position a suitable container beneath the left-hand side of the radiator.
3 The coolant drain plug is located at the bottom of the radiator left-hand end tank. Unscrew the drain plug and allow the coolant to drain.
4 When the flow of coolant stops, refit and tighten the drain plugs.
5 As no cylinder block drain plug is fitted, it is not possible to drain all of the coolant. Due consideration must be made for this when refilling the system, in order to maintain the correct concentration of antifreeze.
6 If the coolant has been drained for a reason other than renewal, then provided it is clean and less than two years old, it can be re-used.

Cooling system flushing

7 If coolant renewal has been neglected, or if the antifreeze mixture has become diluted, then in time, the cooling system may gradually lose efficiency, as the coolant passages become restricted due to rust, scale deposits, and other sediment. The cooling system efficiency can be restored by flushing the system clean.
8 The radiator should be flushed independently of the engine, to avoid unnecessary contamin-ation.

Radiator flushing

9 Disconnect the top and bottom hoses and any other relevant hoses from the radiator, with reference to Chapter 3, Section 2.
10 Insert a garden hose into the radiator top inlet. Direct a flow of clean water through the radiator, and continue flushing until clean water emerges from the radiator bottom outlet.
11 If after a reasonable period, the water still does not run clear, the radiator can be flushed with a good proprietary cleaning agent. It is important that the manufacturer's instructions are followed carefully. If the contamination is particularly bad, remove the radiator, insert the hose in the radiator bottom outlet, and reverse-flush the radiator.

Engine flushing

12 To flush the engine, the thermostat must be removed, because it will be shut, and would otherwise prevent the flow of water around the engine. The thermostat can be removed as

27.17a Unscrew the bleed screw located at the upper right-hand side of the radiator...

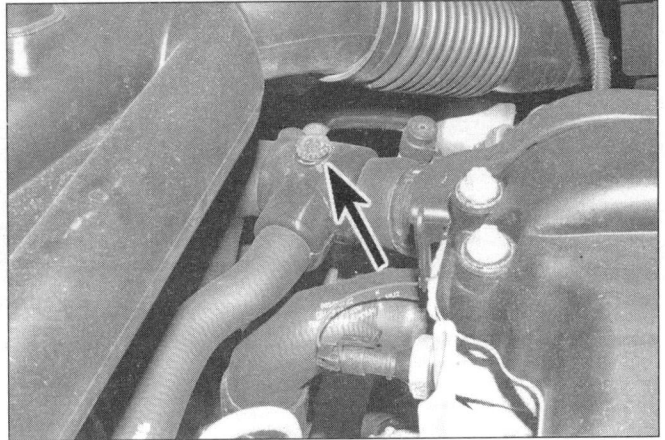

27.17b...and on automatic transmission models, unscrew the additional bleed screw located in the radiator top hose elbow

described in Chapter 3, Section 4. Take care not to introduce dirt or debris into the system if this approach is used.

13 With the bottom hose disconnected from the radiator, insert a garden hose into the thermostat opening. Direct a clean flow of water through the engine, and continue flushing until clean water emerges from the radiator bottom hose.

14 On completion of flushing, refit the thermostat with reference to Chapter 3, and reconnect the hoses.

Cooling system filling

15 Before attempting to fill the cooling system, make sure that all hoses and clips are in good condition, and that the clips are tight. Note that an antifreeze mixture must be used all year round, to prevent corrosion of the engine components.

16 Remove the expansion tank filler cap.

17 Unscrew the bleed screw located at the upper right-hand side of the radiator. There is an opening in the panel above for access. On models with automatic transmission, unscrew the additional bleed screw located in the radiator top hose elbow **(see illustrations)**.

18 Fill the system by slowly pouring the coolant into the expansion tank until it is up to the filler neck.

19 Tighten the bleed screw(s) as soon as coolant emerges from the bleed screw orifice.

20 Refit and tighten the expansion tank filler cap.

21 Start the engine and run it at 2000 to 2500 rpm until the cooling fan switches on. Continue running the engine at between 2000 and 2500 rpm for a further 2 minutes.

22 Stop the engine, and allow it to cool, then re-check the coolant level with reference to *Weekly checks*. Top-up the level if necessary and refit the expansion tank filler cap.

Antifreeze mixture

23 Always use an ethylene-glycol based antifreeze which is suitable for use in mixed-metal cooling systems.

24 Vauxhall/Opel recommend the use of silicate-free coolant (see *Lubricants and fluids* on page 0•17).

25 The quantity of antifreeze and level of protection are given in the Specifications at the start of this Chapter.

26 Before adding antifreeze, the cooling system should be completely drained, preferably flushed, and all hoses checked for condition and security.

27 After filling with antifreeze, a label should be attached to the expansion tank, stating the type and concentration of

antifreeze used, and the date installed. Any subsequent topping-up should be made with the same type and concentration of antifreeze.

Caution: Do not use engine antifreeze in the windscreen/tailgate washer system, as it will cause damage to the vehicle paintwork. A screenwash additive should be added to the washer system in the quantities stated on the bottle.

28 Exhaust emission check

1 The exhaust emission check is carried out initially after 3 years, then every 2 years, however, on vehicles which are subject to intensive use (eg, taxis/hire cars/ambulances) it must be carried out annually. The check involves checking the engine management system operation by plugging an electronic tester into the system diagnostic socket to check the electronic control unit (ECU) memory for faults (see Chapter 4A).

2 In reality, if the vehicle is running correctly and the engine management warning light in the instrument panel is functioning normally, then this check need not be carried out.

Every 40 000 miles or 4 years

29 Air cleaner element renewal

1 The air cleaner is located on the right-hand side of the engine compartment.

2 Disconnect the wiring connector from the inlet air temperature sensor **(see illustration)**.

3 Slacken the retaining clip and detach the air inlet duct from the air cleaner cover **(see illustration)**.

4 Undo the screws and lift off the air cleaner

29.2 Disconnect the inlet air temperature sensor wiring connector

29.3 Slacken the retaining clip and detach the air inlet duct from the air cleaner cover

29.4a Undo the retaining screws and lift off the air cleaner cover...

29.4b...then lift out the filter element

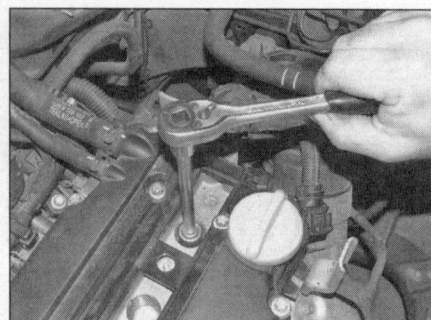
30.5a Unscrew the spark plugs...

30.5b...and remove them

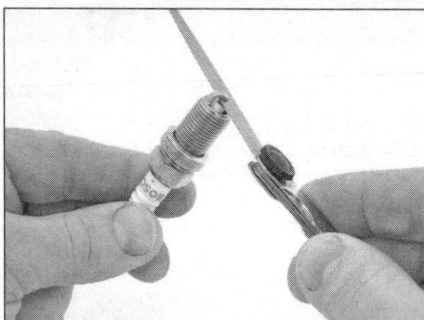
30.10a Measuring a spark plug electrode gap using a feeler blade

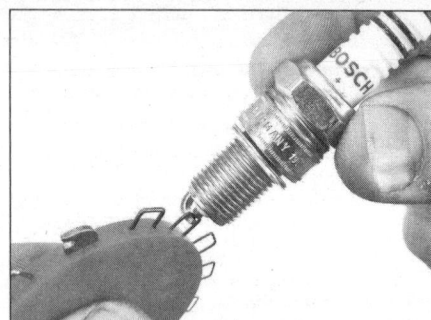
30.10b Measuring a spark plug electrode gap using a wire gauge

cover, then lift out the filter element **(see illustrations)**.

5 Wipe out the casing and the cover.

6 Fit the new filter, noting that the rubber locating flange should be uppermost, and secure the cover with the screws.

7 Reconnect the air inlet duct to the air cleaner cover and reconnect the inlet air temperature sensor wiring connector.

30 Spark plug renewal

1 The correct functioning of the spark plugs is vital for the correct running and efficiency of the engine. It is essential that the plugs fitted are appropriate for the engine, the suitable type being specified at the beginning of this Chapter.

2 If the correct type is used and the engine is in good condition, the spark plugs should not need attention between scheduled renewal intervals. Spark plug cleaning is rarely necessary, and should not be attempted unless specialised equipment is available, as damage can easily be caused to the firing ends.

3 Remove the ignition module from the spark plugs with reference to Chapter 5B, Section 3.

4 It is advisable to remove the dirt from the spark plug recesses using a clean brush, vacuum cleaner or compressed air before removing the plugs, to prevent dirt dropping into the cylinders.

5 Unscrew the spark plugs from the cylinder head using a spark plug spanner, suitable box spanner or a deep socket and extension bar **(see illustrations)**. Keep the socket aligned with the spark plug – if it is forcibly moved to one side, the ceramic insulator may be broken off.

6 Examination of the spark plugs will give a good indication of the condition of the engine. As each plug is removed, examine it as follows. If the insulator nose of the spark plug is clean and white, with no deposits, this is indicative of a weak mixture or too hot a plug (a hot plug transfers heat away from the electrode slowly, a cold plug transfers heat away quickly).

7 If the tip and insulator nose are covered with hard black-looking deposits, then this is indicative that the mixture is too rich. Should the plug be black and oily, then it is likely that the engine is fairly worn, as well as the mixture being too rich.

8 If the insulator nose is covered with light tan to greyish-brown deposits, then the mixture is correct and it is likely that the engine is in good condition.

9 The spark plug electrode gap is of considerable importance. If the gap is too large or too small, the size of the spark and its efficiency will be seriously impaired and it will not perform correctly under all engine speed and load conditions. For the best results, the spark plug gap should be set in accordance with the Specifications at the beginning of this Chapter.

10 To set the gap, measure it with a feeler blade or spark plug gap gauge and then carefully bend the outer plug electrode until the correct gap is achieved. The centre electrode should never be bent, as this may crack the insulator and cause plug failure, if nothing worse. If using feeler blades, the gap is correct when the appropriate-size blade is a firm sliding fit **(see illustrations)**.

11 Special spark plug electrode gap adjusting tools are available from most motor accessory shops, or from some spark plug manufacturers.

12 Before fitting the spark plugs, check that the threaded connector sleeves on the top of the plug are tight, and that the plug exterior surfaces and threads are clean.

13 Screw in the spark plugs by hand where possible, then tighten them to the specified torque. Take extra care to enter the plug threads correctly, as the cylinder head is of light alloy construction.

14 On completion, refit the ignition module as described in Chapter 5B then, where applicable, refit the engine top cover.

31 Automatic transmission fluid renewal

1 Refer to the procedures contained in Chapter 7B, Section 2.

Every 100 000 miles or 6 years

32 Auxiliary drivebelt renewal

1 Refer to the procedures contained in Section 22.

Chapter 1 Part B
Routine maintenance and servicing – diesel models

Contents

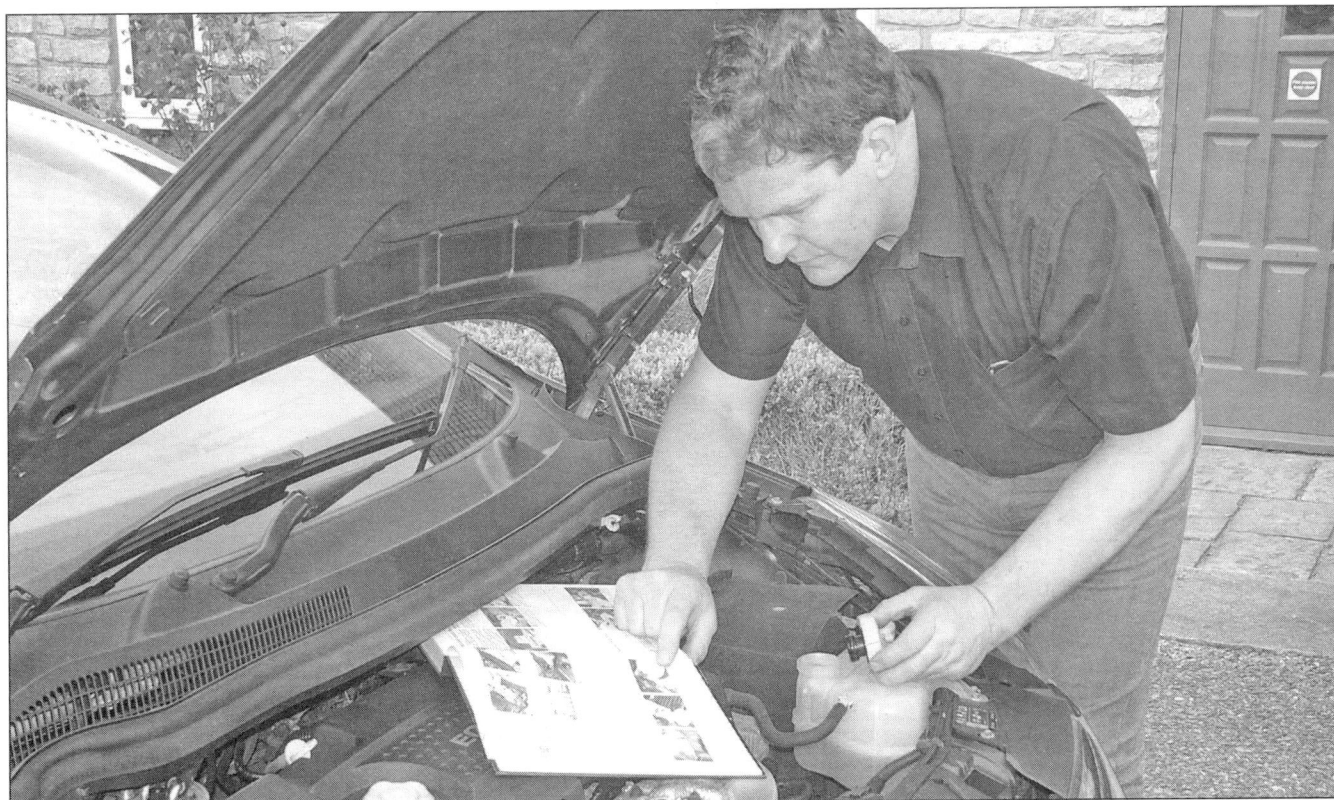

Degrees of difficulty

Easy, suitable for novice with little experience

Fairly easy, suitable for beginner with some experience

Fairly difficult, suitable for competent DIY mechanic

Difficult, suitable for experienced DIY mechanic

Very difficult, suitable for expert DIY or professional

Specifications

Lubricants and fluids........................... Refer to *Lubricants, fluids and tyre pressures* on page 0•17

Capacities

Engine

Engine oil (including oil filter) .... 3.5 litres
Difference between MIN and MAX dipstick marks.................. 1.0 litre

Cooling system

All models.. 6.6 litres

Transmission

5-speed transmission... 1.6 litres
6-speed transmission... 1.8 litres

Washer fluid reservoir

All models.. 2.2 litres

Fuel tank

All models.. 45 litres

Cooling system

Antifreeze mixture:
  50% antifreeze .... Protection down to -40°C

Brakes

Friction material minimum thickness:
  Front brake pads .... 2.0 mm
  Rear brake shoes .... 2.0 mm

Torque wrench settings	Nm	lbf ft
Engine oil filter housing cover	25	18
Roadwheel bolts	110	81
Sump drain plug	20	15

1 Maintenance schedule

1 The maintenance intervals in this manual are provided with the assumption that you, not the dealer, will be carrying out the work. These are the minimum maintenance intervals based on the standard service schedule recommended by the manufacturer for vehicles driven daily. If you wish to keep your vehicle in peak condition at all times, you may wish to perform some of these procedures more often. We encourage frequent maintenance, because it enhances the efficiency, performance and resale value of your vehicle.

2 If the vehicle is driven in dusty areas, used to tow a trailer, or driven frequently at slow speeds (idling in traffic) or on short journeys, more frequent maintenance intervals are recommended.

3 When the vehicle is new, it should be serviced by a dealer service department (or other workshop recognised by the vehicle manufacturer as providing the same standard of service) in order to preserve the warranty. The vehicle manufacturer may reject warranty claims if you are unable to prove that servicing has been carried out as and when specified, using only original equipment parts or parts certified to be of equivalent quality.

Every 250 miles or weekly
☐ Refer to *Weekly checks*

Every 10 000 miles or 6 months – whichever comes first
☐ Renew the engine oil and filter (Section 5)

Note: *Vauxhall/Opel recommend that the engine oil and filter are changed every 20 000 miles or 12 months if the vehicle is being operated under the standard service schedule. However, oil and filter changes are good for the engine and we recommend that the oil and filter are renewed more frequently, especially if the vehicle is used on a lot of short journeys.*

Every 20 000 miles or 12 months – whichever comes first
☐ Check all underbonnet and underbody components, pipes and hoses for leaks (Section 6)
☐ Drain the water from the fuel filter (Section 7)
☐ Check the condition of the front brake pads, the calipers and discs (Section 8)
☐ Check the condition of the rear brake shoes (Section 9)
☐ Check the condition of all brake fluid pipes and hoses (Section 10)
☐ Check the condition of the front suspension and steering components, particularly the rubber gaiters and seals (Section 11)
☐ Check the condition of the driveshaft joint gaiters, and the driveshaft joints (Section 12)
☐ Check the condition of the exhaust system components (Section 13)
☐ Check the condition of the rear suspension components (Section 14)
☐ Check the bodywork and underbody for damage and corrosion, and check the condition of the underbody corrosion protection (Section 15)
☐ Check the tightness of the roadwheel bolts (Section 16)
☐ Lubricate all door, bonnet and tailgate hinges and locks (Section 17)
☐ Check the operation of the horn, all lights, and the wipers and washers (Section 18)
☐ Carry out a road test (Section 19)
☐ Reset the service interval indicator (Section 20)

Every 40 000 miles or 2 years – whichever comes first
☐ Renew the pollen filter (Section 21)
☐ Renew the fuel filter (Section 22)
☐ Check the auxiliary drivebelt and tensioner (Section 23)
☐ Check the operation of the handbrake and adjust if necessary (Section 24)
☐ Check the headlight beam alignment (Section 25)

Every 2 years, regardless of mileage
☐ Renew the battery for the remote control handset (Section 26)
☐ Renew the brake and clutch fluid (Section 27)
☐ Renew the coolant (Section 28)
☐ Exhaust emission test (Section 29)

Note: *Vehicles using Vauxhall/Opel silicate-free coolant do not need the coolant renewed on a regular basis.*

Every 40 000 miles or 4 years – whichever comes first
☐ Renew the air cleaner filter element (Section 30)

Every 100 000 miles or 10 years – whichever comes first
☐ Renew the auxiliary drivebelt (Section 31)

2 Component location

Underbonnet view

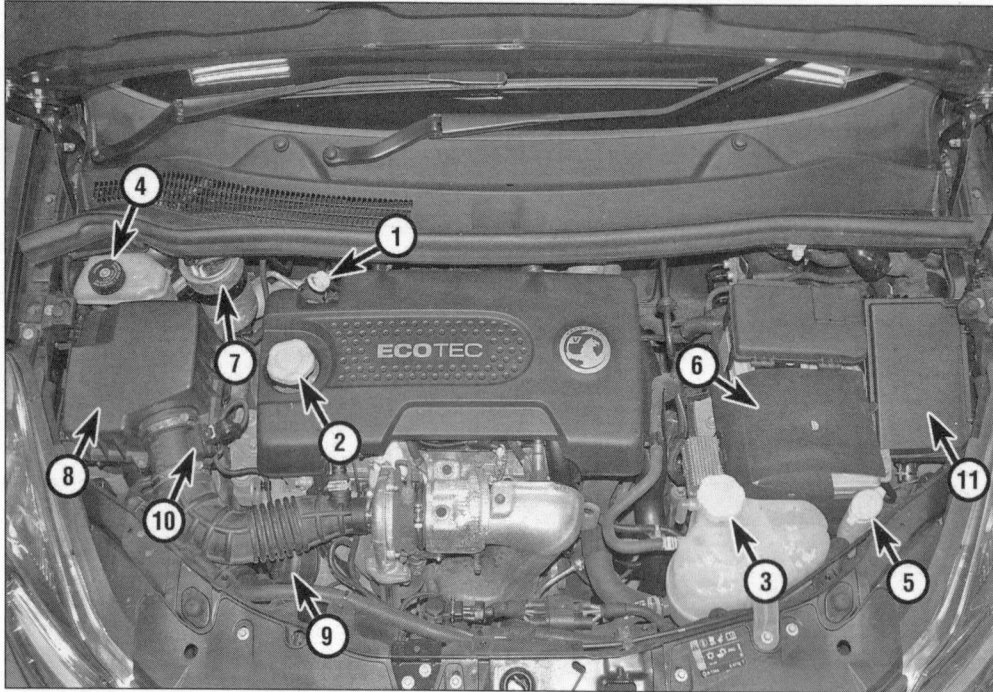

1 Engine oil level dipstick
2 Engine oil filler cap
3 Coolant expansion tank
4 Brake (and clutch) fluid reservoir
5 Screen washer fluid reservoir
6 Battery
7 Fuel filter
8 Air cleaner assembly
9 Oil filter
10 Airflow meter
11 Fuse/relay box

Front underbody view

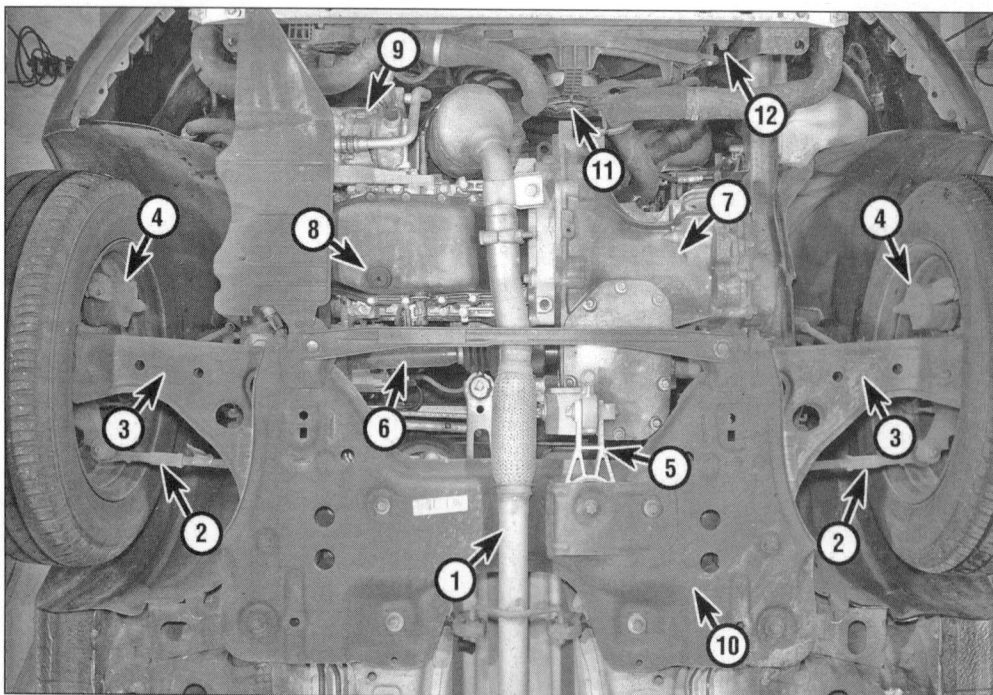

1 Exhaust front pipe
2 Steering track rods
3 Front suspension lower arms
4 Front brake calipers
5 Engine mounting rear torque link
6 Right-hand driveshaft
7 Manual transmission
8 Engine oil drain plug
9 Air conditioning compressor
10 Front subframe
11 Radiator cooling fan
12 Coolant drain plug

Rear underbody view

1 Exhaust tailpipe and silencer
2 Rear suspension torsion beam and trailing arms
3 Fuel tank
4 Handbrake cables
5 Spare wheel well
6 Rear coil springs
7 Rear shock absorber lower mountings
8 Fuel tank heat shield

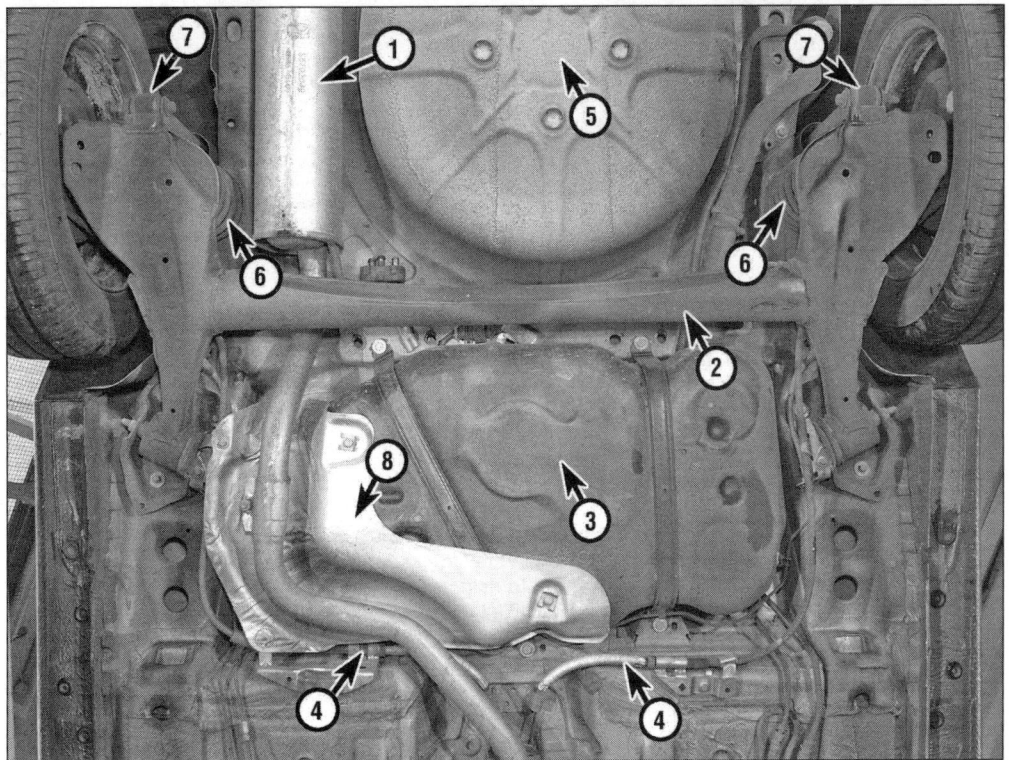

3 General Information

1 This Chapter is designed to help the home mechanic maintain his/her vehicle for safety, economy, long life and peak performance.
2 The Chapter contains a master maintenance schedule, followed by Sections dealing specifically with each task in the schedule. Visual checks, adjustments, component renewal and other helpful items are included. Refer to the accompanying illustrations of the engine compartment and the underside of the vehicle for the locations of the various components.
3 Servicing your vehicle in accordance with the mileage/time maintenance schedule and the following Sections will provide a planned maintenance programme, which should result in a long and reliable service life. This is a comprehensive plan, so maintaining some items but not others at the specified service intervals, will not produce the same results.
4 As you service your vehicle, you will discover that many of the procedures can – and should – be grouped together, because of the particular procedure being performed, or because of the proximity of two otherwise-unrelated components to one another. For example, if the vehicle is raised for any reason, the exhaust can be inspected at the same time as the suspension and steering components.

5 The first step in this maintenance programme is to prepare yourself before the actual work begins. Read through all the Sections relevant to the work to be carried out, then make a list and gather all the parts and tools required. If a problem is encountered, seek advice from a parts specialist, or a dealer service department.

4 Regular maintenance

1 If, from the time the vehicle is new, the routine maintenance schedule is followed closely, and frequent checks are made of fluid levels and high-wear items, as suggested throughout this manual, the engine will be kept in relatively good running condition, and the need for additional work will be minimised.
2 It is possible that there will be times when the engine is running poorly due to the lack of regular maintenance. This is even more likely if a used vehicle, which has not received regular and frequent maintenance checks, is purchased. In such cases, additional work may need to be carried out, outside of the regular maintenance intervals.
3 If engine wear is suspected, a compression test, or leakdown test will provide valuable information regarding the overall performance of the main internal components. Such a test can be used as a basis to decide on the extent of the work to be carried out. If, for example,

the test indicates serious internal engine wear, conventional maintenance as described in this Chapter will not greatly improve the performance of the engine, and may prove a waste of time and money, unless extensive overhaul work is carried out first.
4 The following series of operations are those most often required to improve the performance of a generally poor-running engine:

Primary operations

a) Clean, inspect and test the battery (refer to 'Weekly checks').
b) Check all the engine-related fluids (refer to 'Weekly checks').
c) Check the condition and tension of the auxiliary drivebelt (Section 23).
d) Check the condition of the air cleaner element, and renew if necessary (Section 30).
e) Renew the fuel filter (Section 22).
f) Check the condition of all hoses, and check for fluid leaks (Section 6).
5 If the above operations do not prove fully effective, carry out the following secondary operations:

Secondary operations

6 All items listed under Primary operations, plus the following:
a) Check the charging system (refer to Chapter 5A).
b) Check the pre/post-heating system (refer to Chapter 5A).
c) Check the fuel, exhaust and emission control systems (refer to Chapter 4B or 4C)

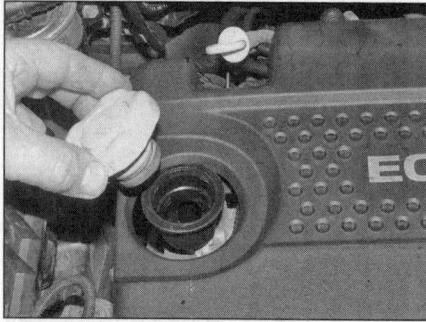

5.4 Remove the oil filler cap from the filler housing

5.5 Sump drain plug

5.7 Oil filter location

Every 10 000 miles or 6 months

5 Engine oil and filter renewal

> **HAYNES HiNT**
> *Frequent oil and filter changes are the most important preventative maintenance procedures which can be undertaken by the DIY owner. As engine oil ages, it becomes diluted and contaminated, which leads to premature engine wear.*

1 Before starting this procedure, gather together all the necessary tools and materials. Also make sure that you have plenty of clean rags and newspapers handy, to mop-up any spills. Ideally, the engine oil should be warm, as it will drain more easily, and more built-up sludge will be removed with it. Take care not to touch the exhaust or any other hot parts of the engine when working under the vehicle. To avoid any possibility of scalding, and to protect yourself from possible skin irritants and other harmful contaminants in used engine oils, it is advisable to wear gloves when carrying out this work.
2 Access to the underside of the vehicle will be greatly improved if it can be raised on a lift, driven onto ramps, or jacked up

and supported on axle stands (see *Jacking and vehicle support*). Whichever method is chosen, make sure that the vehicle remains level, or if it is at an angle, that the drain plug is at the lowest point. Where fitted, remove the screws and clips and remove the engine undertray for access.
3 To gain access to the oil filter, remove the air cleaner and intake duct as described in Chapter 4B, Section 3.
4 Remove the oil filler cap from the oil filler housing on the top of the engine **(see illustration)**.
5 Using a spanner, or preferably a suitable socket and bar, slacken the drain plug about half a turn **(see illustration)**. Position the draining container under the drain plug, then remove the plug completely **(see Haynes Hint)**.

> **HAYNES HiNT**
> *As the drain plug threads release, move it sharply away so the stream of oil issuing from the sump runs into the container, not up your sleeve.*

6 Allow some time for the oil to drain, noting that it may be necessary to reposition the container as the oil flow slows to a trickle.
7 Position another container under the oil filter located at the front of the engine **(see illustration)**.

8 Using a large socket, unscrew the cover and remove it from the top of the oil filter housing. Lift out the old filter element.
9 Wipe clean the oil filter cover and the filter housing, then insert the new filter into the housing.
10 Renew the sealing ring on the oil filter cover, and lubricate the new sealing ring with clean engine oil **(see illustrations)**. Refit the oil filter cover and tighten it to the specified torque.
11 Refit the air cleaner assembly and intake duct as described in Chapter 4B, Section 3.
12 After all the oil has drained, wipe the drain plug and the sealing washer/O-ring with a clean rag. Examine the condition of the sealing washer/O-ring, and renew it if it shows signs of damage which may prevent an oil-tight seal. Clean the area around the drain plug opening, and refit the plug complete with the washer/O-ring. Tighten the plug to the specified torque, using a torque wrench.
13 Remove the old oil and all tools from under the vehicle then refit the undertray (where applicable) and lower the vehicle to the ground.
14 Fill the engine through the filler tube using the correct grade and type of oil (refer to *Weekly checks* for details of topping-up). Pour in half the specified quantity of oil first, then wait a few minutes for the oil to drain into the sump. Continue to add oil, a small quantity at a time, until the level is up to the lower mark on the dipstick. Adding approximately a further 1.0 litre will bring the level up to the upper mark on the dipstick.
15 Start the engine and run it until it reaches normal operating temperature. While the engine is warming-up, check for leaks around the oil filter and the sump drain plug.
16 Stop the engine, and wait at least five minutes for the oil to settle in the sump once more. With the new oil circulated and the filter now completely full, recheck the level on the dipstick, and add more oil as necessary.
17 Dispose of the used engine oil and filter safely, with reference to *General repair procedures*. Do not discard the old filter with domestic household waste. The facility for waste oil disposal provided by many local council refuse tips and/or recycling centres generally has a filter receptacle alongside.

5.10a Renew the sealing ring on the oil filter cover...

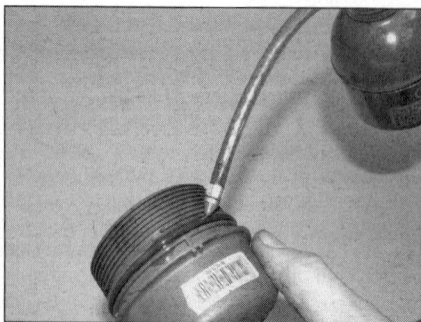

5.10b ...and lubricate the new sealing ring

Every 20 000 miles or 12 months

6 Hose and fluid leak check

Note: *Also refer to Section 10.*

1 Visually inspect the engine joint faces, gaskets and seals for any signs of water or oil leaks. Pay particular attention to the areas around the camshaft cover, cylinder head, oil filter and sump joint faces. Similarly, check the transmission and (where applicable) the air conditioning compressor for oil leakage. Bear in mind that, over a period of time, some very slight seepage from these areas is to be expected; what you are really looking for is any indication of a serious leak. Should a leak be found, renew the offending gasket or oil seal by referring to the appropriate Chapters in this manual.

2 Also check the security and condition of all the engine-related pipes and hoses. Ensure that all cable ties or securing clips are in place, and in good condition. Clips which are broken or missing can lead to chafing of the hoses pipes or wiring, which could cause more serious problems in the future.

3 Carefully check the radiator hoses and heater hoses along their entire length. Renew any hose which is cracked, swollen or deteriorated. Cracks will show up better if the hose is squeezed. Pay close attention to the hose clips that secure the hoses to the cooling system components. Hose clips can pinch and puncture hoses, resulting in cooling system leaks. If wire-type hose clips are used, it may be a good idea to update them with screw-type clips.

4 Inspect all the cooling system components (hoses, joint faces, etc) for leaks. Where any problems of this nature are found on system components, renew the component or gasket with reference to Chapter 3.

5 With the vehicle raised, inspect the fuel tank and filler neck for punctures, cracks and other damage. The connection between the filler neck and tank is especially critical. Sometimes, a rubber filler neck or connecting hose will leak due to loose retaining clamps or deteriorated rubber.

6 Carefully check all rubber hoses and metal or plastic fuel lines leading away from the fuel tank. Check for loose connections, deteriorated hoses, crimped lines and other damage. Pay particular attention to the vent pipes and hoses, which often loop up around the filler neck and can become blocked or crimped. Follow the lines to the front of the vehicle, carefully inspecting them all the way. Renew damaged sections as necessary. Similarly, whilst the vehicle is raised, take the opportunity to inspect all underbody brake fluid pipes and hoses.

7 From within the engine compartment, check the security of all fuel hose attachments and pipe unions, and inspect the fuel hoses and vacuum hoses for kinks, chafing and deterioration.

7 Fuel filter water draining

Caution: Before starting any work on the fuel filter, wipe clean the filter assembly and the area around it; it is essential that no dirt or other foreign matter is allowed into the system. Obtain a suitable container into which the filter can be drained and place rags or similar material under the filter assembly to catch any spillages. Do not allow diesel fuel to contaminate components such as the alternator and starter motor, the coolant hoses and engine mountings, and any wiring.

1 The fuel filter is located at the rear of the engine compartment, towards the right-hand side of the bulkhead.

2 Attach a suitable length of plastic or rubber tube to the drain screw located on top of the fuel filter, ensuring that the tube is a secure fit on the drain screw **(see illustration)**. Place the other end of the tube in a suitable container.

3 Unscrew the drain screw approximately two turns **(see illustration)**.

4 Switch on the ignition for approximately 20 seconds. The in-tank fuel pump will pressurise the system and force water out of the drain screw outlet.

5 On completion, switch off the ignition and tighten the drain screw. Remove the drain tube and dispose of the drained water/fuel safely.

8 Front brake pad and disc check

1 Firmly apply the handbrake, then jack up the front of the vehicle and support it securely on axle stands (see *Jacking and vehicle support*). Remove the front roadwheels.

2 For a quick check, the pad thickness can be carried out via the inspection hole on the caliper **(see Haynes Hint)**. Using a steel rule, measure the thickness of the pad friction linings. This must not be less than that indicated in the Specifications.

3 The view through the caliper inspection hole gives a rough indication of the state of the brake pads. For a comprehensive check, the brake pads should be removed and cleaned. The operation of the caliper can then also be checked, and the condition of the brake disc itself can be fully examined on both sides. Chapter 9, Section 6 contains a detailed description of how the brake disc should be checked for wear and/or damage.

4 If any pad's friction material is worn to the specified thickness or less, all four pads must be renewed as a set. Refer to Chapter 9, Section 4 for details.

5 On completion, refit the roadwheels and lower the vehicle to the ground.

9 Rear brake shoe check

1 Chock the front wheels, then jack up the rear of the vehicle, and support it securely on axle stands (see *Jacking and vehicle support*).

2 For a quick check, the thickness of friction material remaining on one of the brake shoes can be observed through the hole in the

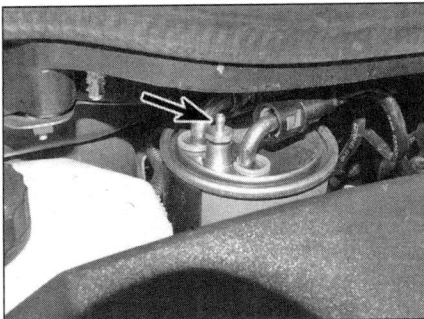

7.2 Fuel filter water drain screw

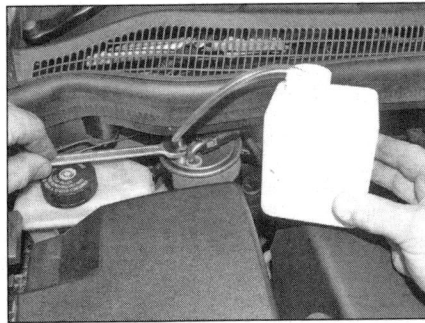

7.3 Unscrew the drain screw approximately two turns

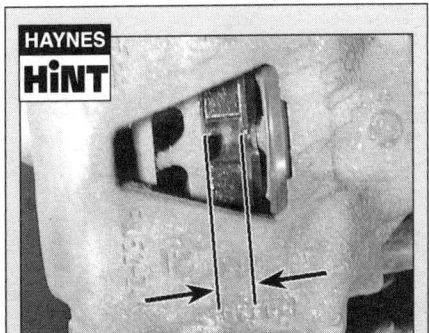

HAYNES HINT

For a quick check, the thickness of friction material remaining on the inner brake pad can be measured through the aperture in the caliper body.

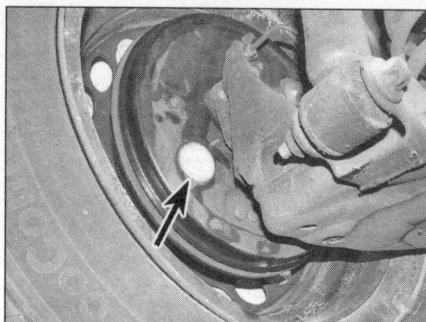

9.2 The rear brake shoe friction material thickness can be observed by prising out the backplate sealing grommet

brake backplate which is exposed by prising out the sealing grommet **(see illustration)**. If a rod of the same diameter as the specified minimum friction material thickness is placed against the shoe friction material, the amount of wear can be assessed. An electric torch or inspection light will probably be required. If the friction material on any shoe is worn down to the specified minimum thickness or less, all four shoes must be renewed as a set.

3 For a comprehensive check, the brake drum should be removed and cleaned. This will allow the wheel cylinders to be checked, and the condition of the brake drum itself to be fully examined (see Chapter 9, Section 7).

10 Brake fluid pipe and hose check

1 The brake hydraulic system includes a number of metal pipes, which run from the master cylinder to the hydraulic modulator of the anti-lock braking system (ABS) and then to the front and rear brake assemblies. Flexible hoses are fitted between the pipes and the front and rear brake assemblies, to allow for steering and suspension movement.

2 When checking the system, first look for signs of leakage at the pipe or hose unions, then examine the flexible hoses for signs of cracking, chafing or deterioration of the rubber. Bend the hoses sharply between the fingers (but do not actually bend them double, or the casing may be damaged) and check

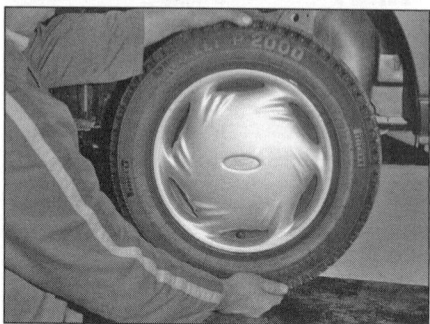

11.4 Check for wear in the hub bearings by grasping the wheel and trying to rock it

that this does not reveal previously-hidden cracks, cuts or splits. Check that the pipes and hoses are securely fastened in their clips.

3 Carefully working along the length of the metal pipes, look for dents, kinks, damage of any sort, or corrosion. Light corrosion can be polished off, but if the depth of pitting is significant, the pipe must be renewed.

11 Front suspension and steering check

1 Apply the handbrake, then raise the front of the vehicle and securely support it on axle stands (see *Jacking and vehicle support*).

2 Inspect the balljoint dust covers and the steering gear gaiters for splits, chafing or deterioration.

3 Any wear of these components will cause loss of lubricant, and may allow water to enter the components, resulting in rapid deterioration of the balljoints or steering gear.

4 Grasp each roadwheel at the 12 o'clock and 6 o'clock positions, and try to rock it **(see illustration)**. Very slight free play may be felt, but if the movement is appreciable, further investigation is necessary to determine the source. Continue rocking the wheel while an assistant depresses the footbrake. If the movement is now eliminated or significantly reduced, it is likely that the hub bearings are at fault. If the free play is still evident with the footbrake depressed, then there is wear in the suspension joints or mountings.

5 Now grasp each wheel at the 9 o'clock and 3 o'clock positions, and try to rock it as before. Any movement felt now may again be caused by wear in the hub bearings or the steering track rod end balljoints. If the track rod end balljoint is worn, the visual movement will be obvious.

6 Using a large screwdriver or flat bar, check for wear in the suspension mounting bushes by levering between the relevant suspension component and its attachment point. Some movement is to be expected, as the mountings are made of rubber, but excessive wear should be obvious. Also check the condition of any visible rubber bushes, looking for splits, cracks or contamination of the rubber.

12.2 Check the condition of the driveshaft gaiters (1) and retaining clips (2)

7 Check for any signs of fluid leakage around the suspension struts, or from the rubber gaiters around the piston rods. Should any fluid be noticed, the suspension strut is defective internally, and should be renewed. **Note:** *Suspension struts should always be renewed in pairs on the same axle.*

8 With the vehicle standing on its wheels, have an assistant turn the steering wheel back-and-forth about an eighth of a turn each way. There should be very little, if any, lost movement between the steering wheel and roadwheels. If this is not the case, closely observe the joints and mountings previously described. In addition, check the steering column universal joints for wear, and also check the rack-and-pinion steering gear itself.

9 The efficiency of each suspension strut may be checked by bouncing the vehicle at each front corner. Generally speaking, the body will return to its normal position and stop after being depressed. If it rises and returns on a rebound, the suspension strut is probably suspect. Also examine the suspension strut upper mountings for any signs of wear.

12 Driveshaft check

1 Firmly apply the handbrake, then jack up the front of the car and support it securely on axle stands (see *Jacking and vehicle support*).

2 Turn the steering onto full lock then slowly rotate the roadwheel. Inspect the condition of the outer constant velocity (CV) joint rubber gaiters while squeezing the gaiters to open out the folds **(see illustration)**. Check for signs of cracking, splits or deterioration of the rubber which may allow the grease to escape and lead to water and grit entry into the joint. Also check the security and condition of the retaining clips. Repeat these checks on the inner CV joints. If any damage or deterioration is found, the gaiters should be renewed as described in Chapter 8, Section 3.

3 At the same time, check the general condition of the CV joints themselves by first holding the driveshaft and attempting to rotate the wheel. Repeat this check by holding the inner joint and attempting to rotate the driveshaft. Any appreciable movement indicates wear in the joints, wear in the driveshaft splines or loose driveshaft retaining nut.

13 Exhaust system check

1 With the engine cold (at least an hour after the vehicle has been driven), check the complete exhaust system from the engine to the end of the tailpipe. The exhaust system is most easily checked with the vehicle raised on a hoist, or suitably-supported on axle

stands, so that the exhaust components are readily visible and accessible (see *Jacking and vehicle*).

2 Check the exhaust pipes and connections for evidence of leaks, severe corrosion and damage. Make sure that all brackets and mountings are in good condition, and that all relevant nuts and bolts are tight. Leakage at any of the joints or in other parts of the system will usually show up as a black sooty stain in the vicinity of the leak.

3 Rattles and other noises can often be traced to the exhaust system, especially the brackets and mountings **(see illustration)**. Try to move the pipes and silencers. If the components are able to come into contact with the body or suspension parts, secure the system with new mountings. Otherwise separate the joints (if possible) and twist the pipes as necessary to provide additional clearance.

14 Rear suspension check

1 Chock the front wheels, then jack up the rear of the vehicle and support securely on axle stands (see *Jacking and vehicle support*).
2 Inspect the rear suspension components for any signs of obvious wear or damage. Pay particular attention to the rubber mounting bushes, and renew if necessary (see Chapter 10).
3 Grasp each roadwheel at the 12 o'clock and 6 o'clock positions **(see illustration 10.4)**, and try to rock it. Any excess movement indicates wear in the wheel hub bearings. Wear may also be accompanied by a rumbling sound when the wheel is spun, or a noticeable roughness if the wheel is turned slowly. The hub bearing can be renewed as described in Chapter 10, Section 9.
4 Check for any signs of fluid leakage around the shock absorber bodies. Should any fluid be noticed, the shock absorber is defective internally, and should be renewed.
Note: *Shock absorbers should always be renewed in pairs on the same axle.*
5 With the vehicle standing on its wheels, the efficiency of each shock absorber may be checked by bouncing the vehicle at each rear corner. Generally speaking, the body will return to its normal position and stop after being depressed. If it rises and returns on a rebound, the shock absorber is probably suspect.

15 Bodywork and underbody condition check

Note: *This work should be carried out by a Vauxhall/Opel dealer in order to validate the vehicle warranty. The work includes a thorough inspection of the vehicle paintwork and underbody for damage and corrosion.*

Bodywork damage and corrosion check

1 Once the car has been washed, and all tar spots and other surface blemishes have been cleaned off, carefully check all paintwork, looking closely for chips or scratches. Pay particular attention to vulnerable areas such as the front panels (bonnet and spoiler), and around the wheel arches. Any damage to the paintwork must be rectified as soon as possible, to comply with the terms of the manufacturer's anti-corrosion warranties; check with a Vauxhall/Opel dealer for details.
2 If a chip or light scratch is found which is recent and still free from rust, it can be touched-up using the appropriate touch-up stick which can be obtained from Vauxhall/Opel dealers. Any more serious damage, or rusted stone chips, can be repaired as described in Chapter 11, Section 4, but if damage or corrosion is so severe that a panel must be renewed, seek professional advice as soon as possible.
3 Always check that the door and ventilation opening drain holes and pipes are completely clear, so that water can drain out.

Corrosion protection check

4 The wax-based underbody protective coating should be inspected annually, preferably just prior to Winter, when the underbody should be washed down as thoroughly as possible without disturbing the protective coating. Any damage to the coating should be repaired using a suitable wax-based sealer. If any of the body panels are disturbed for repair or renewal, do not forget to re-apply the coating. Wax should be injected into door cavities, sills and box sections, to maintain the level of protection provided by the vehicle manufacturer – seek the advice of a Vauxhall/Opel dealer.

16 Roadwheel bolt tightness check

1 Where applicable, remove the wheel trims from the wheels.
2 Using a torque wrench on each wheel bolt in turn, ensure that the bolts are tightened to the specified torque.
3 Where applicable, refit the wheel trims on completion, making sure they are fitted correctly.

17 Hinge and lock lubrication

1 Work around the vehicle and lubricate the hinges of the bonnet, doors and tailgate with a light machine oil.
2 Lightly lubricate the bonnet release mechanism and exposed section of inner cable with a smear of grease.

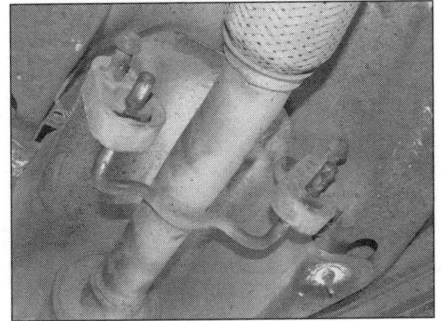

13.3 Exhaust mountings

3 Check the security and operation of all hinges, latches and locks, adjusting them where required. Check the operation of the central locking system.
4 Check the condition and operation of the bonnet and tailgate support struts, renewing them both if either is leaking or no longer able to support the bonnet/tailgate securely when raised.

18 Electrical systems check

1 Check the operation of all the electrical equipment, ie, lights, direction indicators, horn, etc. Refer to the appropriate sections of Chapter 12 for details if any of the circuits are found to be inoperative.
2 Note that the stop-light switch is described in Chapter 9.
3 Check all accessible wiring connectors, harnesses and retaining clips for security, and for signs of chafing or damage. Rectify any faults found.

19 Road test

Instruments and electrical equipment

1 Check the operation of all instruments, warning lights and electrical equipment.
2 Make sure that all instruments read correctly, and switch on all electrical equipment in turn, to check that it functions properly.

Steering and suspension

3 Check for any abnormalities in the steering, suspension, handling or road 'feel'.
4 Drive the vehicle, and check that there are no unusual vibrations or noises.
5 Check that the steering feels positive, with no excessive 'sloppiness', or roughness, and check for any suspension noises when cornering and driving over bumps.

Drivetrain

6 Check the performance of the engine, clutch, transmission and driveshafts.

7 Listen for any unusual noises from the engine, clutch and transmission.

8 Make sure that the engine runs smoothly when idling, and that there is no hesitation when accelerating.

9 Check that, where applicable, the clutch action is smooth and progressive, that the drive is taken up smoothly, and that the pedal travel is not excessive. Also listen for any noises when the clutch pedal is depressed.

10 Check that all gears can be engaged smoothly without noise, and that the gear lever action is smooth and not abnormally vague or 'notchy'.

11 Listen for a metallic clicking sound from the front of the vehicle, as the vehicle is driven slowly in a circle with the steering on full-lock. Carry out this check in both directions. If a clicking noise is heard, this indicates wear in a driveshaft joint (see Chapter 8).

Braking system

12 Make sure that the vehicle does not pull to one side when braking.

13 Check that there is no vibration through the steering when braking. Note: Under heavy braking on models equipped with ABS, vibration may be felt through the brake pedal. This is a normal feature of ABS operation, and does not constitute a fault

14 Check that the handbrake operates correctly, without excessive movement of the lever, and that it holds the vehicle stationary on a slope.

15 Test the operation of the brake servo unit as follows. Depress the footbrake four or five times to exhaust the vacuum, then start the engine. As the engine starts, there should be a noticeable 'give' in the brake pedal as vacuum builds-up. Allow the engine to run for at least two minutes, and then switch it off. If the brake pedal is now depressed again, it should be possible to detect a hiss from the servo as the pedal is depressed. After about four or five applications, no further hissing should be heard, and the pedal should feel considerably harder.

20 Service interval indicator reset

1 With the ignition switched off, depress and hold the trip odometer reset button located on the instrument panel. After approximately 3 seconds, the message 'InSP 0' will appear. Keep the reset button depressed and also depress the brake pedal.

2 Switch on the ignition, with the reset button and brake pedal still depressed, and 'InSP – – – –' will appear, flashing, in the display. Keep the reset button and brake pedal depressed until the display changes.

3 After approximately 10 seconds the display will change to show the maximum mileage before the next required service. Release the reset button and the brake pedal, then switch off the ignition. When the button and brake pedal are released, the odometer will appear again.

Every 40 000 miles or 2 years

21 Pollen filter renewal

1 Remove the glovebox (see Chapter 11, Section 26).

2 Release the plastic expanding rivet and remove the passenger's side footwell air duct **(see illustration)**.

3 Unclip the pollen filter access cover from the side of the heater/ventilation air distribution housing **(see illustration)**.

4 Withdraw the pollen filter from the housing **(see illustration)**.

5 Fit the new filter using a reversal of the removal procedure; make sure that the filter is fitted the correct way up as indicated on the edge of the filter.

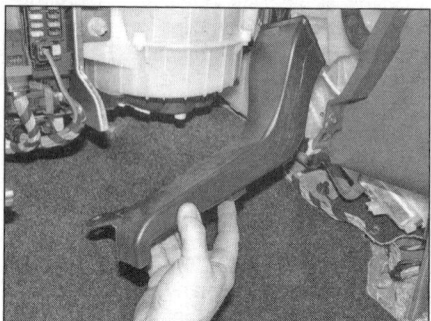

21.2 Release the expanding rivet and remove the passenger's side footwell air duct

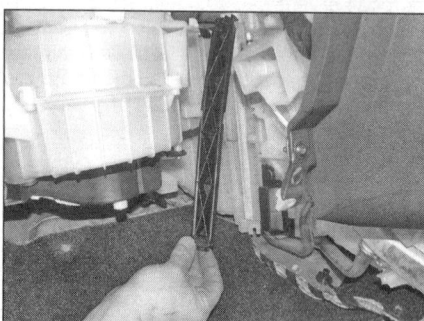

21.3 Unclip the pollen filter access cover from the side of the air distribution housing

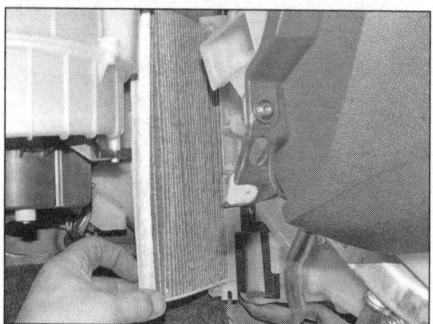

21.4 Withdraw the pollen filter from the housing

22.3 Undo the retaining bolt and lift off the fuel filter mounting bracket clamp

22 Fuel filter renewal

Caution: Before starting any work on the fuel filter, wipe clean the filter assembly and the area around it; it is essential that no dirt or other foreign matter is allowed into the system. Obtain a suitable container into which the filter can be drained and place rags or similar material under the filter assembly to catch any spillages. Do not allow diesel fuel to contaminate components such as the starter motor, the coolant hoses and engine mountings, and any wiring.

1 The fuel filter is located at the rear of the engine compartment, towards the right-hand side of the bulkhead.

2 Remove the air cleaner assembly and air inlet hose as described in Chapter 4B, Section 3.

3 Undo the bolt securing the fuel filter mounting bracket clamp and lift off the clamp **(see illustration)**. Lift the filter out of the mounting bracket.

4 Detach the two fuel hose quick-release connectors and remove the hoses from the fuel filter. A Vauxhall/Opel special tool (KM-796-A) is available to disconnect the hose connectors, but provided care is taken, the connections can be released using two screwdrivers, a pair of long-nosed pliers, or similar, to depress the retaining tangs **(see illustration)**. Suitably cover or plug the open hose connections to prevent dirt entry.

5 Disconnect the heater element/water level sensor wiring connector from the base of the filter, then remove the filter from the car **(see illustration)**.

6 Unscrew the heater element/water level sensor from the base of the filter and transfer it to the new filter. Tighten the element/sensor securely.

7 Connect the fuel hoses and wiring connector to the new filter then locate the filter in the mounting bracket. Make sure the raised projection on the top of the filter engages with the lug on the mounting bracket, then fit and tighten the mounting bracket clamp bolt.

8 Refit the air cleaner assembly and air inlet hose as described in Chapter 4B, Section 3.

9 Bleed the fuel system as described in Chapter 4B, Section 5 and check all disturbed components to ensure that there are no leaks (of air or fuel) when the engine is restarted.

10 On completion, safely dispose of the drained fuel.

23 Auxiliary drivebelt condition check

Note: *The manufacturers recommend that the tensioner roller is checked and if necessary renewed at the same time as the drivebelt.*

Checking

1 Due to their function and material make-up, drivebelts are prone to failure after a long period of time and should therefore be inspected regularly.

2 Apply the handbrake, then jack up the front of the vehicle and support it on axle stands (see *Jacking and vehicle support*). Remove the right-hand front roadwheel and the wheel arch liner cover for access to the right-hand side of the engine.

3 With the engine stopped, inspect the full length of the drivebelt for cracks and separation of the belt plies. It will be necessary to turn the engine (using a spanner or socket and bar on the crankshaft pulley bolt) so that the belt can be inspected thoroughly. Twist the belt between the pulleys so that both

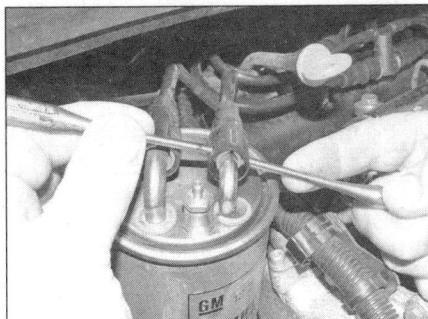

22.4 Using two screwdrivers to detach the fuel hose quick-release connectors

sides can be viewed. Also check for fraying, and glazing which gives the belt a shiny appearance. Check the pulleys for nicks, cracks, distortion and corrosion. If the belt shows signs of wear or damage, it should be renewed as a precaution against breakage in service.

Renewal

4 If not already done, apply the handbrake, then jack up the front of the vehicle and support it on axle stands (see *Jacking and vehicle support*). Remove the right-hand front roadwheel and the wheel arch liner cover for access to the right-hand side of the engine.

5 For additional working clearance, remove the air cleaner assembly and air inlet hose as described in Chapter 4B, Section 3.

6 If the drivebelt is to be re-used, mark it to indicate its normal running direction.

7 Using a spanner on the pulley centre bolt, turn the tensioner clockwise, against the spring tension. Hold the tensioner in this position by inserting a suitable locking pin or drill bit through the special hole provided **(see illustration)**.

8 Slip the drivebelt from the pulleys.

9 Locate the new drivebelt on the pulleys in the correct routing. If the drivebelt is being re-used, make sure it is fitted the correct way around.

10 Turn back the tensioner and remove the locking pin/drill bit, then release it, making

22.5 Disconnect the heater element/water level sensor wiring connector from the base of the fuel filter

sure that the drivebelt ribs locate correctly on each of the pulley grooves.

11 Refit the air cleaner housing (if removed), then refit the wheel arch liner and roadwheel, and lower the vehicle to the ground.

24 Handbrake operation and adjustment check

1 With the vehicle on a slight slope, apply the handbrake lever by up to 3 clicks of the ratchet, and check that it holds the vehicle stationary, then release the lever and check that there is no resistance to movement of the vehicle.

2 If necessary, adjust the handbrake as follows.

3 Chock the front wheels then jack up the rear of the car and securely support it on axle stands (see *Jacking and vehicle support*).

4 Fully depress, then release the brake pedal at least five times. Similarly, fully apply, then release the handbrake at least five times.

5 Unclip the handbrake lever gaiter from the centre console and fold it up the handbrake lever **(see illustration)**. The handbrake cable adjuster nut is situated by the handbrake lever inside the vehicle.

6 Move the handbrake lever to the fully released position, then turn the cable adjuster nut anti-clockwise to remove all tension from the cables **(see illustration)**.

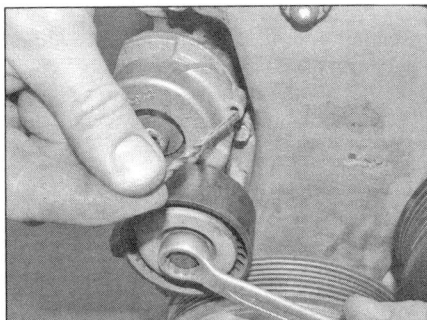

23.7 Lock the tensioner in the released position by inserting a drill bit or similar through the hole provided

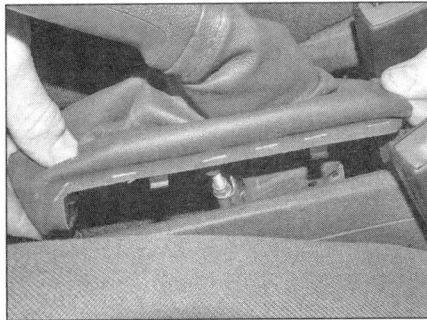

24.5 Unclip the handbrake lever gaiter from the centre console...

24.6...for access to the handbrake cable adjuster nut

7 With the handbrake lever set on the second notch of the ratchet mechanism, rotate the adjuster nut clockwise until a reasonable amount of force is required to turn each wheel. Note: The force required should be equal for each wheel.

8 Now pull the handbrake lever up to the third notch of the ratchet mechanism and check that both rear wheels are locked. Once this

is so, fully release the handbrake lever and check that the wheels rotate freely. Check the adjustment by applying the handbrake fully whilst counting the clicks emitted from the handbrake ratchet and, if necessary, re-adjust.

9 On completion of adjustment, refit the handbrake lever gaiter, then lower the vehicle to the ground.

25 Headlight beam alignment check

1 Accurate adjustment of the headlight beam is only possible using optical beam- setting equipment, and this work should therefore be carried out by a Vauxhall/Opel dealer or service station with the necessary facilities. Refer to Chapter 12, Section 8 for further information.

Every 2 years

26 Remote control battery renewal

1 Using a screwdriver, prise the battery cover from the ignition key fob **(see illustration)**.
2 Note how the circular battery is fitted, then carefully remove it from the contacts **(see illustration)**.
3 Fit the new battery (type CR 2032) and refit the cover making sure that it clips fully onto the base.
4 After changing the battery, lock and unlock the driver's door with the key in the lock, then switch on the ignition to synchronise the remote control unit.

27 Hydraulic fluid renewal

⚠ *Warning: Hydraulic fluid can harm your eyes and damage painted surfaces, so use extreme caution when handling and pouring it. Do not use fluid that has been standing open for some time, as it absorbs moisture from the air. Excess moisture can cause a dangerous loss of braking effectiveness.*

1 The procedure is similar to that for the bleeding of the hydraulic system as described in Chapter 9, Section 2 (brake) and Chapter 6, Section 2 (clutch).
2 Working as described in Chapter 9, open the first bleed screw in the sequence, and pump the brake pedal gently until nearly

all the old fluid has been emptied from the master cylinder reservoir. Top-up to the MAX level with new fluid, and continue pumping until only the new fluid remains in the reservoir, and new fluid can be seen emerging from the bleed screw. Tighten the screw, and top the reservoir level up to the MAX level line.

> **HAYNES HiNT** *Old hydraulic fluid is invariably much darker in colour than the new, making it easy to distinguish the two.*

3 Work through all the remaining bleed screws in the sequence until new fluid can be seen at all of them. Be careful to keep the master cylinder reservoir topped-up to above the MIN level at all times, or air may enter the system and greatly increase the length of the task.
4 Bleed the fluid from the clutch hydraulic system as described in Chapter 6.
5 When the operation is complete, check that all bleed screws are securely tightened, and that their dust caps are refitted. Wash off all traces of spilt fluid, and recheck the master cylinder reservoir fluid level.
6 Check the operation of the brakes and clutch before taking the car on the road.

28 Coolant renewal

Note: *Vauxhall/Opel do not specify renewal intervals for the antifreeze mixture, as the mixture used to fill the system when*

the vehicle is new is designed to last the lifetime of the vehicle. However, it is strongly recommended that the coolant is renewed at the intervals specified in the Maintenance schedule as a precaution against possible engine corrosion problems. This is particularly advisable if the coolant has been renewed using an antifreeze other than that specified by Vauxhall/Opel. With many antifreeze types, the corrosion inhibitors become progressively less effective with age. It is up to the individual owner whether or not to follow this advice.

⚠ *Warning: Wait until the engine is cold before starting this procedure. Do not allow antifreeze to come in contact with your skin, or with the painted surfaces of the vehicle. Rinse off spills immediately with plenty of water. Never leave antifreeze lying around in an open container, or in a puddle in the driveway or on the garage floor. Children and pets are attracted by its sweet smell, but antifreeze can be fatal if ingested.*

Cooling system draining

1 To drain the cooling system, first cover the expansion tank cap with a wad of rag, and slowly turn the cap anti-clockwise to relieve the pressure in the cooling system (a hissing sound will normally be heard). Wait until any pressure remaining in the system is released, then continue to turn the cap until it can be removed.
2 Remove the engine undertray (where fitted), then position a suitable container beneath the left-hand side of the radiator.
3 The coolant drain plug is located at the bottom of the radiator left-hand end tank. Unscrew the drain plug and allow the coolant to drain.
4 When the flow of coolant stops, refit and tighten the drain plugs.
5 As no cylinder block drain plug is fitted, it is not possible to drain all of the coolant. Due consideration must be made for this when refilling the system, in order to maintain the correct concentration of antifreeze.
6 If the coolant has been drained for a reason other than renewal, then provided it is clean and less than two years old, it can be re-used.

Cooling system flushing

7 If coolant renewal has been neglected, or if the antifreeze mixture has become diluted, then in time, the cooling system may gradually lose

26.1 Prise the battery cover from the ignition key fob

26.2 Carefully remove the battery from the contacts

efficiency, as the coolant passages become restricted due to rust, scale deposits, and other sediment. The cooling system efficiency can be restored by flushing the system clean.

8 The radiator should be flushed independently of the engine, to avoid unnecessary contamination.

Radiator flushing

9 Disconnect the top and bottom hoses and any other relevant hoses from the radiator, with reference to Chapter 3, Section 2.

10 Insert a garden hose into the radiator top inlet. Direct a flow of clean water through the radiator, and continue flushing until clean water emerges from the radiator bottom outlet.

11 If after a reasonable period, the water still does not run clear, the radiator can be flushed with a good proprietary cleaning agent. It is important that the manufacturer's instructions are followed carefully. If the contamination is particularly bad, remove the radiator, insert the hose in the radiator bottom outlet, and reverse-flush the radiator.

Engine flushing

12 To flush the engine, the thermostat must be removed, because it will be shut, and would otherwise prevent the flow of water around the engine. The thermostat can be removed as described in Chapter 3, Section 4. Take care not to introduce dirt or debris into the system if this approach is used.

13 With the bottom hose disconnected from the radiator, insert a garden hose into the thermostat opening. Direct a clean flow of water through the engine, and continue flushing until clean water emerges from the radiator bottom hose.

14 On completion of flushing, refit the thermostat with reference to Chapter 3, and reconnect the hoses.

Cooling system filling

15 Before attempting to fill the cooling system,

make sure that all hoses and clips are in good condition, and that the clips are tight. Note that an antifreeze mixture must be used all year round, to prevent corrosion of the engine components.

16 Remove the expansion tank filler cap.

17 Working through the aperture in the top of the radiator, unscrew the bleed screw located at the upper right-hand side of the radiator **(see illustration)**.

18 Fill the system by slowly pouring the coolant into the expansion tank until it is up to the filler neck.

19 Tighten the bleed screw as soon as coolant emerges from the bleed screw orifice.

20 Refit and tighten the expansion tank filler cap.

21 Start the engine and run it at 2000 to 2500 rpm until the cooling fan switches on. Continue running the engine at between 2000 and 2500 rpm for a further 2 minutes.

22 Stop the engine, and allow it to cool, then recheck the coolant level with reference to *Weekly checks*. Top-up the level if necessary and refit the expansion tank filler cap. Refit the engine undertray (where applicable).

Antifreeze mixture

23 Always use an ethylene-glycol based antifreeze which is suitable for use in mixed-metal cooling systems.

24 Vauxhall/Opel recommend the use of silicate-free coolant (see *Lubricants and fluids* on page 0•17).

25 The quantity of antifreeze and level of protection are given in the Specifications at the start of this Chapter.

26 Before adding antifreeze, the cooling system should be completely drained, preferably flushed, and all hoses checked for condition and security.

27 After filling with antifreeze, a label should be attached to the expansion tank, stating the type and concentration of antifreeze used, and the date installed. Any subsequent

28.17 Unscrew the bleed screw located at the upper right-hand side of the radiator

topping-up should be made with the same type and concentration of antifreeze.

Caution: Do not use engine antifreeze in the windscreen/tailgate washer system, as it will cause damage to the vehicle paintwork. A screenwash additive should be added to the washer system in the quantities stated on the bottle.

29 Exhaust emission check

1 The exhaust emission check is carried out initially after 3 years, then every 2 years, however, on vehicles which are subject to intensive use (eg, taxis/hire cars/ambulances) it must be carried out annually. The check involves checking the engine management system operation by plugging an electronic tester into the system diagnostic socket to check the electronic control unit (ECU) memory for faults (see Chapter 4B).

2 In reality, if the vehicle is running correctly and the engine management warning light in the instrument panel is functioning normally, then this check need not be carried out.

Every 40 000 miles or 4 years

30 Air cleaner element renewal

1 The air cleaner is located in the front right-hand corner of the engine compartment.

2 Undo the screws and lift off the air cleaner cover, complete with upper air inlet hose **(see illustrations)**.

3 Lift out the filter element **(see illustration)**.

4 Wipe out the casing and the cover.

5 Fit the new filter, noting that the rubber locating flange should be uppermost, and secure the cover with the screws.

30.2a Undo the air cleaner cover retaining screws...

30.2b...and lift up the air cleaner cover, complete with upper air inlet hose

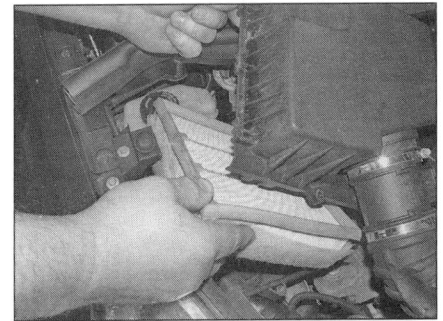

30.3 Lift out the air cleaner filter element

Every 100 000 miles or 10 years

31 Auxiliary drivebelt renewal

1 Refer to the procedures contained in Section 23.

Chapter 2 Part A
1.0 litre petrol engine in-car repair procedures

Contents

Degrees of difficulty

Easy, suitable for novice with little experience	**Fairly easy,** suitable for beginner with some experience	**Fairly difficult,** suitable for competent DIY mechanic	**Difficult,** suitable for experienced DIY mechanic	**Very difficult,** suitable for expert DIY or professional

Specifications

General

Engine type	Three-cylinder, in-line, water-cooled. Double overhead camshafts, chain-driven, acting on rocker arms and hydraulic valve lifters
Manufacturer's engine code	A10XEP (LDB)
Bore	73.40 mm
Stroke	78.60 mm
Capacity	998 cc
Firing order	1-2-3 (No 1 cylinder at timing chain end of engine)
Direction of crankshaft rotation	Clockwise (viewed from timing chain end of engine)
Compression ratio	10.5: 1

Note: *For details of engine code location, see 'Vehicle identification' in Reference.*

Lubrication system

Minimum oil pressure at 80°C	1.5 bars at idle speed
Oil pump type	Gear-type, driven directly from crankshaft
Gear-to-housing clearance (endfloat)	0.020 to 0.065 mm

Flywheel

Maximum permissible lateral run-out of starter ring gear	0.50 mm
Refinishing limit (maximum depth of material which may be removed from clutch friction surface)	0.30 mm

Torque wrench settings

	Nm	lbf ft
Air conditioning compressor to cylinder block	20	15
Auxiliary drivebelt tensioner to cylinder block:		
M8 bolt	20	15
M10 bolt	55	41
Big-end bearing cap bolts: *		
Stage 1	13	10
Stage 2	Angle-tighten a further 60°	
Stage 3	Angle-tighten a further 15°	
Camshaft bearing cap bolts	8	6
Camshaft sprocket bolt: *		
Stage 1	50	37
Stage 2	Angle-tighten a further 60°	
Catalytic converter support bracket bolts	20	15
Catalytic converter-to-exhaust manifold nuts	35	26
Coolant pump bolts	8	6
Coolant pump pulley bolts	20	15
Crankshaft pulley hub-to-crankshaft bolt: *		
Stage 1	150	111
Stage 2	Angle-tighten a further 45°	
Cylinder block baseplate to cylinder block: *		
M6 bolts:		
Stage 1	10	7
Stage 2	Angle-tighten a further 60°	
M8 bolts:		
Stage 1	25	18
Stage 2	Angle-tighten a further 60°	
Cylinder block closure bolt (for TDC setting tool)	60	44
Cylinder head bolts: *		
Stage 1	25	18
Stage 2	Angle-tighten a further 60°	
Stage 3	Angle-tighten a further 60°	
Stage 4	Angle-tighten a further 60°	
Engine mountings:		
Left-hand:		
Mounting-to-body bolts	80	59
Mounting bracket-to-transmission bracket: *		
Stage 1	80	59
Stage 2	Angle-tighten a further 45°	
Transmission bracket-to-transmission*	80	59
Rear mounting/torque link: *		
Stage 1	80	59
Stage 2	Angle-tighten a further 45°	
Rear mounting/torque link bracket-to-transmission: *		
Stage 1	80	59
Stage 2	Angle-tighten a further 45°	
Right-hand:		
Engine bracket-to-engine bolts	60	44
Mounting-to-body bolts	60	44
Mounting-to-engine bracket bolts: *		
Stage 1	80	59
Stage 2	Angle-tighten a further 45°	
Engine-to-transmission bolts	60	44
Exhaust manifold securing nuts*	20	15
Flywheel bolts: *		
Stage 1	35	26
Stage 2	Angle-tighten a further 30°	
Stage 3	Angle-tighten a further 15°	
Front subframe: *		
Stage 1	90	66
Stage 2	Angle-tighten a further 45°	
Stage 3	Angle-tighten a further 15°	
Fuel feed and return hose unions	15	11
Inlet manifold support bracket to cylinder block	20	15
Oil filter housing cap to filter housing	25	18
Oil filter housing to cylinder block	20	15

Torque wrench settings (continued)

	Nm	lbf ft
Sump to cylinder block baseplate/timing cover.	10	7
Sump to transmission	40	30
Timing chain tension rail pivot bolt.	20	15
Timing chain tensioner closure bolt (for locking pin access)	50	37
Timing cover bolts:		
M10	35	26
M6	8	6
Timing cover oil fill channel closure plug	50	37

* Use new fasteners

---

1 General Information

How to use this Chapter

1 This Part of Chapter 2 describes the repair procedures which can reasonably be carried out on the engine while it remains in the vehicle. If the engine has been removed from the vehicle and is being dismantled as described in Chapter 2D, any preliminary dismantling procedures can be ignored.

2 Note that, while it may be possible physically to overhaul items such as the piston/connecting rod assemblies while the engine is in the vehicle, such tasks are not usually carried out as separate operations, and usually require the execution of several additional procedures (not to mention the cleaning of components and of oilways); for this reason, all such tasks are classed as major overhaul procedures, and are described in Chapter 2D.

3 Chapter 2D describes the removal of the engine/transmission unit from the vehicle, and the full overhaul procedures which can then be carried out.

Engine description

4 The engine is of three-cylinder in-line type, with double overhead camshafts (DOHC). The engine is mounted transversely at the front of the vehicle with the transmission attached to its left-hand end.

5 The engine is termed a 'Twinport' engine due to the design of the inlet manifold and cylinder head combustion chambers. Vacuum operated flap valves located in the inlet manifold are opened or closed according to engine operating conditions, to create a variable venturi manifold arrangement. This system has significant advantages in terms of engine power, fuel economy and reduced exhaust emissions.

6 The crankshaft runs in four shell-type main bearings with crankshaft endfloat being controlled by thrustwashers which are an integral part of No 3 main bearing shells.

7 The connecting rods are attached to the crankshaft by horizontally-split shell-type big-end bearings. The pistons are attached to the connecting rods by gudgeon pins, which are an interference fit in the connecting rod small-end bores. The aluminium-alloy pistons are fitted with three piston rings – two compression rings and an oil control ring.

8 The camshafts are driven from the crankshaft by a hydraulically tensioned timing chain. Each cylinder has four valves (two inlet and two exhaust), operated via rocker arms which are supported at their pivot ends by hydraulic self-adjusting valve lifters (tappets). One camshaft operates the inlet valves, and the other operates the exhaust valves.

9 The inlet and exhaust valves are each closed by a single valve spring, and operate in guides pressed into the cylinder head.

10 A rotor-type oil pump is located in the timing cover attached to the cylinder block, and is driven directly from the crankshaft.

11 The coolant pump is located externally on the timing cover, and is driven by the auxiliary drivebelt.

Operations with engine in place

12 The following operations can be carried out without having to remove the engine from the vehicle.

a) *Removal and refitting of the cylinder head.*
b) *Removal and refitting of the timing cover.*
c) *Removal and refitting of the timing chain, tensioner and sprockets.*
d) *Removal and refitting of the camshafts.*
e) *Removal and refitting of the sump.*
f) *Removal and refitting of the big-end bearings, connecting rods, and pistons.**
g) *Removal and refitting of the oil pump.*
h) *Renewal of the crankshaft oil seals.*
i) *Renewal of the engine mountings.*
j) *Removal and refitting of the flywheel.*

Note: Although the operation marked with an asterisk can be carried out with the engine in the vehicle (after removal of the sump), it is preferable for the engine to be removed, in the interests of cleanliness and improved access. For this reason, the procedure is described in Chapter 2D.

2 Compression test – general information

1 When engine performance is down, or if misfiring occurs which cannot be attributed to the ignition or fuel systems, a compression test can provide diagnostic clues as to the engine's condition. If the test is performed regularly, it can give warning of trouble before any other symptoms become apparent.

2 Due to the electronic throttle control system used on these engines, a compression test can only be carried out with the engine management electronic control unit connected to Vauxhall/Opel diagnostic test equipment, or a compatible alternative unit. Without the test equipment, the throttle valve cannot be opened (as there is no accelerator cable) and the test will be inconclusive. Note that even with the accelerator pedal fully depressed, the engine management ECU will only control the throttle valve position when the engine is actually running. The test equipment independently actuates the throttle valve (irrespective of ECU commands) and opens the throttle valve fully.

3 As the equipment needed for the compression test is unlikely to be available to the home mechanic, it is recommended that the test is performed by a Vauxhall/Opel dealer, or suitably-equipped garage.

3 Camshaft cover – removal and refitting

Note: A new camshaft cover rubber seal will be required for refitting, and a suitable silicone sealant will be required to seal the timing cover-to-cylinder head upper joint.

Removal

1 Disconnect the battery negative terminal (refer to Chapter 5A, Section 4).

2 Disconnect the wiring connectors at the coolant temperature sensor, camshaft

3.2a Disconnect the wiring connectors at the airflow meter...

3.2b...coolant temperature sensor (A) and camshaft position sensor (B)...

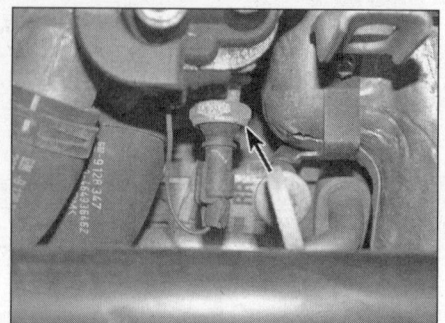

3.2c...and at the oil pressure switch

3.3 Lift the wiring harness trough from the camshaft cover and move it to one side

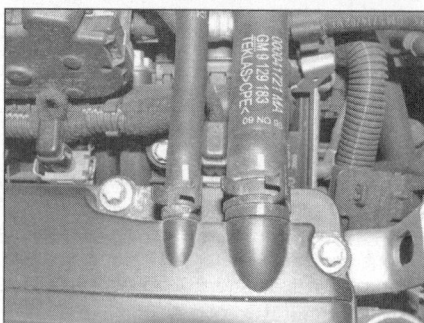

3.4 Breather hoses on the rear of the camshaft cover

3.7 Lift the camshaft cover up and off the cylinder head

position sensor and oil pressure switch (see illustrations).

3 Lift the wiring harness trough from the camshaft cover and move it to one side (see illustration).

4 Disconnect the two breather hoses at the rear of the camshaft cover (see illustration).

5 Remove the ignition module from the centre of the camshaft cover as described in Chapter 5B, Section 3.

6 Progressively slacken the camshaft cover retaining bolts until they are all fully unscrewed. Note that the bolts are captive and will remain in place in the cover as it is removed.

7 Lift the camshaft cover up and off the cylinder head (see illustration).

Refitting

8 Remove the old seal from the camshaft cover, then examine the inside of the cover for a build-up of oil sludge or any other contamination, and if necessary clean the cover with paraffin, or a water-soluble solvent. Dry the cover thoroughly before refitting.

9 Check the condition of the rubber seals on the camshaft cover retaining bolts. If the seals are in any way damaged or deformed, carefully tap the bolts out of the camshaft cover using a soft-faced mallet and fit new seals to the bolts (see illustrations).

10 Fit a new rubber seal to the cover ensuring that it is correctly located in the camshaft cover groove (see illustration).

11 Inspect the joint between the timing cover and cylinder head, and cut off any projecting timing cover gasket using a sharp knife (see illustration).

12 Thoroughly clean the mating faces of the camshaft cover and cylinder head.

13 Apply a 2 mm diameter bead of silicone

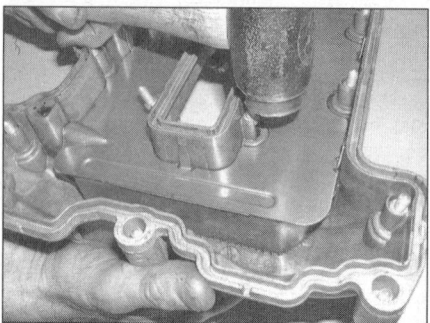

3.9a If necessary, tap the bolts out of the camshaft cover...

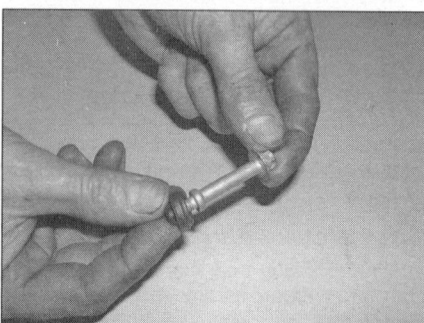

3.9b...and fit new seals to the bolts

3.10 Fit a new rubber seal to the camshaft cover ensuring that it is correctly located in the cover groove

3.11 Cut off any projecting timing cover gasket using a sharp knife

sealant to the joint between the timing cover and cylinder head on each side **(see illustration)**.

14 Locate the camshaft cover on the cylinder head and screw in the retaining bolts. Progressively and evenly tighten the retaining bolts securely.

15 Refit the ignition module from the centre of the camshaft cover as described in Chapter 5B, Section 3.

16 Reconnect the two breather hoses to the right-hand rear of the camshaft cover.

17 Locate the wiring harness trough in the camshaft cover slots then reconnect the coolant temperature sensor, camshaft position sensor and oil pressure switch wiring connectors.

18 Reconnect the battery negative terminal on completion.

4 Valve timing – checking and adjustment

Note: *Certain special tools will be required for this operation. Read through the entire procedure to familiarise yourself with the work involved, then either obtain the manufacturer's special tools, or use the alternatives described. New gaskets and sealing rings will also be required for all disturbed components.*

Checking

1 Disconnect the battery negative terminal (refer to Chapter 5A, Section 4).

2 Remove the air cleaner assembly as described in Chapter 4A, Section 2.

3 Remove the camshaft cover as described in Section 3.

4 Firmly apply the handbrake, then jack up the front of the car and support it securely on axle stands (see *Jacking and vehicle support*). Remove the right-hand front roadwheel and the wheel arch liner for access to the crankshaft pulley.

5 On models with air conditioning, release the tension on the auxiliary drivebelt and lock the tensioner in the released position as described in the auxiliary drivebelt renewal procedure in Chapter 1A, Section 32. Note that it is not necessary to completely remove the drivebelt,

TOOL TiP

A commercially-available clutch aligning tool can be used as a TDC positioning tool.

3.13 Apply a bead of silicone sealant to the joint between the timing cover and cylinder head on each side

as this would entail removal of the right-hand engine mounting bracket. With the drivebelt tension released, slip the belt off the compressor pulley. Unbolt the compressor from the cylinder block, release the refrigerant lines from their brackets and support the compressor clear of the engine. Do not disconnect the refrigerant lines from the compressor.

6 Using a socket or spanner on the crankshaft pulley hub bolt, turn the crankshaft in the normal direction of rotation (clockwise as viewed from the right-hand side of the car) until the TDC notch on the crankshaft pulley is located just before the cast lug on the timing cover **(see illustration)**.

7 Check that No 1 piston is on the compression stroke by observing No 1 cylinder camshaft lobes. All four lobes should

4.6 Turn the crankshaft until the TDC notch (A) on the pulley is located just before the cast lug (B) on the timing cover

4.10a The end of the tool must engage with the slot in the crankshaft web – shown with engine partially dismantled

be pointing outwards (away from the engine) **(see illustration)**. If they are not, No 1 piston is on the exhaust stroke and the crankshaft should be turned through a further full turn, stopping once again just before the TDC notch aligns with the lug on the timing cover.

8 Undo the closure bolt from the crankshaft TDC position setting hole. The plug is located on the front facing side of the cylinder block baseplate, adjacent to the timing cover joint. Note that a new closure bolt sealing ring will be required for refitting.

9 If the Vauxhall/Opel TDC positioning pin KM-952 is available, insert the tool into the TDC position setting hole. Slowly turn the crankshaft in the normal direction of rotation until the tool engages with the TDC slot in the crankshaft, and moves fully in, up to its stop.

10 In the absence of the Vauxhall/Opel tool, a typical commercially-available clutch aligning tool of the type having interchangeable cones and collars of various diameters can be used as an alternative **(see Tool Tip)**. Assemble the tool so that the end collar (the part that normally engages with the crankshaft spigot bearing) is of 12 mm diameter, and the sliding cone (the part that normally engages with the clutch disc hub) is of 17.5 mm diameter. Insert the tool into the TDC position setting hole, and slowly turn the crankshaft in the normal direction of rotation until the end collar engages with the TDC slot in the crankshaft web. Push the cone fully into the setting hole as far as it will go, and the crankshaft should now be locked in the TDC position **(see illustrations)**.

4.7 With No 1 piston on the compression stroke, the camshaft lobes for No 1 cylinder should be pointing outwards

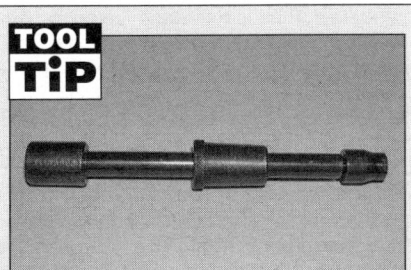

4.10b Clutch aligning tool in position in the TDC setting hole

4.12 Camshaft setting tool made from steel strip and inserted into the camshaft slots

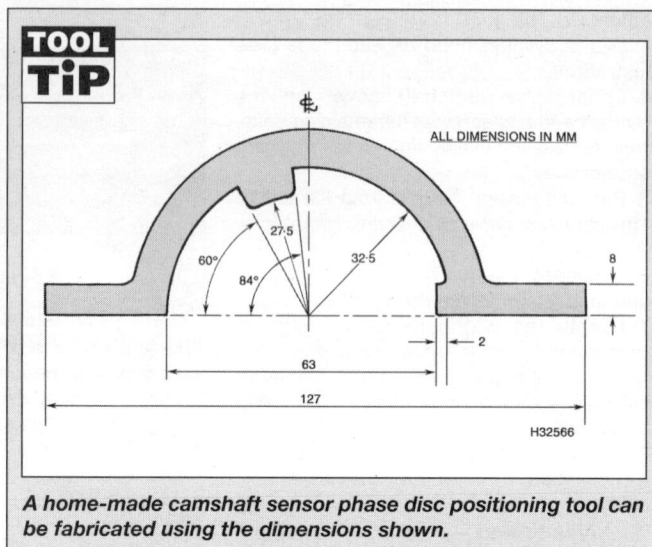

A home-made camshaft sensor phase disc positioning tool can be fabricated using the dimensions shown.

11 If the Vauxhall/Opel camshaft setting tool KM-953 is available, insert the tool into the slots in the left-hand end of the camshafts. Ensure that the tool is inserted fully, up to its stop, to lock both camshafts.

12 In the absence of the Vauxhall/Opel tool, a camshaft setting tool can be made out of 5 mm thick flat steel strip, approximately 20 mm wide and long enough to engage both camshaft slots. Insert the setting tool into the camshaft slots to lock the camshafts in the TDC position **(see illustration)**. Note that a ready-made equivalent is available from tool stockists.

13 If it is not possible to insert the camshaft setting tool, then the valve timing must be adjusted as described in paragraphs 17 to 35 below.

14 If all is satisfactory so far, the position of the camshaft position sensor phase disc on the inlet camshaft should be checked. This check entails the use of Vauxhall/Opel camshaft sensor phase disc positioning

tool KM-954. If this tool is not available, an alternative can be fabricated as follows.

15 The Vauxhall/Opel positioning tool (KM-954) is a relatively substantial die-casting, the purpose of which is to check the position of the phase disc, and also to hold the phase disc in the correct position on the camshaft sprocket if adjustment is required. During the workshop procedures undertaken for the preparation of this manual, we discovered that a tool made from stiff cardboard (such that used for the cover of a Haynes manual) worked just as well as the factory tool **(see Tool Tip and illustrations)**.

16 Using the Vauxhall/Opel positioning tool, or the home-made alternative, check to see if the tool will engage with the phase disc on the camshaft, and also seat squarely on the timing cover surface. If it does, proceed to paragraph 31. If adjustment is required, proceed as follows.

Adjustment

Note: *New camshaft sprocket retaining bolts will be required for this operation.*

17 Remove the camshaft sensor phase disc positioning tool, and the tool used to lock the camshafts in position.

18 Unscrew the timing chain tensioner closure plug from the timing cover, located just below the heater hose union on the coolant pump. Note that a new closure bolt sealing ring will be required for refitting **(see illustration)**.

19 Using a suitable spanner engaged with the flats provided on the inlet camshaft, apply tension in a clockwise direction (as viewed from the right-hand side of the car) to the camshaft, to take up any slack in the timing chain **(see illustration)**. This will push the timing chain tensioner plunger fully into its bore.

20 Hold the camshaft in this position and retain the tensioner plunger in the released position by inserting a 2 mm diameter roll-pin, approximately 30 mm long, through the

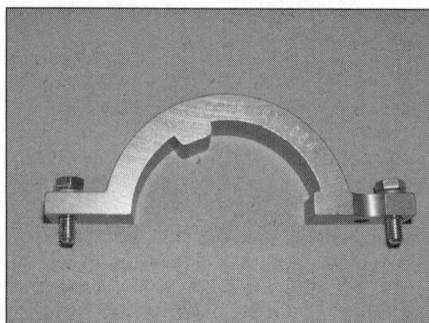

4.15a Vauxhall/Opel camshaft sensor phase disc positioning tool (KM-954)

4.15b Home-made cardboard alternative camshaft sensor phase disc positioning tool in place

4.18 Unscrew the timing chain tensioner closure plug from the timing cover

4.19 Use a spanner on the flats of the inlet camshaft to take up any slack in the timing chain

closure plug aperture and into the hole on the tensioner body (see illustrations).

21 Slacken and remove the sprocket retaining bolts for both camshafts, using a spanner to counterhold each camshaft as the bolts are slackened.

22 Fit the new bolts to both camshaft sprockets and tighten them finger-tight only at this stage. Check that the phase disc on the inlet camshaft can still be turned.

23 Again using the spanner on the camshaft flats, turn the camshafts slightly, as necessary, until the camshaft setting tool can be reinserted into the slots in the ends of the camshafts.

24 Remove the roll-pin used to hold the timing chain tensioner plunger in the retracted position.

25 Turn the camshaft sensor phase disc slightly, as necessary, and locate the Vauxhall/Opel positioning tool (KM-954), or the home-made alternative over the disc and in contact with the timing cover. If the Vauxhall/Opel tool is being used, bolt it into position on the timing cover.

26 Tighten the camshaft sprocket retaining bolts to 10 Nm (7 lbf ft). The inlet camshaft sprocket bolts should be tightened first. Note that this is just an initial torque loading to hold the sprockets and the phase disc in position when the setting tools are removed.

27 Remove the crankshaft, camshaft and phase disc setting tools, then tighten the camshaft sprocket retaining bolts to the specified torque in the stages given in the Specifications. The inlet camshaft sprocket bolts should be tightened first. Counterhold the camshafts using the spanner on the camshaft flats as the sprocket bolts are tightened.

28 Turn the crankshaft through two complete revolutions, stopping just before the TDC notch on the crankshaft pulley aligns with the cast lug on the timing cover (see illustration 4.6). Check that all four lobes for No 1 cylinder are pointing outwards (away from the engine).

29 Slowly turn the crankshaft further until the TDC position setting tool can once again be inserted to lock the crankshaft.

30 It should now be possible to re-insert the camshaft setting tool into the slots in the camshafts, and to fit the camshaft sensor phase disc setting tool over the disc. If this is not possible repeat the entire adjustment procedure.

31 If all is satisfactory, remove all the setting/aligning tools and refit the timing chain tensioner and cylinder block closure bolts using new sealing rings. Tighten both closure bolts to the specified torque.

32 On models with air conditioning, refit the compressor to the cylinder block and tighten the mounting bolts to the specified torque. Refit the refrigerant lines to their relevant clips or brackets, then refit the auxiliary drivebelt as described in Chapter 1A, Section 32.

33 Refit the wheel arch liner and the roadwheel. Tighten the roadwheel bolts to the

4.20a Insert a 2 mm diameter roll-pin, approximately 30 mm long, through the closure plug aperture...

specified torque, then lower the vehicle to the ground.

34 Refit the camshaft cover as described in Section 3.

35 Refit the air cleaner assembly as described in Chapter 4A, Section 2, then reconnect the battery negative terminal.

5 Crankshaft pulley – removal and refitting

Removal

1 Firmly apply the handbrake, then jack up the front of the car and support it securely on axle stands (see Jacking and vehicle support). Remove the right-hand roadwheel and the wheel arch liner. Where necessary remove the engine undertray.

2 Release the tension on the auxiliary drivebelt and lock the tensioner in the released position as described in the auxiliary drivebelt renewal procedure in Chapter 1A, Section 32. Note that it is not necessary to completely remove the drivebelt, as this would entail removal of the right-hand engine mounting bracket.

3 With the drivebelt tension released, slip the belt off the crankshaft pulley.

4 Using quick-drying paint, or similar, make an alignment mark between the crankshaft pulley and the pulley hub. It should only be possible to refit the pulley in one position, but it is advisable to make an alignment mark anyway.

5 Unscrew the six crankshaft pulley retaining bolts and remove the pulley from the hub (see illustration). If necessary, prevent the crankshaft from turning as the pulley bolts are slackened using a spanner or socket on the pulley hub bolt.

Refitting

6 Align the marks made on removal and locate the pulley on the hub.

7 Refit the six retaining bolts and progressively tighten them securely.

8 Refit the auxiliary drivebelt over the crankshaft pulley and ensure that it is correctly seated in the other pulleys.

4.20b ...and into the hole on the tensioner body

9 Unlock the auxiliary drivebelt tensioner as described in Chapter 1A, Section 32 to retension the drivebelt.

10 Refit the wheel arch liner and the roadwheel and tighten the wheel bolts to the specified torque.

11 Lower the car to the ground.

6 Timing cover and chain – removal and refitting

Note: The special tools described in Section 4 will also be required for this operation. Read through the entire procedure and also the procedures contained in Section 4 to familiarise yourself with the work involved, then either obtain the manufacturer's special tools, or use the alternatives described. New gaskets and sealing rings will also be required for all disturbed components, together with new camshaft sprocket retaining bolts. A tube of silicone sealant will be needed to seal the joint between the cylinder block and cylinder head.

Removal

1 Disconnect the battery negative terminal (refer to Chapter 5A, Section 4).

2 Apply the handbrake, then jack up the front of the vehicle and support it on axle stands (see Jacking and vehicle support). Remove the right-hand roadwheel.

3 Drain the cooling system as described in Chapter 1A, Section 27. Tighten the drain plug after draining the system.

5.5 Undo the six bolts and remove the crankshaft pulley from the pulley hub

6.9 Radiator lower hose on the coolant pump

6.17 The coolant pump pulley retaining bolts

6.31 Slacken the crankshaft pulley hub retaining bolt

4 Remove the air cleaner assembly as described in Chapter 4A, Section 2.

5 At the right-hand end of the engine, loosen the clip and disconnect the throttle housing preheater hose from the thermostat housing.

6 Loosen the clip and disconnect the heater feed hose from the coolant pump.

7 Disconnect the wiring from the oil pressure switch, coolant temperature sensor and camshaft position sensor, then unclip the wiring conduit and move it to one side.

8 Loosen the clips and disconnect the radiator upper hose from the radiator and thermostat housing.

9 Loosen the clip and disconnect the radiator lower hose from the coolant pump **(see illustration)**.

10 Remove the ignition module as described in Chapter 5B, Section 3.

11 Disconnect the crankcase ventilation hose from the camshaft cover.

12 Progressively slacken the camshaft cover retaining bolts until they are all fully unscrewed. Note that the bolts are captive and will remain in place in the cover as it is removed. Lift the camshaft cover up and off the cylinder head.

13 Remove the auxiliary drivebelt cover from under the right-hand wheel arch.

14 Position a container beneath the engine sump, then unscrew the drain plug and drain the engine oil. Clean, refit and tighten the drain plug on completion.

15 Refer to Chapter 4A, and disconnect the wiring from the oxygen sensor on the catalytic converter, then unbolt the exhaust front pipe from the exhaust manifold, taking care to support the flexible section.

Note: *Angular movement in excess of 10° can cause permanent damage to the exhaust system flexible section.*

16 Release the mounting rubbers and support the front of the exhaust pipe to one side.

17 Slacken, but do not remove, the three coolant pump pulley retaining bolts **(see illustration)**.

18 On models without air conditioning, turn the auxiliary drivebelt tensioner pulley bolt clockwise then insert a suitable pin through the spring centre shaft to lock the spring in its compressed state. Note the routing of

the drivebelt, then remove it from the pulleys – mark the drivebelt for fitted direction. The drivebelt cannot be removed completely until the right-hand engine mounting has been removed. Unscrew the auxiliary drivebelt tensioner lower mounting bolt and the tensioner roller upper pivot bolt. Remove the tensioner from the timing cover.

19 On models with air conditioning, turn the auxiliary drivebelt tensioner pulley bolt clockwise to tension the spring, then insert a suitable pin through the hole in the tensioner body and into the hole in the timing cover to lock the spring. Note the routing of the drivebelt, then remove it from the pulleys – mark the drivebelt for fitted direction. The drivebelt cannot be removed completely until the right-hand engine mounting has been removed. Turn the tensioner pulley bolt clockwise again and remove the locking pin, then gradually release the tensioner until it is fully released. Unbolt the tensioner from the timing cover.

20 Remove the alternator as described in Chapter 5A, Section 8.

21 Remove the sump as described in Section 11.

22 The engine must now be supported while the right-hand engine mounting is removed. To do this, use a hoist attached to the top of the engine, or make up a wooden frame to locate on the crankcase and use a trolley jack.

23 Remove the right-hand engine mounting bracket with reference to Section 15, then remove the auxiliary drivebelt.

24 Fully unscrew the bolts and remove the coolant pump pulley from its drive flange.

25 On models with air conditioning, unbolt the compressor from the cylinder block, release the refrigerant lines from their brackets and support the compressor clear of the engine. Do not disconnect the refrigerant lines from the compressor.

26 Undo the three bolts securing the thermostat housing cover to the coolant pump. Remove the sealing ring from the housing cover noting that a new one will be required for refitting.

27 Using a socket or spanner on the crankshaft pulley hub bolt, turn the crankshaft in the normal direction of rotation (clockwise as viewed from the right-hand side of the car)

until the TDC notch on the crankshaft pulley is located just before the cast lug on the timing cover **(see illustration 4.6)**.

28 Check that No 1 piston is on the compression stroke by observing No 1 cylinder camshaft lobes. All four lobes should be pointing outwards (away from the engine). If they are not, No 1 piston is on the exhaust stroke and the crankshaft should be turned through a further full turn, stopping once again just before the TDC notch aligns with the lug on the timing cover.

29 Using quick-drying paint, or similar, make an alignment mark between the crankshaft pulley and the pulley hub. It should only be possible to refit the pulley in one position, but it is advisable to make an alignment mark anyway.

30 Unscrew the six crankshaft pulley retaining bolts and remove the pulley from the hub. If necessary, prevent the crankshaft from turning as the pulley bolts are slackened, using a spanner or socket on the pulley hub bolt.

31 Using a suitable socket, initially slacken (but do not remove) the crankshaft pulley hub retaining bolt **(see illustration)**. The crankshaft can be prevented from turning as the bolt is slackened using Vauxhall/Opel special tool KM-956 or a similar tool which will engage with the flats on each side of the pulley hub. Alternatively, remove the starter motor, and lock the flywheel ring gear teeth using a suitable hooked tool bolted to the bellhousing.

32 Undo the closure bolt from the crankshaft TDC position setting hole. The plug is located on the front facing side of the cylinder block baseplate, adjacent to the timing cover joint. Note that a new closure bolt sealing ring will be required for refitting.

33 Temporarily place the crankshaft pulley back on the hub and check that the TDC notch is still positioned just before the lug on the timing cover.

34 Slowly turn the crankshaft in the normal direction of rotation until the TDC positioning pin (or suitable alternative) described in Section 4, engages with the TDC slot in the crankshaft.

35 Remove the crankshaft pulley, if still in place, and check that the punch mark on the pulley hub is in the 11 o'clock position.

6.42 Push back the timing chain tensioner plunger and secure it in the released position with a 2 mm diameter roll-pin

6.43 Undo the two bolts and remove the timing chain sliding rail from the cylinder head

6.44 Undo the two bolts and remove the timing chain guide rail from the cylinder block

36 Insert the camshaft setting tool described in Section 4 into the slots in the ends of the camshafts.

37 Unscrew the coolant pump retaining bolts, noting the locations of the three short bolts. The short bolts secure the pump to the timing cover, and the long bolts secure the pump and the timing cover to the cylinder block and cylinder head.

38 Withdraw the coolant pump from the timing cover, noting that it may be necessary to tap the pump lightly with a soft-faced mallet to free it from the locating dowels.

39 Recover the pump sealing ring/gasket noting that a new one must be used for refitting.

40 Unscrew the previously-slackened crankshaft pulley hub retaining bolt and remove the hub from the crankshaft. Note that a new bolt will be required for refitting.

41 Undo the timing cover retaining bolts and remove the timing cover from the engine. The cover will be initially tight as it is located on dowels and secured by sealant. If necessary, gently tap it off using a soft-faced mallet.

42 Fully push back the timing chain tensioner plunger and secure it in the released position by inserting a 2 mm diameter roll-pin, approximately 30 mm long, in the hole on the tensioner body **(see illustration)**.

43 Undo the two bolts and remove the timing chain sliding rail from the top of the cylinder head **(see illustration)**.

44 Undo the two bolts and remove the timing chain (front) guide rail from the cylinder block **(see illustration)**.

45 Undo the lower pivot bolt and remove the timing chain (rear) tension rail from the cylinder block **(see illustration)**.

46 Lift the timing chain off the sprockets and remove the chain, then remove the drive sprocket from the crankshaft **(see illustrations)**.

47 Remove the composite gasket from the cylinder block baseplate, cylinder block, and cylinder head, using a plastic spatula if necessary to release the sealant **(see illustration)**. Note that if the cylinder head has been previously removed, the gasket will be a two-piece type, with a split at the cylinder head-to cylinder block joint. A new gasket will be required for refitting.

48 Thoroughly clean the timing cover and remove all traces of gasket and sealant from all the mating surfaces. Similarly clean the cylinder block baseplate, cylinder block and cylinder head mating surfaces. Ensure that all traces of old sealant are removed, particularly from the area of the cylinder head-to-cylinder block joint.

49 Inspect the timing chain, sprockets, sliding rail, guide rail and tension rail for any sign of wear or deformation, and renew any suspect components as necessary. Renew the crankshaft timing chain end oil seal in the timing cover as a matter of course using the procedures described in Section 13.

50 It is advisable to check the condition of the timing chain tensioner at this stage, as described in Section 7.

6.45 Undo the lower pivot bolt and remove the timing chain tension rail from the cylinder block

6.46b...then remove the drive sprocket from the crankshaft

51 Obtain all new gaskets and components as necessary ready for refitting.

Refitting

52 Commence refitting by inserting a new coolant pump gasket or rubber seal into the timing cover.

53 Check that the locating dowels are in place, and that the mating surfaces are clean and dry, then locate the pump in position on the timing cover.

54 Refit the three coolant pump short retaining bolts, ensuring that the bolts are fitted to their correct locations (refer to Chapter 3 if necessary). Tighten the bolts to the specified torque.

55 Apply a 2 mm diameter bead of silicone sealant to the joint between the cylinder

6.46a Lift the timing chain off the sprockets and remove the chain...

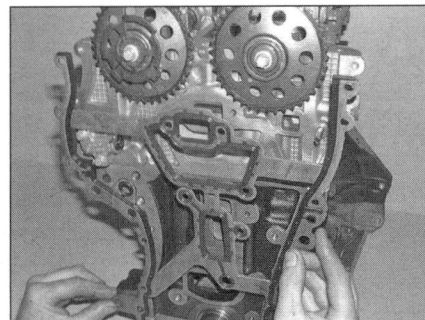

6.47 Remove the timing cover composite gasket from the cylinder block baseplate, cylinder block, and cylinder head

6.55 Apply a 2 mm diameter bead of silicone sealant to the joint between the cylinder block and cylinder head on each side

6.57 Slide the timing chain drive sprocket onto the crankshaft with the markings facing outwards

6.58 Keeping the timing chain tight on the exhaust camshaft side, locate the chain over the sprockets

block and cylinder head on each side (see illustration). The bead should be long enough to fill the joint in the area covered by the timing cover gasket. Similarly, apply silicone sealant to the joint between the cylinder block and baseplate.

56 Ensure that the locating dowels are in position, then locate the new timing cover gasket in place on the cylinder head, cylinder block and baseplate.

57 Slide the timing chain drive sprocket onto the crankshaft with the markings facing outwards (see illustration).

58 Engage the timing chain with the drive sprocket then, keeping it tight on the exhaust camshaft side, feed the chain up and over the camshaft sprockets (see illustration).

59 Place the timing chain tension rail in position, refit the lower pivot bolt and tighten the bolt to the specified torque.

60 Attach the timing chain guide rail to the cylinder block and secure with the two bolts tightened securely.

61 Refit the timing chain sliding rail to the cylinder head and secure with the two bolts tightened securely.

62 Remove the roll-pin used to secure the timing chain tensioner plunger in the released position.

63 Locate the timing cover in position and refit all the retaining bolts, finger-tight only at this stage. Now tighten all the bolts to the specified torque, starting with the bolts around the coolant pump first, followed by the bolts around the periphery of the cover.

64 Refit the sump as described in Section 11.

65 Remove the position setting tools used to lock the crankshaft and camshafts in the TDC position.

66 Lubricate the crankshaft pulley hub with

engine oil, then refit the hub to the crankshaft, ensuring that the punch mark on the hub is in the 11 o'clock position (see illustration).

67 Screw in the new pulley hub retaining bolt and tighten it to the specified torque, in the stages given in the Specifications (see illustrations). Prevent crankshaft rotation as the bolt is tightened, using the method employed for removal.

68 Refit the crankshaft pulley to the pulley hub, with the marks made on removal aligned, and tighten the six bolts securely.

69 Turn the crankshaft through two complete revolutions, stopping just before the TDC notch on the crankshaft pulley aligns with the cast lug on the timing cover. Check that all four lobes for No 1 cylinder are pointing outwards (away from the engine).

70 Slowly turn the crankshaft further until the TDC position setting tool can once again be inserted to lock the crankshaft.

71 It should now be possible to re-insert the camshaft setting tool into the slots in the camshafts. If the setting tool cannot be inserted, carry out the valve timing adjustment procedures contained in Section 4.

72 If all is satisfactory, remove all the setting/aligning tools and refit the closure bolt to the cylinder block using a new sealing ring. Tighten the closure bolt to the specified torque.

73 Refit the coolant pump pulley and tighten the three bolts to the specified torque. To prevent the pulley turning as the bolts are tightened, hold the pulley using a screwdriver engaged with one of the bolts and the pump centre spindle. Alternatively, wait until the auxiliary drivebelt has been refitted and tighten the bolts then.

74 Ensure that the mating surfaces are clean, then fit a new sealing ring to the thermostat housing cover. Refit the cover to the coolant pump and tighten the bolts securely.

75 On models with air conditioning, refit the compressor to the cylinder block and tighten the mounting bolts to the specified torque. Refit the refrigerant lines to their relevant clips or brackets.

76 Refit the alternator as described in Chapter 5A, Section 8.

6.66 Lubricate the crankshaft pulley hub, then refit the hub to the crankshaft

6.67a Screw in the new pulley hub retaining bolt...

6.67b...tighten it to the specified torque...

6.67c...then through the specified angle in the stages given in the Specifications

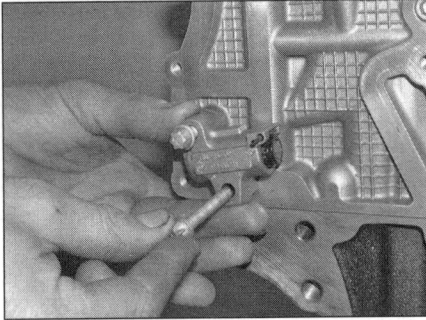

7.2 Undo the two retaining bolts and remove the timing chain tensioner from the cylinder head

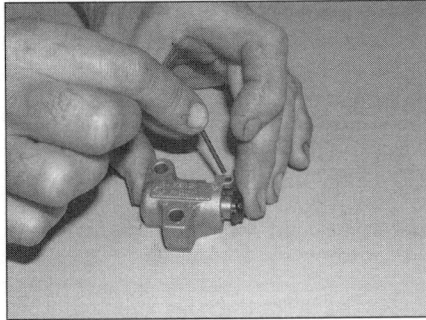

7.3a Extract the roll-pin used to retain the tensioner plunger in the retracted position...

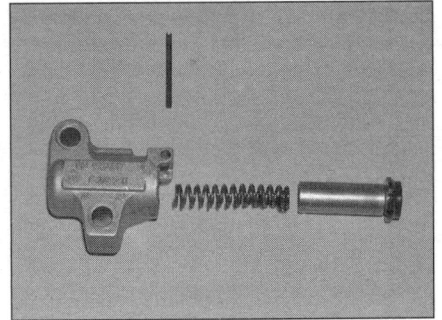

7.3b...and withdraw the tensioner plunger and spring

77 Refit the auxiliary drivebelt tensioner and tighten the mounting bolts to the specified torque.
78 Rotate the tensioner pulley bolt clockwise as for removal, refit the auxiliary drivebelt as previously noted and release the tensioner.
79 Refit the right-hand engine mounting bracket with reference to Section 15.
80 Refit the exhaust front pipe and oxygen sensor with reference to Chapter 4A.
81 Refill the engine with fresh oil as described in Chapter 1A, Section 5.
82 Refit the auxiliary drivebelt cover.
83 Refit the camshaft cover and reconnect the crankcase ventilation hose as described in Section 3.
84 Refit the ignition module and cover.
85 Reconnect the radiator top and bottom hoses and heater hose to their respective connections.
86 Reconnect the wiring to the oil pressure switch, coolant temperature sensor and camshaft position sensor, then clip the wiring conduit in position.
87 Reconnect the throttle housing preheater hose and tighten the clip.
88 Refit the air cleaner assembly as described in Chapter 4A, Section 2.
89 Refill the cooling system as described in Chapter 1A, Section 27, then reconnect the battery negative terminal.
90 Refit the engine undertray as necessary, then refit the roadwheel and lower the vehicle to the ground.

7 Timing chain tensioner – removal, inspection and refitting

Removal

1 Remove the timing cover as described in Section 6.
2 Undo the two tensioner retaining bolts and remove the tensioner from the cylinder head (see illustration).
3 Extract the roll-pin used to retain the tensioner plunger in the retracted position and withdraw the tensioner plunger and spring (see illustrations).

Inspection

4 Examine the components for any sign of wear, deformation or damage and, if evident, renew the complete tensioner assembly.

Refitting

5 Lubricate the tensioner spring and plunger, then insert the spring, followed by the plunger into the tensioner body.
6 Fully compress the tensioner plunger and reinsert the retaining roll-pin (see illustration).
7 Refit the tensioner assembly to the cylinder head and tighten the retaining bolts securely.

8 Camshaft sprockets – removal and refitting

Note: *The special tools described in Section 4 will also be required for this operation. Read through the entire procedure and also the procedures contained in Section 4 to familiarise yourself with the work involved, then either obtain the manufacturer's special tools, or use the alternatives described. New gaskets and sealing rings will also be required for all disturbed components, together with new camshaft sprocket retaining bolts.*

Removal

1 Disconnect the battery negative terminal (refer to *Disconnecting the battery* in Chapter 5A, Section 4).
2 Remove the air cleaner assembly as described in Chapter 4A, Section 2.

7.6 Timing chain tensioner plunger fully retracted and locked with the roll-pin

3 Disconnect the wiring from the oil pressure switch, coolant temperature sensor and camshaft position sensor, then unclip the wiring conduit and move it to one side.
4 Remove the ignition module as described in Chapter 5B, Section 3.
5 Disconnect the crankcase ventilation hoses from the camshaft cover.
6 Progressively slacken the camshaft cover retaining bolts until they are all fully unscrewed. Note that the bolts are captive and will remain in place in the cover as it is removed. Lift the camshaft cover up and off the cylinder head.
7 Firmly apply the handbrake, then jack up the front of the car and support it securely on axle stands (see *Jacking and vehicle support*). Remove the right-hand front roadwheel and the wheel arch liner for access to the crankshaft pulley.
8 On models with air conditioning, release the tension on the auxiliary drivebelt and lock the tensioner in the released position as described in the auxiliary drivebelt renewal procedure in Chapter 1A, Section 32. Note that it is not necessary to completely remove the drivebelt, as this entails removal of the right-hand engine mounting bracket. With the drivebelt tension released, slip the belt off the compressor pulley. Unbolt the compressor from the cylinder block, release the refrigerant lines from their brackets and support the compressor clear of the engine. Do not disconnect the refrigerant lines from the compressor.
9 Using a socket or spanner on the crankshaft pulley hub bolt, turn the crankshaft in the normal direction of rotation (clockwise as viewed from the right-hand side of the car) until the TDC notch on the crankshaft pulley is located just before the cast lug on the timing cover (see illustration 4.6).
10 Check that No 1 piston is on the compression stroke by observing No 1 cylinder camshaft lobes. All four lobes should be pointing outwards (away from the engine). If they are not, No 1 piston is on the exhaust stroke and the crankshaft should be turned through a further full turn, stopping once again just before the TDC notch aligns with the lug on the timing cover.

8.16 Slacken the camshaft sprocket retaining bolts using a spanner to counterhold each camshaft as the bolts are slackened

11 Unscrew the timing chain tensioner closure bolt from the front of the timing cover, below the heater hose union on the coolant pump. Note that a new closure bolt sealing ring will be required for refitting.

12 Obtain a suitable roll-pin or similar of 2 mm diameter and approximately 30 mm long to use as a timing chain tensioner locking tool.

13 Using a suitable spanner engaged with the flats provided on the inlet camshaft, apply tension in a clockwise direction (as viewed from the right-hand side of the car) to the camshaft, to take up any slack in the timing chain. This will push the timing chain tensioner plunger fully into its bore.

14 Hold the camshaft in this position and retain the tensioner plunger in the released position by inserting the roll-pin through the closure plug aperture and into the hole on the tensioner body.

15 Undo the two bolts and remove the timing chain sliding rail from the top of the cylinder head.

16 Slacken the sprocket retaining bolts for both camshafts, using the spanner to counterhold each camshaft as the bolts are slackened **(see illustration)**. Remove the bolt for the sprocket(s) being removed together with the camshaft position sensor phase disc, if removing the inlet camshaft. Withdraw the relevant sprocket(s) from the camshaft(s), disengage the timing chain and remove the sprocket(s) from the engine.

9.2 Camshaft bearing cap identification numbers

Refitting

17 Engage the sprocket(s) with the timing chain and locate the sprocket(s) on the camshaft(s). Fit the new retaining bolt(s) together with the phase disc, if working on the inlet camshaft. Note that new retaining bolts must be fitted to both sprockets, even if only one sprocket was removed. Tighten the bolts finger-tight only at this stage and check that the phase disc on the inlet camshaft can still be turned.

18 Refit the timing chain sliding rail to the top of the cylinder head and secure with the two bolts tightened securely.

19 Using the spanner on the camshaft flats, turn the camshafts slightly, as necessary, until the camshaft setting tool described in Section 4 can be inserted into the slots in the ends of the camshafts.

20 Turn the camshaft sensor phase disc as necessary until the phase disc positioning tool (or suitable alternative) described in Section 4 can be located over the phase disc. If the Vauxhall/Opel tool is being used, bolt it to the top of the timing cover. If the alternative tool described is being used, ensure that its base is in contact with the timing cover.

21 Remove the roll-pin used to hold the timing chain tensioner plunger in the retracted position.

22 Undo the closure bolt from the crankshaft TDC position setting hole. The plug is located on the front facing side of the cylinder block baseplate, adjacent to the timing cover joint. Note that a new closure bolt sealing ring will be required for refitting.

23 Slowly turn the crankshaft in the normal direction of rotation until the TDC positioning pin (or suitable alternative), described in Section 4, engages with the TDC slot in the crankshaft.

24 Tighten the camshaft sprocket retaining bolts to 10 Nm (7 lbf ft). Note that this is just an initial torque loading to hold the sprockets and the phase disc in position when the setting tools are removed.

25 Remove the crankshaft, camshaft and phase disc setting tools, then tighten the camshaft sprocket retaining bolts to the specified torque in the stages given in the Specifications. Counterhold the camshafts using the spanner on the camshaft flats as the sprocket bolts are tightened.

26 Turn the crankshaft through two complete revolutions, stopping just before the TDC notch on the crankshaft pulley aligns with the cast lug on the timing cover. Check that all four lobes for No 1 cylinder are pointing outwards (away from the engine).

27 Slowly turn the crankshaft further until the TDC position setting tool can once again be inserted to lock the crankshaft.

28 It should now be possible to re-insert the camshaft setting tool into the slots in the camshafts, and to fit the camshaft sensor phase disc setting tool over the disc. If this is not possible carry out the valve timing adjustment procedure contained in Section 4.

29 If all is satisfactory, remove all the setting/aligning tools and refit the timing chain tensioner and cylinder block closure bolts using new sealing rings. Tighten both closure bolts to the specified torque.

30 On models with air conditioning, refit the compressor to the cylinder block and tighten the mounting bolts to the specified torque. Refit the refrigerant lines to their relevant clips or brackets, then refit the auxiliary drivebelt as described in Chapter 1A, Section 32.

31 Refit the wheel arch liner and the roadwheel. Tighten the roadwheel bolts to the specified torque, then lower the vehicle to the ground.

32 Refit the camshaft cover as described in Section 3.

33 Refit the ignition module and cover, and reconnect the wiring.

34 Reconnect the wiring to the oil pressure switch, coolant temperature sensor and camshaft position sensor, then clip the wiring conduit into position.

35 Refit the air cleaner assembly as described in Chapter 4A, Section 2, then reconnect the battery negative terminal.

9 Camshafts, hydraulic tappets and rocker arms – removal and refitting

Removal

1 Remove the camshaft sprocket(s) as described in Section 8.

2 Observe the identification numbers and markings on the camshaft bearing caps **(see illustration)**. On the project car used during the compilation of this manual, the bearing caps with odd numbers were fitted to the exhaust camshaft, and the caps with the even numbers were fitted to the inlet camshaft. However, this may not be the case on other engines. Also, as it is possible to fit the caps either way round, it will be necessary to mark the caps with quick-drying paint, or identify them in some way, so that they can be refitted in exactly the same position. On the project car, all the numbers could be read the correct way up, when viewed from the exhaust camshaft side of the engine. Again, this may not always be the case.

3 With the bearing caps correctly identified, and working in a spiral pattern from the outside to the inside, initially slacken the bearing cap bolts, one at a time, by half a turn. When all the bolts have been initially slackened, repeat the procedure, slackening the bolts by a further half a turn. Continue until all the bolts have been fully-slackened. The camshaft will rise up under the action of the valve springs as the bolts are slackened. Ensure that the camshaft rises uniformly and does not jam in its bearings.

4 When all the bolts have been slackened, remove the bolts and lift off the bearing caps, keeping them in order according to

9.4 Lift off the camshaft bearing caps, keeping them in order – shown with cylinder head removed

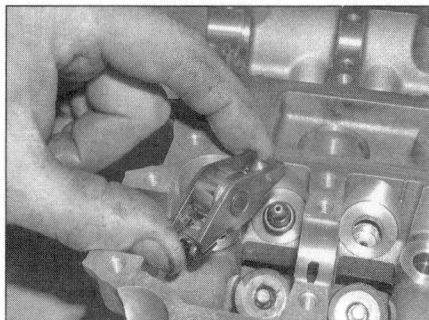

9.6a Withdraw each rocker arm...

9.6b...and hydraulic tappet in turn, and place them in their respective containers – shown with cylinder head removed

the identification method decided on **(see illustration)**.

5 Note the installed position of the camshafts before removal – the cam lobes for No 1 cylinder should be pointing outwards (ie, away from the centre). Carefully lift the camshafts from their locations in the cylinder head. If both camshafts are removed, identify them as exhaust and inlet.

6 Obtain twelve small, clean plastic containers, and number them inlet 1 to 6 and exhaust 1 to 6. Alternatively, divide a larger container into twelve compartments and number each compartment accordingly. Withdraw each rocker arm and hydraulic tappet in turn, and place them in their respective container **(see illustrations)**. Do not interchange the rocker arms and tappets, or the rate of wear will be much increased.

Inspection

7 Examine the camshaft bearing surfaces and cam lobes for signs of wear ridges and scoring. Renew the camshaft if any of these conditions are apparent. Examine the condition of the bearing surfaces, both on the camshaft journals and in the cylinder head/bearing caps. If the head bearing surfaces are worn excessively, the cylinder head will need to be renewed.

8 Examine the rocker arm and hydraulic tappet bearing surfaces for wear ridges and scoring. Renew any rocker arm or tappet on which these conditions are apparent.

9 If either camshaft is being renewed, it will be necessary to renew all the rocker arms and tappets for that particular camshaft also.

Refitting

10 Before refitting, thoroughly clean all the components and the cylinder head and bearing cap journals.

11 Liberally oil the cylinder head hydraulic tappet bores and the tappets. Carefully refit the tappets to the cylinder head, ensuring that each tappet is refitted to its original bore.

12 Lay each rocker arm in position over its respective tappet.

13 Liberally oil the camshaft bearings in the cylinder head and the camshaft lobes, then place the camshafts in the cylinder head. Turn the camshafts so that the cam lobes for No 1

cylinder are pointing outwards as noted during removal.

14 Refit all the bearing caps to their respective locations ensuring they are fitted the correct way round as noted during removal.

15 Working in a spiral pattern from the inside to the outside, initially tighten the bearing cap bolts, one at a time, by half a turn. When all the bolts have been initially tightened, repeat the procedure, tightening the bolts by a further half a turn. Continue until all the bearing caps are in contact with the cylinder head and the bolts are lightly tightened.

16 Again, working in a spiral pattern from inside to outside, tighten all the bolts to the specified torque.

17 Refit the camshaft sprockets as described in Section 8.

10 Cylinder head – removal and refitting

Note: *The engine must be cold when removing the cylinder head. A new cylinder head gasket, timing cover gasket, cylinder head bolts, camshaft sprocket bolts together with seals and sealing rings will be required for refitting. A suitable sealant will also be needed to seal the timing cover-to-cylinder block joint.*
Note: *The special tools described in Section 4 will also be required for this operation. Read through the entire procedure and also the procedures contained in Section 4 to familiarise yourself with the work involved, then either obtain the manufacturer's special tools, or use the alternatives described.*

Removal

1 Apply the handbrake, then jack up the front of the vehicle and support it on axle stands (see *Jacking and vehicle support*). Remove the right-hand roadwheel.

2 Disconnect the battery negative terminal (refer to Chapter 5A, Section 4), then remove the battery and battery tray as also described in Chapter 5A, Section 4.

3 Drain the cooling system as described in Chapter 1A, Section 27.

4 Remove the air cleaner assembly as described in Chapter 4A, Section 2.

5 Unscrew the retaining bolt and remove the air inlet duct from the front of the engine compartment.

6 Remove the throttle housing as described in Chapter 4A, Section 10.

7 Disconnect the heater feed hose from the coolant pump and position it to one side.

8 Disconnect the brake servo vacuum line from the inlet manifold. Where applicable, also disconnect the evaporative system hose from the manifold.

9 Where applicable, undo the two bolts and remove the cover over the fuel rail. Similarly, undo the two bolts and release the wiring harness support bracket from the rear of the inlet manifold.

10 From under the car, undo the bolt securing the support bracket to the base of the inlet manifold. Slacken the bolt securing the bracket to the cylinder block and twist the bracket to one side **(see illustration)**.

11 Detach the additional lower wiring harness bracket from the inlet manifold.

12 Disconnect the heater return hose from the EGR coolant flange, and unclip the wiring harness.

13 Depressurise the fuel system as described in Chapter 4A, Section 4, then disconnect the fuel feed hose quick-release fitting from the fuel rail. Be prepared for fuel spillage, and take adequate precautions. Clamp or plug the open end of the hose, to minimise further fuel loss.

10.10 Undo the bolt securing the support bracket to the base of the inlet manifold

10.30 Undo the two bolts and remove the exhaust manifold heat shield

10.32 Undo the three bolts and remove the oil filter housing from the cylinder block

14 Disconnect the wiring from the following components:
a) *Oil pressure switch.*
b) *Coolant temperature sensor.*
c) *Camshaft position sensor.*
d) *Fuel injectors.*
e) *Throttle valve adjuster.*
f) *Engine electronic control unit (LH end of engine).*
g) *Wiring combination plug (LH end of engine).*
h) *EGR valve.*

15 Release the ignition module cover from the centre of the camshaft cover and remove it toward the transmission end of the engine. Disconnect the wiring plug from the left-hand end of the module.

16 Disconnect the earth cables from the electronic control unit bracket.

17 Undo the two bolts, one at each end, securing the plastic fuel injector wiring trough to the top of the fuel rail. Note that these bolts also secure the fuel rail to the inlet manifold. With the injector wiring disconnected, lift the wiring trough up and off the injectors. Place the trough to one side.

18 Remove the auxiliary drivebelt cover from under the right-hand wheel arch.

19 Refer to Chapter 4A, and disconnect the wiring from the oxygen sensor on the catalytic converter, then unbolt the exhaust front pipe/catalytic converter from the exhaust manifold, taking care to support the flexible section.

Note: *Angular movement in excess of 10° can cause permanent damage to the exhaust system flexible section.*

20 Release the mounting rubbers and support the front of the exhaust pipe to one side.

21 Slacken, but do not remove, the three coolant pump pulley retaining bolts.

22 Unscrew the nuts and disconnect the wiring from the starter motor. Also, release the cable ties.

23 Unbolt the two wiring harness brackets from the inlet manifold.

24 On models without air conditioning, turn the auxiliary drivebelt tensioner pulley bolt clockwise then insert a suitable pin through the spring centre shaft to lock the spring in its compressed state. Note the routing of the drivebelt, then remove it from the pulleys – mark

the drivebelt for fitted direction. The drivebelt cannot be removed completely until the right-hand engine mounting has been removed. Unscrew the auxiliary drivebelt tensioner lower mounting bolt and the tensioner roller upper pivot bolt. Remove the tensioner from the timing cover.

25 On models with air conditioning, turn the auxiliary drivebelt tensioner pulley bolt clockwise to tension the spring, then insert a suitable pin through the hole in the tensioner body and into the hole in the timing cover to lock the spring. Note the routing of the drivebelt, then remove it from the pulleys – mark the drivebelt for fitted direction. The drivebelt cannot be removed completely until the right-hand engine mounting has been removed. Turn the tensioner pulley bolt clockwise again and remove the locking pin, then gradually release the tensioner until it is fully released. Unbolt the tensioner from the timing cover.

26 Undo the bolt securing the oil dipstick guide tube to the exhaust manifold and withdraw the dipstick and guide tube from the cylinder block baseplate. To do this, turn the guide tube forward. Suitably cover or plug the guide tube aperture in the cylinder block baseplate to prevent dirt ingress.

27 Disconnect the wiring from the oxygen sensor on the exhaust manifold at the left-hand front of the engine, then unscrew the sensor from the head. Refer to Chapter 4A if necessary.

28 Unbolt the left-hand engine lifting eye from the cylinder head, complete with attached wiring harness.

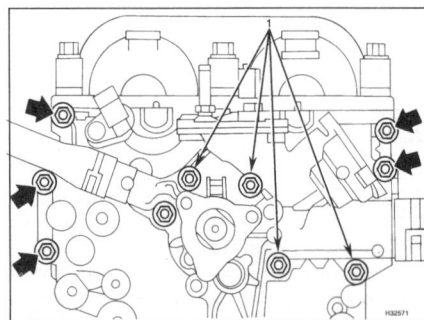

10.38 Undo the bolts (1) securing the coolant pump, and the bolts (arrowed) securing the timing cover to the cylinder head

29 On models with air conditioning, unbolt the compressor from the cylinder block, release the refrigerant lines from their brackets and support the compressor clear of the engine. Do not disconnect the refrigerant lines from the compressor.

30 Unbolt the exhaust manifold heat shield **(see illustration)**, then unscrew the mounting nuts and withdraw the exhaust manifold from the cylinder head. Recover the gasket.

31 Remove the oil filter from the filter housing as described in Chapter 1A, Section 5. Remove as much of the oil remaining in the filter housing as possible using clean rags.

32 Undo the three bolts and remove the oil filter housing from the cylinder block **(see illustration)**. Place absorbent rags below the housing as it is removed to catch any remaining oil. Recover the filter housing seal noting that a new seal will be required for refitting.

33 Loosen the clips and disconnect the radiator upper hose from the radiator and thermostat housing.

34 The engine must now be supported while the right-hand engine mounting is removed. To do this, use a hoist attached to the top of the engine, or make up a wooden frame to locate beneath the sump and use a trolley jack.

35 Remove the right-hand engine mounting bracket with reference to Section 15, then remove the auxiliary drivebelt.

36 Fully unscrew the bolts and remove the coolant pump pulley from its drive flange.

37 Undo the three bolts securing the thermostat housing cover to the coolant pump. Remove the sealing ring from the housing cover noting that a new one will be required for refitting.

38 Undo the bolts securing the coolant pump and timing cover to the cylinder head **(see illustration)**. Note that it is not necessary to remove all the coolant pump bolts as three are shorter than the rest, and only secure the pump to the timing cover.

39 Remove the camshaft cover as described in Section 3.

40 Using a socket or spanner on the crankshaft pulley hub bolt, turn the crankshaft in the normal direction of rotation (clockwise as viewed from the right-hand side of the car) until the TDC notch on the crankshaft pulley is located just before the cast lug on the timing cover (see Section 4).

41 Check that No 1 piston is on the compression stroke by observing No 1 cylinder camshaft lobes. All four lobes should be pointing outwards (away from the engine). If they are not, No 1 piston is on the exhaust stroke and the crankshaft should be turned through a further full turn, stopping once again just before the TDC notch aligns with the lug on the timing cover.

42 Undo the closure bolt from the crankshaft TDC position setting hole. The plug is located on the front facing side of the cylinder block baseplate, adjacent to the timing cover joint. Note that a new closure bolt sealing ring will be required for refitting.

43 Slowly turn the crankshaft in the normal direction of rotation until the TDC positioning pin (or suitable alternative), described in Section 4, engages with the TDC slot in the crankshaft.

44 Obtain a suitable roll-pin, or similar, of 2 mm diameter and approximately 30 mm long, to use as a timing chain tensioner locking tool.

45 Using a suitable spanner engaged with the flats provided on the inlet camshaft, apply tension in a clockwise direction (as viewed from the right-hand side of the car) to the camshaft, to take up any slack in the timing chain. This will push the timing chain tensioner plunger fully into its bore.

46 Hold the camshaft in this position and retain the tensioner plunger in the released position by inserting the roll-pin through the closure plug aperture and into the hole on the tensioner body.

47 Undo the two bolts and remove the timing chain sliding rail from the top of the cylinder head.

48 Slacken the sprocket retaining bolts for both camshafts, using the spanner to counterhold each camshaft as the bolts are slackened. Remove both sprocket bolts together with the camshaft position sensor phase disc from the inlet camshaft. Ease the sprockets and chain off the camshafts and rest the sprockets on the top of the timing cover.

49 Undo the retaining bolt and remove the camshaft position sensor from the front of the timing cover.

50 Working in the specified sequence, progressively slacken the cylinder head retaining bolts half a turn at a time until all the bolts are loose **(see illustration)**. Remove the bolts from their locations noting that new bolts will be required for refitting.

51 Slightly raise the cylinder head so it just clears the cylinder block face and move the head toward the transmission end of the engine. The head will be initially tight due to the sealant on the timing cover gasket and head gasket. Note that the locating dowel holes on the cylinder head are elongated to allow the head to move sideways slightly.

52 As soon as sufficient clearance exists, lift the cylinder head up and off the cylinder block. At the same time, release the timing chain guide rail from the peg on the cylinder head, and guide the chain tensioner clear of the tensioning rail. Check that the tensioner locking pin is not dislodged as the cylinder head is lifted up. Place the cylinder head on wooden blocks after removal to avoid damage to the valves. Recover the cylinder head gasket.

Preparation for refitting

53 The mating faces of the cylinder head and cylinder block must be perfectly clean before refitting the head. Scouring agents are available for this purpose, but acceptable results can be achieved by using a hard plastic or wood scraper to remove all traces

of gasket and carbon. The same method can be used to clean the piston crowns. Take particular care to avoid scoring or gouging the cylinder head mating surfaces during the cleaning operations, as aluminium alloy is easily damaged. Make sure that the carbon is not allowed to enter the oil and water passages – this is particularly important for the lubrication system, as carbon could block the oil supply to the engine's components. Using adhesive tape and paper, seal the water, oil and bolt holes in the cylinder block. To prevent carbon entering the gap between the pistons and bores, smear a little grease in the gap. After cleaning each piston, use a small brush to remove all traces of grease and carbon from the gap, then wipe away the remainder with a clean rag.

54 Check the mating surfaces of the cylinder block and the cylinder head for nicks, deep scratches and other damage. If slight, they may be removed carefully with a file, but if excessive, machining may be the only alternative to renewal. If warpage of the cylinder head gasket surface is suspected, use a straight-edge to check it for distortion. Refer to Chapter 2D, Section 8 if necessary.

55 Thoroughly clean the threads of the cylinder head bolt holes in the cylinder block. Ensure that the bolts run freely in their threads, and that all traces of oil and water are removed from each bolt hole.

56 Using a sharp knife, partially cut through the timing cover gasket flush with the top of the cylinder block. Release the gasket from the timing cover and bend it in half to break it off at the cut line. Remove the upper part of the gasket, and thoroughly clean the mating surface, paying particular attention to the cylinder block edge where it contacts the timing cover.

57 Before refitting the cylinder head, using the spanner on the camshaft flats, turn the camshafts slightly, as necessary, until the camshaft setting tool described in Section 4 can be inserted into the slots in the ends of the camshafts **(see illustration)**. With the tool in position, the camshaft lobes for No 1 cylinder should be pointing outward.

Refitting

58 Prior to locating the cylinder head

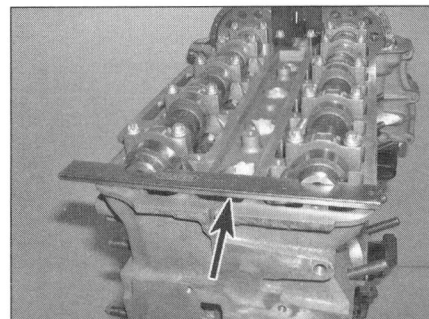

10.57 Before refitting the cylinder head, insert the camshaft setting tool into the slots in the ends of the camshafts

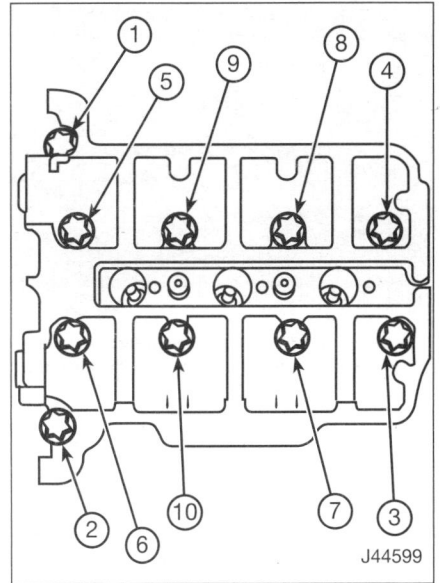

10.50 Cylinder head bolt slackening sequence

gasket on the cylinder block, cut off the two protruding tabs at the timing cover end of the gasket, flush with the gasket edge.

59 Apply a 2 mm diameter bead of silicone sealant to the joint between the cylinder block and the timing cover on each side.

60 Check that the locating dowels are in position in the cylinder block, then lay the new gasket on the block face, with the words OBEN/TOP uppermost **(see illustration)**. Push the gasket hard up against the timing cover so that it engages with the sealant.

61 Position the new timing cover gasket upper part on the timing cover, so that its lower ends engage with the sealant. Temporarily insert the left- and right-hand upper timing cover mounting bolts to locate the gasket in the correct position.

62 Apply a further 2 mm diameter bead of silicone sealant to the joint between the cylinder block and the timing cover on each side.

63 Carefully lower the cylinder head into position on the gasket, guiding the chain tensioner past the tensioning rail and guiding

10.60 Position the cylinder head gasket on the block with the words OBEN/TOP uppermost

10.67a Tighten the cylinder head bolts to the Stage 1 torque setting using a torque wrench

10.67b Tighten the cylinder head bolts through the Stage two, three and four angles using an angle tightening gauge

the tensioner locking pin into the timing cover access hole. Check also that the timing chain guide rail engages with cylinder head peg.

64 Once the head is seated on its dowels, tap it towards the timing cover with a rubber mallet.

65 Refit the three lower timing cover retaining bolts (one at each side, and one below the coolant pump). Tighten the three bolts to the specified torque.

66 Remove the camshaft setting tool from the camshaft slots.

67 Fit the new cylinder head retaining bolts and screw in the bolts until they contact the cylinder head. Working in the reverse order to the loosening sequence shown earlier in this Section, tighten the cylinder head bolts to the Stage one torque setting given in the Specifications, using a torque wrench. Again working in the correct order, tighten all the bolts through the Stage two angle using an angle measuring gauge **(see illustrations)**. Repeat for Stage three and Stage four.

68 Slacken the three previously-fitted bolts securing the timing cover to the cylinder head.

69 Refit the bolts around the coolant pump and tighten them securely.

70 Refit the remaining timing cover retaining bolts and tighten them to the specified torque.

71 Using the spanner on the camshaft flats, turn the camshafts slightly, as necessary, until the camshaft setting tool can once again be inserted into the camshaft slots.

72 Engage the camshaft sprockets with their respective camshafts, and fit the new retaining bolts together with the phase disc on the inlet camshaft. Tighten the bolts finger-tight only at this stage and check that the phase disc on the inlet camshaft can still be turned.

73 Refit the timing chain sliding rail to the top of the cylinder head and secure with the two bolts tightened securely.

74 Remove the roll-pin used to hold the timing chain tensioner plunger in the retracted position.

75 Turn the camshaft sensor phase disc as necessary until the phase disc positioning tool (or suitable alternative), described in Section 4, can be located over the phase disc. If the Vauxhall/Opel tool is being used, bolt it to the top of the timing cover. If the alternative tool

described is being used, ensure that its base is in contact with the timing cover.

76 Tighten the camshaft sprocket retaining bolts to 10 Nm (7 lbf ft). Note that this is just an initial torque loading to hold the sprockets and the phase disc in position when the setting tools are removed. Tighten the inlet camshaft sprocket bolt first, followed by the exhaust camshaft sprocket bolt.

77 Remove the crankshaft, camshaft and phase disc setting tools, then tighten the camshaft sprocket retaining bolts to the specified torque in the stages given in the Specifications. Counterhold the camshafts using the spanner on the camshaft flats as the sprocket bolts are tightened.

78 Turn the crankshaft through two complete revolutions, stopping just before the TDC notch on the crankshaft pulley aligns with the cast lug on the timing cover. Check that all four lobes for No 1 cylinder are pointing outwards (away from the engine).

79 Slowly turn the crankshaft further until the TDC position setting tool can once again be inserted to lock the crankshaft.

80 It should now be possible to re-insert the camshaft setting tool into the slots in the camshafts, and to fit the camshaft sensor phase disc setting tool over the disc. If this is not possible carry out the valve timing adjustment procedure contained in Section 4.

81 If all is satisfactory, remove all the setting/aligning tools and refit the timing chain tensioner and cylinder block closure bolts using new sealing rings. Tighten both closure bolts to the specified torque.

82 Refit the camshaft position sensor using a new sealing ring and tighten the retaining bolt securely.

83 On models with air conditioning, refit the compressor to the cylinder block and tighten the mounting bolts to the specified torque. Refit the refrigerant lines to their relevant clips or brackets.

84 Refit the camshaft cover as described in Section 3.

85 Ensure that the mating surfaces are clean, then fit a new sealing ring to the thermostat housing cover. Refit the cover to the coolant pump and tighten the bolts securely.

86 Refit the coolant pump pulley and tighten

the three bolts to the specified torque. To prevent the pulley turning as the bolts are tightened, hold the pulley using a screwdriver engaged with one of the bolts and the pump centre spindle. Alternatively, wait until the auxiliary drivebelt has been refitted and tighten the bolts then.

87 Refit the right-hand engine mounting bracket together with the auxiliary drivebelt with reference to Section 15. Remove the hoist or trolley jack supporting the engine.

88 Reconnect the radiator top hose and tighten the clips.

89 Thoroughly clean the mating surfaces of the oil filter housing and cylinder block, and refit the housing using a new seal. Refit and tighten the retaining bolts to the specified torque.

90 Fit a new sealing O-ring to the oil filter housing cap, then clip the new oil filter element to the cap.

91 Fit the cap and filter element assembly to the oil filter housing and screw the cap into position. Finally, tighten the cap to the specified torque.

92 Refit the exhaust manifold, together with a new gasket, and tighten the mounting nuts to the specified torque. Refit the exhaust manifold heat shield.

93 Refit the left-hand engine lifting eye to the cylinder head and tighten the bolts securely. Attach the wiring harness.

94 Refer to Chapter 4A and refit the oxygen sensor to the exhaust manifold. Reconnect the wiring.

95 Renew the oil dipstick guide tube O-rings and lubricate the O-rings with petroleum jelly. Insert the guide tube into the cylinder block baseplate then secure the tube to the exhaust manifold with the retaining bolt.

96 Refit the auxiliary drivebelt tensioner and tighten the mounting bolts to the specified torque.

97 Rotate the tensioner pulley bolt clockwise as for removal, refit the auxiliary drivebelt as previously noted and release the tensioner.

98 Refit the wiring harness brackets to the inlet manifold.

99 Reconnect the wiring to the starter motor and tighten the nuts. Secure the cable with ties.

100 Reconnect the catalytic converter to the exhaust manifold using a new flange gasket. Tighten the converter-to-manifold nuts to the specified torque first, followed by the support bracket bolts. Refit the mounting rubbers, then refit the oxygen sensor with reference to Chapter 4A. Reconnect the wiring.

101 Refit the auxiliary drivebelt cover under the right-hand wheel arch.

102 Refit the injector wiring and trough to the top of the fuel rail.

103 Reconnect the earth cables to the electronic control unit bracket.

104 Refit the ignition module with reference to Chapter 5B, and reconnect the wiring.

105 Reconnect the wiring to the following components:

a) Oil pressure switch.

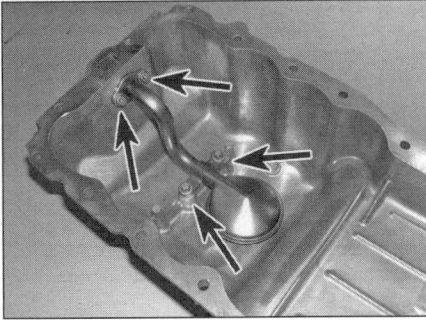

11.7a Undo the bolts...

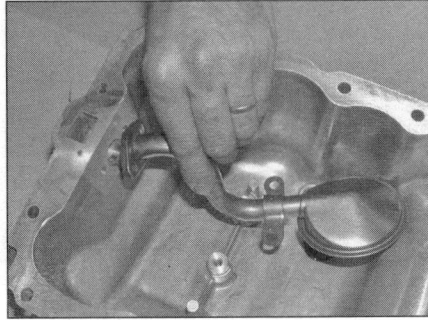

11.7b...remove the oil pick-up pipe...

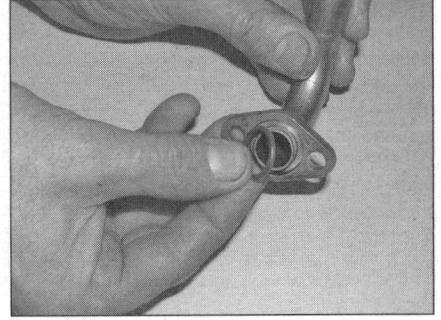

11.7c...and recover the O-ring from the flange

b) *Coolant temperature sensor.*
c) *Camshaft position sensor.*
d) *Fuel injectors.*
e) *Throttle valve adjuster.*
f) *Engine electronic control unit (LH end of engine).*
g) *Wiring combination plug (LH end of engine).*
h) *EGR valve.*

106 Reconnect the fuel feed hose to the fuel rail.

107 Disconnect the heater return hose to the EGR coolant flange, and secure the wiring harness.

108 Attach the lower wiring harness bracket to the inlet manifold.

109 Refit and tighten the bolt securing the support bracket to the base of the inlet manifold.

110 Refit the wiring harness support bracket to the rear of the inlet manifold.

111 Reconnect the brake servo vacuum line to the inlet manifold.

112 Where applicable, refit the cover over the fuel rail.

113 Reconnect the heater feed hose to the coolant pump and tighten the clip.

114 Refit the throttle housing as described in Chapter 4A, Section 10.

115 Refit the air cleaner assembly with reference to Chapter 4A, Section 2. Also refit the air inlet duct to the front of the engine compartment.

116 Refit or reconnect the battery as applicable.

117 Top-up the engine oil, then refill the cooling system with reference to Chapter 1A, Section 27.

118 Refit the roadwheel then lower the vehicle to the ground.

11 Sump and oil pick-up pipe – removal and refitting

Note: *A new sump gasket must be used on refitting. If the oil pick-up pipe is removed, a new O-ring should be used on refitting.*

Removal

1 Firmly apply the handbrake, then jack up

the front of the car and support it securely on axle stands (see *Jacking and vehicle support*). Remove the right-hand roadwheel.

2 Drain the engine oil, with reference to Chapter 1A, Section 5, then refit and tighten the sump drain plug.

3 Refer to Chapter 4A, and disconnect the wiring from the oxygen sensor on the catalytic converter, then unbolt the exhaust front pipe from the exhaust manifold, taking care to support the flexible section. Release the mounting rubbers and support the front of the exhaust pipe to one side to allow removal of the sump.

Note: *Angular movement in excess of 10° can cause permanent damage to the exhaust system flexible section.*

4 Remove the auxiliary drivebelt cover from under the right-hand wheel arch.

5 Undo the bolts securing the sump to the cylinder block baseplate, timing cover and transmission bellhousing, then withdraw the sump. If necessary, tap the sump with a soft-faced mallet to free it from its location – do not lever between the sump and cylinder block baseplate mating faces. Recover the gasket.

6 To remove the oil baffle plate, undo the retaining bolts and remove the baffle plate from the cylinder block baseplate.

7 If desired, the oil pick-up pipe can be removed from the sump by unscrewing the two support bracket retaining bolts and the two bolts securing the flange to the end

face of the sump. Lift out the pick-up pipe and recover the O-ring from the flange **(see illustrations)**. Note that a new O-ring will be required for refitting.

Refitting

8 Thoroughly clean the inside and outside of the sump ensuring that all traces of old gasket are removed from the mating face. Also clean the cylinder block baseplate mating face to remove all traces of old gasket.

9 If the oil pick-up pipe has been removed, fit a new O-ring to the flange, then refit the pipe to the sump. Refit the flange bolts and support bracket bolts, then tighten the flange bolts securely. Tighten the support bracket bolts securely.

10 If removed, refit the oil baffle plate and secure with the retaining bolts tightened securely.

11 Apply a 2 mm diameter bead of silicone sealant to the joint between the timing cover and cylinder block, on each side. Place a new gasket on the sump, then locate the sump on the cylinder block baseplate **(see illustrations)**. Refit the securing bolts and tighten them finger-tight at this stage.

12 If the engine has been removed from the car and separated from the transmission, use a straight-edge to check that the transmission mating face is aligned with the cylinder block baseplate mating face **(see illustration)**.

13 Tighten the bolts securing the sump to the cylinder block baseplate and timing cover progressively and securely. Now tighten the

11.11a Apply a 2 mm diameter bead of silicone sealant to the joint between the timing cover and cylinder block on each side...

11.11b...then place a new gasket on the sump and locate the sump on the cylinder block baseplate – shown with engine removed

bolts securing the sump to the transmission bellhousing to the specified torque.

14 Refit the auxiliary drivebelt cover under the right-hand wheel arch.

15 Reconnect the exhaust system front pipe/catalytic converter to the manifold as described in Chapter 4A. Also, reconnect the wiring to the oxygen sensor.

16 Refit the roadwheel, and where necessary the engine undertray sections, then lower the car to the ground and refill the engine with oil as described in Chapter 1A, Section 5.

12 Oil pump –
removal, inspection and refitting

Note: *A new pressure relief valve cap sealing ring and new oil fill channel closure plug sealing ring will be required for refitting.*

Removal

1 Remove the timing cover and chain as described in Section 6.

2 Remove the securing screws/bolts and withdraw the oil pump cover from the rear of the timing cover **(see illustration)**.

3 Remove the inner and outer rotor from the timing cover and wipe them clean. Also clean the rotor location in the timing cover.

4 The oil pressure relief valve components can also be removed from the timing cover by unscrewing the cap. Withdraw the cap and sealing ring, the spring and plastic pin, and the plunger **(see illustrations)**.

11.12 If the engine has been separated from the transmission, use a straight-edge to check the transmission mating face alignment when refitting the sump

Inspection

5 Locate the inner and outer rotor back in the timing cover, noting that the chamfer on the outer rotor outside diameter must face the timing cover.

6 Check the clearance between the end faces of the gears and the housing (endfloat) using a straight-edge and a feeler gauge **(see illustration)**.

7 If the clearance is outside the specified limits, renew the components as necessary.

8 Examine the pressure relief valve spring and plunger, and renew if any sign of damage or wear is evident.

9 Ensure that the rotor location in the interior of the timing cover is scrupulously clean before commencing reassembly.

Refitting

10 Thoroughly clean the pressure relief valve components, and lubricate them with clean engine oil before refitting. Insert the plunger, the spring and plastic pin, then refit the cap using a new sealing ring. Tighten the cap securely.

11 Ensure that the gears are clean, then lubricate them with clean engine oil, and refit them to the pump body. Ensure that the chamfer on the outer rotor outside diameter faces the timing cover.

12 Ensure that the mating faces of the rear cover and the pump housing are clean, then refit the rear cover. Refit and tighten the securing screws securely.

13 Fit a new crankshaft oil seal to the timing cover as described in Section 13.

14 Refit the timing chain and cover to the engine as described in Section 6.

15 After refitting the timing cover, unscrew the oil fill channel closure bolt from the lower front facing side of the timing cover. Using a pump type oil can filled with clean engine oil, insert the oil can spout into the oil channel, so that the spout pushes back the internal ball valve. Prime the pump by filling it with oil until the oil runs out of the fill channel. Refit the closure plug using a new sealing ring and tighten it to the specified torque.

13 Crankshaft oil seals –
renewal

Timing chain end oil seal

Note: *A new crankshaft pulley hub retaining bolt will be required for refitting.*

1 Disconnect the battery negative terminal (refer to Chapter 5A, Section 4).

2 Remove the air cleaner assembly as described in Chapter 4A, Section 2.

3 Firmly apply the handbrake, then jack up the front of the car and support it securely on axle stands (see *Jacking and vehicle support*). Remove the right-hand front roadwheel and the wheel arch liner for access to the crankshaft pulley.

4 Release the tension on the auxiliary drivebelt and lock the tensioner in the released

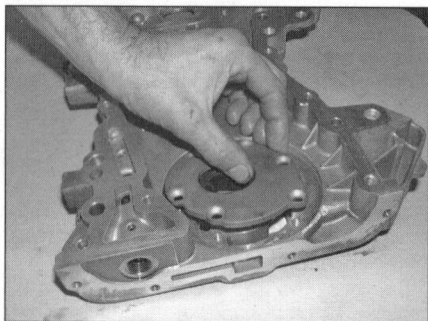

12.2 Remove the securing screws and withdraw the oil pump cover from the rear of the timing cover

12.4a Unscrew the oil pressure relief valve cap and sealing ring...

12.4b...then withdraw the spring and plastic pin...

12.4c...and the plunger

12.6 Check the oil pump gear endfloat using a straight-edge and feeler gauge

position as described in the auxiliary drivebelt renewal procedure in Chapter 1A, Section 32. Note that it is not necessary to completely remove the drivebelt, as this would entail removal of the right-hand engine mounting bracket. With the drivebelt tension released, slip the belt off the crankshaft pulley.

5 Using a socket or spanner on the crankshaft pulley hub bolt, turn the crankshaft in the normal direction of rotation (clockwise as viewed from the right-hand side of the car) until the TDC notch on the crankshaft pulley is located just before the cast lug on the timing cover **(see illustration 4.6)**.

6 Using quick-drying paint, or similar, make an alignment mark between the crankshaft pulley and the pulley hub. It should only be possible to refit the pulley in one position, but it is advisable to make an alignment mark anyway.

7 Unscrew the six crankshaft pulley retaining bolts and remove the pulley from the hub. If necessary, prevent the crankshaft from turning as the pulley bolts are slackened, using a spanner or socket on the pulley hub bolt.

8 Using a suitable socket, slacken the crankshaft pulley hub retaining bolt. The crankshaft can be prevented from turning as the bolt is slackened, using Vauxhall/Opel special tool KM-956 or a similar tool which will engage with the flats on each side of the pulley hub. Alternatively, remove the starter motor, and lock the flywheel ring gear teeth using a suitable hooked tool bolted to the bellhousing.

9 Unscrew the slackened crankshaft pulley hub retaining bolt and remove the hub from the crankshaft. Note that a new bolt will be required for refitting.

10 The seal can now be carefully prised out with a screwdriver or similar hooked tool **(see illustration)**.

11 Clean the oil seal seat with a wooden or plastic scraper.

12 Grease the lips of the new seal, and tap it into position until it is flush with the outer face of the timing cover, using a suitable socket or tube, or a wooden block **(see illustration)**.

13 Refit the crankshaft pulley hub to the crankshaft, ensuring that the punch mark on the pulley hub is in the 11 o'clock position.

14 Screw in the new pulley hub retaining bolt and tighten it to the specified torque, in the stages given in the Specifications. Prevent crankshaft rotation as the bolt is tightened, using the method employed for removal.

15 Refit the crankshaft pulley to the pulley hub, with the marks made on removal aligned, and tighten the six bolts securely.

16 Refit the auxiliary drivebelt as described in Chapter 1A, Section 32.

17 Refit the air cleaner assembly as described in Chapter 4A, Section 2.

18 Refit the wheel arch liner and roadwheel, tightening the wheel bolts to the specified torque.

19 Lower the car to the ground, then reconnect the battery negative terminal.

13.10 Carefully prise out the crankshaft oil seal from the timing cover – shown with timing cover removed

13.23 Locate the seal over the crankshaft and into the recess – shown with engine removed

Transmission end oil seal

20 Remove the flywheel as described in Section 14.

21 Carefully prise out the old seal from its location using a screwdriver or similar hooked tool.

22 Clean the oil seal seat with a wooden or plastic scraper.

23 Grease the lips of the new seal, then carefully locate the seal over the crankshaft and into the recess in the cylinder block and baseplate **(see illustration)**.

24 Tap the seal into position using a suitable socket or tube, or a wooden block, until it is flush with the outer faces of the cylinder block and baseplate **(see illustration)**.

25 Refit the flywheel as described in Section 14.

14 Flywheel – removal, inspection and refitting

Note: New flywheel retaining bolts will be required on refitting.

Removal

1 Remove the transmission as described in Chapter 7A, Section 8 (manual transmission) or Chapter 7C, Section 7 (Easytronic transmission), then remove the clutch assembly as described in Chapter 6, Section 6.

2 Prevent the flywheel from turning by locking the ring gear teeth with a similar arrangement to that shown **(see illustration)**. Alternatively,

13.12 Tap the new seal into position until it is flush with the outer face of the timing cover – shown with timing cover removed

13.24 Tap the seal into position until it is flush – shown with engine removed

bolt a strap between the flywheel and the cylinder block/crankcase. Make alignment marks between the flywheel and crankshaft using paint or a suitable marker pen.

3 Slacken and remove the retaining bolts and remove the flywheel. Do not drop it, as it is very heavy.

Inspection

4 Examine the flywheel for scoring of the clutch face. If the clutch face is scored, the flywheel may be surface-ground, but renewal is preferable.

5 If there is any doubt about the condition of the flywheel, seek the advice of a Vauxhall/Opel dealer or engine reconditioning specialist. They will be able to advise if it is possible to recondition it or whether renewal is necessary.

14.2 If the engine is removed, lock the flywheel with a suitable tool

14.8a Tighten the flywheel bolts to the specified torque using a torque wrench...

14.8b...then through the specified angle using an angle tightening gauge

Refitting

6 Clean the mating surfaces of the flywheel and crankshaft.

7 Apply a drop of locking compound to each of the new retaining bolt threads (unless they are pre-coated) then offer up the flywheel, if the original is being refitted align the marks made prior to removal. Screw in the retaining bolts.

8 Lock the flywheel by the method used on removal, and tighten the retaining bolts to the specified Stage 1 torque setting then angle-tighten the bolts through the specified Stage 2 angle. It is recommended that an angle-measuring gauge is used during the final stage of the tightening, to ensure accuracy (see illustrations). If a gauge is not available, use white paint to make alignment marks between the bolt head and flywheel prior to tightening, the marks can then be used to check that the bolt has been rotated through the correct angle.

9 Refit the clutch as described in Chapter 6, Section 6 then remove the locking tool, and refit the transmission as described in Chapter 7A, Section 8 or Chapter 7C, Section 7 as applicable.

15 Engine/transmission mountings – inspection and renewal

Inspection

1 To improve access, firmly apply the handbrake, then jack up the front of the vehicle and support it on axle stands (see *Jacking and vehicle support*).

2 Check the mounting blocks (rubbers) to see if they are cracked, hardened or separated from the metal at any point. Renew the mounting block if any such damage or deterioration is evident.

3 Check that all the mounting securing nuts and bolts are securely tightened, using a torque wrench to check if possible.

4 Using a large screwdriver, or a similar tool, check for wear in the mounting blocks by carefully levering against them to check for free play. Where this is not possible, enlist the aid of an assistant to move the engine/ transmission unit back-and-forth, and from side-to-side, while you observe the mountings. While some free play is to be expected, even from new components, excessive wear should be obvious. If excessive free play is found, check first to see that the securing nuts and bolts are correctly tightened, then renew any worn components as described in the following paragraphs.

Renewal

Note: *Before slackening any of the engine mounting bolts/nuts, the relative positions of the mountings to their various brackets should be marked to ensure correct alignment upon refitting.*

Right-hand mounting

5 Remove the air cleaner assembly as described in Chapter 4A, Section 2.

6 Support the weight of the engine using a trolley jack with a block of wood placed on its head.

7 Undo the two bolts securing the right-hand engine mounting to the mounting bracket on the engine (see illustration).

8 Undo the three bolts securing the mounting to the body, and remove the mounting. If necessary, the mounting bracket on the engine may be unbolted from the cylinder block.

9 Refitting is a reversal of removal. Tighten the bolts to the specified torque.

Left-hand mounting

10 Remove the battery and battery tray as described in Chapter 5A, Section 4.

11 Support the weight of the transmission using a trolley jack with a block of wood placed on its head.

12 Unscrew the two bolts securing the mounting bracket to the transmission bracket (see illustration).

13 Unscrew the two bolts securing the mounting to the body, slightly lower the engine, then remove the mounting assembly from the car.

14 Refitting is a reversal of removal. Ensure all bolts are tightened to their specified torques.

Rear mounting/torque link

15 Apply the handbrake, then jack up the front of the vehicle and support it on axle stands (see *Jacking and vehicle support*).

16 Working under the vehicle, undo the bolt securing the torque link to the mounting on the transmission bracket (see illustration).

17 Undo the bolt securing the torque link to the subframe, and remove the link.

18 Undo the bolts securing the torque link rubber mounting bracket to the transmission and remove the bracket and mounting.

19 Locate the new mounting bracket in position. Insert the bolts and tighten to the specified torque.

20 Refit the torque link to the subframe and mounting, insert the bolts and tighten to the specified torque.

21 On completion, lower the vehicle to the ground.

15.7 Right-hand engine mounting-to-engine bracket bolts (A) and mounting-to-body bolts (B)

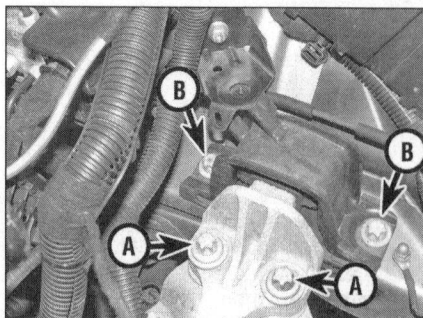

15.12 Left-hand engine mounting-to-transmission bracket bolts (A) and mounting-to-body bolts (B)

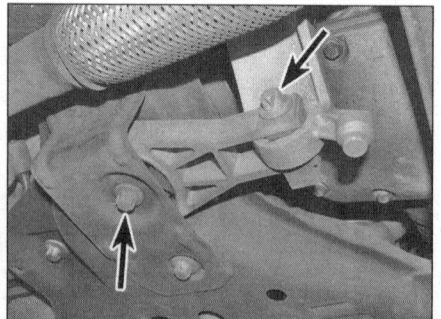

15.16 Rear engine mounting/torque link retaining bolts

Chapter 2 Part B
1.2 and 1.4 litre petrol engine in-car repair procedures

Contents

Degrees of difficulty

Easy, suitable for novice with little experience	**Fairly easy,** suitable for beginner with some experience	**Fairly difficult,** suitable for competent DIY mechanic	**Difficult,** suitable for experienced DIY mechanic	**Very difficult,** suitable for expert DIY or professional

Specifications

General

Engine type.	Four-cylinder, in-line, water-cooled. Double overhead camshafts, chain-driven, acting on rocker arms and hydraulic valve lifters
Manufacturer's engine codes:	
1.2 litre engines	A12XEL (LWD) and A12XER (LDC)
1.4 litre engines	A14XEL (L2Z) and A14XER (LDD)
Bore	73.40 mm
Stroke	
1.2 litre engines	72.60 mm
1.4 litre engines	80.60 mm
Capacity:	
1.2 litre engines	1229 cc
1.4 litre engines	1398 cc
Firing order.	1-3-4-2 (No 1 cylinder at timing chain end of engine)
Direction of crankshaft rotation	Clockwise (viewed from timing chain end of engine)
Compression ratio	10.5: 1

Note: *For details of engine code location, see 'Vehicle identification' in Reference.*

Lubrication system

Minimum oil pressure at 80°C	1.5 bar at idle speed
Oil pump type.	Variable displacement vane-type, driven directly from crankshaft
Oil pump slide pin spring free length	76.5 mm
Oil pump clearances:	
Maximum vane rotor-to-housing axial clearance.	0.1 mm
Maximum vane-to-housing axial clearance	0.09 mm
Maximum vane ring-to-housing axial clearance.	0.04 mm
Maximum pump slide-to-housing axial clearance.	0.08 mm
Maximum pump slide seal-to-housing axial clearance	0.09 mm
Maximum vane rotor-to-vane radial clearance.	0.05 mm
Maximum vane-to-pump slide radial clearance.	0.2 mm

Torque wrench settings

	Nm	lbf ft
Air conditioning compressor mounting bracket bolts	22	16
Air conditioning compressor-to-mounting bracket	22	16
Auxiliary drivebelt tensioner mounting bolts:		
M8 bolt	20	15
M10 bolt	55	41
Big-end bearing cap bolts*:		
Stage 1	25	18
Stage 2	Angle-tighten a further 60°	
Camshaft bearing cap bolts	8	6
Camshaft cover bolts	8	6
Camshaft sprocket bolt*:		
Stage 1	50	37
Stage 2	Angle-tighten a further 60°	
Camshaft VVT solenoid valve bolts	8	6
Coolant pump bolts	8	6
Coolant pump pulley bolts	20	15
Crankshaft pulley bolt*:		
Stage 1	150	111
Stage 2	Angle-tighten a further 60°	
Cylinder block baseplate-to-cylinder block*:		
M6 bolts:		
Stage 1	10	7
Stage 2	Angle-tighten a further 60°	
Stage 3	Angle-tighten a further 15°	
M8 bolts:		
Stage 1	25	18
Stage 2	Angle-tighten a further 60°	
Stage 3	Angle-tighten a further 15°	
Cylinder block closure bolt (for TDC setting tool)	40	30
Cylinder head bolts*:		
Stage 1	32	26
Stage 2	Angle-tighten a further 180°	
Driveplate bolts*	60	44
Engine mountings:		
Left-hand:		
Mounting-to-body bolts	80	59
Mounting bracket-to-transmission bracket*:		
Stage 1	80	59
Stage 2	Angle-tighten a further 45°	
Transmission bracket-to-transmission*	80	59
Rear mounting/torque link: *		
Stage 1	80	59
Stage 2	Angle-tighten a further 45°	
Rear mounting/torque link bracket-to-transmission: *		
Stage 1	80	59
Stage 2	Angle-tighten a further 45°	
Right-hand:		
Mounting bracket-to-timing cover*	60	44
Mounting-to-body	60	44
Mounting-to-mounting bracket*:		
Stage 1	80	59
Stage 2	Angle-tighten a further 45°	
Engine-to-transmission bolts:		
M10 bolts	40	32
M12 bolts	60	44
Exhaust front pipe-to-catalytic converter nuts*	20	15
Flywheel bolts*:		
Stage 1	35	26
Stage 2	Angle-tighten a further 30°	
Stage 3	Angle-tighten a further 15°	
Oil filter housing cap to filter housing	25	18
Oil filter housing to cylinder block	20	15
Oil pressure relief valve cap	50	37
Oil pump cover bolts	8	6
Roadwheel bolts	110	81

Torque wrench settings

	Nm	lbf ft
Sump-to-cylinder block baseplate/timing cover	10	7
Sump-to-transmission	40	30
Timing chain guide rail bolts.	8	6
Timing chain sliding rail-to-cylinder head	8	6
Timing chain tension rail pivot bolt.	20	15
Timing chain tensioner bolts	8	6
Timing chain tensioner closure bolt (for locking pin access)	50	37
Timing cover bolts:		
M6 bolts	8	6
M10 bolts	35	26

* Use new fasteners

1 General Information

How to use this Chapter

1 This Part of Chapter 2 describes the repair procedures which can reasonably be carried out on the engine while it remains in the vehicle. If the engine has been removed from the vehicle and is being dismantled as described in Chapter 2D, any preliminary dismantling procedures can be ignored.

2 Note that, while it may be possible physically to overhaul items such as the piston/connecting rod assemblies while the engine is in the vehicle, such tasks are not usually carried out as separate operations, and usually require the execution of several additional procedures (not to mention the cleaning of components and of oil ways); for this reason, all such tasks are classed as major overhaul procedures, and are described in Chapter 2D.

3 Chapter 2D describes the removal of the engine/transmission unit from the vehicle, and the full overhaul procedures which can then be carried out.

Engine description

4 The engine is of four-cylinder in-line type, with double overhead camshafts (DOHC). The engine is mounted transversely at the front of the vehicle.

5 The power unit is known as a 'Twinport' engine due to the design of the inlet manifold and cylinder head combustion chambers. Vacuum operated flap valves located in the inlet manifold are opened or closed according to engine operating conditions, to create a variable venturi manifold arrangement. This system has significant advantages in terms of engine power, fuel economy and reduced exhaust emissions.

6 The cylinder block is made of cast iron and the cylinder bores are an integral part of the block. An cast iron baseplate is bolted to the cylinder block and forms the lower half of the crankcase.

7 The crankshaft runs in five shell-type main bearings with crankshaft endfloat being controlled by thrust-washers which are an integral part of No 4 main bearing shells.

8 The connecting rods are attached to the crankshaft by horizontally-split shell-type big-end bearings. The pistons are attached to the connecting rods by gudgeon pins, which are an interference fit in the connecting rod small-end bores. The aluminium-alloy pistons are fitted with three piston rings – two compression rings and an oil control ring.

9 The camshafts are driven from the crankshaft by a hydraulically tensioned timing chain. Each cylinder has four valves (two inlet and two exhaust), operated via rocker arms which are supported at their pivot ends by hydraulic self-adjusting valve lifters (tappets). One camshaft operates the inlet valves, and the other operates the exhaust valves.

10 The inlet and exhaust valves are each closed by a single valve spring, and operate in guides pressed into the cylinder head.

11 A variable valve timing (VVT) system is employed. The VVT system allows the inlet and exhaust camshaft timing to be varied under the control of the engine management system, to boost both low-speed torque and top-end power, as well as reducing exhaust emissions. The VVT camshaft adjuster is integral with each camshaft timing chain sprocket, and is supplied with two pressurised oil feeds through passages in the camshaft itself. Two electro-magnetic solenoid valves, one for each camshaft and operated by the engine management system, are fitted to the timing cover, and are used to control the supply of oil to each camshaft adjuster through the two oil feeds. Each adjuster contains two chambers – depending on which of the two oil feeds is enabled by the solenoid valve, the oil pressure will turn the camshaft clockwise (advance) or anti-clockwise (retard) to adjust the valve timing as required. If pressure is removed from both feeds, this induces a timing 'hold' condition. Thus the valve timing is infinitely variable within a given range.

12 A variable displacement vane-type oil pump is located in the timing cover attached to the cylinder block, and is driven directly from the crankshaft.

13 The coolant pump is located externally on the timing cover, and is driven by the auxiliary drivebelt.

Repair operations possible with the engine in the car

14 The following operations can be carried out without having to remove the engine from the vehicle.

a) *Removal and refitting of the cylinder head.*
b) *Removal and refitting of the timing cover.*
c) *Removal and refitting of the timing chain, tensioner and sprockets.*
d) *Removal and refitting of the camshafts.*
e) *Removal and refitting of the sump.*
f) *Removal and refitting of the big-end bearings, connecting rods, and pistons*.*
g) *Removal and refitting of the oil pump.*
h) *Removal and refitting of the oil filter housing.*
i) *Renewal of the crankshaft oil seals.*
j) *Renewal of the engine mountings.*
k) *Removal and refitting of the flywheel.*

Note: *Although the operation marked with an asterisk can be carried out with the engine in the vehicle (after removal of the sump), it is preferable for the engine to be removed, in the interests of cleanliness and improved access. For this reason, the procedure is described in Chapter 2D.*

2 Compression test – general information

1 When engine performance is down, or if misfiring occurs which cannot be attributed to the ignition or fuel systems, a compression test can provide diagnostic clues as to the engine's condition. If the test is performed regularly, it can give warning of trouble before any other symptoms become apparent.

2 Due to the electronic throttle control system used on these engines, a compression test can only be carried out with the engine management electronic control unit connected to Vauxhall/Opel diagnostic test equipment, or a compatible alternative unit. Without the test equipment, the throttle valve cannot be opened (as there is no accelerator cable) and the test will be inconclusive. Note that even with the accelerator pedal fully depressed, the engine management ECU will only control the throttle valve position when the engine is actually running. The test equipment independently actuates the throttle valve (irrespective of ECU commands) and opens the throttle valve fully.

3 As the equipment needed for the compression test is unlikely to be available to the home mechanic, it is recommended that the test is performed by a Vauxhall/Opel dealer, or suitably-equipped garage.

3.3a Disconnect the wiring connectors at the inlet and exhaust camshaft VVT solenoid valves...

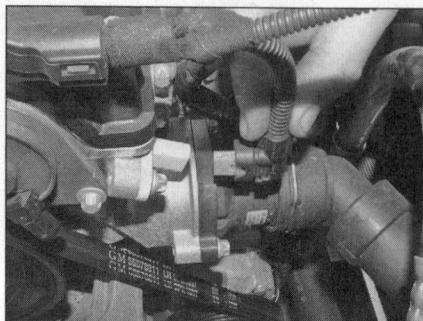

3.3b...inlet and exhaust camshaft position sensors...

3.3c...and thermostat...

3.3d...then unclip the wiring harness trough from the side of the camshaft cover...

3.3e...and from the rear of the cover

3 Camshaft cover – removal and refitting

Note: *A new camshaft cover rubber seal will be required for refitting, and a suitable silicone sealant will be required to seal the timing cover-to-cylinder head upper joint.*

Removal

1 Disconnect the battery negative terminal (refer to *Disconecting the battery* in Chapter 5A, Section 4).
2 Remove the ignition module from the centre of the camshaft cover as described in Chapter 5B, Section 3.
3 Disconnect the wiring connectors at the inlet

and exhaust camshaft VVT solenoid valves, inlet and exhaust camshaft position sensors, thermostat and oil pressure switch. Unclip the wiring harness trough from the camshaft cover and move it to one side (see illustrations).
4 Remove the engine oil level dipstick from the camshaft cover.
5 Progressively slacken the fifteen camshaft cover retaining bolts until they are all fully unscrewed. Note that the bolts are captive and will remain in place in the cover as it is removed.
6 Lift the camshaft cover up and off the cylinder head (see illustration).

Refitting

7 Remove the old seal from the camshaft cover, then examine the inside of the cover

for a build-up of oil sludge or any other contamination, and if necessary clean the cover with paraffin, or a water-soluble solvent. Dry the cover thoroughly before refitting.
8 Fit a new rubber seal to the cover ensuring that it is correctly located in the camshaft cover groove (see illustration).
9 Inspect the joint between the timing cover and cylinder head, and cut off any projecting timing cover gasket using a sharp knife.
10 Thoroughly clean the mating faces of the camshaft cover and cylinder head.
11 Apply a 2 mm diameter bead of silicone sealant to the joint between the timing cover and cylinder head on each side (see illustration).
12 Locate the camshaft cover on the cylinder head and screw in the retaining bolts. Progressively and evenly tighten the retaining bolts securely.
13 Insert the engine oil level dipstick back into its location in the camshaft cover.
14 Reconnect the wiring connectors to the components listed in paragraph 3, then clip the wiring harness trough back into place in the camshaft cover.
15 On turbocharged engines, refit the crankcase ventilation hose and vacuum hose and secure with the retaining clips, then refit the air cleaner outlet air duct.
16 Refit the ignition module to the centre of the camshaft cover as described in Chapter 5B, Section 3.
17 Reconnect the battery negative terminal on completion.

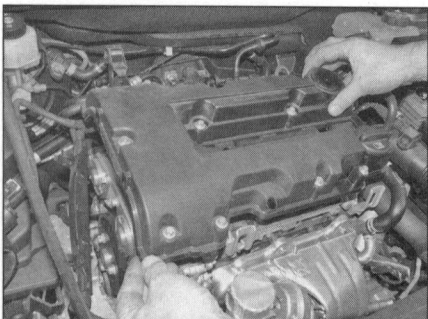

3.6 Lift the camshaft cover up and off the cylinder head

3.8 Fit a new rubber seal to the camshaft cover

3.11 Apply a bead of silicone sealant to the joint between the timing cover and cylinder head on each side

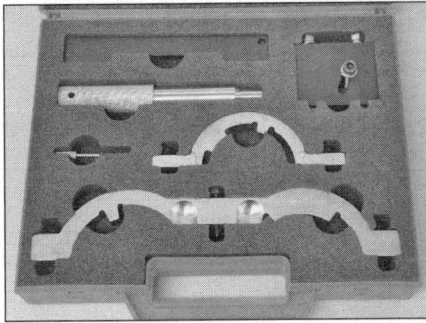

4.3 Typical valve timing checking and adjusting tool set

4.8 Turn the crankshaft until the hole in the crankshaft pulley is located just before the cast lug on the timing cover

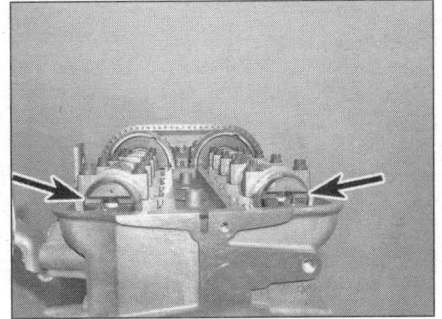

4.9 With No 1 piston on compression, the offset slots in the camshafts should be above the cylinder head mating face

4 Valve timing – checking and adjustment

Note: *Certain special tools will be required for this operation. Read through the entire procedure to familiarise yourself with the work involved, then either obtain the manufacturer's special tools, or suitable alternatives. New gaskets and sealing rings will also be required for all disturbed components.*

General

1 To accurately check, and if necessary adjust, the valve timing, various special tools are required to retain the camshafts, camshaft sprockets, camshaft sensor phase discs and crankshaft in the top dead centre (TDC) position, with No 1 piston on the compression stroke.
2 The Vauxhall/Opel tool numbers are as follows:

Crankshaft TDC positioning tool   EN-952
Camshaft setting tool   EN-953-A
Camshaft sprocket holding
tool   EN-49977-200
Camshaft sensor phase disc
setting tool   EN-49977-100

3 Although the Vauxhall/Opel tools are specifically designed for the purpose, suitable relatively inexpensive aftermarket alternatives are readily available **(see illustration)**. It will be necessary to use the Vauxhall/Opel tools or the aftermarket alternatives for any work on the timing chain, camshafts or cylinder head.

Checking

4 Disconnect the battery negative terminal (refer to *Disconnecting the battery* in Chapter 5A, Section 4).
5 Remove the air cleaner assembly as described in Chapter 4A, Section 2.
6 Remove the camshaft cover as described in Section 3.
7 Firmly apply the handbrake, then jack up the front of the car and support it securely on axle stands (see *Jacking and vehicle support*). Remove the right-hand front roadwheel and the wheel arch liner lower cover for access to the crankshaft pulley.

8 Using a socket or spanner on the crankshaft pulley bolt, turn the crankshaft in the normal direction of rotation (clockwise as viewed from the right-hand side of the car) until the hole in the crankshaft pulley is located just before the cast lug on the timing cover **(see illustration)**.
9 Check that No 1 piston is on the compression stroke by observing the offset slots at the left-hand end of the camshafts. The slots should be positioned above the camshaft cover mating face of the cylinder head **(see illustration)**. If they are not, No 1 piston is on the exhaust stroke and the crankshaft should be turned through a further full turn, stopping once again when the hole in the crankshaft pulley is located just before the cast lug on the timing cover.
10 Undo the closure bolt from the crankshaft TDC position setting hole. The bolt is located on the front facing side of the cylinder block

4.10 Undo the closure bolt from the crankshaft TDC position setting hole

4.12a Insert the camshaft setting tool into the slots in the ends of the camshafts...

baseplate, adjacent to the timing cover joint **(see illustration)**. Note that a new closure bolt sealing ring will be required for refitting.
11 Insert the crankshaft TDC positioning tool into the position setting hole and push it into contact with the crankshaft **(see illustration)**. Slowly turn the crankshaft in the normal direction of rotation until the tool engages with the TDC slot in the crankshaft, and moves fully in, up to its stop.
12 Insert the camshaft setting tool into the slots in the left-hand end of the camshafts. Ensure that the tool is inserted fully, up to its stop, to lock both camshafts **(see illustrations)**.
13 If it is not possible to insert the camshaft setting tool, then the valve timing must be adjusted as described in paragraphs 15 to 34 below.
14 If all is satisfactory so far, the position of the camshaft position sensor phase discs

4.11 Insert the crankshaft TDC positioning tool into the position setting hole

4.12b ...ensuring that the tool is inserted fully, up to its stop

4.16a Undo the VVT solenoid valve retaining bolts...

4.16b...and remove the solenoid valves

4.17a Slacken the camshaft sprocket retaining bolts...

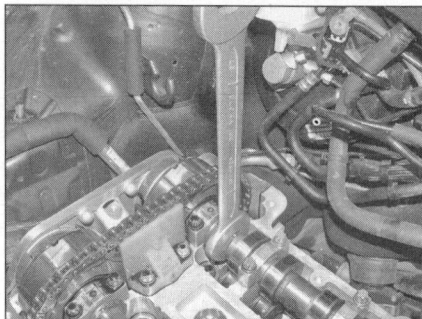

4.17b...while using a spanner to counterhold each camshaft

should be checked. Using the phase disc setting tool, check to see if the tool will engage with the phase disc on each camshaft,

and also seat squarely on the timing cover surface. If it does, proceed to paragraph 31. If adjustment is required, proceed as follows.

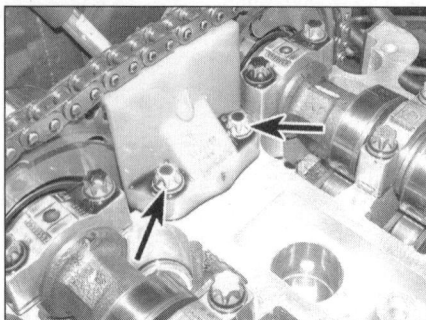

4.21 Undo the two bolts and remove the timing chain sliding rail

4.22a Slacken the bolt at the rear of the camshaft sprocket holding tool and place the tool in position

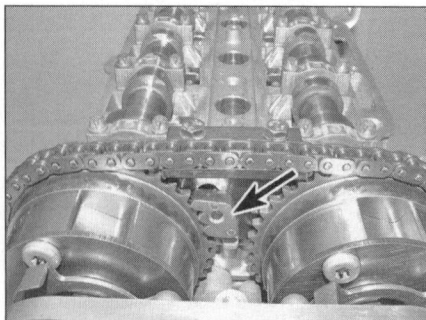

4.22b Slide the toothed portion of the tool to engage with the inlet camshaft sprocket teeth

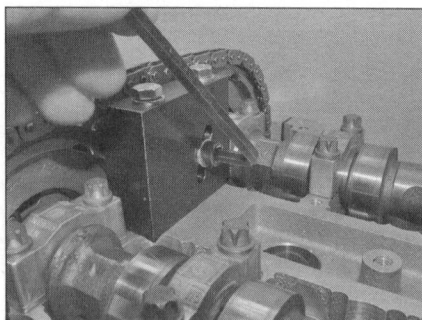

4.22c Hold the toothed portion fully into engagement with the sprocket teeth and tighten the bolt

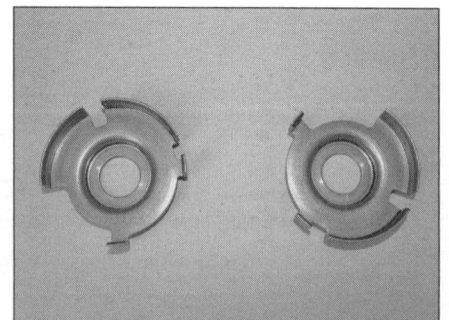

4.23a Correct positioning of the camshaft sensor phase discs...

Adjustment

Note: *New camshaft sprocket retaining bolts will be required for this operation.*

15 Remove the camshaft sensor phase disc setting tool, but leave the camshaft setting tool and the crankshaft TDC positioning tool in place.

16 Undo the four bolts securing the VVT solenoid valves to the timing cover. Carefully rotate the inlet camshaft solenoid valve anti-clockwise slightly while at the same time pulling it squarely out of the timing cover. Repeat this procedure to remove the exhaust camshaft solenoid valve, but this time, rotate it clockwise during removal (see illustrations). Remove the sealing ring from the rear of each solenoid valve, noting that new sealing rings will be required for refitting.

17 Slacken the sprocket retaining bolts for both camshafts, using a spanner to counterhold each camshaft as the bolts are slackened (see illustrations).

18 Unscrew and remove both camshaft sprocket retaining bolts together with the camshaft position sensor phase discs.

19 Fit the phase discs and the new bolts to both camshaft sprockets and tighten them finger tight only at this stage. Check that the phase discs can still be turned.

20 Again, using the spanner on the camshaft flats, turn the camshafts slightly, as necessary, until the camshaft setting tool can be reinserted into the slots in the ends of the camshafts.

21 Undo the two bolts and remove the timing chain sliding rail from the top of the cylinder head (see illustration).

22 Slacken the bolt at the rear of the camshaft sprocket holding tool, place the tool in position on the cylinder head, then fit and tighten the two retaining bolts. Slide the toothed portion of the tool to engage with the inlet camshaft sprocket teeth. Hold the toothed portion fully into engagement with the sprocket teeth and tighten the bolt (see illustrations).

23 Position the camshaft sensor phase discs as shown to allow the phase disc setting tool to locate over them. Fit the phase disc setting tool and secure it to the timing cover with the three bolts (see illustrations). Ensure that

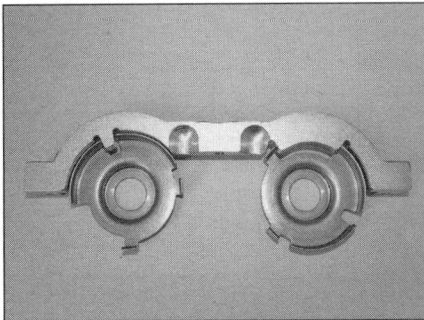
4.23b...to allow the phase disc setting tool to locate over them

4.23c Fit the phase disc setting tool and secure it to the timing cover with the three bolts

4.24a Tighten the camshaft sprocket retaining bolts to the specified torque...

the tool correctly engages with the phase discs and seats squarely on the timing cover surface.

24 Tighten the camshaft sprocket retaining bolts to the specified torque, then through the specified angle in the two stages given in the Specifications **(see illustrations)**. The inlet camshaft sprocket bolt should be tightened first. Counterhold the camshafts using the spanner on the camshaft flats as the sprocket bolts are tightened.

25 Remove the camshaft sensor phase disc setting tool and the camshaft sprocket holding tool.

26 Refit the timing chain sliding rail to the top of the cylinder head and secure with the two bolts, tightened to the specified torque.

27 Remove the camshaft setting tool and the crankshaft TDC positioning tool.

28 Turn the crankshaft through two complete revolutions, stopping just before the hole in the crankshaft pulley aligns with the cast lug on the timing cover **(see illustration 4.8)**.

29 Slowly turn the crankshaft further until the TDC position setting tool can once again be inserted to lock the crankshaft.

30 It should now be possible to re-insert the camshaft setting tool into the slots in the camshafts, and to fit the camshaft sensor phase disc setting tool over the discs. If this is not possible repeat the entire adjustment procedure.

31 If all is satisfactory, remove all the setting/ positioning tools and refit the cylinder block closure bolt using a new sealing ring. Tighten the closure bolt to the specified torque.

32 Locate a new sealing ring on each camshaft VVT solenoid valve. Lubricate the sealing rings with clean engine oil and carefully insert them into their locations in the timing cover. Position the solenoid valves as shown, then insert the four retaining bolts and tighten them securely **(see illustration)**.

33 Refit the wheel arch liner lower cover and the roadwheel. Tighten the roadwheel nuts to the specified torque, then lower the vehicle to the ground.

34 Refit the camshaft cover as described in Section 3.

35 Refit the air cleaner assembly as described in Chapter 4B, Section 3, then reconnect the battery negative terminal.

4.24b...then through the specified angle

5 Crankshaft pulley – removal and refitting

Removal

1 Firmly apply the handbrake, then jack up the front of the car and support it securely on axle stands (see *Jacking and vehicle support*). Remove the right-hand roadwheel and the wheel arch liner lower cover.

2 Using a socket or spanner on the pulley centre bolt, turn the auxiliary drivebelt tensioner clockwise against the spring tension. Hold the tensioner in this position by inserting a suitable locking pin/bolt through the special hole provided **(see illustration)**.

3 With the drivebelt tension released, slip the belt off the crankshaft pulley. Note that it is not

5.2 Turn the tensioner clockwise and insert a suitable locking pin/bolt through the special hole provided

4.32 Correct positioning of the camshaft VVT solenoid valves

necessary to completely remove the drivebelt, as this would entail removal of the right-hand engine mounting.

4 Using a socket or spanner on the crankshaft pulley bolt, turn the crankshaft in the normal direction of rotation (clockwise as viewed from the right-hand side of the car) until the hole in the crankshaft pulley is aligned with the cast lug on the timing cover **(see illustration 4.8)**.

5 It will now be necessary to hold the crankshaft pulley to enable the retaining bolt to be removed. Vauxhall/Opel special tools EN-49979 and EN-956-1are available for this purpose, however, a home-made tool can easily be fabricated **(see Tool Tip)**.

TOOL TIP

To make a sprocket holding tool, obtain two lengths of steel strip about 6 mm thick by about 30 mm wide or similar, one 600 mm long, the other 200 mm long (all dimensions are approximate). Bolt the two strips together to form a forked end, leaving the bolt slack so that the shorter strip can pivot freely. At the other end of each 'prong' of the fork, drill a suitable hole and fit a nut and bolt to allow the tool to engage with the spokes in the sprocket.

5.6a Unscrew the crankshaft pulley retaining bolt...

5.6b...and remove the pulley

6 Using the holding tool to prevent rotation of the crankshaft, slacken the pulley retaining bolt. Remove the holding tool, unscrew the retaining bolt and remove the pulley **(see illustrations)**. Note that a new pulley retaining bolt will be required for refitting.

Refitting

7 Align the hole in the crankshaft pulley with the cast lug on the timing cover and locate the pulley on the crankshaft. Note that the pulley flange must engage with the hexagon of the oil pump vane rotor and the two flats of the crankshaft. It may be necessary to carefully reposition the oil pump vane rotor slightly using a screwdriver, until the pulley flange will fully engage. When the pulley is fully engaged, the distance from the pulley inner rim to the cast lug on the timing cover should be no more than 5.5 mm.

8 Fit the new pulley retaining bolt and tighten it to the specified torque, then through the specified angle while preventing crankshaft rotation using the method employed on removal.

9 Refit the auxiliary drivebelt over the crankshaft pulley and ensure that it is correctly seated in the other pulleys.

10 Turn back the tensioner and remove the locking pin/bolt then release it, making sure that the drivebelt ribs locate correctly on each of the pulley grooves.

11 Refit the wheel arch liner lower cover and the roadwheel and tighten the wheel nuts to the specified torque.

12 Lower the car to the ground.

6.6 Air conditioning compressor mounting bracket retaining bolts

6 Timing cover and chain – removal and refitting

Note: *The special tools described in Section 4 will also be required for this operation. Read through the entire procedure and also the procedures contained in Section 4 to familiarise yourself with the work involved, then either obtain the manufacturer's special tools or suitable alternatives. New gaskets and sealing rings will also be required for all disturbed components, together with new camshaft sprocket retaining bolts, crankshaft pulley retaining bolt and right-hand engine mounting bracket retaining bolts. A tube of silicone sealant will be needed to seal the joint between the cylinder block and cylinder head.*

Removal

1 Carry out the operations described in Section 4, paragraphs 1 to 12 to set the engine at TDC for No 1 piston on the compression stroke.

2 Drain the cooling system as described in Chapter 1A, Section 27. Tighten the drain plug after draining the system.

3 Position a container beneath the engine sump, then unscrew the drain plug and drain the engine oil. Clean, refit and tighten the drain plug on completion.

4 Using a socket or spanner on the pulley centre bolt, turn the auxiliary drivebelt tensioner

6.13 Undo the upper and lower mounting bolts and remove the auxiliary drivebelt tensioner

clockwise against the spring tension. Hold the tensioner in this position by inserting a suitable locking pin/bolt through the special hole provided **(see illustration 5.2)**. Note the routing of the drivebelt, then remove it from the pulleys – mark the drivebelt for fitted direction.

Note: *The drivebelt cannot be removed completely until the right-hand engine mounting has been removed.*

5 Disconnect the wiring from the air conditioning compressor and release the wiring harness from the cable clips. Unbolt the compressor from the cylinder block bracket and support the compressor clear of the engine. Do not disconnect the refrigerant lines from the compressor.

6 Undo the three retaining bolts and remove the air conditioning compressor mounting bracket from the cylinder block and timing cover **(see illustration)**.

7 Remove the crankshaft pulley as described in Section 5.

8 Remove the alternator as described in Chapter 5A, Section 8.

9 Remove the sump as described in Section 11.

10 The engine must now be supported while the right-hand engine mounting is removed. To do this, use a hoist attached to the top of the engine, or make up a wooden frame to locate on the crankcase and use a trolley jack.

11 Remove the right-hand engine mounting as described in Section 16, then remove the auxiliary drivebelt.

12 Undo the three bolts and remove the right-hand engine mounting bracket from the timing cover. Note that new bolts will be required for refitting.

13 Undo the upper and lower mounting bolts and remove the auxiliary drivebelt tensioner from the timing cover **(see illustration)**.

14 Remove the coolant pump as described in Chapter 3, Section 7.

15 Undo the four bolts securing the VVT solenoid valves to the timing cover. Carefully rotate the inlet camshaft solenoid valve anticlockwise slightly while at the same time pulling it squarely out of the timing cover. Repeat this procedure to remove the exhaust camshaft solenoid valve, but this time, rotate it clockwise during removal **(see illustrations 4.16a and 4.16b)**. Remove the sealing ring from the rear of each solenoid valve, noting that new sealing rings will be required for refitting.

16 Slacken the sprocket retaining bolts for both camshafts, using a spanner to counterhold each camshaft as the bolts are slackened **(see illustrations 4.17a and 4.17b)**.

17 Undo the fifteen timing cover retaining bolts and remove the timing cover from the engine **(see illustration)**. The cover will be initially tight as it is located on dowels and secured by sealant. If necessary, gently tap it off using a soft-faced mallet.

18 Fully push back the timing chain tensioner plunger and secure it in the released position

6.17 Undo the fifteen retaining bolts and remove the timing cover from the engine

6.18 Secure the timing chain tensioner plunger in the released position by inserting a drill or roll pin in the tensioner body hole

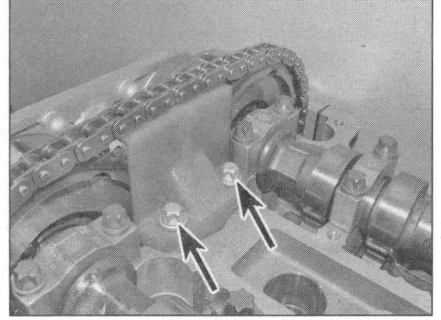

6.19a Undo the two bolts...

6.19b...and remove the timing chain sliding rail

6.20a Undo the two bolts...

6.20b...and remove the timing chain (front) guide rail

by inserting a 2 mm diameter drill or roll pin in the hole on the tensioner body **(see illustration)**.

19 Undo the two bolts and remove the timing chain sliding rail from the top of the cylinder head **(see illustrations)**.

20 Undo the two bolts and remove the timing chain (front) guide rail from the cylinder block **(see illustrations)**.

21 Undo the lower pivot bolt and remove the timing chain (rear) tension rail from the cylinder block **(see illustrations)**.

22 Slide the drive sprocket and timing chain off the crankshaft, then lift the chain off the camshaft sprockets **(see illustrations)**.

23 Remove the composite gasket from the cylinder block baseplate, cylinder block, and cylinder head, using a plastic spatula if necessary to release the sealant. Note that if the cylinder head has ever been previously removed, the gasket will be a two-piece type, with a split at the cylinder head-to cylinder block joint. A new gasket will be required for refitting.

24 Thoroughly clean the timing cover and remove all traces of gasket and sealant from all the mating surfaces. Similarly clean the cylinder block baseplate, cylinder block and cylinder head mating surfaces. Ensure that all traces of old sealant are removed, particularly from the area of the cylinder head-to-cylinder block joint.

25 Inspect the timing chain, sprockets, sliding rail, guide rail and tension rail for any sign of wear or deformation, and renew any suspect components as necessary. Renew

the crankshaft timing chain end oil seal in the timing cover as a matter of course using the procedures described in Section 13.

26 It is advisable to check the condition of

6.21a Undo the lower pivot bolt...

6.22a Slide the drive sprocket and timing chain off the crankshaft...

the timing chain tensioner at this stage, as described in Section 7.

27 Obtain all new gaskets and components as necessary ready for refitting.

6.21b...and remove the timing chain (rear) tension rail from the cylinder block

6.22b...then lift the chain off the camshaft sprockets

6.29 Locate the new timing cover gasket in place on the cylinder head, cylinder block and baseplate

6.30 Engage the timing chain with the camshaft sprockets, then place the drive sprocket in the chain

6.31 Place the timing chain tension rail in position, refit the lower pivot bolt and tighten it to the specified torque

6.32 Attach the timing chain guide rail to the cylinder block and tighten the two bolts securely

6.33 Remove the drill bit or roll pin used to secure the timing chain tensioner plunger in the released position

Refitting

28 Apply a 2 mm diameter bead of silicone sealant to the joint between the cylinder block and cylinder head on each side. The bead should be long enough to fill the joint in the area covered by the timing cover gasket. Similarly, apply silicone sealant to the joint between the cylinder block and baseplate.

29 Ensure that the locating dowels are in position, then locate the new timing cover gasket in place on the cylinder head, cylinder block and baseplate **(see illustration)**.

30 Engage the timing chain with the camshaft sprockets, then place the drive sprocket in the chain with the markings facing outward. Slide the drive sprocket onto the crankshaft **(see illustration)**.

31 Place the timing chain tension rail in position, refit the lower pivot bolt and

6.34 Correct location for the longer M6 bolt

tighten the bolt to the specified torque **(see illustration)**.

32 Attach the timing chain guide rail to the cylinder block and secure with the two bolts tightened securely **(see illustration)**.

33 Remove the roll pin used to secure the timing chain tensioner plunger in the released position **(see illustration)**.

34 Locate the timing cover in position and refit all the retaining bolts, finger tight only at this stage. Note that the two M10 bolts are fitted at the lower right-hand side of the timing cover and the longer M6 bolt is fitted adjacent to the crankshaft pulley location **(see illustration)**. Now tighten all the bolts progressively to the specified torque.

35 Align the hole in the crankshaft pulley with the cast lug on the timing cover and locate the pulley on the crankshaft. Note that the pulley

6.46 Auxiliary drivebelt routing

flange must engage with the hexagon of the oil pump rotor and the two flats of the crankshaft. It may be necessary to carefully reposition the oil pump rotor slightly using a screwdriver, until the pulley flange will fully engage. When the pulley is fully engaged, the distance from the pulley inner rim to the cast lug on the timing cover should be no more than 5.5 mm.

36 Fit the new pulley retaining bolt and tighten it to the specified torque and through the specified angle while preventing crankshaft rotation using the method employed on removal.

37 Locate a new sealing ring on each camshaft VVT solenoid valve. Lubricate the sealing rings with clean engine oil and carefully insert them into their locations in the timing cover. Position the solenoid valves as shown, then insert the four retaining bolts and tighten them securely **(see illustration 4.32)**.

38 Adjust the valve timing as described in Section 4, paragraphs 18 to 31.

39 Refit the sump as described in Section 11.

40 Refit the coolant pump as described in Chapter 3, Section 7.

41 Locate the auxiliary drivebelt tensioner on the timing cover and secure with the two bolts tightened to the specified torque.

42 Refit the right-hand engine mounting bracket to the timing cover and secure with the three new bolts, tightened to the specified torque.

43 Refit the alternator as described in Chapter 5A, Section 8.

44 Refit the air conditioning compressor mounting bracket to the cylinder block and timing cover and secure with the three bolts, tightened to the specified torque.

45 Refit the air conditioning compressor to the mounting bracket, then fit and tighten the mounting bolts to the specified torque. Reconnect the wiring and secure the wiring harness with the cable clips.

46 Locate the auxiliary drivebelt onto the pulleys in the correct routing **(see illustration)**. If the drivebelt is being re-used, make sure it is fitted the correct way around.

47 Turn back the tensioner and remove the locking pin/bolt then release it, making sure that the drivebelt ribs locate correctly on each of the pulley grooves.

48 Refit the right-hand engine mounting as described in Section 16.
49 Refit the camshaft cover as described in Section 3.
50 Refit the air cleaner assembly as described in Chapter 4A, Section 2.
51 Refit the wheel arch liner lower cover and the roadwheel and tighten the wheel nuts to the specified torque.
52 Lower the car to the ground and reconnect the battery negative terminal.
53 Refill the engine with fresh oil as described in Chapter 1A, Section 5.
54 Refill the cooling system as described in Chapter 1A, Section 27.

7 Timing chain tensioner – removal, inspection and refitting

Removal

1 Remove the timing cover and chain as described in Section 6.
2 Undo the two tensioner retaining bolts and remove the tensioner from the cylinder head (see illustration).
3 Hold the tensioner plunger, then extract the roll pin used to retain the plunger in the retracted position. Withdraw the tensioner plunger and spring.

Inspection

4 Examine the components for any sign of wear, deformation or damage and, if evident, renew the complete tensioner assembly.

Refitting

5 Lubricate the tensioner spring and plunger, then insert the spring, followed by the plunger into the tensioner body.
6 Fully compress the tensioner plunger and reinsert the retaining roll pin.
7 Refit the tensioner assembly to the cylinder head and tighten the retaining bolts securely.
8 Refit the timing chain and cover as described in Section 6.

8 Camshaft sprockets – removal and refitting

Note: *The special tools described in Section 4 will also be required for this operation. Read through the entire procedure and also the procedures contained in Section 4 to familiarise yourself with the work involved, then either obtain the manufacturer's special tools, or use the alternatives described. New gaskets and sealing rings will also be required for all disturbed components, together with new camshaft sprocket retaining bolts.*

Removal

1 Carry out the operations described in Section 4, paragraphs 1 to 12 to set the engine

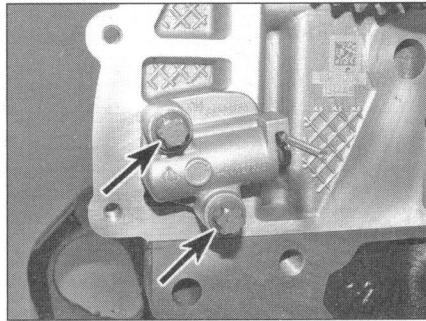
7.2 Timing chain tensioner retaining bolts

at TDC for No 1 piston on the compression stroke.
2 Undo the four bolts securing the VVT solenoid valves to the timing cover. Carefully rotate the inlet camshaft solenoid valve anti-clockwise slightly while at the same time pulling it squarely out of the timing cover. Repeat this procedure to remove the exhaust camshaft solenoid valve, but this time, rotate it clockwise during removal (see illustrations 4.16a and 4.16b). Remove the sealing ring from the rear of each solenoid valve, noting that new sealing rings will be required for refitting.
3 Unscrew the timing chain tensioner closure bolt from the front of the timing cover, below the heater hose union on the coolant pump (see illustration). Note that a new closure bolt sealing ring will be required for refitting.
4 Obtain a suitable roll pin or similar of 2 mm diameter and approximately 30 mm long to use as a timing chain tensioner locking tool.
5 Using a suitable spanner engaged with the flats provided on the inlet camshaft, apply tension in a clockwise direction (as viewed from the right-hand side of the car) to the camshaft, to take up any slack in the timing chain. This will push the timing chain tensioner plunger fully into its bore.
6 Hold the camshaft in this position and retain the tensioner plunger in the released position by inserting the roll pin through the closure bolt aperture and into the hole on the tensioner body (see illustrations).
7 Undo the two bolts and remove the timing chain sliding rail from the top of the cylinder head (see illustration 4.21).

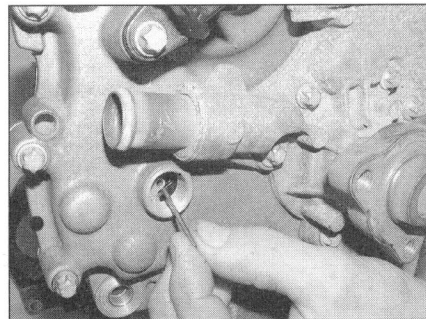
8.3 Unscrew the timing chain tensioner closure bolt from the timing cover

8 Slacken the sprocket retaining bolts for both camshafts, using the spanner to counterhold each camshaft as the bolts are slackened (see illustrations 4.17a and 4.17b).
9 Unscrew and remove both camshaft sprocket retaining bolts together with the camshaft position sensor phase discs.
10 Withdraw both sprockets from the camshaft, then disengage the relevant sprocket from the timing chain and remove it from the engine.

Refitting

11 Engage the relevant sprocket with the timing chain then locate both sprockets on the camshafts. Fit the new retaining bolts together with the phase discs. Tighten the bolts finger tight only at this stage and check that the phase discs can still be turned.
12 Remove the roll pin used to hold the timing chain tensioner plunger in the retracted position.
13 Adjust the valve timing as described in Section 4, paragraphs 20 to 35.

9 Camshafts, hydraulic tappets and rocker arms – removal and refitting

Removal

1 Remove both camshaft sprockets as described in Section 8.
2 Observe the identification numbers and

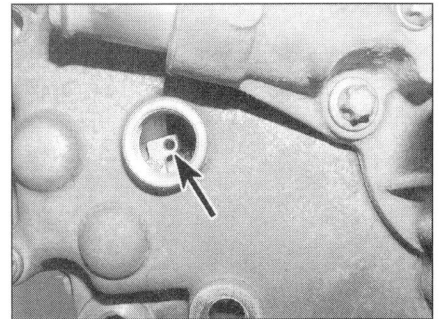
8.6a Insert a 2 mm diameter drill bit or roll pin through the closure bolt aperture...

8.6b...and into the hole in the tensioner body

9.2 Camshaft bearing cap identification numbers

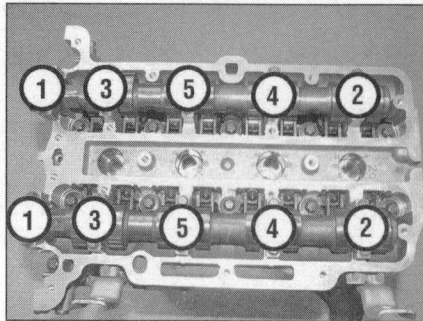

9.3 Camshaft bearing cap retaining bolt slackening sequence

9.4 Remove the retaining bolts and lift off the camshaft bearing caps

markings on the camshaft bearing caps **(see illustration)**. On the project car used during the compilation of this manual, the bearing caps with odd numbers were fitted to the exhaust camshaft, and the caps with the even numbers were fitted to the inlet camshaft. However, this may not be the case on other engines. Also, as it is possible to fit the caps either way round, it will be necessary to mark the caps with quick-drying paint, or identify them in some way, so that they can be refitted in exactly the same position. On the project car, all the numbers could be read the correct way up, when viewed from the exhaust camshaft side of the engine. Again, this may not always be the case.

3 With the bearing caps correctly identified, initially slacken the bearing cap bolts, one at a time, by half a turn, in the sequence shown **(see illustration)**. When all the bolts have

been initially slackened, repeat the procedure, slackening the bolts by a further half a turn. Continue until all the bolts have been fully slackened. The camshaft will rise up under the action of the valve springs as the bolts are slackened. Ensure that the camshaft rises uniformly and does not jam in its bearings.

4 When all the bolts have been slackened, remove the bolts and lift off the bearing caps, keeping them in order according to the identification method decided on **(see illustration)**.

5 Carefully lift the camshafts from their locations in the cylinder head. If both camshafts are removed, identify them as exhaust and inlet **(see illustration)**.

6 Obtain sixteen small, clean plastic containers, and number them inlet 1 to 8 and exhaust 1 to 8; alternatively, divide a larger container into sixteen compartments and

number each compartment accordingly. Fill each container, or each compartment with clean engine oil so that the hydraulic tappets will be completely submerged. Withdraw each rocker arm and hydraulic tappet in turn, and place them in their respective container **(see illustrations)**. Do not interchange the rocker arms and tappets, or the rate of wear will be much increased.

Inspection

7 Examine the camshaft bearing surfaces and cam lobes for signs of wear ridges and scoring. Renew the camshaft if any of these conditions are apparent. Examine the condition of the bearing surfaces, both on the camshaft journals and in the cylinder head/bearing caps. If the head bearing surfaces are worn excessively, the cylinder head will need to be renewed.

8 Examine the rocker arm and hydraulic tappet bearing surfaces for wear ridges and scoring. Renew any rocker arm or tappet on which these conditions are apparent.

9 If either camshaft is being renewed, it will be necessary to renew all the rocker arms and tappets for that particular camshaft also.

Refitting

10 Before refitting, thoroughly clean all the components and the cylinder head and bearing cap journals.

11 Liberally oil the cylinder head hydraulic tappet bores and the tappets. Carefully refit the tappets to the cylinder head, ensuring that each tappet is refitted to its original bore.

12 Lay each rocker arm in position over its respective tappet.

13 Liberally oil the camshaft bearings in the cylinder head and the camshaft lobes, then place the camshafts in the cylinder head.

14 Position the camshafts so that the offset slot in the left-hand end of each camshaft is above the camshaft cover mating face of the cylinder head. The indentations between the camshaft lobes should be facing toward the centre of the engine **(see illustration)**.

15 Refit all the bearing caps to their respective locations ensuring they are fitted the correct way round as noted during removal.

16 Initially tighten the bearing cap bolts,

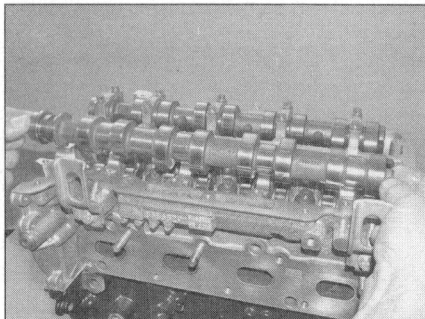

9.5 Carefully lift the camshafts from their locations in the cylinder head

9.6a Withdraw each rocker arm...

9.6b...and hydraulic tappet in turn...

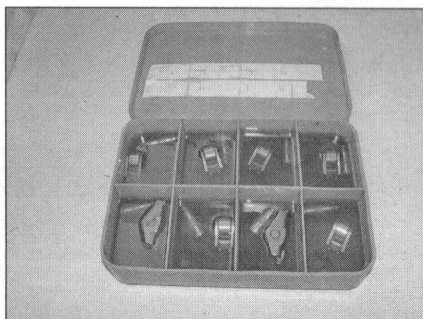

9.6c...and place them in their respective containers

one at a time, by half a turn, in the sequence shown **(see illustration)**. When all the bolts have been initially tightened, repeat the procedure, tightening the bolts by a further half a turn. Continue until all the bearing caps are in contact with the cylinder head and the bolts are lightly tightened.

17 Again, working in the sequence shown, tighten all the bolts to the specified torque.

18 Refit the camshaft sprockets as described in Section 8.

10 Cylinder head – removal and refitting

Note: *The engine must be cold when removing the cylinder head. A new cylinder head gasket, timing cover gasket, cylinder head bolts, camshaft sprocket bolts, right-hand engine mounting bracket bolts, together with seals and sealing rings will be required for refitting. A suitable sealant will also be needed to seal the timing cover-to-cylinder block joint.*

Note: *The special tools described in Section 4 will also be required for this operation. Read through the entire procedure and also the procedures contained in Section 4 to familiarise yourself with the work involved, then either obtain the manufacturer's special tools, or use the alternatives described.*

Removal

1 Disconnect the battery negative terminal (refer to *Disconnecting the battery* in Chapter 5A, Section 4).

2 Remove the air cleaner assembly as described in Chapter 4A, Section 2.

3 Remove the camshaft cover as described in Section 3.

4 Firmly apply the handbrake, then jack up the front of the car and support it securely on axle stands (see *Jacking and vehicle support*). Remove the right-hand front roadwheel and the wheel arch liner lower cover.

5 Drain the cooling system as described in Chapter 1A, Section 27.

6 Remove the inlet manifold as described in Chapter 4A, Section 11.

7 Remove the exhaust manifold as described in Chapter 4A, Section 12.

9.14 The indentations between the camshaft lobes should be facing toward the centre of the engine

8 Extract the retaining spring clip and disconnect the cooling system air bleed hose from the coolant outlet elbow on the left-hand side of the cylinder head **(see illustration)**.

9 Release the retaining clips and disconnect the oil cooler inlet hose, radiator inlet hose and heater matrix inlet hose from the coolant outlet elbow **(see illustrations)**.

10 Disconnect the wiring connector from the coolant temperature sensor on the coolant outlet elbow.

11 Undo the retaining bolt and disconnect the earth lead from the left-hand end of the cylinder head **(see illustration)**.

12 Extract the retaining spring clip and disconnect the radiator outlet hose from the thermostat housing **(see illustration)**.

13 Using a socket or spanner on the pulley

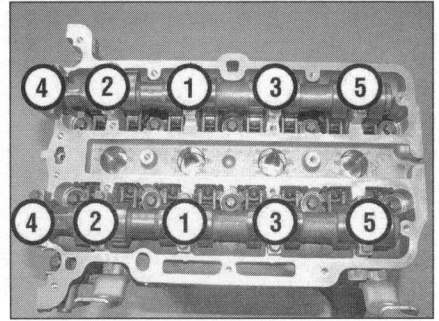

10.8 Extract the retaining spring clip and disconnect the cooling system air bleed hose from the coolant outlet elbow

9.16 Camshaft bearing cap retaining bolt tightening sequence

centre bolt, turn the auxiliary drivebelt tensioner clockwise against the spring tension. Hold the tensioner in this position by inserting a suitable locking pin/bolt through the special hole provided **(see illustration 5.2)**. Note the routing of the drivebelt, then remove it from the pulleys – mark the drivebelt for fitted direction.

Note: *The drivebelt cannot be removed completely until the right-hand engine mounting has been removed.*

14 The engine must now be supported while the right-hand engine mounting is removed. To do this, use a hoist attached to the top of the engine, or make up a wooden frame to locate beneath the sump and use a trolley jack.

15 Remove the right-hand engine mounting

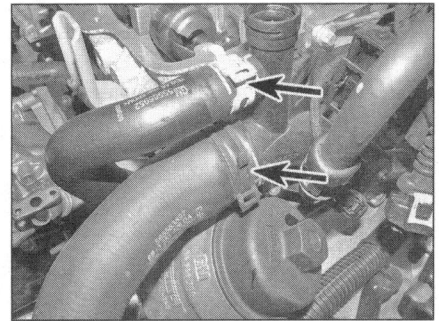

10.9a Release the retaining clips and disconnect the oil cooler inlet hose and radiator inlet hose...

10.9b...and the heater matrix inlet hose from the coolant outlet elbow

10.11 Undo the retaining bolt and disconnect the cylinder head earth lead

10.12 Extract the retaining spring clip and disconnect the radiator outlet hose from the thermostat housing

10.17a Hold the coolant pump shaft and undo the three coolant pump pulley retaining bolts...

10.17b...then remove the pulley

as described in Section 16, then remove the auxiliary drivebelt.

16 Undo the three bolts and remove the right-hand engine mounting bracket from the timing cover. Note that new bolts will be required for refitting.

17 Hold the coolant pump shaft with a suitable spanner, undo the three coolant pump pulley retaining bolts and remove the pulley (see illustrations).

18 Undo the bolts securing the coolant pump and timing cover to the cylinder head (see illustration). Note that it is not necessary to remove all the coolant pump bolts as five are shorter than the rest, and only secure the pump to the timing cover.

19 Remove the camshaft sprockets from the camshafts as described in Section 8. Leave the timing chain engaged and move the chain and both sprockets into the timing cover.

20 Working in the specified sequence, progressively slacken the cylinder head retaining bolts half a turn at a time until all the bolts are loose (see illustration). Remove the bolts from their locations noting that new bolts will be required for refitting.

21 Slightly raise the cylinder head so it just clears the cylinder block face and move the head toward the transmission end of the engine. The head will be initially tight due to the sealant on the timing cover gasket and head gasket. Note that the locating dowel

holes on the cylinder head are elongated to allow the head to move sideways slightly.

22 As soon as sufficient clearance exists, lift the cylinder head up and off the cylinder block. At the same time, release the timing chain guide rail from the peg on the cylinder head, and guide the chain tensioner clear of the tensioning rail. Check that the tensioner locking pin is not dislodged as the cylinder head is lifted up. Place the cylinder head on wooden blocks after removal to avoid damage to the valves. Recover the cylinder head gasket.

Preparation for refitting

23 The mating faces of the cylinder head and cylinder block must be perfectly clean before refitting the head. Scouring agents are available for this purpose, but acceptable results can be achieved by using a hard plastic or wood scraper to remove all traces of gasket and carbon. The same method can be used to clean the piston crowns. Take particular care to avoid scoring or gouging the cylinder head mating surfaces during the cleaning operations, as aluminium alloy is easily damaged. Make sure that the carbon is not allowed to enter the oil and water passages – this is particularly important for the lubrication system, as carbon could block the oil supply to the engine's components. Using adhesive tape and paper, seal the water, oil and bolt holes in the cylinder block. To prevent carbon entering the gap between the pistons and bores, smear a little grease in the gap. After cleaning each piston, use a small brush to remove all traces of grease and carbon from the gap, then wipe away the remainder with a clean rag.

24 Check the mating surfaces of the cylinder block and the cylinder head for nicks, deep scratches and other damage. If slight, they may be removed carefully with a file, but if excessive, machining may be the only alternative to renewal. If warpage of the cylinder head gasket surface is suspected, use a straight-edge to check it for distortion. Refer to Chapter 2D, Section 8 if necessary.

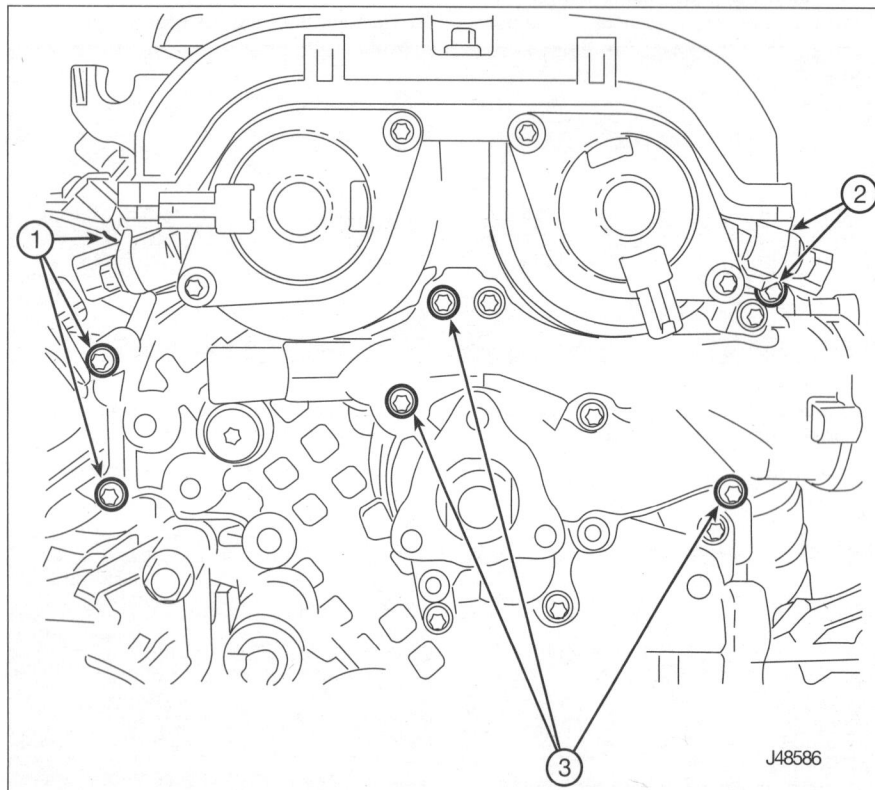

10.18 Undo the bolts securing the coolant pump and timing cover to the cylinder head

1 and 2 Timing cover retaining bolts   *3 Coolant pump retaining bolts*

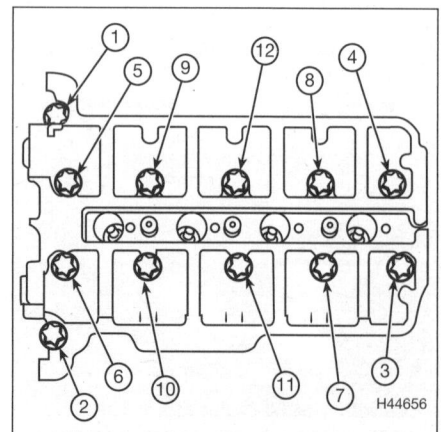

10.20 Cylinder head bolt slackening sequence

25 Thoroughly clean the threads of the cylinder head bolt holes in the cylinder block. Ensure that the bolts run freely in their threads, and that all traces of oil and water are removed from each bolt hole.

26 Using a sharp knife, partially cut through the timing cover gasket flush with the top of the cylinder block. Release the gasket from the timing cover and bend it in half to break it off at the cut line. Remove the upper part of the gasket, and thoroughly clean the mating surface, paying particular attention to the cylinder block edge where it contacts the timing cover.

27 Before refitting the cylinder head, using the spanner on the camshaft flats, turn the camshafts slightly, as necessary, until the camshaft setting tool described in Section 4 can be inserted into the slots in the ends of the camshafts (see illustration).

Refitting

28 Apply a 2 mm diameter bead of silicone sealant to the joint between the cylinder block and the timing cover on each side.

29 Check that the locating dowels are in position in the cylinder block, then lay the new gasket on the block face, with the words OBEN/TOP uppermost (see illustration). Push the gasket hard up against the timing cover so that it engages with the sealant.

30 Position the new timing cover gasket upper part on the timing cover, so that its lower ends engage with the sealant. Temporarily insert the left- and right-hand upper timing cover mounting bolts to locate the gasket in the correct position.

31 Apply a further 2 mm diameter bead of silicone sealant to the joint between the cylinder block and the timing cover on each side.

32 Carefully lower the cylinder head into position on the gasket, guiding the chain tensioner past the tensioning rail and guiding the tensioner locking pin into the timing cover access hole. Check also that the timing chain guide rail engages with cylinder head peg.

33 Once the head is seated on its dowels, tap it towards the timing cover with a rubber mallet.

34 Refit three of the coolant pump and timing cover retaining bolts in the locations shown (see illustration). Tighten the three bolts to the specified torque.

35 Fit the new cylinder head retaining bolts and screw in the bolts until they contact the cylinder head.

36 Remove the camshaft setting tool from the camshaft slots.

37 Working in the reverse order to the loosening sequence shown earlier in this Section, tighten the cylinder head bolts to the Stage one torque setting given in the Specifications, using a torque wrench. Again working in the correct order, tighten all the bolts through the Stage two angle using an angle measuring gauge.

38 Slacken the three previously-fitted bolts

10.27 Turn the camshafts as necessary, until the camshaft setting tool can be inserted into the slots in the ends of the camshafts

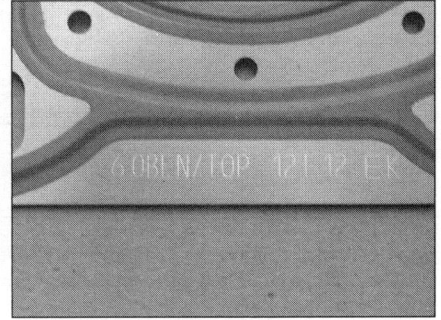

10.29 Lay the new gasket on the block face, with the words OBEN/TOP uppermost

securing the coolant pump and timing cover to the cylinder head.

39 Refit the remaining coolant pump and timing cover retaining bolts and tighten all the bolts to the specified torque.

40 Using the spanner on the camshaft flats, turn the camshafts slightly, as necessary, until the camshaft setting tool can once again be inserted into the camshaft slots.

41 Refit the coolant pump pulley and secure with the three bolts, tightened to the specified torque.

42 Refit the right-hand engine mounting bracket to the timing cover and secure with the three new bolts, tightened to the specified torque, then through the specified angle.

43 Locate the auxiliary drivebelt onto the pulleys in the correct routing (see illustration 6.46). If the drivebelt is being re-used, make sure it is fitted the correct way around.

44 Turn back the tensioner and remove the locking pin/bolt then release it, making sure that the drivebelt ribs locate correctly on each of the pulley grooves.

45 Refit the right-hand engine mounting as described in Section 16.

46 Engage the camshaft sprockets with their respective camshafts and fit the new retaining bolts together with the phase discs. Tighten the bolts finger tight only at this stage and check that the phase discs can still be turned.

47 Remove the roll pin used to hold the

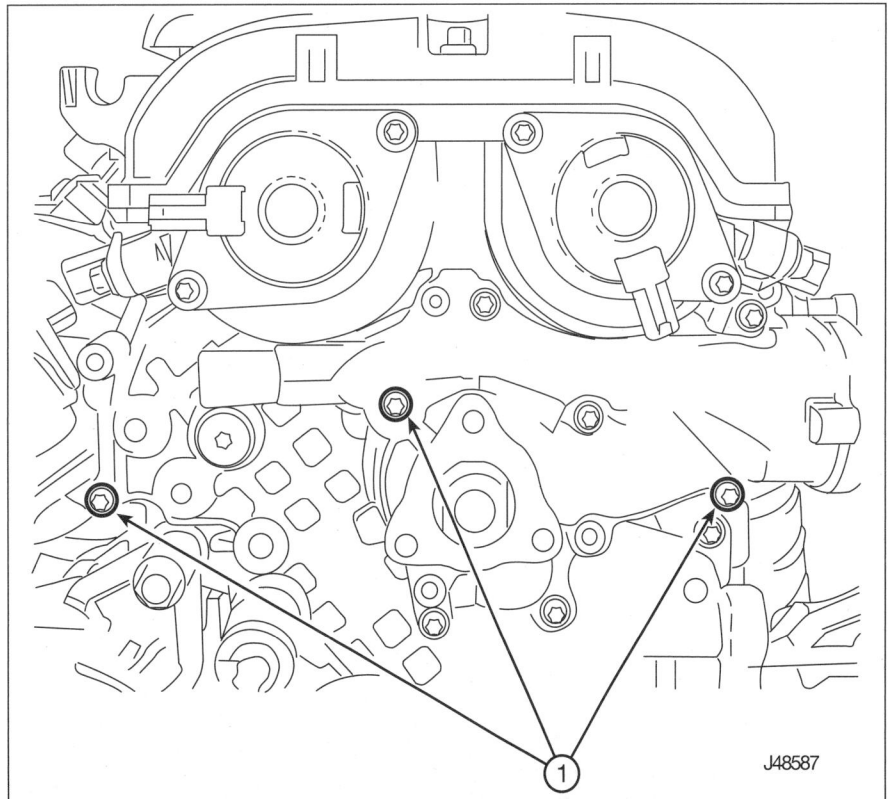

10.34 Refit three of the coolant pump and timing cover retaining bolts (1) in the locations shown

11.11 Screw alignment studs into one of the retaining bolt holes on each side of the cylinder block baseplate

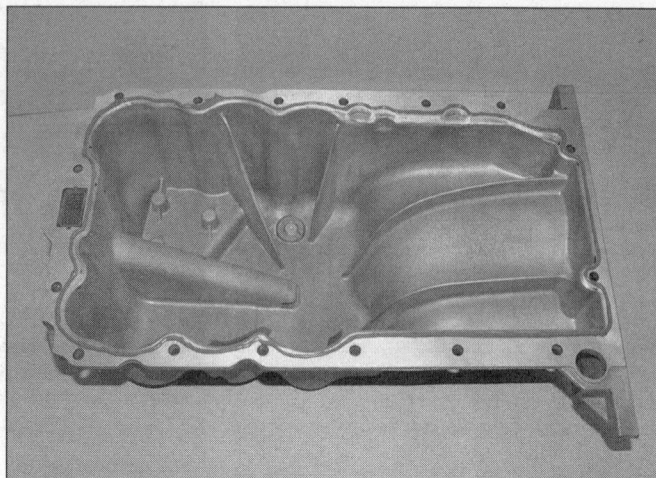

11.12 Apply a bead of silicone sealant to the sump mating face, close to the inner edge of the sump and on the inside of the bolt holes

timing chain tensioner plunger in the retracted position.

48 Adjust the valve timing as described in Section 4, paragraphs 20 to 32.

49 Connect the radiator outlet hose to the thermostat housing and secure with the retaining spring clip.

50 Refit the earth lead to the left-hand end of the cylinder head and tighten the retaining bolt securely.

51 Reconnect the wiring connector to the coolant temperature sensor on the coolant outlet elbow.

52 Connect the heater matrix inlet hose, radiator inlet hose and oil cooler inlet hose to the coolant outlet elbow and secure with the retaining clips.

53 Connect the cooling system air bleed hose to the coolant outlet elbow and secure with the retaining spring clip.

54 Refit the exhaust manifold as described in Chapter 4A, Section 12.

55 Refit the inlet manifold as described in Chapter 4A Section 11.

56 Refit the camshaft cover as described in Section 3.

57 Refit the air cleaner assembly as described in Chapter 4A, Section 2, then reconnect the battery negative terminal.

58 Refill the cooling system as described in Chapter 1A, Section 27.

11 Sump –
removal and refitting

Removal

1 Firmly apply the handbrake, then jack up the front of the car and support it securely on axle stands (see *Jacking and vehicle support*).

2 Drain the engine oil, with reference to Chapter 1A, Section 5 then refit and tighten the sump drain plug.

3 Remove the exhaust system front pipe as described in Chapter 4A, Section 13.

4 Remove the auxiliary drivebelt cover from under the right-hand wheel arch.

5 Undo the three bolts securing the sump to the transmission bellhousing.

6 Undo the sixteen bolts securing the sump to the cylinder block baseplate and timing cover.

7 Engage a screwdriver or similar tool in the slot between the sump and cylinder block baseplate. The slot is located on the front facing side of the sump, at the transmission end. Carefully lever the sump away from the baseplate to release it from the sealant, then manoeuvre the sump out from under the car.

8 To remove the oil baffle plate, undo the retaining bolts and remove the baffle plate from the cylinder block baseplate.

Refitting

9 Thoroughly clean the inside and outside of the sump ensuring that all traces of old sealant are removed from the mating face. Also clean the cylinder block baseplate mating face and the groove in the timing cover to remove all traces of old sealant.

10 If removed, refit the oil baffle plate and secure with the retaining bolts tightened securely.

11 Obtain two M6 studs, approximately 30 mm long to act as alignment pins when offering the sump into position. Cut a slot in the end of each pin to allow them to be unscrewed after the sump is in position. Wrap masking tape around the stud so it is a snug fit in the sump retaining bolt hole. Alternatively, use heat-shrink film. Screw each stud into one of the retaining bolt holes on each side of the cylinder block baseplate **(see illustration)**.

12 Apply a 2 mm continuous bead of silicone sealing compound (available from your Vauxhall/Opel dealer) to the sump mating face. The bead should be close to the inner edge of the sump and on the inside of the retaining bolt holes **(see illustration)**.

13 Apply an additional 2 mm bead of sealant to the groove in the timing cover, and around the bolt hole at the rear of the cylinder block baseplate **(see illustrations)**.

14 Locate the sump in position on the cylinder block baseplate, guiding it over the two centring pins.

15 Refit two of the sump retaining bolts to each side of the sump and tighten them sufficiently to hold the sump in place. Remove the two centring pins, then refit the remaining bolts securing the sump to the timing cover and cylinder block baseplate.

16 Refit the three bolts securing the sump to the transmission bellhousing and tighten them to the specified torque. Now tighten the bolts securing the sump to the timing cover and cylinder block baseplate to the specified torque.

11.13a Apply an additional bead of sealant to the groove in the timing cover...

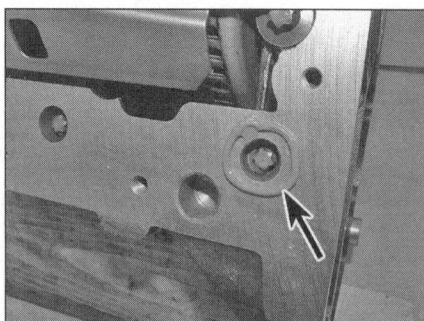

11.13b...and around the bolt hole at the rear of the cylinder block baseplate

12.2 Remove the securing bolts and withdraw the oil pump cover from the rear of the timing cover

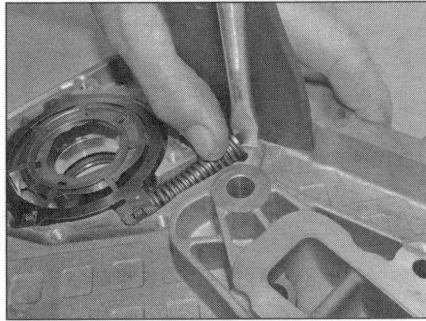

12.3a Compress the oil pump slide pin spring...

12.3b...and carefully lever out the pin and spring

17 Refit the auxiliary drivebelt cover under the right-hand wheel arch.

18 Refit the exhaust system front pipe as described in Chapter 4A, Section 13.

19 Refit the roadwheel, then lower the car to the ground and tighten the wheel bolts to the specified torque.

20 Refill the engine with oil as described in Chapter 1A, Section 5.

12 Oil pump – removal, inspection and refitting

Removal

1 Remove the timing cover and chain as described in Section 6.

2 Remove the securing bolts and withdraw the oil pump cover from the rear of the timing cover **(see illustration)**.

3 Using a screwdriver in contact with the oil pump slide pin, compress the slide pin spring and carefully lever out the pin and spring. Use a suitable piece of plastic or similar to protect the edge of the pump housing as the pin and spring are levered out **(see illustrations)**. It is also advisable to cover the spring with a cloth to prevent a sudden and unexpected release!

4 Lift out the two oil pump slide seal springs, together with the two slide seals **(see illustrations)**.

5 Lift out the outer oil pump vane ring **(see illustration)**.

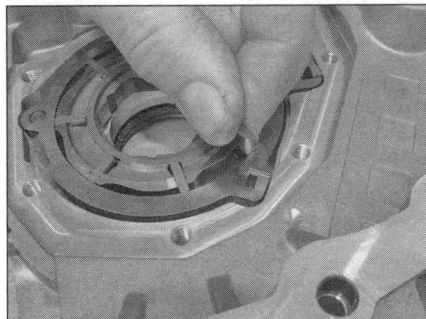

12.4a Lift out the two oil pump slide seal springs...

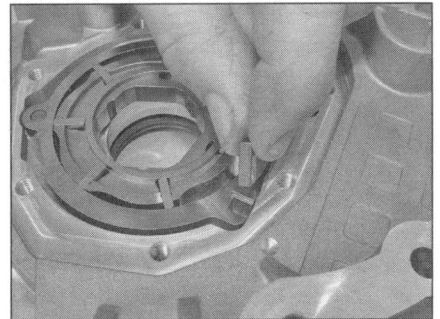

12.4b...together with the two slide seals

6 Remove the seven oil pump vanes, then lift out the oil pump vane rotor **(see illustrations)**.

7 Lift out the inner oil pump vane ring,

followed by the oil pump slide **(see illustrations)**.

8 The oil pressure relief valve components can also be removed from the timing cover by

12.5 Lift out the outer oil pump vane ring

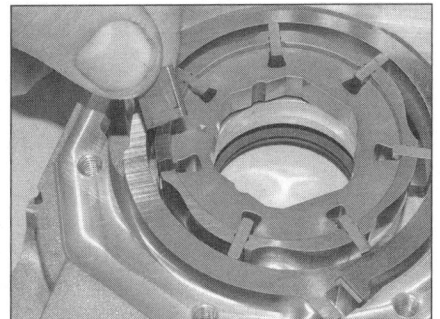

12.6a Remove the seven oil pump vanes...

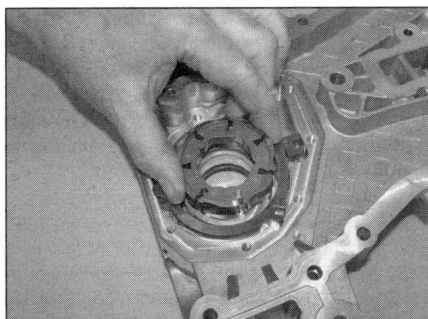

12.6b...then lift out the oil pump vane rotor

12.7a Lift out the inner oil pump vane ring...

12.7b...followed by the oil pump slide

12.8a Unscrew and remove the oil pressure relief valve cap...

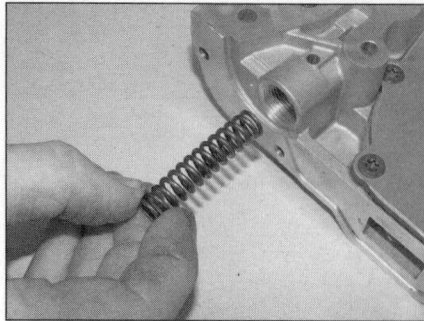

12.8b...then remove the spring...

12.8c...and plunger

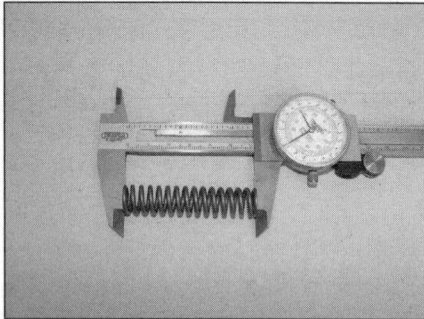

12.11 Measure the free length of the oil pump slide pin spring

12.17 Refit the oil pump vane rotor with the direction mark facing the oil pump cover

12.18 Locate the seven oil pump vanes into the slots in the vane rotor

unscrewing the cap. Withdraw the cap, spring and plunger **(see illustrations)**.

Inspection

9 Thoroughly clean all the individual components and the oil pump housing in the timing cover. Blow out all the oil holes and galleries in the timing cover using compressed air, if possible.

⚠️ *Warning: Wear eye protection when using compressed air.*

10 Check the components for any signs of scuffing, scoring, wear or distortion. If any abnormalities are found, a pump repair kit is available from Vauxhall/Opel parts stockists. If any wear or damage is visible in the pump housing, a new timing cover will be required.

11 Measure the free length of the oil pump slide pin spring and renew it if it is outside the dimension given in the Specifications **(see illustration)**.

12 Examine the pressure relief valve spring and plunger, and renew if any sign of damage or wear is evident.

13 Checking of the oil pump clearances is carried out after reassembly of the pump.

14 Ensure that all the individual components, and the oil pump housing in the interior of the timing cover, are scrupulously clean before commencing reassembly.

Refitting

15 Thoroughly clean the pressure relief valve components, and lubricate them with clean engine oil before refitting. Insert the plunger, and the spring, then refit the cap. Tighten the cap to the specified torque.

16 Refit the oil pump slide to the pivot pin, then place the inner oil pump vane ring in position.

17 Refit the oil pump vane rotor, ensuring that it is fitted with the direction mark facing the oil pump cover **(see illustration)**.

18 Locate the seven oil pump vanes into the slots in the vane rotor, ensuring that they are fitted with the slight scuff marks, caused by the vane rings, facing the vane rotor **(see illustration)**.

19 Place the outer oil pump vane ring in position on the vane rotor.

20 Refit the two oil pump slide seals, followed by the slide seal springs **(see illustration)**.

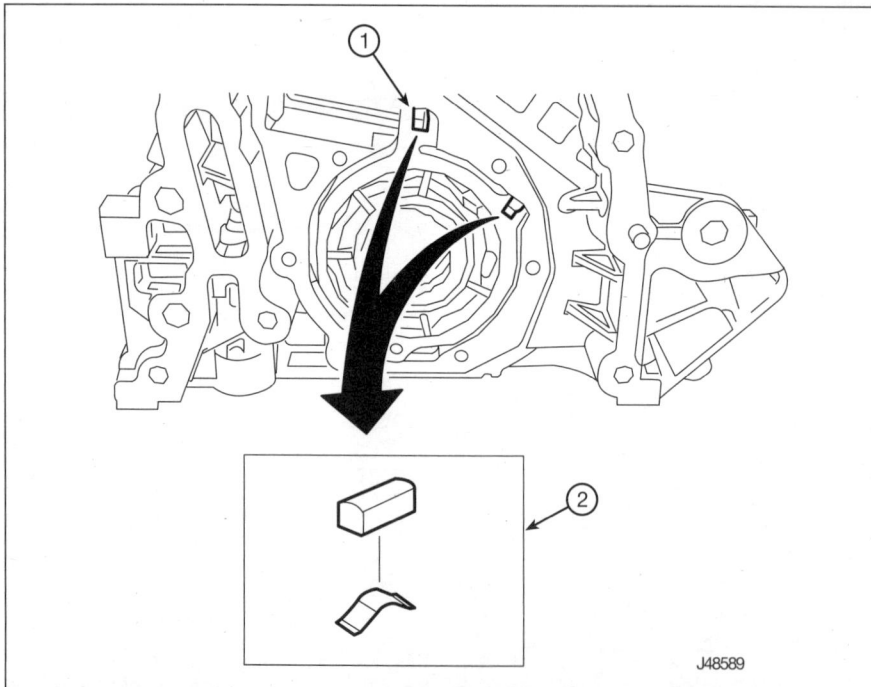

J48589

12.20 Refit the two oil pump slide seals and slide seal springs (2) into the locations shown (1)

21 Fit the oil pump slide pin to the slide pin spring, then refit the spring and pin to the pump housing. Using a screwdriver, compress the slide pin as done during removal, and push the slide pin and spring into position. Ensure that the flat side of the slide pin head is facing toward the top of the timing cover **(see illustration)**.

22 With the oil pump assembled, measure the axial and radial clearances of the various components using a straight-edge and feeler blades **(see illustrations)**. If any of the measurements exceed the clearances given in the specifications, a new pump repair kit or a new timing cover will be required.

23 If all is satisfactory, thoroughly lubricate the pump internal components with clean engine oil, then refit the pump cover **(see illustration)**. Progressively tighten the pump cover retaining bolts in a diagonal sequence to the specified torque.

24 Temporarily refit the crankshaft pulley to the timing cover, engaging the pulley shaft with the oil pump vane rotor. Turn the pulley in the normal direction of rotation to check that the pump operates smoothly and the pulley can be turned easily.

25 Fit a new crankshaft oil seal to the timing cover as described in Section 13.

26 Refit the timing chain and cover to the engine as described in Section 6.

13 Crankshaft oil seals – renewal

Timing chain end oil seal

1 Remove the crankshaft pulley as described in Section 5.

2 The seal can now be carefully prised out with a screwdriver or similar hooked tool **(see illustration)**.

3 Clean the oil seal seat with a wooden or plastic scraper.

4 Tap the new seal into position until it is flush with the outer face of the timing cover, using a wooden block or preferably, an oil seal installer tool **(see illustration)**.

5 Lubricate the sealing lip of the oil seal with clean engine oil, then refit the crankshaft pulley as described in Section 5.

Transmission end oil seal

6 Remove the flywheel/driveplate as described in Section 15.

7 Carefully prise out the old seal from its location using a screwdriver or similar hooked tool.

8 Clean the oil seal seat with a wooden or plastic scraper.

9 If available, fit a protector sleeve over the end of the crankshaft to protect the oil seal lips as the seal is initially fitted **(see illustration)**.

10 Lubricate the lips of the new oil seal and locate it over the protector sleeve. If a protector sleeve is not being used, carefully

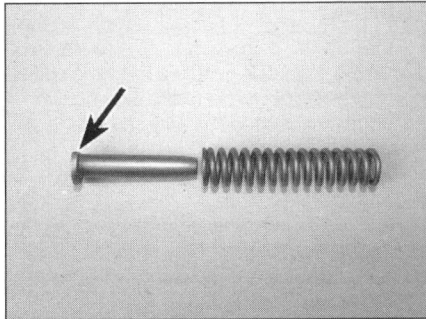

12.21 Ensure that the flat side of the oil pump slide pin head is facing toward the top of the timing cover

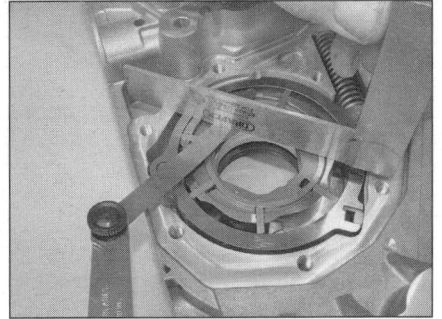

12.22b...and radial clearances of the various components using a straight-edge and feeler blades

guide the oil seal lips over the crankshaft. Push the seal into the recess in the cylinder

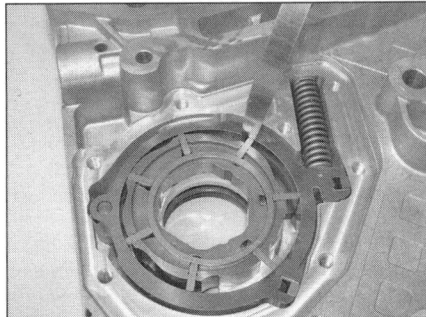

13.2 Carefully prise out the crankshaft oil seal from the timing cover

13.9 If available, fit a protector sleeve over the end of the crankshaft to protect the oil seal lips as the seal is initially fitted

12.22a Measure the axial clearances...

12.23 Thoroughly lubricate the pump internal components with clean engine oil, then refit the pump cover

block and baseplate **(see illustration)**. Where applicable, remove the protector sleeve.

13.4 Tap the new seal into position until it is flush with the outer face of the timing cover

13.10 Lubricate the lips of the new oil seal and locate it over the protector sleeve

13.11 Tap the seal into position until it is flush

11 Tap the seal into position using a suitable socket or tube, or a wooden block, until it is flush with the outer faces of the cylinder block and baseplate **(see illustration)**.
12 Refit the flywheel/driveplate as described in Section 15.

14 Oil filter housing – removal and refitting

Removal

1 Remove the exhaust manifold as described in Chapter 4A, Section 12.
2 Undo the three retaining bolts and withdraw the oil filter housing from the cylinder block. Recover the rubber seal, noting that a new seal will be required for refitting.

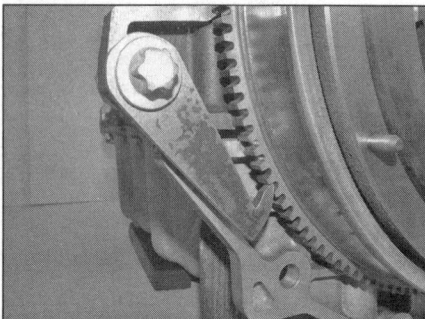

15.4 Prevent the flywheel from turning by using a suitable tool

15.13a Tighten the flywheel retaining bolts to the specified torque...

Refitting

3 Refitting is a reversal of the removal procedure, bearing in mind the following points:
a) *Fit a new rubber seal to the filter housing flange, ensuring that is fully seated in the flange groove.*
b) *Tighten the filter housing retaining bolts to the specified torque.*
c) *Refit the exhaust manifold as described in Chapter 4A, Section 12.*

15 Flywheel/driveplate – removal, inspection and refitting

Removal

Note: *New flywheel/driveplate securing bolts must be used on refitting.*

Manual transmission models

1 Remove the transmission as described in Chapter 7A, Section 8 or Chapter 7C, Section 7.
2 Remove the clutch assembly as described in Chapter 6, Section 6.
3 Although the flywheel bolt holes are offset so that the flywheel can only be fitted in one position, it will make refitting easier if alignment marks are made between the flywheel and the end of the crankshaft.
4 Prevent the flywheel from turning by jamming the ring gear teeth using a suitable tool **(see illustration)**.
5 Unscrew the retaining bolts, and remove the flywheel **(see illustration)**.
Caution: Take care, as the flywheel is heavy.

15.5 Unscrew the retaining bolts and remove the flywheel

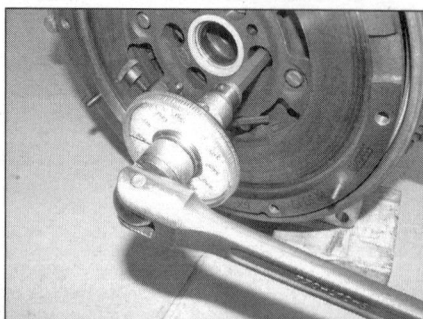

15.13b...then through the specified angles

Automatic transmission models

6 Remove the transmission as described in Chapter 7B, Section 10, then remove the driveplate as described in paragraphs 4 and 5.

Inspection

Flywheel

7 Examine the flywheel for wear or chipping of the ring gear teeth. Renewal of the ring gear is not possible and if the wear or chipping is significant, a new flywheel will be required.
8 Examine the flywheel for scoring of the clutch face. If the clutch face is scored significantly, a new flywheel will be required.
9 If there is any doubt about the condition of the flywheel, seek the advice of a Vauxhall/Opel dealer or engine reconditioning specialist.

Driveplate

10 Closely examine the driveplate and ring gear teeth for signs of wear or damage and check the driveplate surface for any signs of cracks.
11 If there is any doubt about the condition of the driveplate, seek the advice of a Vauxhall/Opel dealer or engine reconditioning specialist.

Refitting

Flywheel

12 Offer the flywheel to the end of the crankshaft, and align the previously-made marks on the flywheel and crankshaft (if applicable).
13 Coat the threads of the new flywheel bolts with thread-locking compound (note that new bolts may be supplied ready-coated), then fit the bolts and tighten them to the specified torque, then through the specified angles whilst preventing the flywheel from turning as during removal **(see illustrations)**.
14 Refit the clutch as described in Chapter 6, Section 6 then refit the transmission as described in Chapter 7A, Section 8 or Chapter 7C, Section 7.

Driveplate

15 Clean the mating surfaces of the driveplate and crankshaft
16 Offer the driveplate and engage it on the crankshaft. Coat the threads of the new retaining bolts with thread-locking compound (note that new bolts may be supplied ready-coated), then fit the bolts and tighten them to the specified torque. Prevent the driveplate from turning as during removal.
17 Remove the locking tool and refit the transmission as described in Chapter 7B, Section 10.

16 Engine/transmission mountings – inspection and renewal

1 Refer to Chapter 2A, Section 15.

Chapter 2 Part C
Diesel engine in-car repair procedures

Contents

Degrees of difficulty

Easy, suitable for novice with little experience	**Fairly easy,** suitable for beginner with some experience	**Fairly difficult,** suitable for competent DIY mechanic	**Difficult,** suitable for experienced DIY mechanic	**Very difficult,** suitable for expert DIY or professional

Specifications

General

Engine type.	Four-cylinder, in-line, water-cooled. Chain-driven double overhead camshafts, 16 valves
Manufacturer's engine code*	A13DTE (LSF), A13DTR (LSF), A13DTC (LDV) and Z13DTJ (LDP)
Bore	69.6 mm
Stroke	82.0 mm
Capacity	1248 cc
Firing order.	1-3-4-2 (No 1 cylinder at timing chain end)
Direction of crankshaft rotation	Clockwise (viewed from timing chain end of engine)
Compression ratio	16.8: 1

Note: *For details of engine code location, see 'Vehicle identification' in Reference.*

Compression pressures

Maximum difference between any two cylinders.	1.5 bar

Lubrication system

Oil pump type.	Gear-type, driven directly from crankshaft
Oil pressure at 80°C (approximate)	1.4 bar at idle speed
Oil pump clearances:	
Outer rotor-to-body clearance	0.10 to 0.23 mm
Rotor endfloat.	0.025 to 0.075 mm

Torque wrench settings

	Nm	lbf ft
Air conditioning compressor mounting bracket and bolts	22	16
Auxiliary drivebelt tensioner-to-cylinder block	50	37
Big-end bearing cap bolts*:		
Stage 1	20	15
Stage 2	Angle-tighten a further 40°	
Camshaft drive gear bolts	150	111
Camshaft housing closure bolts	15	11
Camshaft housing-to-cylinder head:		
M8 stud bolts:		
Stage 1	15	11
Stage 2	25	18
M7 bolts:		
Stage 1	12	9
Stage 2	18	13
Camshaft position sensor retaining bolt	10	7
Camshaft sprocket bolt	150	111
Crankshaft pulley hub-to-crankshaft*†:		
Stage 1	50	37
Stage 2	Angle-tighten a further 90°	
Crankshaft pulley-to-pulley hub	25	18
Cylinder block baseplate bolts*:		
M10 bolts:		
Stage 1	20	15
Stage 2	Angle-tighten a further 80°	
M8 bolts	30	22
Cylinder head bolts*:		
Stage 1	40	30
Stage 2	Angle-tighten a further 90°	
Stage 3	Angle-tighten a further 90°	
EGR pipe-to-EGR cooler bolts	25	18
EGR pipe-to-inlet manifold bolts	10	7
Engine mountings:		
Front mounting/torque link:		
Mounting-to-transmission bolts	100	74
Mounting to subframe	100	74
Left-hand mounting:		
Mounting-to-body bolts/nut	62	46
Mounting bracket-to-transmission bracket*:		
Stage 1	50	37
Stage 2	Angle-tighten a further 60°	
Rear mounting/torque link:		
Mounting-to-transmission bracket	100	74
Mounting-to-subframe	110	82
Right-hand mounting:		
Mounting bracket-to-engine	60	44
Mounting-to-body	62	46
Mounting-to-mounting bracket	60	44
Engine-to-transmission bolts	60	44
Flywheel bolts*:		
Stage 1	15	11
Stage 2	Angle-tighten a further 35°	
Fuel rail mounting bracket-to-camshaft housing	25	18
Fuel rail-to-mounting bracket bolts	25	18
Glow plug wiring harness bracket bolts	10	7
Intercooler intake duct-to-turbocharger	10	7
Oil filter housing cover	25	18
Oil filter housing-to-cylinder block	10	7
Roadwheel bolts	110	81
Sump drain plug	20	15
Sump reinforcement bracket bolts	30	22
Sump-to-cylinder block baseplate	10	7
Thermostat bypass pipe-to-oil filter housing	10	7
Thermostat bypass pipe support bracket bolt	10	7
Timing chain guide rail bolts	10	7
Timing chain tensioner bolts	10	7
Timing chain tensioner rail pivot bolt	25	18
Timing cover retaining nuts/bolts	10	7
Turbocharger oil supply pipe banjo union bolts	22	16

*Use new fasteners
† Left-hand thread

1 General Information

How to use this Chapter

1 This Part of Chapter 2 describes the repair procedures which can reasonably be carried out on the engine while it remains in the vehicle. If the engine has been removed from the vehicle and is being dismantled as described in Chapter 2D, any preliminary dismantling procedures can be ignored.

2 Note that, while it may be possible physically to overhaul items such as the piston/connecting rod assemblies while the engine is in the vehicle, such tasks are not usually carried out as separate operations, and usually require the execution of several additional procedures (not to mention the cleaning of components and of oil ways); for this reason, all such tasks are classed as major overhaul procedures, and are described in Chapter 2D.

3 Chapter 2D describes the removal of the engine/transmission unit from the vehicle, and the full overhaul procedures which can then be carried out.

Engine description

4 The 1.3 litre common-rail diesel engine is of sixteen-valve, in-line four-cylinder, double overhead camshaft (DOHC) type, mounted transversely at the front of the car with the transmission attached to its left-hand end.

5 The crankshaft runs in five main bearings. Thrustwashers are fitted to No 3 main bearing shell (upper half) to control crankshaft endfloat.

6 The cylinder block is made of cast iron and the cylinder bores are an integral part of the block. On this type of engine the cylinder bores are sometimes referred to as having dry liners. An aluminium baseplate is bolted to the cylinder block and forms the lower half of the crankcase.

7 The connecting rods rotate on horizontally-split bearing shells at their big-ends. The pistons are attached to the connecting rods by gudgeon pins, which are a sliding fit in the connecting rod small-end eyes and retained by circlips. The aluminium-alloy pistons are fitted with three piston rings – two compression rings and an oil control ring.

8 The camshafts are situated in a separate housing bolted to the top of the cylinder head. The exhaust camshaft is driven by the crankshaft by a hydraulically tensioned timing chain and drives the inlet camshaft via a spur gear. Each cylinder has four valves (two inlet and two exhaust), operated via rocker arms which are supported at their pivot ends by hydraulic self-adjusting valve lifters (tappets). One camshaft operates the inlet valves, and the other operates the exhaust valves.

9 The inlet and exhaust valves are each closed by a single valve spring, and operate in guides pressed into the cylinder head.

10 A rotor-type oil pump is located in the timing cover attached to the cylinder block, and is driven directly from the crankshaft. An oil cooler (heat exchanger) is fitted to keep the oil temperature stable under arduous operating conditions.

11 The coolant pump is located externally on the timing cover, and is driven by the auxiliary drivebelt.

Operations with engine in place

12 The following operations can be carried out without having to remove the engine from the vehicle.
a) Removal and refitting of the cylinder head.
b) Removal and refitting of the timing cover.
c) Removal and refitting of the timing chain, tensioner, sprockets and guide rails.
d) Removal and refitting of the camshaft housing.
e) Removal and refitting of the hydraulic tappets and rocker arms.
f) Removal and refitting of the camshafts.
g) Removal and refitting of the sump.
h) Removal and refitting of the big-end bearings, connecting rods, and pistons*.
i) Removal and refitting of the oil pump.
j) Removal and refitting of the oil filter housing.
k) Renewal of the crankshaft oil seals.
l) Renewal of the engine mountings.
m) Removal and refitting of the flywheel.
Note: Although the operation marked with an asterisk can be carried out with the engine in the vehicle (after removal of the sump), it is preferable for the engine to be removed, in the interests of cleanliness and improved access. For this reason, the procedure is described in Chapter 2D.

2 Compression test – description and interpretation

Compression test

Note: A compression tester specifically designed for diesel engines must be used for this test.

1 When engine performance is down, or if misfiring occurs which cannot be attributed to the fuel system, a compression test can provide diagnostic clues as to the engine's condition. If the test is performed regularly, it can give warning of trouble before any other symptoms become apparent.

2 A compression tester specifically intended for diesel engines must be used, because of the higher pressures involved. The tester is connected to an adapter which screws into the glow plug or injector hole. On these models, an adapter suitable for use in the injector holes will be required. It is unlikely to be worthwhile buying such a tester for occasional use, but it may be possible to borrow or hire one – if not, have the test performed by a garage.

3 Unless specific instructions to the contrary are supplied with the tester, observe the following points:
a) *The battery must be in a good state of charge, the air filter must be clean, and the engine should be at normal operating temperature.*
b) *All the fuel injectors must be removed before starting the test (see Chapter 4B, Section 13).*
c) *Open the cover on the engine compartment fuse/relay box and remove the fuel pump relay* **(see illustration)**.

4 Screw the compression tester and adapter in to the fuel injector hole of No 1 cylinder.

5 With the help of an assistant, crank the engine on the starter motor; after one or two revolutions, the compression pressure should build-up to a maximum figure, and then stabilise. Record the highest reading obtained.

6 Repeat the test on the remaining cylinders, recording the pressure in each.

7 All cylinders should produce very similar pressures; any difference greater than that specified indicates the existence of a fault. Note that the compression should build-up quickly in a healthy engine; low compression on the first stroke, followed by gradually-increasing pressure on successive strokes, indicates worn piston rings. A low compression reading on the first stroke, which does not build-up during successive strokes, indicates leaking valves or a blown head gasket (a cracked head could also be the cause).

Note: *The cause of poor compression is less easy to establish on a diesel engine than on a petrol one. The effect of introducing oil into the cylinders ('wet' testing) is not conclusive, because there is a risk that the oil will sit in the recess on the piston crown instead of passing to the rings.*

8 On completion of the test, refit the fuel pump relay, then refit the fuel injectors as described in Chapter 4B, Section 13.

Leakdown test

9 A leakdown test measures the rate at which compressed air fed into the cylinder is lost. It is an alternative to a compression test, and in many ways it is better, since the escaping air

2.3 Fuel pump relay location

3.2 Camshaft timing slot for use with the camshaft locking tools

3.3a Inserting the Vauxhall/Opel crankshaft locking tool through the timing hole in the bellhousing – 5-speed transmission shown

3.3b Using a drill bit to lock the crankshaft through the additional timing hole provided in the flywheel

3.8 Remove the engine lifting bracket and fuel rail mounting bracket from the camshaft housing

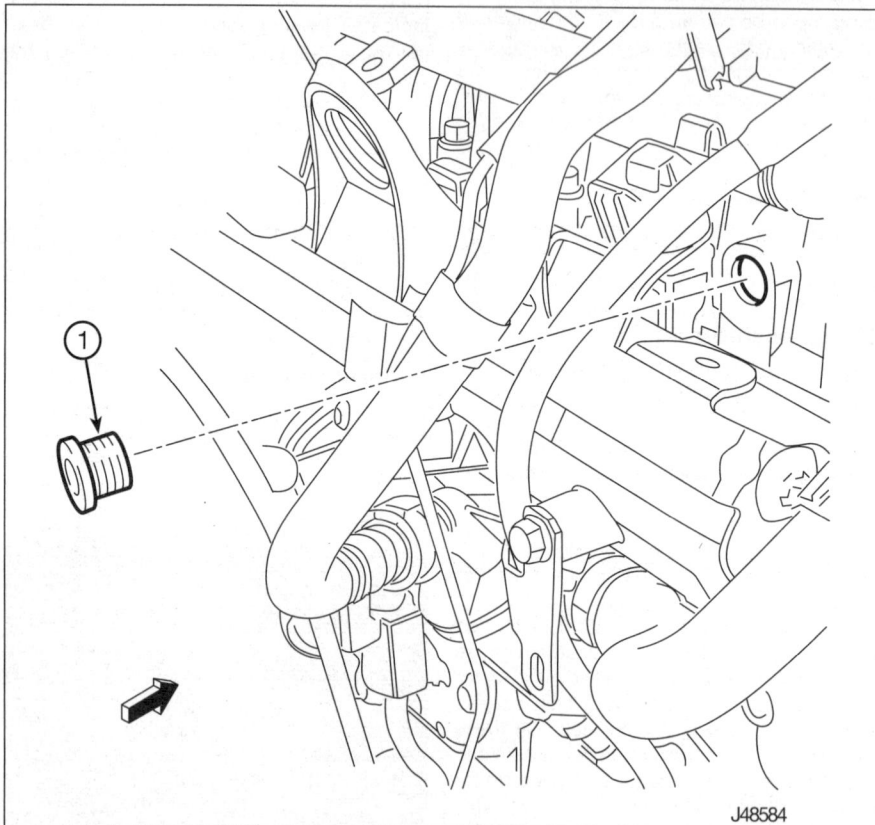

3.9 Unscrew the closure bolt (1) from the valve timing checking hole on the inlet camshaft side of the camshaft housing

provides easy identification of where pressure loss is occurring (piston rings, valves or head gasket).

10 The equipment needed for leakdown testing is unlikely to be available to the home mechanic. If poor compression is suspected, have the test performed by a dealership.

3 Engine assembly/ valve timing holes – general information and usage

Note: *Do not attempt to rotate the engine whilst the camshafts are locked in position. If the engine is to be left in this state for a long period of time, it is a good idea to place suitable warning notices inside the car, and in the engine compartment. This will reduce the possibility of the engine being accidentally cranked on the starter motor, which is likely to cause damage with the locking tools in place.*

1 To accurately set the valve timing for all operations requiring removal and refitting of the timing chain, timing slots are machined in the camshafts and corresponding holes are drilled in the camshaft housing. Timing holes are also drilled in the flywheel, and transmission bellhousing. The holes are used in conjunction with camshaft and crankshaft locking tools to lock the camshafts and crankshaft when all the pistons are positioned at the mid-point of their stroke. This arrangement prevents the possibility of the valves contacting the pistons when refitting the cylinder head or timing chain, and also ensures that the correct valve timing can be obtained. The design of the engine is such that there are no conventional timing marks on the crankshaft or camshaft sprockets to indicate the normal TDC position. Therefore, for any work on the timing chain, camshafts or cylinder head, the locking tools must be used.

2 The Vauxhall/Opel special tool for locking the camshafts comprises a spring loaded plunger free to slide in the bore of the tool body. The tool body is screwed into the camshaft housing timing hole (after removal of a closure plug) so that the sliding plunger contacts the inlet camshaft. The plunger is retained in contact with the camshaft by the spring. The crankshaft is then rotated by means of the crankshaft pulley bolt until a machined slot in the camshaft aligns with the tool plunger **(see illustration)**. The spring then forces the plunger into engagement with the slot, locking the camshaft in the timing position. To accurately check the valve timing, or for any work that entails removal of the camshafts or their drive gears, two of these tools will be required, one for each camshaft.

3 The Vauxhall/Opel special tool for locking the crankshaft is simply a 6 mm diameter pin which is inserted through a hole in the base of the bellhousing (5-speed transmissions) or in the front facing side of the bellhousing (6-speed transmissions) to engage with a corresponding hole in the rim of the flywheel.

An additional hole is provided in the inner face of the flywheel with a corresponding hole in the cylinder block, for use when the transmission has been removed (see illustrations).

4 The Vauxhall/Opel tool numbers are as follows:

Camshaft locking tools   EN-46781
Crankshaft locking tool
    (bellhousing into flywheel)   EN-46785
Crankshaft locking tool
    (flywheel into cylinder block)   EN-46778

5 Although the Vauxhall/Opel camshaft locking tools (or aftermarket equivalents) are relatively inexpensive and should be readily available, it is possible to fabricate suitable alternatives, with the help of a local machine shop, as described below. Once the tools have been made up, their usage is described in the relevant Sections of this Chapter where the tools are required.

Camshaft locking tool

6 Lift off the plastic cover over the top of the engine.
7 Disconnect the wiring connectors at the fuel injectors, at the charge pressure sensor and at the fuel pressure sensor on the fuel rail.
8 Undo the five retaining bolts and remove the engine lifting bracket and fuel rail mounting bracket from the camshaft housing (see illustration). After removal of the mounting bracket, take care not to apply any force to the fuel rail otherwise damage could be caused to the high-pressure fuel pipes.
9 Unscrew the closure bolt from the valve timing checking hole on the inlet camshaft side of the camshaft housing. The bolt is located approximately in line with No 2 fuel injector (see illustration).
10 Using the closure bolt as a pattern, obtain a length of threaded dowel rod, or suitable bolt to screw into the closure bolt hole. With the help of a machine shop or engineering works, make up the camshaft locking tool by having the dowel rod or bolt machined (see illustrations). Note that for some of the procedures described in this Chapter, two locking tools will be needed, one for each camshaft.
11 To refit the closure bolt, thoroughly clean the bolt threads and apply suitable thread locking compound. Screw the bolt into the camshaft housing and tighten to the specified torque.
12 Place the engine lifting bracket and fuel rail mounting bracket in position on the camshaft housing and locate the fuel rail on the mounting bracket. Refit the five retaining bolts and tighten to the specified torque.
13 Reconnect the wiring connectors at the fuel injectors, at the charge pressure sensor and at the fuel pressure sensor on the fuel rail. Refit the engine cover on completion.

Crankshaft locking tools

14 Suitable drill bits or dowel rods can be used as alternatives for the Vauxhall/Opel

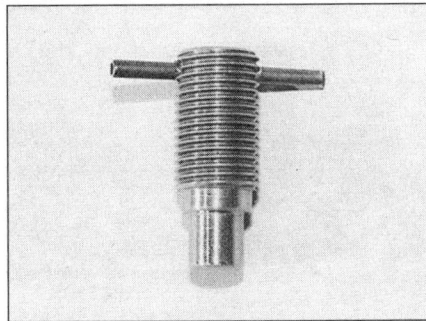

3.10a To make an alternative camshaft locking tool...

special tools described previously. Their respective diameters are as follows:
Crankshaft locking tool
    (bellhousing into flywheel) 6.0 mm diameter
Crankshaft locking tool
    (flywheel into cylinder
    block)   9.0 mm diameter

4 Crankshaft pulley – removal and refitting

Removal

1 Apply the handbrake, then jack up the front of the vehicle and support it on axle stands (see Jacking and vehicle support). Remove the right-hand front roadwheel and the inner wheel arch liner for access to the crankshaft pulley.
2 Remove the auxiliary drivebelt as described in Chapter 1B, Section 31. Prior to removal, mark the direction of rotation on the belt to ensure the belt is refitted the same way around.
3 Slacken and remove the four retaining bolts securing the pulley to the pulley hub. If necessary, prevent the crankshaft from turning by holding the pulley hub retaining bolt with a socket.

Refitting

4 Refit the crankshaft pulley to the pulley hub. Refit the pulley retaining bolts, tightening them to the specified torque.
5 Refit the auxiliary drivebelt as described in Chapter 1B, Section 31 using the mark made prior to removal to ensure the belt is fitted the correct way around.
6 Refit the wheel arch liner and roadwheel, then lower the car to the ground and tighten the roadwheel nuts to the specified torque.

5 Timing cover – removal and refitting

Note: The special tools described in Section 3, together with additional tools will be required for this operation. Read through the entire procedure and also the procedures

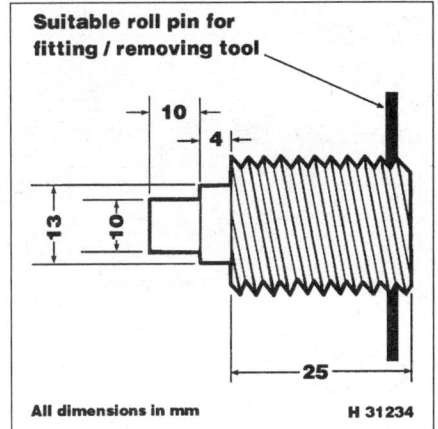

3.10b...have suitable dowel rods or bolts machined to the dimensions shown

contained in Section 3 to familiarise yourself with the work involved, then either obtain the manufacturer's special tools, or use the alternatives described, where applicable. New gaskets and sealing rings will be needed for all disturbed components, together with a tube of suitable gasket sealant.

Removal

1 Disconnect the battery negative terminal (refer to Disconnecting the battery in Chapter 5A, Section 4).
2 Lift off the plastic cover over the top of the engine.
3 Remove the air cleaner assembly as described in Chapter 4B, Section 3.
4 Remove the coolant pump as described in Chapter 3, Section 7.
5 Remove the crankshaft pulley as described in Section 4.
6 Remove the sump as described in Section 11.
7 Undo the centre retaining bolt and remove the auxiliary drivebelt tensioner from the timing cover.
8 Release the retaining clip and disconnect the crankcase ventilation hose from the oil filler housing at the top of the timing cover. Undo the two retaining bolts and remove the oil filler housing. Release the wiring harness from the timing cover support clips.
9 Undo the two retaining bolts securing the fuel rail to the mounting bracket.
10 Undo the remaining bolts and remove the engine lifting bracket and fuel rail mounting bracket from the camshaft housing (see illustration 3.8). After removal of the mounting bracket, take care not to apply any force to the fuel rail otherwise damage could be caused to the high-pressure fuel pipes.
11 Unscrew the closure bolt from the valve timing checking hole on the inlet camshaft side of the camshaft housing. The bolt is located approximately in line with No 2 fuel injector (see illustration 3.9).
12 If the Vauxhall/Opel camshaft locking tool or similar alternative is available (see Section 3), screw the tool into the valve timing checking hole. Ensure that the mark

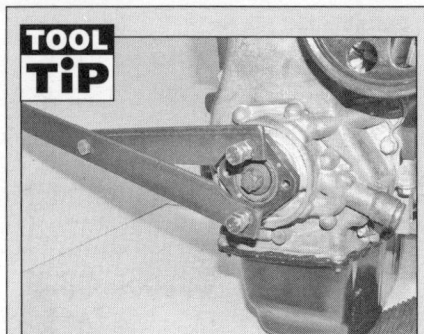

TOOL TiP

To make a sprocket holding tool, obtain two lengths of steel strip about 6 mm thick by about 30 mm wide or similar, one 600 mm long, the other 200 mm long (all dimensions are approximate). Bolt the two strips together to form a forked end, leaving the bolt slack so that the shorter strip can pivot freely. At the other end of each 'prong' of the fork, drill a suitable hole and fit a nut and bolt to allow the tool to be bolted to the crankshaft pulley hub.

on the tool plunger is facing upwards. Using a socket or spanner on the crankshaft pulley hub bolt, turn the crankshaft in the normal direction of rotation (clockwise as viewed from the right-hand side of the car) until the spring-loaded plunger of the locking tool slides into engagement with the slot on the camshaft. There will be an audible click from the tool when this happens, and the plunger will be seen to move in, towards the camshaft.
13 If the home-made locking tool described in Section 3 is being used, insert a screwdriver through the valve timing checking hole on the inlet camshaft side of the camshaft housing, and into contact with the inlet camshaft. Using a socket or spanner on the crankshaft pulley hub bolt, turn the crankshaft in the normal direction of rotation (clockwise as viewed from the right-hand side of the car) until the screwdriver can be felt to engage with the slot in the camshaft. Screw the tool into the camshaft housing until resistance is felt, then turn the crankshaft slightly until the camshaft slot is correctly aligned, and the tool can be screwed fully in.

5.20a Using a flat-bladed screwdriver inserted behind the lugs on the edge of the timing cover...

5.18 Right-hand engine mounting retaining bolts

14 Insert the Vauxhall/Opel crankshaft locking tool or suitable alternative (see Section 3) into the timing hole at the base or at the front of the transmission bellhousing and into engagement with the flywheel **(see illustration 3.3a)**. It may be necessary to turn the crankshaft very slightly one way or the other, by means of the pulley retaining bolt, to allow the tool to fully engage.
15 It will now be necessary to hold the crankshaft pulley hub to enable the retaining bolt to be removed. Vauxhall/Opel special tool EN-662-C is available for this purpose, however, a home-made tool can easily be fabricated **(see Tool Tip)**.
16 Using the Vauxhall/Opel tool or the home-made alternative, hold the pulley hub stationary and unscrew the retaining bolt. The pulley hub retaining bolt has a left-hand thread and is unscrewed by turning it clockwise. Withdraw the pulley hub from the crankshaft. Discard the retaining bolt; a new bolt will be required for refitting.
17 Connect a suitable hoist and lifting tackle to the right-hand end of the engine and support its weight. If available, the type of support bar which locates in the engine compartment side channels is to be preferred. Alternatively, support the engine on a jack with a block of wood positioned between the jack head and cylinder block baseplate.
18 Undo the three bolts securing the right-hand engine mounting to the engine mounting bracket. Similarly, undo the three bolts securing the mounting to the body, and remove the mounting **(see illustration)**.

5.20b...carefully prise the cover free and remove it from the engine

5.19 Undo the four bolts and remove the engine bracket

19 Undo the four bolts securing the engine bracket to the cylinder block and cylinder head and remove the engine bracket, together with the engine lifting eye **(see illustration)**.
20 Undo the fourteen bolts and three nuts securing the timing cover to the cylinder block, cylinder block baseplate, cylinder head and camshaft housing. Using a flat-bladed screwdriver inserted behind the lugs on the edge of the timing cover, carefully prise the cover free and remove it from the engine **(see illustrations)**. Recover the timing cover gasket, a new gasket will be required for refitting.
21 Carefully prise out the old crankshaft oil seal with a screwdriver or similar hooked tool. Clean the oil seal seat with a wooden or plastic scraper.
22 Thoroughly clean the timing cover and remove all traces of gasket and sealant from all the mating surfaces. Similarly clean the cylinder block baseplate, cylinder block, cylinder head and camshaft housing mating surfaces. Ensure that all traces of old sealant are removed, particularly from the joint areas between these components.
23 Obtain all new gaskets and components as necessary ready for refitting. In addition, a new crankshaft oil seal will be required together with a tube of Loctite 5900 sealant, or equivalent. Vauxhall/Opel special tool EN-46775, or a suitable alternative, will be required to centralise the timing cover during refitting.

Refitting

24 Prior to refitting the timing cover, ensure that the face of the timing chain sprocket on the crankshaft is free from oil or grease.
25 Apply a 2 mm bead of Loctite 5900 across the camshaft housing-to-cylinder head joint, the cylinder head-to-cylinder block joint and the cylinder block-to-baseplate joint **(see illustration)**.
26 Place the new gasket in position on the engine then locate the timing cover over the gasket. Insert the Vauxhall/Opel centring tool (EN-46775) or a suitable equivalent, over the crankshaft and into engagement with the timing cover.
27 Refit the fourteen bolts and three nuts securing the timing cover to the engine, and tighten them progressively to the specified

5.25 Apply a bead of sealant across the housing joints

torque, in the sequence shown **(see illustration)**. Remove the centring tool.

28 Tap a new crankshaft oil seal into position until it is flush with the outer face of the timing cover, using a suitable socket or tube, or a wooden block.

29 Thoroughly clean the crankshaft pulley hub, ensuring that the timing chain sprocket contact face is free from oil or grease.

30 Refit the pulley hub to the crankshaft, then fit the new retaining bolt. Using the method employed on removal to hold the pulley hub stationary, tighten the retaining bolt to the specified torque, then through the specified angle.

31 Locate the engine bracket in position, together with the engine lifting eye, refit the four retaining bolts and tighten to the specified torque.

32 Refit the right-hand engine mounting and secure the mounting to the body with the retaining bolts tightened to the specified torque. Fit the bolts securing the mounting to the engine bracket and tighten the bolts to the specified torque. Remove the hoist or jack used to support the engine.

33 Refit the crankshaft pulley as described in Section 4.

34 Remove the camshaft and crankshaft locking tools. Turn the engine through two complete revolutions, then check that the locking tools can be reinserted. Remove the locking tools.

35 Thoroughly clean the threads of the closure bolt and apply suitable thread locking compound. Screw the bolt into the camshaft housing and tighten to the specified torque.

5.27 Timing cover tightening sequence. Arrows indicate the location of the three nuts

36 Place the engine lifting bracket and fuel rail mounting bracket in position on the camshaft housing and locate the fuel rail on the mounting bracket.

37 Refit the five fuel rail and mounting bracket retaining bolts and tighten to the specified torque.

38 Refit the oil filler to the timing cover and tighten the two retaining bolts securely. Reconnect the crankcase ventilation hose and clip the wiring harness back into place.

39 Refit the auxiliary drivebelt tensioner ensuring that the lug on the tensioner body engages with the hole in the cylinder block **(see illustration)**. Refit the retaining bolt and tighten the bolt to the specified torque.

5.39 Refit the auxiliary drivebelt tensioner ensuring that the lug engages with the hole in the cylinder block

40 Refit the sump as described in Section 11.

41 Refit the coolant pump as described in Chapter 3, Section 7.

42 Refit the air cleaner assembly as described in Chapter 4B, Section 3.

43 Refit the plastic cover over the top of the engine.

44 Refit the wheel arch liner and roadwheel, then lower the car to the ground and tighten the roadwheel nuts to the specified torque.

45 Refill the engine with fresh oil as described in Chapter 1B, Section 5, then reconnect the battery negative terminal.

46 Refill the cooling system as described in Chapter 1B, Section 28.

6 Timing chain, sprockets, tensioner and guide rails – removal and refitting

Removal

1 Remove the timing cover as described in Section 5.

2 Push the timing chain tensioner plunger back into its bore and insert a suitable drill bit or similar tool to retain it in the released position **(see illustration)**.

3 Undo the two retaining bolts and remove the tensioner from the cylinder head **(see illustration)**.

4 Undo the lower pivot bolt and remove the chain tensioner rail **(see illustrations)**.

5 Slide the crankshaft sprocket off the end of

6.2 Push the timing chain tensioner plunger back into its bore and retain it using a suitable drill bit

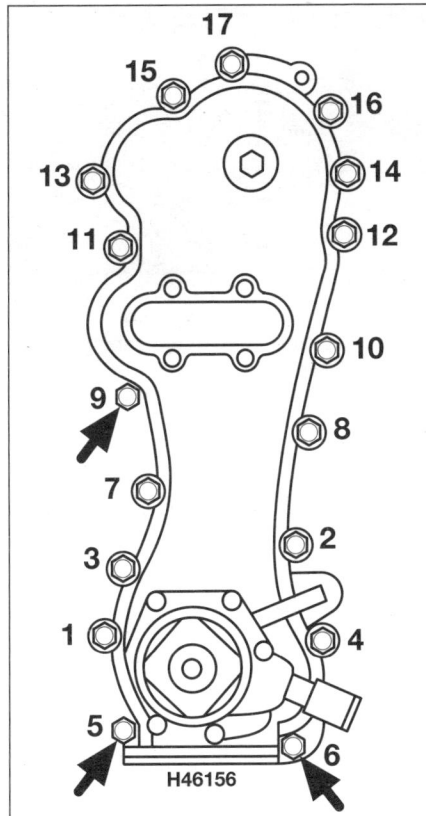

6.3 Undo the two bolts and remove the tensioner from the cylinder head

6.4a Undo the lower pivot bolt...

6.4b...and remove the chain tensioner rail

6.5 Slip the chain off the camshaft sprocket and remove it together with the crankshaft sprocket

6.7a Using the holding tool to prevent rotation, slacken the camshaft sprocket retaining bolt...

the crankshaft. Slip the chain off the camshaft sprocket and remove it together with the crankshaft sprocket **(see illustration)**.

6 It will now be necessary to hold the camshaft sprocket to enable the retaining bolt to be removed. Vauxhall/Opel special tools EN-956-1 and EN-6347 are available for this purpose, however, a home-made tool can easily be fabricated (see *Tool Tip* in Section 5).

7 Using the holding tool to prevent rotation of the camshaft, slacken the sprocket retaining bolt. Remove the holding tool, unscrew the retaining bolt and remove the sprocket **(see illustrations)**.

8 Undo the two retaining bolts and remove the timing chain guide rail **(see illustration)**.

9 Inspect the timing chain, sprockets, tensioner rail and guide rail for any sign of wear or deformation, and renew any suspect components as necessary.

10 Push the timing chain tensioner plunger into the tensioner body and remove the locking drill bit. Check that the tensioner plunger is free to move in out of the tensioner body with no trace of binding. If any binding or sticking of the plunger is felt, renew the tensioner assembly. On completion of the check, or if a new tensioner is being fitted, Compress the plunger and refit the locking drill bit.

Refitting

11 Locate the timing chain guide rail in position, refit the two retaining bolts and tighten the bolts to the specified torque.

12 Fit the sprocket to the camshaft and

screw in the retaining bolt. Tighten the bolt finger tight only at this stage.

13 Thoroughly clean the crankshaft and crankshaft sprocket, ensuring that there is no oil or grease on the contact faces.

14 Place the sprocket in the timing chain, then engage the chain over the camshaft sprocket. Slide the crankshaft sprocket over the end of the crankshaft.

15 Refit the timing chain tensioner rail, screw in the lower pivot bolt and tighten the bolt to the specified torque.

16 Refit the timing chain tensioner and tighten the two retaining bolts to the specified torque. Depress the tensioner plunger, withdraw the locking drill bit and release the plunger.

17 Using the method employed on removal to hold the camshaft sprocket, tighten the retaining bolt to the specified torque.

18 Refit the timing cover as described in Section 5.

7 Camshaft housing – removal and refitting

Removal

1 Disconnect the battery negative terminal (refer to *Disconnecting the battery* in Chapter 5A, Section 4).

2 Lift off the plastic cover over the top of the engine.

3 Remove the air cleaner assembly and intake

ducts as described in Chapter 4B, Section 3.

4 Disconnect the wiring connector from the crankcase ventilation pipe heating element (where fitted).

5 Undo the two bolts securing the crankcase ventilation pipe and vacuum hose to the brackets on the top of the engine. Disconnect the vacuum hose from the vacuum tank connector and from the turbocharger wastegate actuator solenoid valve. Release the crankcase ventilation pipe connector from the vacuum tank and remove the pipe and vacuum hose from the engine.

6 Disconnect the two vacuum hoses from the vacuum tank at the rear of the engine. Undo the two retaining bolts and remove the vacuum tank from its mounting bracket.

7 Unclip the vacuum hose from the vacuum tank mounting bracket, then undo the two retaining bolts and remove the mounting bracket from the cylinder block.

8 Undo the two bolts securing the engine wiring harness to the brackets on the camshaft housing.

9 Disconnect all the engine wiring harness connectors at the front, top and rear of the engine. To avoid confusion when refitting, label each connector as it is disconnected, or alternatively, take a series of photos. Release the wiring harness from all the retaining clips and cable ties, then move the harness to one side, clear of the camshaft cover.

10 Disconnect the wiring connectors from the four glow plugs. Undo the two retaining bolts and remove the glow plug wiring harness and mounting bracket from the camshaft housing.

11 Remove the timing cover as described in Section 5.

12 Remove the high-pressure fuel pump as described in Chapter 4B, Section 11.

13 Remove the fuel rail as described in Chapter 4B, Section 12.

14 Remove the fuel injectors as described in Chapter 4B, Section 13.

15 Remove the vacuum pump as described in Chapter 9, Section 20.

16 Remove the timing chain, sprockets and tensioner as described in Section 6.

17 Undo the sixteen bolts, and two stud bolts, securing the camshaft housing to the cylinder head.

6.7b...then unscrew the bolt and remove the sprocket

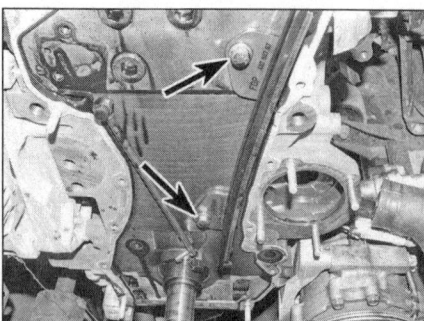
6.8 Undo the two retaining bolts and remove the timing chain guide rail

18 Lift the camshaft housing off the cylinder head and recover the gasket.

19 Thoroughly clean the mating faces of the cylinder head and camshaft housing and obtain a new gasket for refitting.

Refitting

20 Check that all the hydraulic tappets and rocker arms are correctly positioned in the cylinder head and none have been disturbed.

21 Place a new gasket on the cylinder head, then locate the camshaft housing in position. Refit the two stud bolts to align the assembly but only tighten them finger tight at this stage **(see illustrations)**.

22 Using a straight-edge, align the front face of the camshaft housing with the front face of the cylinder head. Lightly tighten the two stud bolts to retain the housing and maintain the alignment.

23 Refit the sixteen camshaft housing retaining bolts, noting that the longer bolt is fitted at the flywheel end of the housing between the high-pressure fuel pump and vacuum pump locations. Progressively screw in the retaining bolts to gradually draw the housing down and into contact with the cylinder head.

24 Using the straight-edge, check the alignment of the camshaft housing and cylinder head once more and correct if necessary.

25 Working in the sequence shown, tighten the camshaft housing retaining bolts to the specified torque in the two Stages given in the Specifications **(see illustration)**. Note that the torque setting for the two stud bolts is different from the other bolts.

26 Refit the timing chain, sprockets and tensioner as described in Section 6.

27 Refit the timing cover as described in Section 5.

28 Refit the vacuum pump as described in Chapter 9, Section 20.

29 Refit the fuel injectors as described in Chapter 4B, Section 13.

30 Refit the fuel rail as described in Chapter 4B, Section 12.

31 Refit the high-pressure fuel pump as described in Chapter 4B, Section 11.

32 Place the glow plug wiring harness and mounting bracket in position on the camshaft housing and secure with the two retaining bolts tightened to the specified torque. Reconnect the wiring connectors to the glow plugs.

33 Reconnect the engine wiring harness to the various engine components, then secure the harness with the two bolts, retaining clips and cable ties.

34 Refit the vacuum tank mounting bracket and the vacuum tank to the rear of the engine and reconnect the two vacuum hoses.

35 Locate the crankcase ventilation pipe and vacuum hose in position on the camshaft housing. Secure the pipe with the two retaining bolts, then reconnect the pipe to

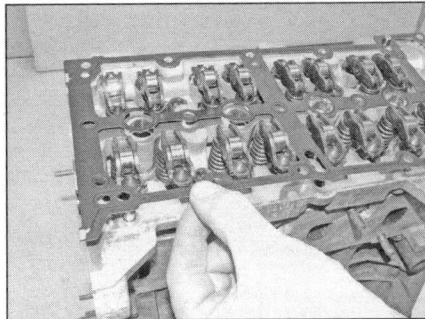

7.21a Place a new gasket on the cylinder head...

7.21b...locate the camshaft housing in position...

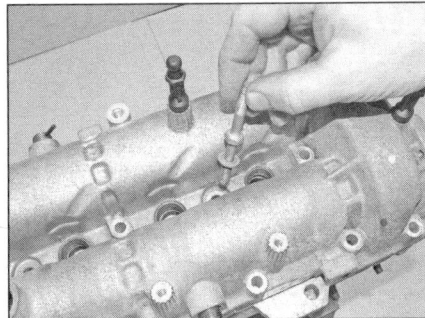

7.21c...then refit the two stud bolts to align the assembly

the vacuum tank. Reconnect the vacuum hose and the pipe heating element wiring connector.

36 Refit the air cleaner assembly and intake ducts as described in Chapter 4B, Section 3.

37 Refit the plastic cover to the top of the engine, then reconnect the battery negative terminal.

---

8 Camshafts –
removal, inspection and refitting

Removal

Note: *An additional camshaft locking tool (two in total) will be required for this operation (see Section 3).*

1 Carry out the operations described in Section 7, paragraphs 1 to 15.

2 Before removing the camshaft housing completely, the retaining bolts for the camshaft drive gears and sprocket should be slackened as follows.

3 It will be necessary to hold the camshaft sprocket to enable the drive gear and sprocket retaining bolts to be slackened. Vauxhall/Opel special tools EN-956-1 and EN-6347 are available for this purpose, however, a home-made tool can easily be fabricated (see Tool-Tip in Section 5).

4 Working through the vacuum pump aperture, and using the holding tool to prevent rotation of the camshaft, slacken the inlet camshaft drive gear retaining bolt. Working through the high-pressure fuel pump aperture,

7.25 Camshaft housing retaining bolt tightening sequence

slacken the exhaust camshaft drive gear retaining bolt in the same way.

5 Again, using the holding tool, slacken the camshaft sprocket retaining bolt.

6 Continue with the camshaft housing removal procedure as described in Section 7, paragraphs 16 to 19.

7 With the camshaft housing removed, unscrew the retaining bolt and withdraw the camshaft position sensor from the top of the housing.

8 Turn the housing over and remove the camshaft locking tool.

9 Unscrew the previously slackened retaining bolt, lift off the drive gear and carefully withdraw the inlet camshaft from the camshaft housing **(see illustrations)**. Using quick-drying paint, correction fluid or a label, suitably mark the drive gear and camshaft to identify them as the inlet components.

10 At the exhaust camshaft, unscrew the

8.9a Unscrew the previously slackened retaining bolt...

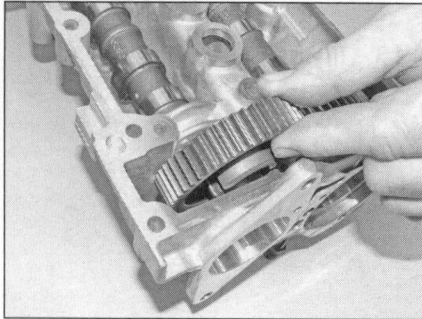
8.9b...lift off the drive gear...

8.9c...and carefully withdraw the inlet camshaft from the camshaft housing

8.10a Unscrew the retaining bolt...

8.10b...lift off the drive gear...

8.10c...and carefully withdraw the exhaust camshaft from the camshaft housing

8.17 Insert the locking tools to lock the camshafts in the timing position

previously slackened retaining bolt, lift off the drive gear and carefully withdraw the exhaust camshaft from the camshaft housing (see illustrations). Using quick-drying paint, correction fluid or a label, suitably mark the drive gear and camshaft to identify them as the exhaust components.

Inspection

11 Examine the camshaft bearing surfaces and cam lobes for signs of wear ridges and scoring. Renew the camshaft if any of these conditions are apparent. Examine the condition of the bearing surfaces in the camshaft housing. If the any wear or scoring is evident, the camshaft housing will need to be renewed.
12 If either camshaft is being renewed, it will be necessary to renew all the rocker arms and tappets for that particular camshaft also (see Section 9).
13 Check the condition of the camshaft drive

gears for chipped or damaged teeth, wear ridges and scoring. Renew any components as necessary.

Refitting

14 Prior to refitting, thoroughly clean all components and dry with a lint-free cloth. Ensure that all traces of oil and grease are removed from the contact faces of the drive gears, sprocket and camshafts.
15 Lubricate the exhaust camshaft bearing journals in the camshaft housing and carefully insert the exhaust camshaft. Ensuring that the contact faces are clean and dry, refit the drive gear to the camshaft and insert the retaining bolt. Screw in the bolt two or three turns at this stage.
16 Lubricate the inlet camshaft bearing journals in the camshaft housing and carefully insert the inlet camshaft. Ensuring that the contact faces are clean and dry, refit the drive gear to the camshaft and insert the retaining bolt. Screw in the bolt two or three turns at this stage.

17 Turn each camshaft to align the timing slot with the valve timing checking hole in the camshaft housing. Insert the camshaft locking tools (either the Vauxhall/Opel tool or the home-made equivalent described in Section 3) ensuring that the tools fully engage with the camshaft slots (see illustration).
18 With the camshafts locked in the timing position, tighten the inlet and exhaust camshaft drive gear retaining bolts to the specified torque.
19 Remove the locking tool from the exhaust camshaft, but leave the inlet camshaft locking tool in place.
20 Refit the camshaft position sensor to the camshaft housing and tighten the retaining bolt securely.
21 Refit the camshaft housing to the cylinder head as described in Section 7.

9 Hydraulic tappets and rocker arms – removal, inspection and refitting

Removal

1 Remove the camshaft housing as described in Section 7.
2 Obtain sixteen small, oil tight clean plastic containers, and number them inlet 1 to 8 and exhaust 1 to 8; alternatively, divide a larger container into sixteen compartments and number each compartment accordingly.
3 Withdraw each rocker arm and hydraulic tappet in turn, unclip the rocker arm from the tappet, and place them in their respective container (see illustrations). Do not

9.3a Withdraw each rocker arm and hydraulic tappet in turn...

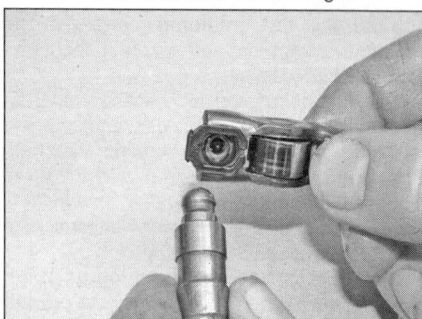
9.3b...then unclip the rocker arm from the tappet

interchange the rocker arms and tappets, or the rate of wear will be much increased. Fill each container with clean engine oil and ensure that the tappet is submerged.

Inspection

4 Examine the rocker arm and hydraulic tappet bearing surfaces for wear ridges and scoring. Renew any rocker arm or tappet on which these conditions are apparent.
5 If any new hydraulic tappets are obtained, they should be immersed in a container of clean engine oil prior to refitting.

Refitting

6 Liberally oil the cylinder head hydraulic tappet bores and the tappets. Working on one assembly at a time, clip the rocker arm back onto the tappet, then refit the tappet to the cylinder head, ensuring that it is refitted to its original bore. Lay the rocker arm over its respective valve.
7 Refit the remaining tappets and rocker arms in the same way.
8 With all the tappets and rocker arms in place, refit the camshaft housing as described in Section 7.

10 Cylinder head – removal and refitting

Removal

Note: *New cylinder head retaining bolts will be required for refitting.*
1 Remove the camshaft housing as described in Section 7, and the hydraulic tappets and rocker arms as described in Section 9.
2 Remove the catalytic converter as described in Chapter 4B, Section 20.
3 Remove the thermostat as described in Chapter 3, Section 4.
4 Remove the turbocharger wastegate solenoid as described in Chapter 4B, Section 10.
5 Undo the bolt securing the oil level dipstick guide tube to the rear of the inlet manifold. Remove the guide tube and collect the sealing ring.
6 Release the retaining clips at each end of the exhaust pressure pipe at the rear of the engine. Undo the two mounting bolts, unclip the vacuum hose and remove the pressure pipe.
7 Undo the two bolts securing the exhaust gas recirculation (EGR) pipe to the EGR valve cooler.
8 Undo the three bolts securing the EGR pipe to the manifold. Remove the pipe and collect the gasket and O-ring seal.
9 Undo the two bolts and remove the throttle housing support bracket.
10 Release the retaining clip and disconnect the heater matrix coolant hose from the EGR valve cooler.
11 Disconnect the EGR valve wiring connector.
12 Disconnect the wiring connector and vacuum hose from the EGR valve vacuum solenoid.

13 Unscrew the turbocharger oil supply pipe banjo unions from the top of the turbocharger and from the oil filter housing. Collect the two copper washers at each union and remove the oil supply pipe.
14 Release the two retaining clips and remove the turbocharger oil return hose from the turbocharger and oil filter housing.
15 Undo the two bolts securing the intercooler intake duct to the underside of the turbocharger. Separate the flange joint and recover the gasket.
16 Working in the reverse of the tightening sequence **(see illustration 10.37a)**, progressively slacken the cylinder head bolts by half a turn at a time, until all bolts can be unscrewed by hand. Note that an M12 RIBE socket bit will be required to unscrew the bolts. Remove the cylinder head bolts.
17 Engage the help of an assistant and lift the cylinder head from the cylinder block. Take care as it is a bulky and heavy assembly.
18 Remove the gasket and keep it for identification purposes (see paragraph 25).
19 If the cylinder head is to be dismantled for overhaul, then refer to Chapter 2D, Section 7.

Preparation for refitting

20 The mating faces of the cylinder head and cylinder block/crankcase must be perfectly clean before refitting the head. Use a hard plastic or wood scraper to remove all traces of gasket and carbon; also clean the piston crowns. Take particular care, as the surfaces are damaged easily. Also, make sure that the carbon is not allowed to enter the oil and water passages – this is particularly important for the lubrication system, as carbon could block the oil supply to any of the engine's components. Using adhesive tape and paper, seal the water, oil and bolt holes in the cylinder block/crankcase. To prevent carbon entering the gap between the pistons and bores, smear a little grease in the gap. After cleaning each piston, use a small brush to remove all traces of grease and carbon from the gap, then wipe away the remainder with a clean rag. Clean all the pistons in the same way.
21 Check the mating surfaces of the cylinder block/crankcase and the cylinder head for nicks, deep scratches and other damage. If slight, they may be removed carefully with a file, but if excessive, machining may be the only alternative to renewal.
22 Ensure that the cylinder head bolt holes in the crankcase are clean and free of oil. Syringe or soak up any oil left in the bolt holes. This is most important in order that the correct bolt tightening torque can be applied and to prevent the possibility of the block being cracked by hydraulic pressure when the bolts are tightened.
23 The cylinder head bolts must be discarded and renewed, regardless of their apparent condition.
24 If warpage of the cylinder head gasket surface is suspected, use a straight-edge to

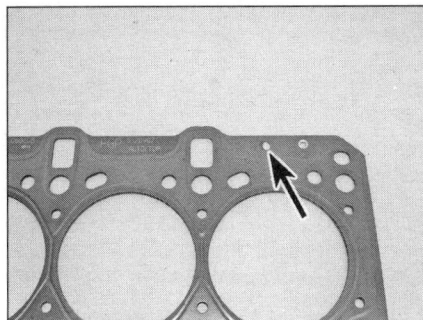
10.25 Cylinder head gasket thickness identification hole

check it for distortion. Refer to Chapter 2D, Section 8 if necessary.
25 On this engine, the cylinder head-to-piston clearance is controlled by fitting different thickness head gaskets. The gasket thickness can be determined by looking at the right-hand front corner of the gasket and checking on the number of holes **(see illustration)**.

Holes in gasket	Gasket thickness
No holes	0.67 to 0.77 mm
One hole	0.77 to 0.87 mm
Two holes	0.87 to 0.97 mm

26 The correct thickness of gasket required is selected by measuring the piston protrusions as follows.
27 Remove the crankshaft locking tool from the base of the bellhousing and temporarily refit the crankshaft pulley hub retaining bolt to enable the crankshaft to be turned.
28 Mount a dial test indicator securely on the block so that its pointer can be easily pivoted between the piston crown and block mating surface. Turn the crankshaft to bring No 1 piston roughly to the TDC position. Move the dial test indicator probe over and in contact with No 1 piston. Turn the crankshaft back and forth slightly until the highest reading is shown on the gauge, indicating that the piston is at TDC.
29 Zero the dial test indicator on the gasket surface of the cylinder block then carefully move the indicator over No 1 piston. Measure its protrusion at the highest point between the valve cut-outs, and then again at its highest point between the valve cut-outs at 90° to the first measurement **(see illustration)**. Repeat this procedure with No 4 piston.

10.29 Using a dial test indicator to measure piston protrusion

10.36 Using a straight-edge, align the front face of the cylinder head with the front face of the cylinder block

10.37a Cylinder head bolt tightening sequence

10.37b Working in sequence, tighten the cylinder head bolts to their Stage 1 torque, using a torque wrench

30 Rotate the crankshaft half a turn (180º) to bring No 2 and 3 pistons to TDC. Ensure the crankshaft is accurately positioned then measure the protrusions of No 2 and 3 pistons at the specified points. Once all pistons have been measured, rotate the crankshaft to position all the pistons at their mid-stroke and refit the crankshaft locking tool. If the tool will not engage the hole in the flywheel, turn the crankshaft one complete turn and try again.

31 Select the correct thickness of head gasket required by determining the largest amount of piston protrusion, and using the following table.

Piston protrusion measurement	Gasket thickness required
0.028 to 0.127 mm	0.67 to 0.77 mm (no holes)
0.128 to 0.227 mm	0.77 to 0.87 mm (one hole)
0.228 to 0.327 mm	0.87 to 0.97 mm (two holes)

Refitting

32 Wipe clean the mating surfaces of the cylinder head and cylinder block/crankcase. Place the new gasket in position with the words ALTO/TOP uppermost.

33 If not already done, rotate the crankshaft to position all the pistons at their mid-stroke and refit the crankshaft locking tool. If the tool will not engage the hole in the flywheel, turn the crankshaft one complete turn and try again. Once the tool is in place, remove the crankshaft pulley hub retaining bolt.

34 With the aid of an assistant, carefully refit the cylinder head assembly to the block, aligning it with the locating dowels.

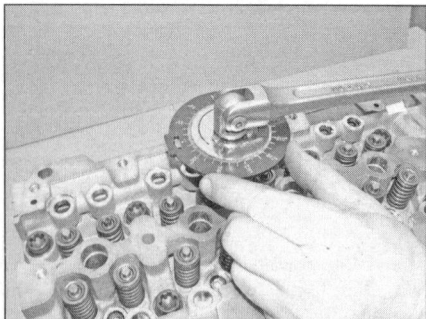

10.38 Tighten the bolts through the Stage 2 and Stage 3 angle using an angle-measuring gauge

35 Carefully enter each new cylinder head bolt into its relevant hole (do not drop them in). Screw all bolts in, by hand only, until finger-tight.

36 Using a straight-edge, align the front face of the cylinder head with the front face of the cylinder block (see illustration). Lightly tighten the cylinder head bolts to retain the head and maintain the alignment.

37 Working progressively in the sequence shown, tighten the cylinder head bolts to their Stage 1 torque setting, using a torque wrench and suitable socket (see illustrations).

38 Once all bolts have been tightened to the Stage 1 torque, working again in the same sequence, go around and tighten all bolts through the specified Stage 2 angle, then through the specified Stage 3 angle using an angle-measuring gauge (see illustration).

39 Place a new gasket on the intercooler intake duct flange and locate the flange on the turbocharger. Refit the two bolts and tighten them to the specified torque.

40 Refit the turbocharger oil return hose and secure with the two retaining clips.

41 Refit the turbocharger oil supply pipe to the turbocharger and oil filter housing using new copper washers at the banjo unions. Tighten the banjo union bolts to the specified torque.

42 Reconnect the wiring connector and vacuum hose to the EGR valve vacuum solenoid.

43 Reconnect the wiring connector to the EGR valve.

44 Refit the heater matrix coolant hose to the EGR valve cooler and secure with the retaining clip.

45 Refit the throttle housing support bracket and secure with the two bolts, tightened securely.

46 Refit the EGR pipe to the manifold and EGR cooler using a new gasket and O-ring. Refit the retaining bolts and tighten them to the specified torque.

47 Refit the exhaust pressure pipe at the rear of the engine and secure with the retaining clips and mounting bolts. Tighten the bolts securely.

48 Using a new seal, refit the oil level dipstick

tube. Refit the retaining bolt and tighten it securely.

49 Refit the turbocharger wastegate solenoid as described in Chapter 4B, Section 10.

50 Refit the thermostat as described in Chapter 3, Section 4.

51 Refit the catalytic converter as described in Chapter 4B, Section 20.

52 Refit the hydraulic tappets and rocker arms as described in Section 9, and the camshaft housing as described in Section 7.

11 Sump – removal and refitting

Removal

1 Disconnect the battery negative terminal (refer to *Disconnecting the battery* in Chapter 5A, Section 4).

2 Apply the handbrake, then jack up the front of the vehicle and support it on axle stands (see *Jacking and vehicle support*).

3 Drain the engine oil, with reference to Chapter 1B, Section 5 then refit and tighten the sump drain plug.

4 Remove the catalytic converter as described in Chapter 4B, Section 20.

5 Remove the auxiliary drivebelt as described in Chapter 1B, Section 31.

6 Disconnect the wiring from the air conditioning compressor and release the wiring harness from the cable clips. Unbolt the compressor from the cylinder block bracket and support the compressor clear of the engine. Do not disconnect the refrigerant lines from the compressor.

7 Undo the four retaining bolts and remove the air conditioning compressor mounting bracket from the cylinder block.

8 Undo the six bolts securing the sump reinforcement bracket to the cylinder block baseplate and transmission bellhousing and remove the bracket (see illustration). Note the locations of the different length bolts to aid refitting.

9 Undo the thirteen bolts and two nuts securing the sump to the cylinder block baseplate and timing cover. Using a wide bladed scraper or similar tool inserted

between the sump and baseplate, carefully break the joint, then remove the sump from under the car.

Refitting

10 Thoroughly clean the inside and outside of the sump ensuring that all traces of old sealant are removed from the mating face. Also clean the cylinder block baseplate mating face to remove all traces of old sealant.

11 Apply a 3 to 4 mm bead of Loctite 5900 to the sump mating face, ensuring the sealant bead runs around the inside of the bolt holes **(see illustration)**. Position the sump on the cylinder block baseplate, then refit the thirteen bolts and two nuts. Progressively tighten the bolts/nuts to the specified torque.

12 Refit the sump reinforcement bracket to the cylinder block baseplate and transmission bellhousing and secure with the six bolts, tightened to the specified torque.

13 Refit the air conditioning compressor mounting bracket and tighten the retaining bolts to the specified torque.

14 Refit the air conditioning compressor to the mounting bracket, then fit and tighten the mounting bolts to the specified torque. Reconnect the wiring and secure the wiring harness with the cable clips.

15 Refit the catalytic converter as described in Chapter 4B, Section 20.

16 Refit the auxiliary drivebelt as described in Chapter 1B, Section 31.

17 Reconnect the battery negative terminal.

18 Lower the vehicle to the ground then fill the engine with fresh oil as described in Chapter 1B, Section 5.

11.8 Remove the sump reinforcement bracket from the cylinder block baseplate and transmission bellhousing

12 Oil pump – removal, inspection and refitting

Removal

1 Remove the timing cover as described in Section 5.

2 Undo the two retaining bolts and remove the oil pick-up pipe from the oil pump cover on the rear of the timing cover. Remove the rubber seal from the pick-up pipe, noting that a new seal will be required for refitting **(see illustrations)**.

3 Remove the securing screws and withdraw the oil pump cover from the rear of the timing cover **(see illustration)**.

4 Remove the inner and outer rotor from the timing cover and wipe them clean. Also clean

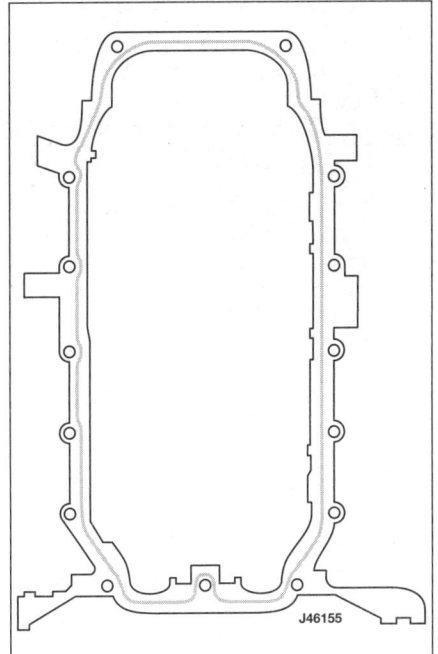

11.11 Apply a bead of sealant to the sump mating face, ensuring the bead runs around the inside of the bolt holes

the rotor location in the timing cover **(see illustrations)**.

5 The oil pressure relief valve components can also be removed from the timing cover by unscrewing the cap. Withdraw the cap, the spring and the plunger **(see illustrations)**.

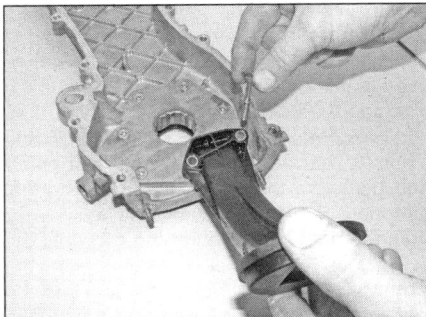

12.2a Remove the oil pick-up pipe from the oil pump cover...

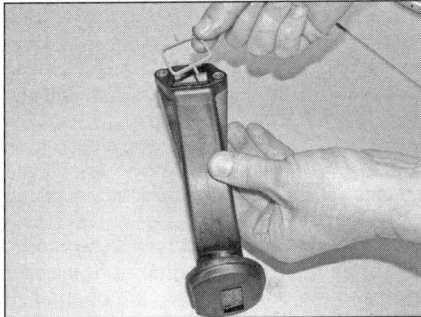

12.2b...then remove the rubber seal from the pick-up pipe

12.3 Remove the screws and withdraw the oil pump cover from the rear of the timing cover

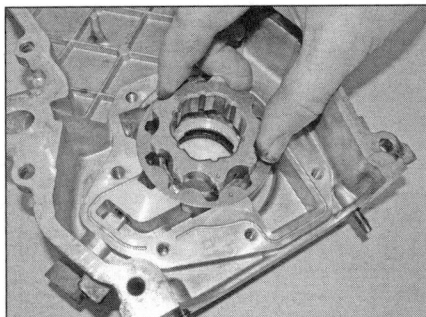

12.4a Remove the oil pump inner rotor...

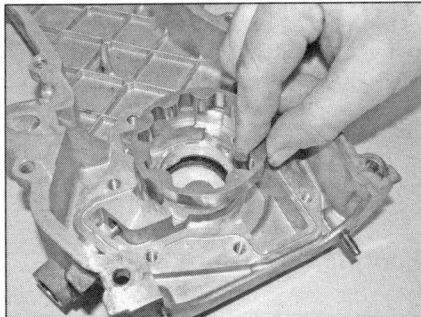

12.4b...and outer rotor from the timing cover

12.5a Unscrew the oil pressure relief valve cap...

12.5b...then withdraw the spring...

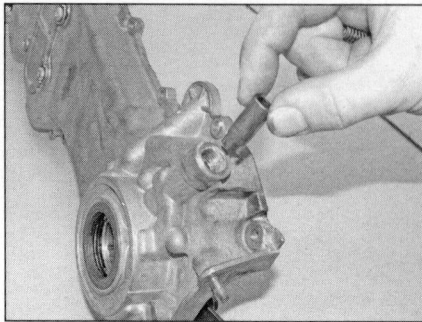

12.5c...and the plunger

12.7 Checking the oil pump rotor endfloat

12.8 Checking the oil pump outer rotor-to-body clearance

Inspection

6 Check for any signs of scoring, pitting, scuffing or general wear on the rotors or their location in the timing cover. Renew any components as necessary. If the pump components are satisfactory, check the rotor clearances as follows.

7 Locate the inner and outer rotor back in the timing cover. Check the clearance between the end faces of the gears and the housing (endfloat) using a straight-edge and a feeler gauge **(see illustration)**.

8 Check the outer rotor-to-body clearance using a feeler gauge **(see illustration)**.

9 If the clearances are outside the specified limits, renew the components as necessary.

10 Examine the pressure relief valve spring and plunger, and renew if any sign of damage or wear is evident.

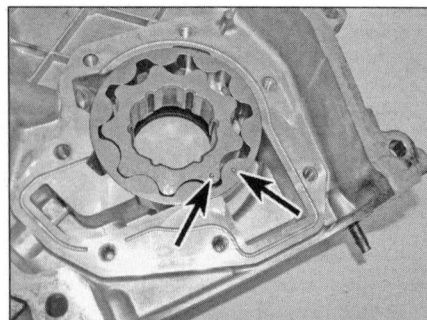

12.13 Locate the rotors in the timing cover with the dot marks aligned and facing away from the timing cover

11 Ensure that the rotor location in the interior of the timing cover is scrupulously clean before commencing reassembly.

Refitting

12 Thoroughly clean the pressure relief valve components, and lubricate them with clean engine oil before refitting. Insert the plunger and spring, then apply thread locking compound to the cap threads and refit the cap. Tighten the cap securely.

13 Ensure that the rotors are clean, then lubricate them with clean engine oil. Locate the inner and outer rotor back in the timing cover, with the dot marks aligned and facing away from the timing cover **(see illustration)**.

14 Ensure that the mating faces of the rear cover and the pump housing are clean, then refit the rear cover. Refit and tighten the securing screws securely.

15 Fit a new rubber seal to the oil pick-up pipe and locate the pipe on the oil pump cover. Refit the two retaining bolts and tighten securely.

16 Refit the timing cover as described in Section 5.

13 Crankshaft oil seals – renewal

Front (timing cover) oil seal

Note: *The design of the engine is such, that once the crankshaft pulley hub bolt is undone the valve timing will be lost unless suitable locking tools are used to retain the camshafts*

and crankshaft in the timing position. Refer to the information contained in Section 3 for further details and obtain the tools described.

1 Disconnect the battery negative terminal (refer to *Disconnecting the battery* in Chapter 5A, Section 4).

2 Lift off the plastic cover over the top of the engine.

3 Remove the crankshaft pulley as described in Section 4.

4 Undo the two retaining bolts securing the fuel rail to the mounting bracket.

5 Undo the remaining bolts and remove the engine lifting bracket and fuel rail mounting bracket from the camshaft housing **(see illustration 3.8)**. After removal of the mounting bracket, take care not to apply any force to the fuel rail otherwise damage could be caused to the high-pressure fuel pipes.

6 Unscrew the closure bolt from the valve timing checking hole on the inlet camshaft side of the camshaft housing. The bolt is located approximately in line with No 2 fuel injector **(see illustration 3.9)**.

7 If the Vauxhall/Opel camshaft locking tool or similar alternative is available (see Section 3), screw the tool into the valve timing checking hole. Ensure that the mark on the tool plunger is facing upwards. Using a socket or spanner on the crankshaft pulley hub bolt, turn the crankshaft in the normal direction of rotation (clockwise as viewed from the right-hand side of the car) until the spring-loaded plunger of the locking tool slides into engagement with the slot on the camshaft. There will be an audible click from the tool when this happens, and the plunger will be seen to move in, towards the camshaft.

8 If the home-made locking tool described in Section 3 is being used, insert a screwdriver through the valve timing checking hole on the inlet camshaft side of the camshaft housing, and into contact with the inlet camshaft. Using a socket or spanner on the crankshaft pulley hub bolt, turn the crankshaft in the normal direction of rotation (clockwise as viewed from the right-hand side of the car) until the screwdriver can be felt to engage with the slot in the camshaft. Screw the tool into the camshaft housing until resistance is felt, then turn the crankshaft slightly until the camshaft slot is correctly aligned, and the tool can be screwed fully in.

9 Insert the Vauxhall/Opel crankshaft locking tool or suitable alternative (see Section 3) into the timing hole at the base or on the front facing side of the transmission bellhousing and into engagement with the flywheel **(see illustration 3.3a)**. It may be necessary to turn the crankshaft very slightly one way or the other, by means of the pulley retaining bolt, to allow the tool to fully engage.

10 It will now be necessary to hold the crankshaft pulley hub to enable the retaining bolt to be removed. Vauxhall/Opel special tool EN-662-C is available for this purpose, however, a home-made tool can easily be fabricated. Refer to the Tool-Tip in Section 5.

11 Using the Vauxhall/Opel tool or the home-made alternative, hold the pulley hub stationary and unscrew the retaining bolt. The pulley hub retaining bolt has a left-hand thread and is unscrewed by turning it clockwise. Withdraw the pulley hub from the crankshaft. Discard the retaining bolt; a new bolt will be required for refitting.

12 Carefully prise out the old crankshaft oil seal with a screwdriver or similar hooked tool. Clean the oil seal seat with a wooden or plastic scraper.

13 Tap the new oil seal into position until it is flush with the outer face of the timing cover, using a suitable socket or tube, or a wooden block.

14 Thoroughly clean the crankshaft pulley hub, ensuring that the timing chain sprocket contact face is free from oil or grease.

15 Refit the pulley hub to the crankshaft, then fit the new retaining bolt. Using the method employed on removal to hold the pulley hub stationary, tighten the retaining bolt to the specified torque, then through the specified angle.

16 Remove the camshaft and crankshaft locking tools.

17 Thoroughly clean the threads of the closure bolt and apply suitable thread locking compound. Screw the bolt into the camshaft housing and tighten to the specified torque.

18 Place the engine lifting bracket and fuel rail mounting bracket in position on the camshaft housing and locate the fuel rail on the mounting bracket. Refit the retaining bolts and tighten to the specified torque.

19 Refit the crankshaft pulley as described in Section 4.

20 Refit the plastic cover to the top of the engine, then reconnect the battery negative terminal.

Rear (transmission end) oil seal

Note: *Vauxhall/Opel special tools EN-4677-10 and EN-4677-20 or a suitable equivalent oil seal fitting tool will be required for this operation.*

21 Remove the flywheel as described in Section 15.

22 Carefully prise out the old seal from its location using a screwdriver or similar hooked tool.

23 Clean the oil seal seat with a wooden or plastic scraper.

24 Fit the new seal to the Vauxhall/Opel tool, or equivalent fitting tool, so that the seal lip is spread open toward the crankshaft side **(see illustration)**.

25 Position the seal, together with the fitting tool over the end of the crankshaft, then tap the seal into position using a suitable socket or tube, or a wooden block, until it is flush with the outer faces of the cylinder block and baseplate **(see illustrations)**.

26 Once the seal is in position, remove the fitting tool **(see illustration)**.

27 Refit the flywheel as described in Section 15.

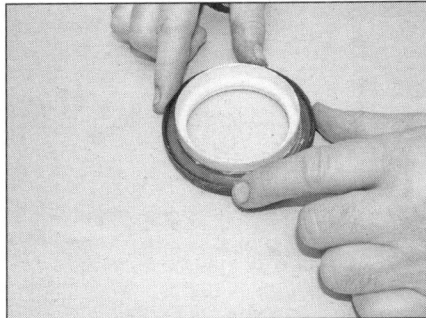
13.24 Fit the oil seal to the fitting tool, so that the seal lip is spread open toward the crankshaft side

13.25b...then tap the seal into position using a suitable wooden block or similar

14 Oil filter housing – removal and refitting

Removal

1 Disconnect the battery negative terminal (refer to *Disconnecting the battery* in Chapter 5A, Section 4).

2 Drain the cooling system as described in Chapter 1B, Section 28.

3 Remove the turbocharger as described in Chapter 4B, Section 19.

4 Undo the two bolts securing the thermostat bypass pipe to the oil filter housing, then undo the bypass pipe support bracket bolt **(see illustration)**. Lift the bypass pipe off the oil filter housing and collect the flange gasket.

14.4 Undo the two bolts securing the thermostat bypass pipe to the oil filter housing

13.25a Position the seal, together with the fitting tool over the end of the crankshaft...

13.26 Once the seal is in position, remove the fitting tool

Note that a new gasket will be required for refitting.

5 Release the retaining clip and disconnect the radiator outlet hose from the oil filter housing.

6 Undo the four retaining bolts and remove the oil filter housing from the cylinder block. Recover the rubber seal from the rear of the housing. Note that a new seal will be required for refitting.

Refitting

7 Place a new rubber seal on the oil filter housing, ensuring the seal is fully engaged with the housing grooves **(see illustration)**.

8 Position the oil filter housing on the cylinder block and fit the four retaining bolts. Tighten the bolts to the specified torque.

9 Connect the radiator outlet hose to the oil

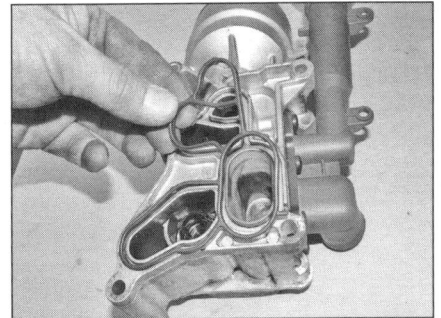
14.7 Place a new rubber seal on the oil filter housing, ensuring the seal is fully engaged with the housing grooves

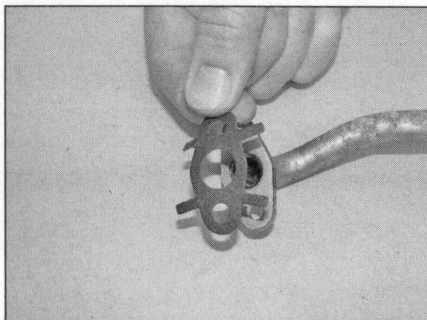

14.10 Locate a new gasket over the thermostat bypass pipe flange and bend over the tabs of the gasket to retain it on the flange

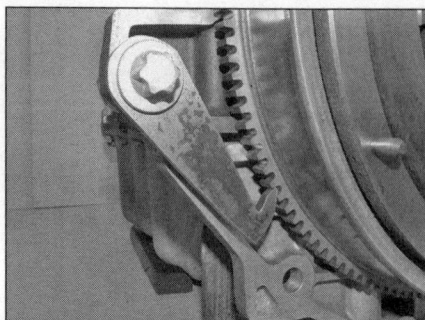

15.3 Prevent the flywheel from turning by jamming the ring gear teeth using a suitable tool

15.4 Flywheel retaining bolts

filter housing and secure with the retaining clip.

10 Locate a new gasket over the thermostat bypass pipe flange and bend over the tabs of the gasket to retain it on the flange **(see illustration)**.

11 Position the pipe flange on the oil filter housing. Refit the two flange bolts and the support bracket bolt and tighten them to the specified torque.

12 Refit the turbocharger as described in Chapter 4B, Section 19.

13 Lower the vehicle to the ground, then reconnect the battery negative terminal.

14 Refill the cooling system as described in Chapter 1B, Section 28.

15 Flywheel –
removal, inspection and refitting

Note: *New flywheel retaining bolts will be required for refitting.*

Removal

1 Remove the transmission as described in Chapter 7A, Section 8.

2 Remove the clutch assembly as described in Chapter 6, Section 6.

3 Prevent the flywheel from turning by jamming the ring gear teeth using a suitable tool **(see illustration)**.

4 Slacken and remove the retaining bolts and remove the flywheel **(see illustration)**.

Caution: Take care, as the flywheel is heavy.

Inspection

5 Examine the flywheel for wear or chipping of the ring gear teeth. Renewal of the ring gear is not possible and if the wear or chipping is significant, a new flywheel will be required.

6 Examine the flywheel for scoring of the clutch face. If the clutch face is scored significantly, a new flywheel will be required.

7 The dual-mass flywheel used on these engines has the effect of reducing engine and transmission vibrations and harshness. The flywheel consists of a primary mass and a secondary mass constructed in such a way that the secondary mass is allowed to rotate slightly in relation to the primary mass. Springs within the assembly restrict this movement to set limits.

8 Dual-mass flywheels have earned an unenviable reputation for unreliability and have been known to fail at quite low mileages (sometimes as low as 20 000 miles). As well as the checks described above in paragraphs 5 and 6, some additional checks should be performed as follows.

9 Look through the bolt hole and inspection openings in the secondary mass and check for any visible damage in the area of the centre bearing.

10 Place your thumbs on the clutch face of the secondary mass at the 3 o'clock and 9 o'clock positions and try to rock it. The maximum movement should not exceed 3 mm. Repeat this check with your thumbs at the 12 o'clock and 6 o'clock positions.

11 Rotate the secondary mass clockwise and anti-clockwise. It should move freely in both directions until spring resistance is felt, with

no abnormal grating or rattling noises. The maximum rotational movement should not exceed a distance of eight teeth of the ring gear.

12 If there is any doubt about the condition of the flywheel, seek the advice of a Vauxhall/Opel dealer or engine reconditioning specialist. They will be able to advise if the flywheel is an acceptable condition, or whether renewal is necessary.

Refitting

13 Clean the mating surfaces of the flywheel and crankshaft.

14 Apply a drop of locking compound to the threads of each of the new flywheel retaining bolts (unless they are already pre-coated) then refit the flywheel and install the new bolts.

15 Lock the flywheel using the method employed on removal then, working in a diagonal sequence, evenly and progressively tighten the retaining bolts to the specified torque setting.

16 Refit the clutch as described in Chapter 6, Section 6, then refit the transmission as described in Chapter 7A, Section 8.

16 Engine/transmission mountings –
inspection and renewal

1 Refer to Chapter 2A, Section 15, noting the slight variation in the retaining bolt arrangement on the right-hand mounting. Also observe the different torque wrench settings given in the Specifications of this Chapter for the right-hand mounting.

Chapter 2 Part D
Engine removal and overhaul procedures

Contents

Degrees of difficulty

Easy, suitable for novice with little experience	**Fairly easy,** suitable for beginner with some experience	**Fairly difficult,** suitable for competent DIY mechanic	**Difficult,** suitable for experienced DIY mechanic	**Very difficult,** suitable for expert DIY or professional

Specifications

Petrol engines

Cylinder block

Material	Cast iron
Cylinder bore diameter.	73.385 to 73.415 mm

Pistons

Piston diameter	73.345 to 73.375 mm

Piston rings

Number of rings (per piston).	2 compression, 1 oil control
Ring end gap:	
Compression	0.30 to 0.45 mm
Oil control	0.25 to 0.75 mm

Cylinder head

Material	Light alloy
Maximum permissible distortion of sealing face	0.025 mm
Overall height of cylinder head (sealing surface-to-sealing surface) . . .	126.0 mm
Valve seat width:	
Inlet	1.00 to 1.40 mm
Exhaust.	1.40 to 1.80 mm
Valve seat angle	45°

Crankshaft and bearings

Number of main bearings:	
1.0 litre engines	4
1.2 and 1.4 litre engines	5
Main bearing journal diameter	50.004 to 50.017 mm (nominal)
Big-end bearing journal diameter.	42.971 to 42.987 mm (nominal)
Crankshaft endfloat	0.100 to 0.200 mm

Valves and guides

	Inlet	Exhaust
Stem diameter (standard).	4.955 to 4.970 mm	4.945 to 4.960 mm
Valve head diameter.	27.900 to 28.100 mm	24.900 to 25.100 mm
Maximum permissible valve stem play in guide.	0.018 to 0.052 mm	0.028 to 0.062 mm
Valve clearances.	Automatic adjustment by hydraulic valve lifters	

Diesel engines

Cylinder block
Material	Cast iron
Cylinder bore diameters	69.600 to 69.630 mm (nominal)

Pistons
Piston diameter	69.520 to 69.550 mm (nominal)

Piston rings
Number of rings (per piston)	2 compression, 1 oil control
Ring end gap:	
Top compression ring	0.20 to 0.30 mm
Second compression ring	1.00 to 1.50 mm
Oil control ring	0.25 to 0.50 mm

Cylinder head
Material	Light alloy
Maximum permissible distortion of sealing face	0.1 mm
Overall height of cylinder head (sealing surface-to-sealing surface)	105.45 to 105.55 mm
Valve seat width	1.5 to 1.7 mm
Valve seat angle	45°

Crankshaft and bearings
Number of main bearings	5
Main bearing journal diameter	50.855 to 51.000 mm (nominal)
Big-end bearing journal diameter	42.455 to 42.600 mm (nominal)
Endfloat	0.055 to 0.265 mm

Valves and guides
Valve stem diameter	5.90 to 5.94 mm
Valve head diameter	22.0 mm
Maximum permissible valve stem play in guide	0.028 to 0.064 mm
Valve clearances	Automatic adjustment by hydraulic valve lifters

Torque wrench settings

1.0 litre petrol engines
Refer to Chapter 2A

1.2 and 1.4 litre petrol engines
Refer to Chapter 2B

Diesel engines
Refer to Chapter 2C

---

1 General Information

1 Included in this Part of Chapter 2 are details of removing the engine/transmission from the car and general overhaul procedures for the cylinder head, cylinder block/crankcase and all other engine internal components.

2 The information given ranges from advice concerning preparation for an overhaul and the purchase of parts, to detailed step-by-step procedures covering removal, inspection, renovation and refitting of engine internal components.

3 After Section 6, all instructions are based on the assumption that the engine has been removed from the car. For information concerning in-car engine repair, as well as the removal and refitting of those external components necessary for full overhaul, refer to Part A, B or C of this Chapter (as applicable) and to Section 6. Ignore any preliminary dismantling operations described in Part A, B or C that are no longer relevant once the engine has been removed from the car.

4 Apart from torque wrench settings, which are given in the Specifications of Part A, B or C (as applicable), all specifications relating to engine overhaul are at the beginning of this Part of Chapter 2.

2 Engine overhaul –
general information

1 It is not always easy to determine when, or if, an engine should be completely overhauled, as a number of factors must be considered.

2 High mileage is not necessarily an indication that an overhaul is needed, while low mileage does not preclude the need for an overhaul. Frequency of servicing is probably the most important consideration. An engine which has had regular and frequent oil and filter changes, as well as other required maintenance, should give many thousands of miles of reliable service. Conversely, a neglected engine may require an overhaul very early in its life.

3 Excessive oil consumption is an indication that piston rings, valve seals and/or valve guides are in need of attention. Make sure that oil leaks are not responsible before deciding that the rings and/or guides are worn. Perform a compression test to determine the likely cause of the problem.

4 Check the oil pressure with a gauge fitted in place of the oil pressure switch, and compare it with that specified. If it is extremely low, the main and big-end bearings, and/or the oil pump, are probably worn out.

5 Loss of power, rough running, knocking or metallic engine noises, excessive valve gear noise, and high fuel consumption may also point to the need for an overhaul, especially if they are all present at the same time. If a complete service does not cure the situation, major mechanical work is the only solution.

6 A full engine overhaul involves restoring all internal parts to the specification of a new engine. During a complete overhaul, the pistons and the piston rings are renewed, and the cylinder bores are reconditioned. New main and big-end bearings are generally fitted; if necessary, the crankshaft may be reground, to compensate for wear in the journals. The valves are also serviced as well, since they are usually in less-than-perfect condition at this point. Always pay careful attention to the condition of the oil pump when overhauling the engine, and renew it if there is any doubt as to its serviceability. The end result should be an as-new engine that will give many trouble-free miles.

7 Critical cooling system components such as the hoses, thermostat and coolant pump should be renewed when an engine is overhauled. The radiator should also be checked carefully, to ensure that it is not clogged or leaking.

8 Before beginning the engine overhaul, read through the entire procedure, to familiarise yourself with the scope and requirements of the job. Check on the availability of parts and make sure that any necessary special tools and equipment are obtained in advance. Most work can be done with typical hand tools, although a number of precision measuring tools are required for inspecting parts to determine if they must be renewed.

9 The services provided by an engineering machine shop or engine reconditioning specialist will almost certainly be required, particularly if major repairs such as crankshaft regrinding or cylinder reboring are necessary. Apart from carrying out machining operations, these establishments will normally handle the inspection of parts, offer advice concerning reconditioning or renewal and supply new components such as pistons, piston rings and bearing shells. It is recommended that the establishment used is a member of the Federation of Engine Re-Manufacturers, or a similar society.

10 Always wait until the engine has been completely dismantled, and until all components (especially the cylinder block/ crankcase and the crankshaft) have been inspected, before deciding what service and repair operations must be performed by an engineering works. The condition of these components will be the major factor to consider when determining whether to overhaul the original engine, or to buy a reconditioned unit. Do not, therefore, purchase parts or have overhaul work done on other components until they have been thoroughly inspected. As a general rule, time is the primary cost of an overhaul, so it does not pay to fit worn or sub-standard parts.

11 As a final note, to ensure maximum life and minimum trouble from a reconditioned engine, everything must be assembled with care, in a spotlessly-clean environment.

3 Engine removal – methods and precautions

1 On all Corsa models, the engine must be removed complete with the transmission as an assembly. There is insufficient clearance in the engine compartment to remove the engine leaving the transmission in the vehicle. The assembly is removed by raising the front of the vehicle, and lowering the assembly from the engine compartment.

2 If you have decided that the engine must be removed for overhaul or major repair work, several preliminary steps should be taken.

3 Locating a suitable place to work is extremely important. Adequate work space, along with storage space for the car, will be needed. If a workshop or garage is not available, at the very least, a flat, level, clean work surface is required.

4 Cleaning the engine compartment and engine/transmission before beginning the removal procedure will help keep tools clean and organised.

5 An engine hoist will also be necessary. Make sure the equipment is rated in excess of the combined weight of the engine and transmission. Safety is of primary importance, considering the potential hazards involved in removing the engine/transmission from the car.

6 The help of an assistant is essential. Apart from the safety aspects involved, there are many instances when one person cannot simultaneously perform all of the operations required during engine/transmission removal.

7 Plan the operation ahead of time. Before starting work, arrange for the hire of or obtain all of the tools and equipment you will need. Some of the equipment necessary to perform engine/transmission removal and installation safely (in addition to an engine hoist) is as follows: a heavy duty trolley jack, complete sets of spanners and sockets as described in the rear of this manual, wooden blocks, and plenty of rags and cleaning solvent for mopping-up spilled oil, coolant and fuel. If the hoist must be hired, make sure that you arrange for it in advance, and perform all of the operations possible without it beforehand. This will save you money and time.

8 Plan for the car to be out of use for quite a while. An engineering machine shop or engine reconditioning specialist will be required to perform some of the work which cannot be accomplished without special equipment. These places often have a busy schedule, so it would be a good idea to consult them before removing the engine, in order to accurately estimate the amount of time required to rebuild or repair components that may need work.

9 During the engine/transmission removal procedure, it is advisable to make notes of the locations of all brackets, cable ties, earthing points, etc, as well as how the wiring harnesses, hoses and electrical connections are attached and routed around the engine and engine compartment. An effective way of doing this is to take a series of photographs of the various components before they are disconnected or removed; the resulting photographs will prove invaluable when the engine/transmission is refitted.

10 Always be extremely careful when removing and refitting the engine/ transmission. Serious injury can result from careless actions. Plan ahead and take your time, and a job of this nature, although major, can be accomplished successfully.

4 Petrol engine and transmission unit – removal, separation and refitting

Note: *The engine can be removed from the car only as a complete unit with the transmission; the two are then separated for overhaul. The engine/transmission unit is lowered out of position, and withdrawn from under the vehicle. Bearing this in mind, ensure the vehicle is raised sufficiently so that there is enough clearance between the front of the vehicle and the floor to allow the engine/ transmission unit to be slid out once it has been lowered out of position.*

Note: Such is the complexity of the power unit arrangement on these vehicles, and the variations that may be encountered according to model and optional equipment fitted, that the following should be regarded as a guide to the work involved, rather than a step-by-step procedure. Where differences are encountered, or additional component disconnection or removal is necessary, make notes of the work involved as an aid to refitting.

Removal

1 Position the steering with the front roadwheels straight-ahead, and lock the steering by removing the ignition key.

2 Apply the handbrake, then jack up the front of the vehicle and support it on axle stands (see *Jacking and vehicle support*). Remove both front roadwheels, and the right-hand inner wheel arch liner for access to the crankshaft pulley. Where necessary, remove the engine compartment undertray and the engine top cover. Note that the vehicle must be raised sufficiently high (approximately 650 mm) to enable the engine/transmission assembly to be withdrawn from under the front of the vehicle.

3 To improve access, remove the bonnet as described in Chapter 11, Section 8.

4 Remove the battery and battery tray as described in Chapter 5A, Section 4.

5 If necessary, drain the engine oil as described in Chapter 1A, Section 5.

6 Working in the driver's footwell, unscrew the two bolts securing the universal joint to the bottom of the steering column intermediate

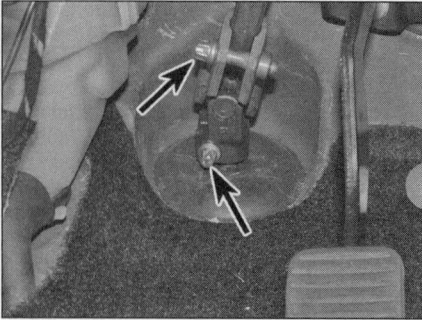

4.6 Unscrew the two bolts securing the universal joint to the intermediate shaft and the steering gear pinion

shaft and the steering gear pinion **(see illustration)**. Discard the bolts; new ones must be used on refitting. Slide the universal joint up the intermediate shaft to disengage it from the steering gear pinion.

Caution: To prevent damage to the airbag wiring contact unit, the steering lock must remain locked until the intermediate shaft is re-attached to the pinion shaft.

7 Remove the front bumper as described in Chapter 11, Section 6.

8 Drain the cooling system as described in Chapter 1A, Section 27, then refit and tighten the drain plug.

9 Remove the air cleaner assembly as described in Chapter 4A, Section 2.

10 Release the clip and disconnect the upper preheater hose from the throttle housing.

11 On the bulkhead at the rear of the engine compartment, release the clips and disconnect the two hoses from the heater matrix.

12 Depressurise the fuel system with reference to Chapter 4A, Section 4, then disconnect the fuel line from the fuel rail. Be prepared for fuel spillage, and take adequate precautions. Clamp or plug the open unions, to minimise further fuel loss.

13 Disconnect the brake vacuum servo hose, and fuel evaporation purge hose.

14 Loosen the clips and remove the upper and lower radiator hoses and the coolant expansion tank hose.

15 Unclip the fuse/relay box from its location, rotate it clockwise and move it to one side.

4.20 Prise out the clip to disconnect the clutch hydraulic hose from the release cylinder pipe

Undo the nut and release the wiring harness bracket, then cut the cable ties securing the wiring harness to the bracket.

16 On models with Easytronic transmission, disconnect the transmission wiring harness connector and release the wiring harness from the clips and cable ties.

17 Disconnect the engine wiring harness at the connector on the left-hand side of the engine and release the wiring harness from the clips and cable ties.

18 Disconnect the wiring connectors for the engine management electronic control unit by releasing them in the direction of the arrow marked on the connector. Release the wiring harness from the clips and cable ties.

19 On standard manual transmission models (not Easytronic), remove the filler cap from the brake/clutch fluid reservoir on the bulkhead, then tighten it onto a piece of polythene. This will reduce the loss of fluid when the clutch hydraulic hose is disconnected. Alternatively, fit a hose clamp to the flexible hose next to the clutch hydraulic connection on the transmission housing.

20 Place some cloth rags beneath the hose, then prise out the retaining clip securing the clutch hydraulic pipe/hose end fitting to the top of the transmission bellhousing and detach the end fitting from the transmission **(see illustration)**. Gently squeeze the two legs of the retaining clip together and re-insert the retaining clip back into position in the end fitting. Discard the sealing ring from the pipe end; a new sealing ring must be used on refitting. Plug/cover both the union and pipe ends to minimise fluid loss and prevent the entry of dirt into the hydraulic system. Whilst the hose/pipe is disconnected, do not depress the clutch pedal.

21 On automatic transmission models, press the selector cable adjuster from the lever on the selector lever position switch at the top of the transmission, then pull back the retaining sleeve and lift the selector outer cable from the mounting bracket on the transmission. On manual transmission models, disconnect the gearchange mechanism from the transmission as described in Chapter 7A.

22 Remove both driveshafts as described in Chapter 8, Section 2.

23 On models with air conditioning, release the auxiliary drivebelt from the pulleys (see Chapter 1A, Section 32), then unbolt the compressor from the engine without disconnecting the refrigerant lines and support the compressor to one side.

24 On automatic transmission models, place a suitable container beneath the fluid cooler hose connections at the transmission. Release the retaining clips and disconnect the hoses from the fluid cooler.

25 Attach a suitable hoist and lifting tackle to the engine lifting brackets on the cylinder head, and support the weight of the engine/transmission.

26 Remove the front subframe as described in Chapter 10, Section 7.

27 Unscrew the two bolts securing the right-hand engine mounting to the engine lower mounting bracket. There is no need to remove the mounting, since the engine/transmission is lowered from the engine compartment.

28 Unscrew the two bolts securing the left-hand engine mounting to the transmission.

29 Make a final check to ensure that all relevant pipes, hoses, wires, etc, have been disconnected, and that they are positioned clear of the engine and transmission.

30 With the help of an assistant, carefully lower the engine/transmission assembly to the ground. Make sure that the surrounding components in the engine compartment are not damaged. Ideally, the assembly should be lowered onto a trolley jack or low platform with castors, so that it can easily be withdrawn from under the car.

31 Ensure that the assembly is adequately supported, then disconnect the engine hoist and lifting tackle, and withdraw the engine/transmission assembly from under the front of the vehicle.

32 Clean away any external dirt using paraffin or a water-soluble solvent and a stiff brush.

33 With reference to Chapter 7A, 7B or 7C, unbolt the transmission from the engine. Carefully withdraw the transmission from the engine. On manual transmission and Easytronic models, ensure that its weight is not allowed to hang on the input shaft while engaged with the clutch friction disc. On automatic transmission models, ensure that the torque converter is removed together with the transmission so that it remains engaged with the oil pump. Note that the transmission locates on dowels positioned in the rear of the cylinder block.

Refitting

34 With reference to Chapter 7A, 7B or 7C, refit the transmission to the engine and tighten the bolts to the specified torque.

35 With the front of the vehicle raised and supported on axle stands, move the engine/transmission assembly under the vehicle, ensuring that the assembly is adequately supported.

36 Reconnect the hoist and lifting tackle to the engine lifting brackets, and carefully raise the engine/transmission assembly up into the engine compartment with the help of an assistant.

37 Reconnect the right- and left-hand engine/transmission mountings and tighten the bolts to the specified torque given in Chapter 2A or 2B.

38 Refit the front subframe as described in Chapter 10, Section 7.

39 Disconnect the hoist and lifting tackle from the engine lifting brackets.

40 Refit the driveshafts as described in Chapter 8, Section 2.

41 Reconnect the gearchange mechanism to the transmission as described in Chapter 7A.

42 On automatic transmission models,

reconnect the coolant hoses to the fluid cooler.

43 On models with air conditioning, refit the compressor with reference to Chapter 3, Section 11, then refit the auxiliary drivebelt with reference to Chapter 1A, Section 32.

44 On standard manual transmission models (not Easytronic), reconnect and bleed the clutch hydraulic connection at the transmission with reference to Chapter 6, Section 2.

45 On automatic transmission models, refit the selector cable adjuster to the lever on the selector lever position switch, then refit the selector outer cable to the mounting bracket on the transmission.

46 Reconnect the wiring to the various components as previously-noted, then refit the fuse/relay box.

47 Reconnect the upper and lower radiator hoses and tighten the clips.

48 Reconnect the brake vacuum servo hose, and fuel evaporation purge hose.

49 Reconnect the fuel line to the fuel rail.

50 Reconnect the heater matrix hoses.

51 Reconnect the upper preheater hose to the throttle housing and tighten the clips.

52 Refit the air cleaner assembly with reference to Chapter 4A, Section 2.

53 Refit the front bumper with reference to Chapter 11, Section 6.

54 Reconnect the universal joint to the steering column intermediate shaft and steering gear pinion and tighten the new bolts with reference to Chapter 10.

55 Check and if necessary top-up the transmission oil level as described in Chapter 7A, Section 2 or Chapter 7C, Section 2, as appropriate.

56 Make a final check to ensure that all relevant hoses, pipes and wires have been correctly reconnected.

57 Refit the battery tray and battery as described in Chapter 5A, Section 4.

58 Refit the right-hand inner wheel arch liner, front roadwheels, and engine compartment undertray (where fitted), then lower the vehicle to the ground.

59 Refill the engine with oil with reference to Chapter 1A, Section 5.

60 Refill and bleed the cooling system with reference to Chapter 1A, Section 27.

61 On automatic transmission models, check and top-up the fluid level with reference to Chapter 7B, Section 2.

62 Refit the bonnet as described in Chapter 11, Section 8.

5 Diesel engine and transmission unit – removal, separation and refitting

Note: *The engine can be removed from the car only as a complete unit with the transmission; the two are then separated for overhaul. The engine/transmission unit is lowered out of position, and withdrawn from under the vehicle. Bearing this in mind, ensure the vehicle is raised sufficiently so that there is enough clearance between the front of the vehicle and the floor to allow the engine/transmission unit to be slid out once it has been lowered out of position.*

Note: Such is the complexity of the power unit arrangement on these vehicles, and the variations that may be encountered according to model and optional equipment fitted, that the following should be regarded as a guide to the work involved, rather than a step-by-step procedure. Where differences are encountered, or additional component disconnection or removal is necessary, make notes of the work involved as an aid to refitting.

Removal

1 Position the steering with the front road-wheels straight-ahead, and lock the steering by removing the ignition key.

2 Apply the handbrake, then jack up the front of the vehicle and support it on axle stands (see *Jacking and vehicle support*). Remove both front roadwheels, and the right-hand inner wheel arch liner for access to the crankshaft pulley. Where necessary, remove the engine compartment undertray and the engine top cover. Note that the vehicle must be raised sufficiently high (approximately 650 mm) to enable the engine/transmission assembly to be withdrawn from under the front of the vehicle.

3 To improve access, remove the bonnet as described in Chapter 11, Section 8.

4 Remove the battery and battery tray as described in Chapter 5A, Section 4.

5 If necessary, drain the engine oil as described in Chapter 1B, Section 5.

6 Working in the driver's footwell, unscrew the two bolts securing the universal joint to the bottom of the steering column intermediate shaft and the steering gear pinion **(see illustration 4.6)**. Discard the bolts; new ones must be used on refitting. Slide the universal joint up the intermediate shaft to disengage it from the steering gear pinion.

Caution: To prevent damage to the airbag wiring contact unit, the steering lock must remain locked until the intermediate shaft is re-attached to the pinion shaft.

7 Remove the front bumper as described in Chapter 11, Section 6.

8 Drain the cooling system as described in Chapter 1B, Section 28, then refit and tighten the drain plug.

9 Remove the air cleaner assembly, intake ducts and charge air ducts/hoses as described in Chapter 4B, Section 3.

10 Remove the fuel filter as described in Chapter 1B, Section 22 and unclip the fuel feed and return hoses from the bulkhead.

11 Disconnect the vacuum hose at the quick-release fitting on the vacuum pump.

12 Unclip the fuse/relay box from its location, rotate it clockwise and move it to one side. Undo the nut and release the wiring harness

bracket, then cut the cable ties securing the wiring harness to the bracket.

13 Disconnect the engine wiring harness at the connector on the bulkhead and release the wiring harness from the clips and cable ties.

14 Withdraw the locking plates, lift the locking levers and disconnect the two wiring connectors from the engine management ECU. Release the wiring harness from the clips and cable ties.

15 On the bulkhead at the rear of the engine compartment, pull out the special locking spring clips and disconnect the quick-release connections for the two hoses from the heater matrix.

16 Loosen the clips and remove the upper and lower radiator hoses and the coolant expansion tank hose.

17 Remove the filler cap from the brake/clutch fluid reservoir on the bulkhead, then tighten it onto a piece of polythene. This will reduce the loss of fluid when the clutch hydraulic hose is disconnected. Alternatively, fit a hose clamp to the flexible hose next to the clutch hydraulic connection on the transmission housing.

18 Place some cloth rags beneath the hose, then prise out the retaining clip securing the clutch hydraulic pipe/hose end fitting to the top of the transmission bellhousing and detach the end fitting from the transmission **(see illustration 4.20)**. Gently squeeze the two legs of the retaining clip together and re-insert the retaining clip back into position in the end fitting. Discard the sealing ring from the pipe end; a new sealing ring must be used on refitting. Plug/cover both the union and pipe ends to minimise fluid loss and prevent the entry of dirt into the hydraulic system. Note: Whilst the hose/pipe is disconnected, do not depress the clutch pedal.

19 Disconnect the gearchange mechanism from the transmission as described in Chapter 7A.

20 Remove both driveshafts as described in Chapter 8, Section 2.

21 On models with air conditioning, remove the auxiliary drivebelt as described in Chapter 1B, Section 31, then unbolt the compressor from the engine without disconnecting the refrigerant lines and support the compressor to one side.

22 Attach a suitable hoist and lifting tackle to the engine lifting brackets on the cylinder head, and support the weight of the engine/transmission.

23 Remove the front subframe as described in Chapter 10, Section 7.

24 Mark the position of the right-hand engine mounting, then unscrew the two bolts securing the upper mounting to the engine bracket. There is no need to remove the mounting, since the engine/transmission is lowered from the engine compartment.

25 Unscrew the three bolts securing the left-hand engine mounting to the transmission bracket.

26 Make a final check to ensure that all relevant pipes, hoses, wires, etc, have been disconnected, and that they are positioned clear of the engine and transmission.

27 With the help of an assistant, carefully lower to the ground the engine/transmission assembly. Make sure that the surrounding components in the engine compartment are not damaged. Ideally, the assembly should be lowered onto a trolley jack or low platform with castors, so that it can easily be withdrawn from under the car.

28 Ensure that the assembly is adequately supported, then disconnect the engine hoist and lifting tackle, and withdraw the engine/transmission assembly from under the front of the vehicle.

29 With the engine/transmission assembly removed, support the assembly on suitable blocks of wood, on a workbench (or failing that, on a clean area of the workshop floor).

30 Clean away any external dirt using paraffin or a water-soluble solvent and a stiff brush.

31 With reference to Chapter 5A, Section 11, remove the starter motor.

32 With reference to Chapter 7A, unbolt the transmission from the engine. Carefully withdraw the transmission and adaptor plate from the engine, ensuring that its weight is not allowed to hang on the input shaft while engaged with the clutch friction disc.

33 Note that the transmission locates on dowels positioned in the rear of the cylinder block. If they are loose, remove them and keep them in a safe place.

Refitting

34 Ensure the locating dowels are correctly positioned then locate the adaptor plate on the engine. Carefully offer the transmission to the engine, until the locating dowels are engaged. Ensure that the weight of the transmission is not allowed to hang on the input shaft as it engages the clutch friction disc. With reference to Chapter 7A, complete the transmission refitting procedure and tighten the bolts to the specified torque.

35 Refit the starter motor with reference to Chapter 5A, Section 11.

36 With the front of the vehicle raised and supported on axle stands, move the engine/transmission assembly under the vehicle, ensuring that the assembly is adequately supported.

37 Reconnect the hoist and lifting tackle to the engine lifting brackets, and carefully raise the engine/transmission assembly up into the engine compartment with the help of an assistant.

38 Reconnect the right- and left-hand engine/transmission mountings, making sure that the previously-made positional marks are complied with, and tighten the bolts to the specified torque given in Chapter.

39 Refit the front subframe as described in Chapter 10, Section 7.

40 Disconnect the hoist and lifting tackle from the engine lifting brackets.

41 Refit both driveshafts as described in Chapter 8, Section 2.

42 Reconnect the gearchange mechanism to the transmission as described in Chapter 7A.

43 On models with air conditioning, refit the compressor with reference to Chapter 3, Section 11, then refit the auxiliary drivebelt with reference to Chapter 1B, Section 31.

44 Reconnect and bleed the clutch hydraulic connection at the transmission with reference to Chapter 6, Section 2 (not Easytronic models).

45 Reconnect the upper and lower radiator hoses.

46 Reconnect the wiring to the various components as previously noted.

47 Reconnect the heater matrix hoses and tighten the clips.

48 Reconnect the vacuum hose to the pump outlet.

49 Refit the fuel filter as described in Chapter 1B, Section 22.

50 Refit the air cleaner assembly, intake ducts and charge air ducts/hoses with reference to Chapter 4B, Section 3.

51 Refit the front bumper with reference to Chapter 11, Section 6.

52 Reconnect the universal joint to the steering column intermediate shaft and steering gear pinion and tighten the new bolts with reference to Chapter 10.

53 Check and if necessary top-up the transmission oil level as described in Chapter 7A, Section 2.

54 Make a final check to ensure that all relevant hoses, pipes and wires have been correctly reconnected.

55 Refit the battery tray and battery as described in Chapter 5A, Section 4.

56 Refit the right-hand inner wheel arch liner, front roadwheels, and engine compartment undertray (where fitted), then lower the vehicle to the ground.

57 Refill the engine with oil with reference to Chapter 1B, Section 5.

58 Refill and bleed the cooling system with reference to Chapter 1B, Section 28.

59 Refit the bonnet as described in Chapter 11, Section 8.

6 Engine overhaul – dismantling sequence

1 It is much easier to dismantle and work on the engine if it is mounted on a portable engine stand. These stands can often be hired from a tool hire shop. Before the engine is mounted on a stand, the flywheel/driveplate should be removed, so that the stand bolts can be tightened into the end of the cylinder block/crankcase.

2 If a stand is not available, it is possible to dismantle the engine with it blocked up on a sturdy workbench, or on the floor. Be extra careful not to tip or drop the engine when working without a stand.

3 If you are going to obtain a reconditioned engine, all the external components must be removed first, to be transferred to the new engine (just as they will if you are doing a complete engine overhaul yourself). These components include the following:

a) *Engine wiring harness and supports (Chapter 2A, 2B or 2C).*
b) *Alternator and air conditioning compressor mounting brackets (as applicable) (Chapter 5A).*
c) *Coolant pump (where applicable) and inlet/outlet housings (Chapter 3).*
d) *Dipstick tube (Chapter 2A, 2B or 2C).*
e) *Fuel system components (Chapter 4A or 4B).*
f) *All electrical switches and sensors (Chapter 4A or 4B).*
g) *Inlet and exhaust manifolds and, where fitted, the turbocharger (Chapter 4A or 4B).*
h) *Oil filter and oil cooler/heat exchanger (Chapter 2A, 2B or 2C).*
i) *Flywheel/driveplate (Chapter 2A, 2B or 2C).*

Note: *When removing the external components from the engine, pay close attention to details that may be helpful or important during refitting. Note the fitted position of gaskets, seals, spacers, pins, washers, bolts, and other small items.*

4 If you are obtaining a 'short' engine (which consists of the engine cylinder block/crankcase, crankshaft, pistons and connecting rods all assembled), then the cylinder head, sump, oil pump, and timing chains will have to be removed also.

5 Before beginning the dismantling and overhaul procedures, make sure that you have all of the correct tools necessary. See *Tools and working facilities* in Reference for further information.

6 If you are planning a complete overhaul, the engine can be dismantled, and the internal components removed, in the order given below.

Petrol engines

a) *Inlet and exhaust manifolds (see Chapter 4A or 4B).*
b) *Coolant pump (see Chapter 3).*
c) *Cylinder head (see Chapter 2A or 2B).*
d) *Flywheel/driveplate (see Chapter 2A or 2B).*
e) *Sump (see Chapter 2A or 2B).*
f) *Oil pump (see Chapter 2A or 2B).*
g) *Timing chain and sprockets (see Chapter 2A or 2B).*
h) *Pistons/connecting rod assemblies (see Section 10).*
i) *Crankshaft (see Section 11).*

Diesel engines

a) *Sump (see Chapter 2C).*
b) *Coolant pump (see Chapter 3).*
c) *Timing chain and sprockets (see Chapter 2C).*
d) *Oil pump (see Chapter 2C).*
e) *Camshaft housing (see Chapter 2C).*
f) *Cylinder head (see Chapter 2C).*
g) *Inlet and exhaust manifolds (see Chapter 4B).*
h) *Flywheel (see Chapter 2C).*
i) *Pistons/connecting rod assemblies (see Section 10).*
j) *Crankshaft (see Section 11).*

7 Cylinder head – dismantling

Note: *New and reconditioned cylinder heads are available from the manufacturer, and from engine overhaul specialists. Due to the fact that some specialist tools are required for the dismantling and inspection procedures, and new components may not be readily available, it may be more practical and economical for the home mechanic to purchase a reconditioned head rather than to dismantle, inspect and recondition the original head. A valve spring compressor tool will be required for this operation.*

1 With the cylinder head removed as described in Chapter 2A, 2B or 2C, clean away all external dirt, and remove the following components as applicable, if not already done:
a) Manifolds (see Chapter 4A or 4B).
b) Spark plugs (petrol engines – see Chapter 1A).
c) Glow plugs (diesel engines – see Chapter 5A).
d) Camshafts and hydraulic tappets (petrol engines – see Chapter 2A or 2B).
e) Hydraulic tappets and rocker arms (diesel engines – see Chapter 2C).
f) Engine lifting brackets.
2 To remove a valve, fit a valve spring compressor tool. Ensure that the arms of the compressor tool are securely positioned on the head of the valve and the spring cap

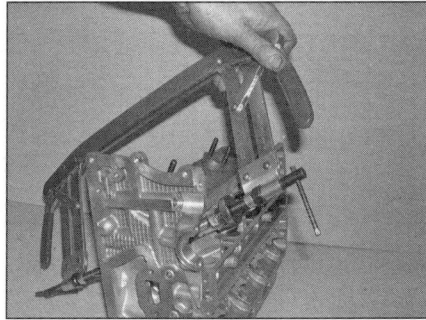
7.2 Fit a valve spring compressor tool, ensuring that the arms of the compressor are securely positioned

(see illustration). The valves are deeply-recessed on petrol engines, and a suitable extension piece may be required for the spring compressor.
3 Compress the valve spring to relieve the pressure of the spring cap acting on the collets.

> **HAYNES HINT** *If the spring cap sticks to the valve stem, support the compressor tool, and give the end a light tap with a soft-faced mallet to help free the spring cap.*

4 Extract the two split collets by hooking them out using a small screwdriver, then slowly release the compressor tool **(see illustration)**.

7.4 Extract the two split collets by hooking them out using a small screwdriver

5 Remove the valve spring cap and the spring, then withdraw the valve through the combustion chamber. Remove the valve stem oil seal (using long-nosed pliers if necessary), and the spring seat **(see illustrations)**.
6 Repeat the procedure for the remaining valves, keeping all components in strict order so that they can be refitted in their original positions, unless all the components are to be renewed. If the components are to be kept and used again, place each valve assembly in a labelled polythene bag or a similar small container **(see illustration)**. Note that as with cylinder numbering, the valves are normally numbered from the timing chain end of the engine. Make sure that the valve components are identified as inlet and exhaust, as well as numbered.

7.5a Remove the valve spring cap...

7.5b...and the spring...

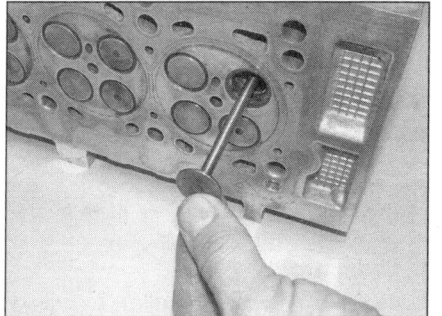
7.5c...then withdraw the valve through the combustion chamber

7.5d Remove the valve stem oil seal...

7.5e...and the spring seat

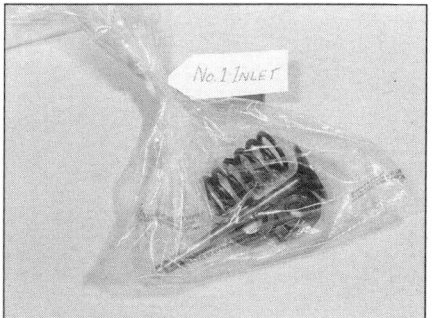
7.6 Place each valve assembly in a labelled polythene bag or similar container

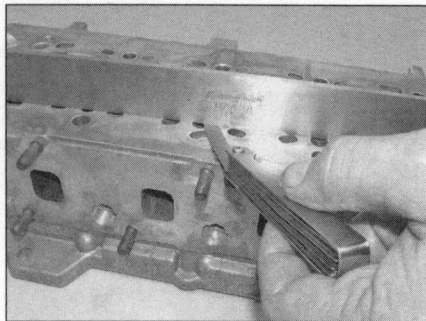

8.6 Checking the cylinder head surface for distortion

8 Cylinder head and valve components – cleaning and inspection

1 Thorough cleaning of the cylinder head and valve components, followed by a detailed inspection, will enable a decision to be made on whether further work is necessary before reassembling the components.

Cleaning

2 Scrape away all traces of old gasket material and sealing compound from the cylinder head surfaces. Take care not to damage the cylinder head surfaces, as the head is made of light alloy.

3 Scrape away the carbon from the combustion chambers and ports, then wash the cylinder head thoroughly with paraffin or a suitable solvent.

4 Scrape off any heavy carbon deposits that may have formed on the valves, then use a power-operated wire brush to remove deposits from the valve heads and stems.

Inspection

Note: *Be sure to perform all the following inspection procedures before concluding that the services of a machine shop or engine overhaul specialist are required. Make a list of all items that require attention.*

Cylinder head

5 Inspect the head very carefully for cracks, evidence of coolant leakage, and other damage. If cracks are found, a new cylinder head should be obtained.

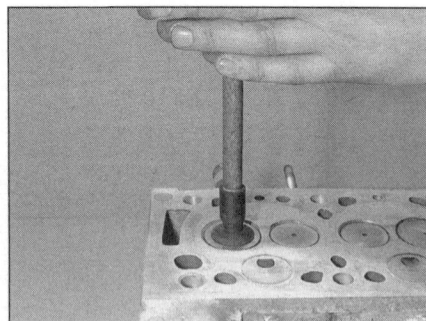

8.12 Grinding-in a valve

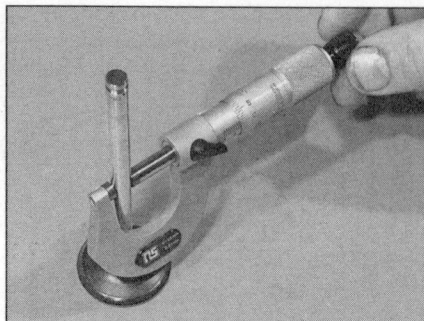

8.10 Measuring a valve stem diameter

6 Use a straight-edge and feeler blade to check that the cylinder head surface is not distorted **(see illustration)**. If the specified distortion limit is exceeded on 1.0 and 1.2 litre petrol engines, the cylinder head must be renewed, as machining is not possible, however, on the 1.4 litre petrol engines and the diesel engines, it may be possible to have the cylinder head resurfaced, provided that the overall height of the head is not reduced to less than the specified minimum.

7 Examine the valve seats in each of the combustion chambers. If the seats are severely pitted, cracked or burned, then they will need to be recut or renewed by an engine overhaul specialist. If only slight pitting is evident, this can be removed by grinding the valve heads and seats together with coarse, then fine, grinding paste, as described later in this Section.

8 If the valve guides are worn, indicated by a side-to-side motion of the valve, oversize valve guides are available, and valves with oversize stems can be fitted. This work is best carried out by an engine overhaul specialist. A dial gauge may be used to determine whether the amount of side play of a valve exceeds the specified maximum.

9 Check the tappet bores in the cylinder head for wear. If excessive wear is evident, the cylinder head must be renewed. Also check the tappet oil holes in the cylinder head for obstructions.

Valves

10 Examine the head of each valve for pitting, burning, cracks and general wear, and check the valve stem for scoring and wear ridges. Rotate the valve, and check for any obvious

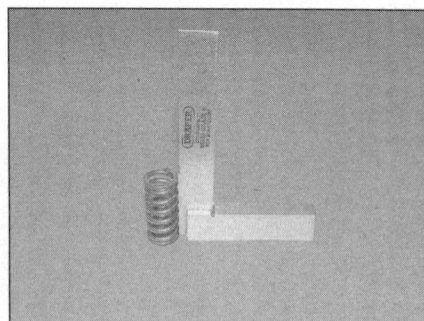

8.14 Check each valve spring for squareness

indication that it is bent. Look for pitting and excessive wear on the end of each valve stem. If the valve appears satisfactory at this stage, measure the valve stem diameter at several points using a micrometer **(see illustration)**. Any significant difference in the readings obtained indicates wear of the valve stem. Should any of these conditions be apparent, the valve(s) must be renewed. If the valves are in satisfactory condition, they should be ground (lapped) onto their respective seats to ensure a smooth gas-tight seal.

11 Valve grinding is carried out as follows. Place the cylinder head upside-down on a bench, with a block of wood at each end to give clearance for the valve stems.

> **HAYNES HiNT** *A light spring placed under the valve head will greatly ease the grinding operation.*

12 Smear a trace of coarse carborundum paste on the seat face in the cylinder head, and press a suction grinding tool onto the relevant valve head. With a semi-rotary action, grind the valve head to its seat, lifting the valve occasionally to redistribute the grinding paste **(see illustration)**. When a dull, matt, even surface is produced on the faces of both the valve seat and the valve, wipe off the paste and repeat the process with fine carborundum paste. When a smooth unbroken ring of light grey matt finish is produced on both the valve and seat faces, the grinding operation is complete. Carefully clean away every trace of grinding paste, taking great care to leave none in the ports or in the valve guides. Clean the valves and valve seats with a paraffin-soaked rag, then with a clean rag, and finally, if an airline is available, blow the valves, valve guides and cylinder head ports clean.

Valve springs

13 Check that all the valve springs are intact. If any one is broken, all should be renewed.

14 If possible, check the free height of the springs against new ones, then stand each spring on a flat surface and check it for squareness **(see illustration)**. If a spring is found to be too short, or damaged in any way, renew all the springs as a set. Springs suffer from fatigue, and it is a good idea to renew them even if they look serviceable.

Rocker arm components

15 Check the rocker arm thrust faces (the areas that contact the tappets and valve stems) for pits, wear, score-marks or any indication that the surface-hardening has worn through. Check the rocker arm camshaft roller in the same manner. Renew any rocker arms which appear suspect.

Hydraulic tappets

16 Inspect the tappets for obvious signs of wear on the contact faces, and check the oil holes for obstructions, particularly for oil sludge. If excessive wear is evident, or if any tappet has been noisy in operation, all the tappets must be renewed as a set.

9 Cylinder head – reassembly

Note: *New valve stem oil seals should be used on reassembly. A valve spring compressor tool will be required for this operation.*

1 With all the components cleaned, starting at one end of the cylinder head, fit the valve components as follows.

2 Insert the appropriate valve into its guide (if new valves are being fitted, insert each valve into the location to which it has been ground), ensuring that the valve stem is well-lubricated with clean engine oil. If the original components are being refitted, all components must be refitted in their original positions.

3 Fit the spring seat.

4 New valve stem oil seals may be supplied with a fitting sleeve, which fits over the collet groove in the valve stem, to prevent damage to the oil seal as it is slid down the valve stem. If no sleeve is supplied, wind a short length of tape round the top of the valve stem to cover the collet groove.

5 Lubricate the valve stem oil seal with clean engine oil, then push the oil seal down the valve stem using a suitable tube or socket, until the seal is fully engaged with the valve guide **(see illustrations)**. Remove the fitting sleeve or the tape, as applicable, from the valve stem.

6 Fit the valve spring and the spring cap.

7 Fit the spring compressor tool, and compress the valve spring until the spring cap passes beyond the collet groove in the valve stem.

8 Refit the split collets to the groove in the valve stem, with the narrow ends nearest the spring.

> **HAYNES HiNT**
> *Apply a little grease to the split collets, then fit the split collets into the groove. The grease should hold the collets in the groove.*

9 Slowly release the compressor tool, ensuring

9.5a Fit the new valve stem oil seal...

9.5b...and push it down using a suitable tube or socket, until the seal is fully engaged with the spring seat

that the collets are not dislodged from the groove. When the compressor is fully released, give the top of the valve assembly a tap with a soft-faced mallet to settle the components.

10 Repeat the procedure for the remaining valves, ensuring that if the original components are being used, they are all refitted in their original positions.

11 Refit the components removed in Section 7, paragraph 1.

10 Piston/connecting rod assemblies – removal

Note: *The mating faces of the connecting rods and the big-end bearing caps are 'rough' (not machined), which ensures perfect mating of each individual rod and bearing cap. When the components have been removed from the engine, extreme care should be taken not to damage the mating surfaces – eg, do not rest the bearing caps on the mating faces. Ensure that each bearing cap is kept together with its respective rod, to prevent any possibility of the components being refitted incorrectly.*

Note: *New big-end cap bolts will be required for reassembly.*

Petrol engines

1 Remove the cylinder head as described in Chapter 2A or 2B.

2 Remove the sump and oil pick-up pipe, as described in Chapter 2A or 2B.

3 Undo the retaining bolts and remove the oil baffle plate from the cylinder block baseplate **(see illustration)**.

4 If the connecting rods and big-end caps are not marked to indicate their positions in the cylinder block (ie, marked with cylinder numbers), suitably mark both the rod and cap with quick-drying paint or similar. Note which side of the engine the marks face and accurately record this also. There may not be any other way of identifying which way round the cap fits on the rod when refitting.

5 Unscrew the big-end cap bolts from the first connecting rod, and remove the cap **(see illustration)**. If the bearing shells are to be re-used, tape the cap and the shell together.

6 Check the top of the cylinder bore for a wear ridge. If evident, carefully scrape it away with a ridge reamer tool, otherwise the piston rings may jam against the ridge as the piston is pushed out of the block.

7 Place the wooden handle of a hammer against the bottom of the connecting rod, and push the piston/rod assembly up and out of the cylinder bore **(see illustration)**. Recover the bearing shell, and tape it to the connecting rod if it is to be re-used.

8 Remove the remaining assemblies in a similar way. Rotate the crankshaft as necessary to bring the big-end bolts to the most accessible position.

Diesel engines

9 Referring to Chapter 2C, remove the following components:

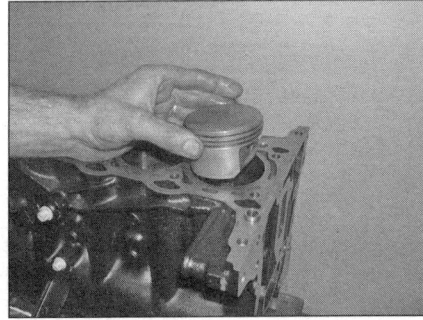

10.3 Undo the bolts and remove the oil baffle plate from the cylinder block baseplate – petrol engines

10.5 Unscrew the big-end cap bolts from the first connecting rod, and remove the cap – petrol engines

10.7 Push the piston/rod assembly up and out of the top of the cylinder bore – petrol engines

11.4 Using a dial gauge to check the crankshaft endfloat

a) *Timing cover (which includes the sump removal procedure).*
b) *Timing chain, sprockets and tensioner.*
c) *Camshaft housing.*
d) *Cylinder head.*

10 Undo the retaining bolts and remove the oil baffle plate from the cylinder block baseplate.

11 If the connecting rods and big-end caps are not marked to indicate their positions in the cylinder block (ie, marked with cylinder numbers), suitably mark both the rod and cap with quick-drying paint or similar. Note which side of the engine the marks face and accurately record this also. There may not be any other way of identifying which way round the cap fits on the rod when refitting.

12 If there is a pronounced wear ridge at the top of any bore, it may be necessary to remove it with a scraper or ridge reamer, to avoid piston damage during removal. Such a ridge indicates excessive wear of the cylinder bore.

13 Turn the crankshaft to bring pistons 1 and 4 to BDC (bottom dead centre).

14 Unscrew the bolts from No 1 piston big-end bearing cap. Take off the cap and recover the bottom half bearing shell. If the bearing shells are to be re-used, tape the cap and the shell together.

15 Using a hammer handle, push the piston up through the bore, and remove it from the top of the cylinder block. Recover the bearing shell, and tape it to the connecting rod for safe-keeping.

16 Loosely refit the big-end cap to the

11.8 Lift the cylinder block baseplate off the cylinder block – petrol engines

11.5a Checking the crankshaft endfloat with a feeler gauge

connecting rod, and secure with the bolts – this will help to keep the components in their correct order.

17 Remove No 4 piston assembly in the same way.

18 Turn the crankshaft through 180° to bring pistons 2 and 3 to BDC (bottom dead centre), and remove them in the same way.

11 Crankshaft – removal

Note: *New cylinder block baseplate retaining bolts will be required for refitting.*

1 Remove the flywheel/driveplate as described in Chapter 2A, 2B or 2C.

2 Remove the pistons and connecting rods, as described in Section 10.

3 Invert the engine so that the crankshaft is uppermost.

4 Before removing the crankshaft, check the endfloat using a dial gauge in contact with the end of the crankshaft. Push the crankshaft fully one way, and then zero the gauge. Push the crankshaft fully the other way, and check the endfloat (see illustration). The result should be compared with the specified limit, and will give an indication as to the size of the main bearing shell thrust journal width which will be required for reassembly.

5 If a dial gauge is not available, a feeler gauge can be used to measure crankshaft endfloat. Push the crankshaft fully towards one end of the crankcase, and insert a feeler gauge between the thrust flange of the main

11.14 Lift the cylinder block baseplate off the cylinder block – diesel engines

bearing shell and the machined surface of the crankshaft web (see illustration). Before measuring, ensure that the crankshaft is fully forced towards one end of the crankcase, to give the widest possible gap at the measuring location.

Note: *Measure at the bearing with the thrustwasher.*

Petrol engines

6 Working in a diagonal sequence, progressively slacken the outer (M6) bolts securing the cylinder block baseplate to the cylinder block.

7 When all the outer bolts have been slackened, repeat the procedure on the inner (M8) retaining bolts.

8 Remove all the bolts and lift the cylinder block baseplate off the cylinder block (see illustration). If the baseplate is initially tight to remove, carefully tap it free using a soft-faced mallet.

9 As the baseplate is withdrawn check that the lower main bearing shells come away with the baseplate. If they remain on the crankshaft journals, lift them off and refit them to their respective locations in the baseplate.

10 Lift the crankshaft from the cylinder block and remove the crankshaft oil seal.

11 Extract the upper bearing shells, and identify them for position if they are to be re-used.

Diesel engines

12 Working in a diagonal sequence, progressively slacken the outer (M8) bolts securing the cylinder block baseplate to the cylinder block.

13 When all the outer bolts have been slackened, repeat the procedure on the inner (M10) retaining bolts.

14 Remove all the bolts and lift the cylinder block baseplate off the cylinder block (see illustration). If the baseplate is initially tight to remove, carefully tap it free using a soft-faced mallet. Alternatively, use a spatula to break the seal between the baseplate and cylinder block.

15 As the baseplate is withdrawn check that the lower main bearing shells come away with the baseplate. If they remain on the crankshaft journals, lift them off and refit them to their respective locations in the baseplate.

16 Lift the crankshaft from the cylinder block and remove the crankshaft oil seal.

17 Extract the upper bearing shells, and identify them for position if they are to be re-used.

12 Cylinder block – cleaning and inspection

Cleaning

1 For complete cleaning, remove all external components (senders, sensors, brackets, oil

pipes, coolant pipes, etc) from the cylinder block.

2 Scrape all traces of gasket and/or sealant from the cylinder block and cylinder block baseplate, taking particular care not to damage the cylinder head and sump mating faces.

3 Remove all oil gallery plugs, where fitted. The plugs are usually very tight – they may have to be drilled out and the holes retapped. Use new plugs when the engine is reassembled. On diesel engines, undo the retaining bolts and remove the piston oil spray nozzles from inside the cylinder block **(see illustration)**. Also remove the timing chain oil spray pipe from the front face of the cylinder block.

4 If the block and baseplate (where applicable) are extremely dirty, they should be steam-cleaned.

5 If the components have been steam-cleaned, clean all oil holes and oil galleries one more time on completion. Flush all internal passages with warm water until the water runs clear. Dry the block and, where necessary, the baseplate thoroughly and wipe all machined surfaces with a light oil. If you have access to compressed air, use it to speed-up the drying process, and to blow out all the oil holes and galleries.

⚠️ *Warning: Wear eye protection when using compressed air.*

6 If the block and baseplate are relatively clean, an adequate cleaning job can be achieved with hot soapy water and a stiff brush. Take plenty of time, and do a thorough job. Regardless of the cleaning method used, be sure to clean all oil holes and galleries very thoroughly, dry everything completely, and coat all cast-iron machined surfaces with light oil.

7 The threaded holes in the cylinder block and baseplate must be clean, to ensure accurate torque readings when tightening fixings during reassembly. Run the correct-size tap (which can be determined from the size of the relevant bolt) into each of the holes to remove rust, corrosion, thread sealant or other contamination, and to restore damaged threads. If possible, use compressed air to clear the holes of debris produced by this operation. Do not forget to clean the threads of all bolts and nuts which are to be re-used, as well.

8 Where applicable, apply suitable sealant to the new oil gallery plugs, and insert them into the relevant holes in the cylinder block. Tighten the plugs securely. On diesel engines, refit the oil spray nozzles into the block and secure with the retaining bolts tightened securely. Refit the timing chain oil spray pipe to the front face of the cylinder block and tighten the two bolts securely.

9 If the engine is to be left dismantled for some time, cover the cylinder block with a large plastic bag to keep it clean and prevent corrosion. Where applicable, refit the baseplate and tighten the bolts finger-tight.

Inspection

10 Visually check the block for cracks, rust and corrosion. Look for stripped threads in the threaded holes. It's also a good idea to have the block checked for hidden cracks by an engine reconditioning specialist that has the equipment to do this type of work, especially if the vehicle had a history of overheating or using coolant. If defects are found, have the block repaired, if possible, or renewed.

11 If in any doubt as to the condition of the cylinder block, have it inspected and measured by an engine reconditioning specialist. If the bores are worn or damaged, they will be able to carry out any necessary reboring (where possible), and supply appropriate oversized pistons, etc.

13 Piston/connecting rod assemblies – inspection

1 Before the inspection process can begin, the piston/connecting rod assemblies must be cleaned, and the original piston rings removed from the pistons.

Note: *Always use new piston rings when the engine is reassembled.*

2 Carefully expand the old rings over the top of the pistons. The use of two or three old feeler gauges will be helpful in preventing the rings dropping into empty grooves **(see illustration)**. Take care, however, as piston rings are sharp.

3 Scrape away all traces of carbon from the top of the piston. A hand-held wire brush, or a piece of fine emery cloth, can be used once the majority of the deposits have been scraped away.

4 Remove the carbon from the ring grooves in the piston, using an old ring. Break the ring in half to do this (be careful not to cut your fingers – piston rings are sharp). Be very careful to remove only the carbon deposits – do not remove any metal, and do not nick or scratch the sides of the ring grooves.

5 Once the deposits have been removed, clean the piston/connecting rod assembly with paraffin or a suitable solvent, and dry thoroughly. Make sure that the oil return holes in the ring grooves are clear.

6 If the pistons and cylinder bores are not damaged or worn excessively, and if the cylinder block does not need to be rebored, the original pistons can be refitted. Normal piston wear shows up as even vertical wear on the piston thrust surfaces, and slight looseness of the top ring in its groove. New piston rings should always be used when the engine is reassembled.

7 Carefully inspect each piston for cracks around the skirt, at the gudgeon pin bosses, and at the piston ring lands (between the ring grooves).

8 Look for scoring and scuffing on the thrust faces of the piston skirt, holes in the piston crown, and burned areas at the edge of

12.3 Undo the retaining bolts and remove the piston oil spray nozzles – diesel engines

the crown. If the skirt is scored or scuffed, the engine may have been suffering from overheating, and/or abnormal combustion ('pinking') which caused excessively-high operating temperatures. The cooling and lubrication systems should be checked thoroughly. A hole in the piston crown, or burned areas at the edge of the piston crown indicates that abnormal combustion (pre-ignition, 'pinking', knocking or detonation) has been occurring. If any of the above problems exist, the causes must be investigated and corrected, or the damage will occur again.

9 Corrosion of the piston, in the form of pitting, indicates that coolant has been leaking into the combustion chamber and/or the crankcase. Again, the cause must be corrected, or the problem may persist in the rebuilt engine.

10 If in any doubt as to the condition of the pistons and connecting rods, have them inspected and measured by an engine reconditioning specialist. If new parts are required, they will be able to supply and fit appropriate-sized pistons/rings, and rebore (where possible) or hone the cylinder block.

14 Crankshaft – inspection

1 Clean the crankshaft using paraffin or a suitable solvent, and dry it, preferably with compressed air if available. Be sure to clean the oil holes with a pipe cleaner or

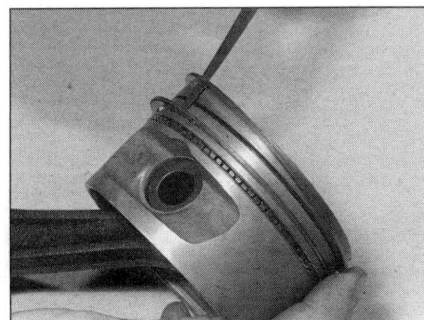

13.2 Using a feeler gauge to aid removal of a piston ring

14.8 Transfer the crankshaft speed/position sensor pulse pick-up ring to the new crankshaft

similar probe, to ensure that they are not obstructed.

⚠️ *Warning: Wear eye protection when using compressed air.*

2 Check the main and big-end bearing journals for uneven wear, scoring, pitting and cracking.

3 Big-end bearing wear is accompanied by distinct metallic knocking when the engine is running (particularly noticeable when the engine is pulling from low revs), and some loss of oil pressure.

4 Main bearing wear is accompanied by severe engine vibration and rumble – getting progressively worse as engine revs increase – and again by loss of oil pressure.

5 Check the bearing journal for roughness by running a finger lightly over the bearing surface. Any roughness (which will be accompanied by obvious bearing wear) indicates that the crankshaft requires regrinding.

6 If the crankshaft has been reground, check for burrs around the crankshaft oil holes (the

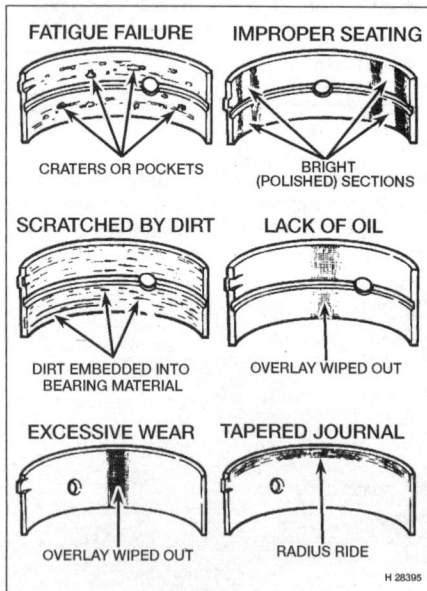

15.2 Typical bearing failures

holes are usually chamfered, so burrs should not be a problem unless regrinding has been carried out carelessly). Remove any burrs with a fine file or scraper, and thoroughly clean the oil holes as described previously.

7 Have the crankshaft journals measured by an engine reconditioning specialist. If the crankshaft is worn or damaged, they may be able to regrind the journals and supply suitable undersize bearing shells. If no undersize shells are available and the crankshaft has worn beyond the specified limits, it will have to be renewed. Consult your Vauxhall/Opel dealer or engine reconditioning specialist for further information on parts availability.

8 If a new crankshaft is to be fitted on petrol engines, undo the screws securing the crankshaft speed/position sensor pulse pick-up ring to the crankshaft, and transfer the ring to the new crankshaft **(see illustration)**.

15 Main and big-end bearings – inspection

1 Even though the main and big-end bearings should be renewed during the engine overhaul, the old bearings should be retained for close examination, as they may reveal valuable information about the condition of the engine.

2 Bearing failure occurs because of lack of lubrication, the presence of dirt or other foreign particles, overloading the engine, or corrosion **(see illustration)**. If a bearing fails, the cause must be found and eliminated before the engine is reassembled, to prevent the failure from happening again.

3 To examine the bearing shells, remove them from the cylinder block, the cylinder block baseplate, the connecting rods and the big-end bearing caps, and lay them out on a clean surface in the same order as they were fitted to the engine. This will enable any bearing problems to be matched with the corresponding crankshaft journal.

4 Dirt and other foreign particles can enter the engine in a variety of ways. Contamination may be left in the engine during assembly, or it may pass through filters or the crankcase ventilation system. Normal engine wear produces small particles of metal, which can eventually cause problems. If particles find their way into the lubrication system, it is likely that they will eventually be carried to the bearings. Whatever the source, these foreign particles often end up embedded in the soft bearing material, and are easily recognised. Large particles will not embed in the bearing, and will score or gouge the bearing and journal. To prevent possible contamination, clean all parts thoroughly, and keep everything spotlessly-clean during engine assembly. Once the engine has been installed in the vehicle, ensure that engine oil and filter changes are carried out at the recommended intervals.

5 Lack of lubrication (or lubrication breakdown) has a number of interrelated causes. Excessive heat (which thins the oil), overloading (which squeezes the oil from the bearing face), and oil leakage (from excessive bearing clearances, worn oil pump or high engine speeds) all contribute to lubrication breakdown. Blocked oil passages, which may be the result of misaligned oil holes in a bearing shell, will also starve a bearing of oil and destroy it. When lack of lubrication is the cause of bearing failure, the bearing material is wiped or extruded from the steel backing of the bearing. Temperatures may increase to the point where the steel backing turns blue from overheating.

6 Driving habits can have a definite effect on bearing life. Full-throttle, low-speed operation (labouring the engine) puts very high loads on bearings, which tends to squeeze out the oil film. These loads cause the bearings to flex, which produces fine cracks in the bearing face (fatigue failure). Eventually the bearing material will loosen in places, and tear away from the steel backing. Regular short journeys can lead to corrosion of bearings, because insufficient engine heat is produced to drive off the condensed water and corrosive gases which form inside the engine. These products collect in the engine oil, forming acid and sludge. As the oil is carried to the bearings, the acid attacks and corrodes the bearing material.

7 Incorrect bearing installation during engine assembly will also lead to bearing failure. Tight-fitting bearings leave insufficient bearing lubrication clearance, and will result in oil starvation. Dirt or foreign particles trapped behind a bearing shell results in high spots on the bearing which can lead to failure.

8 Do not touch any shell's bearing surface with your fingers during reassembly; there is a risk of scratching the delicate surface, or of depositing particles of dirt on it.

9 As mentioned at the beginning of this Section, the bearing shells should be renewed as a matter of course during engine overhaul; to do otherwise is false economy.

16 Engine overhaul – reassembly sequence

1 Before reassembly begins, ensure that all necessary new parts have been obtained (particularly gaskets, and various bolts which must be renewed), and that all the tools required are available. Read through the entire procedure to familiarise yourself with the work involved, and to ensure that all items necessary for reassembly of the engine are to hand. In addition to all normal tools and materials, a thread-locking compound will be required. A tube of suitable sealant will be required to seal certain joint faces which are not fitted with gaskets.

2 At this stage, all engine components should be absolutely clean and dry, with all faults repaired. The components should be laid out

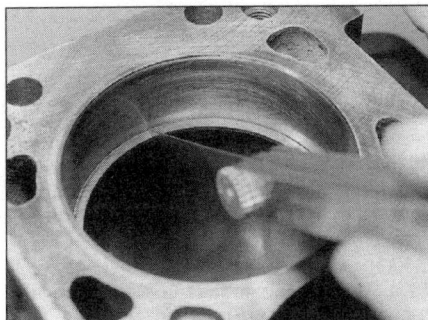

17.4 Measuring a piston ring end gap using a feeler gauge

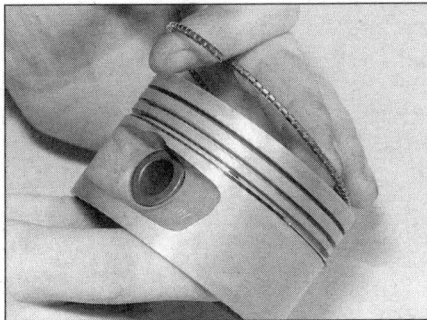

17.9 Fitting an oil control spreader ring

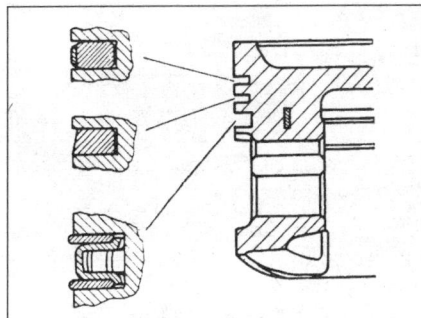

17.11 Sectional view showing correct orientation of piston rings

(or in individual containers) on a completely clean work surface.

3 In order to save time and avoid problems, engine reassembly can be carried out in the following order:

Petrol engines

a) *Piston rings (see Section 17).*
b) *Crankshaft (see Section 18).*
c) *Piston/connecting rod assemblies (see Section 19).*
d) *Timing chain and sprockets (see Chapter 2A or 2B).*
e) *Oil pump (see Chapter 2A or 2B).*
f) *Sump (see Chapter 2A or 2B).*
g) *Flywheel/driveplate (see Chapter 2A or 2B).*
h) *Cylinder head (see Chapter 2A or 2B).*
i) *Coolant pump (see Chapter 3).*
j) *Inlet and exhaust manifolds (see Chapter 4A).*

Diesel engines

a) *Piston rings (see Section 17).*
b) *Crankshaft (see Section 18).*
c) *Pistons/connecting rod assemblies (see Section 19).*
d) *Flywheel (see Chapter 2C).*
e) *Inlet and exhaust manifolds (see Chapter 4B).*
f) *Cylinder head (see Chapter 2C).*
g) *Camshaft housing (see Chapter 2C).*
h) *Oil pump (see Chapter 2C).*
i) *Timing chain and sprockets (see Chapter 2C).*
j) *Coolant pump (see Chapter 3).*
k) *Sump (see Chapter 2C).*

17 Piston rings – refitting

1 Before refitting the new piston rings, the ring end gaps must be checked as follows.
2 Lay out the piston/connecting rod assemblies and the new piston ring sets, so that the ring sets will be matched with the same piston and cylinder during the end gap measurement and subsequent engine reassembly.
3 Insert the top ring into the first cylinder, and push it down the bore slightly using the top of the piston. This will ensure that the ring remains square with the cylinder walls.

4 Measure the end gap using feeler gauges, and compare the measurements with the figures given in the Specifications **(see illustration)**.
5 If the gap is too small (unlikely if genuine Vauxhall/Opel parts are used), it must be enlarged or the ring ends may contact each other during engine operation, causing serious damage. Ideally, new piston rings providing the correct end gap should be fitted, but as a last resort, the end gap can be increased by filing the ring ends very carefully with a fine file. Mount the file in a vice equipped with soft jaws, slip the ring over the file with the ends contacting the file face, and slowly move the ring to remove material from the ends – take care, as piston rings are sharp, and are easily broken.
6 With new piston rings, it is unlikely that the end gap will be too large. If they are too large, check that you have the correct rings for your engine and for the particular cylinder bore size.
7 Repeat the checking procedure for each ring in the first cylinder, and then for the rings in the remaining cylinders. Remember to keep rings, pistons and cylinders matched up.
8 Once the ring end gaps have been checked and if necessary corrected, the rings can be fitted to the pistons.
9 The oil control ring (lowest one on the piston) is composed of three sections, and should be installed first. Fit the lower steel ring, then the spreader ring, followed by the upper steel ring **(see illustration)**.
10 With the oil control ring components installed, the second (middle) ring can be fitted. It is usually stamped with a mark (TOP) which must face up, towards the top of the piston
Note: *Always follow the instructions supplied with the new piston ring sets – different manufacturers may specify different procedures. Do not mix up the top and middle rings, as they have different cross-sections. Using two or three old feeler blades, as for removal of the old rings, carefully slip the ring into place in the middle groove.*
11 Fit the top ring in the same manner, ensuring that, where applicable, the mark on the ring is facing up. If a stepped ring is being fitted, fit the ring with the smaller diameter of the step uppermost **(see illustration)**.

12 Repeat the procedure for the remaining pistons and rings.

18 Crankshaft – refitting

Note: *New cylinder block baseplate bolts must be used when refitting the crankshaft. A tube of sealant (Loctite 5900 or equivalent) will be required when fitting the baseplate to the cylinder block.*
1 Refitting the crankshaft is the first step in the engine reassembly procedure. It is assumed at this point that the cylinder block, baseplate and crankshaft have been cleaned, inspected and repaired or reconditioned as necessary.
2 Position the cylinder block with the baseplate mating face uppermost.
3 Clean the bearing shells and the bearing recesses in both the cylinder block and the baseplate. If new shells are being fitted, ensure that all traces of the protective grease are cleaned off using paraffin. Wipe the shells dry with a clean lint-free cloth.
4 Note that the crankshaft endfloat is controlled by thrustwashers located on one of the main bearing shells. The thrustwashers are incorporated into, or attached to, the bearing shells themselves.
5 If the original bearing shells are being re-used, they must be refitted to their original locations in the block and baseplate **(see illustrations)**.

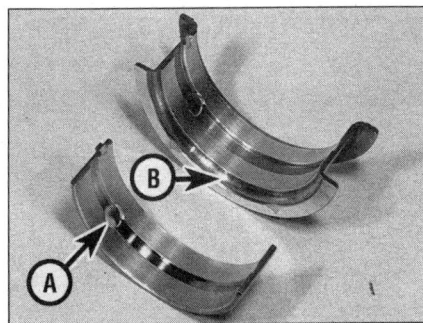

18.5a Main bearing shell (A) and central main bearing shell (B) with thrust flange – petrol engines shown

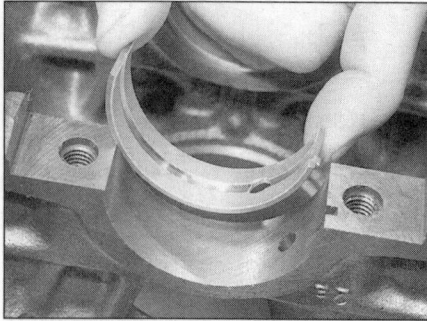

18.5b Fitting a main bearing shell to the cylinder block

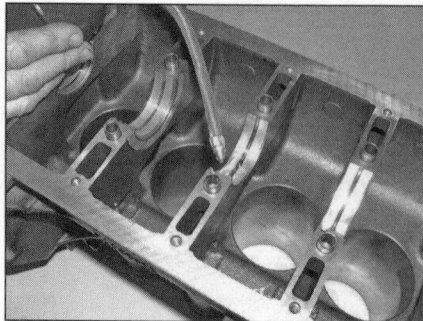

18.7 Liberally lubricate each bearing shell in the cylinder block then lower the crankshaft into position – petrol engines

6 Fit the upper main bearing shells in place in the cylinder block.

Petrol engines

7 Liberally lubricate each bearing shell in the cylinder block, and lower the crankshaft into position (see illustration).
8 If necessary, seat the crankshaft using light taps from a soft-faced mallet on the crankshaft balance webs.
9 Fit the bearing shells in the baseplate.
10 Lubricate the crankshaft journals, and the bearing shells in the baseplate (see illustration).
11 Ensure that the cylinder block and baseplate mating surfaces are clean and dry, then apply a 2 mm diameter bead of sealant to the outside of the groove (not in the groove itself) in the baseplate (see illustration).
12 Locate the baseplate over the crankshaft and onto the cylinder block.
13 Fit the new baseplate retaining bolts, then working progressively and in a diagonal sequence, tighten the inner (M8) bolts to the specified torque, then through the specified angle, in the two stages given in the Specifications. Now similarly tighten the outer (M6) retaining bolts (see illustrations).

Diesel engines

14 Liberally lubricate each bearing shell in the cylinder block, and lower the crankshaft into position (see illustrations).

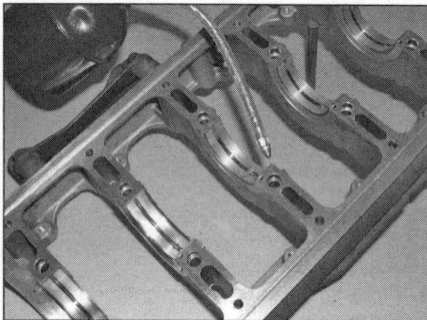

18.10 Lubricate the bearing shells in the baseplate – petrol engines

18.11 Apply a 2 mm diameter bead of silicone sealant to the outside of the groove in the baseplate – petrol engines

18.13a Fit the new baseplate inner bolts...

18.13b...and outer bolts – petrol engines

18.13c Tighten the inner bolts to the specified Stage 1 torque setting using a torque wrench...

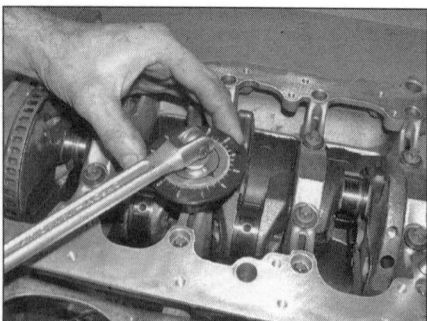

18.13d...then through the specified Stage 2 angle using an angle tightening gauge – petrol engines

18.13e Similarly tighten the outer bolts to the specified torque...

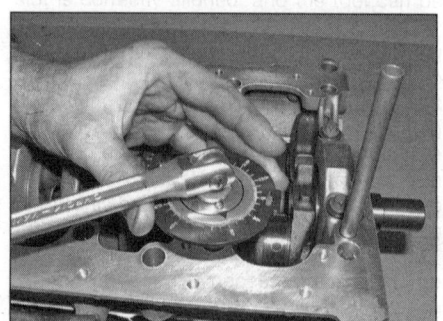

18.13f...and through the specified angle – petrol engines

18.14a Liberally lubricate each bearing shell in the cylinder block...

18.14b...and lower the crankshaft into position – diesel engines

18.16 Fit the bearing shells in the baseplate...

18.17...then lubricate the crankshaft journals, and the bearing shells – diesel engines

18.18a Apply a bead of sealant to the cylinder block mating face...

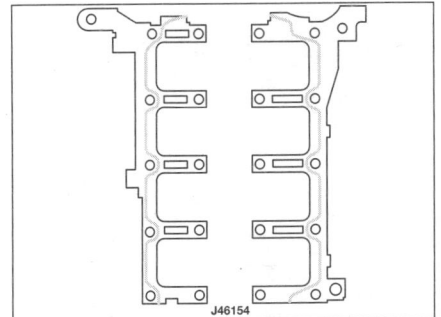

18.18b...ensuring the sealant is applied around the inside of the bolt holes as shown – diesel engines

15 If necessary, seat the crankshaft using light taps from a soft-faced mallet on the crankshaft balance webs.

16 Fit the bearing shells in the baseplate (see illustration).

17 Lubricate the crankshaft journals, and the bearing shells in the baseplate (see illustration).

18 Ensure that the cylinder block and baseplate mating surfaces are clean and dry, then apply a 2.5 mm diameter bead of sealant to the cylinder block face (see illustrations).

19 Locate the baseplate over the crankshaft and onto the cylinder block.

20 Fit the new baseplate retaining bolts, then working progressively and in the sequence shown, tighten the inner (M10) bolts to the specified torque, then through the

specified angle, in the two stages given in the Specifications. Now similarly tighten the outer (M8) retaining bolts to the specified torque in the sequence shown (see illustrations).

All engines

21 Now rotate the crankshaft, and check that it turns freely, with no signs of binding or tight spots.

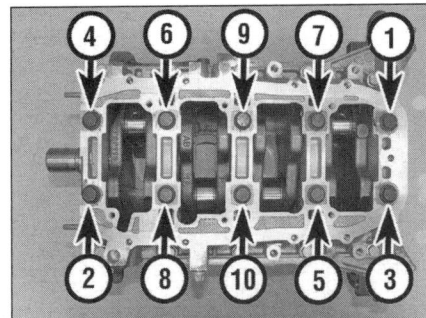

18.20a Tightening sequence for cylinder block baseplate inner (M10) bolts...

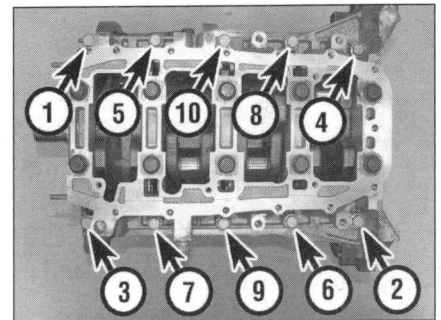

18.20b...and outer (M8) bolts – diesel engines

18.20c Tighten the M10 bolts to the specified torque...

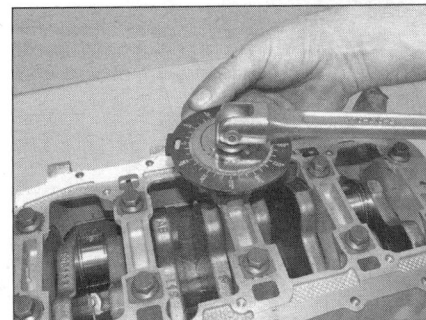

18.20d...then through the specified angle...

18.20e...and tighten the outer M8 bolts to the specified torque – diesel engines

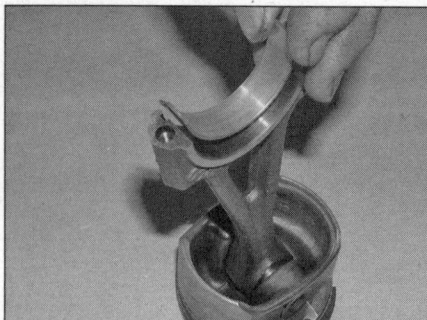

19.2 Press the bearing shells into the connecting rods and caps in their correct positions

19.5a Position the piston with the arrow or notch (as applicable) pointing towards the timing chain end of the engine...

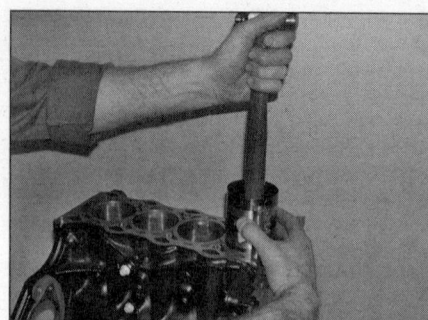

19.5b...then tap the piston carefully into the cylinder bore

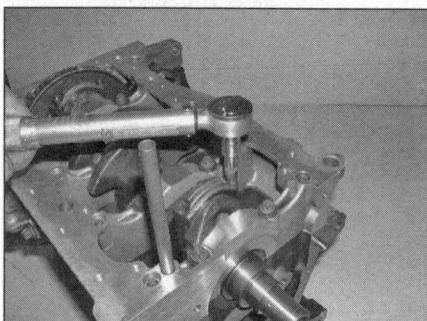

19.7a Tighten the big-end bearing cap bolts to the specified torque...

19.7b...then through the specified angle

22 Check the crankshaft endfloat with reference to Section 11.
23 Fit a new crankshaft transmission end oil seal as described in Chapter 2A, 2B or 2C.
24 Refit the pistons and connecting rods as described in Section 19.
25 Refit the flywheel/driveplate as described in Chapter 2A, 2B or 2C.

19 Pistons/connecting rods – refitting

1 Clean the backs of the big-end bearing shells and the recesses in the connecting rods and big-end caps. If new shells are being fitted, ensure that all traces of the protective grease are cleaned off using paraffin. Wipe the shells, caps and connecting rods dry with a lint-free cloth.
2 Press the bearing shells into the connecting rods and caps in their correct positions **(see illustration)**. When finally refitting the piston/connecting rod assemblies, new big-end bearing cap bolts must be used. Ensure that the mating faces of the connecting rods and big-end bearing caps are clean before refitting (refer to Section 10).
3 Lubricate No 1 piston and piston rings, and check that the ring gaps are correctly positioned. The gaps in the upper and lower steel rings of the oil control ring should be offset by 25 to 50 mm to the right and left of the spreader ring gap. The two upper compression ring gaps should be offset by 180° to each other.

4 Liberally lubricate the cylinder bore with clean engine oil.
5 Fit a ring compressor to No 1 piston, then insert the piston and connecting rod into the cylinder bore so that the base of the compressor stands on the block. With the crankshaft big-end bearing journal positioned at its lowest point, tap the piston carefully into the cylinder bore with the wooden handle of a hammer, and at the same time guide the connecting rod onto the bearing journal. Note that the arrow or notch (as applicable) on the piston crown must point towards the timing chain end of the engine **(see illustrations)**.
6 Fit the bearing shells to the bearing caps.
7 Liberally lubricate the bearing journals and bearing shells, and fit the bearing cap in its original location. Tighten the new bearing cap bolts to the Stage 1 torque setting, then tighten all bolts through the specified angles **(see illustrations)**.
8 After refitting each piston/connecting rod assembly, rotate the crankshaft, and check that it turns freely, with no signs of binding or tight spots.
9 Refit the following components.

Petrol engines

a) Refit the oil baffle plate and tighten the retaining bolts securely.
b) Refit the cylinder head as described in Chapter 2A or 2B.
c) Refit the timing chain, sprockets and tensioner as described in Chapter 2A or 2B.
d) Refit the timing cover as described in Chapter 2A or 2B.

e) Refit the sump and oil pick-up pipe as described in Chapter 2A or 2B.

Diesel engines

a) Refit the oil baffle plate and tighten the retaining bolts securely.
b) Refit the cylinder head as described in Chapter 2C.
c) Refit the camshaft housing as described in Chapter 2C.
d) Refit the timing chain, sprockets and tensioner as described in Chapter 2C.
e) Refit the timing cover (which includes the sump refitting procedure) as described in Chapter 2C.

20 Engine – initial start-up after overhaul

1 With the engine refitted in the vehicle, double-check the engine oil and coolant levels. Make a final check that everything has been reconnected, and that there are no tools or rags left in the engine compartment.
2 On diesel engines, prime and bleed the fuel system as described in Chapter 4B, Section 5.
3 Start the engine, noting that this may take a little longer than usual. Make sure that the oil pressure warning light goes out.
4 While the engine is idling, check for fuel, water and oil leaks. Don't be alarmed if there are some odd smells and smoke from parts getting hot and burning off oil deposits.
5 Assuming all is well, keep the engine idling until hot water is felt circulating through the top hose, then switch off the engine.
6 After a few minutes, recheck the oil and coolant levels as described in *Weekly checks*, and top-up as necessary.
7 Note that there is no need to retighten the cylinder head bolts once the engine has first run after reassembly.
8 If new pistons, rings or crankshaft bearings have been fitted, the engine must be treated as new, and run-in for the first 600 miles. Do not operate the engine at full-throttle, or allow it to labour at low engine speeds in any gear. It is recommended that the oil and filter be changed at the end of this period.

Chapter 3
Cooling, heating and ventilation systems

Contents

Degrees of difficulty

Easy, suitable for novice with little experience	Fairly easy, suitable for beginner with some experience	Fairly difficult, suitable for competent DIY mechanic	Difficult, suitable for experienced DIY mechanic	Very difficult, suitable for expert DIY or professional

Specifications

Thermostat

Opening temperature:	
1.0 litre petrol engines	92°C
1.2 and 1.4 litre petrol engines:	
Electric element	80°C
Wax capsule	103°C
Diesel engines	88°C

Air conditioning system

Refrigerant	R134a
Refrigerant quantity	470g

Torque wrench settings

	Nm	lbf ft
Air conditioning compressor mounting bolts	22	16
Air conditioning refrigerant pipe block connections.	20	15
Coolant pump blanking plug (petrol engines)	15	11
Coolant pump bolts/nuts	9	7
Coolant pump cover bolts (petrol engines)	8	6
Coolant pump pulley bolts (petrol engines)	20	15
Thermostat housing bolts:		
Petrol engines..	8	6
Diesel engines	25	18

1 General information and precautions

General information

1 The cooling system is of pressurised type, comprising a pump driven by the auxiliary drivebelt, an aluminium crossflow radiator, electric cooling fan, and a thermostat. The system functions as follows. Cold coolant from the radiator passes through the hose to the coolant pump, where it is pumped around the cylinder block and head passages. After cooling the cylinder bores, combustion surfaces and valve seats, the coolant reaches the underside of the thermostat, which is initially closed. The coolant passes through the heater, and is returned to the coolant pump.

2 When the engine is cold, the coolant circulates only through the cylinder block, cylinder head, expansion tank and heater. When the coolant reaches a predetermined temperature, the thermostat opens and the coolant passes through to the radiator. As the coolant circulates through the radiator, it is cooled by the inrush of air when the car is in forward motion. Airflow is supplemented by the action of the electric cooling fan when necessary. Once the coolant has passed through the radiator, and has cooled, the cycle is repeated.

3 The electric cooling fan, mounted on the rear of the radiator, is controlled by a thermostatic switch/sensor. At a predetermined coolant temperature, the fan is actuated.

4 On 1.2 and 1.4 litre petrol engines, an electrically assisted thermostat is fitted. Engine coolant temperature is monitored by the engine management system electronic control unit, via the coolant temperature sensor. In conjunction with information received from various other engine sensors, the thermostat opening temperature can be controlled according to engine speed and load. During normal engine operation the thermostat operates conventionally. Under conditions of high engine speed and load, an electric heating element within the thermostat is energised, to cause the thermostat to open at a lower temperature (typically 80°).

5 An expansion tank is fitted to the front, left-hand side of the engine compartment to accommodate expansion of the coolant when it gets hot. The expansion tank is connected to the top of the radiator by a small bore rubber hose.

Precautions

⚠️ *Warning: Do not attempt to remove the expansion tank filler cap, or disturb any part of the cooling system, while the engine is hot; there is a high risk of scalding. If the expansion tank filler cap must be removed before the engine and radiator have fully cooled (even though this is not recommended) the pressure in the cooling system must first be relieved. Cover the cap with a thick layer of cloth, to avoid scalding, and slowly unscrew the filler cap until a hissing sound can be heard. When the hissing has stopped, indicating that the pressure has reduced, slowly unscrew the filler cap until it can be removed; if more hissing sounds are heard, wait until they have stopped before unscrewing the cap completely. At all times, keep well away from the filler cap opening.*

• *Do not allow antifreeze to come into contact with skin, or with the painted surfaces of the vehicle. Rinse off spills immediately, with plenty of water. Never leave antifreeze lying around in an open container, or in a puddle on the driveway or garage floor. Children and pets are attracted by its sweet smell, but antifreeze can be fatal if ingested.*

• *If the engine is hot, the electric cooling fan may start rotating even if the engine is not running; be careful to keep hands, hair and loose clothing well clear when working in the engine compartment.*

• *Refer to Section 10 for precautions to be observed when working on models equipped with air conditioning.*

2 Cooling system hoses – disconnection and renewal

Note: *Refer to the warnings given in Section 1 of this Chapter before proceeding. Do not attempt to disconnect any hose while the system is still hot.*

1 If the checks described in Chapter 1A, Section 6 or Chapter 1B, Section 6 reveal a faulty hose, it must be renewed as follows.

2 First drain the cooling system as described in Chapter 1A, Section 27 or Chapter 1B, Section 28. If the coolant is not due for renewal, it may be re-used if it is collected in a clean container.

3 Before disconnecting a hose, first note its routing in the engine compartment, and whether it is secured by any additional retaining clips or cable-ties. Use a pair of pliers to release the clamp-type clips, or a screwdriver to slacken the screw-type clips, then move the clips along the hose, clear of the relevant inlet/outlet union. Carefully work the hose free.

4 Depending on engine, some of the hose attachments may be of the quick-release type. Where this type of hose is encountered, lift the ends of the wire retaining clip, to spread the clip, then withdraw the hose from the inlet/outlet union **(see illustrations)**.

5 Note that the radiator inlet and outlet unions are fragile; do not use excessive force when attempting to remove the hoses. If a hose proves to be difficult to remove, try to release it by rotating the hose ends before attempting to free it.

> **HAYNES HINT** *If all else fails, cut the coolant hose with a sharp knife, then slit it so that it can be peeled off in two pieces. Although this may prove expensive if the hose is otherwise undamaged, it is preferable to buying a new radiator.*

6 When fitting a hose, first slide the clips onto the hose, then work the hose into position. If clamp-type clips were originally fitted, it is a good idea to use screw-type clips when refitting the hose. If the hose is stiff, use a little soapy water (washing-up liquid is ideal) as a lubricant, or soften the hose by soaking it in hot water.

7 Work the hose into position, checking that it is correctly routed and secured. Slide each clip along the hose until it passes over the flared end of the relevant inlet/outlet union, before tightening the clips securely.

8 Refill the cooling system with reference to Chapter 1A, Section 27 or Chapter 1B, Section 28.

9 Check thoroughly for leaks as soon as possible after disturbing any part of the cooling system.

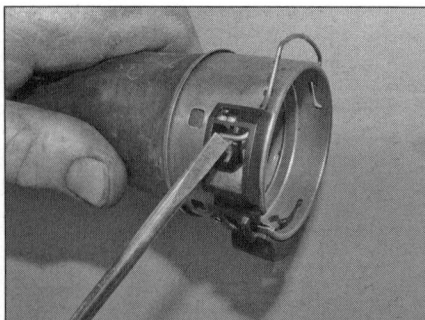

2.4a To disconnect quick-release hose fittings, lift the ends of the wire retaining clip, to spread the clip...

2.4b...then withdraw the hose from the inlet/outlet union

3 Radiator –
removal, inspection
and refitting

Removal

Petrol engines

1 Disconnect the battery negative terminal (refer to *Disconnecting the battery* in Chapter 5A, Section 4).

2 Firmly apply the handbrake, then jack up the front of the car and support it securely on axle stands (see *Jacking and vehicle support*).

3 Remove the front bumper as described in Chapter 11, Section 6.

4 Drain the cooling system as described in Chapter 1A, Section 27.

5 Slacken the retaining clips, and disconnect the coolant top and bottom hoses from the radiator.

6 Unclip the expansion tank hoses from the cooling fan shroud **(see illustration)**.

7 Disconnect the cooling fan wiring connector located above the radiator **(see illustration)**.

8 Undo the retaining bolt, release the two clips and move the coolant expansion tank to one side **(see illustrations)**.

9 Undo the retaining nut and disconnect the two earth leads from the chassis side member, just in front of the battery.

10 On automatic transmission models, release the retaining clips and disconnect the fluid cooler hoses from the radiator.

11 On models equipped with air conditioning, unclip the four mounting brackets and separate the condenser from the radiator. Suitably suspend the condenser from the bonnet lock platform using cable-ties, to avoid straining the refrigerant lines.

12 Also on models equipped with air conditioning, disconnect the wiring connector from the compressor.

13 With the help of an assistant, undo the retaining bolt each side securing the radiator support crossmember to the underbody **(see illustration)**. Lower the radiator out through the bottom of the vehicle, disengaging it from its upper mountings.

14 If required, the electric cooling fan can

3.6 Unclip the expansion tank hoses from the cooling fan shroud – petrol engines

3.7 Disconnect the cooling fan wiring connector located above the radiator – petrol engines

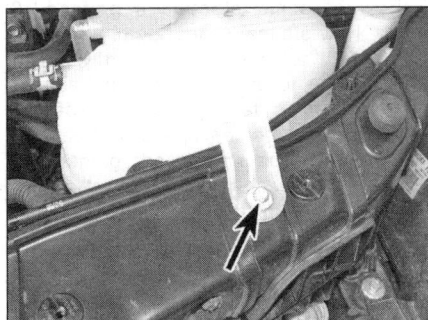
3.8a Undo the retaining bolt...

3.8b...then release the two clips and move the coolant expansion tank to one side – petrol engines

be detached after and releasing the wiring harness.

Diesel engines

15 Disconnect the battery negative terminal (refer to *Disconnecting the battery* in Chapter 5A, Section 4).

16 Firmly apply the handbrake, then jack up the front of the car and support it securely on axle stands (see *Jacking and vehicle support*).

17 Remove the front bumper as described in Chapter 11, Section 6.

18 Drain the cooling system as described in Chapter 1A, Section 27.

19 Disconnect the quick-release fittings and remove the two charge air hoses from the intercooler. Undo the bolt each side securing

the charge air hose clamps to the radiator support crossmember **(see illustrations)**.

20 Disconnect the wiring connectors from the cooling fan and the cooling fan resistor, then release the wiring harness from the cable-ties on the fan shroud **(see illustrations)**.

21 Disconnect the quick-release fitting and remove the coolant bottom hose from the right-hand side of the radiator.

22 Slacken the retaining clip and disconnect the coolant expansion tank hose from the right-hand side of the radiator.

23 Unclip the expansion tank hoses from the cooling fan shroud **(see illustration 3.6)**.

24 Disconnect the quick-release fitting and remove the coolant top hose from the left-hand side of the radiator.

3.13 Undo the retaining bolt each side securing the radiator support crossmember to the underbody – petrol engines

3.19a Disconnect the two charge air hoses from the intercooler...

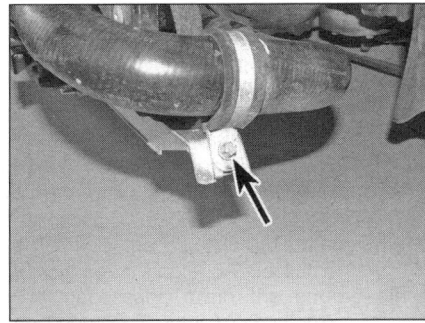
3.19b...then undo the bolt each side securing the charge air hose clamps to the radiator support crossmember – diesel engines

3.20a Disconnect the wiring connectors from the cooling fan...

3.20b...and the cooling fan resistor...

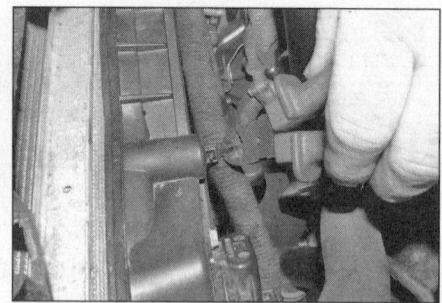
3.20c...then release the wiring harness from the cable ties on the fan shroud – diesel engines

25 On models equipped with air conditioning, undo the two bolts securing the condenser to the radiator (see illustrations). Release the condenser from its mounting bracket and suitably suspend it from the bonnet lock platform using cable-ties, to avoid straining the refrigerant lines.

26 Slacken the retaining bolt each side securing the radiator support crossmember to the underbody and lower the crossmember slightly (see illustration 3.13).

27 Working through the small gap between the underside of the radiator and the top of the support crossmember, undo the two bolts securing the charge air pipe to the crossmember. Release the charge air pipe from the crossmember (see illustrations).

28 With the help of an assistant, remove the two previously-slackened support crossmember retaining bolts and lower the radiator out through the bottom of the vehicle, disengaging it from its upper mountings (see illustration).

29 If required, the electric cooling fan and intercooler can be removed after undoing the mounting bolts and releasing the wiring harness.

Inspection

30 If the radiator has been removed due to suspected blockage, reverse-flush it as described in Chapter 1A, Section 27 or Chapter 1B, Section 28. Clean dirt and debris from the radiator fins, using an airline (in which case, wear eye protection) or a soft brush.

Caution: Be careful, as the fins are easily damaged, and are sharp.

31 If necessary, a radiator specialist can perform a 'flow test' on the radiator, to establish whether an internal blockage exists.

32 A leaking radiator must be referred to a specialist for permanent repair. Do not attempt DIY repairs to a leaking radiator, as damage may result.

33 In an emergency, minor leaks from the radiator can be cured by using a suitable radiator sealant (in accordance with its manufacturer's instructions) with the radiator in situ.

34 Inspect the radiator mounting rubbers, and renew them if necessary.

Refitting

35 Refitting is a reversal of removal, bearing in mind the following points:

a) Ensure that all hoses are correctly reconnected, and their retaining clips securely tightened.

b) On completion, refill the cooling system as described in Chapter 1A, Section 27 or Chapter 1B, Section 28.

3.25a Undo the upper left-hand bolt...

3.25b...and lower right-hand bolt securing the condenser to the radiator – diesel engines

---

4 Thermostat – removal, testing and refitting

Removal

Petrol engines

1 The thermostat housing is attached to the coolant pump at the right-hand side of the engine.

3.27a Undo the two bolts securing the charge air pipe to the crossmember...

3.27b...then release the charge air pipe from the crossmember

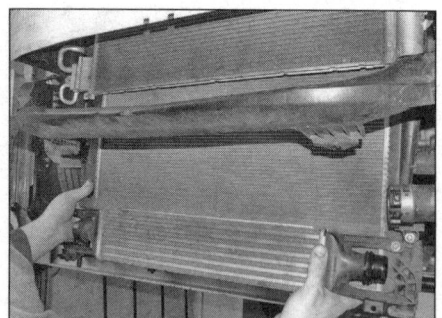
3.28 Lower the radiator out through the bottom of the vehicle, disengaging it from its upper mountings

4.4a Release the retaining clip...

4.4b...or pull out the retaining spring clip and disconnect the coolant hose from the thermostat housing – petrol engines

4.5 Remove the thermostat housing from the coolant pump – 1.0 litre petrol engine shown

2 Disconnect the battery negative terminal (refer to *Disconnecting the battery* in Chapter 5A, Section 4).
3 Drain the cooling system as described in Chapter 1A, Section 27.
4 Slacken the retaining clip or pull out the retaining spring clip and disconnect the coolant hose from the thermostat housing **(see illustrations)**.
5 Where applicable, disconnect the wiring connector from the thermostat housing, then slacken and remove the three retaining bolts, and remove the housing **(see illustration)**.
6 Remove the thermostat. Note that on some models, the thermostat is an integral part of the housing and cannot be renewed separately.
7 Remove the sealing ring from the housing cover and discard it; a new one should be used on refitting **(see illustration)**.

Diesel engines

8 Lift off the engine cover.
9 Drain the cooling system as described in Chapter 1B, Section 28.
10 Remove the battery and battery tray as described in Chapter 5A, Section 4.
11 Slacken the retaining clips, and disconnect the four coolant hoses from the thermostat housing.
12 Disconnect the coolant temperature sensor wiring connector and release the wiring harness from the thermostat housing.
13 Undo and remove the two retaining bolts and remove the thermostat housing from the engine **(see illustration)**.
14 Remove the sealing ring from the housing and discard it; a new one should be used on refitting **(see illustration)**.
15 Note that the thermostat is an integral part of the housing, and cannot be renewed separately.

Testing

16 Where it is possible to separate the thermostat from the cover, a rough test of the thermostat's operation may be made by suspending it with a piece of string in a container full of water. Heat the water to bring it to the boil – the thermostat must open by the time the water boils. If not, renew it **(see illustration)**.
Note: *If there is any question about the*

operation of the thermostat, it's best to renew it – they are not usually expensive items. Testing involves heating in, or over, an open pan of boiling water, which carries with it the risk of scalding. A thermostat which has seen more than five years' service may well be past its best already.
17 The opening temperature is marked on the thermostat. If a thermometer is available, the precise opening temperature of the thermostat may be determined, and compared with the value mark on the thermostat.
18 A thermostat which fails to close as the water cools must also be renewed.

Refitting

19 Refitting is a reversal of removal, bearing in mind the following points:
a) *Fit the new sealing rings to all applicable mating faces.*

4.7 Remove the sealing ring from the thermostat housing – petrol engines

4.14 Remove the sealing ring from the thermostat housing – diesel engines

b) *Tighten the thermostat housing bolts to the specified torque.*
c) *On completion, refill the cooling system as described in Chapter 1A, Section 27 or Chapter 1B, Section 28.*

5 Electric cooling fan – removal and refitting

⚠ *Warning: If the engine is hot, the cooling fan may start up at any time. Take extra precautions when working in the vicinity of the fan.*

Removal

Petrol engines

1 Disconnect the battery negative terminal

4.13 Undo the two retaining bolts and remove the thermostat housing – diesel engines

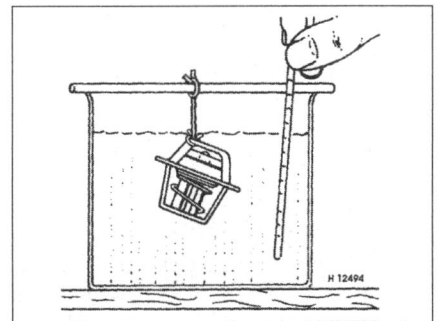
4.16 Testing the thermostat opening temperature

5.9 Fan motor retaining bolts/nuts

(refer to *Disconnecting the battery* in Chapter 5A, Section 4).

2 Firmly apply the handbrake, then jack up the front of the car and support it securely on axle stands (see *Jacking and vehicle support*).

3 Unclip the expansion tank hoses from cooling fan housing **(see illustration 3.6)**.

4 Disconnect the cooling fan wiring connector located above the radiator **(see illustration 3.7)**.

5 Undo the retaining bolt, release the two clips and move the coolant expansion tank to one side **(see illustrations 3.8a and 3.8b)**.

6 Undo the retaining nut and disconnect the two earth leads from the chassis sidemember, just in front of the battery.

7 On models equipped with air conditioning, disconnect the wiring connector from the compressor.

8 Depress the tab at the top of the fan shroud at each side and move the shroud away from the radiator. Lift the fan shroud out of the lower retainers, then lower the fan and shroud assembly and remove it from under the vehicle.

9 To remove the fan motor, disconnect the motor wiring connector, then unscrew the three retaining bolts/nuts and remove the motor from the shroud **(see illustration)**.

Diesel engines

10 Disconnect the battery negative terminal (refer to *Disconnecting the battery* in Chapter 5A, Section 4).

11 Firmly apply the handbrake, then jack up the front of the car and support it securely on axle stands (see *Jacking and vehicle support*).

**6.2 Coolant temperature sensor location –
1.0 litre petrol engines**

12 Remove the front bumper as described in Chapter 11, Section 6.

13 Drain the cooling system as described in Chapter 1B, Section 28.

14 Disconnect the quick-release fittings and remove the two charge air hoses from the intercooler. Undo the bolt each side securing the charge air hose clamps to the radiator support crossmember.

15 Disconnect the wiring connectors from the cooling fan and the cooling fan resistor, then release the wiring harness from the cable-ties on the fan shroud **(see illustrations 3.20a to 3.20c)**.

16 Unclip the expansion tank hoses from cooling fan shroud **(see illustration 3.6)**.

17 Disconnect the quick-release fitting and remove the coolant bottom hose from the right-hand side of the radiator.

18 Slacken the retaining clip and disconnect the coolant expansion tank hose from the right-hand side of the radiator.

19 Suitably suspend the radiator from the bonnet lock platform using cable-ties or similar.

20 Slacken the retaining bolt each side securing the radiator support crossmember to the underbody and lower the crossmember slightly **(see illustration 3.13)**.

21 Working through the small gap between the underside of the radiator and the top of the support crossmember, undo the two bolts securing the charge air pipe to the crossmember. Release the charge air pipe from the crossmember **(see illustrations 3.27a and 3.27b)**.

22 Remove the two previously-slackened support crossmember retaining bolts and remove the crossmember.

23 Undo the two left-hand bolts and one lower right-hand bolt securing the fan shroud to the radiator.

24 Ease the fan shroud away from the radiator and lower it down and out from under the car.

25 To remove the fan motor, unscrew the three retaining bolts and remove the motor from the shroud **(see illustration 5.9)**.

Refitting

26 Refitting is a reversal of removal, bearing in mind the following points:

**6.6 Coolant temperature sensor located in the coolant outlet housing –
1.2 and 1.4 litre petrol engines**

a) *Ensure that the shroud is correctly located on the radiator.*

b) *Use new cable-ties to secure all disturbed wiring harnesses.*

c) *Where removed, refit the front bumper as described in Chapter 11, Section 6.*

d) *On diesel engines refill the cooling system as described in Chapter 1B, Section 28.*

e) *On completion, start the engine and run it until it reaches normal operating temperature; continue to run the engine, and check that the cooling fan cuts in and functions correctly.*

6 Coolant temperature sensor
– testing, removal and refitting

Testing

1 Testing of the coolant temperature sensor circuit is best entrusted to a Vauxhall/Opel dealer, who will have the necessary specialist diagnostic equipment.

Removal

1.0 litre petrol engines

2 The coolant temperature sensor is located at the top of the coolant pump housing **(see illustration)**.

3 Drain the cooling system as described in Chapter 1A, Section 27.

4 With the engine cold, unscrew the cap from the coolant expansion tank to release the pressure, then refit and tighten it. This will reduce the loss of coolant when the sensor is removed. Have a suitable plug available to insert in the sensor hole.

5 Disconnect the wiring connector from the temperature sensor, then unscrew and remove it from the coolant pump housing. If the cooling system has not been drained, either insert the new sensor or fit a blanking plug to prevent further loss of coolant.

1.2 and 1.4 litre petrol engines

6 Two temperature sensors are fitted; one located in the side of the coolant outlet housing at the left-hand end of the cylinder head, and one located in the radiator right-hand side tank **(see illustration)**. The removal and refitting procedures are the same for both sensors.

7 Drain the cooling system as described in Chapter 1A, Section 27.

8 With the engine cold, unscrew the cap from the coolant expansion tank to release the pressure, then refit and tighten it. This will reduce the loss of coolant when the sensor is removed. Have a suitable plug available to insert in the sensor hole.

9 Disconnect the wiring connector, then extract the wire retaining clip. Remove the sensor from the outlet housing or radiator. If the cooling system has not been drained, either insert the new sensor or fit a blanking plug to prevent further loss of coolant.

Diesel engines

10 The coolant temperature sensor is located on the thermostat housing on the left-hand end of the cylinder head **(see illustration)**.
11 Lift off the engine cover.
12 Drain the cooling system as described in Chapter 1B, Section 28.
13 Remove the intercooler left-hand charge air pipe as described in Chapter 4B, Section 3.
14 Disconnect the wiring connector from the temperature sensor, then unscrew and remove it from the thermostat housing.

Refitting

15 Refitting is a reversal of removal, bearing in mind the following points:
a) *Where applicable fit a new sealing O-ring to the sensor. Where the sensor is fitted without an O-ring, ensure the sensor threads are clean, and apply a smear of suitable sealant to them.*
b) *On completion, refill the cooling system as described in Chapter 1A, Section 27 or Chapter 1B, Section 28.*

7 Coolant pump – removal and refitting

Removal

1.0 litre petrol engines

1 Disconnect the battery negative terminal (refer to *Disconnecting the battery* in Chapter 5A, Section 4).
2 Remove the air cleaner assembly and air intake ducts as described in Chapter 4A, Section 2.
3 Remove the auxiliary drivebelt as described in Chapter 1A, Section 32.
4 Drain the cooling system as described in Chapter 1A, Section 27.
5 Support the engine and remove the right-hand engine mounting and engine mounting bracket as described in Chapter 2A, Section 15.
6 Unscrew the three coolant pump pulley bolts and withdraw the pulley from the pump.
7 Disconnect the coolant temperature sensor wiring connector.

6.10 Coolant temperature sensor location – diesel engines

8 Release the retaining clips and disconnect the hoses from the coolant pump and thermostat housing **(see illustrations)**.
9 Unscrew the coolant pump retaining bolts, noting the locations of the three short bolts **(see illustration)**. The short bolts secure the pump to the timing cover, and the long bolts secure the pump and the timing cover to the cylinder block and cylinder head.
10 Withdraw the coolant pump from the timing cover, noting that it may be necessary to tap the pump lightly with a soft-faced hammer to free it from the locating dowels.
Note: *Coolant which is trapped in the cylinder block will leak out when the pump is removed.*
11 Recover the pump sealing ring/gasket, and discard it; a new one must be used on refitting **(see illustration)**.

7.8a Release the clips and disconnect the hoses from the front...

7.9 Coolant pump short retaining bolt locations – 1.0 litre petrol engines

7.11 Remove the sealing ring from the timing cover groove – 1.0 litre petrol engines

12 Note that it is not possible to overhaul the pump. If it is faulty, the unit must be renewed complete.
13 If the pump is being renewed, remove the thermostat and temperature sensor then transfer them to the new pump.
14 Similarly, unscrew the two bolts and withdraw the coolant pump top cover from the old pump and fit the cover to the new pump using a new seal. Tighten the cover bolts to the specified torque.

1.2 and 1.4 litre petrol engines

15 Disconnect the battery negative terminal (refer to *Disconnecting the battery* in Chapter 5A, Section 4).
16 Remove the air cleaner assembly and air intake ducts as described in Chapter 4A, Section 2.
17 Remove the auxiliary drivebelt as described in Chapter 1A, Section 32.
18 Drain the cooling system as described in Chapter 1A, Section 27.
19 Support the engine and remove the right-hand engine mounting and engine mounting bracket as described in Chapter 2B, Section 16.
20 Pull out the retaining spring clip and disconnect the radiator inlet hose from the thermostat housing **(see illustration 4.4b)**.
21 Disconnect the thermostat wiring connector.
22 Release the retaining clip and disconnect the heater outlet hose from the coolant pump **(see illustration)**.
23 Hold the coolant pump pulley hub using a

7.8b...and rear of the coolant pump housing – 1.0 litre petrol engines

7.22 Release the retaining clip and disconnect the heater outlet hose from the coolant pump – 1.2 and 1.4 litre petrol engines

7.23a Hold the coolant pump pulley hub using a spanner on the flats provided, then undo the three pulley retaining bolts...

7.23b...and remove the pulley from the pump – 1.2 and 1.4 litre petrol engines

7.24 Unscrew the coolant pump retaining bolts noting the locations of the different length bolts – 1.2 and 1.4 litre petrol engines

spanner on the flats provided. Undo the three pulley retaining bolts and remove the pulley **(see illustrations)**.

24 Unscrew the ten coolant pump retaining bolts, noting the locations of the different length bolts **(see illustration)**. The short bolts secure the pump to the timing cover, and the long bolts secure the pump and the timing cover to the cylinder block and cylinder head.

25 Withdraw the coolant pump from the timing cover, noting that it may be necessary to tap the pump lightly with a soft-faced hammer to free it from the locating dowels **(see illustration)**.

Note: *Coolant which is trapped in the cylinder block will leak out when the pump is removed.*

26 Recover the pump sealing gasket, and discard it; a new one must be used on refitting.

27 Note that it is not possible to overhaul the pump. If it is faulty, the unit must be renewed complete.

28 If the pump is being renewed, remove the thermostat (referring to the procedures in Section 4) and transfer it to the new pump.

Diesel engines

29 Disconnect the battery negative terminal (refer to *Disconnecting the battery* in Chapter 5A, Section 4).

30 Remove the air cleaner assembly and air intake ducts as described in Chapter 4B, Section 3.

31 Drain the cooling system with reference to Chapter 1B, Section 28.

32 Remove the auxiliary drivebelt as described in Chapter 1B, Section 31.

33 Working through the apertures in the pulley, unscrew and remove the four coolant pump retaining nuts **(see illustration)**.

34 Withdraw the coolant pump from the cylinder block studs.

Note: *Coolant which is trapped in the cylinder block will leak out when the pump is removed.*

35 Recover the pump sealing ring, and discard it; a new one must be used on refitting **(see illustration)**.

36 Note that it is not possible to overhaul the pump. If it is faulty, the unit must be renewed complete.

Refitting

37 Refitting is a reversal of the removal procedure, bearing in mind the following points:

Petrol engines

a) Ensure that the pump and timing cover mating faces are clean and dry and locate a new seal/gasket in the pump or timing cover groove.

b) Tighten all retaining nuts/bolts to the specified torque.

c) Refit the auxiliary drivebelt as described in Chapter 1A, Section 32.

d) Refit the right-hand engine mounting bracket and engine mounting as described in Chapter 2A, Section 15 or Chapter 2B, Section 16.

e) Refit the air cleaner assembly and air

intake ducts as described in Chapter 4A, Section 2.

f) Refill the cooling system as described in Chapter 1A, Section 27.

Diesel engines

a) Ensure that the pump and cylinder block mating surfaces are clean and dry and fit a new sealing ring to the pump.

b) Tighten all retaining nuts/bolts to the specified torque.

c) Refit the auxiliary drivebelt as described in Chapter 1B, Section 31.

d) Refit the air cleaner assembly and air intake ducts as described in Chapter 4B, Section 3.

e) Refill the cooling system as described in Chapter 1B, Section 28.

8 Heater/ventilation system – general information

1 The heater/ventilation system consists of a four-speed blower motor which is inside the vehicle behind the facia to the left-hand side of the heater housing, face-level vents in the centre and at each end of the facia, and air ducts to the front footwells and windscreen.

2 The control unit is located in the facia to the right-hand side of the heater housing assembly. The controls operate flap valves to deflect and mix the air flowing through the various parts of the heater/ventilation system.

7.25 Withdraw the coolant pump from the timing cover – 1.2 and 1.4 litre petrol engines

7.33 Working through the pulley apertures, unscrew and remove the coolant pump retaining nuts – diesel engines

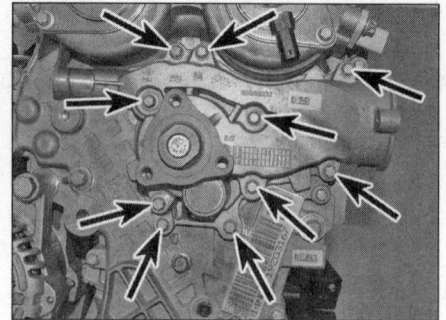

7.35 Remove the sealing ring from the coolant pump – diesel engines

The flap valves are contained in the air distribution housing, which acts as a central distribution unit, passing air to the various ducts and vents.

3 Cold air enters the system through the grille at the rear of the engine compartment. A pollen filter is fitted to the ventilation intake, to filter out dust, soot, pollen and spores from the air entering the vehicle.

4 The air (boosted by the blower fan if required) then flows through the various ducts, according to the settings of the controls. Stale air is expelled through ducts behind the doors. If warm air is required, the cold air is passed through the heater matrix, which is heated by the engine coolant.

5 A recirculation lever enables the outside air supply to be closed off, while the air inside the vehicle is recirculated. This can be useful to prevent unpleasant odours entering from outside the vehicle, but should only be used briefly, as the recirculated air inside the vehicle will soon deteriorate.

9 Heater/ventilation system components – removal and refitting

Heater control assembly

Removal

1 Disconnect the battery negative terminal (refer to *Disconnecting the battery* in Chapter 5A, Section 4).

2 Remove the following components as described in Chapter 11 :
a) *Centre console.*
b) *Glovebox.*
c) *Driver's side lower trim panel.*
d) *Footwell centre trim panel on both sides.*

3 Extract the expanding rivet and remove the footwell air ducts on both sides **(see illustrations)**.

4 Remove the radio/CD player as described in Chapter 12, Section 17.

5 Mark the position of the heater control cables in their respective retaining clips on the air distribution housing, then release the outer cable retaining clips and disconnect the inner cables from their attachments **(see illustrations)**.

6 From within the radio/CD player aperture, undo the two screws securing the heater control assembly to the facia **(see illustration)**.

7 Using a screwdriver, carefully lift the facia support above the heater control assembly, while at the same time pulling the assembly away from the facia to release the two retaining clips each side **(see illustrations)**.

8 Disconnect the wiring connectors and the heater control illumination bulbholders from the rear of the panel **(see illustrations)**.

9.3a Extract the expanding rivet and remove the right-hand footwell air duct...

9.3b...and left-hand footwell air duct

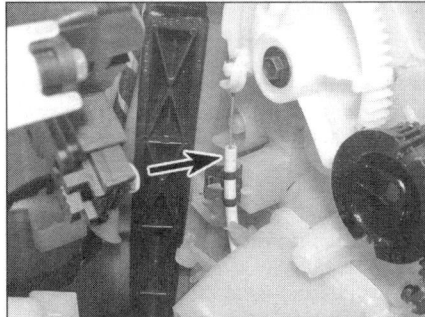
9.5a Mixed air valve control cable...

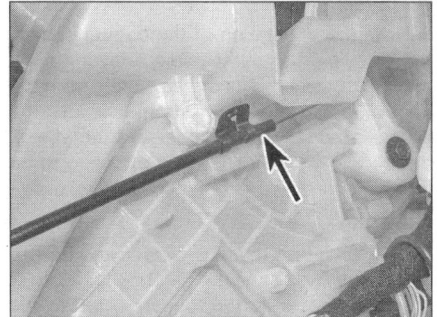
9.5b...and centre air valve control cable

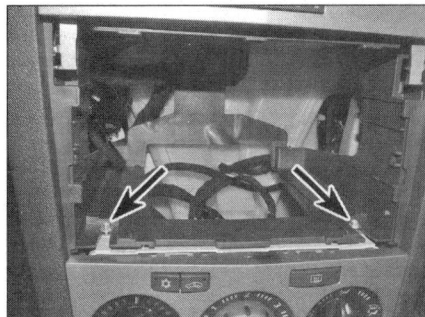
9.6 Undo the two screws securing the heater control assembly to the facia

9.7a Carefully lift the facia support above the heater control assembly...

9.7b...while at the same time pulling the assembly away from the facia to release the two clips each side

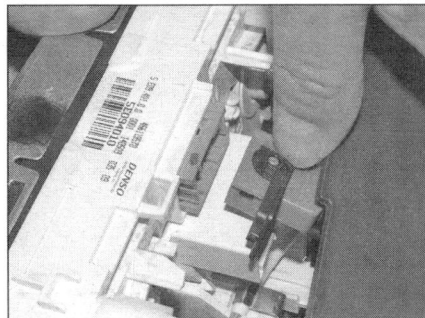
9.8a Disconnect the wiring connectors...

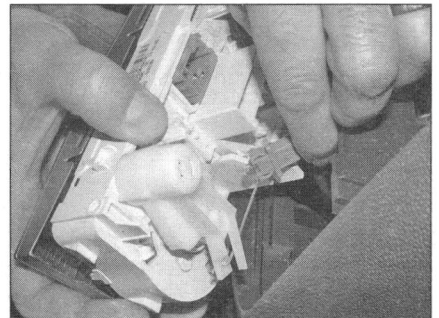
9.8b...and the heater control illumination bulbholders from the rear of the panel

9.9 Release the outer cable retaining clips and disconnect the inner cable ends from the control levers

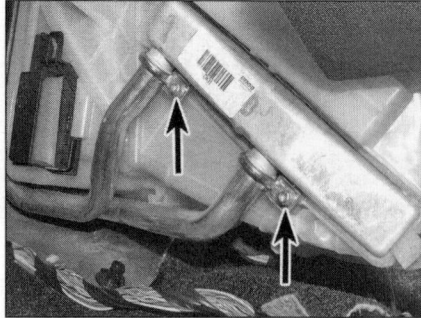

9.20 Undo the two screws and remove the clamps securing the coolant pipes to the heater matrix

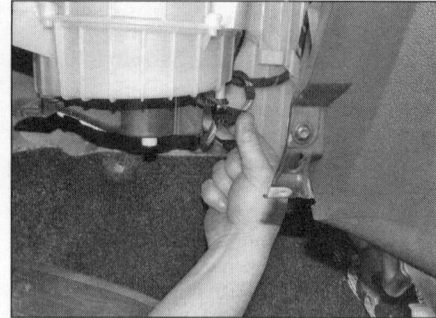

9.27 Disconnect the wiring connector from the fan motor

9 Note the orientation of the control cables, then release the outer cable retaining clips and disconnect the inner cable ends from the control levers **(see illustration)**. Remove the control assembly from the facia. Alternatively, the control cables can be left attached to be removed complete with the control assembly.

Refitting

10 Refitting is a reversal of removal. Ensure that the wiring connectors and control cables are correctly routed and reconnected to the control assembly, as noted before removal. Clip the outer cable(s) in position, and check the operation of each knob/lever before refitting the components removed for access.

Heater control assembly cables

Removal

11 Proceed as described previously in paragraphs 1 to 9 according to cable.

Refitting

12 Refitting is a reversal of removal. Ensure that the wiring connectors and control cables are correctly routed and reconnected to the control assembly, as noted before removal. Clip the outer cable(s) in position, and check the operation of each knob/lever before refitting the components removed for access.

Heater matrix

Removal

13 Disconnect the battery negative terminal

(refer to *Disconnecting the battery* in Chapter 5A, Section 4).
14 With the engine cold, unscrew the expansion tank cap (referring to the warning note in Section 1) to release any pressure present in the cooling system, then securely refit the cap.
15 Clamp both heater hoses as close to the bulkhead as possible, to minimise coolant loss. Alternatively, drain the cooling system as described in Chapter 1A, Section 27 or Chapter 1B, Section 28.
16 Working in the engine compartment, release the retaining clips, and disconnect both hoses from the heater matrix unions.
17 Remove the following components as described in Chapter 11 :
a) *Centre console.*
b) *Glovebox.*
c) *Footwell centre trim panel on the passenger's side.*
18 Extract the expanding rivet and remove the footwell air duct on the passenger's side **(see illustration 9.3b)**.
19 Cover the carpet directly underneath the air distribution housing, to catch any coolant which may be spilt from the matrix as it is removed.
20 Undo the two screws and remove the clamps securing the coolant pipes to the heater matrix **(see illustration)**.
21 Unclip the heater matrix and slide it out from the air distribution housing, then remove the matrix from the vehicle.
Note: *Keep the matrix unions uppermost*

as the matrix is removed, to prevent coolant spillage. Mop-up any spilt coolant immediately, and wipe the affected area with a damp cloth to prevent staining.
22 Where necessary, recover the sealing rings from the matrix unions and hoses, and renew them.

Refitting

23 Refitting is a reversal of the removal procedure. On completion, top-up/refill the cooling system as described in Chapter 1A, Section 27 or Chapter 1B, Section 28.

Heater blower motor

Removal

24 Disconnect the battery negative terminal (refer to *Disconnecting the battery* in Chapter 5A, Section 4).
25 Remove the glovebox as described in Chapter 11, Section 26.
26 Extract the expanding rivet and remove the footwell air duct on the passenger's side **(see illustration 9.3b)**.
27 Disconnect the wiring connector from the fan motor **(see illustration)**.
28 Undo the three retaining screws, and withdraw the motor from the housing **(see illustration)**.

Refitting

29 Refitting is a reversal of the removal procedure.

Heater blower motor resistor

Removal

30 Disconnect the battery negative terminal (refer to *Disconnecting the battery* in Chapter 5A, Section 4).
31 Remove the glovebox as described in Chapter 11, Section 26.
32 Extract the expanding rivet and remove the footwell air duct on the passenger's side **(see illustration 9.3b)**.
33 Reach up behind the heater blower motor and disconnect the wiring connector from the underside of the blower motor resistor **(see illustration)**.
34 Undo the retaining screw and unclip the resistor from the blower motor housing **(see illustrations)**.

9.28 Undo the three retaining screws, and withdraw the motor from the housing

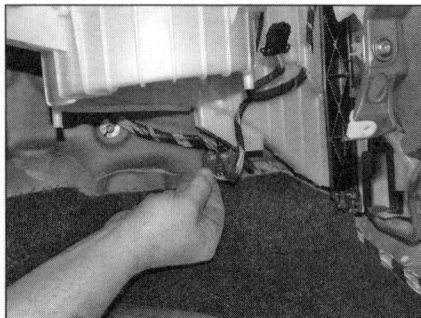

9.33 Disconnect the wiring connector from the underside of the blower motor resistor

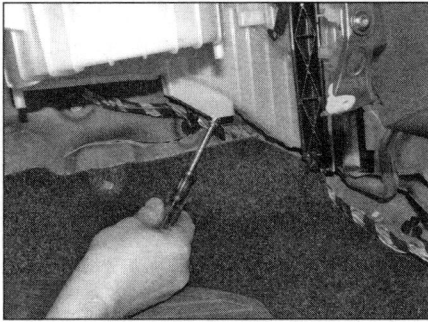

9.34a Undo the retaining screw...

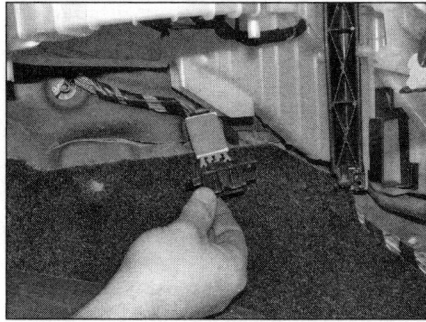

9.34b...and unclip the resistor from the blower motor housing

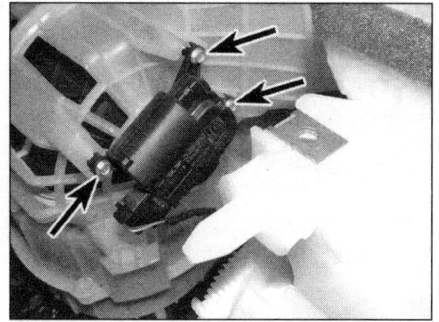

9.39 Mixed air valve servo motor retaining bolts

Refitting

35 Refitting is the reverse of removal.

Mixed air valve servo motor

Removal

36 Disconnect the battery negative terminal (refer to *Disconnecting the battery* in Chapter 5A, Section 4).
37 Remove the following components as described in Chapter 11 :
a) *Centre console.*
b) *Glovebox.*
c) *Footwell centre trim panel on the passenger's side.*
38 Extract the expanding rivet and remove the footwell air duct on the passenger's side **(see illustration 9.3b)**.
39 Disconnect the wiring connector, then undo the three bolts and remove the servo motor from the side of the air distribution housing **(see illustration)**.

Refitting

40 Refitting is the reverse of removal.

Recirculating air valve servo motor

Removal

41 Carry out the operations described previously in paragraphs 36 to 38.
42 Disconnect the wiring connector, then undo the three bolts and remove the recirculating air valve servo motor located above the heater matrix.

Refitting

43 Refitting is the reverse of removal.

Air distribution housing

Note: *On models with air conditioning, it is not possible to remove the air distribution housing without opening the refrigerant circuit (see Section 10 and Section 11). Have the refrigerant discharged at a dealer service department or an automotive air conditioning repair facility before proceeding.*

Removal

44 Remove the complete facia assembly and the facia crossmember as described in Chapter 11 Section 26.

45 Drain the cooling system as described in Chapter 1A, Section 27 or Chapter 1B, Section 28.
46 Working in the engine compartment, release the retaining clips, and disconnect both hoses from the heater matrix unions.
47 Disconnect the four wiring connectors, extract the five cable-ties or retaining clips and release the wiring harness from the air distribution housing.
48 On models with air conditioning, working in the engine compartment, undo the bolt securing the refrigerant pipe block connection to the expansion valve and withdraw the refrigerant pipes from the valve. Note that new seals for the refrigerant pipes will be required for refitting. Suitably plug or cover the disconnected pipes.
49 Cover the carpet directly underneath the air distribution housing, to catch any coolant which may be spilt from the matrix as the housing assembly is removed.
Note: *Keep the matrix unions uppermost as the housing is removed, to prevent coolant spillage. Mop-up any spilt coolant immediately, and wipe the affected area with a damp cloth to prevent staining.*
50 Working inside the vehicle withdraw the air distribution housing from the bulkhead.

Refitting

51 Refitting is the reverse of removal. On completion, refill the cooling system as described in Chapter 1A, Section 27 or Chapter 1B, Section 28. On models with air

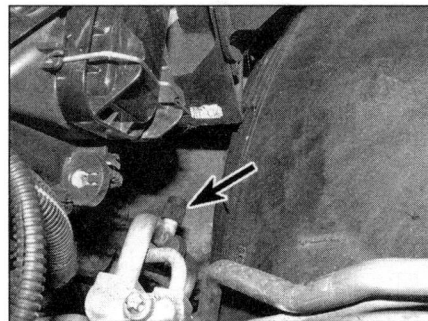

10.6a Air conditioning system low-pressure service port...

conditioning, have the system evacuated, charged and leak-tested by the specialist who discharged it.

10 Air conditioning system – general information and precautions

General information

1 Air conditioning is available on certain models. It enables the temperature of incoming air to be lowered, and also dehumidifies the air, which makes for rapid demisting and increased comfort.
2 The cooling side of the system works in the same way as a domestic refrigerator. Refrigerant gas is drawn into a belt-driven compressor, and passes into a condenser mounted in front of the radiator, where it loses heat and becomes liquid. The liquid passes through an expansion valve to an evaporator, where it changes from liquid under high pressure to gas under low pressure. This change is accompanied by a drop in temperature, which cools the evaporator. The refrigerant returns to the compressor, and the cycle begins again.
3 Air blown through the evaporator passes to the air distribution unit, where it is mixed with hot air blown through the heater matrix, to achieve the desired temperature in the passenger compartment.
4 The heating side of the system works in the same way as on models without air conditioning (see Section 8).
5 The operation of the system is controlled electronically. Any problems with the system should be referred to a Vauxhall/Opel dealer.

Air conditioning service ports

6 The low-pressure and high-pressure service ports are located in the engine compartment behind the right-hand headlight **(see illustrations)**. It may be necessary to remove the air cleaner inlet duct for improved access.

Precautions

7 It is necessary to observe special precautions whenever dealing with any part of the system, its associated components, and

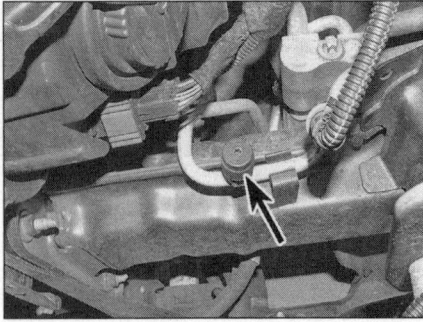

10.6b...and high-pressure service port

any items which necessitate disconnection of the system.

⚠️ **Warning: The refrigeration circuit contains a liquid refrigerant. This refrigerant is potentially dangerous, and should only be handled by qualified persons. If it is splashed onto the skin, it can cause frostbite. It is not itself poisonous, but in the presence of a naked flame it forms a poisonous gas; inhalation of the vapour through a lighted cigarette could prove fatal. Uncontrolled discharging of the refrigerant is dangerous, and potentially damaging to the environment. It is therefore dangerous to disconnect any part of the system without specialised knowledge and equipment. If for any reason the system must be disconnected, entrust this task to your Vauxhall/Opel dealer or air conditioning specialist.**

Caution: Do not operate the air conditioning system if it is known to be short of refrigerant, as this may damage the compressor.

11 Air conditioning system components – removal and refitting

⚠️ **Warning: The air conditioning system is under high pressure. Do not loosen any fittings or remove any components until**

after the system has been discharged. **Air conditioning refrigerant should be properly discharged into an approved type of container at a dealer service department or an automotive air conditioning repair facility capable of handling R134a refrigerant. Cap or plug the pipe lines as soon as they are disconnected, to prevent the entry of moisture. Always wear eye protection when disconnecting air conditioning system fittings.**

Note: *This Section refers to the components of the air conditioning system itself – refer to Section 9 for details of components common to the heating/ventilation system.*

Condenser

Petrol engines

1 Have the refrigerant discharged at a dealer service department or an automotive air conditioning repair facility.

2 Disconnect the battery negative terminal (refer to *Disconnecting the battery* in Chapter 5A, Section 4).

3 Firmly apply the handbrake, then jack up the front of the car and support it securely on axle stands (see *Jacking and vehicle support*).

4 Remove the front bumper as described in Chapter 11, Section 6.

5 With the system discharged, undo the retaining bolt and disconnect the refrigerant pipe connector block. Discard the O-ring seals – new ones must be used when refitting. Suitably cap the open fittings immediately to keep moisture and contamination out of the system.

6 Unclip the four mounting brackets and separate the condenser from the radiator. Lower the condenser out from under the vehicle and store it upright, to prevent fluid loss. Take care not to damage the condenser fins.

7 Refitting is the reverse of removal. Renew the O-rings and lubricate with refrigerant oil.

8 Have the system evacuated, charged and leak-tested by the specialist who discharged it.

Diesel engines

9 Have the refrigerant discharged at a dealer

service department or an automotive air conditioning repair facility.

10 Disconnect the battery negative terminal (refer to *Disconnecting the battery* in Chapter 5A, Section 4).

11 Firmly apply the handbrake, then jack up the front of the car and support it securely on axle stands (see *Jacking and vehicle support*).

12 Remove the front bumper as described in Chapter 11, Section 6.

13 With the system discharged, undo the retaining bolt and disconnect the refrigerant pipe connector block **(see illustration)**. Discard the O-ring seals – new ones must be used when refitting. Suitably cap the open fittings immediately to keep moisture and contamination out of the system.

14 Undo the two bolts securing the condenser to the radiator **(see illustration)**. Release the condenser from its mounting bracket, lower it out from under the vehicle and store it upright, to prevent fluid loss. Take care not to damage the condenser fins.

15 Refitting is the reverse of removal. Renew the O-rings and lubricate with refrigerant oil.

16 Have the system evacuated, charged and leak-tested by the specialist who discharged it.

Evaporator

17 Have the refrigerant discharged at a dealer service department or an automotive air conditioning repair facility.

18 Remove the air distribution housing as described in Section 9.

19 Undo the two screws and remove the clamps securing the coolant pipes to the heater matrix. Undo the guide plate retaining bolt and remove the heater pipes.

20 Undo the two bolts, release the two clips and open the air distribution housing.

21 Unscrew the two bolts and remove the expansion valve.

22 Lift the evaporator upward and remove it from the air distribution housing.

23 Refitting is the reverse of removal ensuring that all disturbed seals are renewed.

24 Have the system evacuated, charged and leak-tested by the specialist who discharged it.

Compressor

25 Have the refrigerant discharged at a dealer service department or an automotive air conditioning repair facility.

26 Disconnect the battery negative terminal (refer to *Disconnecting the battery* in Chapter 5A, Section 4).

27 Firmly apply the handbrake, then jack up the front of the car and support it securely on axle stands (see *Jacking and vehicle support*).

28 Release the auxiliary drivebelt from the pulleys as described in Chapter 1A, Section 32 or Chapter 1B, Section 31.

29 With the system discharged, undo the retaining bolt and disconnect the refrigerant pipes from the compressor. Discard the O-ring seals – new ones must be used when refitting.

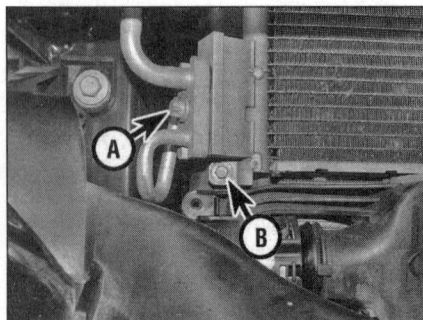

11.13 Refrigerant pipe connector block retaining bolt (A) and condenser right-hand mounting bolt (B)

11.14 Condenser left-hand mounting bolt

Suitably cap the open fittings immediately to keep moisture and contamination out of the system.

30 Disconnect the compressor wiring connector.

31 Unbolt the compressor from the cylinder block/crankcase, then withdraw the compressor downwards from under the vehicle **(see illustration)**.

32 Refit the compressor in the reverse order of removal; renew all seals disturbed.

33 If you are installing a new compressor, refer to the compressor manufacturer's instructions for adding refrigerant oil to the system.

34 Have the system evacuated, charged and leak-tested by the specialist that discharged it.

35 After installing a new compressor, always observe the following running-in procedure:

a) *Open all instrument panel air outlet flaps.*

b) *Start vehicle engine and stabilise idle speed for approximately 5 seconds.*

c) *Switch fan to maximum speed.*

d) *Switch on the air conditioning and let it run for at least 2 minutes without interruption at engine speed under 1500 rpm.*

11.31 Compressor mounting bolts

Chapter 4 Part A
Fuel and exhaust systems – petrol engines

Contents

Degrees of difficulty

Easy, suitable for novice with little experience	Fairly easy, suitable for beginner with some experience	Fairly difficult, suitable for competent DIY mechanic	Difficult, suitable for experienced DIY mechanic	Very difficult, suitable for expert DIY or professional

Specifications

General
System type . . . .   GMPT-E83 sequential multi-point fuel injection

Fuel pump
Type . . . .   Electric, mounted in fuel tank

Fuel injection system data
System pressure. . . . .   3.8 bar
Idle speed. . . . .   Not adjustable – controlled by ECU
Idle mixture CO content . . . .   Not adjustable – controlled by ECU

Torque wrench settings	Nm	lbf ft
Camshaft position sensor bolt(s)	6	4
Catalytic converter support bracket nuts/bolts:		
1.0 litre engines	22	16
1.2 and 1.4 litre engines	10	7
Crankshaft speed/position sensor bolt	8	6
Exhaust front pipe to catalytic converter*	25	18
Exhaust manifold securing nuts*:		
1.0 litre engines:		
With cast iron manifold.	20	15
With sheet metal manifold	15	11
1.2 and 1.4 litre engines	22	16
Front subframe cross-brace bolts	60	44
Fuel tank	20	15
Inlet manifold securing nuts:		
1.0 litre engines	10	7
1.2 and 1.4 litre engines	20	15
Knock sensor	20	15
Throttle housing bolts.	8	6

Use new fasteners

1 General information and precautions

General information

1 The fuel supply system consists of a fuel tank (which is mounted under the rear of the car, with an electric fuel pump immersed in it) and fuel feed lines. The fuel pump supplies fuel to the fuel rail, which acts as a reservoir for the fuel injectors which inject fuel into the inlet tracts. The fuel pressure regulator is located on the fuel pump module in the fuel tank.

2 The electronic control unit controls both the fuel injection system and the ignition system, integrating the two into a complete engine management system. Refer to Section 8 for further information on the operation of the fuel system and to Chapter 5B for details of the ignition side of the system.

3 All engines utilise a 'Twinport' inlet manifold configuration. Vacuum operated flap valves located in the inlet manifold are opened or closed according to engine operating conditions to create a variable venturi manifold arrangement. This layout has significant advantages in terms of engine power, fuel economy and reduced exhaust emissions.

4 The exhaust manifold incorporates an integral catalytic converter to reduce harmful exhaust gas emissions. The remaining exhaust system is in two sections. Further details can be found in Chapter 4C, along with details of the other emission control systems and components.

Precautions

5 Refer to Chapter 4C, Section 4 for general information and precautions relating to the catalytic converter.

Before disconnecting any fuel lines, or working on any part of the fuel system, the system must be depressurised as described in Section 4.

Care must be taken when disconnecting the fuel lines. When disconnecting a fuel union or hose, loosen the union or clamp screw slowly, to avoid sudden uncontrolled fuel spillage. Take adequate fire precautions.

When working on fuel system components, scrupulous cleanliness must be observed, and care must be taken not to introduce any foreign matter into fuel lines or components.

After carrying out any work involving disconnection of fuel lines, it is advisable to check the connections for leaks; pressurise the system by switching the ignition on and off several times.

Electronic control units are very sensitive components, and certain precautions must be taken to avoid damage to these units as follows:

a) When carrying out welding operations on the vehicle using electric welding equipment, the battery and alternator should be disconnected.

b) Although the underbonnet-mounted control units will tolerate normal underbonnet conditions, they can be adversely affected by excess heat or

moisture. If using welding equipment or pressure-washing equipment in the vicinity of an electronic control unit, take care not to direct heat, or jets of water or steam, at the unit. If this cannot be avoided, remove the control unit from the vehicle, and protect its wiring plug with a plastic bag.

c) Before disconnecting any wiring, or removing components, always ensure that the ignition is switched off.

d) Do not attempt to improvise fault diagnosis procedures using a test light or multimeter, as irreparable damage could be caused to the control unit.

e) After working on fuel injection/engine management system components, ensure that all wiring is correctly reconnected before reconnecting the battery or switching on the ignition.

6 Many of the procedures in this Chapter require the disconnection of fuel line connections, and the removal of components, which may result in some fuel spillage. Before carrying out any operation on the fuel system, refer to the precautions given in *Safety first!*, and follow them implicitly. Petrol is a highly-dangerous and volatile liquid, and the precautions necessary when handling it cannot be overstressed.

2 Air cleaner assembly – removal and refitting

Removal

1 Disconnect the wiring connector from the inlet air temperature sensor, then release the wiring harness from the air cleaner body **(see illustrations)**.

2 Slacken the retaining clamp securing the inlet air temperature sensor housing to the air cleaner lid **(see illustration)**.

3 Undo the screws securing the air cleaner lid to the air cleaner housing.

4 Lift off the air cleaner lid and detach it from the inlet air temperature sensor housing **(see illustration)**.

5 Remove the air cleaner element from the housing **(see illustration)**.

6 Disconnect the air inlet duct from the front of the air cleaner housing.

2.1a Disconnect the wiring connector from the inlet air temperature sensor...

2.1b...then release the wiring harness clip from the air cleaner body

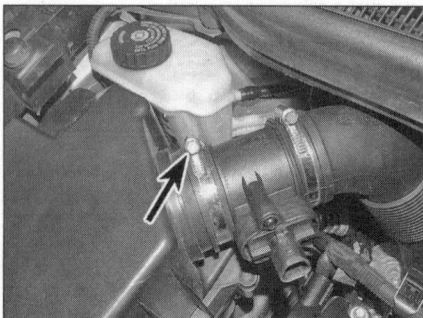

2.2 Slacken the inlet air temperature sensor housing retaining clamp

2.4 Lift off the air cleaner lid

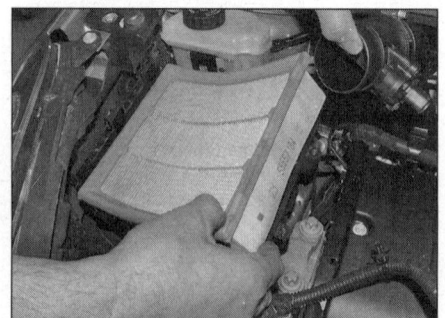

2.5 Lift the air cleaner element out of the housing

2.7 Lift the air cleaner housing upward and inward to free it from the mounting rubbers

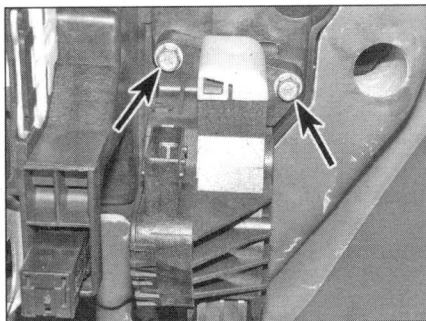
2.8a Undo the resonator retaining bolt...

2.8b...and lift the resonator out of the engine compartment

7 Lift the air cleaner housing upward and inwards to free it from the mounting rubbers, and withdraw the assembly from the engine compartment **(see illustration)**.

8 If necessary, the air intake pipe (resonator) can be removed from the front body panel after unscrewing the retaining bolt **(see illustrations)**.

9 If necessary the throttle housing inlet duct can be removed after slackening the clamp securing it to the throttle housing.

Refitting

10 Refitting is a reversal of removal.

3 Accelerator pedal position sensor – removal and refitting

Removal

1 Disconnect the battery negative terminal (as described in *Disconnecting the battery* in Chapter 5A, Section 4).
2 Remove the driver's side lower trim panel as described in Chapter 11, Section 26.
3 Working in the driver's footwell, remove the plastic expanding rivet and remove the footwell air duct **(see illustration)**.
4 Disconnect the wiring connector from the top of the accelerator pedal position sensor **(see illustration)**.
5 Unscrew the two mounting bolts, and withdraw the sensor from the bulkhead **(see illustration)**.

Refitting

6 Refitting is a reversal of removal.

4 Fuel system – depressurising

⚠ *Warning: The fuel system is pressurised all the time the ignition is switched on, and a high pressure will remain in the system even 20 minutes after switching off. It is therefore essential to depressurise the system before disconnecting fuel lines, or carrying out any work on the fuel system components. Failure to do this before carrying out work may result in a sudden release of pressure which may cause fuel spray – this constitutes a fire hazard, and a health risk. Note that, even when the system has been depressurised, fuel will still be present in the system fuel lines and components, and adequate precautions should still be taken when carrying out work.*

1 The fuel system referred to in this Section is defined as the tank-mounted fuel pump and pressure regulator, the fuel injectors, the fuel rail, and the metal pipes and flexible hoses of the fuel lines between these components. All these contain fuel which will be under pressure while the engine is running, and/or while the ignition is switched on. High pressure will remain for at least 20 minutes after the ignition has been switched off, and must be relieved in a controlled fashion when any of these components are disturbed for servicing work.
2 Unscrew the cap from the fuel pressure testing point valve on the top right-hand side of the fuel rail and position a container beneath the valve **(see illustrations)**.

3.3 Remove the plastic expanding rivet and remove the footwell air duct

3.4 Disconnect the wiring connector from the accelerator pedal position sensor

3.5 Unscrew the two mounting bolts, and withdraw the sensor from the bulkhead

4.2a Fuel pressure connection valve on the fuel rail on 1.0 litre engines...

4.2b...and on 1.2 and 1.4 litre engines

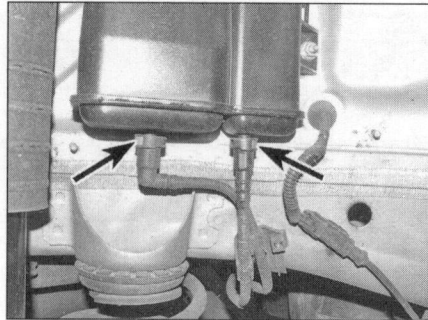
5.6 Disconnect the two vent hoses at the quick-release connectors

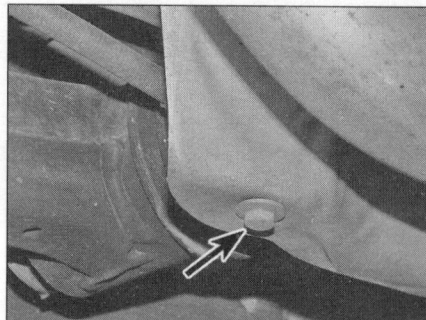
5.10a Undo the bolt...

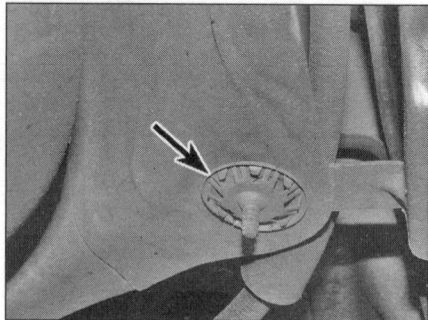
5.10b...the sheet metal nut...

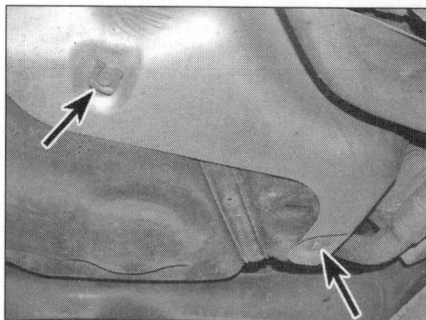
5.10c...and two clamps and remove the fuel tank heat shield

3 Hold a wad of rag over the valve and relieve the pressure in the fuel system by depressing the valve core with a suitable screwdriver. Be prepared for the squirt of fuel as the valve core is depressed and catch it with the rag.

Hold the valve core down until no more fuel is expelled from the valve.
4 Once all pressure is relieved, refit the valve cap and dispose of the expelled fuel and the rag safely.

5.12 Disconnect the fuel pump and fuel gauge sender unit wiring at the underbody connector

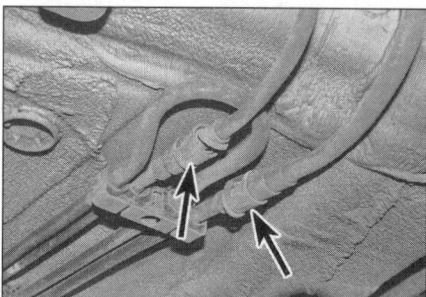
5.13 Disconnect the fuel feed line and the evaporative vent line at the quick-release connectors on the underbody

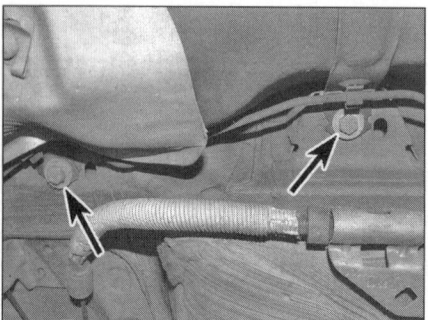
5.15a Fuel tank securing strap front retaining bolts...

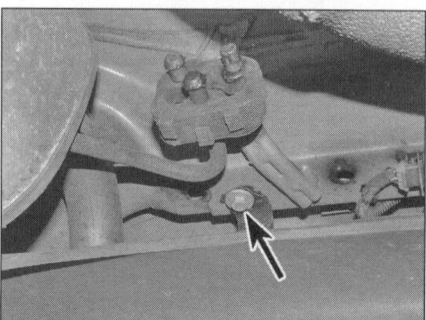
5.15b...left-hand rear retaining bolt...

5 Fuel tank – removal and refitting

⚠️ **Warning: Refer to the precautions in Section 1 before proceeding. Since a fuel tank drain plug is not provided, it is preferable to carry out this work when the tank is nearly empty.**

Removal

1 Disconnect the battery negative terminal (refer to *Disconnecting the battery* in Chapter 5A, Section 4).
2 Depressurise the fuel system (see Section 4).
3 Hand-pump any remaining fuel in the tank out through the filler pipe into a clean metal container which can be sealed.
4 Chock the front wheels then jack up the rear of the vehicle and support on axle stands (see *Jacking and vehicle support*). Remove both rear wheels.
5 Unscrew the five nuts and two bolts and remove the right-hand rear wheel arch liner for access to the charcoal canister.
6 Disconnect the two vent hoses at the quick-release connectors on the charcoal canister **(see illustration)**. A Vauxhall/Opel special tool is available to release the connectors, but provided care is taken, the connectors can be released using a pair of long-nosed pliers, or a similar tool, to depress the retaining tangs. Suitably seal the vent hoses and canister unions to prevent dirt ingress.
7 Release the two disconnected vent hoses from the retaining bracket located below the charcoal canister.
8 Position a suitable container beneath the fuel filler hose connection on the fuel tank. Loosen the retaining clip and disconnect the filler hose from the tank. Be prepared for some loss of fuel.
9 Disconnect the rear of the exhaust system from its rubber mountings, and lower the system, then move it to one side sufficiently to enable removal of the fuel tank. Alternatively, remove the exhaust system completely to provide greater clearance (refer to Section 13).
10 Undo the bolt, sheet metal nut and two clamps, and remove the heat shield from the base of the fuel tank **(see illustrations)**.
11 Unclip the brake hydraulic pipes from the brackets on the fuel tank and tank retaining straps.
12 Disconnect the fuel pump and fuel gauge sender unit wiring at the connector on the underbody **(see illustration)**.
13 Disconnect the fuel feed line and the evaporative vent line at the quick-release connectors on the underbody, then release the feed line and vent line from the clips on the fuel tank bracket **(see illustration)**. Suitably seal the fuel and vent lines to prevent dirt ingress.
14 Support the weight of the fuel tank on a jack with interposed block of wood.
15 Unbolt and remove the two securing straps from the fuel tank **(see illustrations)**.

16 Lower the tank sufficiently to enable access to the remaining fuel and vent hoses on the tank, then disconnect them. Be prepared for some loss of fuel.

17 Continue to lower the tank, guiding the fuel and vent hoses over the handbrake cables, until it can be removed from under the vehicle.

18 Plug or clamp the fuel and vent hoses to prevent entry of dust and dirt.

19 If necessary, remove the fuel lines, hoses and wiring from the tank for transfer to the new tank.

20 If the tank contains sediment or water, it may cleaned out with two or three rinses of clean fuel. Remove the fuel tank module as described in Section 6. Shake the tank vigorously, and change the fuel as necessary to remove all contamination from the tank.

> **Warning: This procedure should be carried out in a well-ventilated area, and it is vital to take adequate fire precautions.**

21 Any repairs to the fuel tank should be carried out by a professional. Do not under any circumstances attempt any form of DIY repair to a fuel tank.

Refitting

22 Refitting is a reversal of removal, bearing in mind the following points:
a) Ensure that all hoses are securely reconnected to their correct locations.
b) On completion, fill the fuel tank, then run the engine and check for leaks. If leakage is evident, stop the engine immediately and rectify the problem without delay.

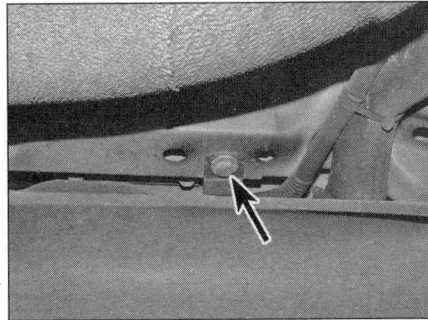
5.15c...and right-hand rear retaining bolt

6 Fuel gauge sender unit – removal and refitting

Note: Refer to the precautions given in Section 1 before proceeding.
Note: The fuel tank should be as empty as possible when carrying out this procedure.

Removal

1 Disconnect the battery negative terminal (refer to Disconnecting the battery in Chapter 5A, Section 4).

2 Depressurise the fuel system as described in Section 4.

3 Hand-pump any remaining fuel in the tank out through the filler pipe into a clean metal container which can be sealed.

4 Remove the rear seat cushion as described in Chapter 11, Section 21.

5 Fold up the acoustic insulation, then, using a screwdriver, carefully lever out the plastic cover to expose the tank module cover (see illustration).

6 Disconnect the main wiring plug from the cover (see illustration).

7 Disconnect the fuel feed hose at the quick-release fitting (see illustration). Be prepared for some loss of fuel. A Vauxhall/Opel special tool is available to release the fuel hose fitting, but provided care is taken, the fitting can be released using a pair of long-nosed pliers, or a similar tool, to depress the retaining tangs. Clamp or plug the open end of the hose and the fuel pump union, to prevent dirt ingress and further fuel spillage.

8 Using a suitable pen, mark the position of the tank module cover locking ring on the fuel tank and locking ring, then release the locking ring. A special tool (Vauxhall/Opel tool CH-48378) is available for this, but suitable alternatives are readily available (see illustration).

9 Remove the locking ring, then carefully lift out the tank module (see illustrations).

10 Collect the O-ring seal from the top of the fuel tank (see illustration). It is advisable to temporarily refit the tank module cover locking ring to the tank until the module is ready for refitting. This will prevent any possibility of the tank distorting (a common problem) which would prevent the locking ring from being correctly refitted.

6.5 Carefully prise the plastic access cover from the floor

6.6 Disconnect the wiring connector from the tank module cover

6.7 Disconnect the fuel feed hose at the quick-release fitting

6.8 Using the Vauxhall/Opel special tool, or commercially available alternative, unscrew the tank module cover locking ring

6.9a Remove the locking ring...

6.9b...then carefully lift out the tank module

11 Press the fuel gauge sender unit inwards slightly to release the retaining tags, then lift the sender upwards and out of the tank module **(see illustrations)**.

12 Suitably identify the sender unit wiring orientation to aid refitting. Using an electrician's screwdriver or similar tool, press the tab on the end of each wire and carefully pull the wires free **(see illustration)**. Note that on some versions, the sender unit wiring is disconnected at the wiring connector on the underside of the module cover.

Refitting

13 Refitting is a reversal of removal, bearing in mind the following points:

a) Ensure that the sender unit engages correctly with the clips on the tank module

b) Check the condition of the tank module cover sealing ring and renew if necessary.

c) Ensure that the arrow on the edge of the tank module cover points toward the mark on the fuel tank when refitting.

d) Tighten the locking ring to its original position as marked during removal. When tightening the locking ring, press down on the tank module cover and ensure it doesn't rotate.

7 Fuel pump – removal and refitting

1 The fuel pump is located in the tank module in the fuel tank. The removal and refitting procedures are the same as for the fuel gauge sender unit described in Section 6. The pump is integral with the tank module and cannot be renewed separately.

8 Fuel Injection system – general information

1 The fuel injection system is integrated with the emissions control system and ignition system to form a combined engine management system under the control of one electronic control unit (ECU).

2 All the systems operate in a similar manner and comply with the latest emission control standards. The fuel injection side of the systems operate as follows. Refer to Chapter 4C for information on the emissions control systems, and to Chapter 5B for information on the ignition system.

3 Fuel is supplied from the rear-mounted tank, via a pressure regulator to the fuel rail. The fuel rail acts as a reservoir for the fuel injectors, which inject fuel into the cylinder inlet tracts, upstream of the inlet valves. The systems are of the 'sequential' injection type, which means that each of the fuel injectors is triggered individually, just before the inlet valve on the relevant cylinder opens.

4 The duration of the electrical pulses to the fuel injectors determines the quantity of fuel injected. The pulse duration is computed by the ECU on the basis of information received from the following sensors:

a) Accelerator pedal position sensor – informs the ECU of accelerator pedal position, and the rate of throttle opening/closing.

b) Throttle potentiometer (integral with the throttle housing) – informs the ECU of the throttle position, and confirms the signals received from the accelerator pedal position sensor.

c) Coolant temperature sensor – informs the ECU of engine temperature.

d) Airflow meter (with inlet air temperature sensor) – informs the ECU of the temperature and amount of air passing from the air cleaner to the throttle housing.

e) Oxygen sensors (two) – inform the ECU of the oxygen content of the exhaust gases (explained in greater detail in Chapter 4C).

f) Manifold pressure sensor – informs the ECU of the engine load by monitoring the pressure in the inlet manifold.

g) Crankshaft speed/position sensor – informs the ECU of the crankshaft speed and position.

h) Camshaft sensor(s) – inform the ECU of speed and position of the camshaft).

i) Knock sensor – informs the ECU when pre-ignition ('pinking') is occurring.

j) ABS control unit – informs the ECU of the vehicle speed, based on wheel speed sensor signals (explained in greater detail in Chapter 9).

5 The signals from the various sensors are processed by the ECU, and the optimum fuelling and ignition settings are selected for the prevailing engine operating conditions.

6 Idle speed and throttle position is controlled by the throttle valve control motor, which is an integral part of the throttle housing. The motor is controlled by the ECU, in conjunction with signals received from the accelerator pedal position sensor.

7 A catalytic converter is incorporated in the exhaust manifold, to reduce harmful exhaust gas emissions. Details of this and other emissions control system equipment are given in Chapter 4C.

8 If certain sensors fail, and send abnormal signals to the ECU, the ECU has a back-up programme. In this event, the abnormal signals are ignored, and a pre-programmed value is substituted for the sensor signal, allowing the engine to continue running, albeit at reduced efficiency. If the ECU enters its back-up mode, a warning light on the instrument panel will illuminate, and a fault code will be stored in the ECU memory. This fault code can be read using suitable specialist test equipment.

9 Fuel injection system components – testing

1 If a fault appears in the engine management system, first ensure that all the system wiring connectors are securely connected and free of corrosion. Ensure that the fault is not due to poor maintenance; ie, check that the air

6.10 Collect the O-ring seal from the top of the fuel tank

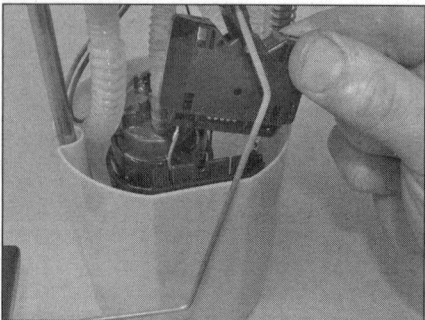

6.11a Press the fuel gauge sender unit inwards slightly to release the retaining tags...

6.11b...then lift the sender upwards and out of the tank module

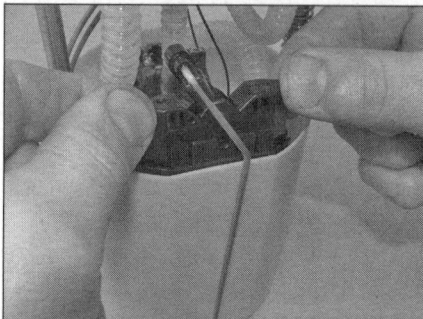

6.12 Press the tab on the end of each wire and carefully pull the sender unit wires free

cleaner filter element is clean, the spark plugs are in good condition and correctly gapped, the cylinder compression pressures are correct and that the engine breather hoses are clear and undamaged, referring to Chapters 1A, 2A, 2B and 4C for further information.

2 If these checks fail to reveal the cause of the problem, the vehicle should be taken to a suitably-equipped Vauxhall/Opel dealer or engine management diagnostic specialist for testing. Using a fault code reader or similar diagnostic equipment, the engine management ECU can be interrogated, and any stored fault codes can be retrieved. Live data can also be captured from the various system sensors and actuators, indicating their operating parameters. This will allow the fault to be quickly and simply traced, alleviating the need to test all the system components individually, which is a time-consuming operation that carries a risk of damaging the ECU.

10 Fuel injection system components – removal and refitting

1.0 litre engines

Throttle housing

1 Disconnect the battery negative terminal (refer to *Disconnecting the battery* in Chapter 5A, Section 4).
2 Remove the air cleaner assembly and intake ducts as described in Section 2.
3 Disconnect the wiring connector from the throttle housing (see illustration).
4 Partially drain the cooling system as described in Chapter 1A, Section 27 (drain sufficient coolant to empty the coolant expansion tank).
5 Release the retaining clips and disconnect the two coolant hoses from the rear of the throttle housing.
6 Undo the four bolts and lift the throttle housing off the inlet manifold (see illustration). Recover the gasket.
7 It is not possible to obtain the throttle valve control motor or throttle valve position sensor separately, so if either is faulty, the complete throttle housing must be renewed.

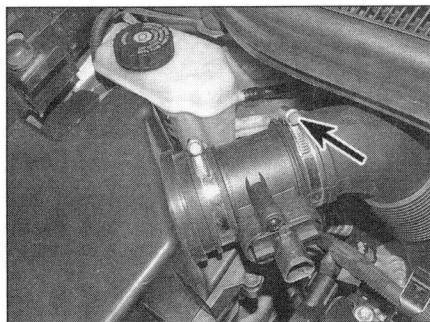

10.3 Disconnect the wiring connector from the throttle housing

8 Refitting is a reversal of removal, but thoroughly clean the mating faces and use a new gasket. Tighten the bolts progressively to the specified torque. Top-up the coolant level as described in *Weekly checks*. Finally, switch on the ignition for 30 seconds without starting the engine to allow ECU matching.

Airflow meter

9 Disconnect the wiring connector from the inlet air temperature sensor located in the airflow meter.
10 Slacken the hose clamp and disconnect the inlet air duct from the airflow meter (see illustration).
11 Slacken the remaining hose clamp and detach the airflow meter from the air cleaner lid.
12 Refitting is a reversal of removal.

Fuel injectors and fuel rail

Note: *Refer to the precautions given in Section 1 before proceeding. The seals at both ends of the fuel injectors must be renewed on refitting.*

13 Disconnect the battery negative terminal (refer to *Disconnecting the battery* in Chapter 5A, Section 4).
14 Depressurise the fuel system as described in Section 4.
15 Remove the throttle housing as described previously in this Section, however, it is not necessary to drain the cooling system, as the housing can be placed to one side with the hoses still attached.
16 Loosen the clip and disconnect the engine breather hose from the camshaft cover.

10.6 Throttle housing retaining bolts

17 If not already done, undo the two screws and remove the cover over the fuel rail.
18 Disconnect the wiring connector from each fuel injector (see illustration).
19 Disconnect the fuel feed hose quick-release connector at the fuel rail. Be prepared for some loss of fuel. A Vauxhall/Opel special tool is available to release the connector, but provided care is taken, it can be released using a pair of long-nosed pliers, or a similar tool, to depress the retaining tangs. Clamp or plug the open end of the hose, to prevent dirt ingress and further fuel spillage.
20 Unscrew the mounting bolts, then lift the fuel rail complete with the injectors off of the inlet manifold.
21 To remove an injector from the fuel rail, prise out the metal securing clip using a screwdriver or a pair of pliers, and pull the injector from the fuel rail. Remove and discard the injector sealing rings; new ones must be fitted on refitting.
22 Overhaul of the fuel injectors is not possible, as no spares are available. If faulty, an injector must be renewed.
23 Before refitting, clean thoroughly the mating surfaces of the throttle housing and inlet manifold.
24 Commence refitting by fitting new O-ring seals to both ends of the fuel injectors (see illustration). Coat the seals with a thin layer of petroleum jelly before fitting.
25 Refitting is a reversal of removal, bearing in mind the following points:
a) *When refitting the injectors to the fuel rail, note that the groove in the metal securing*

10.10 Slacken the hose clamp and disconnect the inlet air duct

10.18 Fuel injector wiring connectors

10.24 Fit new O-rings to the fuel injectors before refitting

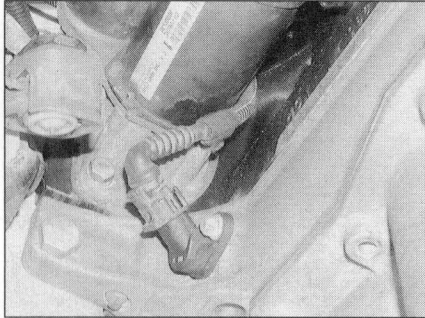

10.26 Crankshaft speed/position sensor location

clip must engage with the lug on the injector body.

b) Make sure that the quick-release connector audibly engages on the fuel rail.

c) Refit the throttle housing as described previously in this Section.

d) Ensure that all wiring connectors are securely reconnected, and that the wiring is secured in the relevant clips and brackets.

Crankshaft speed/position sensor

Note: A new O-ring seal must be used on refitting.

26 The crankshaft speed/position sensor is located at the rear left-hand end of the cylinder block baseplate, below the starter motor **(see illustration)**.

27 Apply the handbrake, then jack up the front of the vehicle and support it on axle stands (see Jacking and vehicle support).

28 Disconnect the sensor wiring connector, then undo the retaining bolt and withdraw the sensor from the cylinder block baseplate.

29 Refitting is a reversal of removal, but ensure that the mating surfaces of the sensor and baseplate are clean and fit a new O-ring seal to the sensor before refitting. Tighten the bolt to the specified torque.

Camshaft position sensor

30 The camshaft position sensor is located on the timing cover, on the inlet camshaft side.

31 Disconnect the sensor wiring connector.

32 Undo the retaining bolt and withdraw the sensor from the timing cover.

10.61 Throttle housing retaining bolts

33 Refitting is a reversal of removal, but ensure that the mating surfaces of the sensor and timing cover are clean before fitting.

Coolant temperature sensor

34 The coolant temperature sensor is located in the top of the coolant pump housing.

35 Removal and refitting procedures are given in Chapter 3, Section 6.

Knock sensor

36 The knock sensor is located on the rear of the cylinder block, just above the starter motor.

37 Disconnect the battery negative terminal (refer to Disconnecting the battery in Chapter 5A, Section 4).

38 Apply the handbrake, then jack up the front of the vehicle and support it on axle stands (see Jacking and vehicle support).

39 On the left-hand side of the engine, disconnect the wiring connectors for the engine electronic control unit by releasing them in the direction of the arrow marked on the connector.

40 Unscrew the bolt securing the earth wire to the cylinder head, then unbolt and remove the electronic control unit.

41 Reach up behind the engine and disconnect the wiring from the knock sensor.

42 Note its position, then unscrew the bolt and remove the knock sensor from the block.

43 Clean the contact surfaces of the sensor and block. Also clean the threads of the sensor mounting bolt.

44 Locate the sensor on the block and insert the mounting bolt. Position the sensor as previously noted, then tighten the bolt to the specified torque. Note that the torque setting is critical for the sensor to function correctly.

45 Reconnect the wiring, then refit the engine control unit together with its wiring and earth wire.

46 Lower the vehicle to the ground and reconnect the battery.

Manifold pressure sensor

47 The manifold pressure sensor is located on the inlet manifold at the rear of the engine.

48 Disconnect the battery negative terminal (refer to Disconnecting the battery in Chapter 5A, Section 4).

49 Disconnect the sensor wiring plug.

50 Unscrew the bolt and remove the sensor from the manifold. Recover the sealing ring.

51 Refitting is a reversal of removal, but use a new sealing ring, and tighten the retaining bolt securely.

Electronic control unit (ECU)

Note: If a new ECU is to be fitted, this work must be entrusted to a Vauxhall/Opel dealer or suitably-equipped specialist as it is necessary to program the new ECU after installation. This work requires the use of dedicated Vauxhall/Opel diagnostic equipment or a compatible alternative.

52 The engine management electronic control unit is located on the rear, left-hand side of the engine.

53 Disconnect the battery negative terminal (refer to Disconnecting the battery in Chapter 5A, Section 4).

54 Disconnect the wiring connectors for the electronic control unit by releasing them in the direction of the arrow marked on the connector.

55 Where fitted, unscrew the bolt securing the earth wire to the cylinder head, then release the retaining tabs and lift the control unit from the mounting bracket.

56 Refitting is a reversal of removal.

Oxygen sensors

57 Refer to Chapter 4C, Section 2 for removal and refitting details.

1.2 and 1.4 litre engines

Throttle housing

58 Disconnect the battery negative terminal (refer to Disconnecting the battery in Chapter 5A, Section 4).

59 Remove the throttle housing intake duct as described in Section 2.

60 Disconnect the wiring connector from the throttle housing and release the wiring from the retaining clip.

61 Undo the four bolts and lift the throttle housing off the inlet manifold **(see illustration)**. Recover the O-ring seal.

62 It is not possible to obtain the throttle valve control motor or throttle valve position sensor separately, so if either is faulty, the complete throttle housing must be renewed.

63 Refitting is a reversal of removal but thoroughly clean the mating surfaces and use a new O-ring seal. Tighten the bolts progressively and securely.

Airflow meter

64 Disconnect the wiring connector from the airflow meter.

65 Slacken the hose clamp and disconnect the inlet air duct from the airflow meter **(see illustration 10.10)**.

66 Slacken the remaining hose clamp and detach the airflow meter from the air cleaner lid.

67 Refitting is a reversal of removal.

Fuel injectors and fuel rail

Note: Refer to the precautions given in Section 1 before proceeding. The seals at both ends of the fuel injectors must be renewed on refitting.

68 Disconnect the battery negative terminal (refer to Disconnecting the battery in Chapter 5A, Section 4).

69 Remove the plastic cover over the top of the engine **(see illustrations)**.

70 Depressurise the fuel system as described in Section 4.

71 Undo the two screws and remove the cover over the fuel rail.

72 Disconnect the fuel feed hose quick-release connector at the fuel rail **(see**

10.69a Using a plastic spatula or similar tool, release the retaining tabs...

10.69b...and remove the plastic cover over the top of the engine

10.72 Disconnect the fuel feed hose quick-release connector at the fuel rail

illustration). Be prepared for some loss of fuel. Clamp or plug the open end of the hose, to prevent dirt ingress and further fuel spillage.
73 Release the wiring harness from the retaining clips on the camshaft cover and fuel rail (see illustration).
74 Disconnect the wiring connectors from the fuel injectors and move the wiring harness clear of the fuel rail.
75 Unscrew the two mounting bolts, then lift the fuel rail complete with the injectors off of the inlet manifold (see illustration).
76 To remove an injector from the fuel rail, prise out the metal securing clip using a screwdriver or a pair of pliers, and pull the injector from the fuel rail (see illustrations). Remove and discard the injector sealing rings; new ones must be fitted on refitting.

77 Overhaul of the fuel injectors is not possible, as no spares are available. If faulty, an injector must be renewed.
78 Commence refitting by fitting new O-ring seals to both ends of the fuel injectors (see illustrations). Coat the seals with a thin layer of petroleum jelly before fitting.
79 Refitting is a reversal of removal, bearing in mind the following points:
a) When refitting the injectors to the fuel rail, note that the groove in the metal securing clip must engage with the lug on the injector body.
b) Make sure that the fuel hose quick-release connector(s) audibly engages on the fuel rail.
c) Ensure that all wiring connectors are securely reconnected, and that the

wiring is secured in the relevant clips and brackets.

Crankshaft speed/position sensor

Note: A new O-ring seal must be used on refitting.
80 The crankshaft speed/position sensor is located at the rear left-hand end of the cylinder block baseplate, below the starter motor (see illustration).
81 Apply the handbrake, then jack up the front of the vehicle and support it on axle stands (see Jacking and vehicle support).
82 Disconnect the sensor wiring connector, then undo the retaining bolt and withdraw the sensor from the cylinder block baseplate.
83 Refitting is a reversal of removal, but ensure that the mating surfaces of the sensor

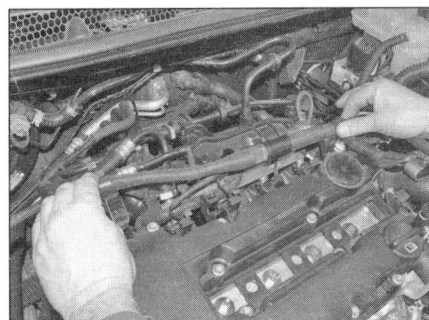

10.73 Release the wiring harness from the retaining clips on the camshaft cover and fuel rail

10.75 Unscrew the two mounting bolts, then lift the fuel rail complete with injectors off of the inlet manifold

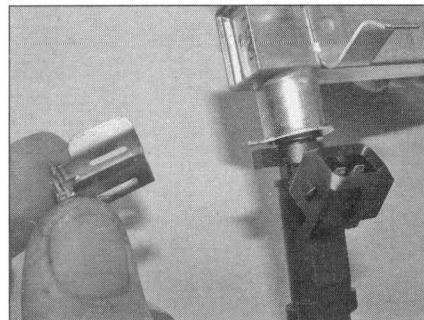

10.76a Remove the metal securing clip...

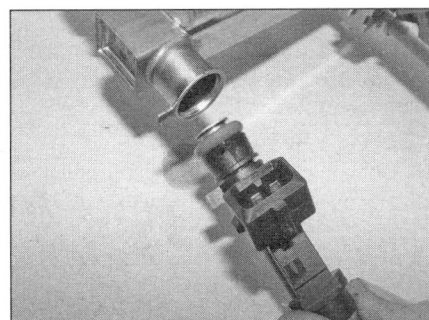

10.76b...and pull the injector from the fuel rail

10.78a Fit a new O-ring seal to the upper end...

10.78b...and lower end of each injector

10.80 Crankshaft speed/position sensor location

10.84 Inlet camshaft position sensor location

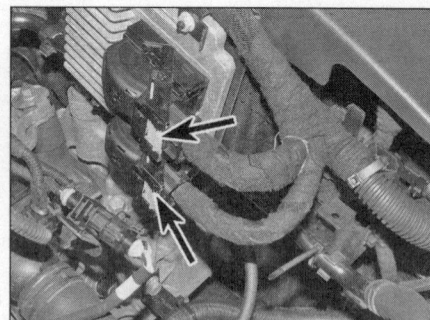

10.108 Lift up the locking bars and disconnect the two ECU wiring connectors

and baseplate are clean and fit a new O-ring seal to the sensor before refitting. Tighten the bolt to the specified torque.

Camshaft position sensor

84 Two sensors are fitted, one for each camshaft. Both sensors are located at the right-hand end of the cylinder head **(see illustration)**.
85 Disconnect the wiring connector from the relevant sensor.
86 Undo the retaining bolt and remove the sensor from the cylinder head.
87 Refitting is a reversal of removal, tightening the sensor retaining bolt to the specified torque.

Coolant temperature sensor

88 The coolant temperature sensor is located in the top of the coolant pump housing.
89 Removal and refitting procedures are given in Chapter 3, Section 6.

Manifold absolute pressure sensor

90 The manifold absolute pressure sensor is located on the left-hand side of the inlet manifold.
91 Disconnect the wiring connector, then undo the retaining bolt and remove the sensor from the inlet manifold.
92 Refit the sensor to the manifold, then refit the retaining bolt and tighten it securely.
93 Reconnect the sensor wiring connector.

Knock sensor

94 The knock sensor is located on the rear of the cylinder block, just above the starter motor.
95 Disconnect the battery negative terminal (refer to *Disconnecting the battery* in Chapter 5A, Section 4).
96 Apply the handbrake, then jack up the front of the vehicle and support it on axle stands (see *Jacking and vehicle support*).
97 Remove the starter motor as described in Chapter 5A, Section 11.
98 Undo the two bolts and remove the inlet manifold support bracket.
99 Disconnect the wiring connector from the knock sensor.
100 Note its position, then unscrew the bolt and remove the knock sensor from the block.
101 Clean the contact surfaces of the sensor

and block. Also clean the threads of the sensor mounting bolt.
102 Locate the sensor on the block and insert the mounting bolt. Position the sensor as previously noted, then tighten the bolt to the specified torque. Note that the torque setting is critical for the sensor to function correctly.
103 Refit the inlet manifold support bracket, then refit the starter motor as described in Chapter 5A, Section 11.
104 Lower the vehicle to the ground and reconnect the battery.

Electronic control unit (ECU)

Note: *If a new ECU is to be fitted, this work must be entrusted to a Vauxhall/Opel dealer or suitably-equipped specialist as it is necessary to program the new ECU after installation. This work requires the use of dedicated Vauxhall/Opel diagnostic equipment or a compatible alternative.*

105 The ECU is located on the left-hand side of the engine compartment, attached to the side of the battery tray.
106 Disconnect the battery negative terminal (refer to *Disconnecting the battery* in Chapter 5A, Section 4).
107 Unclip the ECU wiring harness from the side of the battery tray.
108 Lift up the locking bars and disconnect the two ECU wiring connectors **(see illustration)**.
109 Release the retaining tab and carefully lift the ECU mounting bracket off the battery tray.
110 If required, undo the four retaining bolts and remove the ECU from the mounting bracket.
111 Refitting is a reversal of removal.

Oxygen sensors

112 Refer to Chapter 4C, Section 2 for removal and refitting details.

---

11 Inlet manifold – removal and refitting

Removal

1.0 litre engines

1 Apply the handbrake, then jack up the front of the vehicle and support it on axle stands (see *Jacking and vehicle support*).

2 Disconnect the battery negative terminal (refer to *Disconnecting the battery* in Chapter 5A, Section 4).
3 Drain the coolant as described in Chapter 1A, Section 27.
4 Remove the windscreen cowl panel as described in Chapter 11, Section 20.
5 Remove the throttle housing as described in Section 10.
6 Disconnect the fuel evaporation system hose from the inlet manifold.
7 Depressurise the fuel system as described in Section 4.
8 Disconnect the fuel supply line from the fuel rail and release it from the support clip. A quick-release connector is fitted and Vauxhall/Opel technicians use a special tool to release it, however, provided care is taken, the connector can be released using a pair of long-nosed pliers, or a similar tool, to depress the retaining tangs.
9 Disconnect the crankcase ventilation hose from the camshaft cover, and the brake servo vacuum line from the inlet manifold.
10 Disconnect the wiring from the injectors and engine electronic control unit, also unbolt the earth cable and unclip the wiring conduit. Place the wiring harness to one side.
11 Disconnect the wiring connectors from the manifold pressure sensor and twinport vacuum unit.
12 Working beneath the vehicle, disconnect the wiring from the starter motor and release it from the supports on the inlet manifold.
13 Unbolt the EGR valve pipe from the EGR valve housing and position to one side. Discard the gasket; a new one must be used for refitting.
14 Unscrew the bolts and withdraw the inlet manifold from the cylinder head. Discard the seals; new ones must be used for refitting.

1.2 and 1.4 litre engines

15 Disconnect the battery negative terminal (refer to *Disconnecting the battery* in Chapter 5A, Section 4).
16 Depressurise the fuel system as described in Section 4.
17 Remove the throttle housing as described in Section 10.
18 Remove the windscreen cowl panel as described in Chapter 11, Section 20.

11.23a Disconnect the wiring connectors at the inlet and exhaust camshaft VVT solenoid valves...

11.23b...inlet and exhaust camshaft position sensors...

11.23c...thermostat, and oil pressure switch

11.23d Unclip the wiring harness trough from the camshaft cover...

11.23e...and move it to one side

19 Firmly apply the handbrake, then jack up the front of the car and support it securely on axle stands (see *Jacking and vehicle support*).
20 Remove the starter motor as described in Chapter 5A, Section 11.
21 Undo the two bolts and remove the inlet manifold support bracket.
22 From under the car, unclip the coolant hose and the wiring harness from the inlet manifold.
23 Disconnect the wiring connectors at the inlet and exhaust camshaft VVT solenoid valves, inlet and exhaust camshaft position sensors, thermostat and oil pressure switch. Unclip the wiring harness trough from the camshaft cover and move it to one side **(see illustrations)**.
24 Disconnect the wiring connectors from the evaporative emission control system purge valve and the inlet manifold flap valve solenoid.
25 Release the wiring harness from the retaining clips on the inlet manifold and fuel rail. Disconnect the wiring connectors from the fuel injectors and move the wiring harness to one side.
26 Disconnect the quick-release fitting and detach the brake servo vacuum hose from the inlet manifold.
27 Disconnect the wiring connector from the manifold absolute pressure sensor, and release the wiring harness from the retaining clips.
28 Disconnect the fuel feed hose quick-release connector at the fuel rail. Be prepared for some loss of fuel. Clamp or plug the open end of the hose, to prevent dirt ingress and further fuel spillage. Release the hose from the support bracket.
29 Remove the ventilation pipe from the evaporative emission control system purge valve and release the pipe from the retainer clip.
30 Slacken and remove the six retaining bolts and manoeuvre the manifold assembly away from the cylinder head. Remove and discard the seal rings.

Refitting
31 Refitting is the reverse of removal noting the following.
a) Ensure the manifold and cylinder head mating surfaces are clean and dry and fit the new seal rings. Refit the manifold

and tighten the retaining bolts evenly and progressively to the specified torque.
b) Ensure that all relevant hoses are reconnected to their original positions, and are securely held (where necessary) by their retaining clips.

12 Exhaust manifold/catalytic converter – removal and refitting

Removal

1.0 litre engines
Note: *New manifold retaining nuts, a new manifold gasket, exhaust front pipe gasket and oil dipstick guide tube O-rings must be used on refitting.*
Note: *Either a cast iron, or a pressed steel*

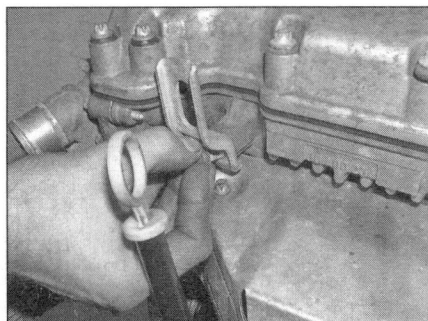
12.5 Remove the engine lifting brackets from the front of the cylinder head

manifold may be fitted according to engine type. The following procedures are applicable to both types, but the pressed steel manifold does not have a separate heat shield.
1 Disconnect the battery negative terminal (refer to *Disconnecting the battery* in Chapter 5A, Section 4).
2 Apply the handbrake, then jack up the front of the vehicle and support it on axle stands (see *Jacking and vehicle support*).
3 Release the air intake pipe (resonator) from the front of the air cleaner, then unscrew the retaining bolt and remove the pipe from the front body panel.
4 Remove the oxygen sensor (mixture regulation) from the exhaust manifold with reference to Chapter 4C, Section 2.
5 Unbolt the engine lifting eye from the cylinder head **(see illustration)**.
6 Disconnect the wiring from the oxygen sensor (mixture regulation) on the catalytic converter, then unbolt the exhaust front pipe from the exhaust manifold/catalytic converter, taking care to support the flexible section. Recover the gasket.
Note: *Angular movement in excess of 10° can cause permanent damage to the flexible section.*
7 Release the mounting rubbers and support the front of the exhaust pipe to one side.
8 Where applicable, undo the two lower exhaust manifold support bolts.
9 On models with air conditioning, unbolt the compressor from the front of the engine and support it to one side. Do not disconnect the refrigerant lines from the compressor.

12.11a Remove the exhaust manifold heat shield...

12.11b...then undo the exhaust manifold retaining nuts...

12.11c...and withdraw the manifold from the cylinder head studs

10 Unbolt and remove the oil dipstick guide tube, and withdraw it from the baseplate. Remove and discard the O-ring seals.

11 Unbolt the heat shield (where fitted), then undo the retaining nuts and withdraw the exhaust manifold/catalytic converter from the cylinder head studs **(see illustrations)**. Remove the manifold/converter from the engine compartment and recover the gasket.

1.2 and 1.4 litre engines

Note: *New manifold and exhaust front pipe retaining nuts, a new manifold gasket and exhaust front pipe gasket must be used on refitting.*

12 Disconnect the battery negative terminal (refer to *Disconnecting the battery* in Chapter 5A, Section 4).

13 Release the air intake pipe (resonator) from the front of the air cleaner, then unscrew the retaining bolt and remove the pipe from the front body panel.

14 Remove the oxygen sensor (mixture regulation) from the exhaust manifold with reference to Chapter 4C, Section 2.

15 Apply the handbrake, then jack up the front of the vehicle and support it on axle stands (see *Jacking and vehicle support*).

16 Unbolt the exhaust front pipe from the catalytic converter, taking care to support the flexible section. Recover the gasket.

Note: *Angular movement in excess of 10° can cause permanent damage to the flexible section.*

17 Undo the two lower catalytic converter support bolts.

18 Undo the nine retaining nuts and withdraw the exhaust manifold upwards from the cylinder head studs. Recover the gasket.

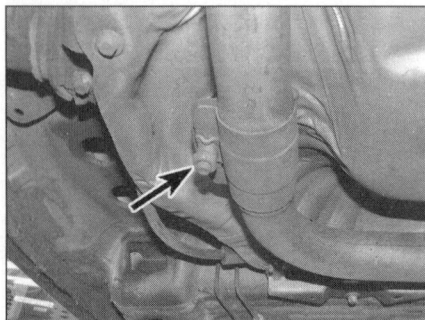

13.6 Exhaust front pipe-to-tailpipe retaining clamp bolt

Refitting

19 Refitting is the reverse of removal noting the following:

a) *Examine all the exhaust manifold studs for signs of damage and corrosion; remove all traces of corrosion, and repair or renew any damaged studs.*

b) *Ensure that the manifold and cylinder head sealing faces are clean and flat, and fit the new gasket.*

c) *Tighten the new manifold retaining nuts progressively, in a diagonal sequence, to the specified torque.*

13 Exhaust system – general information and component renewal

General information

1 The exhaust system is in two sections. The front section includes the exhaust front pipe, the oxygen sensor (catalytic converter control) and, on 1.0 litre models, the front silencer. The rear section consists of the tailpipe and silencer.

2 Periodically, the exhaust system should be checked for signs of leaks or damage. Also inspect the system rubber mountings, and renew if necessary.

3 Small holes or cracks can be repaired using proprietary exhaust repair products.

4 Before renewing an individual section of the exhaust system, it is wise to inspect the remaining section. If corrosion or damage is evident, it may prove more economical to renew the entire system.

13.8 Exhaust front pipe-to-catalytic converter/exhaust manifold joint

Component renewal

5 If either part of the system is to be renewed, it is important to ensure that the correct component is obtained.

6 To remove the rear tailpipe and silencer, chock the front wheels then jack up the rear of the vehicle and support on axle stands (see *Jacking and vehicle support*). Loosen the clamp securing the front pipe to the tailpipe **(see illustration)**, then release the rubber mountings and slide the tailpipe from the front pipe. If the tailpipe is rusted onto the front pipe, apply liberal amounts of penetrating oil and tap around the joint with a hammer to free it. Twist the tailpipe in both directions while holding the front pipe.

7 To remove the front section of the exhaust, jack up the front and rear of the vehicle and support it on axle stands (see *Jacking and vehicle support*). Undo the two bolts and remove the cross-brace from the front subframe.

8 Remove the tailpipe and silencer as described in paragraph 6, then remove the oxygen sensor from the front pipe as described in Chapter 4C, Section 2. Unbolt the exhaust front pipe from the catalytic converter/exhaust manifold **(see illustration)**, taking care to support the flexible section. Recover the gasket. Release the rubber mountings and withdraw the exhaust from under the vehicle.

Note: *Angular movement in excess of 10° can cause permanent damage to the flexible section.*

9 Refitting is a reversal of removal, but renew all gaskets and tighten the front pipe flange nuts to the specified torque. When refitting the cross-brace to the front subframe, note that the side marked LH must be toward the left-hand side of the car. Tighten the cross-brace retaining bolts to the specified torque.

Heat shield(s)

10 The heat shields are secured to the underside of the body by various nuts and bolts. Each shield can be removed once the relevant exhaust section has been removed. If a shield is being removed to gain access to a component located behind it, it may prove sufficient in some cases to remove the retaining nuts and/or bolts, and simply lower the shield, without disturbing the exhaust system.

Chapter 4 Part B
Fuel and exhaust systems – diesel engines

Contents

Degrees of difficulty

Easy, suitable for novice with little experience	**Fairly easy,** suitable for beginner with some experience	**Fairly difficult,** suitable for competent DIY mechanic	**Difficult,** suitable for experienced DIY mechanic	**Very difficult,** suitable for expert DIY or professional

Specifications

General

System type:

Z13DTJ engines . . . . Magneti-Marelli MULTIJET 6X3 high-pressure direct injection 'common-rail' system, electronically controlled

All other engines. . . . . Bosch EDC 17 high-pressure direct injection 'common-rail' system, electronically controlled

Firing order . . . . 1–3–4–2 (No 1 at timing chain end)
Fuel system operating pressure . . . . 1400 to 1600 bar at 2200 rpm
Idle speed. . . . . 850 rpm – controlled by ECU
Maximum speed. . . . . 5200 rpm – controlled by ECU

High-pressure fuel pump

Type . . . . Bosch CP1

Fuel supply pump

Type . . . . Electric, mounted in fuel tank
Delivery pressure . . . . 3.3 bar (maximum)

Injectors

Type . . . . Bosch CRIP 2-MI

Torque wrench settings

	Nm	lbf ft
Camshaft position sensor retaining bolt.	7	5
Catalytic converter support bracket to sump reinforcement bracket . .	25	18
Catalytic converter-to-turbocharger bolts	30	22
Coolant pipe-to-heat exchanger bolts	9	7
Crankshaft speed/position sensor retaining bolt	9	7
EGR valve bolts	22	16
Exhaust manifold nuts: *		
Stage 1	15	11
Stage 2	Angle-tighten a further 30º	
Exhaust system clamp nuts	50	37
Front subframe cross-brace bolts	60	44
Fuel injector clamp bracket nuts	20	15
Fuel pressure regulating valve to fuel rail	9	7
Fuel pressure sensor to fuel rail	70	52
Fuel rail mounting bracket-to-camshaft housing bolts	25	18
Fuel rail-to-mounting bracket bolts	25	18
High-pressure fuel pipe unions:		
M12 union nuts.	25	18
M14 union nuts.	28	21
High-pressure fuel pump mounting bolts.	15	11
Inlet manifold bolts.	25	18
Injection pump to camshaft housing	15	11
Injector retaining clamp nut	20	15
Oil filter housing to cylinder block	9	7
Turbocharger oil return pipe bolts	9	7
Turbocharger oil supply pipe banjo union bolts	12	9
Turbocharger to exhaust manifold	25	18

* Use new fastenings

1 General Information

1 The diesel engine covered in this manual is equipped with a High-pressure Diesel injection (HDi) system which incorporates the very latest in diesel injection technology. On the HDi system, the high-pressure fuel pump is used purely to provide the pressure required for the injection system and has no control over the injection timing (unlike conventional diesel injection systems). The injection timing is controlled by the electronic control unit (ECU) via the electrically-operated injectors. The system operates as follows.

2 The fuel system consists of a fuel tank (which is mounted under the rear of the car, with an electric fuel supply pump immersed in it, a fuel filter with integral water separator, a high-pressure fuel pump, injectors and associated components.

3 Fuel is supplied by the tank-mounted supply pump to the fuel filter which is located in the engine compartment. The fuel filter removes all foreign matter and water, and ensures that the fuel supplied to the high-pressure pump is clean. Excess fuel is returned from the outlet on the filter housing lid to the tank via the fuel cooler. The fuel cooler is fitted to the underside of the vehicle and is cooled by the passing airflow to ensure the fuel is cool before it enters the fuel tank.

4 The fuel is heated to ensure no problems occur when the ambient temperature is very low. An electrically-operated fuel heater is fitted to the fuel filter housing, and the heater is controlled by the ECU.

5 The high-pressure fuel pump is driven directly from the rear of the exhaust camshaft. The high pressure required in the system (up to 1400 bar) is produced by the three pistons in the pump. The pump supplies high-pressure fuel to the fuel rail, which acts as a reservoir for the four injectors.

6 The electrical control system consists of the ECU, along with the following sensors:

a) *Accelerator pedal position sensor – informs the ECU of the accelerator pedal position, and the speed of pedal travel.*

b) *Coolant temperature sensor – informs the ECU of engine temperature.*

c) *Airflow meter – informs the ECU of the amount and temperature of air passing through the inlet duct.*

d) *Crankshaft speed/position sensor – informs the ECU of the crankshaft position and speed of rotation.*

e) *Camshaft position sensor – informs the ECU of the positions of the pistons.*

f) *Charge (boost) pressure sensor – informs the ECU of the pressure in the inlet manifold.*

g) *Fuel pressure sensor – informs the ECU of the fuel pressure present in the fuel rail.*

h) *ABS control unit – informs the ECU of the vehicle speed, based on wheel speed sensor signals (explained in greater detail in Chapter 9, Section 18).*

7 All the above signals (in addition to signals from various other systems on the vehicle) are analysed by the ECU which selects the fuelling response appropriate to those values. The ECU controls the fuel injectors (varying the pulse width – the length of time the injectors are held open – to provide a richer or weaker mixture, as appropriate). The mixture is constantly varied by the ECU, to provide the best setting for cranking, starting (with either a hot or cold engine), warm-up, idle, cruising and acceleration.

8 The ECU also has full control over the fuel pressure present in the system via the pressure regulating valve located on the fuel rail. To reduce the fuel pressure, the ECU opens the pressure regulating valve which allows the excess fuel to return directly to the fuel tank.

9 The ECU also controls the exhaust gas recirculation (EGR) system, described in detail in Chapter 4C, Section 1, and the engine cooling fan.

10 A turbocharger is fitted to increases engine efficiency. It does this by raising the pressure in the inlet manifold above atmospheric pressure. Instead of the air simply being sucked into the cylinders, it is forced in.

11 Energy for the operation of the turbocharger comes from the exhaust gas. The gas flows through a specially-shaped housing (the turbine housing) and in so doing, spins the turbine wheel. The turbine wheel is attached to a shaft, at the end of which is another vaned wheel known as the compressor wheel. The compressor wheel spins in its own housing, and compresses the inlet air on the way to the inlet manifold. The turbo shaft is pressure-lubricated by an oil feed pipe from the main oil gallery. The shaft 'floats' on a cushion of oil. A drain pipe returns the oil to the sump. Boost pressure (the pressure in the inlet manifold) is limited by a wastegate, which diverts the exhaust gas away from the turbine wheel in response to a pressure-sensitive actuator.

12 If there is an abnormality in any of the readings obtained from the various sensors, the ECU enters its back-up mode. In this event, it ignores the abnormal sensor signal and assumes a pre-programmed value which will allow the engine to continue running (albeit at reduced efficiency). If the ECU enters this back-up mode, the warning light on the instrument panel will come on, and the relevant fault code will be stored in the ECU memory. The fault code can be read using specialist test equipment.

2 High-pressure diesel injection system – special information

Warnings and precautions

1 It is essential to observe strict precautions when working on the fuel system components, particularly the high-pressure side of the system. Before carrying out any operations on the fuel system, refer to the precautions given in *Safety first!*, and to the following additional information.

a) *Do not carry out any repair work on the high-pressure fuel system unless you are competent to do so, have all the necessary tools and equipment required, and are aware of the safety implications involved.*

b) *Before starting any repair work on the fuel system, wait at least 30 seconds after switching off the engine to allow the fuel circuit to return to atmospheric pressure.*

c) *Never work on the high-pressure fuel system with the engine running.*

d) *Keep well clear of any possible source of fuel leakage, particularly when starting the engine after carrying out repair*

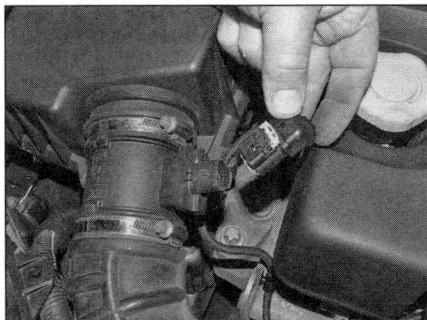

2.4 Typical plastic plug and cap set for sealing disconnected fuel pipes and components

work. A leak in the system could cause an extremely high pressure jet of fuel to escape, which could result in severe personal injury.

e) *Never place your hands or any part of your body near to a leak in the high-pressure fuel system.*

f) *Do not use steam cleaning equipment or compressed air to clean the engine or any of the fuel system components.*

Repair procedures and general information

2 Strict cleanliness must be observed at all times when working on any part of the fuel system. This applies to the working area in general, the person doing the work, and the components being worked on.

3 Before working on the fuel system components, they must be thoroughly cleaned with a suitable degreasing fluid. Cleanliness is particularly important when working on the fuel system connections at the following components:

a) Fuel filter.
b) High-pressure fuel pump.
c) Fuel rail.
d) Fuel injectors.
e) High-pressure fuel pipes.

4 After disconnecting any fuel pipes or components, the open union or orifice must be immediately sealed to prevent the entry of dirt or foreign material. Plastic plugs and caps in various sizes are available in packs from motor factors and accessory outlets, and are

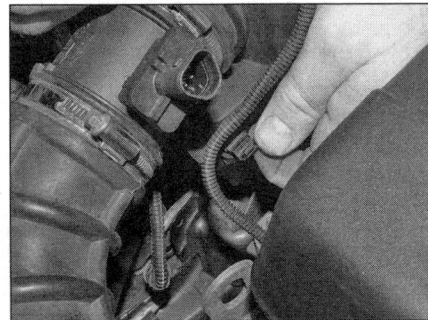

2.6 Two crow-foot adaptors will be necessary for tightening the fuel pipe unions

particularly suitable for this application **(see illustration)**. Fingers cut from disposable rubber gloves should be used to protect components such as fuel pipes, fuel injectors and wiring connectors, and can be secured in place using elastic bands.

5 Whenever any of the high-pressure fuel pipes are disconnected or removed, a new pipe(s) must be obtained for refitting.

6 The torque wrench settings given in the Specifications must be strictly observed when tightening component mountings and connections. This is particularly important when tightening the high-pressure fuel pipe unions. To enable a torque wrench to be used on the fuel pipe unions, two crow-foot adaptors are required. Suitable types are available from motor factors and accessory outlets **(see illustration)**.

3 Air cleaner assembly and intake ducts – removal and refitting

Air cleaner assembly

1 Disconnect the wiring connector from the airflow meter on the air cleaner cover **(see illustration)**.

2 Unclip the wiring harness from the base of the air cleaner **(see illustration)**.

3 Slacken the retaining clamp and disconnect the turbocharger air inlet hose from the airflow meter **(see illustration)**. Move the hose clear of the air cleaner assembly.

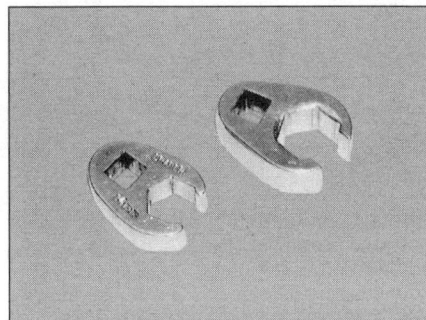

3.1 Disconnect the airflow meter wiring connector

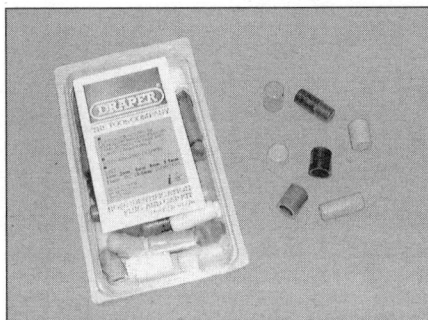

3.2 Unclip the wiring harness from the base of the air cleaner

3.3 Slacken the clamp and disconnect the air inlet hose from the airflow meter

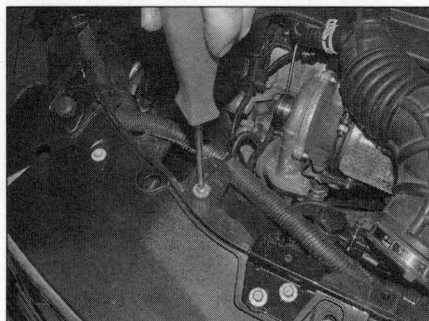

3.4 Undo the screw securing the resonator to the front body panel

3.5a Release the wiring harness retaining clip from the resonator...

3.5b...then remove the resonator

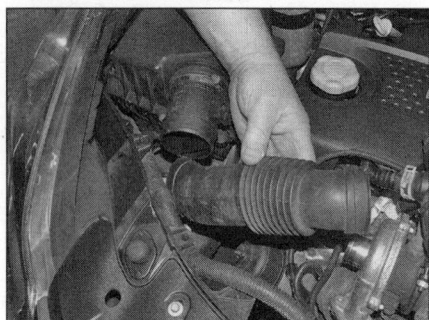

3.6 Disconnect and remove the air cleaner air inlet hose

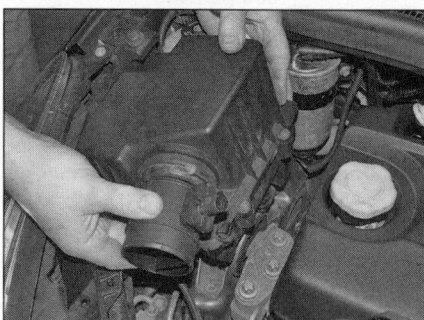

3.8 Lift the air cleaner upward and inward to free it from the rubber mountings

4 Undo the screw securing the resonator to the front body panel **(see illustration)**.

5 Release the wiring harness retaining clip from the resonator. Detach the resonator from the air cleaner air inlet hose, then remove the resonator from the engine compartment **(see illustrations)**.

6 Disconnect the air inlet hose from the air cleaner and remove it from the engine compartment **(see illustration)**.

7 Where applicable, disconnect the water drain hose from the base of the air cleaner.

8 Lift the air cleaner upward and inward to free it from the rubber mountings and remove the air cleaner from the engine compartment **(see illustration)**.

9 If necessary, slacken the clamp and detach the airflow meter and upper air inlet hose from the air cleaner cover.

10 Refitting is a reversal of removal.

Air inlet hoses/ducts

11 Various flexible hoses and rigid ducts are used to circulate the inlet air through the air cleaner, turbocharger, intercooler and inlet manifold. Depending on the particular hose, duct or pipe being removed, it may be necessary to move aside or disconnect additional components for access, and to release cable-ties and harness clips to allow complete removal. Refer to the accompanying illustrations and proceed as described under the relevant sub-heading below.

Turbocharger air inlet hose

12 Remove the plastic cover over the top of the engine.

13 Slacken the clamp and disconnect the right-hand end of the upper air inlet hose from the airflow meter **(see illustration 3.3)**.

14 Where fitted, disconnect the wiring connector at the crankcase ventilation hose heating element.

15 Release the retaining clip and disconnect the crankcase ventilation hose from the turbocharger air inlet hose **(see illustration)**.

16 Slacken the clamp and disconnect the inlet hose from the turbocharger. Lift the hose up and out of the engine compartment.

17 Suitably cover the turbocharger air inlet to prevent the possible entry of foreign material.

18 Refitting is a reversal of removal.

Resonator

19 Undo the screw securing the resonator to the front body panel **(see illustration 3.4)**.

20 Release the wiring harness retaining clip from the resonator. Detach the resonator from the air cleaner air inlet hose, then remove the resonator from the engine compartment **(see illustrations 3.5a and 3.5b)**.

21 Refitting is a reversal of removal.

Intercooler left-hand charge air pipe

22 Disconnect the battery negative terminal (refer to *Disconnecting the battery* in Chapter 5A, Section 4).

23 Firmly apply the handbrake, then jack up the front of the car and support it securely on axle stands (see *Jacking and vehicle support*).

24 Lift off the plastic cover over the top of the engine.

25 Remove the front bumper as described in Chapter 11, Section 6.

26 Remove the battery and battery tray as described in Chapter 5A, Section 4.

27 Disconnect the quick-release fitting and remove the charge air hose from the intercooler **(see illustration)**.

28 Undo the bolts securing the charge air hose clamps to the radiator support crossmember and transmission **(see illustrations)**.

29 Undo the bolts securing the charge air pipe to the throttle housing or inlet manifold flange and, where fitted, the bolt securing the pipe support to the thermostat housing **(see illustration)**. Manipulate the charge air pipe from its location and recover the sealing ring.

30 Refitting is a reversal of removal.

3.15 Release the retaining clip and disconnect the crankcase ventilation hose from the air inlet hose

3.27 Disconnect the quick-release fitting and remove the charge air hose from the intercooler

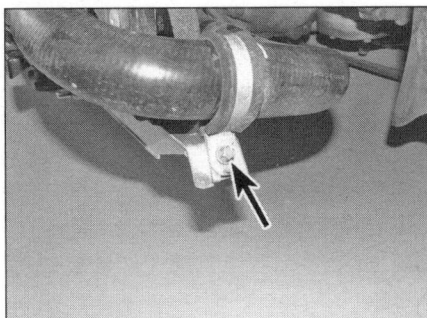

3.28a Undo the bolts securing the charge air hose clamps to the radiator support crossmember...

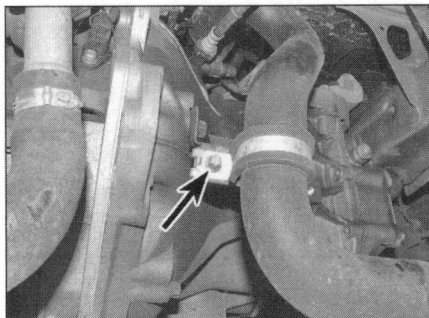

3.28b...and transmission

3.29 Undo the bolt securing the charge air pipe support to the thermostat housing

Intercooler right-hand charge air pipe

31 Disconnect the battery negative terminal (refer to *Disconnecting the battery* in Chapter 5A, Section 4).

32 Firmly apply the handbrake, then jack up the front of the car and support it securely on axle stands (see *Jacking and vehicle support*).

33 Lift off the plastic cover over the top of the engine.

34 Remove the front bumper as described in Chapter 11, Section 6.

35 Disconnect the quick-release fitting and remove the charge air hose from the intercooler.

36 Undo the bolt securing the charge air hose clamp to the radiator support crossmember.

37 Retain the radiator in position by securing it to the bonnet lock platform using cable-ties.

38 Slacken the retaining bolt each side securing the radiator support crossmember to the underbody and lower the crossmember slightly **(see illustration)**.

39 Working through the small gap between the underside of the radiator and the top of the support crossmember, undo the two bolts securing the charge air pipe to the crossmember. Release the charge air pipe from the crossmember **(see illustrations)**.

40 On models equipped with air conditioning, unclip the compressor wiring harness from the charge air pipe.

41 Release the retaining clip and disconnect the charge air pipe connecting hose from the turbocharger elbow **(see illustration)**. Remove the charge air pipe assembly from under the car.

42 Refitting is a reversal of removal.

4 Accelerator pedal position sensor – removal and refitting

1 Refer to Chapter 4A, Section 3.

5 Fuel system – priming and bleeding

1 After disconnecting part of the fuel supply

system or running out of fuel, it is necessary to prime the fuel system and bleed off any air which may have entered the system components, as follows.

2 Prime the system by switching on the ignition three times for approximately 15 seconds each time. Operate the starter for a maximum of 30 seconds. If the engine does not start within this time, wait 5 seconds and repeat the procedure.

3 When the engine starts, run it at a fast idle speed for a minute or so to purge any trapped air from the fuel lines. After this time the engine should idle smoothly at a constant speed.

4 If the engine idles roughly, then there is still some air trapped in the fuel system. Increase

the engine speed again for another minute or so then allow it to idle. Repeat this procedure as necessary until the engine is idling smoothly.

6 Fuel gauge sender unit – removal and refitting

Note: *Refer to the warnings and precautions contained in Section 2 before proceeding.*

1 Removal and refitting of the fuel gauge sender unit is the same as described in Chapter 4A, Section 6 for petrol engines.

2 On completion, prime and bleed the fuel system as described in Section 5.

3.38 Slacken the retaining bolt each side securing the radiator support crossmember to the underbody

3.39a Undo the two bolts securing the charge air pipe to the crossmember...

3.39b...then release the charge air pipe from the crossmember

3.41 Release the retaining clip and disconnect the charge air pipe connecting hose from the turbocharger elbow

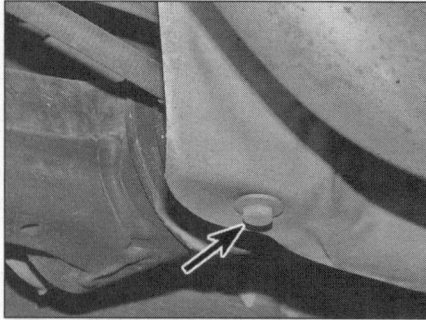

7.6a Undo the bolt...

7.6b...the sheet metal nut...

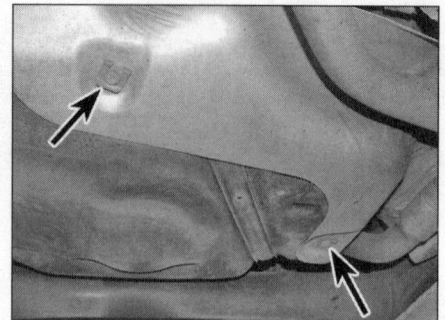

7.6c...and two clamps and remove the fuel tank heat shield

7.8 Disconnect the fuel pump and fuel gauge sender unit wiring at the underbody connector

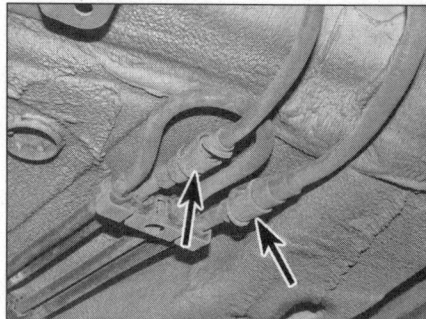

7.9 Disconnect the fuel feed and return lines at the quick-release connectors on the underbody

7 Fuel tank – removal and refitting

Note: *Refer to the warnings and precautions contained in Section 2 before proceeding.*
Note: *The fuel tank should be as empty as possible when carrying out this procedure.*

Removal

1 Disconnect the battery negative terminal (refer to *Disconnecting the battery* in Chapter 5A, Section 4).
2 Hand-pump any remaining fuel in the tank out through the filler pipe into a clean metal container which can be sealed.
3 Chock the front wheels then jack up the rear of the vehicle and support on axle stands

(see *Jacking and vehicle support*). Remove both rear wheels.
4 Position a suitable container beneath the fuel filler hose connection on the fuel tank. Loosen the retaining clip and disconnect the filler hose from the tank. Be prepared for some loss of fuel.
5 Disconnect the rear of the exhaust system from its rubber mountings, and lower the system, then move it to one side sufficiently to enable removal of the fuel tank. Alternatively, remove the exhaust system completely to provide greater clearance (refer to Section 20).
6 Undo the bolt, sheet metal nut and two clamps, and remove the heat shield from the base of the fuel tank **(see illustrations)**.
7 Unclip the brake hydraulic pipes from the brackets on the fuel tank and tank retaining straps.

8 Disconnect the fuel pump and fuel gauge sender unit wiring at the connector on the underbody **(see illustration)**.
9 Disconnect the fuel feed and return lines at the quick-release connectors on the underbody, then release the feed and return lines from the clips on the fuel tank bracket **(see illustration)**. Suitably seal the fuel lines to prevent dirt ingress.
10 Support the weight of the fuel tank on a jack with interposed block of wood.
11 Unbolt and remove the two securing straps from the fuel tank **(see illustrations)**.
12 Lower the tank sufficiently to enable access to the remaining fuel hoses on the tank, then disconnect them. Be prepared for some loss of fuel.
13 Continue to lower the tank, guiding the fuel hoses over the handbrake cables, until it can be removed from under the vehicle.
14 Plug or clamp the fuel hoses to prevent entry of dust and dirt.
15 If necessary, remove the fuel lines, hoses and wiring from the tank for transfer to the new tank. If a new tank is being fitted, it is recommended that the filter is renewed at the same time.
16 If the tank contains sediment or water, it may cleaned out with two or three rinses of clean fuel. Remove the fuel tank module as described in Section 6. Shake the tank vigorously, and change the fuel as necessary to remove all contamination from the tank.

⚠ *Warning: This procedure should be carried out in a well-ventilated area, and it is vital to take adequate fire precautions.*

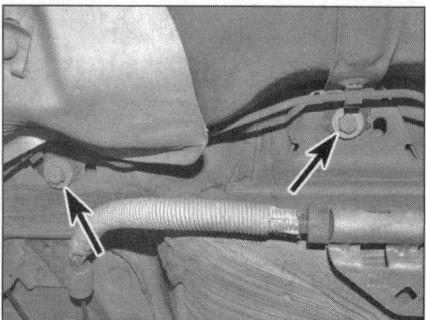

7.11a Fuel tank securing strap front retaining bolts...

7.11b...left-hand rear retaining bolt...

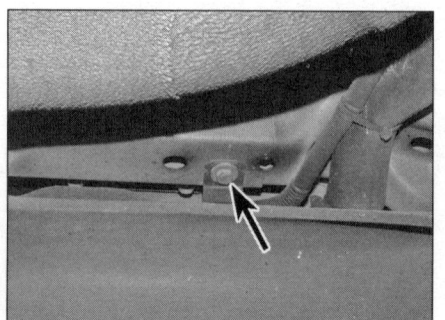

7.11c...and right-hand rear retaining bolt...

17 Any repairs to the fuel tank should be carried out by a professional. Do not under any circumstances attempt any form of DIY repair to a fuel tank.

Refitting

18 Refitting is a reversal of removal, bearing in mind the following points:
a) *Ensure that all hoses are securely reconnected to their correct locations.*
b) *On completion, fill the fuel tank, then run the engine and check for leaks. If leakage is evident, stop the engine immediately and rectify the problem without delay.*

8 Fuel supply pump – removal and refitting

1 The diesel fuel supply pump is located in the tank module in the fuel tank. The removal and refitting procedures are the same as for the fuel gauge sender unit described in Section 6. The pump is integral with the tank module and cannot be renewed separately.

9 Fuel injection system electrical components – testing

1 If a fault is suspected in the electronic control side of the system, first ensure that all the wiring connectors are securely connected and free of corrosion. Ensure that the suspected problem is not of a mechanical nature, or due to poor maintenance; ie, check that the air cleaner filter element is clean, the engine breather hoses are clear and undamaged, and that the cylinder compression pressures are correct, referring to Chapters 1B, 2C and 4C.
2 If these checks fail to reveal the cause of the problem, the vehicle should be taken to a suitably-equipped Vauxhall/Opel dealer or engine management diagnostic specialist for testing. Using a fault code reader or similar diagnostic equipment, the engine management ECU can be interrogated, and any stored fault codes can be retrieved. Live data can also be captured from the various system sensors and actuators, indicating their operating parameters. This will allow the fault to be quickly and simply traced, alleviating the need to test all the system components individually, which is a time-consuming operation that carries a risk of damaging the ECU.

10 Fuel injection system electrical components – removal and refitting

Airflow meter

Removal

1 Disconnect the wiring from the airflow meter at the right-hand side of the engine compartment **(see illustration 3.1)**.
2 Slacken the retaining clamp and disconnect the turbocharger air inlet hose from the airflow meter **(see illustration 3.3)**.
3 Slacken the retaining clamp and remove the airflow meter from the air cleaner lid.

Refitting

4 Refitting is a reversal of removal, but ensure that the arrow on the airflow meter body points away from the air cleaner when refitting.

Throttle housing

Note: *A throttle housing is not fitted to Z13DTJ engines.*

Removal

5 Lift off the plastic cover over the top of the engine.
6 Remove the battery and battery tray as described in Chapter 5A, Section 4.
7 Undo the two bolts securing the charge air pipe to the throttle housing. Withdraw the pipe and recover the seal.
8 Release the clamp and detach the charge air pipe from the charge air hose.
9 Disconnect the vacuum hose from the throttle housing solenoid valve.
10 Undo the three retaining bolts and remove the throttle housing from the inlet manifold. Note the location of any wiring harness support brackets also secured by the retaining bolts.

Refitting

11 Refitting is a reversal of removal, but thoroughly clean the mating faces and use a new seal on the charge air pipe.

Crankshaft speed/position sensor

Removal

12 Lift off the plastic cover over the top of the engine.
13 The crankshaft speed/position sensor is located on the front of the cylinder block, in-line with the flywheel.
14 Disconnect the sensor wiring connector, then undo the retaining bolt and remove the sensor from the cylinder block **(see illustration)**.

Refitting

15 Refitting is a reversal of removal, tightening the retaining bolt securely.

Camshaft position sensor

Removal

16 Lift off the plastic cover over the top of the engine.
17 The camshaft position sensor is located on the front right-hand side of the camshaft housing, above the exhaust camshaft **(see illustration)**.
18 Disconnect the sensor wiring connector, then undo the retaining bolt and remove the sensor from the camshaft housing.

10.14 Undo the retaining bolt and remove the crankshaft speed/position sensor from the cylinder block

Refitting

19 Refitting is a reversal of removal, tightening the retaining bolt securely.

Fuel pressure sensor

Removal

20 Lift off the plastic cover over the top of the engine.
21 The fuel pressure sensor is located at the right-hand end of the fuel rail.
22 Disconnect the sensor wiring connector, then unscrew the sensor from the fuel rail.

Refitting

23 Refitting is a reversal of removal, tightening the sensor to the specified torque.

Charge (boost) pressure sensor

Removal

24 Remove the windscreen cowl panel as described in Chapter 11, Section 20.
25 Lift off the plastic cover over the top of the engine.
26 The charge pressure sensor is located on the upper face of the inlet manifold, near the centre.
27 Using a small screwdriver, lift up the locking catch and disconnect the sensor wiring connector **(see illustration)**.
28 Undo the retaining bolt and withdraw the sensor from the manifold. Recover the sealing O-ring.

10.17 Camshaft position sensor location

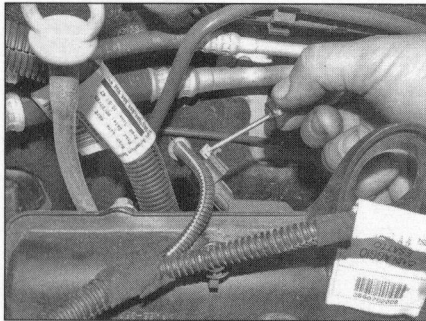

10.27 Lift up the locking catch to disconnect the charge pressure sensor wiring connector

10.33 Withdraw the locking plate, lift the locking levers and disconnect the ECU wiring connectors

Coolant temperature sensor

38 Refer to the procedures contained in Chapter 3, Section 6.

Turbocharger wastegate solenoid

39 The wastegate (charge pressure) solenoid valve is located at the front of the engine compartment above the radiator **(see illustration)**.
40 Disconnect the wiring connector and the two vacuum hoses from the valve then undo the two bolts and remove the valve together with its mounting bracket.
41 Refitting is the reverse of removal.

---

11 High-pressure fuel pump – removal and refitting

10.34 Undo the four nuts securing the ECU mounting frame to the body

Refitting

29 Renew the sealing O-ring, then refit the sensor and tighten the retaining bolt securely. Reconnect the wiring connector and secure with the locking catch.
30 Refit the windscreen cowl panel as described in Chapter 11, Section 20, then refit the engine cover.

Electronic control unit (ECU)

Note: *If a new ECU is to be fitted, this work must be entrusted to a Vauxhall/Opel dealer or suitably-equipped specialist as it is necessary to program the new ECU after installation. This work requires the use of dedicated Vauxhall/Opel diagnostic equipment or a compatible alternative.*

Removal

31 Disconnect the battery negative terminal

11.4 Fuel supply and return hose connections at the high-pressure fuel pump

10.39 Turbocharger wastegate solenoid location.

(refer *Disconnecting the battery* in Chapter 5A, Section 4).
32 Remove the windscreen cowl panel as described in Chapter 11, Section 20.
33 Withdraw the locking plate, lift the locking levers and disconnect the two wiring connectors from the ECU **(see illustration)**.
34 Undo the four nuts securing the ECU mounting frame to the body **(see illustration)**.
35 Move the wiring harness to one side and lift the ECU and mounting frame from the engine compartment.
36 Undo the four nuts and separate the ECU from the mounting frame.

Refitting

37 Refitting is a reversal of removal, ensuring that the wiring connectors are securely connected and locked with the locking levers.

11.7a Unscrew the three mounting bolts...

Note: *Refer to the warnings and precautions contained in Section 2 before proceeding.*
Note: *A new fuel pump-to-fuel rail high-pressure fuel pipe will be required for refitting.*

Removal

1 Disconnect the battery negative terminal (refer to *Disconnecting the battery* in Chapter 5A, Section 4).
2 Lift off the plastic cover over the top of the engine.
3 Undo the two bolts securing the charge air pipe to the throttle housing or inlet manifold. Withdraw the pipe and recover the seal. Release the clamp and detach the charge air pipe from the charge air hose.
4 Release the retaining clip and disconnect the fuel supply hose from the fuel pump **(see illustration)**. Cover the hose end and the pump outlet to prevent dirt entry.
5 Release the retaining clip and disconnect the fuel return hose from the fuel pump. Cover the hose end and the pump outlet to prevent dirt entry.
6 Thoroughly clean the fuel pipe unions on the fuel pump and fuel rail. Using an open-ended spanner, unscrew the union nuts securing the high-pressure fuel pipe to the fuel pump and fuel rail. Counterhold the unions on the pump with a second spanner while unscrewing the union nuts. Withdraw the high-pressure fuel pipe and plug or cover the open unions to prevent dirt entry.
7 Disconnect the pump wiring connector, then unscrew the three mounting bolts and withdraw the pump from the camshaft housing. Recover the sealing O-ring **(see illustrations)**.
Caution: The high-pressure fuel pump is manufactured to extremely close tolerances and must not be dismantled in any way. No parts for the pump are available separately and if the unit is in any way suspect, it must be renewed.

Refitting

8 Thoroughly clean the fuel pump and camshaft housing mating faces.

11.7b...withdraw the fuel pump from the camshaft housing...

11.7c...and recover the sealing O-ring

Removal

1 Disconnect the battery negative terminal (refer to *Disconnecting the battery* in Chapter 5A, Section 4).

2 Lift off the plastic cover over the top of the engine.

3 Disconnect the wiring connector at the at the fuel pressure sensor **(see illustration)**. Unclip the wiring trough and move it clear of the fuel rail.

4 Thoroughly clean all the high-pressure fuel pipe unions on the fuel rail, fuel pump and injectors. Using two spanners, hold the unions and unscrew the union nuts securing the high-pressure fuel pipes to the fuel injectors. Unscrew the union nuts securing the high-pressure fuel pipes to the fuel rail, withdraw the pipes and plug or cover the open unions to prevent dirt entry **(see illustrations)**. It is advisable to label each fuel pipe (1 to 4) to avoid confusion when refitting.

5 Using an open-ended spanner, unscrew the union nuts securing the high-pressure fuel pipe to the fuel pump and fuel rail. Counterhold the unions on the pump with a second spanner, while unscrewing the union nuts **(see illustrations)**. Withdraw the high-pressure fuel pipe and plug or cover the open unions to prevent dirt entry.

6 Release the retaining clip and disconnect the fuel return hose from the fuel rail. Cover the hose end and the pump outlet to prevent dirt entry.

7 Undo the two retaining bolts and lift the fuel rail off the mounting bracket **(see illustrations)**.

9 Locate a new sealing O-ring on the pump flange and lubricate the O-ring with clean diesel fuel.

10 Align the pump drive dog with the slot on the camshaft, then place the pump in position. Refit the three mounting bolts and tighten them to the specified torque.

11 Remove the blanking plugs from the fuel pipe unions on the pump and fuel rail. Locate the new high-pressure fuel pipe over the unions and screw on the union nuts finger-tight at this stage.

12 Using a torque wrench and crow-foot adaptor, tighten the fuel pipe union nuts to the specified torque. Counterhold the unions on the pump with an open-ended spanner while tightening the union nuts.

13 Reconnect the fuel return hose and supply hose and secure with the retaining clips.

14 Refit the charge air pipe to the throttle housing or inlet manifold and charge air hose.

15 Observing the precautions listed in Section 2, prime the fuel system as described in Section 5, then start the engine and allow it to idle. Check for leaks at the high-pressure fuel pipe unions with the engine idling. If satisfactory, increase the engine speed to 4000 rpm and check again for leaks. If any leaks are detected, obtain and fit a new high-pressure fuel pipe.

16 Refit the engine cover on completion.

12 Fuel rail – removal and refitting

Note: *Refer to the warnings and precautions contained in Section 2 before proceeding.*

Note: *A complete set of high-pressure fuel pipes will be required for refitting.*

12.3 Disconnect the wiring connector at the at the fuel pressure sensor

12.4a Unscrew the union nuts securing the high-pressure fuel pipes to the fuel injectors...

12.4b...and the fuel rail

12.5a Unscrew the union nuts securing the high-pressure fuel pipe to the fuel pump...

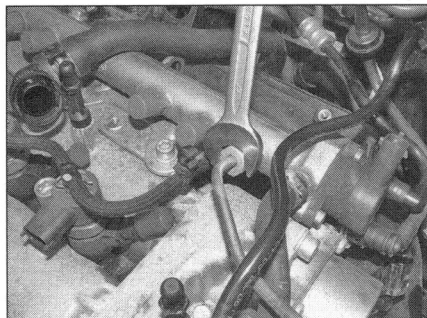

12.5b...and fuel rail

12.7a Undo the two fuel rail retaining bolts...

12.7b...and lift the fuel rail off the mounting bracket

12.10 Tighten the fuel pipe union nuts using a torque wrench and crow-foot adaptor

13 Fuel injectors –
removal and refitting

Note: *Refer to the warnings and precautions contained in Section 2 before proceeding.*
Note: *The following procedure describes the removal and refitting of the injectors as a complete set, however, the injectors may be removed in pairs if required. New copper sealing washers will be required for each disturbed injector when refitting.*

Refitting

8 Locate the fuel rail on the mounting bracket, refit the two retaining bolts and tighten them to the specified torque.
9 Refit the fuel return hose and secure with the retaining clip.
10 Working on one fuel injector at a time, remove the blanking plugs from the fuel pipe unions on the fuel rail and the relevant injector. Locate the new high-pressure fuel pipe over the unions and screw on the union nuts finger-tight. Tighten the union nuts to the specified torque using a torque wrench and crow-foot adaptor **(see illustration)**. Counterhold the union on the injector with an open-ended spanner while tightening the union nut. Repeat this operation for the remaining three injectors.

11 Similarly, fit the high-pressure fuel pipe to the fuel pump and fuel rail, and tighten the union nuts to the specified torque. Counterhold the union on the pump with an open-ended spanner while tightening the union nut.
12 Reconnect the wiring connectors at the fuel pressure sensor.
13 Observing the precautions listed in Section 2, prime the fuel system as described in Section 5, then start the engine and allow it to idle. Check for leaks at the high-pressure fuel pipe unions with the engine idling. If satisfactory, increase the engine speed to 4000 rpm and check again for leaks. If any leaks are detected, obtain and fit a new high-pressure fuel pipe(s).
14 Refit the engine cover on completion.

Removal

1 Disconnect the battery negative terminal (refer to *Disconnecting the battery* in Chapter 5A, Section 4).
2 Lift off the plastic cover over the top of the engine.
3 Thoroughly clean all the high-pressure fuel pipe unions on the fuel rail and injectors.
4 Release the locking catches securing the wiring connectors to the four injectors, then disconnect the injector wiring.
5 Using two spanners, hold the unions and unscrew the union nuts securing the high-pressure fuel pipes to the fuel injectors. Unscrew the union nuts securing the high-pressure fuel pipes to the fuel rail, withdraw the pipes and plug or cover the open unions to prevent dirt entry **(see illustrations 12.4a and 12.4b)**. It is advisable to label each fuel pipe (1 to 4) to avoid confusion when refitting.
6 Disconnect the fuel leak-off hose connection at each injector by pushing in the locking clip and lifting out the hose fitting. Slip a plastic bag over the disconnected leak-off hose to prevent dirt entry **(see illustrations)**.
7 Unscrew the retaining nut then remove the two washers from the injector clamp brackets **(see illustrations)**. There are two clamp brackets, one securing injectors one and two, and the other securing injectors three and four.
8 Working on one pair of injectors at a time (one and two, or three and four) withdraw the two injectors together with the clamp bracket from the camshaft housing and cylinder head. If difficulty is experienced removing the injectors, liberally apply penetrating oil to

13.6a Disconnect the fuel leak-off hose connection at each injector...

13.6b...and slip a plastic bag over the disconnected leak-off hose to prevent dirt entry

13.7a Unscrew the retaining nut...

13.7b...then remove the upper washer...

13.7c...and lower washer from the injector clamp brackets

the base of each injector and allow time for the oil to penetrate. If the injectors are still reluctant to free, it will be necessary to use a small slide hammer engaged under the flange of the injector body casting, and gently tap them free. Note that it is not possible to twist the injectors from side-to-side to free them due to the design of the clamp bracket which positively engages in slots in the injector body **(see illustrations)**.

9 Once the injector pair has been removed, separate them from the clamp bracket and remove the copper washer from each injector **(see illustration)**. The copper washers may have remained in place at the base of the injector orifice in the cylinder head. If so, hook them out with a length of wire. Remove the upper injector seals from the camshaft housing.

10 Examine each injector visually for any signs of obvious damage or deterioration. If any defects are apparent, renew the injector(s).

Caution: The injectors are manufactured to extremely close tolerances and must not be dismantled in any way. Do not unscrew the fuel pipe union on the side of the injector, or separate any parts of the injector body. Do not attempt to clean carbon deposits from the injector nozzle or carry out any form of ultrasonic or pressure testing.

11 If the injectors are in a satisfactory condition, plug the fuel pipe union (if not already done) and suitably cover the electrical element and the injector nozzle.

12 Prior to refitting, obtain a new copper washer and camshaft housing seal for each removed injector.

Refitting

13 Locate a new copper washer on the base of each injector, and fit a new seal to the injector location in the camshaft housing.

14 Place the injector clamp bracket in the slot on each injector body and refit the injectors to the cylinder head in pairs. Guide the clamp bracket over the mounting stud as each injector pair is inserted.

15 Fit the two washers and the injector clamp bracket retaining nut to the mounting stud of each injector pair. Tighten the nuts finger-tight only at this stage.

16 Working on one fuel injector at a time, remove the blanking plugs from the fuel pipe unions on the fuel rail and the relevant injector. Locate the high-pressure fuel pipe over the unions and screw on the union nuts. Take care not to cross-thread the nuts or strain the fuel pipes as they are fitted. Once the union nut threads have started, tighten the nuts moderately tight only at this stage.

17 When all the fuel pipes are in place, tighten the injector clamp bracket retaining nuts to the specified torque.

18 Tighten the fuel pipe union nuts to the specified torque using a torque wrench and crow-foot adaptor **(see illustration 12.10)**.

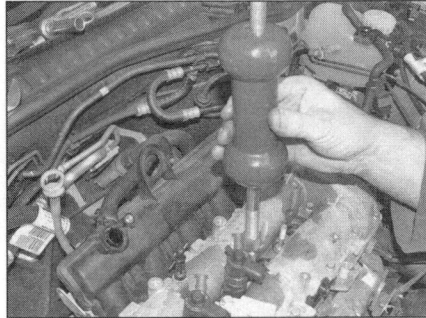
13.8a If necessary, use a slide hammer to free the injectors...

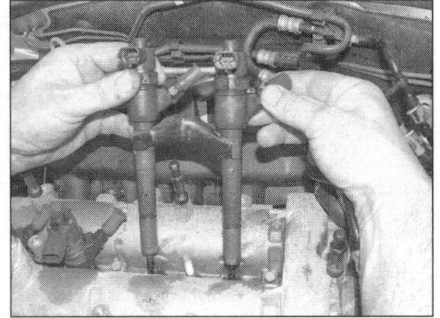
13.8b...then withdraw the two injectors together with the clamp bracket

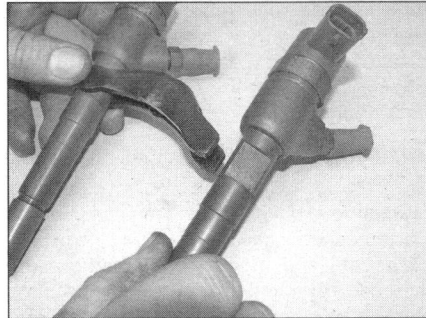
13.8c The clamp bracket engages with slots in the injector body

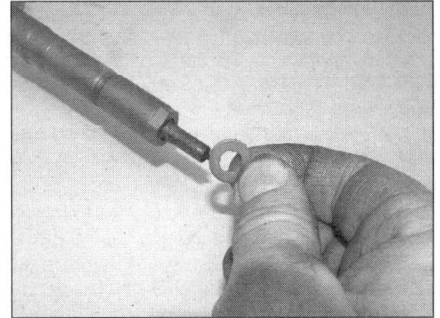
13.9 Remove the copper washer from each injector

Counterhold the union on the injector with an open-ended spanner, while tightening the union nut. Repeat this operation for the remaining three injectors.

19 Reconnect the fuel leak-off hose fittings to the injectors by pushing in the locking clip, attaching the fitting, then releasing the locking clip. Ensure that each fitting is securely connected and retained by the clip.

20 Reconnect the fuel injector wiring connectors and secure with the locking catches.

21 Observing the precautions listed in Section 2, prime the fuel system as described in Section 5, then start the engine and allow it to idle. Check for leaks at the high-pressure fuel pipe unions with the engine idling. If satisfactory, increase the engine speed to 4000 rpm and check again for leaks. If any leaks are detected, obtain and fit a new high-pressure fuel pipe(s).

22 Refit the engine cover on completion.

14 Fuel pressure regulating valve – removal and refitting

Note: *Refer to the warnings and precautions contained in Section 2 before proceeding.*

Removal

1 The fuel pressure regulating valve is located on the left-hand end of the fuel rail.

2 Disconnect the battery negative terminal (refer to *Disconnecting the battery* in Chapter 5A, Section 4).

3 Lift off the plastic cover over the top of the engine.

4 Disconnect the pressure regulating valve wiring connector.

5 Undo the two retaining bolts and remove the valve from the fuel rail. Recover the sealing O-ring.

Refitting

6 Thoroughly clean the fuel rail and pressure regulating valve mating faces.

7 Locate a new sealing O-ring on the pressure regulating valve and lubricate the O-ring with clean diesel fuel.

8 Refit the valve to the fuel rail and secure with the two retaining bolts tightened to the specified torque.

9 Reconnect the wiring connector and refit the engine cover.

15 Inlet manifold – removal and refitting

Removal

1 Disconnect the battery negative terminal (refer to *Disconnecting the battery* in Chapter 5A, Section 4).

2 Drain the cooling system as described in Chapter 1B, Section 28.

3 Remove the windscreen cowl panel as described in Chapter 11, Section 20.

4 Remove the battery and battery tray as described in Chapter 5A, Section 4.

5 Undo the bolts securing the charge air pipe

15.8 Undo the two bolts and free the oil separator from the inlet manifold

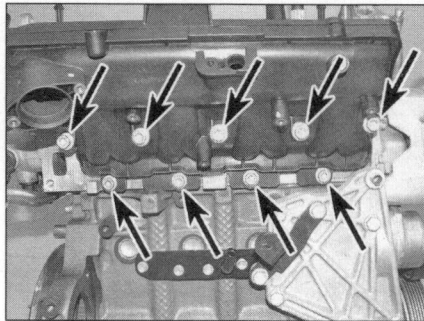
15.15a Undo the retaining bolts and remove the inlet manifold...

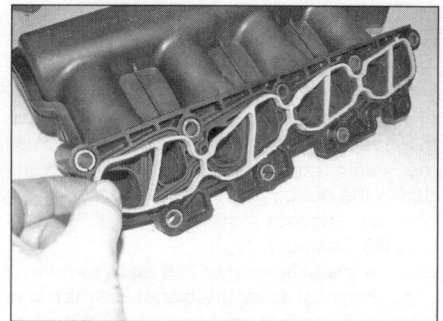
15.15b...then remove the rubber gasket from the manifold flange

to the throttle housing or inlet manifold flange and the bolt securing the pipe support to the thermostat housing. Manipulate the charge air pipe from its location and recover the sealing ring.

6 Detach the two cable-ties and release the wiring harness from the engine oil dipstick guide tube.

7 Trace the all the fuel and return hoses back to their relevant connectors and either disconnect the quick-release fittings or release the hose clamps. Release all the hoses from their retaining clips.

8 Undo the two bolts and free the crankcase ventilation system oil separator from the inlet manifold **(see illustration)**.

9 Withdraw the engine oil dipstick, then undo the retaining bolt securing the dipstick guide tube to the inlet manifold.

10 Disconnect the wiring harness connectors at the EGR valve, fuel pressure regulating valve, charge pressure sensor, fuel pressure sensor, and throttle housing solenoid valve. Release the wiring harness from the retaining clips and cable-ties.

11 Undo the retaining bolts and detach the crankcase ventilation hose attachment from the timing cover.

12 Remove the throttle housing as described in Section 10.

13 Remove the exhaust gas recirculation (EGR) valve as described in Chapter 4C, Section 3.

14 Check that all hoses, wiring and component attachments have been released to allow removal of the manifold.

15 Undo the nine retaining bolts (noting their different lengths) and remove the inlet manifold from the cylinder head. Remove the rubber gasket from the manifold flange **(see illustrations)**.

Refitting

16 Thoroughly clean the inlet manifold and cylinder head mating faces, then locate a new rubber gasket on the inlet manifold flange.

17 Locate the manifold in position and refit the retaining bolts. Diagonally and progressively, tighten the bolts to the specified torque.

18 The remainder of refitting is a reversal of removal, with reference to the Sections and Chapters indicated.

16 Intercooler – removal and refitting

Removal

1 Remove the front bumper as described in Chapter 11, Section 6.

2 Disconnect the quick-release fittings and remove the two charge air hoses from the intercooler. Undo the bolt each side securing the charge air hose clamps to the radiator support crossmember **(see illustrations)**.

3 Undo the retaining bolt on the left-hand side of the intercooler, and pull the intercooler out of the radiator mounting bracket **(see illustration)**.

Refitting

4 Refitting is a reversal of removal.

17 Exhaust manifold – removal and refitting

Removal

1 Remove the turbocharger as described in Section 19.

2 Remove the oil filter housing as described in Chapter 2C, Section 14.

3 Undo the bolt and two nuts securing the heat shield to the manifold. Lift off the heat shield and collect the engine lifting eye.

4 Undo the ten nuts securing the exhaust manifold to the cylinder head. Withdraw the manifold from the cylinder head studs and remove it from the engine. Recover the manifold gasket, noting that a new gasket and new manifold retaining nuts will be required for refitting.

Refitting

5 Thoroughly clean the mating faces of the exhaust manifold then locate the exhaust manifold over the cylinder head studs. Secure with the new nuts tightened progressively to the specified torque.

6 The remainder of refitting is a reversal of removal.

16.2a Disconnect the two charge air hoses from the intercooler...

16.2b...then undo the bolt each side securing the charge air hose clamps to the radiator support crossmember

16.3 Intercooler retaining bolt

18 Turbocharger – description and precautions

Description

1 The turbocharger increases engine efficiency by raising the pressure in the inlet manifold above atmospheric pressure. Instead of the air simply being sucked into the cylinders, it is forced in.

2 Energy for the operation of the turbocharger comes from the exhaust gas. The gas flows through a specially-shaped housing (the turbine housing) and, in so doing, spins the turbine wheel. The turbine wheel is attached to a shaft, at the end of which is another vaned wheel known as the compressor wheel. The compressor wheel spins in its own housing, and compresses the inlet air on the way to the inlet manifold.

3 The turbocharger operates on the principle of variable vane geometry. At low engine speeds the vanes close to give less flow cross-section, then as the speed increases the vanes open to give an increased flow cross-section. This helps improve the efficiency of the turbocharger.

4 Boost pressure (the pressure in the inlet manifold) is limited by a wastegate, which diverts the exhaust gas away from the turbine wheel in response to a pressure-sensitive actuator.

5 The turbo shaft is pressure-lubricated by an oil feed pipe from the main oil gallery. The shaft 'floats' on a cushion of oil. A drain pipe returns the oil to the sump.

Precautions

6 The turbocharger operates at extremely high speeds and temperatures. Certain precautions must be observed, to avoid premature failure of the turbo, or injury to the operator.

7 Do not operate the turbo with any of its parts exposed, or with any of its hoses removed. Foreign objects falling onto the rotating vanes could cause excessive damage, and (if ejected) personal injury.

8 Do not race the engine immediately after start-up, especially if it is cold. Give the oil a few seconds to circulate.

9 Always allow the engine to return to idle speed before switching it off – do not blip the throttle and switch off, as this will leave the turbo spinning without lubrication.

10 Allow the engine to idle for several minutes before switching off after a high-speed run.

11 Observe the recommended intervals for oil and filter changing, and use a reputable oil of the specified quality. Neglect of oil changing, or use of inferior oil, can cause carbon formation on the turbo shaft, leading to subsequent failure.

19 Turbocharger – removal, inspection and refitting

Removal

1 Disconnect the battery negative terminal (refer to *Disconnecting the battery* in Chapter 5A, Section 4).

2 Lift off the plastic cover over the top of the engine.

3 Remove the air cleaner assembly and turbocharger air inlet hose as described in Section 3.

4 Remove the turbocharger wastegate solenoid as described in Section 10.

5 Remove the oxygen sensor as described in Chapter 4C, Section 3.

6 Undo the two upper nuts and one lower nut, then lift off the turbocharger heat shield.

7 Unscrew the turbocharger oil supply pipe banjo union bolt from the top of the turbocharger and collect the two sealing washers.

8 Similarly, unscrew the turbocharger oil supply pipe banjo union bolt from the oil filter housing and collect the two sealing washers. Remove the oil supply pipe.

9 Release the retaining clips and remove the turbocharger oil return hose from the turbocharger and oil filter housing.

10 Undo the two bolts and separate the intercooler intake air duct flange from the turbocharger. Collect the gasket.

11 Remove the catalytic converter/diesel particulate filter as described in Section 20.

12 Undo the three nuts (one from above and two from below) securing the turbocharger to the exhaust manifold. Lift off the turbocharger and recover the gasket.

Inspection

13 With the turbocharger removed, inspect the housing for cracks or other visible damage.

14 Spin the turbine or the compressor wheel, to verify that the shaft is intact and to feel for excessive shake or roughness. Some play is normal, since in use, the shaft is 'floating' on a film of oil. Check that the wheel vanes are undamaged.

15 If oil contamination of the exhaust or induction passages is apparent, it is likely that turbo shaft oil seals have failed.

16 No DIY repair of the turbo is possible and none of the internal or external parts are available separately. If the turbocharger is suspect in any way a complete new unit must be obtained.

Refitting

17 Refitting is the reverse of removal, noting the following points.
a) Ensure all mating surfaces are clean and dry and renew all gaskets and sealing washers.
b) Tighten all retaining nuts and bolts to the specified torque (where given).

20 Exhaust system – general information and component renewal

General information

1 On models without a diesel particulate filter, or with a diesel particulate filter integral with the catalytic converter, the exhaust system is in two sections. The front section comprises the front pipe and flexible section and the rear section consists of the tailpipe and silencer.

2 On models with a separate diesel particulate filter, a three-section exhaust system is used. The front section comprises the front pipe and flexible section, the intermediate section contains the particulate filter and the rear section consists of the tailpipe and silencer.

3 Periodically, the exhaust system should be checked for signs of leaks or damage. Also inspect the system rubber mountings, and renew if necessary.

4 Small holes or cracks can be repaired using proprietary exhaust repair products.

5 Before renewing an individual section of the exhaust system, it is wise to inspect the remaining section. If corrosion or damage is evident, it may prove more economical to renew the entire system.

Component renewal

Models without a particulate filter or with a particulate filter integral with the catalytic converter

6 If either part of the system is to be renewed, it is important to ensure that the correct component is obtained.

7 To remove the rear tailpipe and silencer, chock the front wheels then jack up the rear of the vehicle and support on axle stands (see *Jacking and vehicle support*). Loosen the clamp securing the front pipe to the tailpipe, then release the rubber mountings and slide the tailpipe from the front pipe (see illustration). If the tailpipe is rusted onto the front pipe, apply liberal amounts of penetrating oil and tap around the joint with a hammer to free it. Twist the tailpipe in both directions while holding the front pipe.

8 To remove the front section of the exhaust, jack up the front and rear of the vehicle

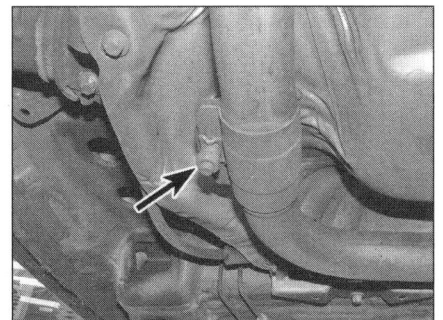

20.7 Exhaust front pipe-to-tailpipe retaining clamp bolt

20.9 Removing the exhaust system front pipe from the catalytic converter/ particulate filter

and support it on axle stands (see *Jacking and vehicle support*). Undo the two bolts and remove the cross-brace from the front subframe.

9 Remove the tailpipe and silencer as described in paragraph 7. Loosen the clamp securing the exhaust front pipe to the catalytic converter/particulate filter then release the rubber mountings and slide the front pipe from the catalytic converter **(see illustration)**. While doing this, take care to support the flexible section. Angular movement in excess of 10° can cause permanent damage to the flexible section. If the front pipe is rusted onto the catalytic converter, apply liberal amounts of penetrating oil and tap around the joint with a hammer to free it. Twist the front pipe in both directions until free.

10 Refitting is a reversal of removal, tightening the clamp nuts to the specified torque. When refitting the cross-brace to the front subframe, note that the side marked LH must be toward the left-hand side of the car. Tighten the cross-brace retaining bolts to the specified torque.

Models with a separate particulate filter

11 If any part of the system is to be renewed, it is important to ensure that the correct component is obtained.

12 To remove the rear tailpipe and silencer, chock the front wheels then jack up the rear of the vehicle and support on axle stands (see *Jacking and vehicle support*). Loosen the clamp securing the intermediate pipe to the tailpipe, then release the rubber mountings and slide the tailpipe from the intermediate pipe. If the tailpipe is rusted onto the intermediate pipe, apply liberal amounts of penetrating oil and tap around the joint with a hammer to free it. Twist the tailpipe in both directions while holding the intermediate pipe.

13 To remove the intermediate section of the exhaust, jack up the front and rear of the vehicle and support it on axle stands (see *Jacking and vehicle support*). Remove the tailpipe and silencer as described in paragraph 12.

14 Undo the three nuts and separate the front pipe flange from the intermediate pipe flange.

15 Suitably support the intermediate section and undo the two bolts securing the rubber mounting support crossmember to the underbody. Lower the intermediate section and remove it from under the car.

16 To remove the front section of the exhaust, jack up the front and rear of the vehicle and support it on axle stands (see *Jacking and vehicle support*). Undo the two bolts and remove the cross-brace from the front subframe.

17 Undo the two union nuts and detach the particulate filter temperature sensor and the differential pressure sensor from the front pipe.

18 Undo the two bolts securing the rubber mounting support crossmember to the underbody.

19 Suitably support the intermediate section, then undo the three nuts and separate the front pipe flange from the intermediate pipe flange.

20 Loosen the clamp securing the exhaust front pipe to the catalytic converter and slide the front pipe from the catalytic converter **(see illustration 20.9)**. While doing this, take care to support the flexible section. Angular movement in excess of 10° can cause permanent damage to the flexible section. If the front pipe is rusted onto the catalytic converter, apply liberal

amounts of penetrating oil and tap around the joint with a hammer to free it. Twist the front pipe in both directions until free.

21 Refitting is a reversal of removal, tightening all fastenings to the specified torque. When refitting the cross-brace to the front subframe, note that the side marked LH must be toward the left-hand side of the car. Tighten the cross-brace retaining bolts to the specified torque.

Catalytic converter

22 Disconnect the battery negative terminal (refer to *Disconnecting the battery* in Chapter 5A, Section 4).

23 Remove the plastic cover from the top of the engine.

24 Remove the front section of the exhaust system as described previously in this Section.

25 Remove the oxygen sensor as described in Chapter 4C, Section 3.

26 Undo the three nuts and lift off the turbocharger heat shield.

27 Disconnect the exhaust temperature sensor, then unscrew the temperature sensor from the catalytic converter.

28 Undo the five retaining bolts and remove the catalytic converter heat shield.

29 Undo the two nuts securing the catalytic converter to the support bracket.

30 Disconnect the oxygen sensor wiring connector.

31 Release the retaining clip and disconnect the exhaust pressure sensor hose from the catalytic converter pipe.

32 Undo the catalytic converter lower mounting bolt.

33 Slacken the catalytic converter clamp bolt nut. Expand the clamp and disconnect the catalytic converter from the exhaust manifold. Lift the catalytic converter up and out of the engine compartment. Collect the front pipe-to-catalytic converter gasket.

34 Refitting is a reversal of removal. When refitting the cross-brace to the front subframe, note that the side marked LH must be toward the left-hand side of the car. Tighten the cross-brace retaining bolts to the specified torque.

Chapter 4 Part C
Emissions control systems

Contents

Degrees of difficulty

Easy, suitable for novice with little experience	Fairly easy, suitable for beginner with some experience	Fairly difficult, suitable for competent DIY mechanic	Difficult, suitable for experienced DIY mechanic	Very difficult, suitable for expert DIY or professional

Specifications

Torque wrench settings	Nm	lbf ft
EGR pipe bolts	10	7
EGR valve bolts	25	18
EGR valve cooler bolts	22	16
Oxygen sensor	45	33
Catalytic converter temperature sensor	45	33

1 General information and precautions

1 All petrol engine models use unleaded petrol and also have various other features built into the fuel/exhaust system to help minimise harmful emissions. All models are equipped with a crankcase emission control system, a catalytic converter and an evaporative emission control system to keep fuel vapour/exhaust gas emissions down to a minimum.

2 Diesel engine models are also designed to meet strict emission requirements. A crankcase emission control system, a catalytic converter and, on some models, a diesel particulate filter are fitted to keep exhaust emissions down to a minimum. An exhaust gas recirculation (EGR) system is also used to further decrease exhaust emissions.

3 The emission control systems function as follows.

Petrol engines

Crankcase emissions control

4 To reduce the emission of unburned hydrocarbons from the crankcase into the atmosphere, the engine is sealed and the blow-by gases and oil vapour are drawn from the camshaft cover into the inlet manifold to be burned by the engine during normal combustion.

5 The gases are forced out of the crankcase by the relatively higher crankcase pressure; if the engine is worn, the raised crankcase pressure (due to increased blow-by) will cause some of the flow to return under all manifold conditions.

Exhaust emission control

6 To minimise the amount of pollutants which escape into the atmosphere, all models are fitted with a catalytic converter which is integral with the exhaust manifold. The system is of the closed-loop type, in which oxygen sensors in the exhaust system provide the fuel injection/ignition system ECU with constant feedback, enabling the ECU to adjust the mixture to provide the best possible conditions for the converter to operate.

7 On all petrol engines covered by this manual, there are two heated oxygen sensors fitted to the exhaust system. The sensor on the top of the exhaust manifold/catalytic converter determines the residual oxygen content of the exhaust gases for mixture correction. The sensor in the exhaust front pipe (after the catalytic converter) monitors the function of the catalytic converter to give the driver a warning signal if there is a fault.

8 The oxygen sensor's tip is sensitive to oxygen and sends the ECU a varying voltage depending on the amount of oxygen in the exhaust gases. Peak conversion efficiency of all major pollutants occurs if the inlet air/fuel mixture is maintained at the chemically-correct ratio for the complete combustion of petrol of 14.7 parts (by weight) of air to 1 part of fuel (the 'stoichiometric' ratio). The sensor output voltage alters in a large step at this point, the ECU using the signal change as a reference point and correcting the inlet air/fuel mixture accordingly by altering the fuel injector pulse width.

Fuel evaporation emission control

9 To minimise the escape into the atmosphere of unburned hydrocarbons, a fuel evaporation emission control system is fitted. The fuel tank filler cap is sealed and a charcoal canister is mounted behind the wheel arch liner under the right-hand rear wing. The canister collects the petrol vapours generated in the tank when the car is parked and stores them until they can be cleared from the canister (under the control of the fuel injection/ignition system ECU) via the purge valve into the inlet manifold to be burned by the engine during normal combustion.

10 To ensure that the engine runs correctly when it is cold and/or idling and to protect the catalytic converter from the effects of an over-rich mixture, the purge control valve is not opened by the ECU until the engine has warmed-up, and the engine is under load; the valve solenoid is then modulated on and off to allow the stored vapour to pass into the inlet manifold.

Diesel engines

Crankcase emission control

11 Refer to paragraphs 4 and 5.

Exhaust emission control

12 To minimise the level of exhaust pollutants released into the atmosphere, a catalytic converter and, on some models, a diesel particulate filter are fitted in the exhaust system.

13 The catalytic converter consists of a canister containing a fine mesh impregnated with a catalyst material, over which the hot exhaust gases pass. The catalyst speeds up the oxidation of harmful carbon monoxide and unburned hydrocarbons, effectively reducing the quantity of harmful products released into the atmosphere via the exhaust gases.

14 On engines without a diesel particulate filter, a heated oxygen sensor is fitted to the exhaust system, upstream of the primary catalytic converter. The sensor monitors the quality of the exhaust gases and provides a signal to the ECU which is then used for mixture correction.

15 On engines with a diesel particulate filter, the filter is either integral with the catalytic converter or incorporated in the exhaust system intermediate section. The filter contains a silicon carbide honeycomb block containing microscopic channels in which the exhaust gases flow. As the gases flow through the honeycomb channels, soot particles are deposited on the channel walls. To prevent clogging of the honeycomb channels, the soot particles are burned off at regular intervals

during what is known as a 'regeneration phase'. Under the control of the injection system ECU, the injection characteristics are altered to raise the temperature of the exhaust gases to approximately 600°C. At this temperature, the soot particles are effectively burned off the honeycomb walls as the exhaust gases pass through. A differential pressure sensor and temperature sensor are used to inform the ECU of the condition of the particulate filter, and the temperature of the exhaust gases during the regeneration phase. When the ECU detects that soot build-up is reducing the efficiency of the particulate filter, it will instigate the regeneration process. This occurs at regular intervals under certain driving conditions and will normally not be detected by the driver.

Exhaust gas recirculation system

16 This system is designed to recirculate small quantities of exhaust gas into the inlet manifold, and therefore into the combustion process. This reduces the level of unburnt hydrocarbons present in the exhaust gas before it reaches the catalytic converter. The system is controlled by the injection system ECU, using the information from its various sensors, via the electrically-operated EGR valve.

---

2 Petrol engine emissions control systems – testing and component renewal

---

Crankcase emission control

1 The components of this system require no attention other than to check that the hose(s) are clear and undamaged at regular intervals.

Evaporative emission control

Testing

2 If the system is thought to be faulty, disconnect the hoses from the charcoal canister and purge control valve and check that they are clear by blowing through them. Full testing of the system can only be carried out using specialist electronic equipment which is connected to the engine management

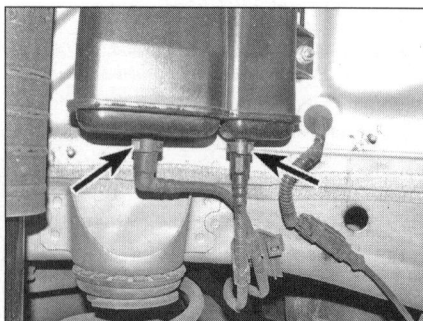

2.5 Disconnect the two vent hoses at the quick-release connectors on the charcoal canister

system diagnostic wiring connector. If the purge control valve or charcoal canister are thought to be faulty, they must be renewed.

Charcoal canister renewal

3 Chock the front wheels then jack up the rear of the vehicle and support on axle stands (see *Jacking and vehicle support*). Remove the right-hand rear wheel.

4 Unscrew the five nuts and two bolts and remove the right-hand rear wheel arch liner for access to the charcoal canister.

5 Disconnect the two vent hoses at the quick-release connectors on the charcoal canister **(see illustration)**. A Vauxhall/Opel special tool is available to release the connectors, but provided care is taken, the connectors can be released using a pair of long-nosed pliers, or a similar tool, to depress the retaining tangs. Suitably seal the vent hoses and canister unions to prevent dirt ingress.

6 Release the two disconnected vent hoses from the retaining bracket located below the charcoal canister.

7 Unscrew the two retaining nuts and remove the canister from under the wheel arch **(see illustration)**.

8 Refitting is a reversal of the removal procedure. Make sure the hoses are correctly and securely reconnected.

Purge valve renewal

9 The purge valve is mounted on the top of the inlet manifold.

10 Remove the air cleaner assembly as described in Chapter 4B, Section 3.

11 Release the purge valve pipe from the clip on the bulkhead, then disconnect the pipe from the purge valve hose.

12 Disconnect the wiring connector from the purge valve.

13 Using a suitable tool, open the purge valve mounting bracket and withdraw the valve from the bracket.

14 Refitting is a reversal of the removal procedure.

Exhaust emission control

Testing

15 The performance of the catalytic converter can be checked only by measuring the exhaust gases using a good-quality, carefully-calibrated exhaust gas analyser.

16 If the CO level at the tailpipe is too high, the vehicle should be taken to a Vauxhall/Opel dealer so that the complete fuel injection and ignition systems, including the oxygen sensors, can be thoroughly checked using the special diagnostic equipment. Once these have been checked and are known to be free from faults, the fault must be in the catalytic converter, which must be renewed.

Catalytic converter renewal

17 The catalytic converter is welded to the exhaust manifold, and the removal and refitting procedure is described in Chapter 4A, Section 12.

2.7 Unscrew the two retaining nuts and remove the canister from under the wheel arch

Mixture regulation oxygen sensor renewal

Caution: The sensor will be very hot if the engine has been running.

18 The mixture regulation oxygen sensor is located on the exhaust manifold **(see illustration)**. First, trace the wiring back from the sensor to the connector on the left-hand side of the cylinder head and disconnect it. Release the wiring from the clip.

19 Unscrew the sensor from the exhaust manifold. Ideally, a special 'split' socket should be used, as this will locate over the sensor wiring.

20 Clean the threads of the sensor then coat them with Vauxhall/Opel special grease for oxygen sensors. If a new sensor is being fitted, it will be supplied with the threads already coated with the special grease to prevent it seizing in the manifold.

21 Screw the sensor into the exhaust manifold and tighten to the specified torque.

22 Reconnect the wiring and clip it in place.

Catalytic converter control oxygen sensor renewal

Caution: The sensor will be very hot if the engine has been running.

23 The catalytic converter control oxygen sensor is located in the exhaust front pipe, just behind the flexible section **(see illustration)**. First, apply the handbrake, then jack up the front of the vehicle and support it on axle stands (see *Jacking and vehicle support*).

24 Trace the wiring back from the sensor to the connector above the right-hand driveshaft, and disconnect it. Release the wiring from the clips.

25 Unscrew the sensor from the exhaust front pipe. Ideally, a special 'split' socket should be used, as this will locate over the sensor wiring.

26 Clean the threads of the sensor then coat them with Vauxhall/Opel special grease for oxygen sensors. If a new sensor is being fitted, it will be supplied with the threads already coated with the special grease to prevent it seizing in the pipe.

27 Screw the sensor into the exhaust front pipe and tighten to the specified torque.

28 Reconnect the wiring and clip it in place.

---

3 Diesel engine emissions control systems – testing and component renewal

---

Crankcase emission control

1 The components of this system require no attention other than to check that the hose(s) are clear and undamaged at regular intervals.

Exhaust emission control

Testing

2 The performance of the catalytic converter and diesel particulate filter can only be checked using special diagnostic equipment. If a system fault is suspected, the vehicle should be taken to a Vauxhall/Opel dealer so

2.18 Mixture regulation oxygen sensor location

that the complete fuel injection system can be thoroughly checked.

Catalytic converter/ diesel particulate filter renewal

3 Refer to Chapter 4B, Section 20, for removal and refitting details.

Oxygen sensor renewal

4 Warm the engine up to normal operating temperature then stop the engine and disconnect the battery negative terminal (refer to Disconnecting the battery in Chapter 5A, Section 4). Remove the plastic cover from the top of the engine.

5 Disconnect the oxygen sensor wiring connector, then unclip the wiring plug from the support bracket.

6 Trace the wiring back to the sensor and release the wiring from the cable clips.

Caution: Take great care not burn yourself on the hot manifold/sensor.

7 Unscrew the sensor and remove it from the exhaust manifold **(see illustration)**.

8 Refitting is a reverse of the removal procedure. Prior to installing the sensor, apply a smear of high-temperature grease to the sensor threads (Vauxhall/Opel recommend the use of a special grease available from your dealer). Tighten the sensor to the specified torque and ensure that the wiring is correctly routed and in no danger of contacting either the exhaust system or engine.

Particulate filter temperature sensor renewal

9 Proceed as described in paragraphs 4 to 8 **(see illustration)**.

3.7 Unscrew the oxygen sensor and remove it from the exhaust manifold

2.23 Catalytic converter control oxygen sensor

Exhaust gas recirculation system

Testing

10 Comprehensive testing of the system can only be carried out using specialist electronic equipment which is connected to the injection system diagnostic wiring connector (see Chapter 4B). If the EGR valve or solenoid valve are thought to be faulty, they must be renewed.

EGR valve renewal

All engines except Z13DTJ

11 Disconnect the battery negative terminal (refer to Disconnecting the battery in Chapter 5A, Section 4). Remove the plastic cover over the top of the engine.

12 Remove the windscreen cowl panel as described in Chapter 11, Section 20.

13 Firmly apply the handbrake, then jack up the front of the vehicle and support it securely on axle stands (see *Jacking and vehicle support*).

14 Disconnect the EGR valve wiring connector.

15 Unscrew the two bolts and remove the valve from the EGR cooler. Recover the gasket.

16 Refitting is the reverse of removal using a new gasket and tightening the retaining bolts to the specified torque.

Z13DTJ engines

17 Disconnect the battery negative terminal (refer toDisconnecting the batteryin Chapter 5A, Section 4). Remove the plastic cover over the top of the engine.

3.9 Particulate filter temperature sensor

3.27 Slacken the retaining screw and release the EGR pipe clamp

3.28 Undo the two bolts and remove the EGR valve and cooler assembly

18 Drain the cooling system as described in Chapter 1B, Section 28.
19 Remove the windscreen cowl panel as described in Chapter 11, Section 20.
20 Working below the thermostat housing, slacken the retaining clip and disconnect the air hose connecting the intercooler to the inlet manifold charge air pipe.
21 Undo the bolts securing the charge air pipe to the inlet manifold flange and the bolt securing the pipe support to the thermostat housing. Manipulate the charge air pipe out from its location and recover the sealing ring.
22 Slacken the retaining clips or disconnect the quick-release fittings and detach the two coolant hoses for the EGR valve cooler.
23 Slacken the retaining clip and detach the coolant hose from the thermostat housing.
24 Release the quick-release fittings and disconnect the brake servo vacuum hose from the vacuum pump.
25 Undo the bolt and detach the wiring harness bracket located above the starter motor.
26 Disconnect the wiring connector from the top of the EGR valve.
27 Slacken the retaining screw and release the clamp securing the EGR pipe to the inlet manifold **(see illustration)**.
28 Undo the two mounting bolts and one support bracket bolt, then remove the EGR valve and cooler assembly from the engine **(see illustration)**. Recover the gasket.
29 Refitting is the reverse of removal, bearing in mind the following points:
a) Thoroughly clean the mating faces and use a new gasket. It will be necessary to insert the mounting bolts into the valve prior to refitting, to retain the gasket in position.
b) Refit the windscreen cowl panel as described in Chapter 11, Section 20.
c) Refill the cooling system as described in Chapter 1B, Section 28.

EGR valve cooler renewal

All engines except Z13DTJ

30 Drain the cooling system as described in Chapter 1B, Section 28.
31 Remove the windscreen cowl panel as described in Chapter 11, Section 20.

32 Remove the battery and battery tray as described in Chapter 5A, Section 4.
33 Remove the intercooler outlet air duct as described in Chapter 4B, Section 3.
34 Undo the bolt securing the exhaust pressure sensor pipe to the throttle housing support bracket.
35 Undo the bolt securing the pressure sensor pipe to the pressure sensor mounting bracket. Release the hose retaining clip, disconnect the pressure sensor hose and remove the pressure sensor pipe.
36 Undo the two bolts securing the EGR pipe to the EGR cooler.
37 Undo the three bolts securing the EGR pipe to the inlet manifold. Lift off the pipe and collect the gasket and O-ring seal.
38 Undo the two bolts and remove the throttle housing support bracket.
39 Release the retaining clip and disconnect the coolant hose from the EGR valve cooler.
40 Disconnect the wiring connectors at the EGR valve and the EGR valve actuator. Disconnect the vacuum hose from the EGR valve actuator.
41 Undo the three retaining bolts and remove the EGR valve cooler. Collect the gasket.
42 Refitting is the reverse of removal, bearing in mind the following points:
a) Renew all disturbed gaskets and seals.
b) Tighten the retaining bolts/nuts to the specified torque (where given).
c) Refit the intercooler outlet air duct as described in Chapter 4B, Section 3.
d) Refit the battery tray and battery as described in Chapter 5A, Section 4.
e) Refit the windscreen cowl panel as described in Chapter 11, Section 20.
f) Refill the cooling system as described in Chapter 1B, Section 28.

Z13DTJ engines

43 Remove the EGR valve as described previously in this Section.
44 Release the retaining clips and disconnect all the coolant hoses from the EGR valve cooler.
45 Undo the retaining bolts and detach the EGR cooler from the EGR valve.

46 Refitting is the reverse of removal, bearing in mind the following points:
a) Renew all disturbed gaskets and seals.
b) Refit the EGR valve as described previously in this Section.

4 Catalytic converter – general information and precautions

1 The catalytic converter is a reliable and simple device which needs no maintenance in itself, but there are some facts of which an owner should be aware if the converter is to function properly for its full service life.

Petrol engines

a) DO NOT use leaded petrol or LRP in a car equipped with a catalytic converter – the lead will coat the precious metals, reducing their converting efficiency and will eventually destroy the converter.
b) Always keep the ignition and fuel systems well-maintained in accordance with the manufacturer's schedule.
c) If the engine develops a misfire, do not drive the car at all (or at least as little as possible) until the fault is cured.
d) DO NOT push- or tow-start the car – this will soak the catalytic converter in unburned fuel, causing it to overheat when the engine does start.
e) DO NOT switch off the ignition at high engine speeds.
f) DO NOT use fuel or engine oil additives – these may contain substances harmful to the catalytic converter.
g) DO NOT continue to use the car if the engine burns oil to the extent of leaving a visible trail of blue smoke.
h) Remember that the catalytic converter operates at very high temperatures. DO NOT, therefore, park the car in dry undergrowth, over long grass or piles of dead leaves after a long run.
i) Remember that the catalytic converter is FRAGILE – do not strike it with tools during servicing work.
j) In some cases a sulphurous smell (like that of rotten eggs) may be noticed from the exhaust. This is common to many catalytic converter-equipped cars and once the car has covered a few thousand miles the problem should disappear.
k) The catalytic converter, used on a well-maintained and well-driven car, should last for between 50 000 and 100 000 miles – if the converter is no longer effective it must be renewed

Diesel engines

2 Refer to the information given in parts f, g, h, i and k of the petrol engines information given above.

Chapter 5 Part A
Starting and charging systems

Contents

Degrees of difficulty

Easy, suitable for novice with little experience	Fairly easy, suitable for beginner with some experience	Fairly difficult, suitable for competent DIY mechanic	Difficult, suitable for experienced DIY mechanic	Very difficult, suitable for expert DIY or professional

Specifications

General
Electrical system type .... 12 volt negative earth

Battery
Type .... Lead-acid, 'maintenance-free' (sealed for life)
Battery capacity.. 36, 44, 55 or 60 Ah (depending on model)
Charge condition:
   Poor .... 12.5 volts
   Normal .... 12.6 volts
   Good .... 12.7 volts

Alternator
Type .... Bosch or Delco-Remy
Regulated voltage .... 13.7 to 14.7 volts (approximately)

Starter motor
Type .... Pre-engaged, Delco-Remy or Valeo

Torque wrench settings	Nm	lbf ft
Alternator:		
Petrol engines..	35	26
Diesel engines	22	16
Auxiliary drivebelt tensioner:		
Petrol engines:		
M8 bolt.....................................	20	15
M10 bolt....................................	55	41
Diesel engines	50	37
Glow plugs......................................	10	7
Oil pressure warning light switch:		
Petrol engines..	20	15
Diesel engines	32	24
Roadwheel bolts..	110	81
Starter motor	25	18

1 General information and precautions

General information

1 The engine electrical system consists mainly of the charging and starting systems. Because of their engine-related functions, these components are covered separately from the body electrical devices such as the lights, instruments, etc (which are covered in Chapter 12). On petrol engine models refer to Part B for information on the ignition system.
2 The electrical system is of 12 volt negative earth type.
3 The battery is of the maintenance-free (sealed for life) type, and is charged by the alternator, which is belt-driven from the crankshaft pulley.
4 The starter motor is of pre-engaged type incorporating an integral solenoid. On starting, the solenoid moves the drive pinion into engagement with the flywheel/driveplate ring gear before the starter motor is energised. Once the engine has started, a one-way clutch prevents the motor armature being driven by the engine until the pinion disengages.
5 Further details of the various systems are given in the relevant Sections of this Chapter. While some repair procedures are given, the usual course of action is to renew the component concerned.

Precautions

6 It is necessary to take extra care when working on the electrical system to avoid damage to semi-conductor devices (diodes and transistors), and to avoid the risk of personal injury. In addition to the precautions given in *Safety first!*, observe the following when working on the system:
a) *Always remove rings, watches, etc, before working on the electrical system. Even with the battery disconnected, capacitive discharge could occur if a component's live terminal is earthed through a metal object. This could cause a shock or nasty burn.*
b) *Do not reverse the battery connections. Components such as the alternator, electronic control units, or any other components having semi-conductor circuitry could be irreparably damaged.*
c) *If the engine is being started using jump leads and a slave battery, connect the batteries positive-to-positive and negative-to-negative (see 'Jump starting'). This also applies when connecting a battery charger but in this case both of the battery terminals should first be disconnected.*
d) *Never disconnect the battery terminals, the alternator, any electrical wiring or any test instruments when the engine is running.*
e) *Do not allow the engine to turn the alternator when the alternator is not connected.*
f) *Never test for alternator output by flashing the output lead to earth.*
g) *Never use an ohmmeter of the type incorporating a hand-cranked generator for circuit or continuity testing.*
h) *Always ensure that the battery negative lead is disconnected when working on the electrical system.*
i) *Before using electric-arc welding equipment on the car, disconnect the battery, alternator and components such as the fuel injection/ignition electronic control unit to protect them from the risk of damage.*

2 Electrical fault finding – general information

1 Refer to Chapter 12, Section 2.

3 Battery – testing and charging

Testing

Traditional and low maintenance battery

1 If the vehicle covers a small annual mileage, it is worthwhile checking the specific gravity of the electrolyte every three months to determine the state of charge of the battery. Use a hydrometer to make the check and compare the results with the following table. Note that the specific gravity readings assume an electrolyte temperature of 15°C; for every 10°C below 15°C subtract 0.007. For every 10°C above 15°C add 0.007.

| | Ambient temperature | |
	above 25°C	below 25°C
Fully-charged	1.210 to 1.230	1.270 to 1.290
70% charged	1.170 to 1.190	1.230 to 1.250
Discharged	1.050 to 1.070	1.110 to 1.130

2 If the battery condition is suspect, first check the specific gravity of electrolyte in each cell. A variation of 0.040 or more between any cells indicates loss of electrolyte or deterioration of the internal plates.
3 If the specific gravity variation is 0.040 or

3.5 Battery condition indicator

more, the battery should be renewed. If the cell variation is satisfactory but the battery is discharged, it should be charged as described later in this Section.

Maintenance-free battery

4 Where a 'sealed for life' maintenance-free battery is fitted, topping-up and testing of the electrolyte in each cell is not possible. The condition of the battery can therefore only be tested using a battery condition indicator or a voltmeter.
5 Some models are fitted with a maintenance-free battery with a built-in 'magic-eye' charge condition indicator. The indicator is located in the top of the battery casing, and indicates the condition of the battery from its colour **(see illustration)**. If the indicator shows green, then the battery is in a good state of charge. If the indicator turns darker, eventually to black, then the battery requires charging, as described later in this Section. If the indicator shows clear/yellow, then the electrolyte level in the battery is too low to allow further use, and the battery should be renewed. Do not attempt to charge, load or jump start a battery when the indicator shows clear/yellow.

All battery types

6 If testing the battery using a voltmeter, connect the voltmeter across the battery and compare the result with those given in the Specifications under 'charge condition'. The test is only accurate if the battery has not been subjected to any kind of charge for the previous six hours. If this is not the case, switch on the headlights for 30 seconds, then wait four to five minutes before testing the battery after switching off the headlights. All other electrical circuits must be switched off, so check that the doors and tailgate are fully shut when making the test.
7 If the voltage reading is less than 12.2 volts, then the battery is discharged, whilst a reading of 12.2 to 12.4 volts indicates a partially-discharged condition.
8 If the battery is to be charged, remove it from the vehicle (Section 4) and charge it as described later in this Section.

Charging

Note: *The following is intended as a guide only. Always refer to the manufacturer's recommendations (often printed on a label attached to the battery) before charging a battery.*

Traditional and low maintenance battery

9 Charge the battery at a rate of 3.5 to 4 amps and continue to charge the battery at this rate until no further rise in specific gravity is noted over a four hour period.
10 Alternatively, a trickle charger charging at the rate of 1.5 amps can safely be used overnight.
11 Specially rapid 'boost' charges which are claimed to restore the power of the battery in

1 to 2 hours are not recommended, as they can cause serious damage to the battery plates through overheating.

12 While charging the battery, note that the temperature of the electrolyte should never exceed 38°C.

Maintenance-free battery

13 This battery type takes considerably longer to fully recharge than the standard type, the time taken being dependent on the extent of discharge, but it will take anything up to three days.

14 A constant voltage type charger is required, to be set, when connected, to 13.9 to 14.9 volts with a charger current below 25 amps. Using this method, the battery should be usable within three hours, giving a voltage reading of 12.5 volts, but this is for a partially-discharged battery and, as mentioned, full charging can take considerably longer.

15 If the battery is to be charged from a fully-discharged state (condition reading less than 12.2 volts), have it recharged by your Vauxhall/Opel dealer or local automotive electrician, as the charge rate is higher and constant supervision during charging is necessary.

4 Battery – disconnection, reconnection, removal and refitting

Battery

Disconnection and reconnection

1 Numerous systems fitted to the vehicle require battery power to be available at all times, either to ensure their continued operation (such as the clock) or to maintain control unit memories which would be erased if the battery were to be disconnected. Whenever the battery is to be disconnected therefore, first note the following, to ensure that there are no unforeseen consequences of this action:

a) First, on any vehicle with central locking, it is a wise precaution to remove the key from the ignition, and to keep it with you, so that it does not get locked in, if the central locking should engage accidentally when the battery is reconnected.

b) Depending on model and specification, the Vauxhall/Opel anti-theft alarm system may be of the type which is automatically activated when the vehicle battery is disconnected and/or reconnected. To prevent the alarm sounding on models so equipped, switch the ignition on, then off, and disconnect the battery within 15 seconds. If the alarm is activated when the battery is reconnected, switch the ignition on then off to deactivate the alarm.

c) The engine management electronic control unit is of the 'self-learning' type, meaning that as it operates, it also monitors and stores the settings which give optimum engine performance under

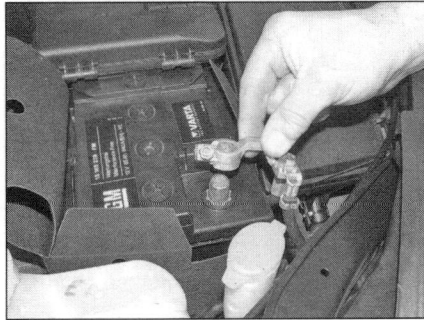
4.3 Disconnect the lead at the battery negative (–) terminal

all operating conditions. When the battery is disconnected, these settings are lost and the ECU reverts to the base settings programmed into its memory at the factory. On restarting, this may lead to the engine running/idling roughly for a short while, until the ECU has re-learned the optimum settings. This process is best accomplished by taking the vehicle on a road test (for approximately 15 minutes), covering all engine speeds and loads, concentrating mainly in the 2500 to 3500 rpm region.

d) On models equipped with automatic transmission, the transmission selector lever assembly incorporates an electrically-operated selector lever lock mechanism that prevents the lever being moved out of the P position unless the ignition is switched on and the brake pedal is depressed. If the selector lever is in the P position and the battery is disconnected, it will not be possible to move the selector lever out of position P by the normal means. Although it is possible to manually override the system (see Chapter 7B, Section 6), it is sensible to move the selector lever to the N position before disconnecting the battery.

e) On models with electric windows, it will be necessary to reprogramme the motors to restore the one-touch function of the buttons, after reconnection of the battery. To do this, fully close both front windows.

4.5a Disengage the legs of the junction box from the battery...

4.4 Unscrew the bolt securing the junction box terminal strip to the battery positive terminal

With the windows closed, depress the up button of the driver's side window for approximately 5 seconds, then release it and depress the passenger side window up button for approximately 5 seconds.

f) On models with an electric sliding sunroof, it will be necessary to fully open and fully close the sunroof after battery reconnection, to recalibrate the sensors.

g) On all models, when reconnecting the battery after disconnection, switch on the ignition and wait 10 seconds to allow the electronic vehicle systems to stabilise and re-initialise.

2 The battery is located at the front, left-hand side of the engine compartment.

3 Open the battery jacket (where fitted) and disconnect the lead at the negative (–) terminal by unscrewing the retaining nut and removing the terminal clamp **(see illustration)**. If necessary, the auxiliary lead may also be unbolted from the terminal. Note that the battery negative (–) and positive (+) terminal connections are stamped on the battery case.

4 Lift up the lid of the positive cable junction box on top of the battery, then unscrew the bolt securing the junction box terminal strip to the battery positive terminal **(see illustration)**.

5 Disengage the legs of the junction box from the battery, then lift off the junction box and place it to one side **(see illustrations)**.

6 Disconnect the lead at the battery positive (+) terminal by unscrewing the retaining

4.5b...then lift off the junction box and place it to one side

4.6 Disconnect the lead at the battery positive (+) terminal

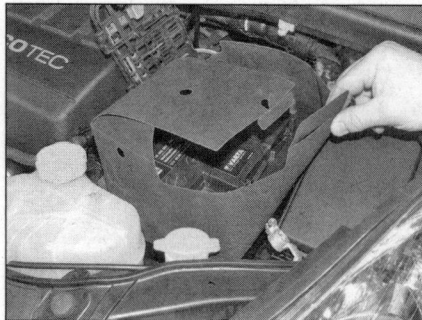

4.10 Where fitted, lift the battery jacket up and off the battery

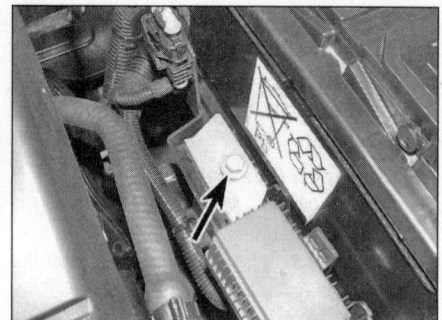

4.11 Unscrew the bolt and remove the battery retaining clamp

nut and removing the terminal clamp **(see illustration)**.

7 Reconnection is a reversal of disconnection, ensuring that the battery positive (+) lead is reconnected first.

8 After both leads have been reconnected, carry out the relevant procedures described in paragraph 1, as applicable.

Removal

9 Disconnect the battery terminals as described previously in this Section.

10 Where fitted, lift the battery jacket up and off the battery **(see illustration)**.

11 On the inner side of the battery, unscrew the bolt and remove the retaining clamp **(see illustration)**.

12 Carefully lift the battery from its location and remove from the car. Make sure the battery is kept upright at all times.

Refitting

13 Refitting is a reversal of removal. Reconnect the battery terminals as described previously in this Section.

Battery tray

Removal

14 Remove the battery as described previously in this Section.

15 Release the wiring harness cable ties from the battery tray and move the harness to one side **(see illustration)**.

16 Unclip the wiring harness connector and release it from the battery tray **(see illustration)**.

17 Unclip the pre/post-heating system control unit from the side of the battery tray and move it to one side **(see illustration)**.

18 On automatic transmission models, release the retaining lug and unclip the

transmission electronic control unit and mounting bracket from the battery tray.

19 Release the battery negative cable from the clip on the front of the battery tray **(see illustration)**.

20 Undo the three retaining bolts and remove the battery tray from the engine compartment **(see illustrations)**.

Refitting

21 Refitting is a reversal of removal.

5 Charging system – testing

Note: *Refer to the precautions given in 'Safety first!' and in Section 1 of this Chapter before starting work.*

4.15 Release the wiring harness cable ties from the battery tray

4.16 Unclip the wiring harness connector and release it from the battery tray

4.17 Unclip the pre/post-heating system control unit from the side of the battery tray

4.19 Release the battery negative cable from the clip on the front of the battery tray

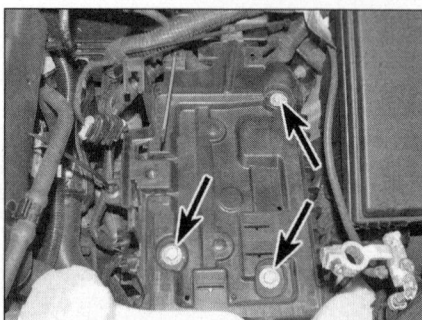

4.20a Undo the three retaining bolts...

4.20b ...and remove the battery tray from the engine compartment

7.3 Auxiliary drivebelt tensioner mounting bolts – petrol engines

7.7 Unscrew the tensioner body retaining bolt and withdraw the tensioner assembly – diesel engines

7.8 Ensure that the lug on the tensioner body engages with the cylinder block – diesel engines

1 If the ignition no-charge warning light fails to illuminate when the ignition is switched on, first check the alternator wiring connections for security. If satisfactory, check that the warning light bulb has not blown, and that the bulbholder is secure in its location in the instrument panel. If the light still fails to illuminate, check the continuity of the warning light feed wire from the alternator to the bulbholder. If all is satisfactory, the alternator is at fault, and should be renewed, or taken to an auto-electrician for testing and repair.

2 If the ignition warning light illuminates when the engine is running, stop the engine and check the condition of the auxiliary drivebelt (see Chapter 1A, Section 22 or Chapter 1B, Section 23) and that the alternator connections are secure. If all is so far satisfactory, the alternator should be taken to an auto-electrician for testing and repair.

3 If the alternator output is suspect even though the warning light functions correctly, the regulated voltage may be checked as follows.

4 Connect a voltmeter across the battery terminals, and start the engine.

5 Increase the engine speed until the voltmeter reading remains steady; the reading should be approximately 12 to 13 volts, and no more than 14 volts.

6 Switch on as many electrical accessories (eg, the headlights, heated rear window and heater blower) as possible, and check that the alternator maintains the regulated voltage at around 13.5 to 14.5 volts.

7 If the regulated voltage is not as stated, the fault may be due to worn brushes, weak brush springs, a faulty voltage regulator, a faulty diode, a severed phase winding, or worn or damaged slip-rings. The alternator should be renewed or taken to an auto-electrician for testing and repair.

6 Auxiliary drivebelt – removal and refitting

1 Refer to Chapter 1A, Section 32 or Chapter 1B, Section 31.

7 Auxiliary drivebelt tensioner – removal and refitting

Petrol engines

Removal

1 Firmly apply the handbrake, then jack up the front of the car and support it securely on axle stands (see Jacking and vehicle support). Remove the right-hand front roadwheel.

2 Release the tension on the auxiliary drivebelt and lock the tensioner in the released position as described in Chapter 1A, Section 32. Note that it is not necessary to completely remove the drivebelt, as this would entail removal of the right-hand engine mounting bracket.

3 Unscrew the upper and lower mounting bolts and withdraw the tensioner pulley and spring assembly **(see illustration)**.

Refitting

4 Refitting is a reversal of removal, but tighten the mounting bolts to the specified torque. Refit the auxiliary drivebelt as described in Chapter 1A, Section 32.

Diesel engines

Removal

5 Firmly apply the handbrake, then jack up the front of the car and support it securely on axle stands (see Jacking and vehicle support). Remove the right-hand front roadwheel.

6 Remove the auxiliary drivebelt as described in Chapter 1B, Section 31.

7 Unscrew the tensioner body retaining bolt and withdraw the tensioner assembly **(see illustration)**.

Refitting

8 Refitting is a reversal of removal, but tighten the mounting bolt to the specified torque. Ensure that the lug on the tensioner body engages with the corresponding hole on the cylinder block as the tensioner is refitted **(see illustration)**. Refit the auxiliary drivebelt as described in Chapter 1B, Section 31.

8 Alternator – removal and refitting

Petrol engines

Removal

1 The alternator is located on the rear of the cylinder block. First, apply the handbrake, then jack up the front of the vehicle and support it on axle stands (see Jacking and vehicle support). Remove the right-hand front roadwheel and the wheel arch liner cover for access to the right-hand side of the engine. Where necessary, remove the engine undertray.

2 Disconnect the battery negative terminal (refer to Disconnecting the battery in Section 4).

3 Release the tension on the auxiliary drivebelt and lock the tensioner in the released position as described in Chapter 1A, Section 32. Note that it is not necessary to completely remove the drivebelt, as this would entail removal of the right-hand engine mounting bracket. With the drivebelt tension released, slip the belt off the alternator pulley.

4 Unscrew the auxiliary drivebelt tensioner lower mounting bolt and pivot the tensioner away from the alternator

5 Disconnect the alternator wiring plug, then unscrew the nut and disconnect the wiring connector.

6 Unscrew the upper and lower mounting bolts/nuts and withdraw the alternator downwards from the block **(see illustration)**.

8.6 Alternator upper and lower mounting bolts/nuts – petrol engines

Refitting

7 Refitting is a reversal of removal, but tighten the mounting bolts to the specified torque. Refit the auxiliary drivebelt as described in Chapter 1A, Section 32.

Diesel engines

Removal

8 The alternator is located on the rear of the cylinder block. First apply the handbrake, then jack up the front of the vehicle and support it on axle stands (see *Jacking and vehicle support*). Remove the right-hand front roadwheel and the wheel arch liner cover for access to the right-hand side of the engine.

9 Disconnect the battery negative terminal (refer to *Disconnecting the battery* in Section 4).

10 Remove the auxiliary drivebelt as described in Chapter 1B, Section 31.

11 Unscrew the three nuts and disconnect the wiring from the rear of the alternator.

12 Unscrew the upper mounting bolt and the two lower mounting bolts, then withdraw the alternator downwards from the block **(see illustration)**.

Refitting

13 Refitting is a reversal of removal, but tighten the mounting bolts to the specified torque. Refit the auxiliary drivebelt as described in Chapter 1B, Section 31.

9 Alternator – testing and overhaul

1 If the alternator is thought to be suspect, it should be removed from the vehicle and taken to an auto-electrician for testing. Most auto-electricians will be able to supply and fit brushes at a reasonable cost. However, check on the cost of repairs before proceeding as it may prove more economical to obtain a new or exchange alternator.

10 Starting system – testing

1 Refer to the precautions given in *Safety first!* and in Section 1 of this Chapter before starting work.

2 If the starter motor fails to operate when the ignition key is turned to the appropriate position, the possible causes are as follows:

a) The engine immobiliser is faulty.
b) The battery is faulty.
c) The electrical connections between the switch, solenoid, battery and starter motor are somewhere failing to pass the necessary current from the battery through the starter to earth.
d) The solenoid is faulty.
e) The starter motor is mechanically or electrically defective.

8.12 Alternator mounting bolts – diesel engines

3 To check the battery, switch on the headlights. If they dim after a few seconds, this indicates that the battery is discharged – recharge (see Section 3) or renew the battery. If the headlights glow brightly, operate the starter switch while watching the headlights. If they dim, then this indicates that current is reaching the starter motor, therefore the fault must lie in the starter motor. If the lights continue to glow brightly (and no clicking sound can be heard from the starter motor solenoid), this indicates that there is a fault in the circuit or solenoid – see the following paragraphs. If the starter motor turns slowly when operated, but the battery is in good condition, then this indicates either that the starter motor is faulty, or there is considerable resistance somewhere in the circuit.

4 If a fault in the circuit is suspected, disconnect the battery leads (including the earth connection to the body), the starter/solenoid wiring and the engine/transmission earth strap. Thoroughly clean the connections, and reconnect the leads and wiring. Use a voltmeter or test light to check that full battery voltage is available at the battery positive lead connection to the solenoid. Smear petroleum jelly around the battery terminals to prevent corrosion – corroded connections are among the most frequent causes of electrical system faults.

5 If the battery and all connections are in good condition, check the circuit by disconnecting the switched feed wire from the solenoid (the thinner wire). Connect a voltmeter or test light between the wire end and a good earth (such

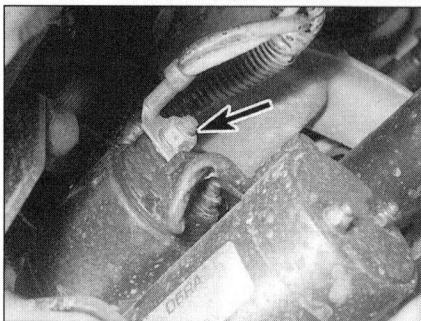

11.4 Battery positive cable connection on the starter motor – petrol engines

as the battery negative terminal), and check that the wire is live when the ignition switch is turned to the 'start' position. If it is, then the circuit is sound – if not, there is a fault in the ignition/starter switch or wiring.

6 The solenoid contacts can be checked by connecting a voltmeter or test light between the battery positive feed connection on the starter side of the solenoid and earth. When the ignition switch is turned to the 'start' position, there should be a reading or lighted bulb, as applicable. If there is no reading or lighted bulb, the solenoid is faulty and should be renewed.

7 If the circuit and solenoid are proved sound, the fault must lie in the starter motor. In this event, it may be possible to have the starter motor overhauled by a specialist, but check on the cost of spares before proceeding, as it may prove more economical to obtain a new or exchange motor.

11 Starter motor – removal and refitting

Petrol engines

Removal

1 Disconnect the battery negative terminal (refer to *Disconnecting the battery* in Section 4).

2 Apply the handbrake, then jack up the front of the vehicle and support it on axle stands (see *Jacking and vehicle support*).

3 On 1.0 litre engines, remove the alternator as described in Section 8.

4 Unscrew the two nuts and disconnect the battery positive cable and the starter trigger wire from the starter **(see illustration)**.

5 Unscrew the nut and disconnect the earth cable from the starter mounting bolt.

6 Unscrew the two mounting bolts and withdraw the starter motor from the rear of the engine.

Refitting

7 Refitting is a reversal of removal, but tighten the mounting bolts to the specified torque. On 1.0 litre engines, refit the alternator as described in Section 8.

Diesel engines

Removal

8 Disconnect the battery negative terminal (refer to *Disconnecting the battery* in Section 4).

9 On manual transmission models with a cable-operated gearchange mechanism, using a suitable forked tool, release the gear selector inner cable end fittings from the transmission selector levers. Pull back the retaining sleeves and detach the outer cables from the mounting bracket on the transmission.

10 Extract the rubber plug (where fitted) at the top of the transmission bellhousing for access to the starter upper mounting bolt.

11 Using a long socket bit inserted through the

access hole, unscrew and remove the upper mounting bolt **(see illustration)**. Take great care not to drop the bolt in the bellhousing.

12 Apply the handbrake, then jack up the front of the vehicle and support it on axle stands (see *Jacking and vehicle support*).

13 Where applicable, disconnect the two vacuum hoses from the vacuum reservoir at the rear of the cylinder block. Unscrew the nut and detach the earth cable, then undo the two bolts and remove the vacuum reservoir complete with its mounting bracket.

14 Undo the two nuts and disconnect the wiring from the starter solenoid **(see illustration)**.

15 Unscrew the lower mounting bolt and withdraw the starter motor from the engine.

Refitting

16 Refitting is a reversal of removal, but tighten the mounting bolts to the specified torque.

12 Starter motor – testing and overhaul

1 If the starter motor is thought to be suspect, it should be removed from the vehicle and taken to an auto-electrician for testing. Most auto-electricians will be able to supply and fit brushes at a reasonable cost. However, check on the cost of repairs before proceeding as it may prove more economical to obtain a new or exchange motor.

13 Ignition switch – removal and refitting

1 The ignition switch, steering column lock and airbag rotary connector are an integral part of the steering column electronics module and cannot be individually removed.

2 Removal and refitting details for the steering column electronics module are contained in Chapter 12, Section 16.

14 Oil pressure warning light switch – removal and refitting

Removal

1 On petrol engines, the oil pressure warning light switch is screwed into the front right-hand side of the cylinder head **(see illustration)**. On diesel engines it is screwed into the front left-hand end of the cylinder head.

2 Pull back the cover and disconnect the wiring from the switch.

3 Place some cloth rags beneath the switch, then unscrew the switch from the block.

Refitting

4 Refitting is a reversal of removal, and tighten the switch to the specified torque.

11.11 Working through the access hole, unscrew and remove the starter upper mounting bolt – diesel engines

15 Oil level sensor – removal and refitting

Note: *An oil level sensor is only fitted to certain engines.*

Removal

1 The oil level sensor is located inside the sump which must first be removed (see Chapter 2C, Section 11).

2 With the sump removed, slide off the retaining clip and free the sensor wiring connector from the sump **(see illustration)**.

3 Where fitted, undo the retaining bolts and remove the oil baffle plate from inside the sump **(see illustration)**.

4 Note the correct routing of the wiring then undo the retaining bolts and remove

14.1 Oil pressure warning light switch location – petrol engines

15.3 Where fitted, undo the retaining bolts and remove the oil baffle plate

11.14 Battery positive cable connection on the starter motor – diesel engines

the sensor assembly from the sump **(see illustration)**. Check the wiring connector seal for signs or damage and renew if necessary.

Refitting

5 Prior to refitting remove all traces of locking compound from the sensor retaining bolt and sump threads. Apply a drop of fresh locking compound to the bolt threads and lubricate the wiring connector seal with a smear of engine oil.

6 Fit the sensor, making sure the wiring is correctly routed, and securely tighten its retaining bolts. Ease the wiring connector through the sump, taking care not to damage its seal, and secure it in position with the retaining clip.

7 Ensure the sensor is correctly refitted then, where applicable, refit the oil baffle plate.

8 Refit the sump as described in Chapter 2C, Section 11.

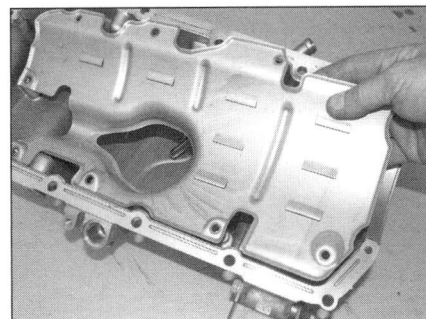

15.2 Slide off the retaining clip and free the oil level sensor wiring connector from the sump

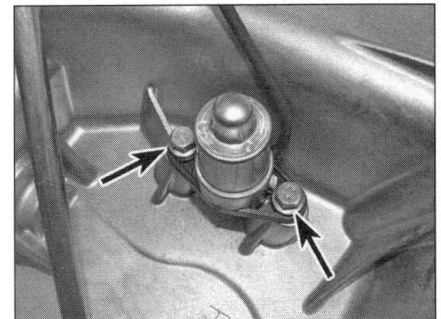

15.4 Undo the two bolts and remove the oil level sensor from the sump

16 Pre/post-heating system (diesel engines) – description and testing

Description

1 Each cylinder of the engine is fitted with a heater plug (commonly called a glow plug) screwed into it. The plugs are electrically-operated before and during start-up when the engine is cold. Electrical feed to the glow plugs is controlled via the pre/post-heating system control unit.

2 A warning light in the instrument panel tells the driver that pre/post-heating is taking place. When the light goes out, the engine is ready to be started. The voltage supply to the glow plugs continues for several seconds after the light goes out. If no attempt is made to start, the timer then cuts off the supply, in order to avoid draining the battery and overheating the glow plugs.

3 The glow plugs also provide a 'post-heating' function, whereby the glow plugs remain switched on after the engine has started. The length of time 'post-heating' takes place is also determined by the control unit, and is dependent on engine temperature.

4 The fuel filter is fitted with a heating element to prevent the fuel 'waxing' in extreme cold temperature conditions and to improve combustion. The heating element is an integral part of the fuel filter housing and is controlled by the pre/post-heating system control unit.

Testing

5 If the system malfunctions, testing is ultimately by substitution of known good units, but some preliminary checks may be made as follows.

6 Connect a voltmeter or 12 volt test lamp between the glow plug supply cable and earth (engine or vehicle metal). Make sure that the live connection is kept clear of the engine and bodywork.

7 Have an assistant switch on the ignition, and check that voltage is applied to the glow plugs. Note the time for which the warning light is lit, and the total time for which voltage is applied before the system cuts out. Switch off the ignition.

8 At an underbonnet temperature of 20°C, typical times noted should be approximately 3 seconds for warning light operation. Warning light time will increase with lower temperatures and decrease with higher temperatures.

9 If there is no supply at all, the control unit or associated wiring is at fault.

10 To locate a defective glow plug, disconnect the wiring connector from each plug.

11 Use a continuity tester, or a 12 volt test lamp connected to the battery positive terminal, to check for continuity between each glow plug terminal and earth. The resistance of a glow plug in good condition is very low (less than 1 ohm), so if the test lamp does not light or the continuity tester shows a high resistance, the glow plug is certainly defective.

12 If an ammeter is available, the current draw of each glow plug can be checked. After an initial surge of 15 to 20 amps, each plug should draw 12 amps. Any plug which draws much more or less than this is probably defective.

13 As a final check, the glow plugs can be removed and inspected as described in Section 17.

17 Glow plugs – removal, inspection and refitting

Caution: If the pre/post-heating system has just been energised, or if the engine has been running, the glow plugs will be very hot.

Removal

1 The glow plugs are located at the front of the cylinder head above the exhaust manifold.

2 Remove the turbocharger as described in Chapter 4B, Section 19. It is not necessary to remove the turbocharger if only No 1 cylinder glow plug is to be removed.

3 Disconnect the wiring from the glow plugs by squeezing the connectors with thumb and forefinger, and pulling them from the plugs.

4 Unscrew the glow plugs and remove them from the cylinder head.

Inspection

5 Inspect each glow plug for physical damage. Burnt or eroded glow plug tips can be caused by a bad injector spray pattern. Have the injectors checked if this type of damage is found.

6 If the glow plugs are in good physical condition, check them electrically using a 12 volt test lamp or continuity tester as described in the previous Section.

7 The glow plugs can be energised by applying 12 volts to them to verify that they heat up evenly and in the required time. Observe the following precautions.

a) Support the glow plug by clamping it carefully in a vice or self-locking pliers. Remember it will become red-hot.

b) Make sure that the power supply or test lead incorporates a fuse or overload trip to protect against damage from a short-circuit.

c) After testing, allow the glow plug to cool for several minutes before attempting to handle it.

8 A glow plug in good condition will start to glow red at the tip after drawing current for 5 seconds or so. Any plug which takes much longer to start glowing, or which starts glowing in the middle instead of at the tip, is defective.

Refitting

9 Carefully refit the plugs and tighten to the specified torque. Do not overtighten, as this can damage the glow plug element. Push the electrical connectors firmly onto the glow plugs.

10 The remainder of refitting is a reversal of removal, checking the operation of the glow plugs on completion.

18 Pre/post-heating system control unit – removal and refitting

Removal

1 The pre/post-heating system control unit is located on the left-hand side of the engine compartment where it is mounted onto the battery tray.

2 Disconnect the battery negative terminal (refer to *Disconnecting the battery* in Section 4).

3 Unclip the control unit and slide it up and off the battery tray (see illustration 4.17).

4 Disconnect the wiring connectors and remove the unit from the engine compartment.

Refitting

5 Refitting is a reversal of removal.

Chapter 5 Part B
Ignition system – petrol engines

Contents

Degrees of difficulty

Easy, suitable for novice with little experience	Fairly easy, suitable for beginner with some experience	Fairly difficult, suitable for competent DIY mechanic	Difficult, suitable for experienced DIY mechanic	Very difficult, suitable for expert DIY or professional

Specifications

General

System type	GMPT-E83
Location of No 1 cylinder	Timing chain end of engine
Firing order:	
All except 1.0 litre engines	1-3-4-2
1.0 litre engines	1-2-3

Torque wrench setting	Nm	lbf ft
Ignition module retaining bolts.	8	6

1 General Information

1 The ignition system is integrated with the fuel injection system to form a combined engine management system under the control of one ECU (See Chapter 4A, Section 8 for further information). The ignition side of the system is of the distributorless type, and consists of the ignition module (mounted on top of the cylinder head) and the knock sensor (mounted on the rear of the cylinder block).

2 The ignition module consists of ignition coils, one per cylinder, in one casing mounted directly above the spark plugs. This module eliminates the need for any HT leads as the coils locate directly onto the relevant spark plug. The ECU uses its inputs from the various sensors to calculate the required ignition advance setting.

3 The knock sensor is mounted onto the cylinder block and informs the ECU when the engine is 'pinking' under load. The sensor is sensitive to vibration and detects the knocking which occurs when the engine starts to 'pink' (pre-ignite). The knock sensor sends an electrical signal to the ECU which in turn retards the ignition advance setting until the 'pinking' ceases.

4 The ignition system operates under the overall control of the engine management electronic control unit. The system has various sensors (whose inputs also provide data to control the fuel injection system), and the electronic control unit, in addition to the ignition module and spark plugs. Details of system sensors and the electronic control unit are given in Chapter 4A, Section 8.

5 The electronic control unit selects the optimum ignition advance setting based on the information received from the various sensors, and fires the relevant ignition coil accordingly. The degree of advance can thus be constantly varied to suit the prevailing engine operating conditions.

⚠ **Warning: Due to the high voltages produced by the electronic ignition system, extreme care must be taken when working on the system with the ignition switched on.**

Persons with surgically-implanted cardiac pacemaker devices should keep well clear of the ignition circuits, components and test equipment.

2 Ignition system – testing

1 If a fault appears in the engine management system, first ensure that all the system wiring connectors are securely connected and free of corrosion. Ensure that the fault is not due to poor maintenance; ie, check that the air cleaner filter element is clean, the spark plugs are in good condition and correctly gapped, the cylinder compression pressures are correct and that the engine breather hoses are clear and undamaged, referring to Chapters 1A, 2A and 2B for further information.

2 If these checks fail to reveal the cause of the problem, the vehicle should be taken to a suitably-equipped Vauxhall/Opel dealer or engine management diagnostic specialist for testing. Using a fault code reader or similar

3.2a Release the ignition module cover by sliding it towards the transmission...

3.2b...then lift it off – 1.0 litre engines

3.3a Using a plastic spatula or similar tool, release the retaining tabs...

3.3b...and remove the plastic cover over the top of the engine – 1.2 and 1.4 litre engines

diagnostic equipment, the engine management ECU can be interrogated, and any stored fault codes can be retrieved. Live data can also be captured from the various system sensors and actuators, indicating their operating parameters. This will allow the fault to be quickly and simply traced, alleviating the need to test all the system components individually, which is a time-consuming operation that carries a risk of damaging the ECU.

3 The only ignition system checks which can be carried out by the home mechanic are those described in Chapter 1A relating to the spark plugs. If necessary, the system wiring and wiring connectors can be checked as described in Chapter 12, ensuring that the ECU wiring connector(s) have first been disconnected.

3 Ignition module – removal and refitting

Removal

1 The ignition module is mounted in the centre of the camshaft cover, directly above the spark plugs.
2 On 1.0 litre engines, remove the cover from the ignition module by sliding it towards the transmission and lifting off (see illustrations).
3 On 1.2 and 1.4 litre engines, lift the plastic cover up and off the top of the engine (see illustrations)).
4 Disconnect the wiring connector from the left-hand end of the ignition module (see illustration).
5 Undo the two ignition module mounting bolts (see illustration).
6 Insert two long 8 mm bolts into the threaded holes in the top of the module, and pull up on the bolts to free the module from the spark plugs (see illustrations).

Refitting

7 Refitting is a reversal of removal, and tighten the mounting bolts to the specified torque.

3.4 Disconnecting the ignition module wiring connector

3.5 Undo the two ignition module retaining bolts

4 Knock sensor – removal and refitting

1 Refer to the procedures contained in Chapter 4A, Section 10.

5 Ignition timing – checking and adjustment

1 Due to the nature of the ignition system, the ignition timing is constantly being monitored and adjusted by the engine management ECU.
2 The only way in which the ignition timing can be checked is by using specialist diagnostic test equipment, connected to the engine management system diagnostic socket. No adjustment of the ignition timing is possible. Should the ignition timing be incorrect, then a fault is likely to be present in the engine management system.

3.6a Insert two long 8 mm bolts into the threaded holes in the top of the module, and pull up on the bolts...

3.6b...to free the module from the spark plugs

Chapter 6
Clutch

Contents

Degrees of difficulty

Easy, suitable for novice with little experience	**Fairly easy,** suitable for beginner with some experience	**Fairly difficult,** suitable for competent DIY mechanic	**Difficult,** suitable for experienced DIY mechanic	**Very difficult,** suitable for expert DIY or professional

Specifications

Type	. . . .	Single dry plate with diaphragm spring, hydraulically-operated

Friction disc

Diameter:
Petrol engines:
1.0 and 1.2 litre engines . . . . 200 mm
1.4 litre engines:
A14XEL engines . . . . 200 mm
A14XER engines . . . . 200 or 205 mm
Diesel engines . . . . 216 mm
New lining thickness:
Petrol engines. . . . . 7.65 mm
Diesel engines:
A13DTC and A13DTE engines . . . . 8.2 mm
A13 DTR and Z13DTJ engines . . . . 7.2 mm

Torque wrench settings	**Nm**	**lbf ft**
Master cylinder retaining bolts	10	7
Pressure plate retaining bolts: *		
M6 bolts	12	9
M7 bolts	15	11
M8 bolts	28	21
Release cylinder mounting bolts	5	4
Universal joint-to-intermediate shaft clamp bolt*	40	30
Universal joint-to-steering pinion clamp bolt*	55	41

* *Use new fastenings*

1 General Information

1 The clutch consists of a friction disc, a pressure plate assembly, and the hydraulic release cylinder (which incorporates the release bearing); all of these components are contained in a large cast-aluminium alloy bellhousing, sandwiched between the engine and the transmission.
2 The friction disc is fitted between the engine flywheel and the clutch pressure plate, and is allowed to slide on the transmission input shaft splines.
3 The pressure plate assembly is bolted to the engine flywheel. When the engine is running, drive is transmitted from the crankshaft, via the flywheel, to the friction disc (these components being clamped securely together by the pressure plate assembly) and from the friction disc to the transmission input shaft.
4 To interrupt the drive, the spring pressure must be relaxed. This is achieved using a hydraulic release mechanism which consists of the master cylinder, the release cylinder and the pipe/hose linking the two components. Depressing the pedal pushes on the master cylinder pushrod which hydraulically forces the release cylinder piston against the pressure plate spring fingers. This causes the springs to deform and releases the clamping force on the friction disc.
5 The clutch is self-adjusting and requires no manual adjustment.

Semi-automatic clutch

6 Models equipped with the Easytronic MTA (Manual Transmission with Automatic shift), are fitted with a semi-automatic clutch. The clutch may be operated either fully automatically or semi-automatically by means of the gear selector lever. There is no conventional clutch pedal fitted.
7 The Easytronic system essentially consists of a conventional manual gearbox and clutch fitted with electrical and hydraulic controls, the clutch being operated by a clutch module attached to the side of the transmission casing. Refer to Chapter 7C for more information. The clutch component removal

2.8 Clutch bleed screw

and refitting procedures are included in this Chapter as they are very similar to those for the standard manual transmission.

2 Clutch hydraulic system – bleeding

Note: *On models equipped with the Easytronic transmission, the following manual method of bleeding the clutch is not possible since the hydraulic control unit is integral with the transmission. On these models, bleeding is carried out using the Vauxhall/Opel TECH2 diagnostic instrument, therefore this work should be entrusted to a Vauxhall/Opel dealer.*

⚠️ *Warning: Hydraulic fluid is poisonous; wash off immediately and thoroughly in the case of skin contact, and seek immediate medical advice if any fluid is swallowed or gets into the eyes. Certain types of hydraulic fluid are flammable, and may ignite when allowed into contact with hot components; when servicing any hydraulic system, it is safest to assume that the fluid is flammable, and to take precautions against the risk of fire as though it is petrol that is being handled. Hydraulic fluid is also an effective paint stripper, and will attack plastics; if any is spilt, it should be washed off immediately, using copious quantities of fresh water. Finally, it is hygroscopic (it absorbs moisture from the air) – old fluid may be contaminated and unfit for further use. When topping-up or renewing the fluid, always use the recommended type, and ensure that it comes from a freshly-opened sealed container.*

General information

1 The correct operation of any hydraulic system is only possible after removing all air from the components and circuit; this is achieved by bleeding the system.
2 The manufacturer stipulates that the system must be initially bled by the 'back-bleeding' method using Vauxhall/Opel special bleeding equipment. This entails connecting a pressure bleeding unit containing fresh brake fluid to the release cylinder bleed screw, with a collecting vessel connected to the brake fluid master cylinder reservoir. The pressure bleeding unit is then switched on, the bleed screw is opened and hydraulic fluid is delivered under pressure, backwards, to be expelled from the reservoir into the collecting vessel. Final bleeding is then carried out in the conventional way.
3 In practice, this method would normally only be required if new hydraulic components have been fitted, or if the system has been completely drained of hydraulic fluid. If the system has only been disconnected to allow component removal and refitting procedures to be carried out, such as removal and refitting of the transmission (for example for clutch

renewal) or engine removal and refitting, then it is quite likely that normal bleeding will be sufficient.
4 Our advice would therefore be as follows:
a) *If the hydraulic system has only been partially disconnected, try bleeding by the conventional methods described in paragraphs 10 to 15, or 16 to 19.*
b) *If the hydraulic system has been completely drained and new components have been fitted, try bleeding by using the pressure bleeding method described in paragraphs 20 to 22.*
c) *If the above methods fail to produce a firm pedal on completion, it will be necessary to 'back-bleed' the system using Vauxhall/ Opel bleeding equipment, or suitable alternative equipment as described in paragraphs 23 to 28.*
5 During the bleeding procedure, add only clean, unused hydraulic fluid of the recommended type; never re-use fluid that has already been bled from the system. Ensure that sufficient fluid is available before starting work.
6 If there is any possibility of incorrect fluid being already in the system, the hydraulic circuit must be flushed completely with uncontaminated, correct fluid.
7 If hydraulic fluid has been lost from the system, or air has entered because of a leak, ensure that the fault is cured before continuing further.
8 The bleed screw is located in the hose end fitting which is situated on the top of the transmission housing **(see illustration)**. On some models access to the bleed screw is limited and it may be necessary to jack up the front of the vehicle and support it on axle stands (see *Jacking and vehicle support*) so that the screw can be reached from below, or remove the battery and battery tray as described in Chapter 5A, Section 4, so that the screw can be reached from above.
9 Check that all pipes and hoses are secure, unions tight and the bleed screw is closed. Clean any dirt from around the bleed screw.

Bleeding procedure

Conventional method

10 Collect a clean glass jar, a suitable length of plastic or rubber tubing which is a tight fit over the bleed screw, and a ring spanner to fit the screw. The help of an assistant will also be required.
11 Unscrew the master cylinder fluid reservoir cap (the clutch shares the same fluid reservoir as the braking system), and top the master cylinder reservoir up to the upper (MAX) level line. Ensure that the fluid level is maintained at least above the lower level line in the reservoir throughout the procedure.
12 Remove the dust cap from the bleed screw. Fit the spanner and tube to the screw, place the other end of the tube in the jar, and pour in sufficient fluid to cover the end of the tube.

13 Have the assistant fully depress the clutch pedal several times to build-up pressure, then maintain it on the final downstroke.

14 While pedal pressure is maintained, unscrew the bleed screw (approximately one turn) and allow the compressed fluid and air to flow into the jar. The assistant should maintain pedal pressure and should not release it until instructed to do so. When the flow stops, tighten the bleed screw again, have the assistant release the pedal slowly, and recheck the reservoir fluid level.

15 Repeat the steps given in paragraphs 13 and 14 until the fluid emerging from the bleed screw is free from air bubbles. If the master cylinder has been drained and refilled allow approximately five seconds between cycles for the master cylinder passages to refill.

Using a one-way valve kit

16 As their name implies, these kits consist of a length of tubing with a one-way valve fitted, to prevent expelled air and fluid being drawn back into the system; some kits include a translucent container, which can be positioned so that the air bubbles can be more easily seen flowing from the end of the tube.

17 The kit is connected to the bleed screw, which is then opened.

18 The user returns to the driver's seat, depresses the clutch pedal with a smooth, steady stroke, and slowly releases it; this is repeated until the expelled fluid is clear of air bubbles.

19 Note that these kits simplify work so much that it is easy to forget the clutch fluid reservoir level; ensure that this is maintained at least above the lower level line at all times.

Pressure-bleeding method

20 These kits are usually operated by the reservoir of pressurised air contained in the spare tyre. However, note that it will probably be necessary to reduce the pressure to a lower level than normal; refer to the instructions supplied with the kit.

21 By connecting a pressurised, fluid-filled container to the clutch fluid reservoir, bleeding can be carried out simply by opening the bleed screw and allowing the fluid to flow out until no more air bubbles can be seen in the expelled fluid.

22 This method has the advantage that the large reservoir of fluid provides an additional safeguard against air being drawn into the system during bleeding.

'Back-bleeding' method

23 The following procedure describes the bleeding method using Vauxhall/Opel equipment. Alternative equipment is available and should be used in accordance with the maker's instructions.

24 Connect the pressure hose (MKM-6174-1) to the bleed screw located in the hose end fitting situated on the top of the transmission housing **(see illustration 2.8)**. Connect

the other end of the hose to a suitable pressure bleeding device set to operate at approximately 2.0 bar.

25 Attach the cap (MKM-6174-2) to the master cylinder reservoir, and place the hose in a collecting vessel.

26 Switch on the pressure bleeding equipment, open the bleed screw, and allow fresh hydraulic fluid to flow from the pressure bleeding unit, through the system and out through the top of the reservoir and into the collecting vessel. When fluid free from air bubbles appears in the reservoir, close the bleed screw and switch off the bleeding equipment.

27 Disconnect the bleeding equipment from the bleed screw and reservoir.

28 Carry out a final conventional bleeding procedure as described in paragraphs 10 to 15, or 16 to 19.

All methods

29 When bleeding is complete, no more bubbles appear and correct pedal feel is restored, tighten the bleed screw securely (do not overtighten). Remove the tube and spanner, and wash off any spilt fluid. Refit the dust cap to the bleed screw.

30 Check the hydraulic fluid level in the master cylinder reservoir, and top-up if necessary.

31 Discard any hydraulic fluid that has been bled from the system; it will not be fit for re-use.

32 Check the operation of the clutch pedal. If the clutch is still not operating correctly, air must still be present in the system, and further bleeding is required. Failure to bleed satisfactorily after a reasonable repetition of the bleeding procedure may be due to worn master cylinder/release cylinder seals.

3 Master cylinder – removal and refitting

Note: *New master cylinder retaining bolts will be required for refitting.*
Note: *This procedure does not apply to models fitted with the Easytronic transmission.*

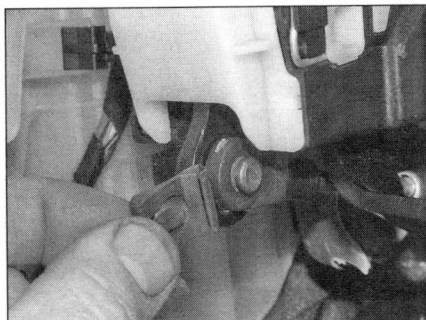
3.7a Extract the spring clip...

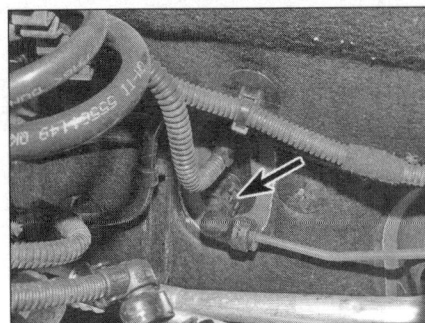
3.3 Extract the retaining clip and disconnect the hydraulic pipe from the master cylinder connector

Removal

1 Unscrew the brake/clutch hydraulic fluid reservoir filler cap, and top-up the reservoir to the MAX mark (see *Weekly checks*). Place a piece of polythene over the filler neck, and secure the polythene with the filler cap. This will minimise brake fluid loss during subsequent operations.

2 Remove all traces of dirt from the outside of the master cylinder, then position some cloth beneath the cylinder to catch any spilt fluid.

3 Extract the retaining clip and disconnect the hydraulic pipe from the connector on the end of the master cylinder **(see illustration)**. Plug the pipe end and master cylinder port to minimise fluid loss and prevent the entry of dirt.

4 Disconnect the fluid supply hose from the clutch master cylinder.

5 From inside the car, remove the driver's side lower trim panel as described in Chapter 11, Section 26.

6 Unscrew the two bolts securing the universal joint to the bottom of the steering column intermediate shaft and the steering gear pinion. Discard the bolts; new ones must be used on refitting. Slide the universal joint up the intermediate shaft to disengage it from the steering gear pinion.

7 Extract the spring clip and withdraw the clevis pin securing the master cylinder pushrod to the clutch pedal **(see illustrations)**.

8 Unscrew the two bolts securing the master cylinder to the pedal support bracket and

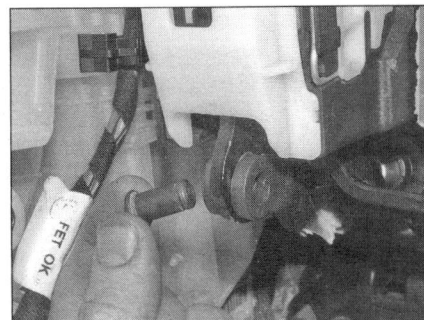
3.7b...and withdraw the clevis pin securing the master cylinder pushrod to the clutch pedal

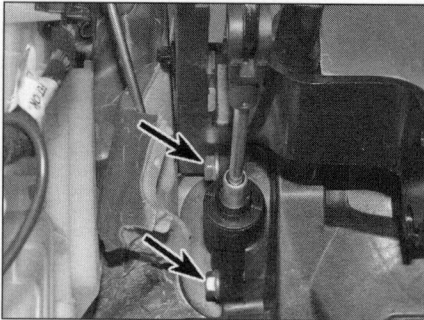

3.8 Unscrew the two bolts securing the master cylinder to the pedal support bracket

remove the master cylinder from inside the car **(see illustration)**. It may be necessary to slacken the five nuts securing the pedal support bracket to the bulkhead and ease the bracket away slightly to allow clearance for removal.

9 If the master cylinder is faulty it must be renewed; overhaul of the unit is not possible.

Refitting

10 Manoeuvre the master cylinder into position and refit the two retaining bolts. Tighten the bolts to the specified torque.

11 Where applicable, tighten the pedal support bracket retaining nuts.

12 Refit the master cylinder pushrod-to-clutch pedal clevis pin, and secure it in position with the spring clip.

13 Refit the universal joint to the steering gear pinion and intermediate shaft, noting that

4.2 Clutch release cylinder hydraulic pipe union nut

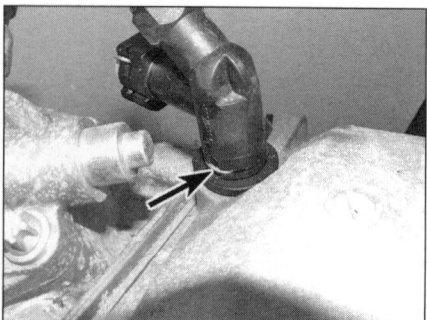

4.5 Extract the retaining clip and remove the hydraulic hose end fitting from the fastening sleeve

the components incorporate master splines and it will only be possible to fit the universal joint in one position. Apply thread-locking compound to the new universal joint retaining bolts and tighten them to the specified torque.

14 Refit the driver's side lower trim panel as described in Chapter 11, Section 26.

15 Connect the fluid supply hose to the master cylinder.

16 Press the hydraulic pipe back into the connector on the end of the master cylinder and secure with the clip.

17 Bleed the clutch hydraulic system as described in Section 2.

---

4 Release cylinder – removal and refitting

Note: *Due to the amount of work necessary to remove and refit clutch components, it is usually considered good practice to renew the clutch friction disc, pressure plate assembly and release cylinder as a matched set, even if only one of these is actually worn enough to require renewal. It is also worth considering the renewal of the clutch components on a preventative basis if the engine and/or transmission have been removed for some other reason.*

Note: *Refer to the warning concerning the dangers of asbestos dust at the beginning of Section 6.*

Note: *On models equipped with the Easytronic transmission, Vauxhall/Opel TECH2 diagnostic equipment will be required to bleed the clutch*

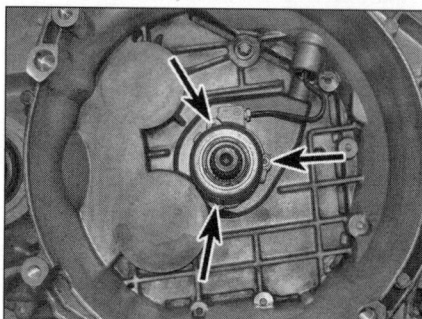

4.3 Clutch release cylinder retaining bolts

4.10 Make sure the lug on the fastening sleeve is located correctly in the transmission housing

hydraulic system and carry out a clutch Contact Point Determination program. If this equipment is not available, the following procedure should be entrusted to a Vauxhall/Opel dealer.

Removal

1 Unless the complete engine/transmission unit is to be removed from the car and separated for major overhaul (see Chapter 2D), the clutch release cylinder can be reached by removing the transmission only, as described in Chapter 7A, Section 8 or Chapter 7C, Section 7.

2 Wipe clean the outside of the release cylinder then slacken the union nut and disconnect the hydraulic pipe **(see illustration)**. Wipe up any spilt fluid with a clean cloth.

3 Unscrew the three retaining bolts and slide the release cylinder off from the transmission input shaft **(see illustration)**. Remove the sealing ring which is fitted between the cylinder and transmission housing and discard it; a new one must be used on refitting. Whilst the cylinder is removed, take care not to allow any debris to enter the transmission unit.

4 The release cylinder is a sealed unit and cannot be overhauled. If the cylinder seals are leaking or the release bearing is noisy or rough in operation, then the complete unit must be renewed.

5 To remove the hydraulic pipe, extract the retaining clip and remove the hydraulic hose end fitting from the fastening sleeve on top of the transmission housing **(see illustration)**. Gently squeeze the legs of the retaining clip together and re-insert the clip back into position in the end fitting.

6 Using a small screwdriver, carefully spread the retaining lugs of the fastening sleeve to release the hydraulic pipe connection, and remove the pipe from inside the transmission housing. Check the condition of the sealing ring on the hydraulic pipe and renew if necessary.

7 If required, the fastening sleeve can be removed by squeezing the lower retaining lugs together with pointed-nose pliers, then withdrawing the sleeve upwards and out of the transmission. Note that if the fastening sleeve is removed, a new one must be obtained for refitting.

Refitting

8 Ensure the release cylinder and transmission mating surfaces are clean and dry and fit the new sealing ring to the transmission recess.

9 Lubricate the release cylinder seal with a smear of transmission oil then carefully ease the cylinder along the input shaft and into position. Vauxhall/Opel technicians use a special tapered sleeve on the input shaft to prevent damage to the seal. If necessary, wrap suitable tape around the end of the shaft. Ensure the sealing ring is still correctly seated in its groove then refit the release cylinder retaining bolts and tighten them to the specified torque.

10 If removed, fit the new fastening sleeve, engaging the lug on the sleeve with the cut-out in the housing **(see illustration)**.

Ensure that the sleeve can be felt to positively lock in position.

11 Insert the hydraulic pipe into the fastening sleeve until the end fitting can be felt to positively lock in position.

12 Reconnect the hydraulic pipe to the release cylinder, tightening its union nut securely.

13 Refit the hydraulic hose end fitting to the fastening sleeve ensuring that it is positively retained by its clip.

14 Refit the transmission unit as described in Chapter 7A, Section 8 or Chapter 7C, Section 7.

15 On models equipped with a conventional transmission, bleed the clutch hydraulic system as described in Section 2.

16 On models equipped with the Easytronic transmission, bleed the clutch hydraulic system and carry out a clutch Contact Point Determination program using Vauxhall/Opel TECH2 diagnostic equipment.

5 Clutch pedal –
removal and refitting

1 The clutch pedal is an integral part of the brake pedal and mounting bracket assembly and cannot be individually removed. Removal and refitting details for the brake pedal and mounting bracket assembly are contained in Chapter 9, Section 11.

6 Clutch assembly –
removal, inspection and refitting

⚠️ *Warning: Dust created by clutch wear and deposited on the clutch components may contain asbestos, which is a health hazard. DO NOT blow it out with compressed air, or inhale any of it. DO NOT use petrol or petroleum-based solvents to clean off the dust. Brake system cleaner or methylated spirit should be used to flush the dust into a suitable receptacle. After the clutch components are wiped clean with rags, dispose of the contaminated rags and cleaner in a sealed, marked container.*

Note: *To prevent possible damage to the ends of the pressure plate diaphragm spring fingers, Vauxhall/Opel recommend the use of a special jig (KM-6263) to remove the clutch assembly, however, with care it is possible to carry out the work without the jig.*

Note: *On models equipped with the Easytronic transmission, Vauxhall/Opel TECH2 diagnostic equipment will be required to carry out a clutch Contact Point Determination program after the transmission has been refitted. If this equipment is not available, the following procedure should be entrusted to a Vauxhall/Opel dealer.*

Removal

1 Unless the complete engine/transmission unit is to be removed from the car and separated for major overhaul (see Chapter 2D), the clutch release cylinder can be reached by removing the transmission only, as described in Chapter 7A, Section 8 or Chapter 7C, Section 7.

2 Before disturbing the clutch, use chalk or a marker pen to mark the relationship of the pressure plate assembly to the flywheel.

3 At this stage, Vauxhall/Opel technicians fit the special jig KM-6263 to the engine and compress the diaphragm spring fingers until the friction disc is released (see illustrations). The pressure plate mounting bolts are then unscrewed, and the jig spindle backed off.

4 If the jig is not available, progressively unscrew the pressure plate retaining bolts in diagonal sequence by half a turn at a time, until spring pressure is released and the bolts can be unscrewed by hand.

5 Remove the pressure plate assembly and collect the friction disc, noting which way round the disc is fitted. It is recommended that new pressure plate retaining bolts are obtained.

Inspection

Note: *Due to the amount of work necessary to remove and refit clutch components, it is usually considered good practice to renew the clutch friction disc, pressure plate assembly and release cylinder as a matched set, even if only one of these is actually worn enough to require renewal. It is also worth considering the renewal of the clutch components on*

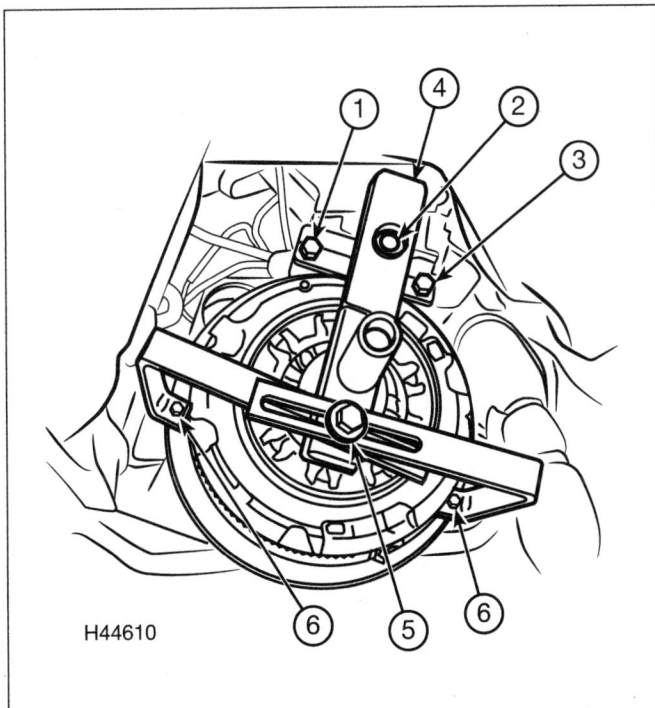

6.3a Vauxhall special jig KM-6263 for removing the clutch pressure plate and friction disc

1, 3 and 6 Bolts securing the jig to the engine
2 and 5 Bolts for adjusting the jig to the centre of the crankshaft

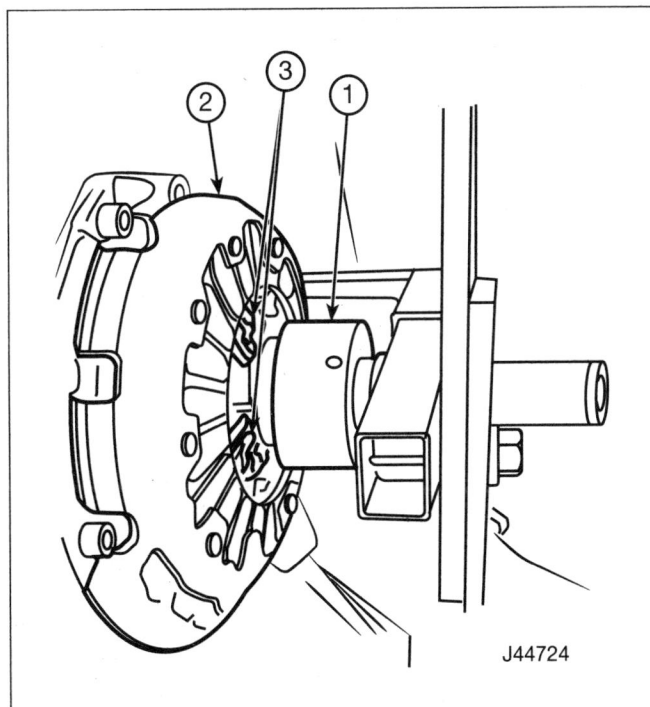

6.3b Thrust piece (1) in contact with the diaphragm spring fingers (3) of the pressure plate (2)

6.15 Mount a large bolt and washer into a vice, then fit the pressure plate over it

6.16 Fit large washers and a nut to the bolt and hand-tighten

6.17a Tighten the nut until the spring adjuster is free to turn...

6.17b...then open up the jaws of suitable pliers to compress the springs

a preventative basis if the engine and/or transmission have been removed for some other reason.

6 When cleaning clutch components, read first the warning at the beginning of this Section; remove dust using a clean, dry cloth, and working in a well-ventilated atmosphere.

7 Check the friction disc facings for signs of wear, damage or oil contamination. If the friction material is cracked, burnt, scored or damaged, or if it is contaminated with oil or grease (shown by shiny black patches), the friction disc must be renewed.

8 If the friction material is still serviceable, check that the centre boss splines are unworn, that the torsion springs are in good condition and securely fastened, and that all the rivets are tight. If any wear or damage is found, the friction disc must be renewed.

9 If the friction material is fouled with oil, this must be due to an oil leak from the crankshaft oil seal, from the sump-to-cylinder block joint, or from the release cylinder assembly (either the main seal or the sealing ring). Renew the crankshaft oil seal or repair the sump joint as described in Chapter 2A, 2B or 2C before installing the new friction disc. The clutch release cylinder is covered in Section 4.

10 Check the pressure plate assembly for obvious signs of wear or damage; shake it to check for loose rivets, or worn or damaged fulcrum rings, and check that the drive straps securing the pressure plate to the cover do not show signs of overheating (such as a deep yellow or blue discoloration). If the diaphragm

spring is worn or damaged, or if its pressure is in any way suspect, the pressure plate assembly should be renewed.

11 Examine the machined bearing surfaces of the pressure plate and of the flywheel; they should be clean, completely flat, and free from scratches or scoring. If either is discoloured from excessive heat, or shows signs of cracks, it should be renewed – although minor damage of this nature can sometimes be polished away using emery paper.

12 Check that the release cylinder bearing rotates smoothly and easily, with no sign of noise or roughness. Also check that the surface itself is smooth and unworn, with no signs of cracks, pitting or scoring. If there is any doubt about its condition, the clutch release cylinder should be renewed (it is not possible to renew the bearing separately).

6.21 The lettering 'transmission side' or 'Getriebeseite' on the friction disc must point towards the transmission

Refitting

13 On certain models, the clutch pressure plate is unusual, as there is a pre-adjustment mechanism to compensate for wear in the friction disc (this is termed by Vauxhall/Opel as a self-adjusting clutch (SAC), which is slightly ambiguous as all clutches fitted to these models are essentially self-adjusting). However, this mechanism must be reset before refitting the pressure plate. A new plate may be supplied preset, in which case this procedure can be ignored.

14 A large diameter bolt (M14 at least) long enough to pass through the pressure plate, a matching nut, and several large diameter washers, will be needed for this procedure. Mount the bolt head in the jaws of a sturdy bench vice, with one large washer fitted.

15 Offer the plate over the bolt, friction disc surface facing down, and locate it centrally over the bolt and washer – the washer should bear on the centre hub (**see illustration**).

16 Fit several further large washers over the bolt, so that they bear on the ends of the spring fingers, then add the nut and tighten by hand to locate the washers (**see illustration**).

17 The purpose of the procedure is to turn the plate's internal adjuster disc so that the three small coil springs visible on the plate's outer surface are fully compressed. Tighten the nut just fitted until the adjuster disc is free to turn. Using a pair of thin-nosed or circlip pliers in one of the three windows in the top surface, open the jaws of the pliers to turn the adjuster disc anti-clockwise, so that the springs are fully compressed (**see illustrations**).

18 Hold the pliers in this position, then unscrew the centre nut. Once the nut is released, the adjuster disc will be gripped in position, and the pliers can be removed. Take the pressure plate from the vice, and it is ready to fit.

19 On reassembly, ensure that the friction surfaces of the flywheel and pressure plate are completely clean, smooth, and free from oil or grease. Use solvent to remove any protective grease from new components.

20 Lightly grease the teeth of the friction disc hub with high melting-point grease. Do not apply too much, otherwise it may eventually contaminate the friction disc linings.

Using the Vauxhall jig

21 Fit the special Vauxhall guide bush to the centre of the crankshaft, and locate the friction disc on it, making sure that the lettering 'transmission side' or 'Getriebeseite' points towards the transmission (**see illustration**).

22 Locate the pressure plate on the special centring pins on the flywheel, then compress the diaphragm spring fingers with the jig, until the friction disc is in full contact with the flywheel.

23 Insert new pressure plate retaining bolts, and progressively tighten them to the specified torque. If necessary, hold the flywheel stationary while tightening the bolts, using a screwdriver engaged with the teeth of the starter ring gear.

24 Back off the jig spindle so that the diaphragm spring forces the pressure plate against the friction disc and flywheel, then remove the jig and guide bush from the engine.
25 Refit the transmission as described in Chapter 7A, Section 8 or Chapter 7C, Section 7.

Without using the Vauxhall jig

26 Locate the friction disc on the flywheel, making sure that the lettering 'transmission side' or 'Getriebeseite' points towards the transmission **(see illustration 6.21)**.
27 Refit the pressure plate assembly, aligning the marks made on dismantling (if the original pressure plate is re-used). Fit new pressure plate bolts, but tighten them only finger-tight so that the friction disc can still be moved **(see illustration)**.
28 The friction disc must now be centralised so that, when the transmission is refitted, its input shaft will pass through the splines at the centre of the friction disc.
29 Centralisation can be achieved by passing a

6.27 Fit the pressure plate assembly over the friction disc

screwdriver or other long bar through the friction disc and into the hole in the crankshaft. The friction disc can then be moved around until it is centred on the crankshaft hole. Alternatively, a clutch-aligning tool can be used to eliminate the guesswork; these can be obtained from most accessory shops **(see illustration)**.

6.29 Centralise the friction disc using a clutch aligning tool or similar

30 When the friction disc is centralised, tighten the pressure plate bolts evenly and in a diagonal sequence to the specified torque setting.
31 Refit the transmission as described in Chapter 7A, Section 8 or Chapter 7C, Section 7.

Chapter 7 Part A
Manual transmission

Contents

Degrees of difficulty

Easy, suitable for novice with little experience	Fairly easy, suitable for beginner with some experience	Fairly difficult, suitable for competent DIY mechanic	Difficult, suitable for experienced DIY mechanic	Very difficult, suitable for expert DIY or professional

Specifications

General

Type . . . . 5 or 6 forward speeds and reverse. Synchromesh on all forward speeds and reverse. Integral differential

Manufacturer's designation:
Petrol engine models . . . . F13 (5-speed) or F17 (5-speed)
Diesel engine models:
A13DTC, A13DTE and Z13DTJ engines. F17 (5-speed)
A13 DTR engines M20 (6-speed)

Lubrication
Lubricant type . . . . See *Lubricants and fluids* on page 0•17
Lubricant capacity . . . . See Chapter 1A or Chapter 1B

Torque wrench settings

	Nm	lbf ft
F13 and F17 transmissions		
Differential housing cover plate:		
Alloy plate.	18	13
Steel plate.	30	22
Engine/transmission mountings.	See Chapter 2A or 2B	
Engine-to-transmission bolts.	See Chapter 2A or 2B	
Gear lever housing bolts	22	16
Gearchange mechanism selector rod clamp bolt:		
Stage 1	12	9
Stage 2	Angle-tighten a further 180°	
Stage 3	Angle-tighten a further 45°	
Oil level plug.	22	16
Reversing light switch	20	15
Roadwheel bolts.	110	81
Transmission breather	30	22
M20 transmissions		
Engine/transmission mountings.	See Chapter 2C	
Engine-to-transmission bolts.	See Chapter 2C	
Oil drain plug	20	15
Oil filler plug	30	22
Oil seal carrier to differential:		
Stage 1	20	15
Stage 2	Angle-tighten a further 45°	
Reversing light switch	20	15
Roadwheel bolts.	110	81

**2.5 Differential cover plate securing bolts –
F13 and F17 transmissions**

1 General Information

1 The transmission is contained in a cast-aluminium alloy casing bolted to the engine's left-hand end, and consists of the gearbox and final drive differential – often called a transaxle.
2 Drive is transmitted from the crankshaft via the clutch to the input shaft, which has a splined extension to accept the clutch friction disc, and rotates in sealed ball-bearings. From the input shaft, drive is transmitted to the output shaft, which rotates in a roller bearing at its right-hand end, and a sealed ball-bearing at its left-hand end. From the output shaft, the drive is transmitted to the differential crownwheel, which rotates with the differential case and planetary gears, thus driving the sun gears and driveshafts. The rotation of the planetary gears on their shaft allows the inner roadwheel to rotate at a slower speed than the outer roadwheel when the car is cornering.
3 The input and output shafts are arranged side-by-side, parallel to the crankshaft and driveshafts, so that their gear pinion teeth are in constant mesh. In the neutral position, the output shaft gear pinions rotate freely, so that drive cannot be transmitted to the crownwheel.
4 Gear selection is via a floor-mounted lever and either a rod-operated, or cable-operated selector linkage mechanism. The selector linkage causes the appropriate selector fork to move its respective synchro-sleeve along the shaft, to lock the gear pinion to the

synchro-hub. Since the synchro-hubs are splined to the output shaft, this locks the pinion to the shaft, so that drive can be transmitted. To ensure that gearchanging can be made quickly and quietly, a synchromesh system is fitted to all forward gears, consisting of baulk rings and spring-loaded fingers, as well as the gear pinions and synchro-hubs. The synchromesh cones are formed on the mating faces of the baulk rings and gear pinions.

2 Transmission oil – draining and refilling

1 This operation is much more efficient if the car is first taken on a journey of sufficient length to warm the engine/transmission up to normal operating temperature.
Caution: If the procedure is to be carried out on a hot transmission unit, take care not to burn yourself on the hot exhaust or the transmission/engine unit.
2 Position the vehicle over an inspection pit, on vehicle ramps, or jack it up and support it securely on axle stands (see *Jacking and vehicle support*), but make sure that it is level. Where fitted, remove the clips and bolts and remove the undertray from beneath the engine.

F13 and F17 transmissions

Note: *A new differential lower cover plate gasket will be required for this operation.*

Draining

3 Since the transmission oil is not renewed as part of the manufacturer's maintenance schedule, no drain plug is fitted to the transmission. If for any reason the transmission needs to be drained, the only way of doing so is to remove the differential lower cover plate.
4 Wipe clean the area around the differential cover plate and position a suitable container underneath the cover.
5 Evenly and progressively slacken and remove the retaining bolts then withdraw the cover plate and allow the transmission oil to drain into the container **(see illustration)**. Remove the gasket and discard it; a new one should be used on refitting.
6 Allow the oil to drain completely into the

container. If the oil is hot, take precautions against scalding. Remove all traces of dirt and oil from the cover and transmission mating surfaces and wipe clean the inside of the cover plate.
7 Once the oil has finished draining, ensure the mating surfaces are clean and dry then refit the cover plate to the transmission unit, complete with a new gasket. Refit the retaining bolts and evenly and progressively tighten them to the specified torque.

Refilling

8 Wipe clean the area around the level plug. The level plug is located behind the driveshaft inner joint on the left-hand side of the transmission **(see illustration)**. Unscrew the plug and clean it.
9 The transmission is refilled via the transmission breather aperture adjacent to the selector mechanism on the top of the transmission **(see illustration)**. Wipe clean the area around the transmission breather and remove the cap. Unscrew the breather and remove it from the transmission. Refill the transmission with the specified grade of oil (see *Lubricants and fluids*) until it reaches the bottom of the level plug aperture. Allow any excess oil to drain, then refit and tighten the level plug to the specified torque.
10 Refit the transmission breather and tighten it to the specified torque. Where applicable, refit the engine undertray, then lower the vehicle to the ground.

M20 transmissions

Note: *A new transmission oil drain plug will be required.*

Draining

11 Wipe clean the area around the drain plug, located on the lower left-hand side of the differential housing, and position a suitable container under the plug.
12 Undo the drain plug and allow the oil to drain.
13 Once the oil has finished draining, fit the new drain plug and tighten the plug to the specified torque.

Refilling

14 The transmission is refilled via the oil filler plug on the top of the casing **(see illustration)**.

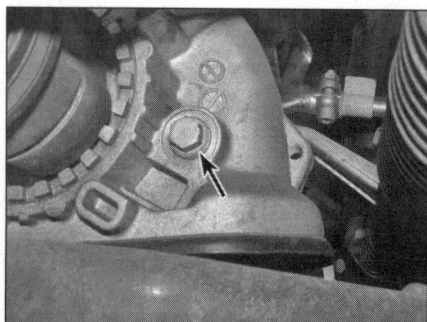

**2.8 Transmission oil level plug –
F13 and F17 transmissions**

**2.9 Fill the transmission through the
transmission breather aperture –
F13 and F17 transmissions**

**2.14 Transmission oil filler plug –
M20 transmissions**

To gain access to the plug, remove the battery and battery tray as described in Chapter 5A, Section 4.

15 Wipe clean the area around the plug and unscrew it. Refill the transmission with exactly 2.2 litres of the specified grade of oil given in *Lubricants and fluids* then refit and tighten the oil filler plug to the specified torque **(see illustration)**.

16 Where applicable, refit the engine undertray, then lower the vehicle to the ground.

17 Refit the battery tray and battery as described in Chapter 5A, Section 4.

3 Gearchange linkage/ mechanism – adjustment

F13 and F17 transmissions

1 Adjustment of the gearchange linkage/ mechanism should only be needed if the mechanism has been disconnected or removed. The mechanism is adjusted at the clamp bolt which secures the selector rod to the transmission linkage at the rear of the engine compartment. Access is best from under the vehicle.

2 Remove the battery and battery tray as described in Chapter 5A, Section 4.

3 Apply the handbrake, then jack up the front of the vehicle and support it on axle stands (see *Jacking and vehicle support*). Remove the engine undertray where fitted.

2.15 Use a graduated container to fill the transmission with the specified quantity of oil – M20 transmissions

4 Slacken the gearchange selector rod clamp bolt which is situated at the front of the rod **(see illustration)**. Do not remove the bolt completely.

5 From inside the vehicle, unclip the storage compartment at the front of the centre console, then unclip the gear lever gaiter from the storage compartment **(see illustration)**. Disconnect the wiring connector (where applicable), then fold the gaiter up over the gear lever knob and remove the storage compartment.

6 Unclip the reverse gear inhibit connection from the gear lever knob **(see illustration)**.

7 Lift the reverse gear locking block on the gear lever upward and rotate it clockwise by 90°. Move the gear lever to the left and engage the lug at the base of the locking block with the slot on the side of the gear lever housing

(see illustrations). The lever is now locked in the adjustment position.

8 Working in the engine compartment, with the selector mechanism in neutral, turn the selector shaft anti-clockwise against the spring pressure towards the third gear position, and lock the selector mechanism by pressing in the spring-loaded locking pin which is located on the top of the transmission unit **(see illustration)**. Ensure that the locking pin is pressed fully in so that the spring is completely compressed.

9 With both the lever and transmission locked in position, tighten the selector rod clamp bolt to the specified Stage 1 torque, then through the Stage 2 and Stage 3 angles.

10 Lift the locking block on the gear lever out of the slot on the lever housing, rotate it back through 90° to its original position and push it down. Refit the reverse gear inhibit connection to the gear lever knob.

11 Check the operation of the gearchange mechanism; the transmission locking pin will automatically release when the lever is moved into the reverse position.

12 Ensure the transmission locking pin has released, then refit the engine undertray (where necessary) and lower the vehicle to the ground.

13 Refit the battery tray and battery as described in Chapter 5A, Section 4.

14 Check that all gears can be engaged easily, first with the engine off, then with the engine running and the clutch disengaged.

15 On completion, refit the gear lever gaiter to the centre console.

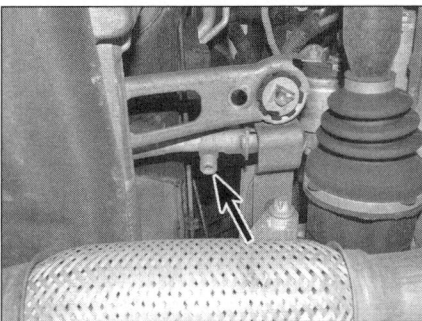
3.4 Gearchange selector rod clamp bolt – F13 and F17 transmissions

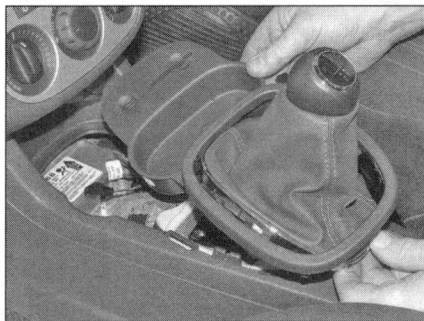
3.5 Unclip the centre console storage compartment, then unclip the gear lever gaiter – F13 and F17 transmissions

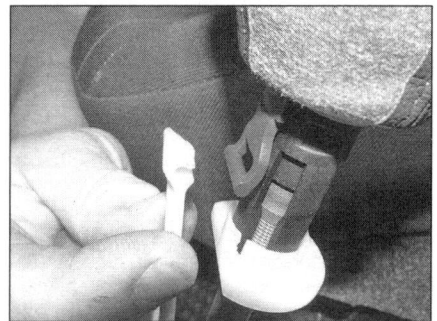
3.6 Unclip the reverse gear inhibit connection from the gear lever knob – F13 and F17 transmissions

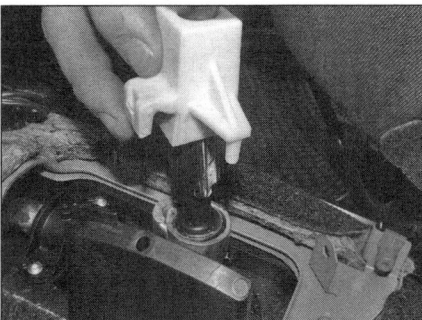
3.7a Lift the reverse gear locking block on the gear lever upward and rotate it clockwise by 90° – F13 and F17 transmissions

3.7b Engage the lug at the base of the locking block with the slot on the side of the gear lever housing – F13 and F17 transmissions

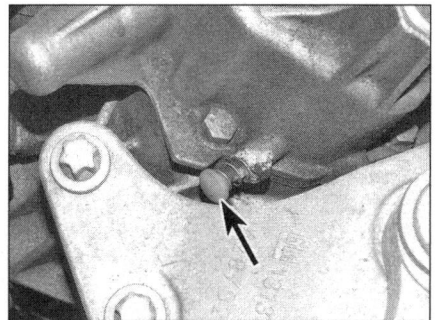
3.8 Lock the selector mechanism by pressing in the spring-loaded locking pin – F13 and F17 transmissions

3.19 Using a 5 mm drill bit to lock the selector mechanism in the adjustment position – M20 transmissions

M20 transmissions

Note: *A 5 mm drill bit or dowel rod will be required to carry out this procedure.*

16 Adjustment of the gearchange linkage/mechanism should only be needed if the mechanism has been disconnected or removed. Adjustment is carried out by means of an adjuster incorporated into the selector cable at the transmission end.

17 Remove the battery and battery tray as described in Chapter 5A, Section 4.

18 Working at the transmission end of the selector cable, push down the spring-loaded plunger on the cable adjuster, until it locks in position.

19 Set the gearchange selector on the transmission to the 'neutral' position. Pull the selector up and lock it in the adjustment position by inserting a 5 mm drill bit or dowel rod through the hole in the side of the housing **(see illustration)**. Ensure that the drill bit or dowel rod fully engages with the selector.

20 From inside the vehicle, unclip the storage compartment at the front of the centre console, then unclip the gear lever gaiter from the storage compartment **(see illustration 3.5)**. Disconnect the wiring connector (where applicable), then fold the gaiter up over the gear lever knob and remove the storage compartment.

21 Unclip the reverse gear inhibit connection from the gear lever knob **(see illustration 3.6)**.

22 Push the locking ring at the base of the gear lever upwards and pull off the gear lever knob.

23 Lift the reverse gear locking block on the

gear lever upward and rotate it anti-clockwise by 90°. Move the gear lever to the left and engage the lug at the base of the locking block with the slot on the side of the gear lever housing. The lever is now locked in the adjustment position.

24 Return to the engine compartment and push the plunger tab on the cable adjuster rearward to release the adjuster.

25 From inside the vehicle, lift the locking block on the gear lever out of the slot on the lever housing, rotate it back through 90° to its original position and push it down.

26 Locate the gear lever knob on the gear lever and push it on as far as it will go. Push the locking ring down and refit the reverse gear inhibit connection to the knob.

27 Remove the drill bit or dowel rod used to lock the gearchange selector on the transmission.

28 Refit the battery tray and battery as described in Chapter 5A, Section 4.

29 Check that all gears can be engaged easily, first with the engine off, then with the engine running and the clutch disengaged.

30 On completion, refit the gear lever gaiter trim to the centre console.

4 Gearchange mechanism (F13 and F17 transmissions) – removal and refitting

1 The gearchange mechanism consists of the gear lever housing and selector rod, and the linkage assembly on the transmission. The lever housing and selector rod, and the linkage assembly can be removed separately.

Gear lever housing and selector rod

Removal

2 From inside the vehicle, unclip the storage compartment at the front of the centre console, then unclip the gear lever gaiter from the storage compartment **(see illustration 3.5)**. Disconnect the wiring connector (where applicable), then fold the gaiter up over the gear lever knob and remove the storage compartment.

3 Unclip the reverse gear inhibit connection from the gear lever knob **(see illustration 3.6)**.

4 Push the locking ring at the base of the gear lever upwards and pull off the gear lever knob **(see illustration)**.

5 Apply the handbrake, then jack up the front of the vehicle and support it on axle stands (see *Jacking and vehicle support*). Where fitted, remove the engine undertray.

6 Reach up behind the transmission and slacken the gearchange selector rod clamp bolt which is situated at the front of the rod **(see illustration 3.4)**. Do not remove the bolt completely. Push the selector rod rearwards and separate it from the shift guide.

7 Remove the complete exhaust system as described in Chapter 4A, Section 13 or Chapter 4B, Section 20.

8 Where fitted, release the four sheet metal nuts securing the exhaust heat shield to the underbody.

9 Undo the four bolts securing the gear lever housing (and heat shield, where fitted) to the underbody **(see illustration)**. Remove the gear lever housing (and heat shield, where fitted) from under the car. Once removed, separate the housing from the heat shield, if applicable.

10 Release the rubber gaiter from the front of the gear lever housing.

11 Undo the two bolts and lift off the selector rod retaining plate. Detach the selector rod from the gear lever and remove the selector rod.

12 Undo the two bolts securing the gear lever retaining plate to the lever housing and remove the gear lever.

Refitting

13 Refitting is a reversal of removal, tightening the housing mounting bolts securely. Adjust the linkage as described in Section 3.

Linkage assembly

Removal

14 Apply the handbrake, then jack up the front of the vehicle and support it on axle stands (see *Jacking and vehicle support*). Where fitted, remove the engine undertray.

15 Reach up behind the transmission and slacken the gearchange selector rod clamp bolt which is situated at the front of the rod **(see illustration 3.4)**. Do not remove the bolt completely. Push the selector rod rearwards and separate it from the shift guide.

16 Remove the two clips and disconnect the linkage from the shift guide brackets **(see illustration)**.

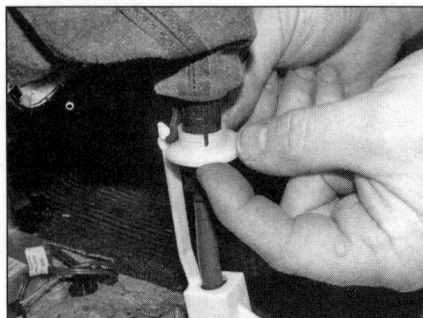

4.4 Push the locking ring at the base of the gear lever upwards and pull off the gear lever knob

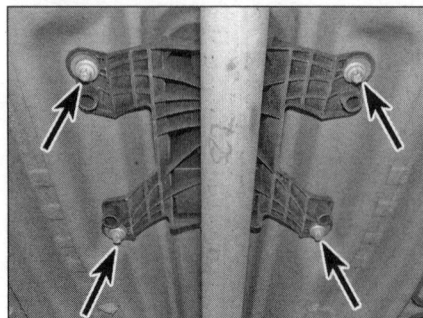

4.9 Undo the four bolts securing the gear lever housing to the underbody

4.16 Gearchange linkage-to-shift guide bracket retaining clip

17 Depress the retaining spring and lever out the pin. Detach the universal joint from the shift rod **(see illustration)**.
18 Withdraw the linkage assembly upwards and out of position.

Refitting

19 Refitting is a reversal of removal, but adjust the linkage as described in Section 3.

5 Gearchange mechanism (M20 transmissions) – removal and refitting

Gear lever housing

Removal

1 From inside the vehicle, unclip the storage compartment at the front of the centre console, then unclip the gear lever gaiter from the storage compartment **(see illustration 3.5)**. Disconnect the wiring connector (where applicable), then fold the gaiter up over the gear lever knob and remove the storage compartment.
2 Unclip the reverse gear inhibit connection from the gear lever knob **(see illustration 3.6)**.
3 Push the locking ring at the base of the gear lever upwards and pull off the gear lever knob **(see illustration 4.4)**.
4 Apply the handbrake, then jack up the front of the vehicle and support it on axle stands (see *Jacking and vehicle support*). Where fitted, remove the engine undertray.
5 Remove the complete exhaust system as described in Chapter 4B, Section 20.
6 Where fitted, release the four sheet metal nuts securing the exhaust heat shield to the underbody.
7 Undo the four bolts securing the gear lever housing (and heat shield, where fitted) to the underbody. Withdraw the gear lever housing (and heat shield, where fitted) from under the car. Once removed, separate the housing from the heat shield, if applicable.
8 Remove the cover from the base of the gear lever housing.
9 Unclip the selector cables from the selector housing linkages, and release the outer cables from the housing. Remove the housing from the car.

Refitting

10 Refitting is a reversal of removal, but adjust the linkage as described in Section 3.

Selector cables

Removal

11 Carry out the operations described in paragraphs 1 to 9 above.
12 Remove the battery and battery tray as described in Chapter 5A, Section 4.
13 Working in the engine compartment, note the fitted locations of the cables at their transmission attachments.
14 Using a suitable forked tool, release the inner cable end fittings from the transmission selector levers **(see illustration)**.
15 Pull back the retaining sleeves and detach the outer cables from the mounting bracket on the transmission, then remove the cables from the car.

Refitting

16 Refitting is a reversal of removal, but adjust the linkage as described in Section 3.

6 Oil seals – renewal

Driveshaft oil seals

F13 and F17 transmissions

1 Firmly apply the handbrake, then jack up the front of the car and support it securely on axle stands (see *Jacking and vehicle support*). Where fitted, remove the engine undertray.
2 Drain the transmission oil as described in Section 2.
3 Remove the driveshaft as described in Chapter 8, Section 2.
4 Note the correct fitted depth of the seal in its housing then carefully prise it out of position using a large flat-bladed screwdriver **(see illustration)**.
5 Remove all traces of dirt from the area around the oil seal aperture, then apply a smear of grease to the outer lip of the new oil seal. Ensure the seal is correctly positioned, with its sealing lip facing inwards, and tap it squarely into position, using a suitable tubular

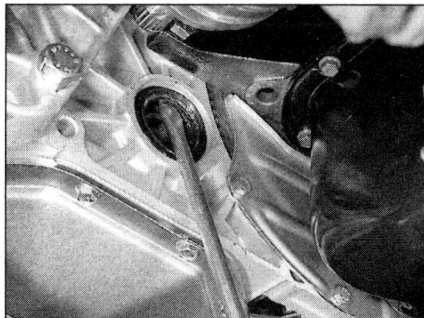

4.17 Gearchange universal joint removal
Arrow shows position of hollow pin retaining spring

drift (such as a socket) which bears only on the hard outer edge of the seal **(see illustration)**. Ensure the seal is fitted at the same depth in its housing that the original was.
6 Refit the driveshaft as described in Chapter 8, Section 2.
7 Refill the transmission with the specified type and amount of oil, as described in Section 2.

M20 transmissions – right-hand oil seal

8 Proceed as described above in paragraphs 1 to 7.

M20 transmissions – left-hand oil seal

Note: *A hydraulic press, together with tubes and mandrels of suitable diameters will be needed for this operation.*
9 Firmly apply the handbrake, then jack up the front of the car and support it securely on axle stands (see *Jacking and vehicle support*). Where fitted, remove the engine undertray.
10 Drain the transmission oil as described in Section 2.
11 Remove the driveshaft as described in Chapter 8, Section 2.
12 Undo the four bolts and remove the oil seal carrier from the side of the differential housing.
13 Place the oil seal carrier on the press bed

5.14 Release the inner cable end fittings from the transmission selector levers

6.4 Prising out a driveshaft oil seal

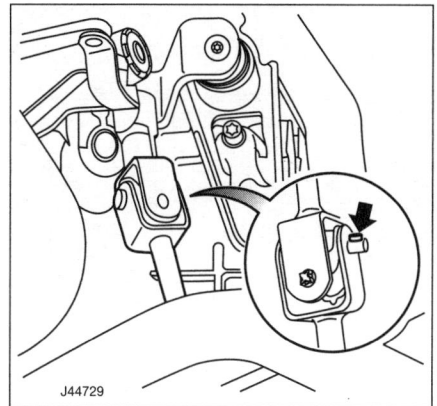

6.5 Fitting a new driveshaft oil seal using a socket as a tubular drift

8.5 Prise out the clip to disconnect the clutch hydraulic hose from the release cylinder pipe

with its outer surface facing down. Using a suitable mandrel, press the oil seal out of the carrier.

14 Using a small screwdriver, remove the sealing O-ring from the oil seal carrier.

15 Support the inner surface of the oil seal carrier on the press bed. Lubricate the new oil seal with transmission oil, then press it fully into position in the carrier using a suitable tube which bears only on the hard outer edge of the seal.

16 Fit a new O-ring to the oil seal carrier, then refit the carrier to the differential housing, tightening the retaining bolts to the specified torque.

17 Refit the driveshaft as described in Chapter 8, Section 2.

18 Refill the transmission with the specified type and amount of oil, as described in Section 2.

Input shaft oil seal

19 The input shaft oil seal is an integral part of the clutch release cylinder; if the seal is leaking the complete release cylinder assembly must be renewed. Before condemning the release cylinder, check that the leak is not coming from the sealing ring which is fitted between the cylinder and the transmission housing; the sealing ring can be renewed once the release cylinder assembly has been removed. Refer to Chapter 6, Section 4 for removal and refitting details.

---

7 Reversing light switch –
testing, removal and refitting

Testing

1 The reversing light circuit is operated by a plunger-type switch, mounted on the upper/front of the transmission casing.

2 To test the switch, disconnect the wiring, and use a suitable meter or a battery-and-bulb test circuit to check for continuity between the switch terminals. Continuity should only exist when reverse gear is selected. If this is not the case, and there are no obvious breaks or other damage to the wires, the switch is faulty and must be renewed.

Removal

3 The reversing light switch is located on the front of the transmission casing, and is accessible from the left-hand side of the engine compartment or from beneath the vehicle.

4 Disconnect the wiring from the switch, then unscrew the switch from the transmission. Recover the O-ring seal.

Refitting

5 Refitting is a reversal of removal, but tighten the switch to the specified torque.

---

8 Manual transmission –
removal and refitting

Note: *This is an involved procedure, and it may well prove easier to remove the transmission complete with the engine as an assembly (see Chapter 2D, Section 4, or 2D Section 5), then separate the transmission. However, this Section describes removing the transmission leaving the engine in position. Suitable equipment will be required to support the engine and transmission, and the help of an assistant will be required.*

Removal

1 Apply the handbrake, then jack up the front of the vehicle and support it on axle stands (see *Jacking and vehicle support*). Allow sufficient working room to remove the transmission from under the left-hand side of the engine compartment. Remove both front roadwheels then, where necessary, undo the retaining clips/screws and remove the engine undertray. Also remove the engine top cover where fitted.

2 Remove the air cleaner assembly and intake ducts (see Chapter 4A, Section 2 or Chapter 4B, Section 3). Remove the battery and battery tray as described in Chapter 5A, Section 4.

3 Drain the transmission oil as described in Section 2 or be prepared for oil loss as the transmission is removed.

4 Remove the filler cap from the brake/clutch fluid reservoir on the bulkhead, then tighten it onto a piece of polythene. This will reduce the loss of fluid when the clutch hydraulic hose is disconnected. Alternatively, fit a hose clamp to the flexible hose next to the clutch hydraulic connection on the transmission housing.

5 Place some cloth rags beneath the hose, then prise out the retaining clip securing the clutch hydraulic pipe/hose end fitting to the top of the transmission bellhousing and detach the end fitting from the transmission **(see illustration)**. Gently squeeze the two legs of the retaining clip together and re-insert the retaining clip back into position in the end fitting. Discard the sealing ring from the pipe end; a new sealing ring must be used on refitting. Plug/cover both the union and pipe ends to minimise fluid loss and prevent the entry of dirt into the hydraulic system.

Note: *Whilst the hose/pipe is disconnected, do not depress the clutch pedal.*

6 Disconnect the wiring from the reversing lamp switch on the front of the transmission.

7 Attach a suitable hoist and lifting tackle to the lifting bracket(s) located on the left-hand side of the cylinder head, and support the weight of the engine/transmission.

8 Refer to Chapter 10, Section 7 and remove the front subframe.

9 Disconnect the inner ends of both driveshafts from the differential as described in Chapter 8, Section 2. There is no need to disconnect the driveshafts from the swivel hub. Support the driveshafts by suspending them with wire or string – do not allow the driveshafts to hang down under their own weight, or the joints may be damaged.

10 Refer to Section 4 or Section 5, as applicable, and disconnect the gearchange linkage/cables from the transmission.

11 Unscrew and remove the three upper bolts securing the transmission to the rear of the engine. Where necessary, pull up the coolant hoses and secure them away from the transmission using plastic cable-ties.

12 Unbolt and remove the left-hand engine/transmission mounting bracket from the transmission with reference to Chapter 2A, Section 15, Chapter 2B, Section 16 or Chapter 2C, Section 16 as applicable.

13 Lower the engine and transmission by approximately 5 cm making sure that the coolant hoses and wiring harnesses are not stretched.

14 Unbolt and remove the rear engine/transmission mounting torque link brackets with reference to Chapter 2A, Section 15, Chapter 2B, Section 16 or Chapter 2C, Section 16 as applicable.

15 Unscrew the four lower bolts securing the transmission to the engine.

16 Support the weight of the transmission on a trolley jack, then unscrew the remaining transmission-to-engine bolts, noting the location of the earth cable.

17 Make a final check that all components have been disconnected, and are positioned clear of the transmission so that they will not hinder the removal procedure.

18 With the help of an assistant, carefully withdraw the transmission (and adaptor plate on diesel engine models) from the engine. Take care not to allow the weight of the transmission to hang on the input shaft otherwise the clutch friction disc hub may be damaged. Note that there are two locating dowels which may be tight, and it may be necessary to rock the transmission from side-to-side to release it from them. Once the transmission is free, lower the jack and manoeuvre the unit out from under the car.

Refitting

19 Commence refitting by positioning the transmission on the trolley jack beneath the engine compartment. With the help of an assistant, raise the transmission and locate

it on the engine, making sure that the input shaft engages accurately with the splines of the friction disc hub. With the transmission located on the dowels, insert all of the retaining bolts and tighten to the specified torque.

20 The remaining refitting procedure is a reversal of removal, noting the following points:

a) *Tighten all nuts and bolts to the specified torque (where given).*

b) *Renew the driveshaft oil seals (see Section 6) before refitting the driveshafts.*

c) *Refit the front subframe assembly as described in Chapter 10, Section 7.*

d) *Fit a new sealing ring to the transmission clutch hydraulic pipe before clipping the hose/pipe end fitting into position. Ensure the end fitting is securely retained by its clip then bleed the hydraulic system as described in Chapter 6, Section 2.*

e) *Refill the transmission with the specified type and quantity of oil, as described in Section 2.*

f) *On completion, adjust the gearchange linkage/mechanism as described in Section 3.*

9 Manual transmission overhaul – general information

1 Overhauling a manual transmission unit is a difficult and involved job for the DIY home mechanic. In addition to dismantling and reassembling many small parts, clearances must be precisely measured and, if necessary, changed by selecting shims and spacers. Internal transmission components are also often difficult to obtain, and in many instances, extremely expensive. Because of this, if the transmission develops a fault or becomes noisy, the best course of action is to have the unit overhauled by a specialist repairer, or to obtain an exchange reconditioned unit.

2 Nevertheless, it is not impossible for the more experienced mechanic to overhaul the transmission, provided the special tools are available, and the job is done in a deliberate step-by-step manner, so that nothing is overlooked.

3 The tools necessary for an overhaul include internal and external circlip pliers, bearing pullers, a slide hammer, a set of pin punches, a dial test indicator, and possibly a hydraulic press. In addition, a large, sturdy workbench and a vice will be required.

4 During dismantling of the transmission, make careful notes of how each component is fitted, to make reassembly easier and more accurate.

5 Before dismantling the transmission, it will help if you have some idea what area is malfunctioning. Certain problems can be closely related to specific areas in the transmission, which can make component examination and renewal easier. Refer to *Fault finding* information in Reference for more information.

Chapter 7 Part B
Automatic transmission

Contents

Degrees of difficulty

Easy, suitable for novice with little experience	Fairly easy, suitable for beginner with some experience	Fairly difficult, suitable for competent DIY mechanic	Difficult, suitable for experienced DIY mechanic	Very difficult, suitable for expert DIY or professional

Specifications

General

Type	Hydrodynamic torque converter with electronically-controlled mechanical lock-up system, two epicyclic gearsets giving four forward speeds and reverse, integral final drive. Gearchanging under full electronic control
Manufacturer's designation	AF 13 II

Lubrication

Lubricant type	See *Lubricants and fluids* on page 0•17
Lubricant capacity	See Chapter 1A

Torque wrench settings

	Nm	lbf ft
Engine/transmission mountings	See Chapter 2B	
Engine-to-transmission bolts	See Chapter 2B	
Fluid cooler mounting bolts/nuts	20	15
Roadwheel bolts	110	81
Selector lever housing bolts	22	16
Selector lever position switch hub-to-shaft nut	8	6
Selector lever position switch-to-transmission	25	18
Selector lever-to-selector lever shaft	16	12
Torque converter-to-driveplate bolts: *		
Stage 1	20	15
Stage 2	45	33
Stage 3	Angle-tighten a further 20°	
Stage 4	Angle-tighten a further 25°	
Transmission fluid drain plug	45	33

* Use new fastenings

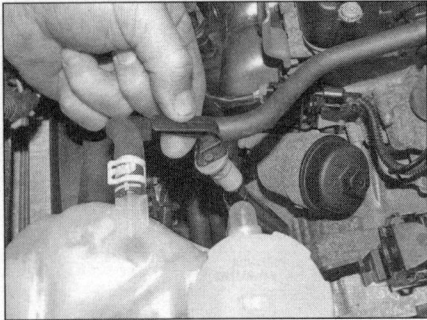

2.6 Pull up the lever on the top of the dipstick to release it from the tube

1 General Information

1 A 4-speed fully-automatic transmission is available as an option on 1.4 litre petrol engine models. The transmission consists of a torque converter, an epicyclic geartrain and hydraulically-operated clutches and brakes. The differential is integral with the transmission, and is similar to that used in manual gearbox models.

2 The torque converter provides a fluid coupling between the engine and transmission which acts as an automatic 'clutch', and also provides a degree of torque multiplication when accelerating.

3 The epicyclic geartrain provides either one of the four forward gear ratios, or reverse gear, according to which of its component parts are held stationary or allowed to turn. The components of the geartrain are held or released by brakes and clutches, which are activated by a hydraulic control unit. A fluid pump within the transmission provides the necessary hydraulic pressure to operate the brakes and clutches.

4 The transmission is electronically-controlled, and two driving modes – Normal and Winter – are provided. The transmission electronic control unit (ECU) operates in conjunction with the engine management ECU to control the gearchanges. The transmission ECU receives information on transmission fluid temperature, throttle position, engine coolant temperature,

and input-versus-output shaft speed. The ECU controls the hydraulically-operated clutches and brakes via four solenoids. The control system can also retard the engine ignition timing, via the engine management ECU, to permit smoother gearchanges.

5 Due to the complexity of the automatic transmission, any repair or overhaul work must be entrusted to a Vauxhall/Opel dealer, who will have the necessary specialist equipment and knowledge for fault diagnosis and repair. See *Fault finding* in Reference for further information.

2 Automatic transmission fluid renewal

Draining

1 This operation is much quicker and more efficient if the vehicle is first taken on a journey of sufficient length to warm the engine/transmission up to normal operating temperature.

2 Apply the handbrake, then jack up the front of the vehicle and support it on axle stands (see *Jacking and vehicle support*).

3 Place a suitable container under the drain plug located centrally at the base of the transmission housing.

4 Wipe clean the area around the drain plug, then unscrew the plug and allow the fluid to drain into the container.

5 After all the fluid has drained, wipe the drain plug and the sealing washer with a clean rag. Examine the condition of the sealing washer, and renew it if it shows signs of scoring or other damage which may prevent a perfect seal. Clean the area around the drain plug opening, and refit the plug complete with the washer. Tighten the plug to the specified torque and lower the car to the ground.

Refilling

6 Withdraw the transmission fluid level dipstick (located at the left-hand side of the engine compartment, next to the engine oil filter). Pull up the lever on the top of the dipstick to release it from the tube **(see illustration)**.

7 Refill the transmission through the dipstick

tube with the correct quantity and type of fluid, then check the level as follows.

8 Lower the vehicle to the ground. Note that the vehicle must be parked on level ground for an accurate level check.

9 If the transmission fluid is cold (ie, if the engine is cold), the level check must be completed within one minute of the engine being started.

10 With the engine idling, fully depress the brake pedal, and move the gear selector lever smoothly through all positions, finishing in position P.

11 With the engine still idling, withdraw the fluid level dipstick. Wipe the dipstick clean with a lint-free rag, re-insert it and withdraw it again.

12 If the transmission fluid was cold at the beginning of the procedure, the fluid level should be between the two marks on the side of the dipstick marked +20°C **(see illustration)**. Note that 0.4 litres of fluid is required to raise the level from the MIN to the MAX mark.

13 If the transmission fluid was at operating temperature at the beginning of the procedure (ie, if the vehicle had been driven for at least 12 miles), the fluid level should be between the two marks on the side of the dipstick marked +80°C **(see illustration)**. Note that 0.2 litres of fluid is required to raise the level from the MIN to the MAX mark.

14 If topping-up is necessary, stop the engine, and top-up with the specified type of fluid through the transmission dipstick tube.

15 Recheck the level, and refit the dipstick on completion.

3 Selector cable – adjustment

1 Operate the selector lever throughout its entire range and check that the transmission engages the correct gear indicated on the selector lever position indicator. If adjustment is necessary, continue as follows.

2 Release the retaining lug and unclip the transmission electronic control unit and mounting bracket from the battery tray **(see illustration)**. Position the control unit and mounting bracket to one side.

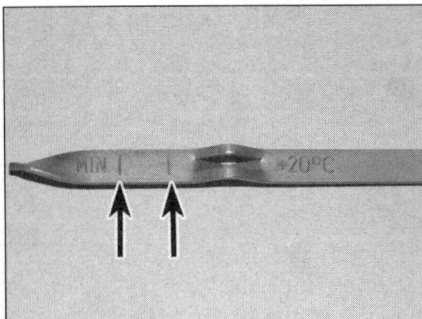

2.12 Transmission fluid level marks on the side of the dipstick marked +20°C

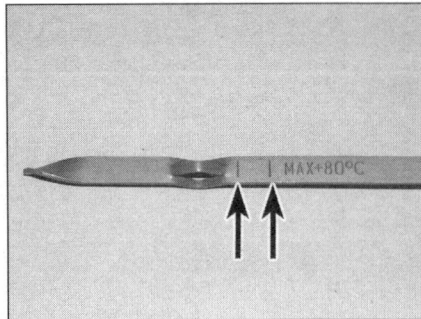

2.13 Transmission fluid level marks (arrowed) on the side of the dipstick marked +80°C

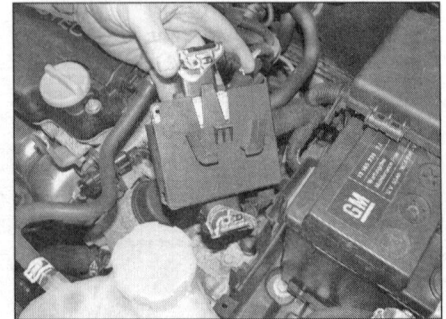

3.2 Unclip the transmission electronic control unit and mounting bracket from the battery tray

3 Using a small screwdriver, open the clamping piece on the selector cable adjuster as far as the notch **(see illustration)**. Opening any further may damage the clamping piece.

4 Move the selector lever inside the car to position P. Check that the lever has engaged properly by moving it back-and-forth without depressing the lock knob.

5 Working at the transmission, move the lever on the position switch clockwise (forward) as far as it will go. Check that the transmission is now in the Park position by releasing the handbrake and pushing the car forward slightly until the parking lock pawl engages.

6 Press down the clamping piece on the selector cable adjuster to lock the cable in position. Ensure that the clamping piece audibly engages.

7 Refit the transmission electronic control unit to the battery tray.

8 Check the selector cable adjustment by selecting P, R, N, D, 3, 2, 1 and checking that the relative positions on the transmission are engaged.

4 Selector cable – removal and refitting

Removal

1 Remove the selector lever housing as described in Section 5.

2 Unscrew the four bolts and separate the selector lever from the lever housing.

3 Using a screwdriver, prise the inner selector cable end fitting off the selector lever then extract the retaining clip and release the outer selector cable from the selector lever housing.

Refitting

4 Insert the selector cable into the selector lever housing and secure the outer cable with the retaining clip.

5 Push the inner selector cable end fitting back onto the selector lever ensuring that it is fully seated.

6 Position the selector lever on the lever housing and secure with the four bolts.

7 Refit the selector lever housing as described in Section 5.

5 Selector lever housing – removal and refitting

Removal

1 Unclip the selector lever cover from the centre console, then unclip the selector lever gaiter from the cover. Disconnect the wiring connector and manoeuvre the cover up and off the selector lever **(see illustrations)**.

2 Release the locking catch and disconnect the wiring connector from the top of the selector lever.

3 Working in the engine compartment, release the retaining lug and unclip the transmission electronic control unit and mounting bracket from the battery tray **(see illustration 3.2)**. Position the control unit and mounting bracket to one side.

4 Using a small screwdriver, open the clamping piece on the selector cable adjuster as far as the notch **(see illustration 3.3)**. Opening any further may damage the clamping piece.

5 Pull back the retaining sleeve and lift the selector outer cable from the mounting bracket on the transmission **(see illustration)**. Pull the cable rearward until the inner cable end disengages from the cable adjuster.

6 Remove the complete exhaust system as described in Chapter 4A, Section 13.

7 From under the car, open the latch and release the selector cable from the bracket on the steering gear.

8 Release the four sheet metal nuts securing the exhaust heat shield to the underbody.

9 Undo the four bolts in the centre of the heat shield and remove the heat shield together with the selector lever housing from under the car. Once removed, separate the housing from the heat shield.

10 If required, the selector cable and selector lever can be removed from the housing as described in Section 4.

Refitting

11 If removed, refit the selector cable and selector lever to the housing as described in Section 4.

3.3 Using a small screwdriver, open the clamping piece on the selector cable adjuster as far as the notch

12 Locate the selector lever housing and heat shield in position on the underbody, ensuring that the selector cable is correctly routed. Insert the four retaining bolts and tighten them to the specified torque.

13 Secure the heat shield to the underbody with the four sheet metal nuts.

14 Guide the selector cable into position on the steering gear bracket and close the latch.

15 Engage the selector inner cable end with the cable adjuster, then refit the outer cable to the transmission bracket. Press down the clamping piece on the selector cable adjuster to lock the cable in position. Ensure that the clamping piece audibly engages.

16 Refit the exhaust system as described in Chapter 4A, Section 13.

17 From inside the car, reconnect the wiring connector to the selector lever, then reconnect the selector lever cover wiring connector and refit the cover. Fold the gaiter back down the selector lever and clip it back into place on the cover.

18 On completion, adjust the selector cable as described in Section 3.

6 Selector lever lock components – removal and refitting

General

1 The transmission selector lever assembly incorporates an electrically-operated selector

5.1a Unclip the selector lever cover from the centre console, then unclip the lever gaiter from the cover

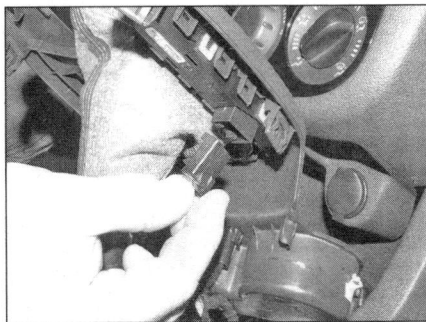

5.1b Disconnect the wiring connector and manoeuvre the cover up and off the selector lever

5.5 Pull back the retaining sleeve and lift the selector outer cable from the transmission bracket

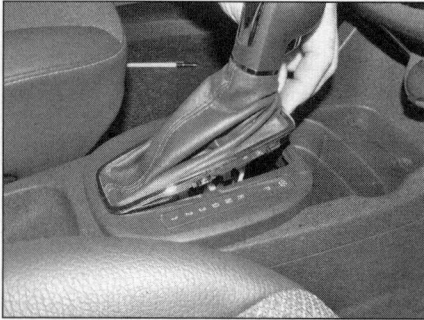
6.11 Unclip the selector lever gaiter from the selector lever cover and fold the gaiter up the lever

6.12 Push the yellow release lever on the lock solenoid downward to release the selector lever lock

7 Refill or top-up the transmission fluid level with reference to Section 2.
8 Refit the roadwheel, then lower the vehicle to the ground.

lever lock mechanism that prevents the lever being moved out of the P position unless the ignition is switched on and the brake pedal depressed. The components associated with the system are as follows:

a) Selector lever lock solenoid.
b) Selector lever lock solenoid switch.
c) Ignition key contact switch.
d) Footbrake stop-light switch.

2 Apart from the stop-light switch, all the components are located on the selector lever housing and are connected by a common wiring harness which cannot be separated. Stop-light switch removal and refitting procedures are given in Chapter 9, Section 16.
3 If the selector lever is in the P position and there is an interruption of the power supply to the ignition switch (ie, if the battery is disconnected, or if the battery is flat) it will not be possible to move the selector lever out of position P by the normal means. To overcome this problem, it is possible, in an emergency, to manually release the selector lever lock solenoid as described in Lever lock manual override later in this Section.

Component renewal

4 Remove the selector lever housing as described in Section 5.
5 Disconnect the lever lock solenoid wiring connector then release the wiring harness from the guides.
6 Unclip the retainer plate and detach the lock solenoid switch and ignition key contact switch from the housing.
7 Unclip the emergency release lever.

8.3 Pipe and hose connections on the transmission fluid cooler

8 On the underside of the housing, release the retaining latch using a small screwdriver and withdraw the lock solenoid from the housing. Remove the solenoid together with the wiring harness and the two switches from the housing.
9 Refitting is a reversal of removal.

Lever lock manual override

10 If it is not possible to move the selector lever out of the P position due to a disconnected or flat battery, proceed as follows.
11 Unclip the selector lever gaiter from the selector lever cover and fold the gaiter up the lever (see illustration).
12 Using a ballpoint pen or small screwdriver, push the yellow release lever on the lock solenoid downward and hold in this position (see illustration). Now depress the knob and move the selector lever out of the P position.
13 Refit the selector lever gaiter.

7 Driveshaft oil seals – renewal

1 Apply the handbrake, then jack up the front of the vehicle and support it on axle stands (see Jacking and vehicle support). Remove the relevant front roadwheel.
2 Drain the transmission fluid as described in Section 2 or be prepared for fluid loss as the seal is changed.
3 Disconnect the inner end of the relevant driveshaft from the differential as described in Chapter 8, Section 2. There is no need to disconnect the driveshaft from the swivel hub. Support the driveshaft by suspending it with wire or string – do not allow the driveshaft to hang down under its own weight, or the joints may be damaged.
4 Prise the now-exposed oil seal from the differential housing, using a screwdriver or similar instrument.
5 Smear the sealing lip of the new oil seal with a little transmission oil, then using a metal tube or socket of suitable diameter, drive the new seal into the differential casing until the outer surface of the seal is flush with the outer surface of the differential casing.
6 Reconnect the driveshaft to the differential as described in Chapter 8, Section 2.

8 Fluid cooler – removal and refitting

Removal

1 Firmly apply the handbrake, then jack up the front of the vehicle and support it securely on axle stands (see Jacking and vehicle support).
2 Drain the cooling system as described in Chapter 1A, Section 27.
3 Take note of the pipe and hose connections on the transmission and fluid cooler before disturbing them, and take note of the hose routing (see illustration).
4 Position a suitable container beneath the fluid cooler pipe connections on the transmission.
5 Pull off the two protective rings over the fluid cooler pipe connections on the transmission. Using a small screwdriver, release the quick-release fittings and disconnect the two fluid pipes from the transmission. Suitably plug or cover the pipe and transmission unions.
6 Reposition the container beneath the pipe connections on the fluid cooler.
7 Pull off the two protective rings over the fluid pipe connections on the fluid cooler. Using a small screwdriver, release the quick-release fittings and disconnect the two fluid pipes from the cooler. Suitably plug or cover the pipe and fluid cooler unions.
8 Unscrew the bolt and two nuts securing the fluid cooler to the transmission and withdraw the cooler from its location.
9 Release the retaining clips and disconnect the two coolant hoses from the fluid cooler, then remove the cooler from the engine compartment.

Refitting

10 Refitting is a reversal of removal, bearing in mind the following points:
a) Ensure that the fluid pipes are correctly routed and that the quick-release fittings audibly engage when reconnected.
b) Refill the cooling system as described in Chapter 1A, Section 27.
c) Check and if necessary top-up the automatic transmission fluid as described in Section 2.

9 Transmission control system electrical components – removal and refitting

Selector lever position switch

Adjustment

1 Adjustment of the switch entails the use of Vauxhall/Opel special tool KM-962, which is

9.3a Press the selector cable adjuster from the lever on the position switch...

9.3b...then pull back the retaining sleeve and lift the outer cable from the transmission bracket

9.20 Automatic transmission electronic control unit location

then connected to the selector lever position switch wiring connector on the transmission. The tool contains a series of LEDs (light emitting diodes), that illuminate in sequence as each selector position is engaged. If the LEDs do not illuminate correctly in each selector lever position, the position switch securing screws must be slackened and the switch repositioned accordingly. As accurate adjustment of the position switch can only be carried out using this tool, the work should be entrusted to a Vauxhall/Opel dealer.

Removal

Note: *It will be necessary to have the adjustment of the switch carried out by a Vauxhall/Opel dealer on completion (see adjustment above). Bearing this in mind, it may be beneficial to have the complete operation (removal, refitting and adjustment) carried out by the dealer at the same time.*

2 Working in the engine compartment, release the retaining lug and unclip the transmission electronic control unit and mounting bracket from the battery tray **(see illustration 3.2)**. Position the control unit and mounting bracket to one side.

3 Press the selector cable adjuster from the lever on the position switch, then pull back the retaining sleeve and lift the selector outer cable from the mounting bracket on the transmission **(see illustrations)**.

4 Release the wiring harness from the support bracket, and disconnect the switch wiring connector.

5 Unscrew the nut and remove the lever from the transmission selector shaft.

6 Bend up the lockplate, then unscrew the switch hub retaining nut and withdraw from the shaft. It is recommended that the lockplate is renewed.

7 Accurately mark the position of the selector lever position switch on the switch and transmission, then unscrew the two retaining bolts and withdraw the switch from the transmission.

Refitting

8 Locate the position switch over the shaft and onto the transmission in the previously-noted position. Insert the retaining bolts and tighten them to the specified torque.

9 Refit the switch hub nut together with a new lockplate and tighten to the specified torque. Bend the lockplate onto the nut to lock it.

10 Locate the lever on selector shaft and tighten the nut to the specified torque.

11 Reconnect the wiring and clip the wiring into the support bracket.

12 Refit the selector outer cable to the transmission bracket.

13 Press the cable adjuster onto the lever on the position switch.

14 Refit the transmission electronic control unit to the battery tray.

15 Have a Vauxhall/Opel dealer adjust the switch.

Winter mode switch

Removal

16 Unclip the selector lever cover from the centre console, then unclip the selector lever gaiter from the cover. Disconnect the wiring connector and manoeuvre the cover up and off the selector lever **(see illustrations 5.1a and 5.1b)**.

17 Unclip the selector lever position display incorporating the winter mode switch. Note that the mode switch is an integral part of the selector lever position display.

Refitting

18 Refitting is a reversal of removal.

Selector lever position display

19 Proceed as described in paragraphs 16 to 18.

Electronic control unit

Note: *If a new ECU is to be fitted, this work must be entrusted to a Vauxhall/Opel dealer or suitably-equipped specialist. It is necessary to reset the transmission electronic control system prior to removal, and to programme the new ECU after installation. This work requires the use of dedicated Vauxhall/Opel diagnostic equipment or a compatible alternative.*

Removal

20 The automatic transmission electronic control unit is located on the left-hand side of the engine compartment, on the side of the battery tray **(see illustration)**.

21 Move the gear selector lever to the N (neutral) position.

22 Disconnect the battery negative terminal (refer to *Disconnecting the battery* in Chapter 5A, Section 4).

23 Open the locking bars and disconnect the wiring plugs from the top and bottom of the electronic control unit.

24 At the top of the unit, press out the retaining tab, then withdraw the control unit upwards from the mounting bracket.

Refitting

25 Refitting is a reversal of removal.

Input and output shaft speed sensors

Removal

26 The input and output speed sensors are located on the rear of the transmission casing, above the left-hand driveshaft **(see illustration)**. Working in the engine compartment, reach down and disconnect the wiring plug from the top of the sensor.

27 Unscrew the retaining bolt and remove the sensor from the casing.

Refitting

28 With a new sealing ring fitted, insert the sensor into the transmission casing aperture.

29 Tighten the retaining bolt securely and reconnect the wiring plug.

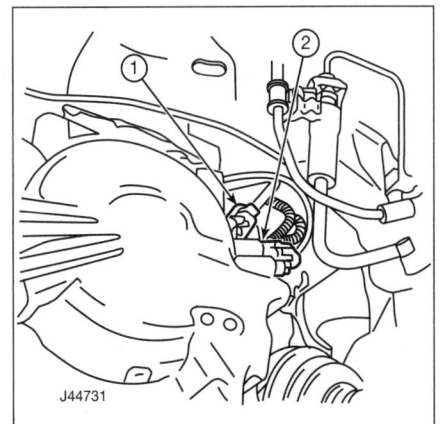

9.26 Transmission output (1) and input (2) speed sensors

10.8 Disconnect the transmission main wiring harness at the connector

10 Automatic transmission – removal and refitting

1 This is an involved procedure, and it may prove easier in many cases to remove the transmission complete with the engine as an assembly, as described in Chapter 2D, Section 4. If removing the transmission on its own, it is suggested that this Section is read through thoroughly before commencing work. Suitable equipment will be required to support the engine and transmission, and the help of an assistant will be required. New torque converter-to-driveplate bolts must be used on refitting, and if the original torque converter is being used, an M10 x 1.25 mm tap will be required.

Removal

2 Apply the handbrake, then jack up the front of the vehicle and support it on axle stands (see *Jacking and vehicle support*). Allow sufficient working room to remove the transmission from under the left-hand side of the engine compartment. Remove both front roadwheels then, where necessary, undo the retaining clips/screws and remove the engine

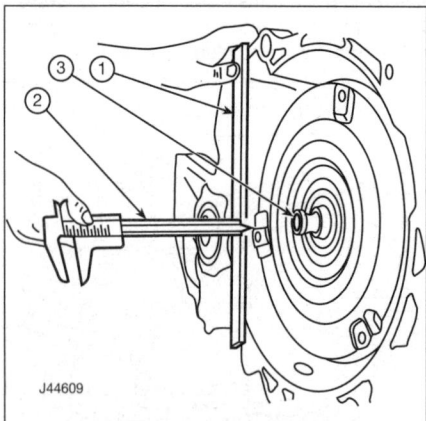

10.30 Check that the torque converter is fully entered

1 Straight-edge
2 Vernier calipers on bolt hole
3 Torque converter centre stub

undertray. Also remove the engine top cover where fitted.
3 Move the gear selector lever to the N (neutral) position.
4 Remove the battery and battery tray as described in Chapter 5A, Section 4.
5 Drain the transmission fluid as described in Section 2.
6 Release the wiring harness from the support bracket, and disconnect the selector lever position switch wiring connector. Undo the retaining bolt and remove the wiring harness support bracket.
7 Press the selector cable adjuster from the lever on the selector lever position switch, then pull back the retaining sleeve and lift the selector outer cable from the mounting bracket on the transmission **(see illustrations 9.3a and 9.3b)**.
8 Disconnect the transmission main wiring harness at the connector on top of the transmission, then unclip the harness from the support bracket **(see illustration)**.
9 Pull off the transmission vent hose located adjacent to the main wiring harness connector.
10 Unscrew the bolt securing the coolant expansion tank to the front body panel. Unclip the tank and position it to one side.
11 Remove the transmission fluid level dipstick, then unscrew the dipstick tube retaining nut. Withdraw the dipstick tube from the transmission and recover the seal.
12 Unscrew the bolt and two nuts, and detach the fluid cooler from the front of the transmission.
13 Pull off the two protective rings over the fluid cooler pipe connections on the transmission. Using a small screwdriver, release the quick-release fittings and disconnect the two fluid pipes from the transmission. Suitably plug or cover the pipe and transmission unions, then secure the pipes clear of the transmission.
14 Unscrew the nut and detach the earth cable from the top of the transmission.
15 Unscrew and remove the three uppermost bolts securing the transmission to the rear of the engine. Remove the wiring harness support bracket.
16 Attach a suitable hoist and lifting tackle to the lifting bracket(s) located on the left-hand side of the cylinder head, and support the weight of the engine/transmission.
17 Refer to Chapter 10, Section 7 and remove the front subframe.
18 Disconnect the inner ends of both driveshafts from the differential as described in Chapter 8, Section 2. There is no need to disconnect the driveshafts from the swivel hub. Support the driveshafts by suspending them with wire or string – do not allow the driveshafts to hang down under their own weight, or the joints may be damaged.
19 Unbolt and remove the rear engine/transmission mounting torque link bracket with reference to Chapter 2B, Section 16.
20 Prise out the two access covers from the driveplate end of the transmission housing.

21 Working through the bellhousing access holes, unscrew the three torque converter-to-driveplate bolts. It will be necessary to turn the engine, using a suitable spanner or socket on the crankshaft pulley or sprocket bolt (as applicable), to gain access to each bolt in turn through the aperture. Use a screwdriver or a similar tool to jam the driveplate ring gear, preventing the driveplate from rotating as the bolts are loosened. Discard the bolts.
22 Unbolt and remove the left-hand engine/transmission mounting bracket from the transmission with reference to Chapter 2B, Section 16.
23 Lower the engine and transmission by approximately 5 cm making sure that the coolant hoses and wiring harnesses are not stretched.
24 Support the weight of the transmission on a trolley jack. Ensure that the engine is adequately supported as previously described.
25 Unscrew and remove the lower transmission-to-engine bolts.
26 Make a final check that all components have been disconnected, and are positioned clear of the transmission so that they will not hinder the removal procedure.
27 With the help of an assistant, carefully withdraw the transmission from the engine, taking care to ensure that the torque converter remains firmly in place in the transmission. Note that there are two locating dowels in the rear of the engine which may be tight, and it may be necessary to rock the transmission from side-to-side to release it from them. If this precaution is not taken, the torque converter could fall out, resulting in fluid spillage and possible damage.
28 Lower the transmission to the ground and withdraw it from under the vehicle. Retain the torque converter while the transmission is removed by bolting a strip of metal across the transmission bellhousing end face.

Refitting

29 If the original torque converter is being refitted, commence refitting by recutting the torque converter-to-driveplate bolt threads in the torque converter using an M10 x 1.25 mm tap. Clean any rust from the centre stub of the torque converter and the hole in the centre of the driveplate. Apply a little grease to the contact surfaces.
30 Check that the torque converter is fully entered inside the transmission bellhousing by measuring the distance from the flange to the bolt holes in the torque converter, using a straight-edge and vernier calipers **(see illustration)**. The distance must measure approximately 12.0 mm.
31 If a new transmission is being fitted, the manufacturers recommend that the fluid cooler passages are flushed clean before the new transmission is installed. Ideally, compressed air should be used (in which case, ensure that adequate safety precautions are taken; in particular, eye protection should be worn).

Alternatively, the cooler can be flushed with clean automatic transmission fluid until all the old fluid has been removed, and fresh fluid runs clear from the cooler outlet.

32 Position the transmission under the front of the vehicle, and support with the trolley jack. Remove the strip of metal retaining the torque converter in the transmission, and hold the torque converter in position as the transmission is located on the engine.

33 With the help of an assistant, raise the transmission and locate it on the engine. Refit all of the engine-to-transmission bolts hand-tight, then tighten them progressively to their specified torque.

34 Raise the engine and transmission, then refit the left-hand mounting and bracket with reference to Chapter 2B, Section 16. Remove the hoist and lifting tackle.

35 Align the holes of the torque converter with the holes in the driveplate. Apply locking fluid to the threads of the new bolts, then insert them separately and tighten to the specified torque while holding the driveplate ring gear stationary with the screwdriver. Refit the two access covers to the transmission housing.

36 Refit the rear engine/transmission mounting torque link bracket with reference to Chapter 2B, Section 16.

37 Reconnect the driveshafts to the transmission with reference to Chapter 8, Section 2.

38 Refit the front subframe assembly with reference to Chapter 10, Section 7.

39 Reattach the earth cable to the top of the transmission.

40 Place the fluid cooler in position on the transmission, then refit and tighten the bolt and two nuts to the specified torque.

41 Reconnect the quick-release fluid cooler hoses together with new O-ring seals to the transmission.

42 Refit the transmission fluid level dipstick tube together with a new O-ring seal to the cylinder block and secure with the retaining nut tightened securely. Reinsert the dipstick.

43 Locate the coolant expansion tank back in position, then refit and tighten the retaining bolt.

44 Refit the transmission vent hose.

45 Clip the transmission wiring harness to the support bracket and reconnect the wiring harness connector.

46 Pull back the retaining sleeve and insert the selector outer cable into the mounting bracket on the transmission. Press the selector cable adjuster back onto the lever on the selector lever position switch.

47 Refit the wiring harness support bracket and retaining bolt and secure the harness to the bracket. Reconnect the selector lever position switch wiring connector.

48 Refit the battery tray and battery as described in Chapter 5A, Section 4.

49 Refill the transmission with the specified fluid as described in Section 2.

50 Where fitted, refit the engine undertray, then refit the roadwheels and lower the vehicle to the ground. Refit the engine top cover where applicable.

11 Automatic transmission overhaul – general information

1 In the event of a fault occurring on the transmission, it is first necessary to determine whether it is of an electrical, mechanical or hydraulic nature, and to achieve this, special test equipment is required. It is therefore essential to have the work carried out by a Vauxhall/Opel dealer if a transmission fault is suspected.

2 Do not remove the transmission from the car for possible repair before professional fault diagnosis has been carried out, since most tests require the transmission to be in the vehicle.

Chapter 7 Part C
Easytronic transmission

Contents

Degrees of difficulty

Easy, suitable for novice with little experience	Fairly easy, suitable for beginner with some experience	Fairly difficult, suitable for competent DIY mechanic	Difficult, suitable for experienced DIY mechanic	Very difficult, suitable for expert DIY or professional

Specifications

General

Type	Five forward speeds and one reverse, automatic or manual selection. Integral differential
Manufacturer's designation	F13 MTA or F17 MTA

Lubrication

Lubricant type	See Lubricants and fluids on page 0•17
Lubricant capacity	See Chapter 1A

Torque wrench settings

	Nm	lbf ft
Clutch module with MTA control unit.	11	8
Differential housing cover plate:		
Alloy plate.	18	13
Steel plate.	30	22
Engine/transmission mountings.	See Chapter 2B	
Engine-to-transmission bolts.	See Chapter 2B	
Transmission oil level plug.	22	16
Transmission shift module	11	8
Transmission vent plug.	13	9

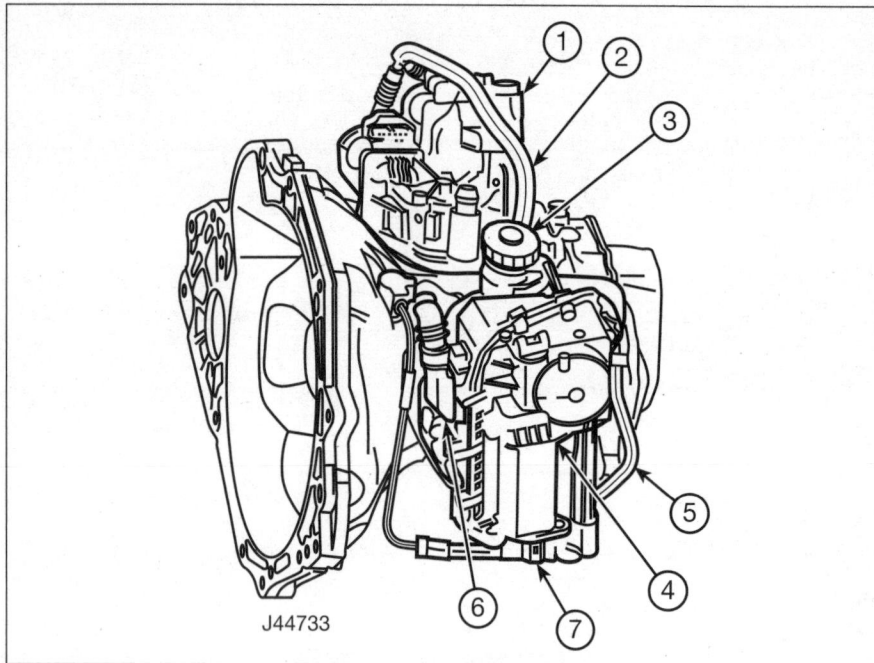

1.1 Easytronic (MTA) transmission

1 *Transmission shift module*
2 *Wiring harness*
3 *Hydraulic fluid reservoir*
4 *Clutch control module*
5 *Hydraulic supply line to clutch control module*
6 *Wiring harness for clutch control module*
7 *Hydraulic pressure line to clutch release cylinder*

1 General Information

1 The Easytronic MTA transmission (Manual Transmission Automatic-shift) is essentially a conventional manual transmission with the addition of a clutch module and shift module, used in conjunction with a self-adjusting clutch plate **(see illustration)**.
2 The description of the MTA transmission is basically as for the manual transmission given in Chapter 7A, Section 1, but with an electronically-operated hydraulic clutch control module and gear selection module. The transmission can be switched between fully automatic and manual mode, even while driving.

3 The clutch control module incorporates its own master cylinder and pushrod, which is operated electrically by a worm gear.
4 The gear selection module is fitted with a shifting motor and a selector motor, which together position the selector lever to move the selector forks in the transmission. It is located in exactly the same position as the gear selection cover fitted to the conventional manual transmission.
5 In the event of a problem, in the first instance the vehicle should be taken to a Vauxhall/Opel dealer or diagnostic specialist who will have the TECH2 diagnostic equipment (or equivalent) necessary to pin-point the faulty area. Note also that if the transmission assembly, shift module or clutch module are renewed, the vehicle must be taken to a Vauxhall/Opel dealer or diagnostic

specialist in order to have the fault memory erased and new parameters programmed into the ECU.

2 Transmission oil – draining and refilling

Note: *Changing the transmission oil is not a specified service operation, however, it may be considered necessary if the vehicle has covered a high mileage or if a new transmission is being fitted. No drain plug is fitted.*

Draining

1 Apply the handbrake, then jack up the front of the vehicle and support it on axle stands (see *Jacking and vehicle support*). Remove the engine undertray where fitted.
2 Unbolt the rear engine/transmission mounting torque link bracket from the transmission and pivot it to one side. If necessary, for improved access, undo the bolt securing the rear engine/transmission mounting torque link to the subframe and remove the torque link and bracket assembly.
3 Undo the two bolts and remove the cross-brace from the front subframe.
4 Place a suitable container under the differential cover plate. Unscrew the securing bolts and withdraw the cover plate, allowing the transmission oil to drain into the container **(see illustration)**. Recover the gasket and, if necessary, renew it.
5 Refit the differential cover plate together with the gasket, and tighten the securing bolts to the specified torque. Refit the rear engine/transmission mounting torque link and tighten the bolts to the specified torque.
6 Refit the cross-brace to the front subframe, ensuring that the mark LH on the end of the brace is toward the left-hand side of the car. Tighten the two retaining bolts securely.

Refilling

7 Wipe clean the area around the level plug. The level plug is located behind the driveshaft inner joint on the left-hand side of the transmission **(see illustration)**. Unscrew the plug and clean it.
8 The transmission is refilled through the vent on top of the transmission. Wipe clean the area around the vent, then unscrew and remove it. Refill the transmission with the specified grade of oil given in *Lubricants and fluids* until it reaches the bottom of the level plug aperture. Allow any excess oil to drain, then refit and tighten the level plug.
Note: *When new, the transmission is originally filled by weight, and the level may be below the level hole.*
9 Refit and tighten the vent, then refit the engine undertray (where fitted) and lower the vehicle to the ground.

2.4 Differential cover plate securing bolts

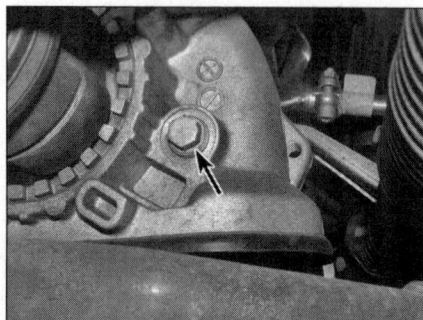

2.7 Transmission oil level plug

3 Selector lever assembly – removal and refitting

Removal

1 From inside the car, pull the gear selector lever knob off the selector lever.
2 Unclip the selector lever cover and disconnect the wiring connector.
3 Release the wiring harness at the front of the selector lever housing and disconnect the wiring connector.
4 Unscrew the four bolts securing the selector lever housing to the floor. Lift the housing up and out of its location and remove it from the car.

Refitting

5 Refitting is a reversal of removal.

4 Transmission shift module – removal and refitting

Removal

1 Switch on the ignition, then depress the footbrake pedal and move the selector lever to position N. Switch off the ignition.
2 Remove the battery and battery tray as described in Chapter 5A, Section 4.
3 Disconnect the two wiring plugs and release the harness from the support cable-ties on the top of the transmission.
4 Unbolt and remove the transmission shift module from the top of the transmission. To do this, lift it and tilt it slightly forwards before removing. Recover the gasket.
5 If the module cannot be removed because of internal jamming, unbolt the selector motor followed by the shifting motor (see illustration), and use a screwdriver to move the selector lever to its neutral position first. The selector motor is the uppermost unit.
Note: The manufacturers recommend that the shift module assembly is never re-used if dismantled.

Refitting

6 Clean the gasket faces of the module and transmission, and obtain a new gasket.
7 Make sure that the selector lever is in neutral, by checking that the mark on the segment is aligned with the pinion tooth. Check also that the lever is fully extended so that the annular groove is visible. The shift forks in the transmission must also be in neutral – use a screwdriver to move them if necessary (see illustrations).
8 Refit the shift module together with a new gasket, then insert the bolts and tighten to the specified torque.
9 Reconnect the wiring and secure with new cable-ties.

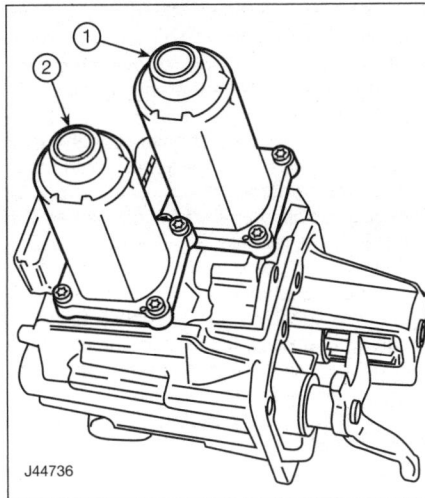

4.5 Shift motor (1) and selector motor (2) on the transmission shift module

10 Refit the battery and battery tray as described in Chapter 5A, Section 4.
11 Finally, it may be necessary to have a Vauxhall/Opel dealer or diagnostic specialist reprogramme all volatile control unit memories. If a new control unit has been fitted, a Vauxhall/Opel dealer or diagnostic specialist must programme the unit specifically for the model to which it is fitted.

5 Clutch module with MTA control unit – removal and refitting

Note: Bleeding the module is carried out using the Vauxhall/Opel TECH2 diagnostic instrument, therefore this work should be entrusted to a Vauxhall/Opel dealer or diagnostic specialist.

Removal

1 Apply the handbrake, then jack up the front of the vehicle and support it on axle stands (see Jacking and vehicle support). Where necessary, remove the engine undertray.

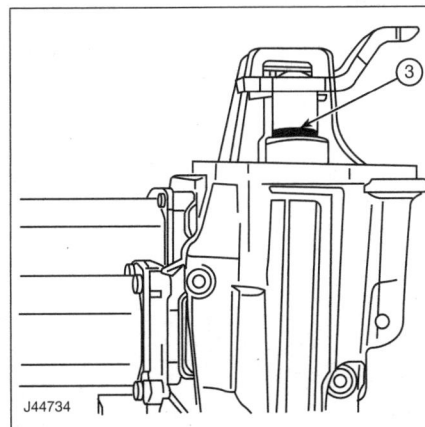

4.7b Groove (3) visible when the shift module is in neutral

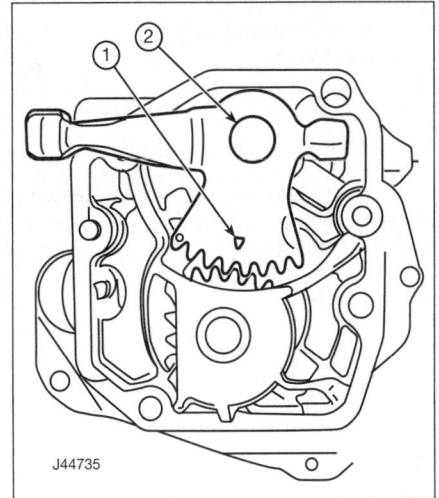

4.7a Neutral mark (1) and shift lever shaft (2) on the transmission shift module

2 Disconnect the wiring from the Easytronic transmission and release it from the cable-tie supports.
3 Place a suitable container beneath the front of the transmission to catch spilt hydraulic fluid.
4 Fit a hose clamp to the hydraulic hose leading from the hydraulic fluid reservoir to the clutch control unit, then disconnect the hose.
5 Disconnect the hydraulic quick-release pressure hose from the clutch control unit.
6 Unscrew the mounting bolts and remove the clutch module with MTA control unit from the transmission.

Refitting

7 Refitting is a reversal of removal, but tighten the mounting bolts to the specified torque. Make sure that the quick-release pressure hose is fully engaged – it must make an audible connection. Bleed the hydraulic circuit. Finally, it may be necessary to reprogramme all volatile control unit memories. If a new control unit has been fitted, a Vauxhall/Opel dealer or diagnostic specialist must programme the unit specifically for the model to which it is fitted.

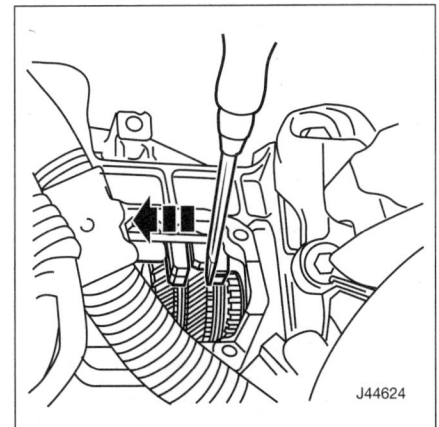

4.7c Using a screwdriver to move the transmission shift forks into neutral

6 Driveshaft oil seals – renewal

1 Apply the handbrake, then jack up the front of the vehicle and support it on axle stands (see *Jacking and vehicle support*). Remove the relevant front roadwheel.

2 Drain the transmission oil as described in Section 2 or be prepared for oil loss as the seal is changed.

3 Disconnect the inner end of the relevant driveshaft from the differential as described in Chapter 8, Section 2. There is no need to disconnect the driveshaft from the swivel hub. Support the driveshaft by suspending it with wire or string – do not allow the driveshaft to hang down under its own weight, or the joints may be damaged.

4 Prise the now-exposed oil seal from the differential housing, using a screwdriver or similar instrument.

5 Smear the sealing lip of the new oil seal with a little transmission oil, then using a metal tube or socket of suitable diameter, drive the new seal into the differential casing until the outer surface of the seal is flush with the outer surface of the differential casing.

6 Reconnect the driveshaft to the differential as described in Chapter 8, Section 2.

7 Refill or top-up the transmission oil level with reference to Section 2.

8 Refit the roadwheel, then lower the vehicle to the ground.

7 Easytronic transmission – removal and refitting

1 This is an involved procedure, and it may well prove easier to remove the transmission complete with the engine as an assembly (see Chapter 2D, Section 4), then separate the transmission. However, this Section describes removing the transmission leaving the engine in position. Suitable equipment will be required to support the engine and transmission, and the help of an assistant will be required.

Removal

2 Apply the handbrake, then jack up the front of the vehicle and support it on axle stands (see *Jacking and vehicle support*). Allow sufficient working room to remove the transmission from under the left-hand side of the engine compartment. Remove both front roadwheels then, where necessary, undo the retaining clips/screws and remove the engine undertray. Also remove the engine top cover where fitted.

3 Remove the air cleaner assembly and inlet ducts as described in Chapter 4A, Section 2.

4 Drain the transmission oil as described in Section 2 or be prepared for oil loss as the transmission is removed.

5 Remove the transmission shift module as described in Section 4.

6 Attach a suitable hoist and lifting tackle to the lifting bracket(s) located on the left-hand side of the cylinder head, and support the weight of the engine/transmission.

7 Refer to Chapter 10, Section 7 and remove the front subframe.

8 Disconnect the inner ends of both driveshafts from the differential as described in Chapter 8, Section 2. There is no need to disconnect the driveshafts from the swivel hub. Support the driveshafts by suspending them with wire or string – do not allow the driveshafts to hang down under their own weight, or the joints may be damaged.

9 Unbolt and remove the rear engine/transmission mounting torque link bracket with reference to Chapter 2B, Section 16.

10 Disconnect the wiring from the transmission clutch and shift modules, and release the wiring from the support cables.

11 Unbolt and remove the left-hand engine/transmission mounting bracket from the transmission with reference to Chapter 2B, Section 16.

12 Lower the engine and transmission by approximately 5 cm making sure that the coolant hoses and wiring harnesses are not stretched.

13 Unscrew and remove the upper bolts securing the transmission to the rear of the engine. Where necessary, pull up the coolant hoses and secure them away from the transmission using plastic cable-ties.

14 Support the weight of the transmission on a trolley jack, then unscrew the remaining transmission-to-engine bolts.

15 Make a final check that all components have been disconnected, and are positioned clear of the transmission so that they will not hinder the removal procedure.

16 With the help of an assistant, carefully withdraw the transmission from the engine. Take care not to allow the weight of the transmission to hang on the input shaft otherwise the clutch friction disc hub may be damaged. Note that there are two locating dowels which may be tight, and it may be necessary to rock the transmission from side-to-side to release it from them. Once the transmission is free, lower the jack and manoeuvre the unit out from under the car.

Refitting

17 Commence refitting by positioning the transmission on the trolley jack beneath the engine compartment. With the help of an assistant, raise the transmission and locate it on the engine, making sure that the input shaft engages accurately with the splines of the friction disc hub. With the transmission located on the dowels, insert all of the retaining bolts and tighten to the specified torque.

18 The remaining refitting procedure is a reversal of removal, noting the following points:

a) *Tighten all nuts and bolts to the specified torque (where given).*

b) *Renew the driveshaft oil seals (see Section 6) before refitting the driveshafts.*

c) *Refit the front subframe assembly with reference to Chapter 10, Section 7.*

d) *Refit the transmission shift module as described in Section 4.*

e) *Refit the air cleaner housing and inlet ducts with reference to Chapter 4A, Section 2.*

f) *Refit the battery tray and battery as described in Chapter 5A, Section 4.*

g) *Refill or top-up the transmission with the specified type and quantity of oil, as described in Section 2.*

h) *Finally, it may be necessary to have a dealer or diagnostic specialist reprogramme all volatile control unit memories.*

8 Easytronic transmission overhaul – general information

1 In the event of a fault occurring on the transmission, it is first necessary to determine whether it is of an electrical, mechanical or hydraulic nature, and to achieve this, special test equipment is required. It is therefore essential to have the work carried out by a Vauxhall/Opel dealer if a transmission fault is suspected.

2 Do not remove the transmission from the car for possible repair before professional fault diagnosis has been carried out, since most tests require the transmission to be in the vehicle.

Chapter 8
Driveshafts

Contents

Degrees of difficulty

Easy, suitable for novice with little experience	Fairly easy, suitable for beginner with some experience	Fairly difficult, suitable for competent DIY mechanic	Difficult, suitable for experienced DIY mechanic	Very difficult, suitable for expert DIY or professional

Specifications

Type . . . . Unequal length shafts with ball-and-cage type constant velocity joint at each end

Lubrication (overhaul only – see text)

Lubricant type/specification. . . . . Use only special grease supplied in sachets with gaiter kits – joints are otherwise pre-packed with grease and sealed

Torque wrench settings Nm — lbf ft

Driveshaft retaining nut: *
Stage 1 . . . . 70 — 52
Stage 2 . . . . Angle-tighten through a further 60°
Stage 3 . . . . Angle-tighten through a further 5°
Lower arm balljoint clamp bolt nut* . . . . 60 — 44
Roadwheel bolts. . . . . 110 — 81
Track rod balljoint-to-swivel hub nut*. . . . . 35 — 26
* Use new fasteners

1 General information

1 Drive is transmitted from the differential to the front wheels by means of two solid steel driveshafts of unequal length. The right-hand driveshaft is longer than the left-hand one, due to the position of the transmission unit.
2 Both driveshafts are splined at their outer ends to accept the wheel hubs, and are threaded so that each hub can be fastened by a large nut. The inner end of each driveshaft is splined to accept the differential sun gear. A vibration damper is attached to the right-hand driveshaft on certain 1.4 litre petrol engine models and certain diesel engine models.
3 Constant velocity (CV) joints are fitted to each end of the driveshafts, to ensure the smooth and efficient transmission of drive at all the angles possible as the roadwheels move up-and-down with the suspension, and as they turn from side-to-side under steering. Both inner and outer constant velocity joints are of the ball-and-cage type.

2 Driveshafts – removal and refitting

Note: *A new driveshaft retaining nut, inner joint circlip, lower arm balljoint clamp bolt and nut and a new track rod end retaining nut will be needed for refitting. The driveshaft outer joint splines may be a tight fit in the hub and it is possible that a puller/extractor will be required to draw the hub assembly off the driveshaft during removal.*

2.2 Carefully tap up the staking securing the driveshaft retaining nut

2.3 Using a fabricated tool to hold the front hub stationary whilst the driveshaft retaining nut is slackened

2.5 Unscrew the retaining nut, then use a balljoint separator tool to remove the track rod end from the swivel hub

Removal

> **HAYNES HINT** *If work is being carried out without the aid of an assistant, remove the wheel trim/hub cap (as applicable) and slacken the driveshaft retaining nut with the vehicle resting on its wheels.*

1 Firmly apply the handbrake, then jack up the front of the car and support it securely on axle stands (see *Jacking and vehicle support*). Remove the relevant front roadwheel.

2 Using a hammer and small chisel, carefully tap up the staking securing the driveshaft retaining nut **(see illustration)**.

3 Refit at least two roadwheel bolts to the front hub, and tighten them securely. Have an assistant firmly depress the brake pedal to prevent the

front hub from rotating, then using a socket and extension bar, slacken the driveshaft retaining nut. Alternatively, a tool can be fabricated from two lengths of steel strip (one long, one short) and a nut and bolt; the nut and bolt forming the pivot of a forked tool. Bolt the tool to the hub using two wheel bolts, and hold the tool to prevent the hub from rotating as the driveshaft retaining nut is undone **(see illustration)**.

4 Unscrew and remove the driveshaft retaining nut. Discard the nut; a new one must be used on refitting.

5 Slacken and remove the nut securing the steering gear track rod balljoint to the swivel hub, and release the balljoint tapered shank using a universal balljoint separator **(see illustration)**. Discard the nut; it should be renewed whenever it is disturbed.

6 Unscrew and remove the lower arm balljoint clamp bolt nut, and withdraw the clamp bolt

from the swivel hub **(see illustration)**. Discard the clamp bolt nut; a new one must be used on refitting.

7 Use a chisel or screwdriver as a wedge to expand the lower portion of the swivel hub **(see illustration)**.

8 Using a lever, push down on the lower arm to free the balljoint from the swivel hub **(see illustration)**, then move the swivel hub to one side and release the balljoint, taking care not to damage the balljoint rubber boot.

9 The swivel hub must now be freed from the end of the driveshaft. It should be possible to pull the hub off the driveshaft, but if the end of the driveshaft is tight in the hub, then tap the end of the driveshaft with a soft-faced hammer while pulling outwards on the swivel hub **(see illustrations)**. Alternatively, use a suitable puller to press the driveshaft through the hub. Support the driveshaft by suspending it with wire or string; Do not allow the driveshaft to hang down under its own weight, or the joints may be damaged.

10 Where fitted, remove the splash shield from under the engine compartment. Position a container beneath the transmission to catch any oil that may be spilt.

11 A suitable lever will now be required to release the inner end of the driveshaft from the differential. To release the right-hand driveshaft, a flat steel bar with a good chamfer on one end can be used. The left-hand driveshaft may prove more difficult to release, and a suitable square- or rectangular-section bar may be required.

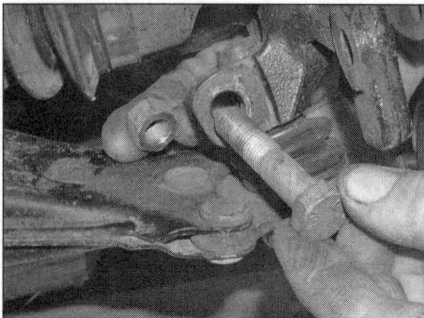

2.6 Unscrew the nut, and withdraw the clamp bolt from the swivel hub

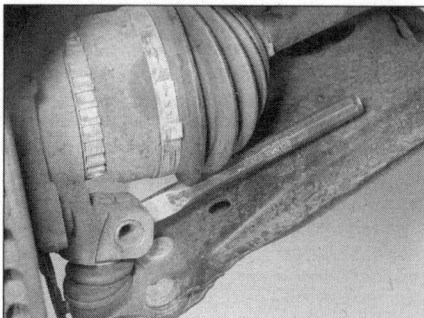

2.7 Use a chisel or screwdriver as a wedge to expand the lower portion of the swivel hub

2.8 Push down the lower suspension arm to free the balljoint from the swivel hub

2.9a Use a soft-faced hammer to drive the driveshaft from the hub splines...

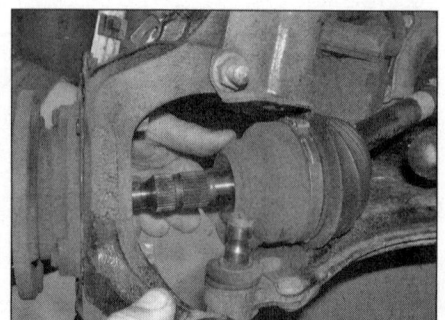

2.9b...then pull the swivel hub outwards

12 Lever between the driveshaft and the differential housing to release the driveshaft circlip from the differential. Carefully withdraw the driveshaft from the transmission unit, taking great care not to damage the driveshaft oil seal, and remove the driveshaft from underneath the vehicle **(see illustration)**.

13 Plug the opening in the differential, to prevent further oil loss and dirt ingress.

Caution: Do not allow the vehicle to rest on its wheels with one or both driveshaft(s) removed, as damage to the wheel bearing(s) may result. If the vehicle must be moved on its wheels, clamp the wheel bearings using a long threaded rod and spacers to take the place of the outer driveshaft joint through the hub.

Refitting

14 Before installing the driveshaft, examine the driveshaft oil seal in the transmission for signs of damage or deterioration. Renew if necessary, referring to Chapter 7A, 7B or 7C for further information.

15 Remove the circlip from the end of the inner constant velocity joint splines and discard it. Fit a new circlip, making sure it is correctly seated in its groove **(see illustration)**.

16 Thoroughly clean the driveshaft splines, and the apertures in the transmission unit and hub assembly. Apply a thin film of grease to the oil seal lips, and to the driveshaft splines and shoulders. Check that all gaiter clips are securely fastened.

17 Remove the plug from the transmission (see paragraph 13) and offer up the driveshaft. Locate the joint splines with those of the differential sun gear, taking great care not to damage the oil seal.

18 Place a screwdriver or similar tool on the slot/weld bead on the inner driveshaft joint, not the rubber cover, and drive the shaft into the differential until the retaining circlip engages positively **(see illustration)**. Pull on the joint, not the shaft, to make sure that the joint is securely retained by the circlip.

19 Locate the outer constant velocity joint splines with those of the swivel hub, and slide the joint back into position in the hub.

20 Using the lever, push down on the lower suspension arm, then relocate the balljoint and release the arm. Make sure that the balljoint stub is fully entered in the swivel hub.

21 Insert the balljoint clamp bolt to the swivel hub, so that its threads are facing to the rear of the vehicle. Fit a new nut to the clamp bolt, and tighten it to the specified torque setting.

22 Engage the track rod balljoint in the swivel hub, then fit the new retaining nut and tighten it to the specified torque.

23 Screw on a new driveshaft nut. Using the method employed on removal to prevent rotation, tighten the new driveshaft retaining nut through the stages given in the Specifications at the start of this Chapter.

24 With the nut correctly tightened, stake it in position by tapping the edge of the nut into

2.12 Lever the driveshaft CV joint out from the transmission to release its circlip from the differential

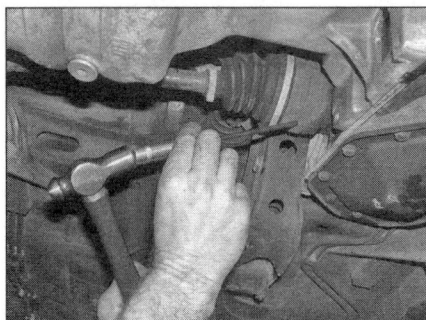

2.18 Using a punch on the CV joint weld bead to drive the joint into the differential until the circlip engages positively

the grooves in the driveshaft in two places **(see illustration)**.

25 Refit the splash shield under the engine (where fitted), then refit the roadwheel, then lower the vehicle to the ground and tighten the roadwheel bolts to the specified torque.

26 Check and if necessary top-up the transmission oil level, using the information given in Chapter 7A, 7B or 7C as applicable.

3 Driveshaft rubber gaiters – renewal

Outer CV joint gaiter

1 Remove the driveshaft from the car as

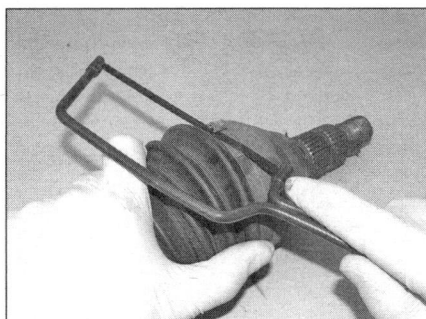

3.2 Release the rubber gaiter retaining clips by cutting through them using a hacksaw

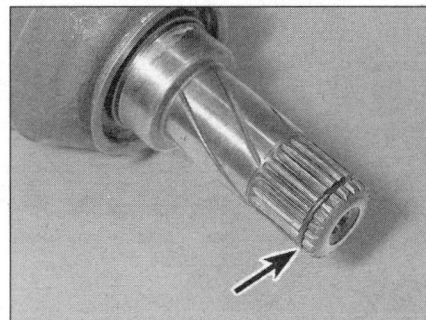

2.15 Prior to refitting, ensure that the circlip is correctly located in the inner CV joint groove

2.24 Stake the driveshaft retaining nut by tapping the edge of the nut into the grooves in the driveshaft in two places

described in Section 2, then secure the shaft in a vice equipped with soft jaws.

2 Release the rubber gaiter inner and outer retaining clips by cutting through them using a junior hacksaw **(see illustration)**. Spread the clips and remove them from the gaiter.

3 Slide the rubber gaiter down the shaft to expose the CV joint or, alternatively, cut the gaiter open using a suitable knife and remove it from the driveshaft **(see illustration)**.

4 Using old rags, clean away as much of the old grease as possible from the CV joint. It is advisable to wear disposable rubber gloves during this operation.

5 The outer CV joint will be retained on the driveshaft either by an external snap-ring, or by an internal circlip **(see illustration)**. If an external snap-ring is fitted, use circlip pliers

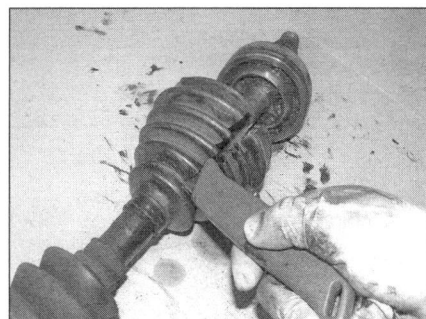

3.3 Cut the gaiter open using a suitable knife and remove it from the driveshaft

3.5 Outer CV joint snap-ring

3.6a Sharply strike the edge of the outer joint to drive it off the end of the shaft

3.6b If an external snap-ring is fitted, use circlip pliers to expand the snap-ring as the joint is removed

3.7 Removing the circlip from the groove in the driveshaft splines

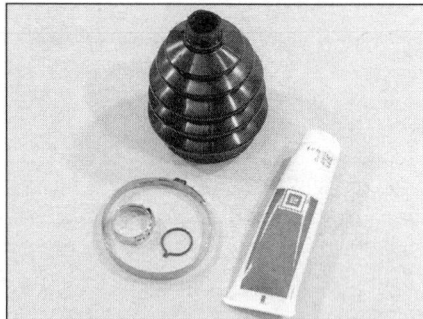

3.12 Components required for driveshaft gaiter renewal

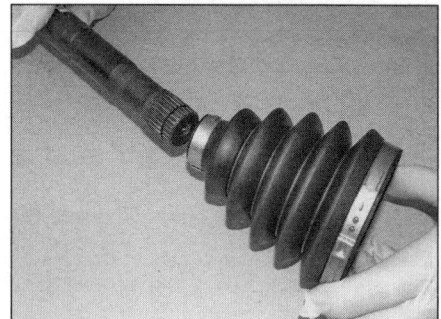

3.13 Slide the new rubber gaiter and retaining clips onto the driveshaft

to expand the snap-ring as the CV joint is removed.

6 Using a mallet, sharply strike the edge of the outer joint to drive it off the end of the shaft **(see illustrations)**.

7 Once the joint has been removed, extract the snap-ring from the joint, or remove the circlip from the groove in the driveshaft splines **(see illustration)**. A new snap-ring or circlip must be fitted on reassembly.

8 If still in place, withdraw the rubber gaiter from the driveshaft.

9 With the CV joint removed from the driveshaft, wipe away the remaining grease (do not use any solvent) to allow the joint components to be inspected.

10 Move the inner splined driving member from side-to-side to expose each ball in turn at the top of its track. Examine the balls for cracks, flat spots, or signs of surface pitting.

11 Inspect the ball tracks on the inner and outer members. If the tracks have widened, the balls will no longer be a tight fit. At the same time, check the ball cage windows for wear or cracking between the windows.

12 If, on inspection, any of the constant velocity joint components are found to be worn or damaged, it will be necessary to renew the complete joint assembly. If the joint is in satisfactory condition, obtain a repair kit consisting of a new gaiter and retaining clips, a constant velocity joint snap-ring or circlip, and the correct type and quantity of grease **(see illustration)**.

13 Slide the new rubber gaiter and retaining clips onto the driveshaft **(see illustration)**.

14 Fit a new snap-ring to the constant velocity joint, or a new circlip to the groove in the driveshaft, as applicable **(see illustrations)**.

15 Pack the joint with the grease supplied in the repair kit **(see illustration)**. Work the grease well into the bearing tracks whilst twisting the joint, and fill the rubber gaiter with any excess.

16 Screw on the driveshaft retaining nut two or three turns to protect the threads, then engage the joint with the driveshaft splines. Tap the joint onto the driveshaft until the snap-ring or circlip engages in its groove **(see illustration)**. Make sure that the joint is securely retained, by pulling on the joint, not the shaft.

17 Ease the gaiter over the joint, and ensure that the gaiter lips are correctly located in the grooves on both the driveshaft and constant velocity joint. Lift the outer sealing lip of the gaiter to equalise air pressure within the gaiter.

18 Pull the large gaiter retaining clip as tight as possible, and locate the hooks on the clip

3.14a Fit a new snap-ring to the constant velocity joint...

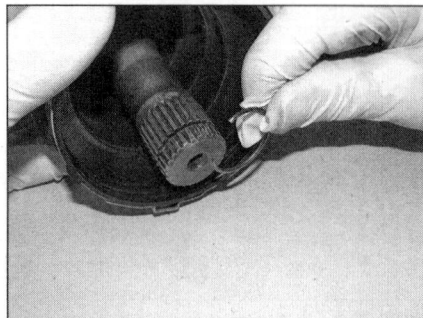

3.14b...or a new circlip to the groove in the driveshaft

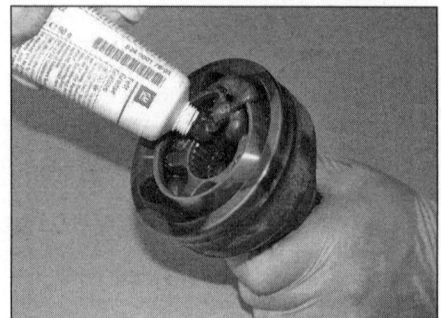

3.15 Pack the joint with the grease supplied in the repair kit

3.16 Tap the joint onto the driveshaft until the snap-ring or circlip engages in its groove

3.18a Secure the large gaiter retaining clip in position by compressing the raised section of the clip

3.18b The small inner retaining clip is secured in the same way

in their slots. Remove any slack in the gaiter retaining clip by carefully compressing the raised section of the clip. In the absence of the special tool, a pair of side-cutters may be used. Secure the small retaining clip using the same procedure **(see illustrations)**.

19 Check that the constant velocity joint moves freely in all directions, then refit the driveshaft to the car as described in Section 2.

Inner CV joint gaiter

Note: *The inner CV joint gaiter is removed from the roadwheel end of the driveshaft after removal of the outer CV joint. If working on the right-hand driveshaft, this will only be possible on models without a vibration damper on the driveshaft. On models with a vibration damper, the complete driveshaft must be renewed as it is not possible to remove the damper (necessary for removal of the gaiter) without damage.*

20 Remove the outer CV joint gaiter as described previously.

21 Mark the fitted position of the inner joint gaiter on both the driveshaft and CV joint.

22 Release the rubber gaiter inner and outer retaining clips by cutting through them using a junior hacksaw. Spread the clips and remove them from the gaiter.

23 Pull the gaiter off the CV joint then slide it down the driveshaft and remove it from the roadwheel end of the shaft.

24 Using old rags, clean away as much of the old grease as possible from the CV joint. It is advisable to wear disposable rubber gloves during this operation.

25 Move the inner splined driving member from side-to-side to expose each ball in turn at the top of its track. Examine the balls for cracks, flat spots, or signs of surface pitting.

26 Inspect the ball tracks on the inner and outer members. If the tracks have widened,

the balls will no longer be a tight fit. At the same time, check the ball cage windows for wear or cracking between the windows.

27 If, on inspection, any of the inner constant velocity joint components are found to be worn or damaged, it will be necessary to renew the complete driveshaft assembly. If the joint is in satisfactory condition, obtain a repair kit consisting of a new gaiter and retaining clips and the correct type and quantity of grease.

28 Slide the new rubber gaiter and retaining clips onto the driveshaft.

29 Pack the CV joint with the grease supplied in the repair kit. Work the grease well into the bearing tracks whilst twisting the joint, and fill the rubber gaiter with any excess.

30 Align the gaiter with the mark made on the driveshaft during removal and ease the gaiter over the joint. Lift the outer sealing lip of the gaiter to equalise air pressure within the gaiter.

31 Pull the large gaiter retaining clip as tight as possible, and locate the hooks on the clip in their slots. Remove any slack in the gaiter retaining clip by carefully compressing the raised section of the clip. In the absence of the special tool, a pair of side-cutters may be used. Secure the small retaining clip using the same procedure.

32 Check that the constant velocity joint moves freely in all directions, then refit the outer constant velocity joint as described previously.

4 Driveshaft joint – checking and renewal

Checking

1 First carry out the checks described in Chapter 1A, Section 12 or Chapter 1B,

Section 12 to reveal if there is any wear in one of the driveshaft joints.

2 If there is any doubt about the tightness of the driveshaft retaining nut, obtain a new nut, then fit and tighten it using the procedures described in Section 2. Once tightened, stake the nut in position and refit the centre cap or wheel trim. Repeat this check on the other driveshaft nut.

3 Road test the vehicle, and listen for a metallic clicking noise from the front as the vehicle is driven slowly in a circle on full-lock. If evident, this indicates wear in the outer constant velocity joint which must be renewed.

4 To check for wear on the inner joint, apply the handbrake then jack up the front of the vehicle and support it on axle stands (see *Jacking and vehicle support*). Attempt to move the inner end of the driveshaft up-and-down, then hold the joint with one hand and attempt to rotate the driveshaft with the other. If excessive wear is evident, the complete driveshaft must be renewed. Note: If vibration, consistent with roadspeed, is felt through the car when accelerating, there is a possibility of wear in the inner constant velocity joints.

Renewal

5 To renew the outer constant velocity joint, follow the procedures in Section 3. If the old gaiter is going to be re-used, it can be left on the driveshaft, take care not to damage the gaiter when removing the retaining clips.

6 The inner constant velocity joints are not available separately and if excessively worn, the complete driveshaft must be renewed.

Chapter 9
Braking system

Contents

Degrees of difficulty

Easy, suitable for novice with little experience	**Fairly easy,** suitable for beginner with some experience	**Fairly difficult,** suitable for competent DIY mechanic	**Difficult,** suitable for experienced DIY mechanic	**Very difficult,** suitable for expert DIY or professional

Specifications

Front brakes

Type	Disc, with single-piston sliding caliper
Disc diameter:	
Petrol models.	257.0 mm
Diesel models.	284.0 mm
Disc thickness:	
New	22.0 mm
Minimum.	19.0 mm
Maximum disc run-out.	0.11 mm
Brake pad minimum thickness (not including backing plate).	2.0 mm
Brake caliper piston diameter	54.0 mm

Rear brakes

Type	Single leading shoe drum	
Drum diameter (inner):	**New**	**Maximum**
1.0 and 1.2 litre 3-door petrol models	203.0 mm	204.5 mm
All other models	228.0 mm	229.5 mm
Brake shoe minimum thickness.	2.0 mm	

Torque wrench settings

	Nm	lbf ft
ABS ECU retaining screws*	3	2
ABS wheel speed sensor bolt	8	6
Brake hose to caliper union	20	15
Brake pedal mounting bracket nuts.	20	15
Brake pipe union nut	16	12
Clutch master cylinder mounting bolts	10	7
Front brake caliper:		
Guide pin bolts*	30	22
Mounting bracket-to-swivel hub bolts	105	77
Front brake disc retaining screw	7	5
Master cylinder mounting nuts*	20	15
Rear hub nut*	280	207
Rear wheel cylinder bolts.	8	6
Roadwheel bolts.	110	81
Vacuum pump mounting bolts:		
Stage 1	5	4
Stage 2	20	15
Vacuum servo unit mounting nuts	20	15

Use new fastenings

1 General Information

1 The braking system is of the servo-assisted, dual-circuit hydraulic type. The arrangement of the hydraulic system is such that each circuit operates one front and one rear brake from a tandem master cylinder. Under normal circumstances, both circuits operate in unison. However, in the event of hydraulic failure in one circuit, full braking force will still be available at two wheels.

2 All models covered in this manual have front disc brakes and rear drum brakes. The disc brakes are actuated by single-piston sliding type calipers, which ensure that equal pressure is applied to each disc pad.

3 The rear drum brakes incorporate leading and trailing shoes, which are actuated by twin-piston wheel cylinders. A self-adjust mechanism is incorporated to automatically compensate for brake shoe wear. As the brake shoe linings wear, the footbrake operation automatically operates the adjuster mechanism, which effectively lengthens the shoe strut, and repositions the brake shoes to maintain the lining-to-drum clearance.

4 An Anti-lock Braking System (ABS) is fitted as standard equipment to all vehicles covered in this manual. On higher specification models, the ABS may also incorporate an electronic stability program and traction control. Refer to Section 18 for further information on ABS operation.

5 The cable-operated handbrake provides an independent mechanical means of rear brake application.

⚠️ *Warning: When servicing any part of the system, work carefully and methodically; also observe scrupulous cleanliness when overhauling any part of the hydraulic system. Always renew components (in axle sets, where applicable) if in doubt about their condition, and use only genuine Vauxhall/Opel parts, or at least those of known good quality. Note the warnings given in 'Safety first!' and at relevant points in this Chapter concerning the dangers of asbestos dust and hydraulic fluid.*

2 Hydraulic system – bleeding

⚠️ *Warning: Hydraulic fluid is poisonous; wash off immediately and thoroughly in the case of skin contact, and seek immediate medical advice if any fluid is swallowed or gets into the eyes. Certain types of hydraulic fluid are inflammable, and may ignite when allowed into contact with hot components. When servicing any hydraulic system, it is safest to assume that the fluid IS inflammable,*

and to take precautions against the risk of fire as though it is petrol that is being handled. Hydraulic fluid is also an effective paint stripper, and will attack plastics; if any is spilt, it should be washed off immediately using copious quantities of water. Finally, it is hygroscopic (it absorbs moisture from the air) – old fluid may be contaminated, and unfit for further use. When topping-up or renewing the fluid, always use the recommended type, and ensure that it comes from a freshly-opened sealed container.

General

1 Any hydraulic system will only function correctly once all the air has been removed from the components and circuit; this is achieved by bleeding the system.

2 During the bleeding procedure, add only clean, fresh hydraulic fluid of the recommended type; never use old fluid, nor re-use any which has already been bled from the system. Ensure that sufficient fresh fluid is available before starting work.

3 If there is any possibility of the wrong fluid being in the system, the brake components and circuit must be flushed completely with uncontaminated, correct fluid, and new seals should be fitted to the various components.

4 If hydraulic fluid has been lost from the system (or if air has entered) because of a leak, ensure that the fault is cured before proceeding further.

5 Park the vehicle on level ground, switch off the engine and select first or reverse gear, then chock the wheels and release the handbrake.

6 Check that all pipes and hoses are secure, that the pipe unions are tight, and that the bleed screws are closed. Clean any dirt from around the bleed screws.

7 Unscrew the master cylinder reservoir cap, and top the master cylinder reservoir up to the MAX level line; refit the cap loosely, and remember to maintain the fluid level at least above the MIN level line throughout the procedure, to avoid the risk of further air entering the system.

8 There are a number of one-man, do-it-yourself brake bleeding kits currently available from motor accessory shops. It is recommended that one of these kits is used whenever possible, as they greatly simplify the bleeding operation, and also reduce the risk of expelled air and fluid being drawn back into the system. If such a kit is not available, the basic (two-man) method must be used, which is described in detail below.

Caution: Vauxhall/Opel recommend using a pressure bleeding kit for this operation (see paragraphs 24 to 27).

9 If a kit is to be used, prepare the vehicle as described previously, and follow the kit manufacturer's instructions, as the procedures may vary slightly according to the type being used; generally, they will be as outlined below in the relevant sub-section.

10 Whichever method is used, the same sequence must be followed (paragraphs 11

and 12) to ensure the removal of all air from the system.

Bleeding sequence

11 If the system has been only partially disconnected, and suitable precautions were taken to minimise fluid loss, it should only be necessary to bleed that part of the system (ie, the primary or secondary circuit).

12 If the complete system is to be bled, then it should be done working in the following sequence:
a) *Right-hand rear brake.*
b) *Left-hand rear brake.*
c) *Right-hand front brake.*
d) *Left-hand front brake.*

Bleeding

Basic (two-man) method

13 Collect a clean glass jar, a suitable length of plastic or rubber tubing which is a tight fit over the bleed screw, and a ring spanner to fit the bleed screw. The help of an assistant will also be required.

14 Remove the dust cap from the first screw in the sequence. Fit the spanner and tube to the screw, place the other end of the tube in the jar, and pour in sufficient fluid to cover the end of the tube.

15 Ensure that the master cylinder reservoir fluid level is maintained at least above the MIN level line throughout the procedure.

16 Have the assistant fully depress the brake pedal several times to build-up pressure, then maintain it on the final stroke.

17 While pedal pressure is maintained, unscrew the bleed screw (approximately one turn) and allow the compressed fluid and air to flow into the jar. The assistant should maintain pedal pressure, following it down to the floor if necessary, and should not release it until instructed to do so. When the flow stops, tighten the bleed screw again; the pedal should then be released slowly, and the reservoir fluid level checked and topped-up.

18 Repeat the steps given in paragraphs 16 and 17 until the fluid emerging from the bleed screw is free from air bubbles. If the master cylinder has been drained and refilled, and air is being bled from the first screw in the sequence, allow approximately five seconds between cycles for the master cylinder passages to refill.

19 When no more air bubbles appear, tighten the bleed screw securely, remove the tube and spanner, and refit the dust cap. Do not overtighten the bleed screw.

20 Repeat the procedure on the remaining screws in the sequence, until all air is removed from the system and the brake pedal feels firm again.

Using a one-way valve kit

21 As their name implies, these kits consist of a length of tubing with a one-way valve fitted, to prevent expelled air and fluid being drawn back into the system; some kits include a translucent container, which can be positioned so that the air bubbles can be more easily seen flowing from the end of the tube.

22 The kit is connected to the bleed screw, which is then opened **(see illustration)**. The user returns to the driver's seat, depresses the brake pedal with a smooth, steady stroke, then slowly releases it; this is repeated until the expelled fluid is clear of air bubbles.

23 These kits simplify work so much that it is easy to forget the master cylinder reservoir fluid level; ensure that this is maintained at least above the MIN level line at all times, or air will be drawn into the system.

Using a pressure bleeding kit

24 These kits are usually operated by the reservoir of pressurised air contained in the spare tyre, noting that it will probably be necessary to reduce the pressure to less than normal; refer to the instructions supplied with the kit.

25 By connecting a pressurised, fluid-filled container to the master cylinder reservoir, bleeding can be carried out simply by opening each screw in turn (in the specified sequence) and allowing the fluid to flow out until no more air bubbles can be seen in the expelled fluid.

26 This method has the advantage that the large reservoir of fluid provides an additional safeguard against air being drawn into the system during bleeding.

27 Pressure bleeding is particularly effective when bleeding 'difficult' systems, or when bleeding the complete system at the time of routine fluid renewal.

All methods

28 When bleeding is complete and firm pedal feel is restored, wash off any spilt fluid, tighten the bleed screws securely, and refit their dust caps.

29 Check the hydraulic fluid level, and top-up if necessary.

30 Discard any hydraulic fluid that has been bled from the system; it will not be fit for re-use. Bear in mind that this fluid may be inflammable.

31 Check the feel of the brake pedal. If it feels at all spongy, air must still be present in the system, and further bleeding is required. Failure to bleed satisfactorily after a reasonable repetition of the bleeding procedure may be due to worn master cylinder seals.

3 Hydraulic pipes and hoses – renewal

Note: *Before starting work, refer to the warning note at the beginning of Section 2 concerning the dangers of hydraulic fluid.*

1 If any pipe or hose is to be renewed, minimise fluid loss by first removing the master cylinder reservoir cap and screwing it down onto a piece of polythene. Alternatively, flexible hoses can be sealed, if required, using a proprietary brake hose clamp. Metal brake pipe unions can be plugged (if care is taken

not to allow dirt into the system) or capped immediately they are disconnected. Place a wad of rag under any union that is to be disconnected, to catch any spilt fluid.

2 If a flexible hose is to be disconnected, unscrew the brake pipe union nut before removing the spring clip which secures the hose to its mounting bracket. Where applicable, unclip the hose from the suspension strut, then unscrew the hose union from the brake caliper.

3 To unscrew the union nuts, it is preferable to obtain a brake pipe spanner of the correct size; these are available from most large motor accessory shops. Failing this, a close-fitting open-ended spanner will be required, though if the nuts are tight or corroded, their flats may be rounded-off if the spanner slips. In such a case, a self-locking wrench is often the only way to unscrew a stubborn union, but it follows that the pipe and the damaged nuts must be renewed on reassembly. Always clean a union and surrounding area before disconnecting it. If disconnecting a component with more than one union, make a careful note of the connections before disturbing any of them.

4 If a brake pipe is to be renewed it can be obtained, cut to length and with the union nuts and end flares in place, from Vauxhall/Opel dealers. All that is then necessary is to bend it to shape, following the line of the original, before fitting it to the car. Alternatively, most motor accessory shops can make up brake pipes from kits, but this requires very careful measurement of the original to ensure that the replacement is of the correct length. The safest answer is usually to take the original to the shop as a pattern.

5 On refitting, securely tighten the union nuts but do not overtighten (it is not necessary to exercise brute force to obtain a sound joint).

6 When refitting hoses to the calipers, make sure that the hoses are positioned so that they will not touch surrounding bodywork or the roadwheels.

7 Ensure that the pipes and hoses are correctly routed, with no kinks, and that they are secured in the clips or brackets provided. After fitting, remove the polythene from the reservoir, and bleed the hydraulic system as described in Section 2. Wash off any spilt fluid, and check carefully for fluid leaks.

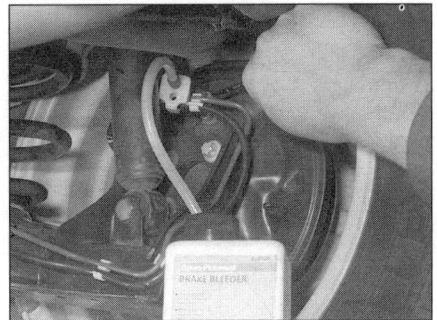

2.22 Using a one-way valve kit to bleed the rear brake

4 Front brake pads – renewal

⚠ *Warning: Renew BOTH sets of front brake pads at the same time – NEVER renew the pads on only one wheel, as uneven braking may result. Note that the dust created by wear of the pads may contain asbestos, which is a health hazard. Never blow it out with compressed air, and don't inhale any of it. An approved filtering mask should be worn when working on the brakes. DO NOT use petroleum-based solvents to clean brake parts – use brake cleaner or methylated spirit only.*

Note: *A new brake caliper lower guide pin bolt will be required for refitting.*

1 Firmly apply the handbrake, then jack up the front of the car and support it securely on axle stands (see *Jacking and vehicle support*). Remove the front roadwheels.

2 Push in the caliper piston by sliding the caliper body towards the outside of the vehicle by hand.

3 Follow the accompanying photos **(see illustrations 4.3a to 4.3m)** for the pad renewal procedure, bearing in mind the additional points listed below. Be sure to stay in order and read the caption under each illustration. Note that if the old pads are to be refitted, ensure that they are identified so that they can be returned to their original positions.

4 If the original brake pads are still

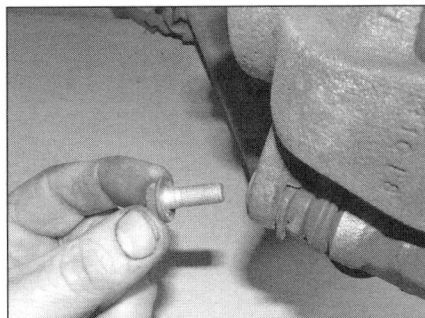

4.3a Unscrew the lower guide pin bolt from the caliper...

4.3b...lift the caliper upwards to gain access to the brake pads...

4.3c ...and tie the caliper in the raised position using string or wire

4.3d Lift out the outer brake pad...

4.3e ...and the inner brake pad

4.3f Remove the anti-rattle springs from the caliper mounting bracket, noting their fitted position

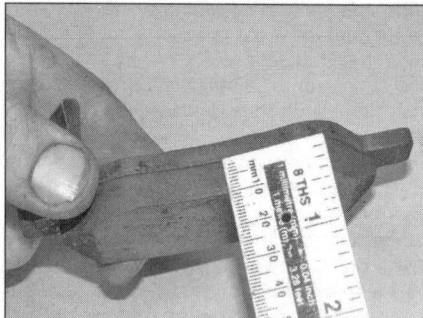

4.3g Measure the thickness of the pad friction material. If any are worn down to the specified minimum, or fouled with oil or grease, all four pads must be renewed

4.3h If new pads are to be fitted, before refitting the caliper, push back the caliper piston whilst opening the bleed screw. This is to prevent any dirt/debris being forced back up the hydraulic circuit in the ABS modulator

4.3i Apply a smear of high-temperature grease to the contact areas of the backing plates

4.3j Refit the anti-rattle springs to the caliper mounting bracket

4.3k Place the inner pad in position...

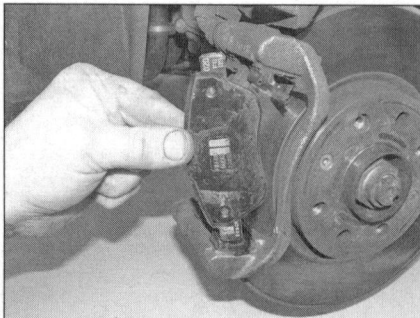

4.3l ...followed by the outer pad

4.3m Lower the caliper and secure with a new guide pin bolt tightened to the specified torque

serviceable, carefully clean them using a clean, fine wire brush or similar, paying particular attention to the sides and back of the metal backing plate. Clean out the grooves in the friction material, and pick out any large embedded particles of dirt or debris. Carefully clean the pad locations in the caliper body/mounting bracket.

5 Prior to fitting the pads, check that the guide pins are a snug fit in the caliper mounting bracket. Brush the dust and dirt from the caliper and piston, but do not inhale it, as it is injurious to health. Inspect the dust seal around the piston for damage, and the piston for evidence of fluid leaks, corrosion or damage. If attention to any of these components is necessary, refer to Section 8.

6 If new brake pads are to be fitted, the caliper piston must be pushed back into the cylinder to allow for the extra pad thickness. Either use a G-clamp or similar tool, or use suitable pieces of wood as levers. Clamp off the flexible brake hose leading to the caliper then connect a brake bleeding kit to the caliper bleed screw. Open the bleed screw as the piston is retracted, the surplus brake fluid will then be collected in the bleed kit vessel **(see illustration 4.3h)**. Close the bleed screw just before the caliper piston is pushed fully into the caliper. This should ensure no air enters the hydraulic system.

Caution: The ABS unit contains hydraulic components that are very sensitive to impurities in the brake fluid. Even the smallest particles can cause the system to fail through blockage. The pad retraction method described here prevents any debris in the brake fluid expelled from the caliper from being passed back to the ABS hydraulic unit, as well as preventing any chance of damage to the master cylinder seals.

7 With the brake pads installed, depress the brake pedal repeatedly, until normal (non-assisted) pedal pressure is restored, and the pads are pressed into firm contact with the brake disc.

8 Repeat the above procedure on the remaining front brake caliper.

9 Refit the roadwheels, then lower the vehicle to the ground and tighten the roadwheel bolts to the specified torque setting.

10 Check the hydraulic fluid level as described in *Weekly checks*.

Caution: New pads will not give full braking efficiency until they have bedded-in. Be prepared for this, and avoid hard braking as far as possible for the first hundred miles or so after pad renewal.

5 Rear brake shoes – renewal

⚠ *Warning: Brake shoes must be renewed on BOTH rear wheels at the same time – NEVER renew the*

shoes on only one wheel, as uneven braking may result. The dust created as the shoes wear may contain asbestos, which is a health hazard. Never blow it out with compressed air, and don't inhale any of it. An approved filtering mask should be worn when working on the brakes. DO NOT use petroleum-based solvents to clean brake parts – use brake cleaner or methylated spirit only.

1 Remove the brake drum as described in Section 7.

2 Working carefully and taking the necessary precautions, remove all traces of brake dust from the brake drum, backplate and shoes.

3 Follow the accompanying photos **(see illustrations 5.3a to 5.3w)** for the brake shoe renewal procedure, bearing in mind the additional points listed below. Be sure to stay in order and read the caption under each illustration.

4 If both brake assemblies are dismantled at the same time, take care not to mix up the components. Note that the left-hand and right-hand adjuster components are 'handed' and must not be interchanged.

5 Prior to refitting the adjuster mechanism, lift the adjuster lever and turn the adjuster strut to shorten the overall length of the mechanism slightly. This will compensate for the additional thickness of the new brake shoes, and allow the brake drum to be fitted easily.

6 On completion, ensure that the handbrake operating lever stop-peg is correctly positioned against the edge of the shoe web, then refit the brake drum as described in Section 7.

7 Repeat the operation on the remaining brake.

8 Once both sets of rear shoes have been renewed, with the handbrake fully released, adjust the lining-to-drum clearance by repeatedly depressing the brake pedal 20 to 25 times. Whilst depressing the pedal, have an assistant listen to the rear drums, to check that the adjuster mechanism is functioning correctly; if so, a clicking sound will be emitted by the adjuster as the pedal is depressed.

9 Check and, if necessary, adjust the handbrake as described in Chapter 1A, Section 23 or Chapter 1B, Section 24.

10 Refit the roadwheels, then lower the vehicle to the ground and tighten the roadwheel bolts to the specified torque setting.

11 Check the hydraulic fluid level as described in *Weekly checks*.

Caution: New brake shoes will not give full braking efficiency until they have bedded-in. Be prepared for this, and avoid hard braking as far as possible for the first hundred miles or so after shoe renewal.

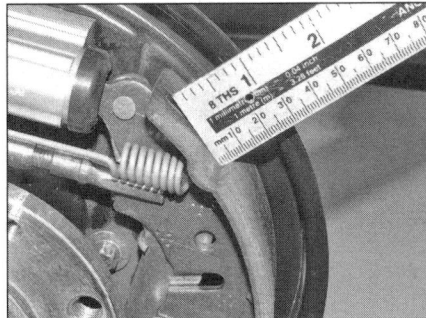

5.3a Measure the thickness of the brake shoe friction material at several points. If any are worn down to the specified minimum, or fouled with oil or grease, all four shoes must be renewed

5.3b Depress the two brake shoe retaining clips and slide them off the retainer pins. With the clips removed, withdraw the retainer pins

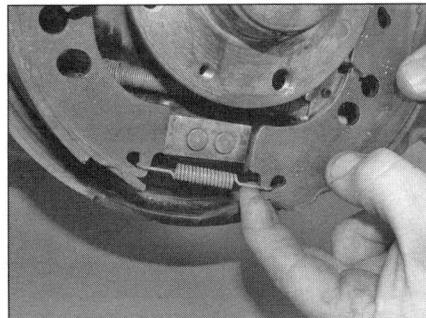

5.3c Pull the lower end of the trailing shoe outward and disengage it from the abutment bracket

5.3d Pull the upper end of the trailing shoe outward and disengage it from the wheel cylinder piston

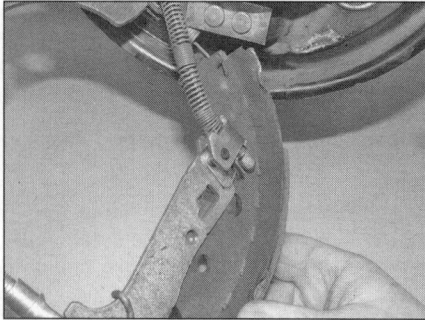

5.3e Similarly disengage the leading shoe from the abutment bracket and wheel cylinder, then turn the shoe assembly over for access to the rear

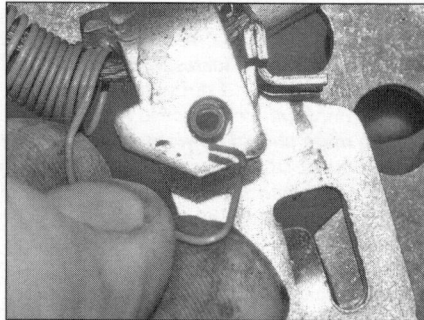

5.3f Unhook the handbrake cable retaining spring from the handbrake lever on the trailing shoe...

5.3g...then lift up the handbrake cable retainer and slip the cable end out of the handbrake lever

5.3h Use a cable-tie or elastic band to retain the wheel cylinder pistons

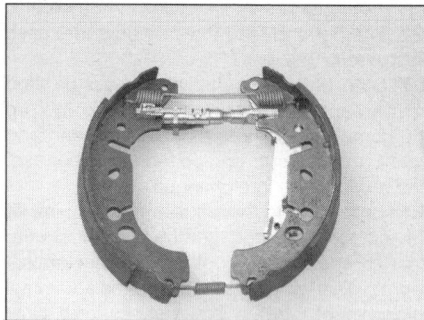

5.3i Prior to disturbing the shoes, note the correct fitted locations of all components, paying particular attention to the adjuster mechanism

5.3j Unhook the lower return spring and remove it from the brake shoes

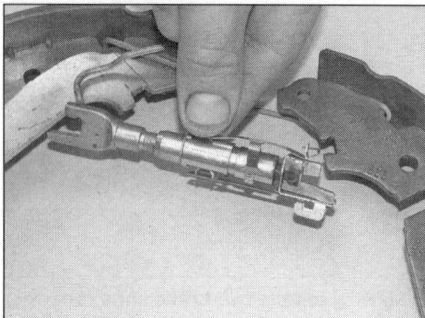

5.3k Spread the brake shoes apart and disengage the adjuster mechanism from the brake shoes

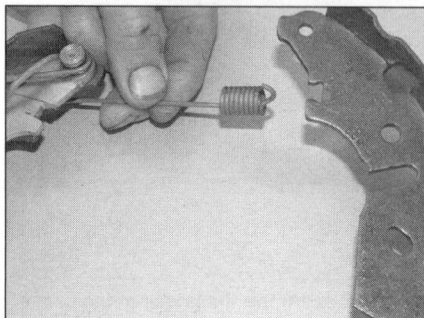

5.3l Now remove the upper return spring from the brake shoes

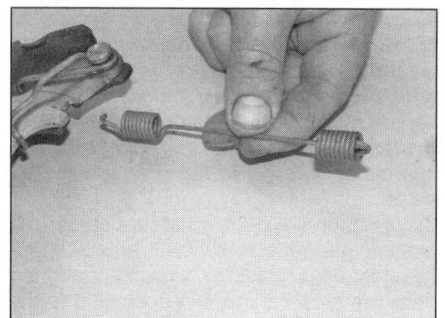

5.3m Place the new brake shoes face down on the bench and engage the upper return spring with the hole in the trailing shoe...

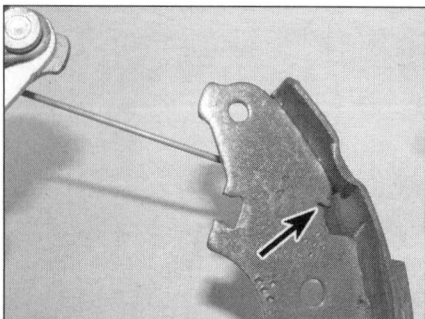

5.3n...and leading shoe

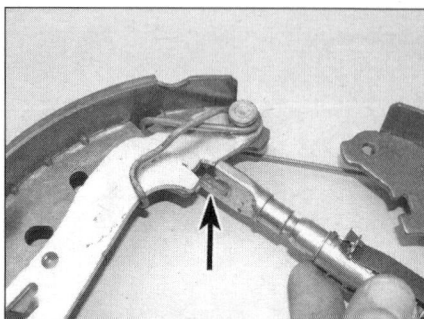

5.3o Spread the brake shoes apart and engage the adjuster mechanism with the trailing brake shoe. Note that the longer part of the fork must be to the front of the shoe

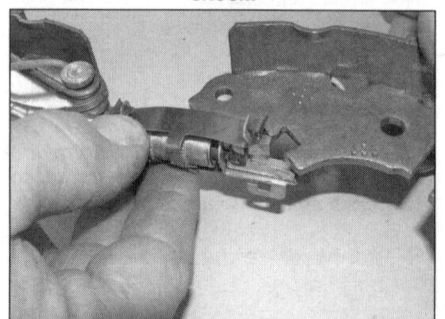

5.3p Engage the other end of the adjuster with the leading shoe noting that the longer part of the fork must also be to the front of the shoe

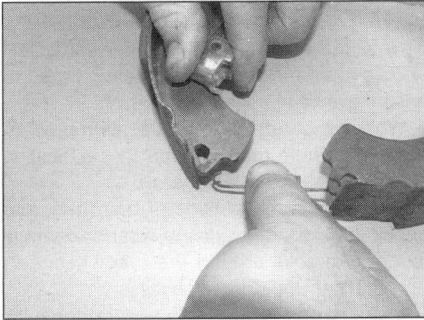

5.3q Pull the shoes together and refit the lower return spring to both shoes

5.3r Thoroughly clean the backplate, then apply a smear of high-temperature brake grease to the contact surfaces

5.3s Engage the handbrake cable with the handbrake lever on the trailing shoe...

5.3t...then refit the cable retaining spring to the cable retainer

5.3u Engage the leading brake shoe with the abutment bracket and wheel cylinder then similarly engage the trailing shoe with the wheel cylinder...

5.3v...and abutment bracket. With the shoes in place, cut off the cable-tie or elastic band used to retain the wheel cylinder pistons

5.3w Refit the retainer pins and retaining clips to both brake shoes

6 Front brake disc – inspection, removal and refitting

Note: *Before starting work, refer to the warning at the beginning of Section 4 concerning the dangers of asbestos dust.*

Inspection

Note: *If either disc requires renewal, BOTH should be renewed at the same time, to ensure even and consistent braking.*

1 Firmly apply the handbrake, then jack up the front of the car and support it securely on axle stands (see *Jacking and vehicle support*). Remove the appropriate front roadwheel.

2 Slowly rotate the brake disc so that the full area of both sides can be checked; remove the brake pads if better access is required to the inner surface. Light scoring is normal in the area swept by the brake pads, but if heavy scoring is found, the disc must be renewed.

3 It is normal to find a lip of rust and brake dust around the disc's perimeter; this can be scraped off if required. If, however, a lip has formed due to excessive wear of the brake pad swept area, then the disc's thickness must be measured using a micrometer. Take measurements at several places around the disc, at the inside and outside of the pad swept area; if the disc has worn at any point to the specified minimum thickness or less, the disc must be renewed.

4 If the disc is thought to be warped, it can be checked for run-out either using a dial gauge mounted on any convenient fixed point, while the disc is slowly rotated, or by using feeler gauges to measure (at several points all around the disc) the clearance between the disc and a fixed point such as the caliper mounting bracket. To ensure that the disc is squarely seated on the hub, fit two wheel bolts, complete with spacers approximately 10 mm thick, and tighten them securely. If the measurements obtained are at the specified maximum or beyond, the disc is excessively warped and must be renewed; however, it is worth checking first that the hub bearing is in

good condition (see Chapter 1A, Section 11 or Chapter 1B, Section 11).

5 Check the disc for cracks, especially around the wheel bolt holes, and for any other wear or damage, and renew if necessary.

Removal

6 Where applicable, remove the roadwheel bolts and spacers used when checking the disc.

7 Unclip the brake hydraulic hose from the suspension strut.

8 Unbolt and remove the front brake caliper complete with disc pads and mounting bracket and suspend it from the coil spring using a cable-tie **(see illustrations)**.

6.8a Unbolt and remove the front brake caliper complete with disc pads and mounting bracket...

6.8b...and suspend it from the coil spring using a cable-tie

6.9 Front brake disc securing screws

9 Remove the two securing screws and withdraw the disc from the hub **(see illustration)**.

Refitting

10 Refitting is the reverse of the removal procedure, noting the following points:
a) Ensure that the mating surfaces of the disc and hub are clean and flat.
b) If a new disc has been fitted, use a suitable solvent to wipe any preservative coating from the disc before refitting the caliper.
c) Remove all traces of old thread-locking compound from the caliper mounting bracket bolts and holes in the swivel hub, ideally by running a tap of the correct size and pitch through them. Apply a suitable thread-locking compound to the threads of the caliper mounting bracket bolts. Slide the caliper assembly into position over the disc, then fit the mounting bolts and tighten them to the specified torque setting.
d) Refit the roadwheel, then lower the vehicle to the ground and tighten the roadwheel bolts to the specified torque. On completion, repeatedly depress the brake pedal until normal (non-assisted) pedal pressure returns.

7 Rear brake drum – removal, inspection and refitting

Note: Before starting work, refer to the

7.2 Undo the two retaining screws, then withdraw the brake drum from the rear hub

warning at the beginning of Section 5 concerning the dangers of asbestos dust.

Removal

1 Chock the front wheels then jack up the rear of the car and securely support it on axle stands (see Jacking and vehicle support). Remove the appropriate rear wheel and release the handbrake.
2 Undo the two brake drum retaining screws, then withdraw the brake drum from the rear hub **(see illustration)**. It may be difficult to remove the drum, due to the brake shoes binding on the inner circumference of the drum. If the brake shoes are binding, first check that the handbrake is fully released, then proceed as follows.
3 Referring to Section 14 for further information, fully slacken the handbrake cable adjuster nut to obtain maximum free play in the cable.
4 Remove the plug from the inspection hole in the brake backplate. Using a screwdriver, pull the handbrake operating lever on the trailing brake shoe inwards, towards the centre of the car. This will release the handbrake lever stop-peg from the edge of the brake shoe, and further collapse the shoes. The brake drum can then be withdrawn from the stub axle.
5 If the brake drum is still difficult to remove, screw two M10 bolts into the holes on the front face of the drum **(see illustration)**. Tighten the bolts while tapping the edge of the drum with a soft-faced mallet until it frees.

7.5 If the brake drum is difficult to remove, screw two bolts into the holes on the drum and tighten them progressively

Inspection

6 Note: If either drum requires renewal, BOTH should be renewed at the same time, to ensure even and consistent braking.
7 Working carefully, remove all traces of brake dust from the drum, but avoid inhaling the dust, as it is a health-hazard.
8 Scrub clean the outside of the drum, and check it for obvious signs of wear or damage (such as cracks around the roadwheel bolt holes); renew the drum if necessary.
9 Examine the inside of the drum carefully. Light scoring of the friction surface is normal, but if heavy scoring is found, the drum must be renewed. It is usual to find a lip on the drum's inboard edge which consists of a mixture of rust and brake dust; this should be scraped away, to leave a smooth surface which can be polished with fine (120- to 150-grade) emery paper. If, however, the lip is due to the friction surface being recessed by excessive wear, then the drum must be renewed.
10 If the drum is thought to be excessively worn, or oval, its internal diameter must be measured at several points using an internal micrometer. Take measurements in pairs, the second at right-angles to the first, and compare the two to check for signs of ovality. Provided that it does not enlarge the drum to beyond the specified maximum diameter, it may be possible to have the drum refinished by skimming or grinding; if this is not possible, the drums on both sides must be renewed. Note that if the drum is to be skimmed, both drums must be refinished, to maintain a consistent internal diameter on both sides.

Refitting

11 If a new brake drum is to be installed, use a suitable solvent to remove any preservative coating that may have been applied to its interior. Note that it may also be necessary to shorten the adjuster strut length by rotating the strut wheel, to allow the new drum to pass over the brake shoes.
12 Ensure that the handbrake lever stop-peg is correctly repositioned against the edge of the brake shoe web.
13 Slide the drum into position, then refit the two retaining screws.
14 With the handbrake fully released, adjust the lining-to-drum clearance by repeatedly depressing the brake pedal 20 to 25 times. Whilst depressing the pedal, have an assistant listen to the rear drums, to check that the adjuster strut is functioning correctly; if so, a clicking sound will be emitted by the strut as the pedal is depressed.
15 With the lining-to-drum clearance set, check and, if necessary, adjust the handbrake as described in Chapter 1A, Section 23 or Chapter 1B, Section 24.
16 Refit the roadwheel, then lower the vehicle to the ground and tighten the roadwheel bolts to the specified torque setting.

8 Front brake caliper – removal, overhaul and refitting

Note: *New caliper guide pin bolts will be required when refitting. Before starting work, refer to the warning at the beginning of Section 2 concerning the dangers of hydraulic fluid, and to the warning at the beginning of Section 4 concerning the dangers of asbestos dust.*

Removal

1 Firmly apply the handbrake, then jack up the front of the car and support it securely on axle stands (see *Jacking and vehicle support*). Remove the appropriate roadwheel.
2 Minimise fluid loss by first removing the master cylinder reservoir cap, then tightening it down onto a piece of polythene to obtain an airtight seal.
3 Clean the area around the caliper brake hose union and also the brake pipe-to-hose union on the inner wheel arch. Unscrew the brake pipe union, then remove the spring clip which secures the hose to its mounting bracket. Unclip the hose from the suspension strut, then unscrew and remove the hose from the brake caliper. Plug the brake pipe end and caliper hole, to minimise fluid loss and prevent the ingress of dirt into the hydraulic system.
4 Slacken and remove the lower and upper caliper guide pin bolts and remove the brake caliper from the vehicle.

Overhaul

Note: *Before starting work, check with your local dealer for the availability of parts to overhaul the caliper.*

5 With the caliper on the bench, wipe away all traces of dust and dirt, but avoid inhaling the dust, as it is a health hazard.
6 Withdraw the partially-ejected piston from the caliper body, and remove the dust seal. The piston can be withdrawn by hand, or if necessary pushed out by applying compressed air to the brake hose union hole. Only low pressure should be required, such as is generated by a foot pump, and as a precaution a block of wood should be positioned to prevent any damage to the piston.
7 Using a small screwdriver, carefully remove the piston seal from the caliper, taking great care not mark the bore **(see illustration)**.
8 Remove the guide pins, then carefully press the guide bushes out of the caliper body.
9 Thoroughly clean all components, using only methylated spirit, isopropyl alcohol or clean hydraulic fluid as a cleaning medium. Never use mineral-based solvents such as petrol or paraffin, which will attack the hydraulic system's rubber components. Dry the components immediately, using compressed air or a clean, lint-free cloth. If compressed air is available, use it to blow through the fluid passages to make sure they are clear
Caution: Always wear eye protection when using compressed air.

10 Check all components, and renew any that are worn or damaged. Check particularly the cylinder bore and piston; these should be renewed if they are scratched, worn or corroded in any way (note that this means the renewal of the complete body assembly). Similarly check the condition of the guide bushes and guide pins; both bushes and pins should be undamaged and (when cleaned) a reasonably tight sliding fit in each other. If there is any doubt about the condition of any component, renew it.
11 If the assembly is fit for further use, obtain the necessary components from your Vauxhall/Opel dealer. Renew the caliper seals as a matter of course; these should never be re-used.
12 On reassembly, ensure that all components are absolutely clean and dry.
13 Soak the piston and the new piston (fluid) seal in clean hydraulic fluid. Smear clean fluid on the cylinder bore surface.
14 Fit the new piston (fluid) seal, using only the fingers to manipulate it into the cylinder bore groove.
15 Fit the new dust seal to the piston, refit it to the cylinder bore using a twisting motion, and ensure that the piston enters squarely into the bore. Press the dust seal fully into the caliper body, and push the piston fully into the caliper bore.
16 Ease the guide bushes into position in the caliper body, then refit the guide pins.

Refitting

17 Using new guide pin bolts, refit the caliper to the mounting bracket and tighten the bolts to the specified torque.
18 Screw the brake hose into the caliper and tighten the hose union to the specified torque. Clip the hose to the suspension strut, then secure the other end of the hose in the mounting bracket with the spring clip. Fit the brake pipe union to the hose and tighten it securely.
19 Remove the polythene, where fitted, and bleed the hydraulic system as described in Section 2. Note that, providing the precautions described were taken to minimise brake fluid loss, it should only be necessary to bleed the relevant front brake.
20 Refit the roadwheel, then lower the vehicle to the ground and tighten the roadwheel bolts to the specified torque.

9 Rear wheel cylinder – removal, overhaul and refitting

Note: *Before starting work, refer to the warning at the beginning of Section 2 concerning the dangers of hydraulic fluid, and to the warning at the beginning of Section 5 concerning the dangers of asbestos dust.*

Removal

1 Remove the brake drum as described in Section 7.
2 Using a chisel, carefully tap out the hub

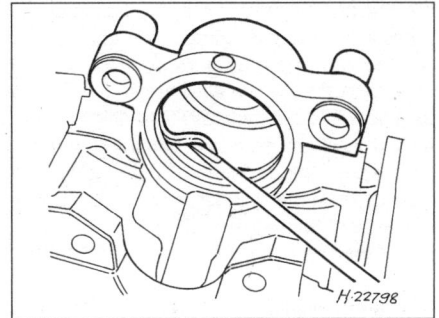

8.7 Removing the piston seal from the caliper body

cap from the centre of the rear hub. If care is taken, it is possible to remove the hub cap without damage. However, if it is damaged or distorted during removal, a new cap will be required for refitting.
3 Slacken and remove the rear hub nut, then slide the hub off the stub axle. Note that a new hub nut will be required for refitting.
4 Remove the brake shoes as described in Section 5.
5 Minimise fluid loss by first removing the master cylinder reservoir cap, then tightening it down onto a piece of polythene to obtain an airtight seal. Alternatively, use a brake hose clamp, a G-clamp or a similar tool to clamp the flexible hose at the nearest convenient point to the wheel cylinder.
6 Wipe away all traces of dirt around the brake pipe union at the rear of the wheel cylinder, and unscrew the union nut. Carefully ease the pipe out of the wheel cylinder, and plug or tape over its end to prevent dirt entry. Wipe off any spilt fluid immediately.
7 Unscrew the wheel cylinder retaining bolts from the rear of the backplate and remove the cylinder, taking great care not to allow surplus hydraulic fluid to contaminate the brake shoe linings.

Overhaul

Note: *Before starting work, check with your local dealer for the availability of parts to overhaul the wheel cylinder.*

8 Brush the dirt and dust from the wheel cylinder, but take care not to inhale it.
9 Pull the rubber dust seals from the ends of the cylinder body **(see illustration)**.

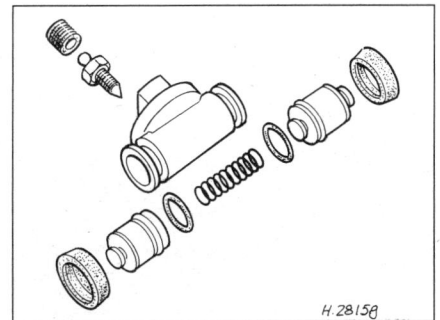

9.9 Exploded view of a typical rear brake wheel cylinder

10 The pistons will normally be ejected by the pressure of the coil spring, but if they are not, tap the end of the cylinder body on a piece of wood, or apply low air pressure (eg, from a foot pump) to the hydraulic fluid union hole to eject the pistons from their bores.

11 Inspect the surfaces of the pistons and their bores in the cylinder body for scoring, or evidence of metal-to-metal contact. If evident, renew the complete wheel cylinder assembly.

12 If the pistons and bores are in good condition, discard the seals and obtain a repair kit, which will contain all the necessary renewable items.

13 Lubricate the piston seals with clean brake fluid, and insert them into the cylinder bores, with the spring between them, using finger pressure only.

14 Dip the pistons in clean brake fluid, and insert them into the cylinder bores.

15 Fit the dust seals, and check that the pistons can move freely in their bores.

Refitting

16 Ensure that the backplate and wheel cylinder mating surfaces are clean, then manoeuvre the wheel cylinder into position.

17 Engage the brake pipe, and screw in the union nut two or three turns to ensure that the thread has started.

18 Insert the wheel cylinder retaining bolts, and tighten them to the specified torque. Now tighten the brake pipe union nut to the specified torque.

19 Refit the brake shoes as described in Section 5.

20 Slide the rear hub onto the stub axle, then screw on the new hub nut. Tighten the nut to the specified torque. Fit the hub cap and tap it fully into position on the hub.

21 Refit the brake drum as described in Section 7.

22 Remove the clamp from the flexible brake hose, or the polythene from the master cylinder reservoir (as applicable).

23 Bleed the brake hydraulic system as described in Section 2. Providing suitable precautions were taken to minimise loss of fluid, it should only be necessary to bleed the relevant rear brake.

11.4a Extract the spring clip...

10 Master cylinder – removal, overhaul and refitting

Note: *New master cylinder retaining nuts will be required when refitting. Before starting work, refer to the warning at the beginning of Section 2 concerning the dangers of hydraulic fluid.*

Removal

1 Remove the master cylinder reservoir cap, and syphon the hydraulic fluid from the reservoir.

Note: *Do not syphon the fluid by mouth, as it is poisonous; use a syringe or an old hydrometer. Alternatively, open any convenient bleed screw in the system, and gently pump the brake pedal to expel the fluid through a plastic tube connected to the screw (see Section 2).*

2 Disconnect the battery negative terminal (refer to *Disconnecting the battery* in Chapter 5A, Section 4).

3 Disconnect the quick-release fittings and detach the two fluid reservoir supply hoses from the side of the master cylinder. On diesel models, access is limited and it may prove beneficial to unbolt and remove the fuel filter bracket and position the filter to one side.

4 Wipe clean the area around the brake pipe unions on the side of the master cylinder, and place absorbent rags beneath the pipe unions to catch any surplus fluid. Make a note of the correct fitted positions of the unions, then unscrew the union nuts and carefully withdraw the pipes. Plug or tape over the pipe ends and master cylinder orifices, to minimise the loss of brake fluid and to prevent the entry of dirt into the system. Wash off any spilt fluid immediately with cold water.

5 Slacken and remove the two nuts securing the master cylinder to the vacuum servo unit. Withdraw the master cylinder assembly from the engine compartment.

6 Where applicable, recover the seal which is fitted between the master cylinder and servo.

Overhaul

7 At the time of writing, master cylinder overhaul is not possible as no spares are available.

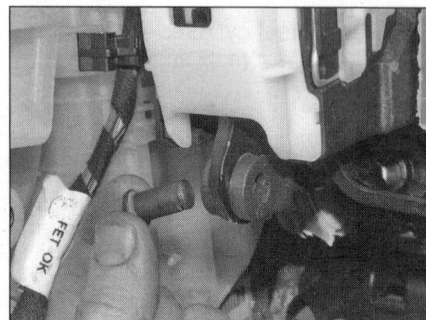
11.4b...withdraw the clutch master cylinder clevis pin...

8 The only parts available individually are the fluid reservoir and the filler cap.

9 If the master cylinder is worn excessively, it must be renewed.

Refitting

10 Remove all traces of dirt from the master cylinder and servo unit mating surfaces. Inspect the master cylinder seal for signs of wear or damage, and renew if necessary.

11 Where applicable, fit a new seal to the servo and refit the master cylinder, ensuring that the pushrod enters the master cylinder bore centrally. Fit the new master cylinder mounting nuts, and tighten them to the specified torque.

12 Wipe clean the brake pipe unions, refit them to the master cylinder ports, and tighten them to the specified torque.

13 Ensure that the brake pipes are correctly clipped back into position in the bulkhead rubber guide/grommet.

14 Reconnect the fluid reservoir supply hoses to the master cylinder, ensuring that the quick-release fittings engage audibly.

15 Reconnect the battery negative terminal.

16 Fill the master cylinder reservoir with new fluid, and bleed the complete hydraulic system as described in Section 2.

11 Brake pedal and mounting bracket – removal and refitting

Note: *The brake pedal (and, where applicable, the clutch pedal) are an integral part of the pedal mounting bracket assembly and cannot be individually removed. Should renewal of the pedal(s), due to wear of the pivot bushes or the pedal itself, be required, it will be necessary to renew the complete mounting bracket assembly.*

Note: *This is a complicated operation that entails removal of the complete facia and facia crossmember. Before starting, read through the entire procedure to familiarise yourself with the work involved and the complications that may be encountered.*

Removal

1 Remove the complete facia and facia crossmember as described in Chapter 11, Section 26.

2 Working in the engine compartment, unscrew the two nuts securing the brake master cylinder to the vacuum servo unit.

3 Carefully ease the vacuum hose out of the servo unit, taking care not to displace the sealing grommet.

4 Working from inside the vehicle on manual transmission models, extract the retaining spring clip and withdraw the clevis pin securing the clutch master cylinder pushrod to the clutch pedal. Unscrew the two bolts securing the clutch master cylinder to the pedal mounting bracket **(see illustrations)**.

11.4c...then unscrew the two bolts securing the master cylinder to the pedal mounting bracket

11.5 Undo the two bolts and remove the accelerator pedal position sensor

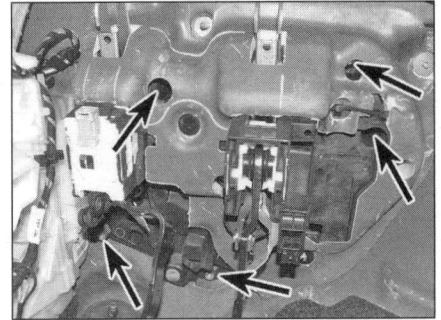
11.7 Unscrew the five nuts securing the pedal mounting bracket to the bulkhead

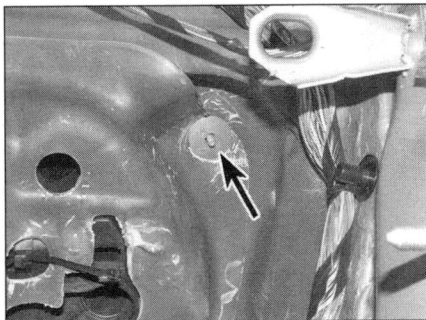
11.8a Extract the right-hand plastic washer...

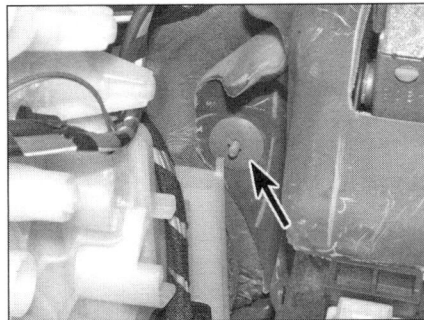
11.8b...and left-hand plastic washer securing the foam sound deadening pad to the studs on the bulkhead

11.9 Collect the bulkhead closure plate from the vacuum servo unit

5 Disconnect the wiring connector, then undo the two bolts and remove the accelerator pedal position sensor (see illustration).
6 Disconnect the wiring connectors from the brake stop-light switch and, where fitted, the clutch pedal switch. Release the wiring harness from the clips and cable-ties on the pedal mounting bracket.
7 Unscrew the five nuts securing the pedal mounting bracket to the bulkhead (see illustration).
8 Extract the two plastic washers securing the foam sound deadening pad to the two studs on the bulkhead (see illustrations).
9 Make a final check that the various wiring harnesses have been released from their clips and ties on the pedal mounting bracket, then withdraw the mounting bracket rearward away from the bulkhead. Collect the bulkhead closure plate from the vacuum servo unit, and remove the pedal and mounting bracket assembly from the car (see illustration).
10 With the pedal mounting bracket removed, if required, the vacuum servo unit can be removed as described in Section 12, and the brake stop-light switch and clutch pedal switch (where fitted) can be removed as described in Section 16.

Refitting

11 If removed, refit the brake stop-light switch and clutch pedal switch (where fitted) as described in Section 16. Refit the vacuum servo unit as described in Section 12.

12 Position the bulkhead closure plate on the vacuum servo unit studs then manoeuvre the pedal mounting bracket assembly into position in the car. Ensure that the vacuum servo unit pushrod enters the brake master cylinder pushrod as the assembly is located in place.
13 Refit the five nuts securing the pedal mounting bracket to the bulkhead and tighten the nuts to the specified torque.
14 Refit the two plastic washers securing the foam sound deadening pad to the two studs on the bulkhead.
15 Reconnect the brake stop-light switch and, where fitted, the clutch switch wiring connectors. Secure the wiring harness with the clips and new cable-ties.
16 Place the accelerator pedal position sensor in position then refit and securely tighten the two bolts. Reconnect the position sensor wiring connector.
17 On manual transmission models, refit the clutch master cylinder retaining bolts and tighten the bolts to the specified torque. Align the clutch pedal hole with the pushrod end, and insert the clevis pin. Secure the pin in position with the spring clip.
18 Locate the brake master cylinder over the servo unit studs then refit and tighten the two retaining nuts to the specified torque.
19 Ease the vacuum hose end piece into place in the servo unit, taking great care not to displace or damage the grommet.
20 Refit the facia crossmember and facia as described in Chapter 11, Section 26.

12 Vacuum servo unit – testing, removal and refitting

Testing

1 To test the operation of the servo unit, with the engine off, depress the footbrake several times to exhaust the vacuum. Now start the engine, keeping the pedal firmly depressed. As the engine starts, there should be a noticeable 'give' in the brake pedal as the vacuum builds-up. Allow the engine to run for at least two minutes, then switch it off. The brake pedal should now feel normal, but further applications should result in the pedal feeling firmer, the pedal stroke decreasing with each application.
2 If the servo does not operate as described, first inspect the servo unit check valve as described in Section 13.
3 If the servo unit still fails to operate satisfactorily, the fault lies within the unit itself. Repairs to the unit are not possible; if faulty, the servo unit must be renewed.

Removal

Note: The servo unit is located inside the car, attached to the pedal mounting bracket. Removal is an involved and complicated operation that entails removal of the complete facia and the facia crossmember. Before starting, read through the entire procedure to familiarise yourself with the work involved and the complications that may be encountered.

12.5a Extract the spring clip (arrowed)...

12.5b...and withdraw the clevis pin securing the servo unit pushrod to the brake pedal

12.6 Slacken and remove the two nuts securing the servo unit to the pedal mounting bracket

4 Remove the brake pedal and mounting bracket as described in Section 11.

5 Extract the retaining spring clip and withdraw the clevis pin securing the servo unit pushrod to the brake pedal **(see illustrations)**.

6 Slacken and remove the two nuts securing the servo unit to the pedal mounting bracket **(see illustration)**. Lift the servo off the pedal mounting bracket and collect the spacer plate.

Refitting

7 Place the spacer plate over the servo unit studs, then locate the servo on the pedal mounting bracket. Ensure that the servo unit pushrod engages around the brake pedal.

8 Refit the two servo unit mounting nuts and tighten them to the specified torque.

9 Refit the servo unit pushrod-to-brake pedal clevis pin, and secure it in position with the spring clip.

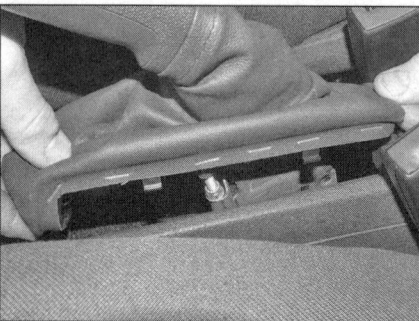

14.1 Unclip the handbrake lever gaiter from the centre console and fold it up the handbrake lever

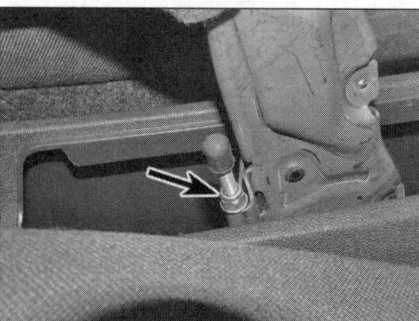

14.2 Fully slacken and remove the handbrake cable adjuster nut

10 Refit the brake pedal mounting bracket as described in Section 11.

13 Vacuum servo unit check valve – removal, testing and refitting

1 The check valve is located in the vacuum hose running from the inlet manifold (or vacuum pump on diesel engine models) to the brake servo. If the valve is faulty, it will need to be renewed with the hose as a complete assembly.

Removal

2 Carefully ease the vacuum hose out of the servo unit, taking care not to displace the grommet.

3 Note the correct routing of the hose, then undo the union nut, or disconnect the quick-release fitting securing the hose to the inlet manifold or vacuum pump. Remove the hose assembly from the vehicle.

Testing

4 Examine the check valve and vacuum hose for signs of damage, and renew if necessary.

5 The valve may be tested by blowing through it in both directions. Air should flow through the valve in one direction only: when blown through from the servo unit end of the valve. Renew the valve if this is not the case.

6 Examine the servo unit rubber sealing grommet for signs of damage or deterioration, and renew as necessary.

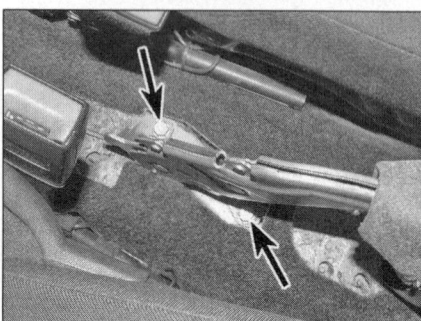

14.4 Unscrew the two handbrake lever mounting bolts

Refitting

7 Ensure that the sealing grommet is correctly fitted to the servo unit.

8 Ease the hose union into position in the servo, taking great care not to displace or damage the grommet.

9 Ensure that the hose is correctly routed, and connect it to the inlet manifold or vacuum pump, tightening its union nut securely (where applicable).

10 On completion, start the engine and check for air leaks at the check valve-to-servo unit connection.

14 Handbrake lever – removal and refitting

Removal

1 Unclip the handbrake lever gaiter from the centre console and fold it up the handbrake lever **(see illustration)**.

2 Remove the protective cap from the end of the handbrake cable, then fully slacken and remove the handbrake cable adjuster nut **(see illustration)**.

3 Disconnect the wiring connector from the handbrake warning light switch.

4 Unscrew the two handbrake lever mounting bolts **(see illustration)**.

5 The handbrake lever can now be withdrawn from inside the vehicle. The warning light switch can be removed from the lever assembly after unscrewing its retaining bolt.

Refitting

6 Refitting is a reversal of the removal procedure, adjusting the handbrake as described in Chapter 1A, Section 23 or Chapter 1B, Section 24, as applicable.

15 Handbrake cables – removal and refitting

Removal

1 The handbrake cable consists of two sections, a short front (primary) section which connects the lever to the compensator plate, and the main cables (secondary) section which links the compensator plate to the rear brake shoes. Each section can be removed individually as follows.

Primary (front) cable

2 Chock the front wheels then jack up the rear of the car and securely support it on axle stands (see *Jacking and vehicle support*). Ensure that the handbrake lever is released (off).

3 Unclip the handbrake lever gaiter from the centre console and fold it up the handbrake lever **(see illustration 14.1)**.

4 Remove the protective cap from the end of the handbrake cable, then fully slacken and remove the handbrake cable adjuster nut **(see illustration 14.2)**. Release the cable from the handbrake lever.

5 Unscrew the bolt and the nut, release the two clamps and remove the exhaust system heatshield from the fuel tank.

6 Detach the front cable from the compensator plate by twisting it through 90° **(see illustration)**.

7 Release the grommet from the lever mounting plate, and withdraw the front cable from under the car. Remove the grommet from the cable.

Secondary (main) cable

Note: *The secondary cables are supplied as one part, together with the compensator plate.*

8 Chock the front wheels then jack up the rear of the car and securely support it on axle stands (see *Jacking and vehicle support*). Remove both rear roadwheels.

9 Release the exhaust system from its rubber mountings, lower it at the rear and support it on an axle stand.

10 Unclip the handbrake lever gaiter from the centre console and fold it up the handbrake lever **(see illustration 14.1)**.

11 Remove the protective cap from the end of the handbrake cable, then slacken the handbrake cable adjuster nut **(see illustration 14.3)**.

12 Unscrew the bolt and the nut, release the two clamps and remove the exhaust system heat shield from the fuel tank.

13 Remove the rear brake shoes as described in Section 5. Release the handbrake outer cable retaining clip and withdraw the handbrake cable from the brake backplate on both sides.

14 Detach the front handbrake cable from the compensator plate by twisting it through 90° **(see illustration 15.6)**.

15 Release the main cable sections from the supports on the underbody and rear axle, and withdraw the cable from under the car.

Refitting

16 Refitting is a reversal of the removal procedure, but adjust the handbrake as described in Chapter 1A, Section 23 or Chapter 1B, Section 24, as applicable. Make sure that the fitting on the rear of the front cable locates correctly in the compensator plate.

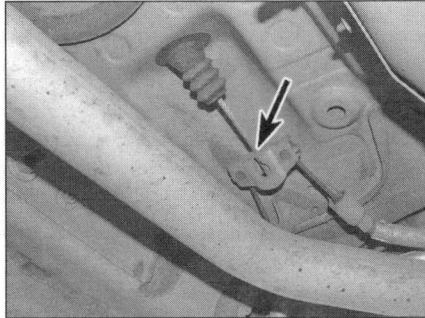

15.6 Detach the front handbrake cable (arrowed) from the compensator plate by twisting it through 90°

16 Stop-light switch – removal and refitting

Removal

1 The stop-light switch is located on the brake pedal mounting bracket in the driver's footwell, behind the facia.

2 Remove the trim panel beneath the facia on the driver's side as described in Chapter 11, Section 26, then remove the expanding rivet and withdraw the footwell air duct.

3 Disconnect the wiring plug from the stop-light switch.

4 Push the brake pedal down, pull out the stop-light switch actuating pin, then unclip the locking sleeve from around the actuating pin **(see illustrations)**.

5 Release the securing clips and pull the switch to disengage it from the pedal mounting bracket.

Refitting and adjustment

6 With the actuating pin pulled out, and the locking sleeve unclipped, refit the switch to the pedal bracket.

7 Secure the switch with the locking sleeve.

8 Release the brake pedal and the pedal will automatically adjust the position of the actuating pin.

9 Reconnect the wiring connector, then refit the footwell air duct and facia trim panel as described in Chapter 11, Section 26.

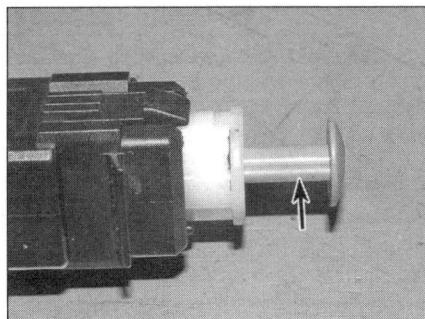

16.4a Pull out the centre actuating pin arrowed (switch removed for clarity)

17 Handbrake warning light switch – removal and refitting

Removal

1 Remove the centre console as described in Chapter 11, Section 25.

2 Disconnect the wiring connector from the warning light switch on the side of the handbrake lever.

3 Unscrew the mounting bolt and remove the switch from the handbrake lever bracket.

Refitting

4 Refitting is a reversal of removal.

18 Anti-lock braking system (ABS) – general information

1 The Bosch 8.1 anti-lock braking system comprises a hydraulic modulator unit and the four wheel speed sensors. The modulator unit contains the electronic control unit (ECU), the hydraulic solenoid valves and the electrically-driven return pump. The purpose of the system is to prevent the wheel(s) locking during heavy braking. This is achieved by automatic release of the brake on the relevant wheel, followed by re-application of the brake.

2 The solenoid valves are controlled by the ECU, which itself receives signals from the four wheel speed sensors which monitor the speed of rotation of each wheel. By comparing these signals, the ECU can determine the speed at which the vehicle is travelling. It can then use this speed to determine when a wheel is decelerating at an abnormal rate, compared to the speed of the vehicle, and therefore predicts when a wheel is about to lock. During normal operation, the system functions in the same way as a non-ABS braking system.

3 If the ECU senses that a wheel is about to lock, it closes the relevant outlet solenoid valves in the hydraulic unit, which then isolates the relevant brake(s) on the wheel(s) which is/are about to lock from the master cylinder, effectively sealing-in the hydraulic pressure.

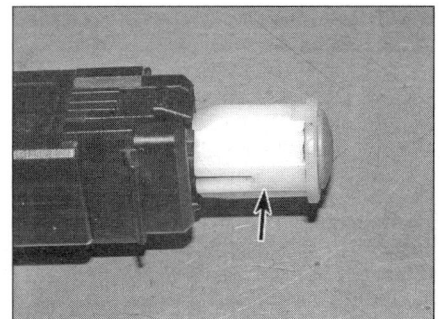

16.4b...and unclip the locking sleeve

19.2 Disconnect the wiring harness plug from the ECU

4 If the speed of rotation of the wheel continues to decrease at an abnormal rate, the ECU opens the inlet solenoid valves on the relevant brake(s), and operates the electrically-driven return pump which pumps the hydraulic fluid back into the master cylinder, releasing the brake. Once the speed of rotation of the wheel returns to an acceptable rate, the pump stops; the solenoid valves switch again, allowing the hydraulic master cylinder pressure to return to the caliper or wheel cylinder, which then re-applies the brake. This cycle can be carried out many times a second.

5 The action of the solenoid valves and return pump creates pulses in the hydraulic circuit. When the ABS system is functioning, these pulses can be felt through the brake pedal.

6 The electronic stability program (ESP) is a further development of ABS. Using additional sensors to monitor steering wheel position, vehicle yaw rate, acceleration and deceleration, in conjunction with the ABS sensors, the ECU can intervene under conditions of vehicle instability. Using the signals from the various sensors, the ECU can determine driver intent (steering wheel position, throttle position, vehicle speed and engine speed). From the sensor inputs from the wheel speed sensors, and yaw rate sensor the ECU can calculate whether the vehicle is responding to driver input, or whether an unstable driving situation is occurring. If instability is detected, the ECU will intervene by applying or releasing the relevant front or rear brake, in conjunction with a power reduction, until vehicle stability returns.

7 The operation of the ABS system is entirely dependent on electrical signals. To prevent the system responding to any inaccurate signals, a built-in safety circuit monitors all signals received by the ECU. If an inaccurate signal or low battery voltage is detected, the ABS system is automatically shut-down, and the warning light on the instrument panel is illuminated to inform the driver that the ABS system is not operational. Normal braking should still be available, however.

8 Additional safety features are also incorporated into the ABS system. These include electronic brake force distribution, which automatically apportions braking effort between the front and rear wheels, and emergency brake assist, which guarantees full braking effort in the event of an emergency stop by monitoring the rate at which the brake pedal is depressed.

9 Should a fault develop in the system, the ECU illuminates a warning light on the instrument panel constantly. To facilitate fault diagnosis, the system is provided with an on-board diagnostic facility. In the event of a fault, the ECU stores a series of fault codes for subsequent read-out and diagnosis. If the instrument panel warning light remains on after the engine has been started, the vehicle must be taken to a Vauxhall/Opel dealer or suitably-equipped diagnostic specialist for fault diagnosis and repair.

19 Anti-lock braking system (ABS) components – removal and refitting

Hydraulic modulator assembly

Note: *Before starting work, refer to the note at the beginning of Section 2 concerning the dangers of hydraulic fluid.*

Removal

1 Remove the battery and battery tray as described in Chapter 5A, Section 4.

2 Pull up the locking bar and disconnect the wiring harness multiplug connector from the electronic control unit located on the hydraulic modulator **(see illustration)**.

3 Unscrew the master cylinder reservoir filler cap, and top-up the reservoir to the MAX mark (see *Weekly checks*). Place a piece of polythene over the filler neck, and secure the polythene with the filler cap. This will minimise brake fluid loss during subsequent operations. As a precaution, place absorbent rags beneath the modulator brake pipe unions when unscrewing them.

4 Wipe clean the area around the modulator brake pipe unions, then make a note of how the pipes are arranged, to use as a reference on refitting. Unscrew the union nuts, and carefully withdraw the pipes.

5 Plug or tape over the pipe ends and modulator orifices, to minimise the loss of brake fluid and to prevent the entry of dirt into the system. Wash off any spilt fluid immediately with cold water.

6 Slacken and remove the three mounting nuts, and remove the modulator complete with mounting bracket from the engine compartment.

7 Undo the two nuts and separate the modulator from the mounting bracket.

Refitting

8 Refitting is the reverse of the removal procedure, noting the following points:

a) *Tighten all mounting nuts securely.*

b) *Refit the brake pipes to their respective unions, and tighten the union nuts to the specified torque.*

c) *Ensure that the wiring is correctly routed, and that the multiplug connector is firmly pressed into position and secured with the locking bar.*

d) *On completion, and prior to refitting the battery, bleed the complete hydraulic system as described in Section 2. Ensure that the system is bled in the correct order, to prevent air entering the modulator return pump.*

Electronic control unit (ECU)

Note: *New ECU retaining screws will be required for refitting.*

Removal

9 Remove the hydraulic modulator from the car as described previously in this Section.

10 Undo the four retaining screws and carefully withdraw the ECU upwards and off the hydraulic modulator. Recover the gasket.

Refitting

11 Prior to refitting, clean and then carefully inspect the condition of the gasket sealing surfaces on the ECU and hydraulic modulator. If the surfaces are in any way deformed, damaged, or rough to the extent that a perfect gasket seal cannot be maintained, the complete modulator and ECU assembly must be renewed.

12 With the gasket in position, and holding the ECU by the outer edges only, carefully lower it over the solenoid valves on the modulator, keeping it square and level.

13 Fit the four new retaining screws, and tighten them evenly and progressively until they all just make contact with the ECU body. Continue tightening the screws alternately and progressively until the ECU body just makes contact with the hydraulic modulator.

14 Progressively, and working in a diagonal sequence, tighten the screws to the specified torque. The ECU must make complete contact with the hydraulic modulator, with no visible gap around any of the sealing area. If this cannot be achieved, release all the screws and tighten them progressively again. If it is still not possible to obtain correct seating of the unit, the complete assembly must be renewed.

15 On completion, refit the hydraulic modulator as described previously in this Section.

Front wheel speed sensor

Note: *The front wheel speed sensors also provide the vehicle roadspeed signal to the various system ECUs as required.*

Removal

16 Disconnect the battery negative terminal (refer to *Disconnecting the battery* in Chapter 5A, Section 4).

17 Firmly apply the handbrake, then jack up the front of the car and support it securely on axle stands (see *Jacking and vehicle support*). Remove the appropriate front roadwheel.

18 Trace the wheel speed sensor wiring back to its wiring connector on the inner wheel arch, and release it from its retaining clip. Disconnect the connector, and work back along the sensor wiring, freeing it from all the relevant retaining clips and ties.

19 Slacken and remove the bolt securing the sensor to the swivel hub, and remove the sensor and lead assembly from the vehicle **(see illustration)**.

Refitting

20 Ensure that the sensor and swivel hub sealing faces are clean, then fit the sensor to the hub. Refit the retaining bolt, and tighten it to the specified torque.

21 Ensure that the sensor wiring is correctly routed, and retained by all the necessary clips. Reconnect it to its wiring connector, and fit the connector into the retaining clip.

22 Refit the roadwheel, then lower the vehicle to the ground and tighten the roadwheel bolts to the specified torque.

Rear wheel speed sensor

Removal

23 Disconnect the battery negative terminal (refer to *Disconnecting the battery* in Chapter 5A, Section 4).

24 Chock the front wheels, then jack up the rear of the vehicle, and support it securely on axle stands (see *Jacking and vehicle support*). Remove the rear roadwheel.

25 Undo the retaining nuts, release the clips and remove the wheel arch liner.

26 Trace the wheel speed sensor wiring back to its wiring connector on the inner wheel arch, and release it from its retaining clip. Disconnect the connector, and work back along the sensor wiring, freeing it from all the relevant retaining clips and ties.

27 Slacken and remove the bolt securing the sensor to the rear axle, and remove the sensor and lead assembly from the vehicle **(see illustration)**.

Refitting

28 Ensure that the sensor and rear axle flange sealing faces are clean, then fit the sensor. Refit the retaining bolt, and tighten it to the specified torque.

29 Ensure that the sensor wiring is correctly routed, and retained by all the necessary clips. Reconnect it to its wiring connector, and fit the connector into the retaining clip.

30 Refit the wheel arch liner and roadwheel, then lower the vehicle to the ground and tighten the roadwheel bolts to the specified torque.

Yaw rate sensor

Note: *The yaw rate sensor is only fitted to vehicles with electronic stability control (ESP). The sensor is located beneath the centre console, just forward of the handbrake lever.*

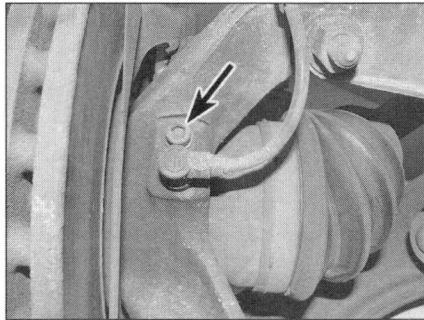

19.19 Front wheel speed sensor retaining bolt

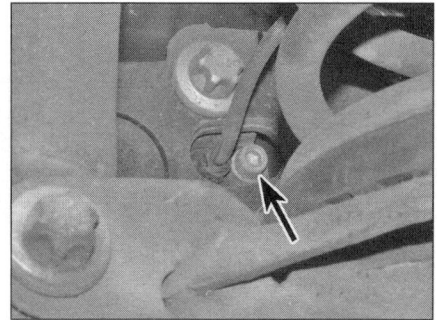

19.27 Rear wheel speed sensor retaining bolt

20.4 Disconnect the quick-release fitting (arrowed) and detach the servo unit vacuum hose

20.8 Undo the two mounting bolts and remove the pump from the camshaft housing

Removal

31 Disconnect the battery negative terminal (refer to *Disconnecting the battery* in Chapter 5A, Section 4).

32 Remove the centre console as described in Chapter 11, Section 25.

33 Disconnect the sensor wiring connector, then undo the two bolts and remove the sensor from the car.

Refitting

34 Refitting is the reverse of the removal procedure.

Steering angle sensor

35 The steering angle sensor is an integral part of the electronic power steering (EPS) column assembly and is not available separately. Removal and refitting details for the steering column are contained in Chapter 10, Section 16.

20 Vacuum pump (diesel engine models) – removal and refitting

Removal

1 Disconnect the battery negative terminal

(refer to *Disconnecting the battery* in Chapter 5A, Section 4).

2 Remove the plastic cover over the top of the engine.

3 Slacken the two retaining clips and disconnect the charge air hose from the intercooler and charge air pipe elbow.

4 Disconnect the quick-release fitting and detach the vacuum servo unit vacuum hose from the pump **(see illustration)**. Disconnect the smaller vacuum hose from the outlet on the side of the pump.

5 Release the retaining clips and disconnect the fuel return hoses at the fuel pump and at the fuel leak-off hose adaptor pipe. Plug or cover the pump union and hose ends to prevent dirt entry.

6 Undo the retaining bolt and free the leak-off hose adaptor pipe from its location.

7 Disconnect the wiring connector at the EGR valve.

8 Undo the two mounting bolts and remove the pump from the camshaft housing **(see illustration)**. Recover the gasket.

Refitting

9 Refitting is a reversal of removal, but clean the mating faces of the pump and camshaft housing and fit a new gasket. Tighten the mounting bolts to the specified torque.

Chapter 10
Suspension and steering

Contents

Degrees of difficulty

Easy, suitable for novice with little experience	**Fairly easy,** suitable for beginner with some experience	**Fairly difficult,** suitable for competent DIY mechanic	**Difficult,** suitable for experienced DIY mechanic	**Very difficult,** suitable for expert DIY or professional

Specifications

Front suspension
Type . . . . Independent, with MacPherson struts and anti-roll bar

Rear suspension
Type . . . . Semi-independent torsion beam, with trailing arms, coil springs and telescopic shock absorbers

Steering
Type . . . . Rack-and-pinion. Electric motor in EPS steering column

Front and rear hub bearings
Bearing play (maximum). . . . . 0.1 mm
Bearing radial run-out. . . . . 0.04 mm
Bearing lateral run-out . . . . 0.05 mm

Torque wrench settings

	Nm	lbf ft
Front suspension		
ABS wheel speed sensor bolt	8	6
Anti-roll bar clamp bolts	25	18
Balljoint-to-lower arm bolts/nuts*	35	26
Brake caliper mounting bracket-to-swivel hub bolts	105	77
Driveshaft retaining nut: *		
Stage 1	70	52
Stage 2	Angle-tighten a further 60°	
Stage 3	Angle-tighten a further 5°	
Front subframe mounting bolts: *		
Stage 1	90	66
Stage 2	Angle-tighten a further 45°	
Link rod-to-strut and anti-roll bar nuts	40	30
Lower arm balljoint clamp bolt nut*	60	44
Lower arm pivot bolts/nut to front subframe: *		
Stage 1	90	66
Stage 2	Angle-tighten a further 75°	
Stage 3	Angle-tighten a further 15°	
Suspension strut piston rod nut	50	37
Suspension strut-to-swivel hub bolts: *		
Stage 1	80	59
Stage 2	Angle-tighten a further 60°	
Stage 3	Angle-tighten a further 15°	
Suspension strut upper mounting nut	45	33
Torque link mounting centre bolt: *		
Stage 1	80	59
Stage 2	Angle-tighten a further 45°	
Rear suspension		
Brake backplate bolts	25	18
Rear axle front mounting bracket:		
Bracket-to-underbody bolts: *		
Stage 1	90	66
Stage 2	Angle-tighten a further 60°	
Stage 3	Angle-tighten a further 15°	
Centre through-bolt	90	66
Rear hub nut*	280	207
Shock absorber:		
Lower bolt	90	66
Upper bolts: *		
Stage 1	55	41
Stage 2	Angle-tighten a further 60°	
Stage 3	Angle-tighten a further 15°	
Stub axle bolts	90	66
Steering		
Intermediate shaft:		
Intermediate shaft to steering column: *		
Stage 1	24	18
Stage 2	Angle tighten a further 60°	
Universal joint-to-steering pinion clamp bolt*	55	41
Universal joint-to-intermediate shaft clamp bolt*	40	30
Steering column mounting bolts	22	16
Steering gear-to-front subframe bolts/nuts: *		
Stage 1	45	33
Stage 2	Angle tighten a further 45°	
Stage 3	Angle tighten a further 15°	
Steering wheel bolt	30	22
Track rod inner balljoint to steering rack	82	61
Track rod balljoint locknut	65	48
Track rod balljoint-to-swivel hub nut*	35	26
Roadwheels		
Roadwheel bolts	110	81

Use new fastenings

1 General Information

1 The independent front suspension is of the MacPherson strut type, incorporating coil springs and integral telescopic shock absorbers. The MacPherson struts are located by transverse lower suspension arms, which utilise rubber inner mounting bushes, and incorporate a balljoint at the outer ends. The front swivel hubs, which carry the wheel bearings, brake calipers and the hub/disc assemblies, are bolted to the MacPherson struts, and connected to the lower arms via the balljoints. A front anti-roll bar is fitted, which has link rods with balljoints at each end to connect it to the strut.

2 The rear suspension is of semi-independent type, consisting of a torsion beam axle and trailing arms, with double-conical coil springs and telescopic shock absorbers. The front ends of the trailing arms are attached to the vehicle underbody by horizontal bushes; the rear ends are located by the shock absorbers, which are bolted to the underbody at their upper ends. The coil springs are mounted independently of the shock absorbers, and act directly between the trailing arms and the underbody.

3 The steering column is linked to the steering gear by an intermediate shaft. The intermediate shaft has a universal joint fitted to its upper end, and is secured to the column by a clamp bolt. The lower end of the intermediate shaft is attached to the steering gear pinion by means of a universal joint and clamp bolts.

4 The rack-and-pinion type steering gear is rubber-mounted onto the engine compartment bulkhead, and is connected by two track rods, with balljoints at their outer ends, to the steering arms projecting rearwards from the swivel hubs. The track rod ends are threaded, to facilitate adjustment.

5 Electric power-assisted steering is fitted as standard, whereby an electric motor, drive gear assembly and torque sensor incorporated in the steering column provide a variable degree of power assistance according to roadspeed. The system is controlled by an electronic control unit with self-diagnostic capability, located on the steering column.

2.2 Using a hammer and small chisel, carefully tap up the staking securing the driveshaft retaining nut

2 Front swivel hub assembly – removal and refitting

Note: *A new driveshaft retaining nut, lower arm balljoint clamp bolt and nut, suspension strut-to-swivel hub nuts and bolts and a new track rod balljoint nut will be needed for refitting. The driveshaft outer joint splines may be a tight fit in the hub and it is possible that a puller/extractor will be required to draw the hub assembly off the driveshaft during removal.*

Caution: The front wheel camber setting is controlled by the bolts securing the swivel hub to the front suspension strut. Before removing the bolts, mark the swivel hub in relation to the strut accurately. On completion, the camber setting must be checked and adjusted by a suitably-equipped garage.

Removal

1 Firmly apply the handbrake, then jack up the front of the car and support it securely on axle stands (see *Jacking and vehicle support*). Remove the appropriate front roadwheel.

2 Using a hammer and small chisel, carefully tap up the staking securing the driveshaft retaining nut **(see illustration)**.

3 Refit at least two roadwheel bolts to the front hub, and tighten them securely. Have an assistant firmly depress the brake pedal

2.3 Using a fabricated tool to hold the front hub stationary whilst the driveshaft retaining nut is slackened

to prevent the front hub from rotating, then using a socket and extension bar, slacken the driveshaft retaining nut. Alternatively, a tool can be fabricated from two lengths of steel strip (one long, one short) and a nut and bolt; the nut and bolt forming the pivot of a forked tool. Bolt the tool to the hub using two wheel bolts, and hold the tool to prevent the hub from rotating as the driveshaft retaining nut is undone **(see illustration)**.

4 Unscrew and remove the driveshaft retaining nut. Discard the nut; a new one must be used on refitting.

5 Remove the brake disc as described in Chapter 9, Section 6. The procedure involves removing the brake caliper and, using a piece of wire or string, tie the caliper to the front suspension coil spring to avoid placing any strain on the hydraulic brake hose.

6 Undo the bolt securing the ABS wheel speed sensor to the swivel hub **(see illustration)**. Withdraw the sensor from the hub and position it to one side.

7 Slacken and remove the nut securing the steering gear track rod balljoint to the swivel hub, and release the balljoint tapered shank using a universal balljoint separator **(see illustration)**. Discard the nut; it should be renewed whenever it is disturbed.

8 Unscrew and remove the lower arm balljoint clamp bolt nut, and withdraw the clamp bolt from the swivel hub, noting which way round it is fitted **(see illustration)**. Discard the clamp bolt nut; a new one must be used on refitting.

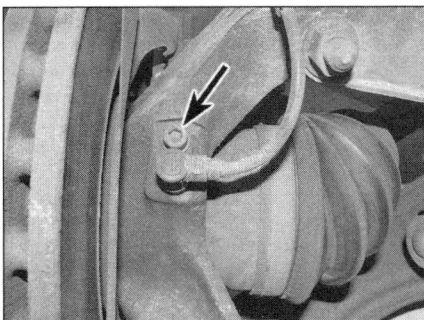

2.6 Undo the bolt securing the ABS wheel speed sensor to the swivel hub

2.7 Use a balljoint separator tool to remove the track rod end

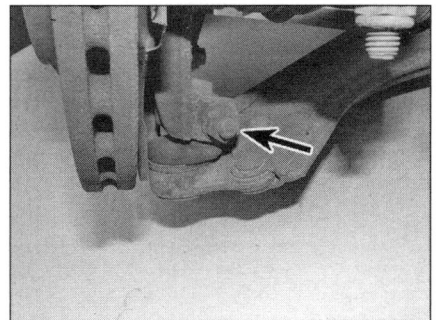

2.8 Unscrew the nut and remove the clamp bolt securing the lower arm balljoint to the swivel hub

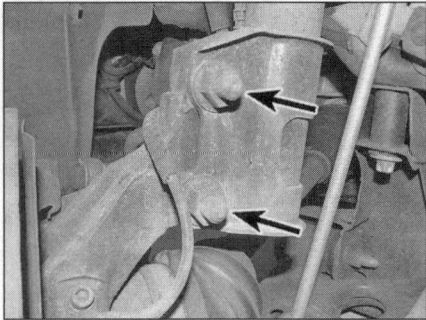

2.11 Unscrew the nuts and withdraw the bolts securing the suspension strut to the swivel hub

2.12a Tap the end of the driveshaft with a soft-faced hammer...

2.12b...then free the driveshaft from the swivel hub

9 Using a suitable lever, push down the lower arm to separate the balljoint from the swivel hub. When releasing the lower arm, take care not to damage the balljoint rubber boot; if necessary protect it with a piece of card or plastic.

Note: *If the balljoint stub is tight in the swivel hub, use a screwdriver or cold chisel as a wedge to force the clamp apart.*

10 Mark the position of the suspension strut on the swivel hub by drawing a circle around the heads of the two retaining bolts.

Note: *This is important to maintain the camber setting.*

11 Slacken and remove the two nuts and bolts securing the suspension strut to the swivel hub, noting that new nuts and bolts will be required for refitting **(see illustration)**.

12 The swivel hub must now be freed from the end of the driveshaft. It should be possible to pull the hub off the driveshaft, but if the end of the driveshaft is tight in the hub, then tap the end of the driveshaft with a soft-faced hammer while pulling outwards on the swivel hub **(see illustrations)**. Alternatively, use a suitable puller to press the driveshaft through the hub. Support the driveshaft by suspending it with wire or string; Do not allow the driveshaft to hang down under its own weight, or the joints may be damaged.

Refitting

13 Ensure that the driveshaft outer constant velocity joint and hub splines are clean, then slide the hub onto the driveshaft splines. Fit

2.21 Stake the driveshaft nut in position by tapping the edge of the nut into the grooves in the driveshaft in two places

the new driveshaft retaining nut, tightening it by hand only at this stage.

14 Engage the swivel hub with the suspension strut, and insert the new bolts from the front of the strut so that their threads are facing to the rear. Fit the new nuts, tightening them by hand only at this stage.

15 Locate the lower arm balljoint in the swivel hub. Insert the clamp bolt from the front of the swivel hub, so that its threads are facing to the rear. Fit the new nut to the clamp bolt, and tighten it to the specified torque setting.

16 With the hub correctly located, align the strut-to-swivel hub bolt heads with the marks made on the strut during removal. Tighten the bolts to the specified torque and through the specified angles given in the Specifications, using a torque wrench and angle-tightening gauge.

17 Engage the track rod balljoint in the swivel hub, then fit the new retaining nut and tighten it to the specified torque setting.

18 Refit the brake disc and caliper to the swivel hub, referring to Chapter 9 for further information.

19 Refit the ABS wheel speed sensor to the hub, making sure it is located correctly, and tighten the retaining bolt to the specified torque.

20 Using the method employed on removal to prevent rotation, tighten the driveshaft retaining nut through the stages given in the Specifications.

21 With the nut correctly tightened, stake it in position by tapping the edge of the nut into the grooves in the driveshaft in two places **(see illustration)**.

22 Refit the roadwheel, then lower the vehicle to the ground and tighten the roadwheel bolts to the specified torque. Refit the wheel trim/hub cap, where applicable.

3 Front hub bearings –
checking and renewal

Checking

1 Firmly apply the handbrake, then jack up the front of the car and support it securely on axle stands (see *Jacking and vehicle support*). Remove the roadwheel.

2 A dial test indicator (DTI) will be required to measure the amount of play in the bearing.

Locate the DTI on the suspension strut and zero the probe on the brake disc.

3 Lever the hub in and out and measure the amount of play in the bearing.

4 To measure the bearing lateral and radial run-out, undo the two bolts securing the brake caliper mounting bracket to the swivel hub. Slide the mounting bracket, complete with brake caliper and pads off the brake disc, and tie it to the coil spring using wire or a cable-tie.

5 Undo the two securing screws and remove the brake disc from the wheel hub.

6 To check the lateral run-out, locate the DTI on the suspension strut and zero the probe on the front face of the hub flange. Rotate the hub and measure the run-out.

7 To check the radial run-out, zero the DTI probe on the upper face of the extended portion at the centre of the hub. Rotate the hub and measure the run-out.

8 If the play or run-out exceeds the specified amounts, renew the hub bearing as described below.

9 If the bearing is satisfactory, refit the brake disc and tighten its retaining screws securely.

10 Slide the brake pads, caliper and mounting bracket over the disc and into position on the swivel hub. Fit the two caliper mounting bracket retaining bolts and tighten them to the specified torque (see Chapter 9).

11 Refit the roadwheel, then lower the vehicle to the ground and tighten the roadwheel bolts to the specified torque.

Renewal

Note: *The bearing is sealed, pre-adjusted and pre-lubricated. Never overtighten the driveshaft nut beyond the specified torque setting in an attempt to 'adjust' the bearing.*

Note: *A press will be required to dismantle and rebuild the assembly; if such a tool is not available, a large bench vice and spacers (such as large sockets) will serve as an adequate substitute. The bearing's inner races are an interference fit on the hub; if the inner race remains on the hub flange when it is pressed out of the swivel hub, a knife-edged bearing puller will be required to remove it.*

12 Remove the swivel hub assembly as described in Section 2.

13 Undo the three screws and remove the brake disc shield from the hub.

3.14a Using a socket to drift out the hub flange out from the bearing

3.14b Use a chisel to remove the inner bearing race from the hub flange

3.15 Use circlip pliers to remove the circlip

3.16 Using a drift to remove the bearing from the swivel hub

3.19 Use a threaded rod and spacers to press the bearing squarely into position

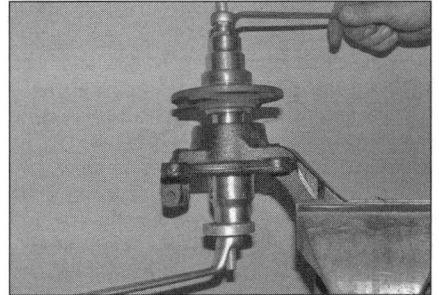
3.21 Using a threaded rod and spacers/ sockets to press the hub flange into the bearing

14 Support the swivel hub securely on blocks or in a vice. Using a tubular spacer/socket which bears only on the inner end of the hub flange, press the hub flange out of the bearing. If the bearing's outboard inner race remains on the hub, remove it using a chisel or bearing puller – see note above (see illustrations).

15 Extract the bearing retaining circlip from the swivel hub assembly (see illustration).

16 Using a drift or tubular spacer which bears only on the inner race, press the complete bearing assembly out of the swivel hub (see illustration).

17 Thoroughly clean the hub and swivel hub, removing all traces of dirt and grease. Polish away any burrs or raised edges which might hinder reassembly. Check both assemblies for cracks or any other signs of wear or damage, and renew as necessary. Renew the circlip regardless of its apparent condition.

18 On reassembly, apply a light film of oil to the bearing outer race and hub flange shaft, to aid installation of the bearing. Remove all traces of old thread-locking compound from the disc shield retaining screw holes, ideally by running a tap of the correct size and pitch through them.

19 Securely support the swivel hub, and locate the bearing in the hub. Ensure that the side of the bearing containing the plastic ABS wheel speed reluctor ring faces the transmission side of the hub. Press the bearing fully into position, ensuring that it enters the hub squarely, using the old wheel bearing or a tubular spacer which bears only on the bearing outer race (see illustration).

20 Once the bearing is correctly seated, secure the bearing in position with the new inner circlip. Make sure that the circlip is correctly located in its groove and with the open ends on either side of the ABS wheel speed sensor opening.

21 Securely support the swivel hub in a vice, then locate the hub flange into the bearing inner race. With the underside of the inner race securely supported, press the flange into the swivel hub bearing, using a tubular spacer/sockets and threaded rod, until it seats against the hub shoulder (see illustration). Check that the hub flange rotates freely, and wipe off any excess oil or grease.

22 Fit the disc shield to the hub assembly, and apply a few drops of thread-locking compound to the new screws. Fit the screws, and tighten them securely.

23 Refit the swivel hub assembly as described in Section 2.

4.3 Unscrew the nut and disconnect the anti-roll bar link rod from the strut

4 Front strut – removal, overhaul and refitting

Note: New strut-to-swivel hub bolts and nuts will be required for refitting. Ideally, both front suspension struts should be renewed at the same time in order to maintain good steering and suspension characteristics.

Caution: The front wheel camber setting is controlled by the bolts securing the swivel hub to the front suspension strut. Before removing the bolts, mark the swivel hub in relation to the strut accurately. On completion, the camber setting must be checked and adjusted by a suitably-equipped garage.

Removal

1 Remove the windscreen cowl panel as described in Chapter 11, Section 20.

2 Firmly apply the handbrake, then jack up the front of the car and support it securely on axle stands (see *Jacking and vehicle support*). Remove the appropriate roadwheel.

3 Unscrew the retaining nut and disconnect the anti-roll bar link rod from the strut. Use a spanner on the flats to hold the link while the nut is being loosened (see illustration).

4 Release the ABS wheel speed sensor wiring from its clip on the suspension strut.

5 Extract the retaining clip and release the brake hydraulic hose from the suspension strut.

6 Mark the position of the suspension strut on the swivel hub by drawing a circle around

4.7 Undo the two nuts and bolts securing the suspension strut to the swivel hub

4.8 Unscrew the suspension strut upper mounting nut and remove the retaining plate

4.10 Fit a spring compressor tool, and compress the coil spring

the heads of the two retaining bolts. This is important to maintain the camber setting.

7 Slacken and remove the two nuts and bolts securing the suspension strut to the swivel hub, noting that new nuts and bolts will be required for refitting **(see illustration)**.

8 Support the front strut assembly then, from within the engine compartment, unscrew the suspension strut upper mounting nut and remove the retaining plate **(see illustration)**.

9 Release the strut from the swivel hub, and withdraw it from under the wheel arch.

Overhaul

Note: *A spring compressor tool will be required for this operation. Before overhaul, mark the position of each component in relationship with each other for reassembly.*

10 With the suspension strut resting on a bench,

or clamped in a vice, fit a spring compressor tool, and compress the coil spring to relieve the pressure on the spring seats. Ensure that the compressor tool is securely located on the spring, in accordance with the tool manufacturer's instructions **(see illustration)**.

11 Mark the position of the spring in relation to the top and bottom mountings, then counterhold the strut piston rod with a spanner, and unscrew the piston rod nut **(see illustration)**.

12 Remove the strut upper mounting, upper spring seat with rubber gaiter, spring and buffer from the strut **(see illustrations)**.

13 With the strut assembly now completely dismantled, examine all the components for wear, damage or deformation, and check the support bearing for smoothness of operation. Renew any of the components as necessary.

14 Examine the strut for signs of fluid leakage.

Check the strut piston for signs of pitting along its entire length, and check the strut body for signs of damage. While holding it in an upright position, test the operation of the strut by moving the piston through a full stroke, and then through short strokes of 50 to 100 mm. In both cases, the resistance felt should be smooth and continuous. If the resistance is jerky or uneven or if there is any visible sign of wear or damage to the strut, renewal is necessary.

15 If any doubt exists as to the condition of the coil spring, carefully remove the spring compressors and check the spring for distortion and signs of cracking. Renew the spring if it is damaged or distorted, or if there is any doubt as to its condition.

16 Inspect all other components for damage or deterioration, and renew any that are suspect.

4.11 Counterhold the strut piston rod with an Allen key or suitable bit, and unscrew the piston rod nut

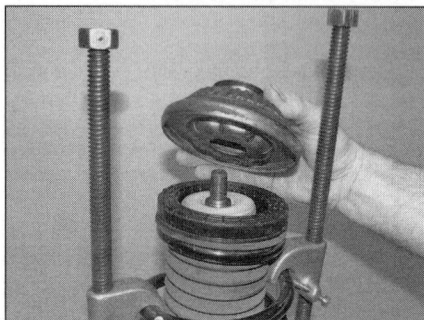

4.12a Remove the strut upper mounting...

4.12b...upper spring seat with rubber gaiter...

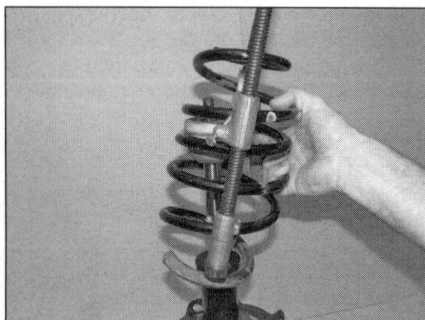

4.12c...spring...

4.12d...and buffer from the strut

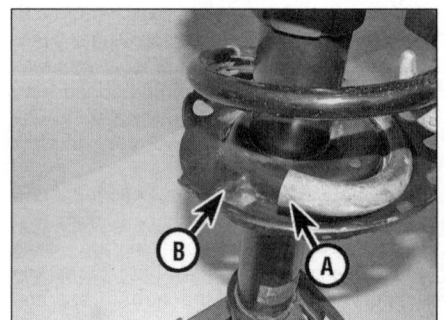

4.17 Locate the spring on the strut making sure that its lower end (A) is against the raised stop (B)

17 With the spring compressed with the compressor tool, locate the spring on the strut making sure that it is correctly seated with its lower end against the raised stop **(see illustration)**.

18 Refit the buffer, rubber gaiter, upper spring seat, and upper damping ring.

19 Refit the piston rod nut and tighten it to the specified torque while counterholding the piston rod with a spanner.

20 Slowly slacken the spring compressor tool to relieve the tension in the spring. Check that the ends of the spring locate correctly against the stops on the spring seats. If necessary, turn the spring and the upper seat so that the components locate correctly before the compressor tool is removed. Remove the compressor tool when the spring is fully seated.

Refitting

21 Manoeuvre the strut assembly into position, ensuring that the top mounting is correctly located in the inner wing panel. Fit the upper mounting plate and retaining nut, and tighten it to the specified torque setting.

22 Engage the swivel hub with the suspension strut, and insert the new bolts from the front of the strut so that their threads are facing to the rear. Fit the new nuts, tightening them by hand only at this stage.

23 Align the strut-to-swivel hub bolt heads with the marks made on the strut during removal. Tighten the bolts to the specified torque and through the specified angles given in the Specifications, using a torque wrench and angle-tightening gauge.

24 Refit the anti-roll bar link rod to the strut. Use a spanner on the flats to hold the link, while the nut is being tightened to the specified torque setting.

25 Clip the ABS wheel speed sensor wiring back into its retaining clip.

26 Clip the brake hydraulic hose to the suspension strut.

27 Refit the roadwheel, then lower the vehicle to the ground and tighten the roadwheel bolts to the specified torque.

28 Refit the windscreen cowl panel as described in Chapter 11, Section 20.

29 If the strut has been renewed, have the front camber angle checked, and if necessary adjusted at the earliest opportunity.

5 Front lower arm – removal and refitting

Note: When refitting, new pivot bolt/nuts, and new lower arm-to-balljoint nut/bolt, will be required.

Removal

1 Firmly apply the handbrake, then jack up the front of the car and support it securely on axle stands (see *Jacking and vehicle support*). Remove the appropriate front roadwheel.

5.4 Front suspension lower arm front mounting...

2 Unscrew and remove the lower arm balljoint clamp bolt nut, and withdraw the clamp bolt from the swivel hub, noting which way round it is fitted **(see illustration 2.8)**. Discard the clamp bolt nut; a new one must be used on refitting.

3 Using a suitable lever, push down the lower arm to separate the balljoint from the swivel hub. When releasing the lower arm, take care not to damage the balljoint rubber boot; if necessary protect it with a piece of card or plastic. Note: If the balljoint stub is tight in the swivel hub, use a screwdriver or cold chisel as a wedge to force the clamp apart.

4 Unscrew the nut and withdraw the pivot bolt securing the front of the lower arm to the front subframe **(see illustration)**. Discard the bolt/nut; new ones should be used on refitting.

5 Unscrew the nut and withdraw the bolt securing the lower arm rear mounting to the front subframe **(see illustration)**. Discard the bolt/nut; new ones should be used on refitting. Remove the lower arm from the vehicle.

6 Thoroughly clean the lower arm and the area around the arm mountings, removing all traces of dirt and underseal if necessary. Check carefully for cracks, distortion, or any other signs of wear or damage, paying particular attention to the pivot bushes. If the pivot bushes are worn, it will be necessary to renew the complete lower arm as the bushes are not available separately. To renew the lower arm balljoint see Section 6.

Refitting

7 Offer up the lower arm, aligning the inner end of the arm with its mountings, insert new pivot bolts and nuts to the front and rear mounting points. Only tighten the mounting bolts/nuts hand tight at this stage.

8 Locate the lower balljoint stub fully in the bottom of the swivel hub, then refit the clamp bolt and tighten to the specified torque. Make sure the bolt head is facing the front of the vehicle.

9 Refit the roadwheel, lower the vehicle to the ground, and tighten the roadwheel bolts to the specified torque setting.

10 With the vehicle lowered to the ground, the lower arm inner mounting bolts/nuts can now be tightened through the various stages given in the Specifications at the start of this Chapter.

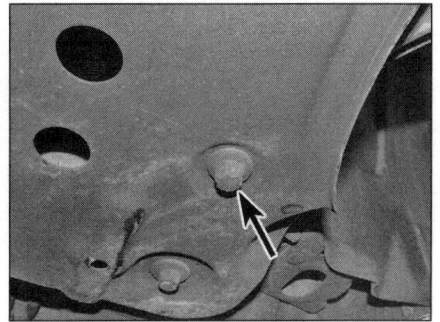
5.5...and rear mounting

11 Have the front wheel alignment settings checked by a suitably-equipped garage at the earliest opportunity.

6 Front lower arm balljoint – renewal

Note: The original balljoint is riveted to the lower arm; service replacements are bolted in position.

1 Remove the front lower arm as described in Section 5.

Note: If the fitted balljoint is a service replacement, it is not necessary to completely remove the arm but only to disconnect the balljoint from the bottom of the swivel hub then unbolt the old balljoint.

2 Mount the lower arm in a vice, then drill the heads from the three rivets that secure the balljoint to the lower arm, using a 10.0 mm diameter drill **(see illustration)**.

3 If necessary, tap the rivets from the lower arm, then remove the balljoint.

4 Clean any rust from the rivet holes, and apply rust inhibitor.

5 The new balljoint must be fitted using three special bolts, spring washers and nuts, available from a Vauxhall/Opel parts stockists.

6 Ensure that the balljoint is fitted the correct way up, noting that the securing nuts are positioned on the underside of the lower arm. Tighten the nuts to the specified torque.

7 Refit the front lower arm as described in Section 5.

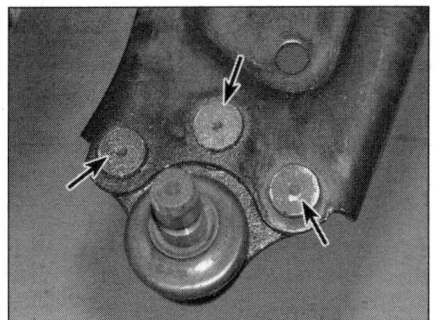
6.2 Front suspension lower balljoint showing rivets securing it to the lower arm

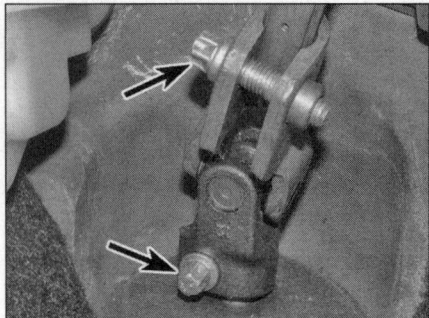

7.2 Unscrew the two bolts securing the universal joint to the intermediate shaft and steering gear pinion

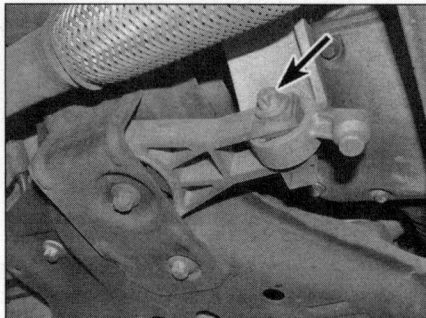

7.10 Undo the centre bolt from the torque link mounting

7.11 On models with a rod-operated gearchange, remove the retaining clip and release the rocker arm from the guide bracket

7 Front subframe – removal and refitting

Caution: Vauxhall/Opel technicians use special jigs to ensure that the front subframe is correctly aligned. Without the use of these tools it is important to note the position of the subframe accurately before removal.

Removal

1 Set the front wheels in the straight-ahead position, then remove the ignition key and lock the column by turning the steering wheel as required.

2 In the driver's footwell, unscrew the two bolts securing the universal joint to the bottom of the steering column intermediate shaft and the steering gear pinion **(see illustration)**. Discard the bolts; new ones must be used on refitting. Slide the universal joint up the intermediate shaft to disengage it from the steering gear pinion.

3 Apply the handbrake, then jack up the front of the vehicle and support it on axle stands (see *Jacking and vehicle support*). Remove both front wheels.

4 Disconnect the steering track rod balljoints from the swivel hubs by unscrewing the nuts and using a balljoint separator tool **(see illustration 2.7)**.

5 Unscrew the nuts and disconnect the anti-roll bar link rods from the struts on both sides. Use a further spanner to hold the studs while the nuts are being loosened **(see illustration 4.3)**.

6 Unscrew and remove the lower arm balljoint clamp bolt nut, and withdraw the clamp bolt from the swivel hub on each side, noting which way round they are fitted **(see illustration 2.8)**. Discard the clamp bolt nuts; new ones must be used on refitting.

7 Using a suitable lever, push down the lower arms to separate the balljoints from the swivel hubs. When releasing the lower arms, take care not to damage the balljoint rubber boots; if necessary protect them with a piece of card or plastic.

Note: *If the balljoint stub is tight in the swivel*

hub, use a screwdriver or cold chisel as a wedge to force the clamp apart.

8 Remove the exhaust system as described in Chapter 4A, Section 13 or Chapter 4B, Section 20.

9 On diesel engine models, where fitted, unscrew the bolt securing the exhaust heat shield to the front subframe.

10 Undo the centre bolt from the torque link mounting at the rear of the engine/transmission **(see illustration)**.

11 On models with a rod-operated gearchange mechanism, remove the retaining clip and release the gearchange rocker arm from the guide bracket **(see illustration)**. On models with a cable-operated gearchange mechanism, open the latch and release the selector cable(s) from the bracket on the steering gear.

12 Support the subframe with a cradle across a trolley jack. Alternatively, two trolley jacks and the help of an assistant will be required.

13 Accurately mark the position of the subframe in relation to the mounting points to ensure correct refitting. Note that Vauxhall-Opel technicians use a special jig with guide pins located through the alignment holes in the subframe and underbody.

14 Unscrew the six subframe mounting bolts and carefully lower the subframe to the ground. Note that new bolts will be required for refitting. As the subframe is lowered, make sure there are no cables or wiring still attached.

15 Remove the lower suspension arms from the subframe with reference to Section 5, the anti-roll bar with reference to Section 8, the rear engine mounting with reference to Chapter 2A, Chapter 2B or Chapter 2C and the steering gear with reference to Section 18.

Refitting

16 Refitting is a reversal of removal, bearing in mind the following points:
a) Tighten all nuts and bolts to the specified torque and, where necessary, in the stages given. Ensure that new nuts/bolts are used where indicated.
b) Make sure that the subframe is correctly aligned with the underbody before fully tightening the mounting bolts.
c) When refitting the universal joint to the

steering gear pinion and intermediate shaft, note that the components incorporate master splines and it will only be possible to fit the universal joint in one position. Apply thread-locking compound to the new universal joint retaining bolts when refitting.

8 Front anti-roll bar – removal and refitting

Note: *A new lower arm balljoint clamp bolt and nut and new track rod balljoint nuts will be needed for refitting.*

Removal

1 Firmly apply the handbrake, then jack up the front of the car and support it securely on axle stands (see *Jacking and vehicle support*).

2 Disconnect the steering track rod balljoints from the swivel hubs by unscrewing the nuts and using a balljoint separator tool **(see illustration 2.7)**.

3 Unscrew and remove the lower arm balljoint clamp bolt nut on the left-hand side, and withdraw the clamp bolt from the swivel hub, noting which way round it is fitted **(see illustration 2.8)**. Discard the clamp bolt and nut; new ones must be used on refitting.

4 Using a suitable lever, push down the lower arm to separate the balljoint from the swivel hub. When releasing the lower arm, take care not to damage the balljoint rubber boot; if necessary protect it with a piece of card or plastic.

Note: *If the balljoint stub is tight in the swivel hub, use a screwdriver or cold chisel as a wedge to force the clamp apart.*

5 Unscrew the nuts and disconnect the anti-roll bar link rods from the suspension struts and anti-roll bar on both sides. Use a further spanner to hold the studs while the nuts are being loosened **(see illustration 4.3)**.

6 On models with a rod-operated gearchange mechanism, remove the retaining clip and release the gearchange rocker arm from the guide bracket **(see illustration 7.11)**. Undo the four retaining bolts and remove the guide bracket from the subframe.

7 Unscrew the two bolts each side securing

9.11 Carefully tap out the dust cap from the centre of the rear hub

9.13a Withdraw the hub from the stub axle...

9.13b...and recover the spacer located behind the hub

the anti-roll bar mountings to the subframe. Move the disconnected suspension components to one side and remove the anti-roll bar from the left-hand side of the car.

Refitting

8 Refitting is a reversal of removal, tightening all nuts and bolts to the specified torque and, where necessary, in the stages given. Ensure that new nuts/bolts are used where indicated.

9 Rear hub bearings – checking and renewal

Note: *The rear hub bearing and integral ABS wheel speed sensor reluctor ring is a sealed unit and no repairs are possible. If the bearing is worn a new bearing assembly must be obtained.*

Checking

1 Chock the front wheels then jack up the rear of the car and securely support it on axle stands (see *Jacking and vehicle support*). Remove the roadwheel.
2 Remove the brake drum as described in Chapter 9, Section 7.
3 A dial test indicator (DTI) will be required to measure the amount of radial and lateral run-out in the bearing. Zero the indicator on the outer edge of the hub flange.
4 Lever the hub in and out and measure the amount of play in the bearing.
5 To measure lateral run-out, locate the probe on the surface of the hub which contacts the drum. To measure radial run-out, locate the probe on the outer perimeter of the hub so that it is pointing towards the centre of the hub.
6 Slowly turn the hub and note the maximum amount of run-out. If the run-out exceeds the amounts given in the Specifications, renew the hub bearing unit as described below.
7 Remove the indicator and refit the brake drum with reference to Chapter 9, Section 7.
8 Refit the roadwheel, then lower the vehicle to the ground and tighten the roadwheel bolts to the specified torque.

Renewal

Note: *A new hub retaining nut will be required for refitting. It may also be necessary to renew the hub dust cap if it is damaged during removal.*

9 Chock the front wheels then jack up the rear of the car and securely support it on axle stands (see *Jacking and vehicle support*). Remove the roadwheel.
10 Remove the brake drum as described in Chapter 9, Section 7.
11 Using a hammer and small chisel, carefully tap out the dust cap from the centre of the hub **(see illustration)**.
12 Unscrew and remove the hub retaining nut and remove the washer.
13 Withdraw the hub from the stub axle and recover the spacer located behind the hub **(see illustrations)**.
14 Lightly lubricate the stub axle and the inner circumference of the hub with clean engine oil.
15 Place the spacer in position then slide the hub onto the stub axle.
16 Fit the washer and new hub retaining nut and tighten the nut to the specified torque.
17 Using a soft-faced hammer, carefully tap the dust cap into position on the hub.
18 Refit the brake drum as described in Chapter 9. Section 7.

10 Rear stub axle – removal and refitting

Removal

1 Remove the rear hub as described in Section 9.
2 Remove the brake shoes, wheel cylinder and ABS wheel speed sensor as described in Chapter 9.
3 Depress the retaining tabs and withdraw the handbrake cable from the brake backplate.
4 Undo the two retaining bolts and remove the brake backplate from the stub axle.
5 Slacken and remove the four retaining bolts, and remove the stub axle from the trailing arm.
6 Inspect the stub axle surface for signs

of damage such as scoring, and renew if necessary.

Refitting

7 Ensure that the mating surfaces of the stub axle and backplate are clean and dry. Check the backplate for signs of damage, and remove any burrs with a fine file or emery cloth.
8 Clean the threads of the stub axle retaining bolts and the bolt holes in the stub axle itself, ensuring that all traces of thread-locking compound are removed.
9 Apply thread-locking compound to the retaining bolt threads, then offer up the stub axle, and refit the bolts. Tighten the retaining bolts to the specified torque.
10 Place the brake backplate in position on the stub axle, then refit the two retaining bolts and tighten them to the specified torque.
11 Insert the handbrake cable into the hole in the backplate and push it through until the cable retainer engages fully.
12 Refit the ABS wheel speed sensor, wheel cylinder and brake shoes as described in Chapter 9.
13 Refit the rear hub as described in Section 9.

11 Rear shock absorber – removal, testing and refitting

Note: *Always renew shock absorbers in pairs and the correct version for model, to maintain good handling.*
Note: *New shock absorber upper mounting bolts will be required for refitting.*

Removal

1 Chock the front wheels then jack up the rear of the car and support it on axle stands (see *Jacking and vehicle support*). Remove the relevant rear roadwheel.
2 Unscrew the two bolts and five nuts and remove the wheel arch liner for access to the shock absorber upper mounting.
3 Position a jack underneath the relevant trailing arm, and raise the jack until it is just supporting the weight of the arm.
4 Undo the two bolts securing the shock

11.4 Undo the two bolts securing the shock absorber upper mounting to the underbody

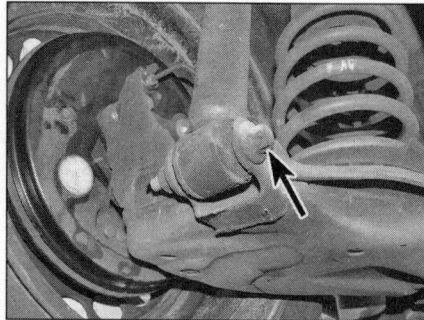

11.5 Undo the nut and remove the shock absorber lower mounting bolt

absorber upper mounting to the underbody **(see illustration)**. Discard the bolts; new ones must be used for refitting.

5 Undo the nut and remove the shock absorber lower mounting bolt, then lower the shock absorber out of position and remove it from underneath the vehicle **(see illustration)**.

Testing

6 Examine the shock absorber for signs of fluid leakage or damage. Test the operation of the strut, while holding it in an upright position, by moving the piston through a full stroke, and then through short strokes of 50 to 100 mm. In both cases, the resistance felt should be smooth and continuous. If the resistance is jerky, or uneven, or if there is any visible sign of wear or damage to the strut, renewal is necessary. Also check the rubber mounting bush(es) for damage and deterioration. If the bushes are damaged or worn, the complete shock absorber will have to be renewed, as the mounting bushes are not available separately. Inspect the shanks of the mounting bolts for signs of wear or damage, and renew as necessary.

7 Examine the upper mounting rubber dampers for signs of damage or deterioration, and renew if necessary.

Refitting

8 Manoeuvre the shock absorber into position and refit the new upper mounting bolts and the lower mounting bolt and nut.

9 Tighten the bolts to the specified torque

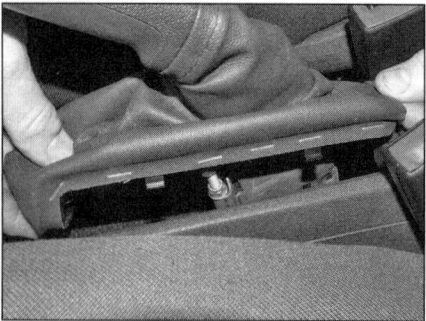

13.3 Unclip the handbrake lever gaiter from the centre console and fold it up the handbrake lever

and through the specified angles given in the Specifications, using a torque wrench and angle-tightening gauge, where applicable.

10 Remove the jack from under the trailing arm and refit the wheel arch liner.

11 Refit the roadwheel, then lower the vehicle to the ground, and tighten the roadwheel bolts to the specified torque.

12 Rear coil spring – removal and refitting

Note: *Always renew coil springs in pairs and the correct version for model, to maintain good handling.*

Removal

1 Chock the front wheels then jack up the rear of the car and support it on axle stands (see *Jacking and vehicle support*). Remove both rear roadwheels.

2 Position a jack underneath the relevant trailing arm, and raise the jack until it is just supporting the weight of the arm.

3 Undo the nut, remove the shock absorber lower mounting bolt, and disengage the shock absorber from the trailing arm.

4 Slowly lower the jack, keeping watch on the brake pipes to ensure no excess strain is placed on them, until it is possible to withdraw the coil spring. Note which way around the spring is installed, and recover the upper damping ring and lower spring seat.

13.4 Fully slacken and remove the handbrake cable adjuster nut

5 If the vehicle is to be left for some time with the spring removed, lift up the trailing arms and refit the shock absorber lower mounting bolts. **Note:** *Do not allow the rear axle assembly to hang unsupported.*

6 Inspect the springs closely for signs of damage, such as cracking, and check the spring seats and damping ring for signs of wear or damage. Renew worn components as necessary.

Refitting

7 Refitting is a reversal of removal, but note the following points.
a) Ensure that the spring locates correctly on the upper and lower seats, as well as on the trailing arm and underbody.
b) Tighten the shock absorber lower mounting bolt to the specified torque.
c) If the spring is being renewed, repeat the procedure on the remaining side of the vehicle.
d) Refit the roadwheels, then lower the vehicle to the ground, and tighten the roadwheel bolts to the specified torque.

13 Rear axle – removal and refitting

Note: *New trailing arm pivot bolts and nuts will be required when refitting.*
Caution: Vauxhall/Opel technicians use special jigs to ensure that the rear axle is correctly aligned. Without the use of these tools it is important to note the position of the axle mounting points accurately before removal.

Removal

1 Chock the front wheels then jack up the rear of the car and support it on axle stands (see *Jacking and vehicle support*). Remove both rear roadwheels.

2 Unscrew the brake master cylinder fluid reservoir cap and screw it down onto a piece of polythene to minimise fluid loss during the following procedure.

3 Unclip the handbrake lever gaiter from the centre console and fold it up the handbrake lever **(see illustration)**.

4 Remove the protective cap from the end of the handbrake cable, then slacken the handbrake cable adjuster nut **(see illustration)**.

5 Remove the rear tailpipe and silencer as described in Chapter 4A, Section 13 or Chapter 4B, Section 20, as applicable.

6 Unscrew the bolt and the nut, release the two clamps and remove the exhaust system heat shield from the fuel tank.

7 Undo the bolt securing the ABS wheel speed sensor to the stub axle on each side **(see illustration)**. Withdraw the sensors from the stub axles and unclip the sensor wiring from the rear brake pipes.

8 Detach the front handbrake cable from the compensator plate by twisting it through 90°,

then release the main cable sections from the supports on the underbody **(see illustration)**.

9 Slacken the union nuts, and disconnect the brake pipes from the flexible hose unions adjacent to the trailing arm mountings. Plug the pipe and hose ends to minimise fluid loss and prevent the entry of dirt into the hydraulic system. Remove the retaining clips, and release the two flexible hoses from their mounting brackets.

10 Remove the rear coil springs as described in Section 13.

11 Accurately mark the position of the axle mounting points in relation with the vehicle underbody to ensure correct refitting. Note that Vauxhall/Opel technicians use a special jig with guide pins located through alignment holes in the underbody.

12 Support the weight of the axle assembly using two trolley jacks. Alternatively, one trolley jack and a length of wood may be used, but the help of an assistant will be required.

13 Undo the three bolts each side securing the axle front mounting brackets to the underbody. Discard the bolts; new ones should be used on refitting.

14 Make a final check that all necessary components have been disconnected and positioned so that they will not hinder the removal procedure. Carefully lower the axle assembly out of position, and remove it from underneath the vehicle.

15 The brake components can be removed from the axle, referring to the relevant Sections of Chapter 9. The hub bearing units can be removed with reference to Section 9.

16 If necessary, the front mounting brackets can be removed after unscrewing the retaining nut and withdrawing the centre through-bolt.

Refitting

17 Refit any components that were removed from the axle, referring to the relevant Sections of this Chapter and Chapter 9, as applicable. If the front mounting brackets were removed, refit the brackets, but only tighten the through-bolt nuts lightly at this stage.

18 Check the condition of the threads in the front mounting bracket captive nuts on the underbody. If necessary, use a tap to clean out the threads.

19 Support the axle on the trolley jacks, and

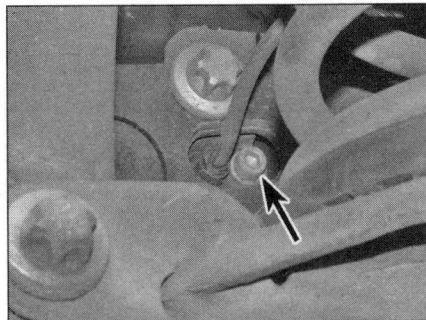

13.7 Rear wheel speed sensor retaining bolt

position the assembly under the rear of the vehicle.

20 Raise the jacks, and fit the new mounting bracket bolts. Do not fully tighten the bolts at this stage.

21 If the front mounting brackets have been removed from the axle, position the axle so that the distance between the upper edge of the shock absorber lower mounting bracket and the underbody chassis member directly above is 146.5 ± 10.0 mm. With the axle in this position, tighten the front mounting bracket through-bolt nuts on each side to the specified torque.

22 Fully tighten the front mounting bracket-to-underbody bolts to the specified torque and angle settings in the stages given.

23 Locate the upper and lower seats on the coil springs, then refit the springs to the axle and underbody.

24 Raise the torsion beam until the shock absorber lower mounting bolts can be inserted. Fit the nuts and tighten to the specified torque.

25 Refit the brake hydraulic pipes and flexible hoses together with the retaining clips and tighten the union nuts to the specified torque (see Chapter 9).

26 Reconnect the handbrake cables to the underbody supports and attach the front cable to the compensator plate.

27 Refit the ABS wheel speed sensors, tightening the retaining bolts to the specified torque (see Chapter 9). Clip the sensor wiring to the brake pipes.

28 Refit the exhaust system heat shield and secure with the bolt, nut and two clamps.

29 Refit the rear tailpipe and silencer as

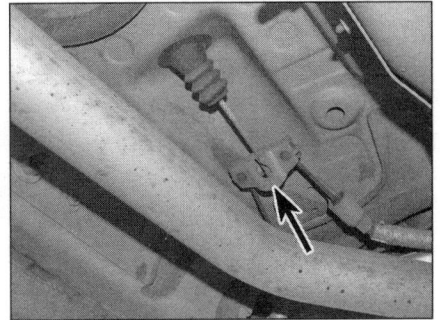

13.8 Detach the front handbrake cable from the compensator plate by twisting it through 90°

described in Chapter 4A, Section 13 or Chapter 4B, Section 20, as applicable.

30 Bleed the complete brake hydraulic system, as described in Chapter 9, Section 2.

31 Adjust the handbrake as described in Chapter 1A, Section 23 or Chapter 1B, Section 24, then refit the protective cap to the cable end and clip the gaiter to the centre console.

32 Refit the roadwheels and lower the vehicle to the ground.

14 Steering wheel – removal and refitting

⚠️ *Warning: Make sure that the airbag safety recommendations given in Chapter 12, Section 22 are followed, to prevent personal injury.*

Removal

1 Remove the airbag as described in Chapter 12, Section 23.

2 Set the front wheels in the straight-ahead position, then lock the column in position after removing the ignition key.

3 Disconnect the wiring harness connector for the steering wheel switches **(see illustration)**.

4 Unscrew the Torx retaining bolt securing the steering wheel to the column **(see illustration)**.

5 Check that there are alignment marks between the steering column shaft and steering wheel **(see illustration)**. If no marks

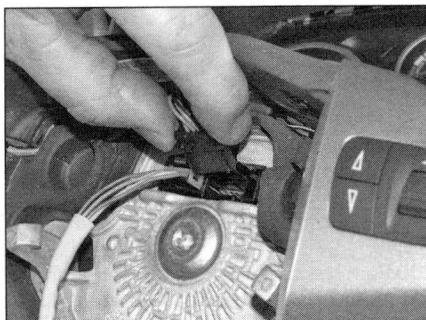

14.3 Disconnect the wiring harness connector for the steering wheel switches

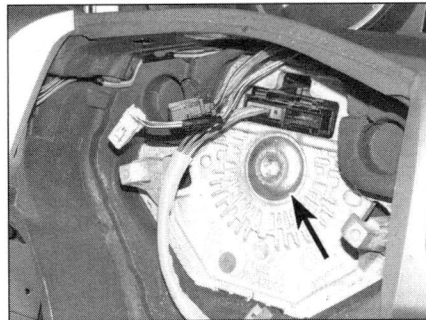

14.4 Unscrew the steering wheel retaining bolt

14.5 Alignment marks between the steering column shaft and steering wheel

16.9a Unscrew the steering column lower mounting bolts...

16.9b...and the upper mounting bolts

are visible, centre punch the wheel and column shaft to ensure correct alignment when refitting.

6 Grip the steering wheel with both hands and carefully rock it from side-to-side to release it from the splines on the steering column.

7 With the steering wheel loose on the splines, the retaining bolt can now be completely removed. As the steering wheel is being removed, guide the wiring for the airbag through the aperture in the wheel, taking care not to damage the wiring connectors.

Refitting

8 Refit the steering wheel, aligning the marks made prior to removal. Route the wiring connectors through the steering wheel aperture.

Note: *Make sure the steering wheel centre hub locates correctly with the contact unit on the steering column.*

9 Clean the threads on the retaining bolt and the threads in the steering column. Coat the retaining bolt with locking compound, then fit the retaining bolt and tighten to the specified torque setting.

10 Reconnect the wiring connector for the steering wheel switches.

11 Release the steering lock, and refit the airbag as described in Chapter 12, Section 23.

15 Ignition switch/ steering column lock – removal and refitting

1 The ignition switch, steering column lock and airbag rotary connector are an integral part of the steering column electronics module and cannot be individually removed.

2 Removal and refitting details for the steering column electronics module are contained in Chapter 12, Section 16.

16 Steering column – removal and refitting

Note: *The steering column also contains the electronic power steering (EPS) motor and electronic control unit. These components are*

an integral part of the column assembly and cannot be separated.

Note: *If a new steering column is to be fitted, this work must be entrusted to a Vauxhall/ Opel dealer or suitably-equipped specialist. It is necessary to initialise and calibrate the new electronic control unit after installation, which requires the use of dedicated diagnostic equipment.*

Removal

1 Disconnect the battery negative terminal (refer to *Disconnecting the battery* in Chapter 5A, Section 4).

2 From inside the car, remove the lower facia panel on the driver's side as described in Chapter 11, Section 26.

3 Working in the driver's footwell under the facia, remove the plastic expanding rivet and remove the footwell ait duct.

4 Set the front wheels in the straight-ahead position, then remove the ignition key and lock the column by turning the steering wheel as required.

5 Remove the steering wheel as described in Section 14 and the steering column electronics module as described in Chapter 12, Section 16.

6 Unscrew the two bolts securing the universal joint to the bottom of the steering column intermediate shaft and the steering gear pinion **(see illustration 7.2)**. Discard the bolts; new ones must be used on refitting. Slide the universal joint up the intermediate shaft to disengage it from the steering gear pinion.

17.6 Align the intermediate shaft upper retaining bolt with the access aperture in the EPS electronic control unit

7 If applicable, make sure the steering column adjustment handle is in the locked position.

8 Disconnect the wiring connector from the EPS control unit on the steering column.

9 Suitably support the column assembly, then und the two lower bolts and two upper bolts securing the column to the facia crossmember **(see illustrations)**.

10 Release the column assembly from its location and remove it from the vehicle. DO NOT release the steering lock while the steering column is off the vehicle.

Refitting

11 Refitting is a reversal of removal, bearing in mind the following points:

a) *Tighten all nuts and bolts to the specified torque.*

b) *When refitting the universal joint to the steering gear pinion and intermediate shaft, note that the components incorporate master splines and it will only be possible to fit the universal joint in one position. Apply thread-locking compound to the new universal joint retaining bolts when refitting.*

c) *Refit the steering column electronics module as described in Chapter 12, Section 16.*

d) *Refit the steering wheel as described in Section 14.*

e) *Refit the facia lower trim panel as described in Chapter 11, Section 26.*

17 Steering column intermediate shaft – removal, inspection and refitting

Removal

1 Disconnect the battery negative terminal (refer to *Disconnecting the battery* in Chapter 5A, Section 4).

2 From inside the car, remove the lower facia panel on the driver's side as described in Chapter 11, Section 26.

3 Working in the driver's footwell under the facia, remove the plastic expanding rivet and remove the footwell ait duct.

4 Set the front wheels in the straight-ahead position, then remove the ignition key and lock the column by turning the steering wheel as required.

5 Unscrew the two bolts securing the universal joint to the bottom of the steering column intermediate shaft and the steering gear pinion **(see illustration 7.2)**. Discard the bolts; new ones must be used on refitting. Slide the universal joint up the intermediate shaft to disengage it from the steering gear pinion.

6 Unlock the steering column with the ignition key and turn the steering wheel 90° anti-clockwise. Align the intermediate shaft upper retaining bolt with the access aperture in the EPS electronic control unit **(see illustration)**.

Unscrew the bolt then return the steering wheel to the straight-ahead position. Discard the bolt; a new one must be used on refitting. Remove the ignition key and lock the column once again.

7 Withdraw the intermediate shaft from the steering column and remove it from the vehicle.

Inspection

8 The steering column intermediate shaft incorporates a telescopic safety section, in the event of a front-end crash, the shaft shortens on the splines and prevents the steering wheel injuring the driver. Inspect the intermediate shaft universal joints for excessive wear or damage. If either joint is worn or damaged in any way, the complete shaft assembly must be renewed.

Refitting

9 Check that the front wheels and steering wheel are still in the straight-ahead position, and that the steering wheel is still locked.

10 Engage the intermediate shaft upper universal joint with the steering column noting that the square end of the universal joint will only engage with the column in one position.

11 Unlock the steering column and turn the steering wheel 90° anti-clockwise. Align the intermediate shaft upper retaining bolt hole with the access aperture and fit the new upper retaining bolt. Tighten the bolt to the specified torque using a torque wrench, then through the specified angle using an angle tightening gauge.

12 Return the steering wheel to the straight-ahead position, then remove the ignition key and lock the column once again.

13 Slide the lower universal joint down the intermediate shaft and engage it with the steering gear pinion. Note that the universal joint, intermediate shaft and steering gear pinion incorporate master splines and it will only be possible to fit the universal joint in one position.

14 Apply thread-locking compound to the threads of the new lower universal joint retaining bolts, fit the bolts and tighten to the specified torque.

15 Refit the footwell air duct and secure with the expanding rivet.

16 Refit the lower facia panel as described in Chapter 11 Section 26 then reconnect the battery.

18 Steering gear assembly – removal, inspection and refitting

Removal

1 Firmly apply the handbrake, then jack up the front of the car and support it securely on axle stands (see *Jacking and vehicle support*). Remove both front roadwheels.

2 Remove the front subframe as described in Section 7.

3 Slacken and remove the two bolts, nuts and washers securing the steering gear to the subframe, then remove the steering gear from the subframe. Discard the bolts, nuts and washers as new ones will be required when refitting.

4 If a new steering gear is to be fitted, then the track rod balljoints will need to be removed from each end of the steering track rod arms (see Section 20).

Inspection

5 Examine the steering gear assembly for signs of wear or damage, and check that the rack moves freely throughout the full length of its travel, with no signs of roughness or excessive free play between the steering gear pinion and rack. Check with your Vauxhall/Opel dealer to see if it is possible to overhaul the steering gear assembly. The only components which can be renewed easily by the home mechanic are the steering gear gaiters, the track rod balljoints and the track rods. Steering gear gaiter, track rod balljoint and track rod renewal procedures are covered in Sections 19, 20 and 21 respectively.

Refitting

6 Refitting is a reverse of the removal procedure, bearing in mind the following points:
a) *Use new nuts bolts and washers when refitting the steering gear to the subframe and tighten the nuts to the specified torque*
b) *Set the steering gear in the straight-ahead position prior to refitting the front subframe.*
c) *Refit the front subframe as described in Section 7.*
d) *On completion, have the front wheel alignment checked and, if necessary, adjusted – see Section 22 for general information.*

19 Steering gear rubber gaiters – renewal

1 Remove the track rod balljoint as described in Section 20.

2 Mark the correct fitted position of the gaiter on the track rod, then release the retaining clips **(see illustration)**, and slide the gaiter off the steering gear housing and track rod.

3 Thoroughly clean the track rod and the steering gear housing, clean off any corrosion, burrs or sharp edges which might damage the new gaiter's sealing lips on installation. Scrape off all the old grease, and apply new grease to the track rod inner balljoint.

4 Carefully slide the new gaiter onto the track rod, and locate it on the steering gear

19.2 Steering gear rubber gaiter outer securing clip

housing. Align the outer edge of the gaiter with the mark made on the track rod prior to removal, then secure it in position with new retaining clips.

5 Refit the track rod balljoint as described in Section 20.

20 Track rod balljoint – removal and refitting

Note: *A new track rod balljoint-to-swivel hub nut will be required when refitting.*

Removal

1 Firmly apply the handbrake, then jack up the front of the car and support it securely on axle stands (see *Jacking and vehicle support*). Remove the appropriate front roadwheel.

2 If the balljoint is to be re-used, use a scriber, or similar, to mark its relationship to the track rod.

3 Hold the track rod arm, and unscrew the balljoint locknut by a quarter of a turn **(see illustration)**.

4 Slacken and remove the nut securing the track rod balljoint to the swivel hub, and release the balljoint tapered shank using a universal balljoint separator **(see illustrations)**. Discard the nut; a new one must be used of refitting.

5 Counting the exact number of turns necessary to do so, unscrew the balljoint from the track rod arm.

20.3 Hold the track rod stationary while loosening the track rod balljoint securing locknut

20.4a Unscrew the nut securing the track rod balljoint to the steering arm...

20.4b...then disconnect the track rod balljoint from the steering arm using a balljoint separator tool

6 Count the number of exposed threads between the end of the track rod and the locknut, and record this figure. If a new gaiter is to be fitted, unscrew the locknut from the track rod.

7 Carefully clean the balljoint and the track rod threads. Renew the balljoint if there is excessive free play of the balljoint shank, or if the shank is excessively stiff. If the balljoint gaiter is damaged, the complete balljoint assembly must be renewed; it is not possible to obtain the gaiter separately.

Refitting

8 If it was removed, screw the locknut onto the track rod threads, and position it so that the same number of exposed threads are visible as was noted prior to removal.

9 Screw the balljoint on to the track rod by the number of turns noted on removal. This should bring the balljoint locknut to within approximately quarter of a turn from the locknut, with the alignment marks that were noted on removal.

10 Refit the balljoint shank to the swivel hub, then fit a new retaining nut and tighten it to the specified torque setting. If the balljoint stud turns as the nut is being tightened, press down on the track rod balljoint to force the tapered part of the stud into the arm on the swivel hub.

11 Tighten the track rod balljoint securing locknut on the track rod arm while holding the track rod arm stationary with a second spanner on the flats provided. Note: If possible tighten the nut to the specified torque using a special crow's-foot adaptor for the torque wrench.

12 Refit the roadwheel, then lower the vehicle to the ground and tighten the roadwheel bolts to the specified torque setting.

13 Have the front wheel alignment checked and if necessary, adjusted at the earliest

opportunity. See Section 22 for general information on wheel alignment

21 Track rod – renewal

Note: *When refitting, a new track rod balljoint-to-swivel hub nut and new gaiter retaining clips will be required. Vauxhall/Opel technicians use a special socket to tighten the track rod inner balljoint to the end of the steering rack.*

1 Remove the track rod balljoint as described in Section 20.

2 Release the retaining clips, and slide the steering gear gaiter off the end of the track rod (see Section 19).

3 Turn the steering on full lock, so that the rack protrudes from the steering gear housing on the relevant side, slide the cover (where fitted) off the inner balljoint.

4 Prevent the rack from rotating using an open-ended spanner located on the rack flats, then unscrew and remove the track rod inner balljoint from the end of the steering rack. Where fitted remove any spacers/washers noting the correct position for refitting.

5 Remove the track rod assembly, and examine the track rod inner balljoint for signs of slackness or tight spots. Check that the track rod itself is straight and free from damage. If necessary, renew the track rod; it is also recommended that the steering gear gaiter/dust cover is renewed.

6 Where applicable, locate the spacer on the end of the steering rack, and screw the balljoint into the end of the steering rack. Tighten the track rod inner balljoint to the specified torque, whilst retaining the steering rack with an open-ended spanner.

7 Install the steering gaiter and track rod balljoint as described in Sections 19 and 20.

22 Wheel alignment and steering angles – general information

Definitions

1 A car's steering and suspension geometry is defined in four basic settings – all angles are expressed in degrees (toe settings are also expressed as a measurement); the steering axis is defined as an imaginary line drawn through the axis of the suspension strut, extended where necessary to contact the ground.

2 Camber is the angle between each roadwheel and a vertical line drawn through its centre and tyre contact patch, when viewed from the front or rear of the car. Positive camber is when the roadwheels are tilted outwards from the vertical at the top; negative camber is when they are tilted inwards. Slight adjustment of the front camber angle is possible, by altering the position of the swivel hub at its attachment to the front suspension strut. The rear camber angle is not adjustable.

3 Castor is the angle between the steering axis and a vertical line drawn through each roadwheel's centre and tyre contact patch, when viewed from the side of the car. Positive castor is when the steering axis is tilted so that it contacts the ground ahead of the vertical; negative castor is when it contacts the ground behind the vertical. The castor angle is not adjustable.

4 Toe is the difference, viewed from above, between lines drawn through the roadwheel centres and the car's centre-line. 'Toe-in' is when the roadwheels point inwards, towards each other at the front, while 'toe-out' is when they splay outwards from each other at the front.

5 The front wheel toe setting is adjusted by screwing the track rod in or out of its balljoints, to alter the effective length of the track rod assembly. The rear wheel toe setting is not adjustable.

Checking and adjustment

6 Due to the special measuring equipment necessary to check the wheel alignment and steering angles, and the skill required to use it properly, the checking and adjustment of these settings is best left to a Vauxhall/Opel dealer or similar expert. Note that most tyre-fitting shops now possess sophisticated checking equipment.

Chapter 11
Bodywork and fittings

Contents

Degrees of difficulty

Easy, suitable for novice with little experience	Fairly easy, suitable for beginner with some experience	Fairly difficult, suitable for competent DIY mechanic	Difficult, suitable for experienced DIY mechanic	Very difficult, suitable for expert DIY or professional

Specifications

Torque wrench settings	Nm	lbf ft
Facia crossmember-to-A-pillar bolts	20	15
Front seat mounting bolts	35	26
Rear seat:		
Seat backrest-to-floor bolts	20	15
Seat cushion-to-floor bolts.	20	15
Seat belt anchorage bolts	35	26
Seat belt inertia reel bolt.	35	26
Seat belt tensioner bolts	35	26

1 General Information

1 The bodyshell is made of pressed-steel sections, and is available in three- and five-door Hatchback versions, and a Van version. Most components are welded together, but some use is made of structural adhesives; the front wings are bolted on.

2 The bonnet, doors, and some other vulnerable panels, are made of zinc-coated metal, and are further protected by being coated with an anti-chip primer, prior to being sprayed.

3 Extensive use is made of plastic materials, mainly on the interior, but also in exterior components. The front and rear bumpers are injection-moulded from a synthetic material which is very strong and yet light. Plastic components such as wheel arch liners are fitted to the underside of the vehicle, to improve the body's resistance to corrosion.

2 Maintenance – bodywork and underframe

1 The general condition of a vehicle's body-work is the one thing that significantly affects its value. Maintenance is easy, but needs to be regular. Neglect, particularly after minor damage, can lead quickly to further deterioration and costly repair bills. It is important also to keep watch on those parts of the vehicle not immediately visible, for instance the underside, inside all the wheel arches, and the lower part of the engine compartment.

2 The basic maintenance routine for the bodywork is washing – preferably with a lot of water, from a hose. This will remove all the loose solids which may have stuck to the vehicle. It is important to flush these off in such a way as to prevent grit from scratching the finish. The wheel arches and underframe need washing in the same way, to remove any accumulated mud, which will retain moisture and tend to encourage rust. Paradoxically enough, the best time to clean the underframe and wheel arches is in wet weather, when the mud is thoroughly wet and soft. In very wet weather, the underframe is usually cleaned of large accumulations automatically, and this is a good time for inspection.

3 Periodically, except on vehicles with a wax-based underbody protective coating, it is a good idea to have the whole of the underframe of the vehicle steam-cleaned, engine compartment included, so that a thorough inspection can be carried out to see what minor repairs and renovations are necessary. Steam-cleaning is available at many garages, and is necessary for the removal of the accumulation of oily grime, which sometimes is allowed to become thick in certain areas. If steam-cleaning facilities are not available, there are some excellent grease solvents available which can be brush-applied; the dirt can then be simply hosed off. Note that these methods should not be used on vehicles with wax-based underbody protective coating, or the coating will be removed. Such vehicles should be inspected annually, preferably just prior to Winter, when the underbody should be washed down, and any damage to the wax coating repaired. Ideally, a completely fresh coat should be applied. It would also be worth considering the use of such wax-based protection for injection into door panels, sills, box sections, etc, as an additional safeguard against rust damage, where such protection is not provided by the vehicle manufacturer.

4 After washing paintwork, wipe off with a chamois leather to give an unspotted clear finish. A coat of clear protective wax polish will give added protection against chemical pollutants in the air. If the paintwork sheen has dulled or oxidised, use a cleaner/polisher combination to restore the brilliance of the shine. This requires a little effort, but such dulling is usually caused because regular washing has been neglected. Care needs to be taken with metallic paintwork, as special non-abrasive cleaner/polisher is required to avoid damage to the finish. Always check that the door and ventilator opening drain holes and pipes are completely clear, so that water can be drained out. Brightwork should be treated in the same way as paintwork. Windscreens and windows can be kept clear of the smeary film which often appears, by the use of proprietary glass cleaner. Never use any form of wax or other body or chromium polish on glass.

3 Maintenance of upholstery and carpets – general

1 Mats and carpets should be brushed or vacuum-cleaned regularly, to keep them free of grit. If they are badly stained, remove them from the vehicle for scrubbing or sponging, and make quite sure they are dry before refitting. Seats and interior trim panels can be kept clean by wiping with a damp cloth. If they do become stained (which can be more apparent on light-coloured upholstery), use a little liquid detergent and a soft nail brush to scour the grime out of the grain of the material. Do not forget to keep the headlining clean in the same way as the upholstery. When using liquid cleaners inside the vehicle, do not over-wet the surfaces being cleaned. Excessive damp could get into the seams and padded interior, causing stains, offensive odours or even rot.

2 If the inside of the vehicle gets wet accidentally, it is worthwhile taking some trouble to dry it out properly, particularly where carpets are involved. Do not leave oil or electric heaters inside the vehicle for this purpose.

4 Minor body damage – repair

Minor scratches

1 If the scratch is very superficial, and does not penetrate to the metal of the bodywork, repair is very simple. Lightly rub the area of the scratch with a paintwork renovator, or a very fine cutting paste, to remove loose paint from the scratch, and to clear the surrounding bodywork of wax polish. Rinse the area with clean water.

2 Apply touch-up paint to the scratch using a fine paint brush; continue to apply fine layers of paint until the surface of the paint in the scratch is level with the surrounding paintwork. Allow the new paint at least two weeks to harden, then blend it into the surrounding paintwork by rubbing the scratch area with a paintwork renovator or a very fine cutting paste. Finally, apply wax polish.

3 Where the scratch has penetrated right through to the metal of the bodywork, causing the metal to rust, a different repair technique is required. Remove any loose rust from the bottom of the scratch with a penknife, then apply rust-inhibiting paint to prevent the formation of rust in the future. Using a rubber or nylon applicator, fill the scratch with bodystopper paste. If required, this paste can be mixed with cellulose thinners to provide a very thin paste which is ideal for filling narrow scratches. Before the stopper-paste in the scratch hardens, wrap a piece of smooth cotton rag around the top of a finger. Dip the finger in cellulose thinners, and quickly sweep it across the surface of the stopper-paste in the scratch; this will ensure that the surface of the stopper-paste is slightly hollowed. The scratch can now be painted over as described earlier in this Section.

Dents

4 When deep denting of the vehicle's bodywork has taken place, the first task is to pull the dent out, until the affected bodywork almost attains its original shape. There is little point in trying to restore the original shape completely, as the metal in the damaged area will have stretched on impact, and cannot be reshaped fully to its original contour. It is better to bring the level of the dent up to a point which is about 3 mm below the level of the surrounding bodywork. In cases where the dent is very shallow anyway, it is not worth trying to pull it out at all. If the underside of the dent is accessible, it can be hammered out gently from behind, using a mallet with a wooden or plastic head. Whilst doing this, hold a suitable block of wood firmly against the outside of the panel, to absorb the impact from the hammer blows and thus prevent a large area of the bodywork from being 'belled-out'.

5 Should the dent be in a section of the

bodywork which has a double skin, or some other factor making it inaccessible from behind, a different technique is called for. Drill several small holes through the metal inside the area – particularly in the deeper section. Then screw long self-tapping screws into the holes, just sufficiently for them to gain a good purchase in the metal. Now the dent can be pulled out by pulling on the protruding heads of the screws with a pair of pliers.

6 The next stage of the repair is the removal of the paint from the damaged area, and from an inch or so of the surrounding 'sound' bodywork. This is accomplished most easily by using a wire brush or abrasive pad on a power drill, although it can be done just as effectively by hand, using sheets of abrasive paper. To complete the preparation for filling, score the surface of the bare metal with a screwdriver or the tang of a file, or alternatively, drill small holes in the affected area. This will provide a really good 'key' for the filler paste.

7 To complete the repair, see the Section on filling and respraying.

Rust holes or gashes

8 Remove all paint from the affected area, and from an inch or so of the surrounding 'sound' bodywork, using an abrasive pad or a wire brush on a power drill. If these are not available, a few sheets of abrasive paper will do the job most effectively. With the paint removed, you will be able to judge the severity of the corrosion, and therefore decide whether to renew the whole panel (if this is possible) or to repair the affected area. New body panels are not as expensive as most people think, and it is often quicker and more satisfactory to fit a new panel than to attempt to repair large areas of corrosion.

9 Remove all fittings from the affected area, except those which will act as a guide to the original shape of the damaged bodywork (eg headlight shells etc). Then, using tin snips or a hacksaw blade, remove all loose metal and any other metal badly affected by corrosion. Hammer the edges of the hole inwards, in order to create a slight depression for the filler paste.

10 Wire-brush the affected area to remove the powdery rust from the surface of the remaining metal. Paint the affected area with rust-inhibiting paint, if the back of the rusted area is accessible, treat this also.

11 Before filling can take place, it will be necessary to block the hole in some way. This can be achieved by the use of aluminium or plastic mesh, or aluminium tape.

12 Aluminium or plastic mesh, or glass-fibre matting, is probably the best material to use for a large hole. Cut a piece to the approximate size and shape of the hole to be filled, then position it in the hole so that its edges are below the level of the surrounding bodywork. It can be retained in position by several blobs of filler paste around its periphery.

13 Aluminium tape should be used for small or very narrow holes. Pull a piece off the roll, trim it to the approximate size and shape required, then pull off the backing paper (if used) and stick the tape over the hole; it can be overlapped if the thickness of one piece is insufficient. Burnish down the edges of the tape with the handle of a screwdriver or similar, to ensure that the tape is securely attached to the metal underneath.

Filling and respraying

14 Before using this Section, see the Sections on dent, deep scratch, rust holes and gash repairs.

15 Many types of bodyfiller are available, but generally speaking, those proprietary kits which contain a tin of filler paste and a tube of resin hardener are best for this type of repair. A wide, flexible plastic or nylon applicator will be found invaluable for imparting a smooth and well-contoured finish to the surface of the filler.

16 Mix up a little filler on a clean piece of card or board – measure the hardener carefully (follow the maker's instructions on the pack), otherwise the filler will set too rapidly or too slowly. Using the applicator, apply the filler paste to the prepared area; draw the applicator across the surface of the filler to achieve the correct contour and to level the surface. As soon as a contour that approximates to the correct one is achieved, stop working the paste – if you carry on too long, the paste will become sticky and begin to 'pick-up' on the applicator. Continue to add thin layers of filler paste at 20-minute intervals, until the level of the filler is just proud of the surrounding bodywork.

17 Once the filler has hardened, the excess can be removed using a metal plane or file. From then on, progressively-finer grades of abrasive paper should be used, starting with a 40-grade production paper, and finishing with a 400-grade wet-and-dry paper. Always wrap the abrasive paper around a flat rubber, cork, or wooden block – otherwise the surface of the filler will not be completely flat. During the smoothing of the filler surface, the wet-and-dry paper should be periodically rinsed in water. This will ensure that a very smooth finish is imparted to the filler at the final stage.

18 At this stage, the 'dent' should be surrounded by a ring of bare metal, which in turn should be encircled by the finely 'feathered' edge of the good paintwork. Rinse the repair area with clean water, until all of the dust produced by the rubbing-down operation has gone.

19 Spray the whole area with a light coat of primer – this will show up any imperfections in the surface of the filler. Repair these imperfections with fresh filler paste or bodystopper, and once more smooth the surface with abrasive paper. Repeat this spray-and-repair procedure until you are satisfied that the surface of the filler, and the feathered edge of the paintwork, are perfect.

Clean the repair area with clean water, and allow to dry fully.

20 The repair area is now ready for final spraying. Paint spraying must be carried out in a warm, dry, windless and dust-free atmosphere. This condition can be created artificially if you have access to a large indoor working area, but if you are forced to work in the open, you will have to pick your day very carefully. If you are working indoors, dousing the floor in the work area with water will help to settle the dust which would otherwise be in the atmosphere. If the repair area is confined to one body panel, mask off the surrounding panels; this will help to minimise the effects of a slight mis-match in paint colours. Bodywork fittings (eg chrome strips, door handles etc) will also need to be masked off. Use genuine masking tape, and several thicknesses of newspaper, for the masking operations.

21 Before commencing to spray, agitate the aerosol can thoroughly, then spray a test area (an old tin, or similar) until the technique is mastered. Cover the repair area with a thick coat of primer; the thickness should be built up using several thin layers of paint, rather than one thick one. Using 400-grade wet-and-dry paper, rub down the surface of the primer until it is really smooth. While doing this, the work area should be thoroughly doused with water, and the wet-and-dry paper periodically rinsed in water. Allow to dry before spraying on more paint.

22 Spray on the top coat, again building up the thickness by using several thin layers of paint. Start spraying at one edge of the repair area, and then, using a side-to-side motion, work until the whole repair area and about 2 inches of the surrounding original paintwork is covered. Remove all masking material 10 to 15 minutes after spraying on the final coat of paint.

23 Allow the new paint at least two weeks to harden, then, using a paintwork renovator, or a very fine cutting paste, blend the edges of the paint into the existing paintwork. Finally, apply wax polish.

Plastic components

24 With the use of more and more plastic body components by the vehicle manufacturers (eg bumpers. spoilers, and in some cases major body panels), rectification of more serious damage to such items has become a matter of either entrusting repair work to a specialist in this field, or renewing complete components. Repair of such damage by the DIY owner is not really feasible, owing to the cost of the equipment and materials required for effecting such repairs. The basic technique involves making a groove along the line of the crack in the plastic, using a rotary burr in a power drill. The damaged part is then welded back together, using a hot-air gun to heat up and fuse a plastic filler rod into the groove. Any excess plastic is then removed, and

6.2a Undo the lower retaining bolt...

6.2b...and upper retaining bolt securing the lower corners and sides of the front bumper to the wheel arch liner

6.3 Unscrew the four bolts securing the top of the bumper to the bonnet lock platform

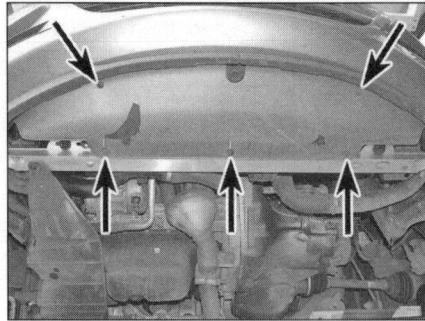
6.4 Unscrew the five bolts securing the lower reinforcement panel to the bumper and radiator crossmember

5 Major body damage repair – general

1 Where serious damage has occurred, or large areas need renewal due to neglect, it means that complete new panels will need welding-in, and this is best left to professionals. If the damage is due to impact, it will also be necessary to check completely the alignment of the bodyshell, and this can only be carried out accurately by a Vauxhall/ Opel dealer, using special jigs. If the body is left misaligned, it is primarily dangerous as the car will not handle properly, and secondly, uneven stresses will be imposed on the steering, suspension and possibly transmission, causing abnormal wear, or complete failure, particularly to such items as the tyres.

6 Front bumper – removal and refitting

Removal

1 Firmly apply the handbrake, then jack up the front of the car and support it securely on axle stands (see *Jacking and vehicle support*).
2 Unscrew the four bolts (two on each side) securing the lower corners and sides of the bumper to the wheel arch liner **(see illustrations)**.
3 Unscrew the four bolts securing the top of the bumper to the bonnet lock platform **(see illustration)**.
4 Unscrew the five bolts securing the lower reinforcement panel to the bumper and radiator crossmember **(see illustration)**.
5 Where applicable, disconnect the left-hand and right-hand foglight wiring connectors **(see illustration)**.
6 With the aid of an assistant, pull the bumper upward and outward at the sides to disengage the guide rails **(see illustration)**.
7 When sufficient clearance exists disconnect the wiring connector from the external temperature sensor, then remove the bumper from the car **(see illustration)**.

the area rubbed down to a smooth finish. It is important that a filler rod of the correct plastic is used, as body components can be made of a variety of different types (eg polycarbonate, ABS, polypropylene).
25 Damage of a less serious nature (abrasions, minor cracks etc) can be repaired by the DIY owner using a two-part epoxy filler repair material. Once mixed in equal proportions, this is used in similar fashion to the bodywork filler used on metal panels. The filler is usually cured in twenty to thirty minutes, ready for sanding and painting.
26 If the owner is renewing a complete component himself, or if he has repaired it with epoxy filler, he will be left with the problem of finding a suitable paint for finishing which is compatible with the type of plastic used. At one time, the use of a

universal paint was not possible, owing to the complex range of plastics encountered in body component applications. Standard paints, generally speaking, will not bond to plastic or rubber satisfactorily. However, it is now possible to obtain a plastic body parts finishing kit which consists of a pre-primer treatment, a primer and coloured top coat. Full instructions are normally supplied with a kit, but basically, the method of use is to first apply the pre-primer to the component concerned, and allow it to dry for up to 30 minutes. Then the primer is applied, and left to dry for about an hour before finally applying the special-coloured top coat. The result is a correctly-coloured component, where the paint will flex with the plastic or rubber, a property that standard paint does not normally possess.

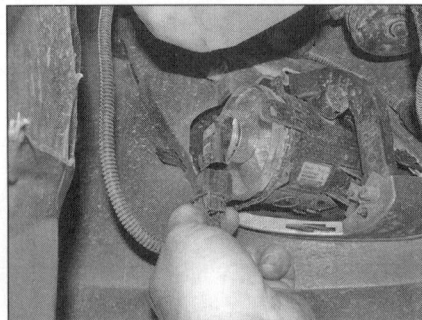
6.5 Where applicable, disconnect the foglight wiring connectors

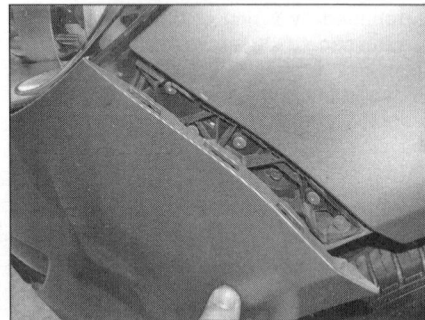
6.6 Pull the bumper upward and outward at the sides to disengage the guide rails

6.7 Disconnect the external temperature sensor wiring connector

7.3a Undo the lower retaining bolt...

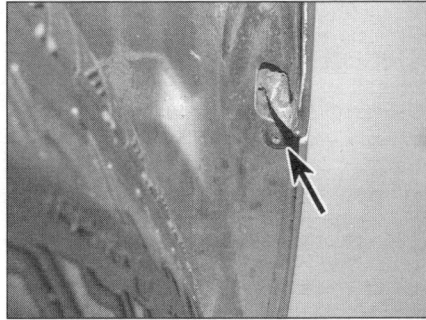
7.3b...and upper retaining bolt securing the lower corners and sides of the rear bumper to the wheel arch liner

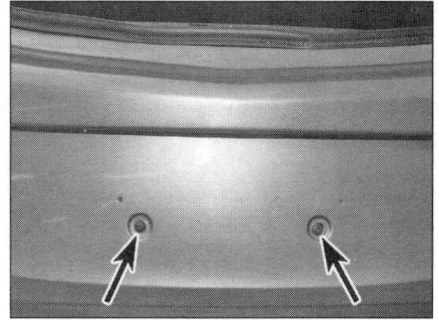
7.4 Undo the two bumper rear retaining screws in the number plate aperture

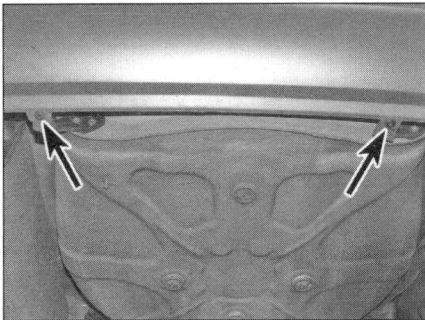
7.5 Undo the two bolts securing the bottom of the bumper to the vehicle body

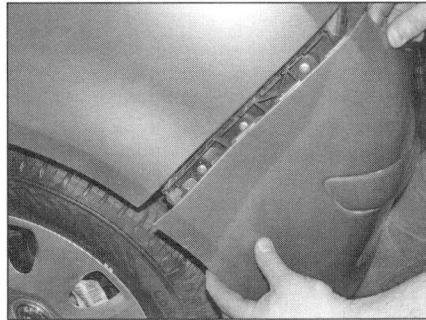
7.6 Pull the bumper upward and outward at the sides to disengage the side guide rails

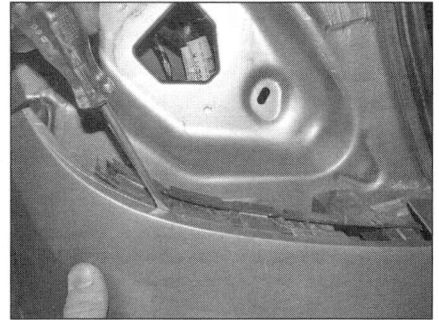
7.7 Pull the bumper rearwards and carefully disengage the rear guide rails and centre guide rails

Refitting

8 Refitting is a reversal of the removal procedure, ensuring that all bumper fasteners are securely tightened.

7 Rear bumper – removal and refitting

Removal

1 Remove the number plate lights and the rear light cluster on each side as described in Chapter 12, Section 7.
2 Remove the rear number plate.
3 Unscrew the four bolts (two on each side) securing the lower corners and sides of the bumper to the wheel arch liner (see illustrations).
4 Undo the two bumper rear retaining screws in the number plate aperture (see illustration).
5 Undo the two bolts securing the bottom of the bumper to the vehicle body (see illustration).
6 With the aid of an assistant, pull the bumper upward and outward at the sides to disengage the side guide rails (see illustration).
7 Pull the bumper rearwards and carefully disengage the rear guide rails and centre guide rails (see illustration).
8 On models with parking distance sensors, when sufficient clearance exists, disconnect the distance sensor main wiring connector from the underside of the bumper.

Refitting

9 Refitting is a reverse of the removal procedure, ensuring that all disturbed fasteners are securely tightened. Before finally bolting the bumper in position, ensure that any wiring is securely connected.

8 Bonnet – removal, refitting and adjustment

Removal

1 Open the bonnet, and have an assistant support it. It may be useful to mark the outline position of each bonnet hinge in relation to the bonnet (using a pencil or felt-tip pen), to use as a guide on refitting.

8.2 Bonnet-to-hinge retaining nuts

2 Undo the bonnet retaining nuts (see illustration) two each side, then with the help of an assistant, carefully lift the bonnet clear. Store the bonnet out of the way, in a safe place.
3 Inspect the hinge for signs of wear or damage. If hinge renewal is necessary, the lower hinge bolts (three each side) will need to be removed from the inner wing panel (see illustration). To gain access to the bolts, remove the windscreen cowl panel as described in Section 20.

Refitting

4 With the aid of an assistant, offer up the bonnet, and loosely fit the retaining bolts. Align the hinges with the marks made on removal, then tighten the retaining bolts securely.

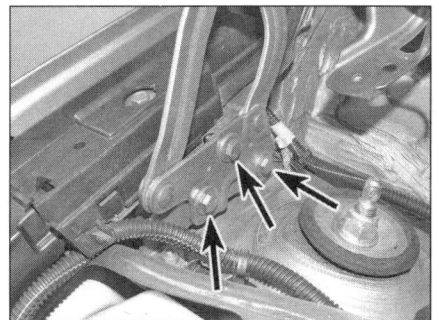
8.3 Bonnet hinge retaining bolts

9.4 Bonnet release lever retaining bolts

Adjustment

5 Close the bonnet, and check that there is an equal gap (approximately 4.0 mm) at each side, between the bonnet and the wing panels. Check also that the bonnet sits flush in relation to the surrounding body panels.
6 The bonnet should close smoothly and positively without excessive pressure. If this is not the case, adjustment will be required.
7 To adjust the bonnet alignment, loosen the bonnet-to-hinge mounting bolts, and move the bonnet on the bolts as required (the bolt holes in the hinges are enlarged). If necessary, the scissor-type hinge mounting bolts may be loosened as well. Access to the hinge retaining bolts can be gained after removing the windscreen cowl panel (see Section 20). To adjust the bonnet front height in relation to the front wings, adjustable rubber bump stops are fitted to the corners of the bonnet. These

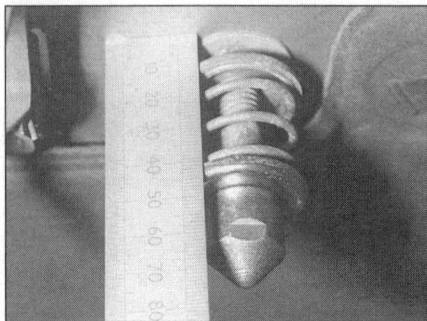
10.5 When refitting, adjust the position of the bonnet lock striker

10.7b...slide the other end off the release cable and remove the spring

may be screwed in or out as necessary. After making an adjustment, the bonnet striker must be adjusted so that the lock spring holds the bonnet firmly against the rubber bump stops. Loosen the locknut and screw the striker in or out as necessary.

9 Bonnet release cable – removal and refitting

Removal

1 Remove the windscreen cowl panel as described in Section 20.
2 Unscrew the clamp bolt from the bonnet lock platform and release the outer cable, then detach the inner cable from the lock spring.
3 From inside the car, remove the front sill trim panel on the left-hand side as described in Section 24.
4 Unclip the wiring harness from the bonnet release lever, then undo the two bolts securing the lever to the body (see illustration).
5 Release the cable from the support clips and brackets in the engine compartment, then release the cable grommet from the bulkhead. Withdraw the cable through the bulkhead and into the passenger compartment. As an aid to refitting, tie a length of string to the cable before removing it and leave the string in position ready for refitting.
6 Disconnect the other end of the cable from the release lever and remove the cable and lever from the car.

10.7a Disengage the bonnet lock spring leg from the bonnet lock platform...

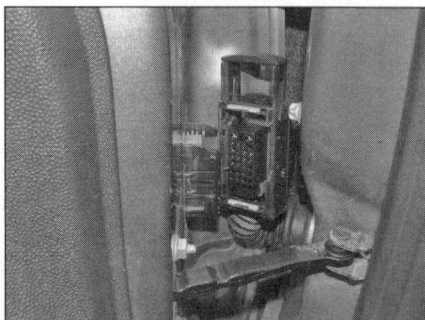
11.2 Lift up the locking bar and disconnect the wiring connector from the front edge of the door

Refitting

7 Refitting is a reversal of removal, but tie the string to the end of the cable, and use the string to pull the cable into position. Ensure that the cable is routed as noted before removal, and make sure that the grommet is correctly seated. On completion, refit the windscreen cowl panel and the sill trim panel as described in Sections 20 and 24.

10 Bonnet lock components – removal and refitting

Bonnet lock hook

1 Drill out the pivot pin, and remove the lock hook and return spring from the bonnet.
2 On refitting, locate the hook and spring in the bonnet bracket, and insert a new pivot pin. Secure the pin in position by flattening its end with a suitable pair of pliers.

Lock striker

3 Slacken the striker locknut, then unscrew the striker from the bonnet and recover the washer. If necessary, unscrew the locknut from the end of the striker, and remove the spring and spring seats.
4 Where necessary, fit the spring and spring seats to the striker, and screw on the locknut. Fit the washer to the striker, and screw the striker into position in the bonnet, tightening it only lightly at this stage.
5 Hold the locknut, and adjust the position of the striker so that the distance from the lower spring seat to the inside of the bonnet is 40 to 45 mm (see illustration).
6 When the striker is correctly positioned, securely tighten the locknut.

Lock spring

7 Unhook the bonnet release cable from the spring (see Section 9), then free the spring from the bonnet lock platform and remove it from the car (see illustrations).
8 On refitting, ensure that the spring is correctly engaged with the cable and lock platform. Check the operation of the bonnet release lever before shutting the bonnet.

11 Door – removal, refitting and adjustment

Front door

Removal

1 To remove a door, open it fully and support it under its lower edge on blocks or axle stands covered with pads of rag.
2 Lift up the locking bar and disconnect the wiring connector from the front edge of the door (see illustration).

11.3 Unscrew the Torx bolt securing the door check arm pivot to the A-pillar

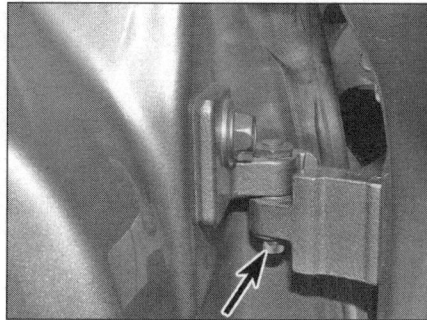

11.4a Door hinge upper retaining bolt...

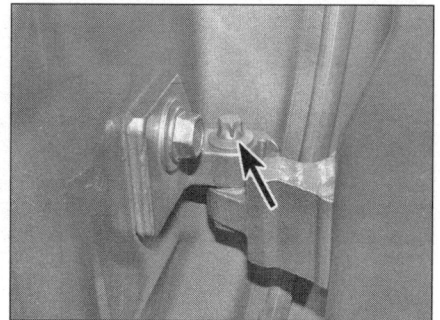

11.4b...and lower retaining bolt

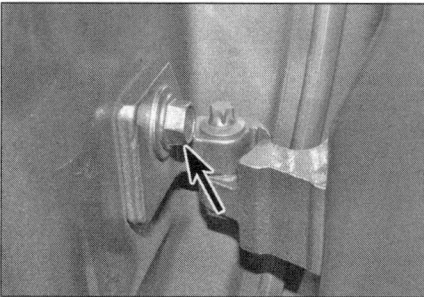

11.9 To adjust the door alignment, loosen the door-to-hinge mounting bolts and move the door as required

11.10 Front door lock striker on the B-pillar

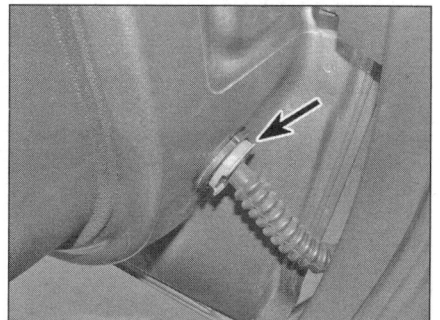

11.11 Disconnect the wiring connector from the front edge of the rear door

3 Unscrew the Torx bolt securing the door check arm pivot to the A-pillar **(see illustration)**.

4 Unscrew the upper and lower door hinge retaining bolts **(see illustrations)**.

5 With the help of an assistant, lift the door up and off the hinge pins. If renewing a door, transfer all the serviceable fixings to the new door.

Refitting

6 Refitting is a reversal of removal.

Adjustment

7 Close the door, and check that there is an equal gap (approximately 4.0 mm) all around the door. Check also that the door sits flush in relation to the surrounding body panels.

8 The door should close smoothly and positively without excessive pressure. If this is not the case, adjustment will be required.

9 To adjust the door alignment, loosen the door-to-hinge mounting bolts, and move the door on the bolts as required (the bolt holes in the hinges are enlarged) **(see illustration)**.

10 Door closure may be adjusted by altering the position of the lock striker on the body pillar, using an Allen key or a hexagon bit **(see illustration)**.

Rear door

Removal

11 Disconnect the wiring connector from the front edge of the door. To release the connector, slide the locking collar in, then carefully withdraw the wiring connector to

disconnect it from the front edge of the door **(see illustration)**.

12 Unscrew the Torx bolt securing the door check arm pivot to the B-pillar **(see illustration 11.3)**.

13 Unscrew the upper and lower door hinge retaining bolts **(see illustrations 11.4a and 11.4b)**.

14 With the help of an assistant, lift the door up and off the hinge pins. If renewing a door, transfer all the serviceable fixings to the new door.

Refitting

15 Refitting is a reversal of removal.

Adjustment

16 Refer to the information contained in paragraphs 7 to 10.

12.1 Carefully prise out the trim cap in the door interior handle aperture and undo the screw now exposed

12 Door inner trim panel – removal and refitting

Front door

Removal

1 Using a small screwdriver, carefully prise out the trim cap in the door interior handle aperture and undo the screw now exposed **(see illustration)**.

2 Where a manual window regulator is fitted, locate a cloth rag between the handle and the trim panel and pull it to one side to release the spring clip. Remove the handle and trim plate from the splined shaft and refit the spring clip to the handle **(see illustrations)**.

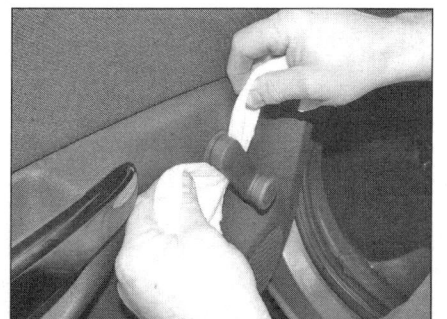

12.2a With a manual window regulator, locate a cloth rag between the handle and the trim panel and pull it to one side to release the spring clip...

12.2b...then remove the handle and trim plate from the splined shaft and refit the spring clip to the handle

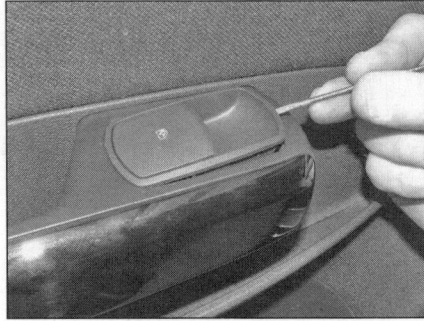

12.3a Where electric windows are fitted, unclip the window switch assembly from the door trim panel...

12.3b...then disconnect the wiring connector

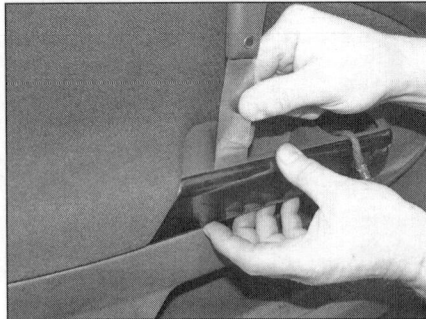

12.4 Using a plastic wedge or similar tool, carefully prise off the door grab handle plastic cover and undo the two screws now exposed

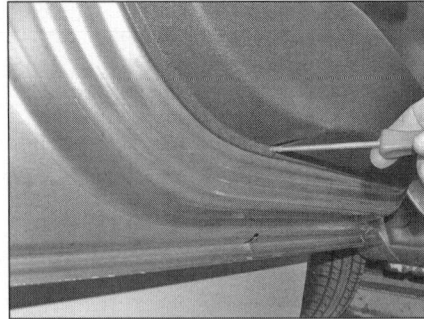

12.5a Undo the lower screw...

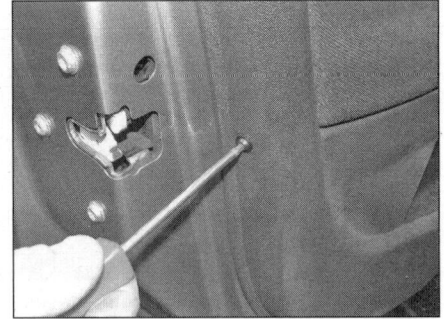

12.5b...and rear screw securing the edge of the trim panel to the door

3 Where electric windows are fitted, unclip the window switch assembly from the door trim panel, then disconnect the wiring connector **(see illustrations)**.

4 Using a plastic wedge or similar tool, carefully prise off the door grab handle plastic cover and undo the two screws now exposed **(see illustration)**.

5 Undo the lower screw and rear screw securing the edge of the trim panel to the door **(see illustrations)**.

6 Using a wide-bladed screwdriver or removal tool, carefully prise the bottom and sides of the panel away from door to release the internal clips. Lift the panel upward to release it from the window aperture.

7 Once the panel is free, reach behind and release the door lock operating cable from the interior handle. Disengage the inner cable end from the handle lever **(see illustration)**. Where fitted, disconnect the wiring connector from the tweeter speaker.

Refitting

8 Refitting is a reversal of removal.

Rear door

Removal

9 Where a manual window regulator is fitted, locate a cloth rag between the handle and the trim panel and pull it to one side to release the spring clip. Remove the handle and trim plate from the splined shaft and refit the spring clip to the handle **(see illustrations 12.2a and 12.2b)**.

10 Where electric windows are fitted, unclip the window switch assembly from the door trim panel, then disconnect the wiring connector **(see illustrations 12.3a and 12.3b)**.

11 Using a small screwdriver, carefully prise out the trim cap in the door interior handle aperture and undo the screw now exposed **(see illustration 12.1)**.

12 Using a plastic wedge or similar tool, carefully prise off the door grab handle plastic cover and undo the two screws now exposed **(see illustrations)**.

13 Using a wide-bladed screwdriver or removal tool, carefully prise the bottom and sides of the panel away from door to release the internal clips. Lift the panel upward to

12.7 Reach behind the panel and release the door lock operating cable from the interior handle

12.12a Using a plastic wedge or similar tool, carefully prise off the door grab handle plastic cover...

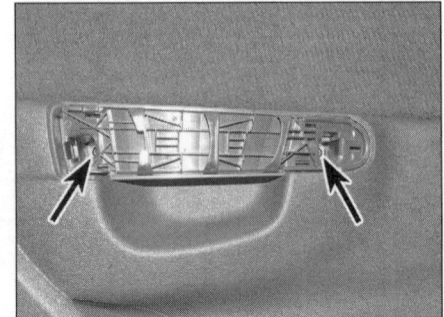

12.12b...and undo the two screws now exposed

release it from the window aperture **(see illustration)**.

14 Once the panel is free, reach behind and release the door lock operating cable from the interior handle. Disengage the inner cable end from the handle lever **(see illustration)**.

Refitting

15 Refitting is a reversal of removal.

13 Door handle and lock components – removal and refitting

Interior handle

Removal

1 The door interior handle is an integral part of the door inner trim panel and cannot be individually removed. If there are any problems with the interior handle, a new inner trim panel will be required.

Exterior handle

Removal

2 Open the door and carefully prise out the blanking cap from the rear edge of the door to gain access to the handle locking screw **(see illustration)**.

3 Pull the exterior door handle outwards and hold it in that position. With the exterior door handle held in the open position, turn the handle locking screw anti-clockwise until it reaches its stop **(see illustration)**. The exterior door handle should now be fixed in the open position.

4 Withdraw the fixed part of the handle from the door **(see illustration)**.

5 Slide the exterior door handle to the rear, disengage the front pivot from the handle frame and remove the handle from the door **(see illustration)**.

Refitting

6 Engage the handle front pivot with the frame and move the handle back into position.

7 Refit the fixed part of the handle to the door.

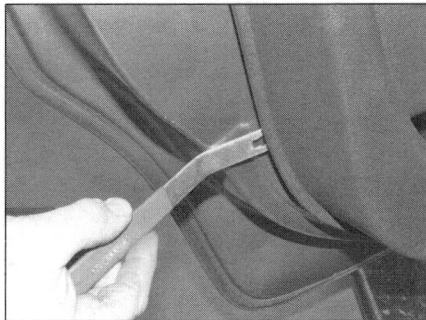
12.13 Using a wide-bladed screwdriver or removal tool, carefully prise the bottom and sides of the panel away from door

8 Hold the exterior handle and turn the handle locking screw clockwise to retain the handle.
9 Check the operation of the handle then refit the blanking cap to the edge of the door.

Lock cylinder

Removal

10 Remove the exterior handle as described previously in this Section.
11 Unclip the trim cap and remove the cap from the lock cylinder housing.
12 The lock cylinder body is an integral part of the housing and no further dismantling is possible.

Refitting

13 Refitting is a reversal of removal.

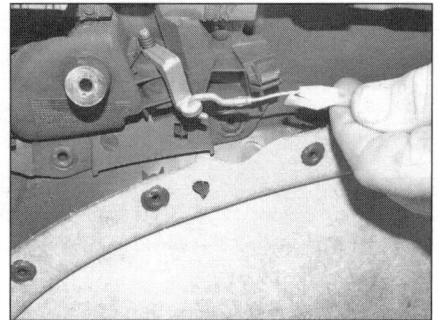
13.2 Open the door and carefully prise out the blanking cap from the rear edge of the door

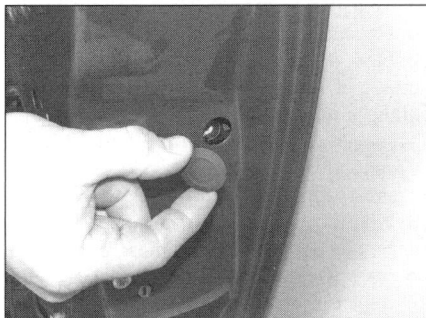
12.14 Once the panel is free, reach behind and release the door lock operating cable from the interior handle

Exterior handle frame

Removal

14 Disconnect the battery negative terminal (refer to *Disconnecting the battery* in Chapter 5A, Section 4).
15 Remove the door inner trim panel as described in Section 12.
16 Remove the exterior handle as described previously in this Section.
17 If working on the front door, remove the inner trim panel plastic guides from the door panel **(see illustration)**. Release the clips securing the wiring harness to the door.
18 Carefully peel back the protective plastic sheet and remove the sheet from the door **(see illustration)**.

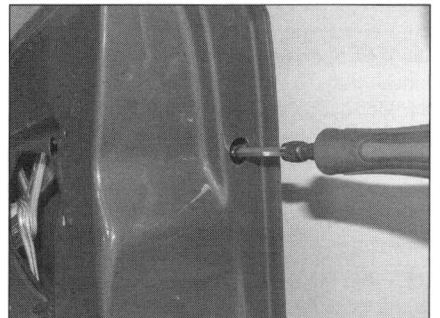
13.3 With the exterior door handle held open, turn the handle locking screw anti-clockwise until it reaches its stop

13.4 Withdraw the fixed part of the handle, containing the lock cylinder, from the door

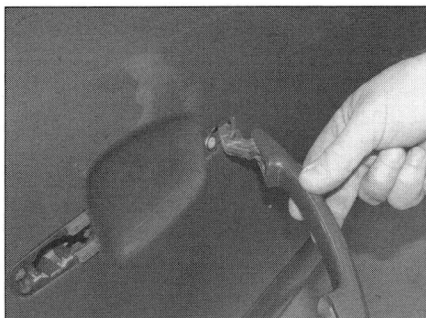
13.5 Disengage the exterior handle front pivot from the frame and remove the handle from the door

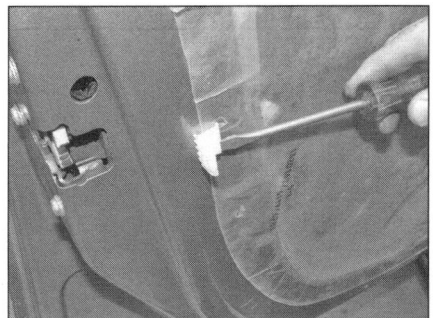
13.17 If working on the front door, remove the inner trim panel plastic guides from the door panel

13.18 Carefully peel back the protective plastic sheet and remove the sheet from the door

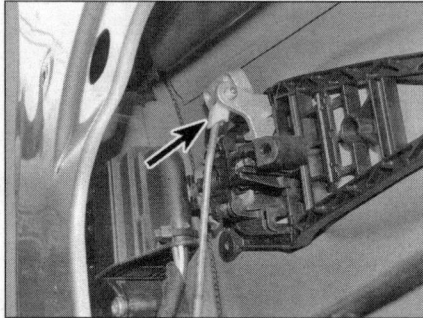

13.20 Release the retaining clip and disconnect the lock operating rod from the lever on the exterior handle frame

13.21a Undo the exterior handle frame front retaining screw and extract the rear guide clip...

13.21b...then slide the handle frame forward to release the rear locating lugs. Remove the frame through the door aperture

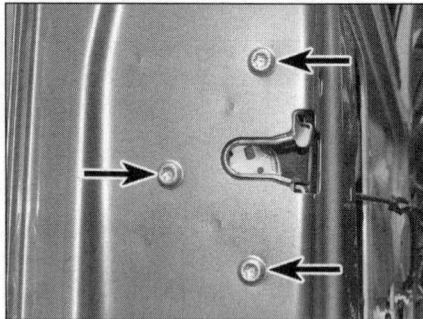

13.34 Undo the three screws securing the lock to the door

19 Where applicable, disconnect the two 'Open and Start' wiring harness connectors located on the exterior handle frame.

20 Release the retaining clip and disconnect the lock operating rod from the lever on the exterior handle frame **(see illustration)**.

21 Undo the exterior handle frame front retaining screw, extract the rear guide clip, then slide the handle frame forward to release the rear locating lugs. Remove the frame through the door aperture **(see illustrations)**.

Refitting

22 Place the exterior handle frame in position in the door. Refit the rear guide clip, then refit and tighten the front retaining screw securely.

23 Engage the lock operating rod with the lever on the exterior handle frame and push the retaining clip back into position on the rod.

24 Where applicable, reconnect the two 'Open and Start' wiring harness connectors.

25 Refit the protective plastic sheet to the door ensuring it is firmly stuck with no air bubbles. If the sheet was damaged during removal it should be renewed. This entails cutting a new sheet to the correct size and shape using the old sheet as a template. The new sheet can then be attached to the door with fresh adhesive.

26 Where applicable, refit the inner trim panel plastic guides and wiring harness clips to the door, ensuring they are firmly attached.

27 Refit the door inner trim panel (Section 12).

28 Refit the exterior handle as described previously in this Section, then reconnect the battery negative terminal.

Door lock

Removal

29 Disconnect the battery negative terminal (refer to *Disconnecting the battery* in Chapter 5A, Section 4).

30 Remove the door inner trim panel as described in Section 12.

31 If working on the front door, remove the inner trim panel plastic guides from the door panel **(see illustration 13.17)**. Release the clips securing the wiring harness to the door.

32 Carefully peel back the protective plastic sheet and remove the sheet from the door.

33 Release the retaining clip and disconnect the lock operating rod from the lever on the exterior handle frame **(see illustration 13.20)**.

34 Undo the three screws securing the lock to the door **(see illustration)**.

35 Withdraw the lock from its location, then lift the locking bar and disconnect the wiring connector **(see illustrations)**.

36 Remove the lock assembly through the door aperture.

Refitting

37 Refitting is a reversal of removal.

14 Door window glass and regulator – removal and refitting

Front door window glass

Removal

1 Open the door window fully.

2 Remove the door inner trim panel as described in Section 12.

3 Remove the inner trim panel plastic guides from the door panel **(see illustration 13.17)**.

4 Release the clips securing the wiring harness to the door.

5 Carefully peel back the protective plastic sheet and remove the sheet from the door **(see illustration 13.18)**.

6 Using a plastic wedge or similar tool, starting from the rear, tap up the door window

13.35a Withdraw the lock from its location...

13.35b...then lift the locking bar and disconnect the wiring connector

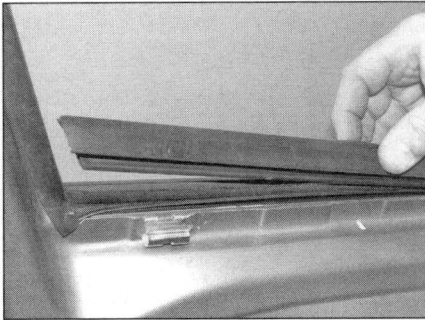

14.6 Using a plastic wedge or similar tool tap up the door window inner waist seal from the door aperture

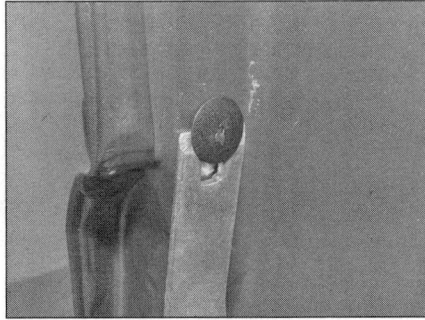

14.7a Extract the clip securing the door window outer waist seal to the door frame...

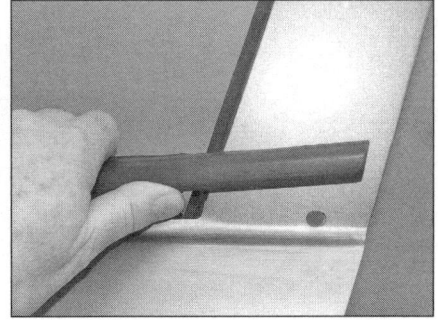

14.7b...starting from the rear, tap up the waist seal from the door aperture...

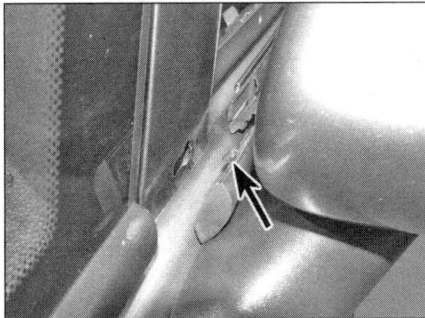

14.7c...lift the seal up, then slide it to the rear slightly to disengage the front locating lug

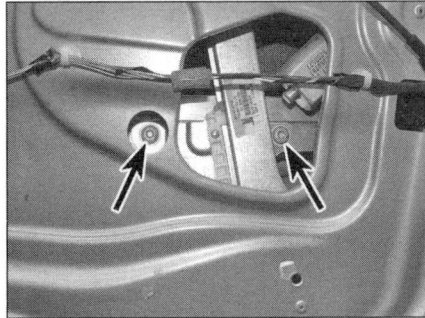

14.8a Undo the two bolts securing the window glass lower frame to the regulator (5-door models shown)...

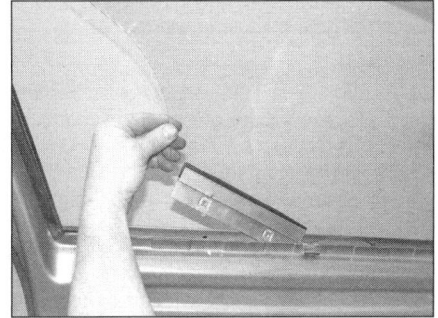

14.8b...then lift the glass up and out of the door

inner waist seal from the door aperture. Lift the seal up and remove it from the door (see illustration).

7 Extract the clip securing the door window outer waist seal to the door frame. Starting from the rear, tap up the waist seal from the door aperture. Lift the seal up, then slide it to the rear slightly to disengage the front locating lug (see illustrations).

8 Undo the two bolts (5-door models) or release the two clips (3-door models) securing the window glass lower frame to the regulator. Lift the glass up and out of the door (see illustrations).

Refitting

9 Carefully lower the window glass into the door and engage the lower frame with the regulator. Refit and tighten the two retaining bolts or attach the two clips, as applicable.

10 Refit the window inner and outer waist seals to the door aperture, ensuring that the retaining clips securely engage.

11 Refit the protective plastic sheet to the door ensuring it is firmly stuck with no air bubbles. If the sheet was damaged during removal it should be renewed. This entails cutting a new sheet to the correct size and shape using the old sheet as a template. The new sheet can then be attached to the door with fresh adhesive.

12 Refit the inner trim panel plastic guides and the wiring harness retaining clips.

13 Refit the door inner trim panel as described in Section 12.

Rear door window glass

Removal

14 Open the door window fully.

15 Remove the door inner trim panel as described in Section 12.

16 On models with manual window regulators, remove the rubber seal from the regulator shaft.

17 On models with electric window regulators, release the clips securing the wiring harness to the door.

18 Carefully peel back the protective plastic sheet and remove the sheet from the door (see illustration 13.18).

19 Using a plastic wedge or similar tool, starting from the rear, tap up the door

window inner waist seal from the door aperture. Lift the seal up and remove it from the door.

20 Similarly, starting from the rear, tap up the door window outer waist seal from the door aperture. Lift the seal up, then slide it to the rear slightly to disengage the front locating lug (see illustrations).

21 Undo the bolt securing the lower end of the window rear guide rail to the door. Pull the guide rail down to disengage the upper locating tongue, then remove the guide rail (see illustrations).

22 Pull the fixed window out of the guide channel and lift it out of the door (see illustration).

23 Release the two clips securing the window

14.20a Starting from the rear, tap up the rear door window outer waist seal from the door aperture...

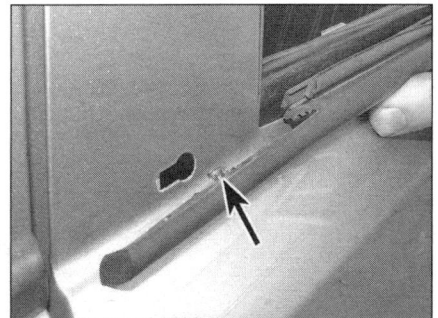

14.20b...then lift the seal up, and slide it to the rear slightly to disengage the front locating lug

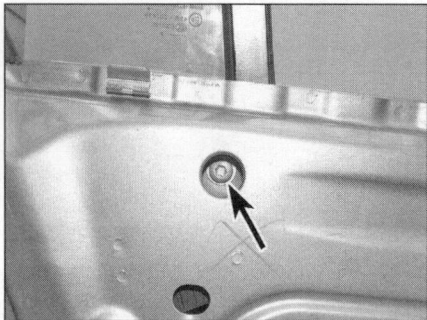

14.21a Undo the bolt securing the lower end of the window rear guide rail to the door...

14.21b...pull the guide rail down to disengage the upper locating tongue...

14.21c... then remove the guide rail

glass to the regulator and lift the glass up and out of the door **(see illustrations)**.

Refitting

24 Carefully lower the window glass into the door and secure the glass to the regulator with the two clips.

25 Locate the fixed window glass in the guide channel then refit the rear guide rail. Ensure that the upper end of the channel correctly engages with the upper locating tongue, then secure the lower end with the retaining bolt.

26 Refit the window inner and outer waist seals to the door aperture, ensuring that the retaining clips securely engage.

27 Refit the protective plastic sheet to the door ensuring it is firmly stuck with no air bubbles. If the sheet was damaged during removal it should be renewed. This entails cutting a new sheet to the correct size and

shape using the old sheet as a template. The new sheet can then be attached to the door with fresh adhesive.

28 Refit the wiring harness retaining clips or regulator shaft rubber seal, as applicable.

29 Refit the door inner trim panel as described in Section 12.

Rear door fixed window glass

Removal

30 Carry out the operations described previously in paragraphs 14 to 22.

Refitting

31 Carry out the operations described previously in paragraphs 25 to 29.

Front and rear window regulator

Note: *A pop-rivet gun and suitable rivets will*

be required when refitting. The rivet heads should be approximately 4.8 mm in diameter and 11 mm in length.

Removal

32 Remove the front or rear door window glass as described previously in this Section.

33 Where applicable, disconnect the wiring connector from the window regulator motor.

34 Using an 8.5 mm drill bit, drill out the four or five rivets (as applicable) securing the window regulator to the door, taking great care not to damage the door panel **(see illustration)**.

35 Remove the regulator through the door aperture.

36 Clean out the remains of the old rivets from inside the door.

Refitting

37 Refit the regulator to the door and secure the regulator with new pop rivets.

38 Reconnect the regulator wiring connector, where applicable.

39 Refit the front or rear door window glass as described previously in this Section.

---

15 Tailgate and support struts
– removal and refitting

Tailgate

Removal

1 Disconnect the battery negative terminal (refer to *Disconnecting the battery* in Chapter 5A, Section 4).

2 Open the tailgate, and detach the parcel shelf lifting cords from the tailgate.

3 Remove the C-pillar trim panel on the left-hand side, as described in Section 24.

4 Disconnect the tailgate wiring harness connector, then unclip the harness from the C-pillar.

5 Disconnect the tailgate washer hose at the connector adjacent to the wiring harness.

6 Release the rubber grommet from the roof frame and withdraw the wiring harness and washer hose from the roof **(see illustration)**.

7 Have an assistant support the tailgate, then

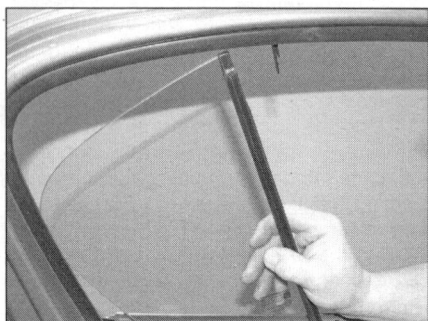

14.22 Pull the fixed window out of the guide channel and lift it out of the door

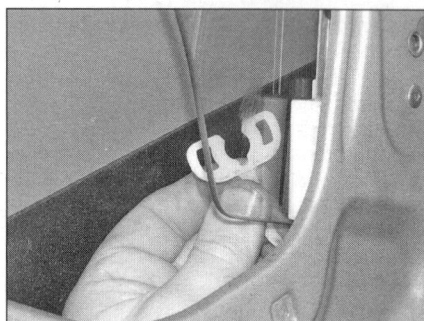

14.23a Release the two clips securing the window glass to the regulator...

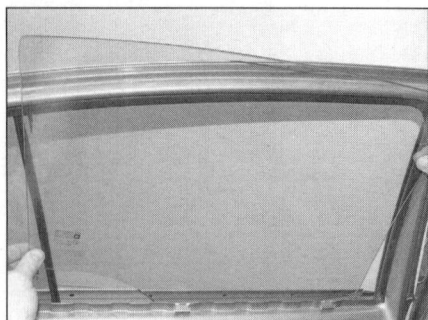

14.23b...and lift the glass up and out of the door

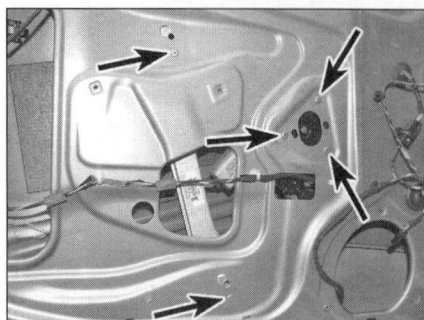

14.34 Door window regulator securing rivets – 5-door models shown

15.6 Release the rubber grommet from the roof frame and withdraw the wiring harness and washer hose from the roof

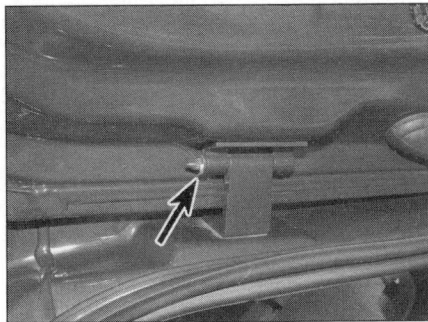
15.8 Extract the clips and carefully drive out the hinge pins from outside to inside

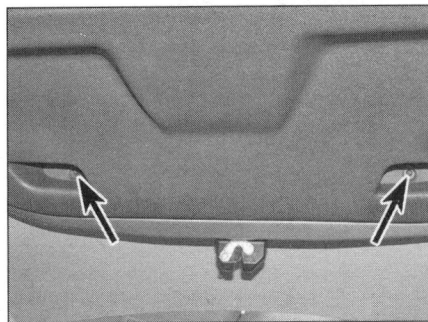
15.11 Prise the spring clip from the top of the strut and disconnect it from the ball on the tailgate

disconnect the tops of the support struts by prising out the spring clips with a small screwdriver. Lower the struts to the body.

8 Extract the clips and carefully drive out the hinge pins from outside to inside, using a small drift, while the assistant supports the tailgate (see illustration). Withdraw the tailgate from the body.

Refitting

9 Refitting is a reversal of removal, but apply a little grease to the pivots, and check that when closed the tailgate is positioned centrally within the body aperture and flush with the surrounding bodywork. If necessary, adjust the position of the rubber supports so that the tailgate is flush with the surrounding bodywork. After making adjustments, check that the striker enters the lock centrally and if necessary loosen the striker bolts to reposition it. Tighten the bolts on completion.

Support struts

Removal

10 Open the tailgate and note which way round the struts are fitted. Have an assistant support the tailgate in its open position.
11 Using a small screwdriver, prise the spring clip from the top of the strut and disconnect it from the ball on the tailgate (see illustration).
12 Similarly prise the spring clip from the bottom of the strut and disconnect it from the ball on the body. Withdraw the strut.

Refitting

13 Refitting is a reversal of removal.

16 Tailgate lock components – removal and refitting

Lock assembly

Removal

1 Disconnect the battery negative terminal (refer to *Disconnecting the battery* in Chapter 5A, Section 4).
2 Open the tailgate, and detach the parcel shelf lifting cords from the tailgate.
3 Undo the two screws securing the tailgate inner trim panel to the tailgate (see

illustration). Carefully prise the trim panel from the tailgate to release the eight retaining clips.
4 Undo the two lock assembly retaining screws (see illustration).
5 Withdraw the lock through the tailgate aperture and disconnect the wiring connector (see illustration).

Refitting

6 Refitting is a reversal of removal.

Exterior handle

Removal

7 Carry out the operations described in paragraphs 1 to 3.
8 Undo the two nuts, disconnect the wiring connector and remove the exterior handle from the tailgate (see illustration).

16.3 Undo the two screws securing the tailgate inner trim panel to the tailgate

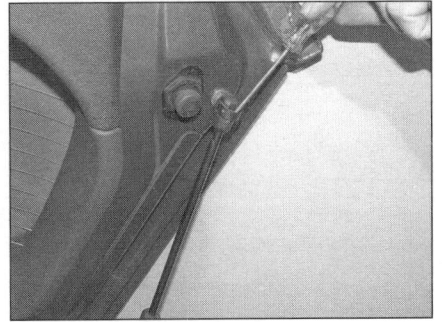
16.5 Withdraw the lock through the tailgate aperture and disconnect the wiring connector

Refitting

9 Refitting is a reversal of removal.

17 Exterior mirror and associated components – removal and refitting

Mirror assembly

Removal

1 Remove the door inner trim panel as described in Section 12.
2 Disconnect the mirror wiring harness at the connector on the inside of the door (see illustration).
3 Remove the mirror glass as described later in this Section.

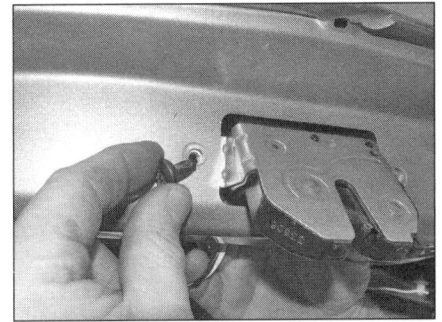
16.4 Undo the two lock assembly retaining screws

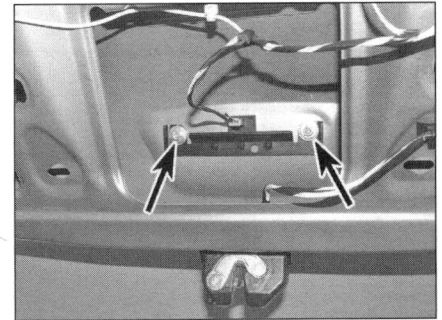
16.8 Undo the two nuts, disconnect the wiring connector and remove the exterior handle from the tailgate

17.2 Disconnect the mirror wiring harness at the connector on the inside of the door

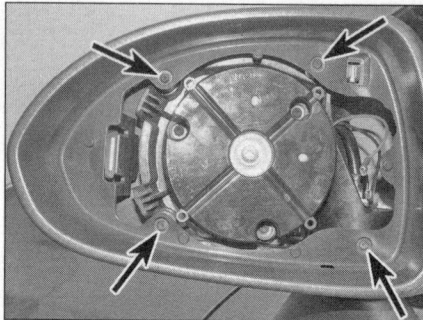

17.4 Undo the four screws securing the rear part of the mirror housing to the mirror body

17.5a Release the inner clips...

17.5b...and outer clips...

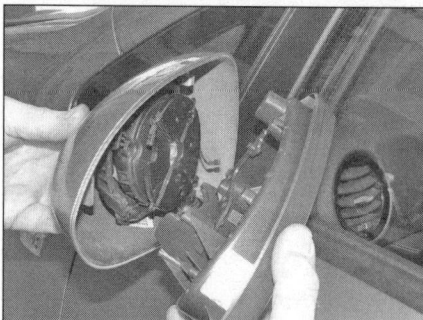

17.5c...and remove the rear part of the mirror housing from the mirror body

6 Release the clips and remove the front part of the mirror housing from the mirror body **(see illustration)**.

7 Tie a suitable length of string to the mirror wiring harness connector inside the door. This can be used to draw the wiring harness back into position when refitting.

8 Undo the bolt securing the mirror body to the door. Release the mirror wiring harness grommet by pushing it inside the door, then withdraw the mirror body, complete with wiring harness and grommet, from the door **(see illustrations)**. When the end of the wiring harness appears, untie the string and leave it in position in the door ready for refitting.

Refitting

9 Tie the string to the end of the wiring harness, and pull the harness back into the inside of the door.

10 Locate the mirror body in position, then fit and securely tighten the retaining bolt.

11 Clip the front part of the mirror housing in position, followed by the rear part. Secure the rear part to the mirror body with the four retaining screws.

12 Refit the mirror glass as described later in this Section.

13 Reconnect the mirror wiring harness connector and ensure that the grommet is correctly seated in the door.

14 Refit the door inner trim panel as described in Section 12.

Mirror glass

Removal

15 Push in the upper inner (nearest the door) corner of the glass so that the lower outer corner of the glass is forced out from the centre.

16 Using a plastic wedge, prise the outer edge of the glass outwards to release the internal retaining clips **(see illustration)**.

17 Withdraw the mirror glass and disconnect the wiring connectors **(see illustration)**.

Refitting

18 Refitting is a reversal of removal. Carefully press the mirror glass into the housing until the centre retainer clips are engaged.

4 Undo the four screws securing the rear part of the mirror housing to the mirror body **(see illustration)**.

5 Release the three clips and remove the rear part of the mirror housing from the mirror body **(see illustrations)**.

17.6 Release the clips and remove the front part of the mirror housing from the mirror body

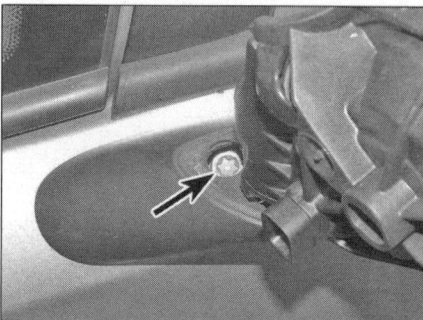

17.8a Undo the bolt securing the mirror body to the door...

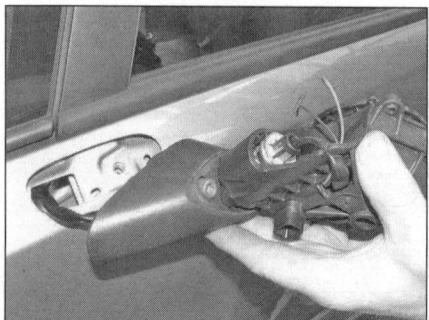

17.8b...then withdraw the mirror body, complete with wiring harness and grommet, from the door

17.16 Using a plastic wedge, prise the outer edge of the glass outwards to release the internal retaining clips

Mirror housing

Removal

19 Remove the mirror glass as described earlier in this Section.

20 Undo the four screws securing the rear part of the mirror housing to the mirror body **(see illustration 17.4)**.

21 Release the three clips and remove the rear part of the mirror housing from the mirror body **(see illustrations 17.5a to 17.5c)**.

22 Release the clips and remove the front part of the mirror housing from the mirror body **(see illustration 17.6)**.

Refitting

23 Refitting is a reversal of removal.

Mirror switch

24 Refer to Chapter 12, Section 4.

---

18 Windscreen, tailgate and fixed window glass – general information

1 The windscreen, tailgate and fixed window glasses are cemented in position with a special adhesive and require the use of specialist equipment for their removal and refitting. Renewal of such fixed glass is considered beyond the scope of the home mechanic. Owners are strongly advised to have the work carried out by one of the many specialist windscreen fitting specialists.

---

19 Sunroof – general information

1 An electric sunroof was offered as an optional extra on most models, and is fitted as standard equipment on some models.

2 Due to the complexity of the sunroof mechanism, considerable expertise is needed to repair, renew or adjust the sunroof components successfully. Removal of the roof first requires the headlining to be removed, which is a complex and tedious operation in itself, and not a task to be undertaken lightly. Therefore, any problems with the sunroof should be referred to a Vauxhall/Opel dealer.

---

20 Body exterior fittings – removal and refitting

Radiator grille

1 Remove the front bumper as described in Section 6. The radiator grille can now be removed after disengaging the nineteen

17.17 Withdraw the mirror glass and disconnect the wiring connectors

fasteners. Clip the grille back into the bumper to refit.

Wheel arch liners and body under-panels

2 The various plastic covers fitted to the underside of the vehicle are secured in position by a mixture of screws, nuts and retaining clips, and removal will be fairly obvious on inspection. Work methodically around the liner/panel, removing its retaining screws and releasing its retaining clips until it is free to be removed from the underside of the vehicle. Most clips used on the vehicle, with the exception of the fasteners which are used to secure the wheel arch liners, are simply prised out of position. The wheel arch liner clips

20.4 Pull up the rubber weatherseal from the flange at the rear of the engine compartment

20.7 Lift the cowl panel upper section up and disengage it from the windscreen guide

are released by tapping their centre pins through the clip, and then removing the outer section of the clip; new clips will be required on refitting if the centre pins are not recovered.

3 When refitting, renew any retaining clips that may have been broken on removal, and ensure that the panel is securely retained by all the relevant clips, nuts and screws. Vauxhall/Opel also recommend that plastic nuts (where used) are renewed, regardless of their apparent condition, whenever they are disturbed.

Windscreen cowl panel

4 Open the bonnet and pull up the rubber weatherseal from the flange at the rear of the engine compartment **(see illustration)**.

5 Remove the windscreen wiper arms as described in Chapter 12, Section 12.

6 Undo the two screws securing the cowl panel upper section to the lower section **(see illustration)**.

7 Lift the cowl panel upper section up and disengage it from the windscreen guide **(see illustration)**.

8 Disconnect the windscreen washer hose at the connector on the underside of the cowl panel and remove the panel from the car **(see illustration)**.

9 Extract the two plastic rivets and remove the support brace from the cowl panel lower section and windscreen flange **(see illustration)**.

20.6 Undo the two screws securing the cowl panel upper section to the lower section

20.8 Disconnect the windscreen washer hose and remove the panel from the car

20.9 Extract the two plastic rivets and remove the support brace from the cowl panel lower section and windscreen flange

20.10a Unscrew the bolts securing the cowl panel lower section to the scuttle (two of six shown)...

20.10b...then withdraw the windscreen washer hose and remove the panel lower section from the car

10 Unscrew the six bolts securing the cowl panel lower section to the scuttle. Withdraw the windscreen washer hose from panel lower section and remove the lower section from the car (see illustrations).

11 Refit the two sections of the cowl panel using the reversal of removal.

Body trim strips and badges

12 The various body trim strips and badges are held in position with a special adhesive tape. Removal requires the trim/badge to be heated, to soften the adhesive, and then cut away from the surface. Due to the high risk of damage to the vehicle's paintwork during this operation, it is recommended that this task should be entrusted to a Vauxhall/Opel dealer.

21 Seats –
removal and refitting

⚠️ **Warning: The front seats are equipped with seat belt tensioners, and side airbags may be built into the outer sides of the seats. The seat belt tensioners and side airbags may cause injury if triggered accidentally. If the tensioner has been triggered due to a sudden impact or accident, the unit must be renewed, as it cannot be reset. If a seat is to be disposed of, the tensioner must be triggered before the seat is removed from the vehicle.**

Due to safety considerations, this work must be entrusted to a Vauxhall/Opel dealer. Where side airbags are fitted, refer to Chapter 12, Section 22 for the precautions which should be observed when dealing with an airbag system.

1 Disconnect the battery negative terminal (refer to *Disconnecting the battery* in Chapter 5A, Section 4). Wait 2 minutes for the capacitors to discharge before working on the seat electrics.

Front seat removal

2 Slide the seat adjustment fully to the rear.
3 Slacken and remove the seat retaining bolts from the front of the seat guide rails (see illustration).
4 Slide the seat fully forwards, then slacken and remove the seat retaining bolts from rear of the guide rails (see illustrations).
5 Pull out the locking bar and disconnect the wiring connector from the underside of the seat, then remove the seat from the car (see illustration).

Rear seat removal

Cushion

6 Unclip and remove the rear side sill trim panels at the base of the seat cushion on each side.
7 Unclip and remove the covers over the three seat mounting brackets at the lower front of the cushion. Unscrew the three cushion mounting bolts (see illustrations).

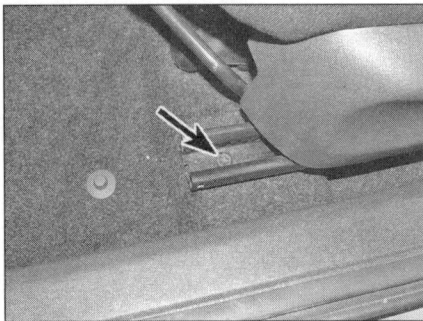

21.3 Front seat front outer retaining bolt

21.4a Front seat rear outer retaining bolt...

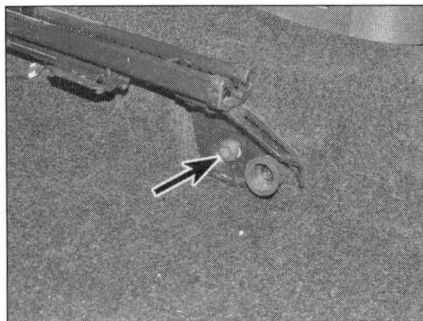

21.4b...and rear inner retaining bolt

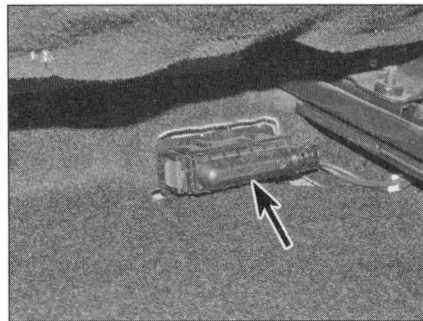

21.5 Pull out the locking bar and disconnect the wiring connector from the underside of the seat

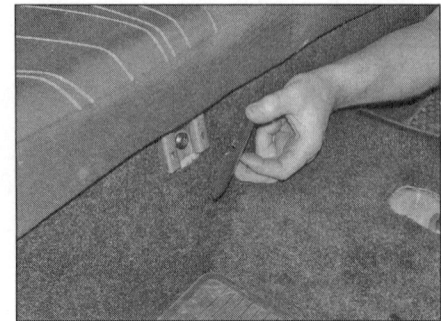

21.7a Unclip and remove the trim covers...

21.7b...then unscrew the rear seat cushion mounting bolts

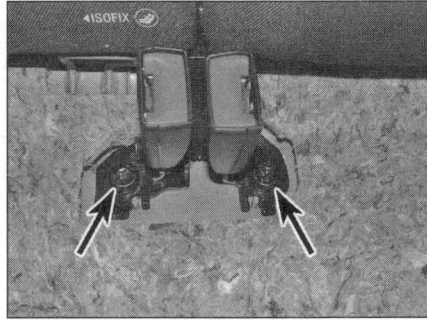

21.10 Rear seat backrest front mounting bolts

21.11 Unclip the hinge access panels from the luggage compartment trim panels

8 Push the seat cushion to the rear and lift it upwards to disengage the rear guides.

Backrest

9 Remove the rear seat cushion as described previously in this Section.
10 Unscrew the single bolt (one-piece backrest) or three bolts (two-piece backrest) securing the seat belt and backrest mounting(s) at the front **(see illustration)**.
11 Fold the backrest forward and unclip the hinge access panels from the luggage compartment trim panels on both sides **(see illustration)**.
12 With the help of an assistant, press the outer hinge pin locking collars in, using a screwdriver, to free the hinge pins on each side, while at the same time pulling upward to release the backrest. Remove the backrest from the car.
13 To separate the two-piece backrest, unzip the upholstery at the centre of the left-hand side backrest to expose the hinge retaining bolts **(see illustration)**.
14 Undo the two bolts and remove the right-hand side backrest and hinge from the left-hand side backrest **(see illustration)**.

Front seat refitting

15 Refitting is a reverse of the removal procedure, noting the following points:
a) *Remove all traces of old thread-locking compound from the threads of the seat retaining bolts, and clean the threaded holes in the vehicle floor, ideally by running a tap of the correct size and pitch down them.*
b) *Apply a suitable thread-locking compound to the threads of the seat bolts. Refit the bolts, and tighten them to the specified torque setting.*
c) *Reconnect the seat wiring block connector making sure it has locked securely, then reconnect the battery negative terminal.*

Rear seat refitting

16 Refitting is a reverse of the removal procedure, tightening the seat mounting bolts to the specified torque.

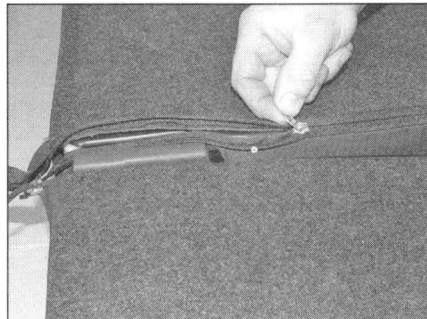

21.13 Unzip the upholstery at the centre of the left-hand side backrest to expose the hinge retaining bolts

22 Front seat belt tensioning mechanism – general information

1 All models covered in this manual are fitted with a front seat belt pyrotechnic tensioner system. The system is designed to instantaneously take up any slack in the seat belt in the case of a sudden frontal impact, therefore reducing the possibility of injury to the front seat occupants. Each front seat belt is fitted with two tensioner units; one mounted on the seat frame attached to the seat belt buckle, and one mounted on the body attached to the seat belt lower mounting.
2 The seat belt tensioner is triggered by a frontal impact causing a deceleration of six

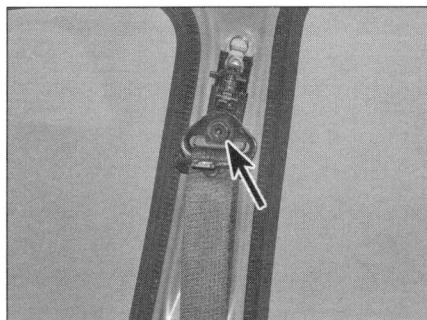

23.3 Front seat belt upper mounting bolt

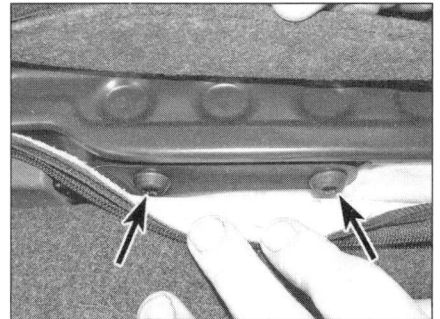

21.14 Undo the two bolts and remove the right-hand backrest and hinge from the left-hand backrest

times the force of gravity or greater. Lesser impacts, including impacts from behind, will not trigger the system.
3 When the system is triggered, a pretensioned spring in each tensioner unit draws back the seat belt via a cable which acts on the seat belt stalk or seat belt lower mounting. The cable can move up to 80.0 mm, which therefore reduces the slack in the seat belt around the shoulders and waist of the occupant by a similar amount.
4 There is a risk of injury if the system is triggered inadvertently when working on the vehicle, and it is therefore strongly recommended that any work involving the seat belt tensioner system is entrusted to a Vauxhall/Opel dealer. Refer to the warning given at the beginning of Section 21 before contemplating any work on the front seats.

23 Seat belt components – removal and refitting

Front belt and reel

Removal

1 On 3-door models, remove the B-pillar lower trim panel as described in Section 24.
2 On 5-door models, remove the side sill trim panel and B-pillar upper trim panel as described in Section 24.
3 Undo the seat belt upper mounting bolt **(see illustration)**.

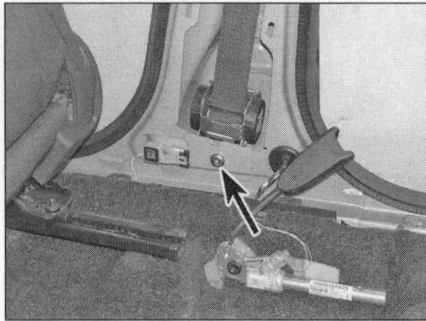

23.4 Front seat belt inertia reel mounting bolt

4 Undo the inertia reel mounting bolt and remove the reel and seat belt from the B-pillar (see illustration).

Refitting

5 Refitting is a reversal of removal, but tighten the mounting bolts to the specified torque.

Front belt stalk and inner tensioner

Removal

6 Remove the front seat as described in Section 21.

7 From underneath the seat, open the clamps and disconnect the tensioner wiring harness from the connector socket. Unclip the wiring harness from the seat.

8 Undo the retaining bolt and withdraw the tensioner from the seat.

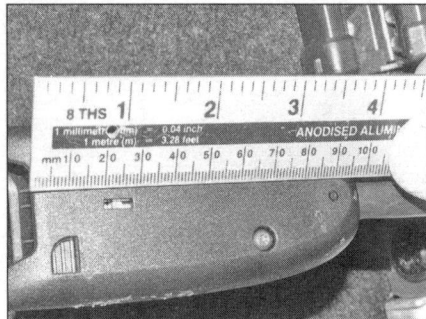

23.13a Measure down approximately 22 mm from the upper edge of the belt tensioner stalk and pierce the stalk protective sheath

23.17a Rear seat belt upper mounting bolt...

Refitting

9 Refitting is a reversal of removal, but tighten the tensioner retaining bolt to the specified torque.

Front belt outer tensioner

Removal

10 Disconnect the battery negative terminal (refer to *Disconnecting the battery* in Chapter 5A, Section 4).

11 On 3-door models, remove the B-pillar lower trim panel as described in Section 24.

12 On 5-door models, remove the side sill front trim panel as described in Section 24.

13 Disconnect the lower end of the seat belt from the tensioner stalk. To do this measure down approximately 22 mm from the upper edge of the tensioner stalk and pierce the stalk protective sheath with a small screwdriver. Push the screwdriver through the pierced hole and depress the locking catch. With the catch depressed, pull the seat belt out of the stalk (see illustrations).

14 Disconnect the tensioner wiring connector, then undo the retaining bolt and remove the tensioner from the sill.

Refitting

15 Refitting is a reversal of removal, but tighten the tensioner retaining bolt to the specified torque.

Rear outer belt and reel

Removal

16 Remove the relevant luggage

23.13b Push a screwdriver through the pierced hole and depress the tensioner stalk locking catch

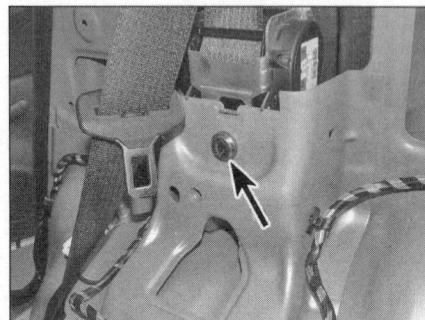

23.17b...and the inertia reel mounting bolt

compartment side trim panels as described in Section 24.

17 Undo the seat belt upper mounting bolt and the inertia reel mounting bolt and remove the reel and belt from the car (see illustrations).

Refitting

18 Refitting is a reversal of removal, but tighten the mounting bolts to the specified torque.

Rear centre belt and reel

19 The inertia reel for the centre rear seat belt is located internally within the rear seat backrest. To gain access, the backrest must be removed and completely dismantled. This is a complex operation and considerable expertise is needed to remove and refit the seat upholstery and internal components without damage. Therefore, any problems with the centre seat belt and reel should be referred to a Vauxhall/Opel dealer.

Rear belt stalk

Removal

20 Remove the rear seat cushion as described in Section 21.

21 Undo the retaining bolt and remove the relevant stalk from the floor (see illustration).

Refitting

22 Refitting is a reversal of removal, but tighten the mounting bolts to the specified torque.

24 Interior trim – removal and refitting

1 The interior trim panels are secured by a combination of clips and screws. Removal and refitting is generally self-explanatory, noting that it may be necessary to remove or loosen surrounding panels to allow a particular panel to be removed. The following paragraphs describe the general removal and refitting details of the major panels on Hatchback models. The procedures are generally similar on Van models, although some differences will be encountered in the load compartment area.

23.21 Undo the retaining bolt and remove the relevant rear seat belt stalk from the floor

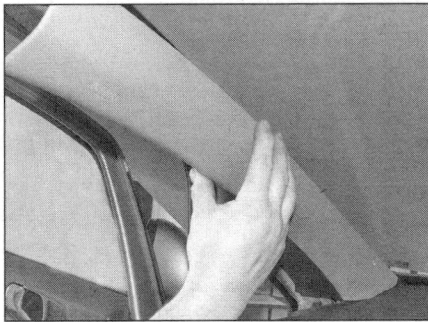
24.2 Pull the trim panel away from the A-pillar to release the two retaining clips

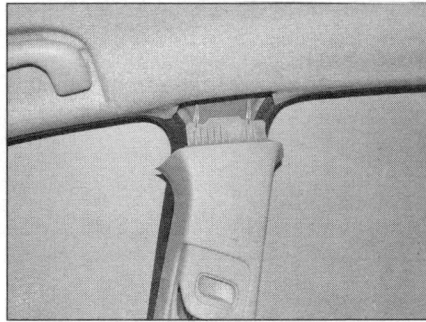
24.8 Prise the centre of the trim panel away from the B-pillar, then disengage the locating lugs at the top

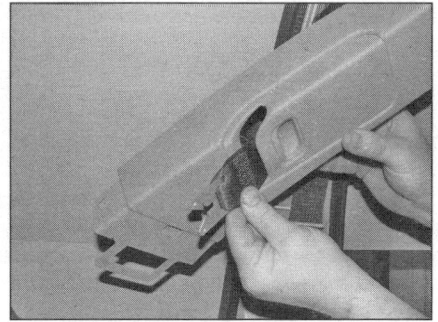
24.9 Feed the seat belt through the opening and remove the panel

24.19 Disengage the top of the lower panel from the B-pillar upper panel and remove the panel

24.25 Lift the side sill rear trim panel upwards to release the clips and remove the panel

24.26 Starting at the rear, lift the side sill main trim upwards to release the clips

A-pillar trim panel

2 Pull the trim panel away from the A-pillar to release the two retaining clips **(see illustration)**.
3 Disengage the panel from the guide and remove it from the car.
4 Refitting is a reversal of removal.

B-pillar upper trim panel

5 Move the front seat fully forward.
6 On 5-door models, remove the B-pillar lower trim panel as described later in this Section.
7 Disconnect the lower end of the front seat belt from the tensioner stalk. To do this measure down approximately 22 mm from the upper edge of the tensioner stalk and pierce the stalk protective sheath with a small screwdriver. Push the screwdriver through the pierced hole and depress the locking catch. With the catch depressed, pull the seat belt out of the stalk **(see illustrations 23.13a and 23.13b)**.
8 Prise the centre of the panel away from the B-pillar, then disengage the locating lugs at the top **(see illustration)**.
9 Feed the seat belt through the opening and remove the panel from the car **(see illustration)**.
10 Refitting is a reversal of removal.

B-pillar lower trim panel

3-door models

11 Remove the rear seat cushion and backrest as described in Section 21.

12 Remove the B-pillar upper trim panel as described previously.
13 Remove the side sill trim panel as described later in this Section.
14 Undo the retaining bolt at the upper front of the panel in the area of the B-pillar upper trim panel attachment.
15 Pull the panel away from the pillar to release the internal clips.
16 Disengage the panel from the seat belt tensioner stalk, then remove the panel from the car.
17 Refitting is a reversal of removal.

5-door models

18 Starting at the bottom, pull the panel away from the pillar to release the internal clips.
19 Disengage the top of the lower panel from the B-pillar upper panel and remove the panel from the car **(see illustration)**.

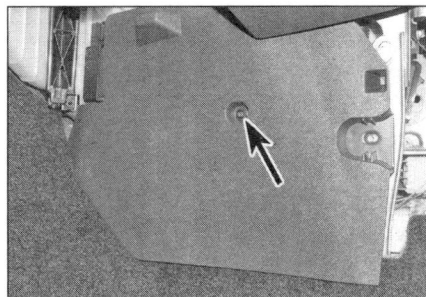
24.29 Undo the screw securing the centre trim panel to the heater air distribution housing

20 Refitting is a reversal of removal.

Side sill trim panel

3-door models

21 Lift the panel upwards to unclip it from the sill and remove the panel from the car.
22 Refitting is a reversal of removal.

5-door models

23 Remove the B-pillar lower trim panel as described previously.
24 Where fitted, carefully prise the footwell lights from the side sill panel using a small screwdriver. Disconnect the wiring connectors and remove the lights from the car.
25 Lift the side sill rear trim panel upwards to release the internal clips and remove the panel **(see illustration)**.
26 Starting at the rear, lift the side sill main trim upwards to release the internal clips. Disengage the panel from the seat belt tensioner stalk, then remove the panel from the car **(see illustration)**.
27 Refitting is a reversal of removal.

Footwell centre trim panel

28 Remove the centre console as described in Section 25.
29 Undo the screw securing the centre trim panel to the heater air distribution housing **(see illustration)**.
30 Disengage the panel at the front and remove it from under the facia.
31 Refitting is a reversal of removal.

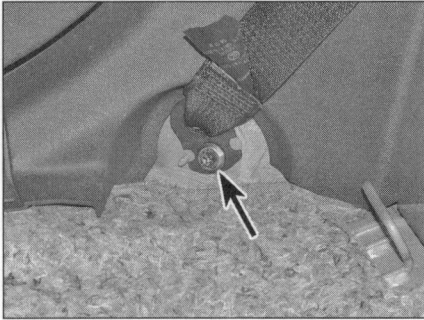

24.33 Undo the rear seat belt lower mounting bolt

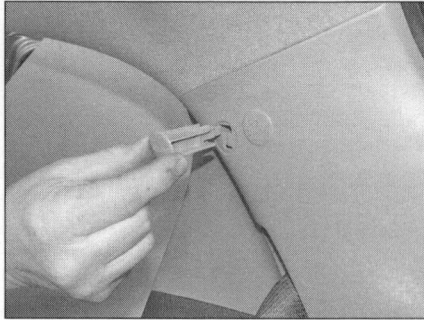

24.34 Prise out the plastic cover at the top of the upper trim panel

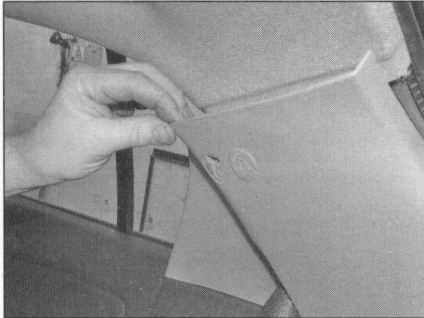

24.35 Pull the panel out to disengage the clips and release the panel from the pillar

24.36 Feed the seat belt through the panel opening and remove the panel

Luggage area upper trim panel

32 Remove the rear seat cushion as described in Section 21.
33 Undo the rear seat belt lower mounting bolt **(see illustration)**.
34 Prise out the plastic cover at the top of the upper trim panel **(see illustration)**.
35 Pull the panel out to disengage the retaining clips and release the panel from the pillar **(see illustration)**.
36 Feed the seat belt through the panel opening and remove the panel from the car **(see illustration)**.
37 Refitting is a reversal of removal, but tighten the seat belt mounting bolt to the specified torque.

Luggage area side trim panel

3-door models

38 Fold down the rear seat backrest.

39 Remove the tailgate aperture lower centre trim panel as described later in this Section.
40 Prise out the plastic cover at the top of the luggage compartment upper trim panel **(see illustration 24.34)**.
41 Pull the upper trim panel out to disengage the retaining clips and release the panel from the pillar.
42 Open the storage compartment cover in the side trim panel.
43 If working on the right-hand side trim panel, remove the jack and tools, then remove the polystyrene tool tray from the storage compartment. On models with a puncture repair kit, remove the repair kit from the storage compartment and disconnect the wiring from the electric pump.
44 From within the storage compartment, undo the two bolts and remove the rear seat backrest locking bracket.

45 Undo the two screws along the upper edge of the trim panel.
46 Pull the panel out to disengage the retaining clips and, where fitted, disconnect the wiring connector at the luggage compartment light. Remove the panel from the car.
47 Refitting is a reversal of removal.

5-door models

48 Remove the rear seat cushion and backrest as described in Section 21.
49 Remove the luggage compartment upper trim panel as described previously.
50 Remove the tailgate aperture lower centre trim panel as described later in this Section.
51 Open the storage compartment cover in the side trim panel.
52 If working on the right-hand side trim panel, remove the jack and tools, then remove the polystyrene tool tray from the storage compartment. On models with a puncture repair kit, remove the repair kit from the storage compartment and disconnect the wiring from the electric pump.
53 From within the storage compartment, undo the two bolts and remove the rear seat backrest locking bracket **(see illustration)**.
54 Undo the three screws along the upper edge of the trim panel **(see illustration)**.
55 Pull the panel out to disengage the aretaining clips and remove the panel from the car **(see illustration)**.
56 Refitting is a reversal of removal.

Tailgate aperture lower centre trim panel

57 Open the tailgate.
58 Remove the luggage compartment floor covering.
59 Pull the panel away to release the six internal clips, and remove the panel from the car **(see illustration)**.
60 Refitting is a reversal of removal.

Interior mirror

61 On models fitted with a rain sensor, unclip and remove the sensor trim panel, then release the retaining clip(s) and disconnect the wiring connectors from the mirror assembly.

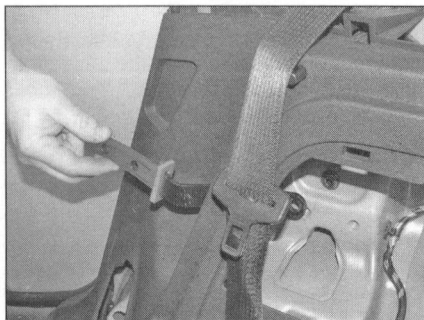

24.53 Undo the two bolts and remove the rear seat backrest locking bracket

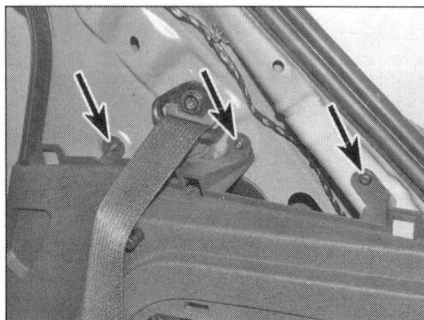

24.54 Undo the three screws along the upper edge of the trim panel

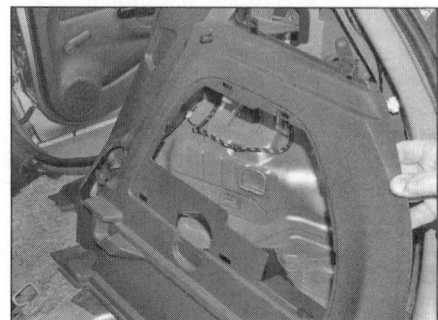

24.55 Pull the panel out to disengage the retaining clips and remove the panel

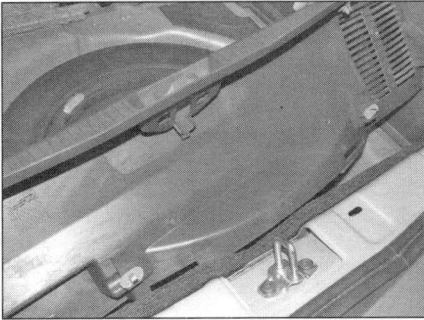

24.59 Pull the panel away to release the six clips and remove the panel

25.1 Unclip the storage compartment from the centre console, then unclip the gear lever gaiter from the storage compartment – manual transmission models

25.2 Unclip the selector lever cover from the centre console – automatic transmission models

62 Press the retaining clip at the top of the interior mirror mounting bracket, then carefully release the interior mirror in the downwards direction to remove it from the windscreen.
63 Refitting is the reverse of removal.

25 Centre console – removal and refitting

Removal

1 On models with manual transmission, unclip the storage compartment at the front of the centre console, then unclip the gear lever gaiter from the storage compartment (see illustration). Disconnect the wiring connector (where applicable), then fold the gaiter up over the gear lever knob and remove the storage compartment.
2 On models with automatic transmission, unclip the selector lever cover from the centre console, then unclip the selector lever gaiter from the cover (see illustration). Disconnect wiring connector from the selector display, fold the gaiter up over the selector knob and remove the selector lever cover.
3 Unclip the handbrake lever gaiter from the centre console, and fold it back over the handbrake lever (see illustration).
4 Unclip and remove the centre console rear storage compartment and undo the console retaining nut now exposed (see illustrations).
5 Reposition the front seats as necessary and undo the two centre console retaining screws each side (see illustrations).
6 Pull the handbrake up as far as possible. Slide the console to the rear and lift it upwards and over the gear/selector lever and handbrake (see illustration).

Refitting

7 Refitting is the reverse of removal.

25.3 Unclip the handbrake lever gaiter from the centre console, and fold it back over the handbrake lever

25.4a Unclip and remove the centre console rear storage compartment...

25.4b...and undo the console retaining nut

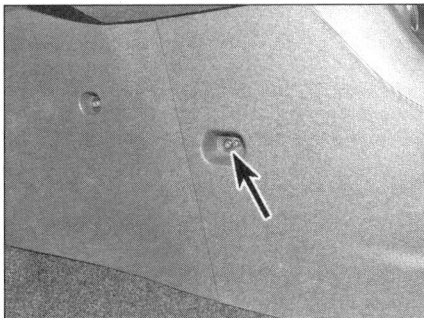

25.5a Centre console front retaining screw...

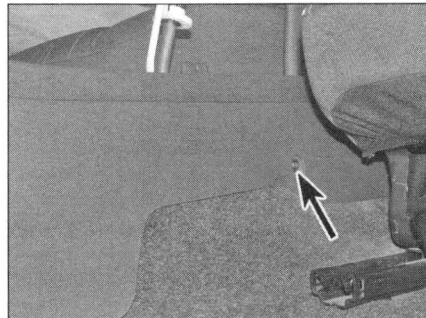

25.5b...and rear retaining screw

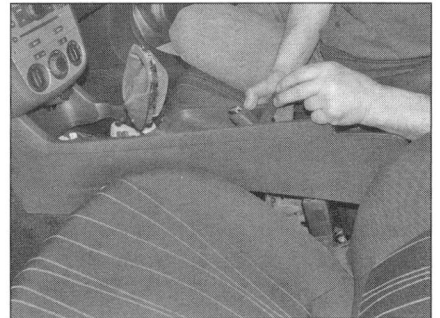

25.6 Slide the console to the rear and lift it upwards and over the gear/selector lever and handbrake

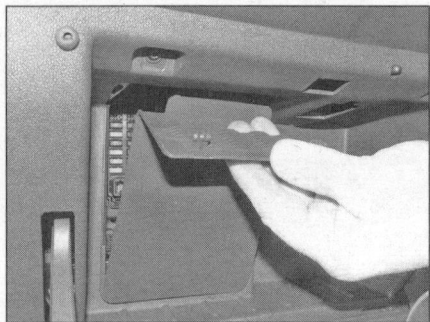
26.1 Open the glovebox lid and remove the fusebox access cover

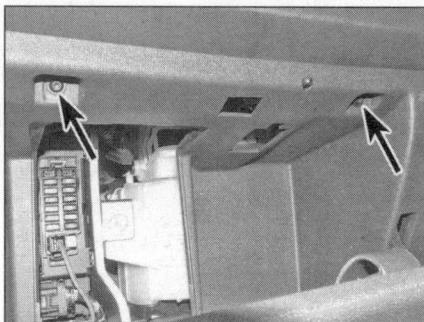
26.2a Undo the two glovebox upper retaining screws...

26.2b...the lower left-hand retaining screw...

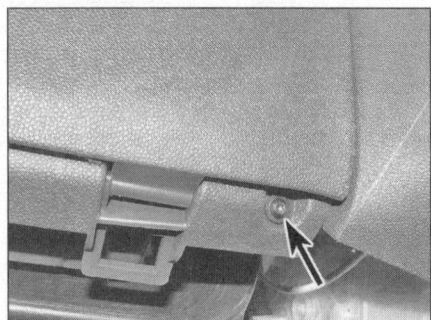
26.2c...and the lower right-hand retaining screw

26.3 Withdraw the glovebox from the facia and disconnect the glovebox light wiring connector (where applicable)

26.7 Carefully prise free the centre speaker panel from the upper centre of the facia

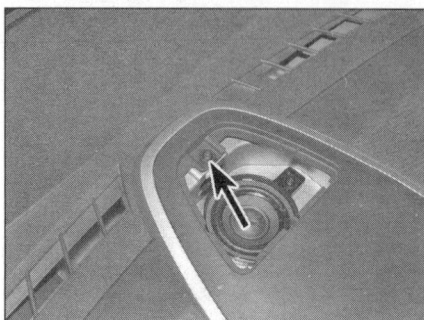
26.8 Undo the retaining screw at the front of the information display cover panel

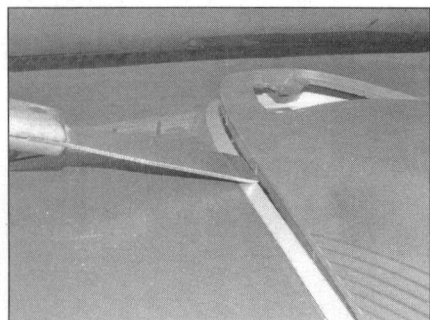
26.9a Carefully prise up the front of the information display cover panel to release the two clips each side

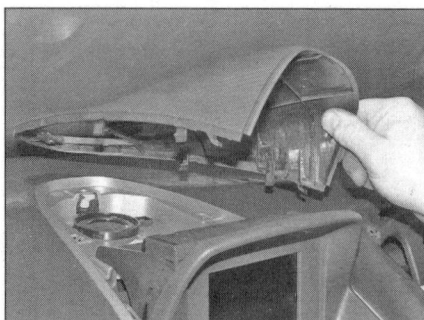
26.9b Once the side clips are released, move the panel forward to disengage the two lugs at the rear

26 Facia panel components – removal and refitting

Glovebox

Removal

1 Open the glovebox lid and remove the fusebox access cover **(see illustration)**.
2 Undo the four screws securing the glovebox to the facia **(see illustrations)**.
3 Withdraw the glovebox from the facia, disconnect the glovebox light wiring connector (where applicable) and remove the glovebox from the car **(see illustration)**.

Refitting

4 Refitting is a reversal of removal.

Facia centre switch/vent panel

Removal

5 Disconnect the battery negative terminal (refer to *Disconnecting the battery* in Chapter 5A, Section 4).
6 Remove the radio/CD player as described in Chapter 12, Section 17.
7 Using a small screwdriver, carefully prise free the centre speaker panel from the upper centre of the facia **(see illustration)**. Where applicable, disconnect the sunlight sensor wiring connector and remove the panel.
8 Undo the retaining screw at the front of the information display cover panel **(see illustration)**.
9 Using a plastic spatula or similar tool, carefully prise up the front of the information display cover panel to release the two clips each side. Once the side clips are released, move the panel forward to disengage the two lugs at the rear **(see illustrations)**.
10 Undo the two screws securing the speaker to the centre switch/vent panel. Lift out the speaker and disconnect the wiring connector **(see illustrations)**.
11 Undo the four screws securing the information display unit to the centre switch/vent panel. Lift the display unit up to release the three clips, then disconnect the wiring connector and remove the unit **(see illustrations)**.

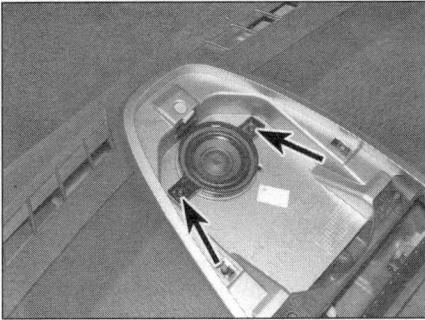
26.10a Undo the two screws securing the speaker to the centre switch/vent panel

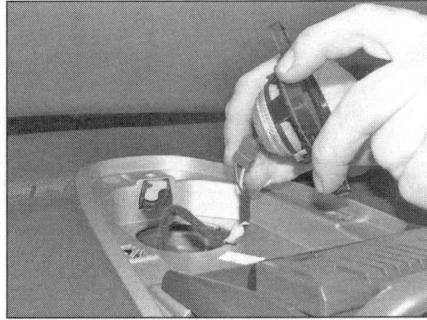
26.10b Lift out the speaker and disconnect the wiring connector

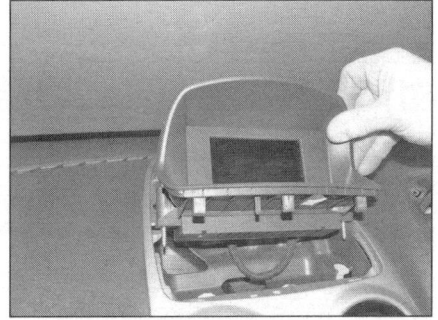
26.11a With the four screws removed, lift the information display unit up to release the three clips...

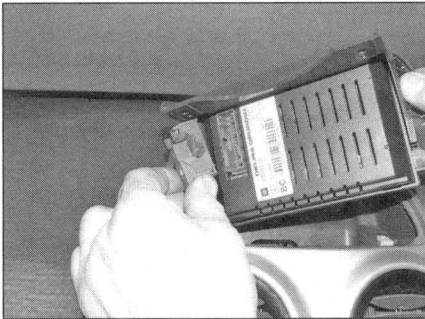
26.11b...then disconnect the wiring connector and remove the unit

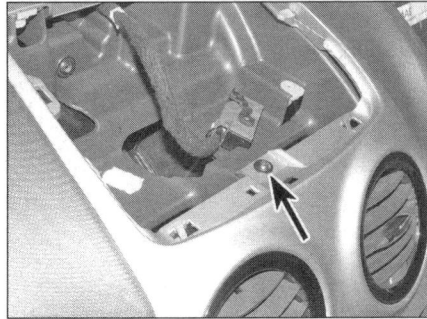
26.12 Undo the remaining screw securing the switch/vent panel to the facia

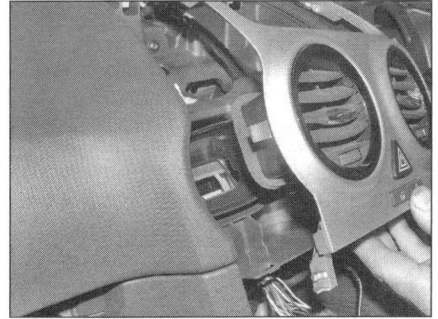
26.13a Carefully release the two side clips and two lower clips and withdraw the switch/vent panel from the facia

12 Undo the remaining screw securing the switch/vent panel to the facia (see illustration).

13 Carefully release the two side clips and two lower clips and withdraw the switch/vent panel from the facia. Disconnect the switch wiring connector and remove the switch/vent panel (see illustrations).

Refitting

14 Refitting is a reversal of removal.

Driver's side lower trim panel

Removal

15 Open the screw trim caps and undo the two screws securing the lower edge of the panel to the facia.

16 Withdraw the panel downwards to disengage the upper lugs, then disconnect the wiring conector from the lighting switch and remove the panel (see illustration).

Refitting

17 Refitting is a reversal of removal.

Steering column shrouds

Removal

18 Turn the steering wheel as necessary to access the left and right front retaining screws.

19 Carefully prise off the screw trim cap and undo the front retaining screw now exposed (see illustrations). Repeat this procedure on the other side of the shroud.

26.13b Disconnect the switch wiring connector and remove the switch/vent panel

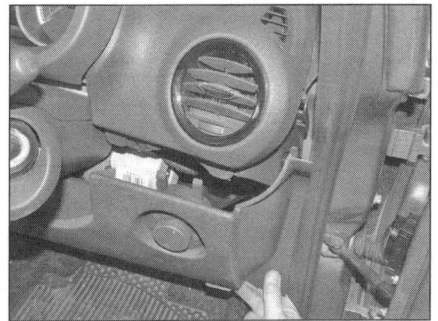
26.16 Withdraw the lower trim panel downwards to disengage the upper lugs

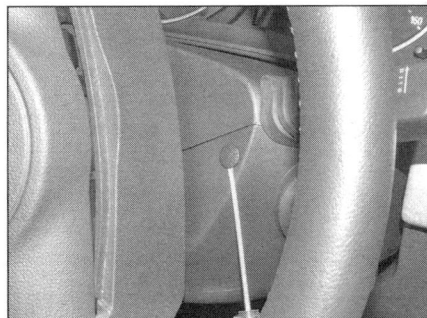
26.19a Carefully prise off the screw trim cap...

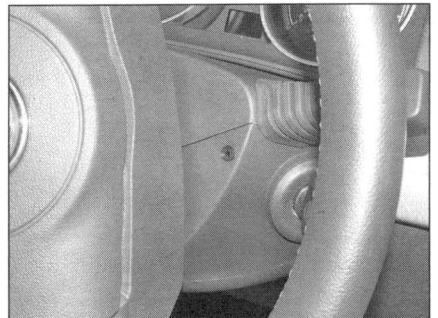
26.19b...and undo the front retaining screw now exposed

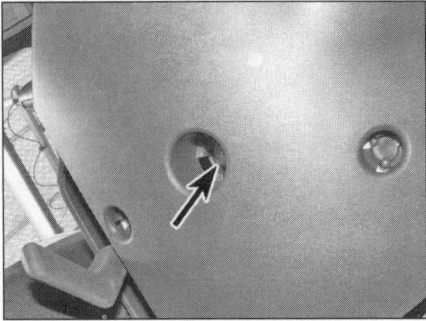

26.20 Undo the lower shroud lower retaining screw

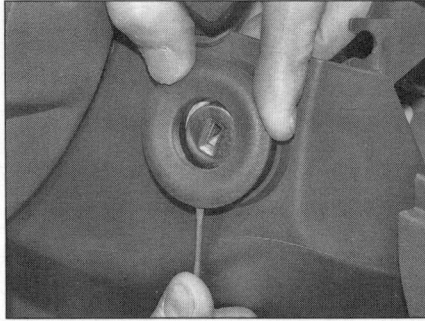

26.21 Carefully prise free the circular trim panel around the ignition switch

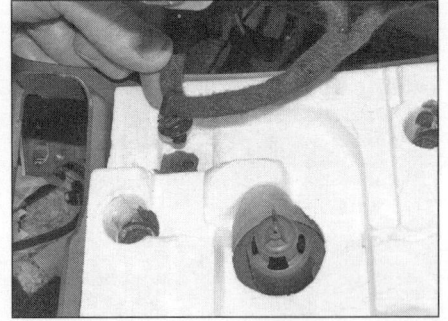

26.22 Withdraw the lower shroud from the steering column and unclip the wiring harness

20 Undo the lower shroud lower retaining screw **(see illustration)**.
21 Carefully prise free the circular trim panel around the ignition switch **(see illustration)**.
22 Withdraw the lower shroud from the steering column, unclip the wiring harness and remove the shroud **(see illustration)**.
23 Lift the upper shroud off the steering column and remove it from the car **(see illustration)**.

Refitting

24 Refitting is a reversal of removal.

Complete facia assembly

Note: *This is an involved operation entailing the removal of numerous components and assemblies, and the disconnection of a multitude of wiring connectors. Make notes on the location of all disconnected wiring,* or attach labels to the connectors, to avoid confusion when refitting.

Removal

25 Disconnect the battery negative terminal (refer to *Disconnecting the battery* in Chapter 5A, Section 4).
26 Remove the centre console as described in Section 25.
27 Remove the following trim panels as described in Section 24.
a) *A-pillar trim panels on both sides.*
b) *Side sill trim panel on both sides.*
c) *Footwell centre trim panel on both sides.*
28 Undo the nut and two bolts and remove the facia lower supports on both sides **(see illustration)**.
29 Remove the steering wheel as described in Chapter 10, Section 14.

30 Remove the following facia panels as described previously in this Section:
a) *Glovebox.*
b) *Facia centre switch/vent panel.*
c) *Driver's side lower trim panel.*
d) *Steering column shrouds.*
31 Extract the expanding rivet and remove the footwell air ducts on both sides **(see illustrations)**.
32 Remove the following components as described in Chapter 12 :
a) *Steering column electronics module.*
b) *Instrument panel.*
c) *Radio/CD player.*
d) *Passenger's airbag.*
33 Unclip and remove the radio/CD player mounting frame from the facia aperture.
34 Remove the heater control assembly as described in Chapter 3, Section 9.
35 Unclip and remove the facia upper end panels on both sides **(see illustration)**.
36 Disconnect the two wiring connectors at the cigarette lighter, where fitted.
37 Undo the following fasteners securing the facia to the facia crossmember **(see illustrations)**:
a) *1 bolt at the left-hand and right-hand end of the facia.*
b) *1 bolt on each side of the facia lower centre section.*
c) *1 bolt in the facia centre switch/vent panel aperture.*
38 With the help of an assistant, carefully lift the facia from its location. Check that all wiring has been disconnected, then remove the facia from the car.

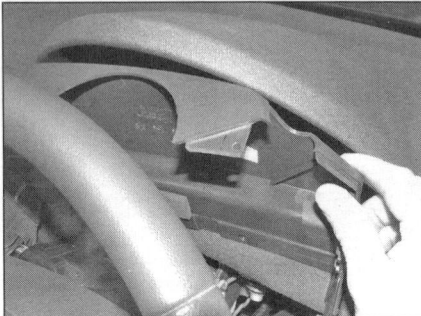

26.23 Lift the upper shroud off the steering column and remove it from the car

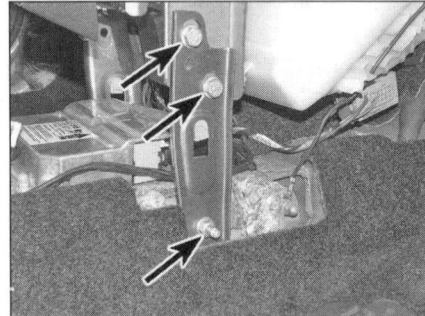

26.28 Undo the nut and two bolts and remove the facia lower supports on both sides

26.31a Extract the expanding rivet...

26.31b...and remove the footwell air ducts on both sides

26.35 Unclip and remove the facia upper end panels on both sides

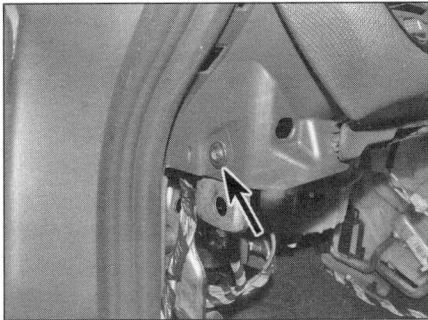
26.37a Undo the bolt at the left-hand and right-hand end of the facia...

26.37b...the bolt on each side of the facia lower centre section...

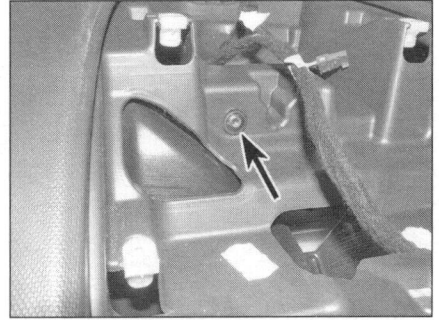
26.37c...and the bolt in the facia centre switch/vent panel aperture

26.42 Open the locking bars and disconnect the three main wiring harness connectors on the fuse/relay box

26.43 Release the wiring harness guide from the base of the fuse/relay box and move the harness to one side

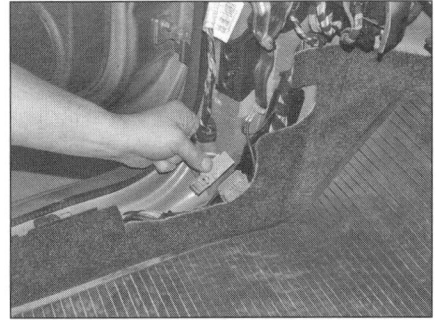
26.44 Open the locking bar and disconnect the wiring harness connector at the left-hand side of the passenger's footwell

Refitting

39 Refitting is a reversal of removal ensuring that all wiring is correctly reconnected and all mountings securely tightened.

Facia crossmember

Note: *This is an involved operation entailing the disconnection of a multitude of wiring connectors. Make notes on the location of all disconnected wiring, or attach labels to the connectors, to avoid confusion when refitting.*

Removal

40 Remove the complete facia assembly as described previously in this Section.
41 Remove the steering column as described in Chapter 10, Section 16.
42 Open the locking bars and disconnect the three main wiring harness connectors on the fuse/relay box **(see illustration)**. Also disconnect the smaller wiring harness plug below the fuses.
43 Release the wiring harness guide from the base of the fuse/relay box and move the harness to one side **(see illustration)**.
44 Open the locking bar and disconnect the wiring harness connector at the left-hand side of the passenger's footwell **(see illustration)**.
45 Open the locking bar and disconnect the wiring harness connector at the front of the airbag control unit **(see illustration)**.
46 Undo the nuts and disconnect the earth lead behind the airbag control unit, and on the right-hand side of the passenger's footwell **(see illustrations)**.

47 Disconnect the wiring harness connector on the right-hand side of the driver's footwell **(see illustration)**.

48 Undo the four bolts securing the facia crossmember to the air distribution housing in the following locations **(see illustrations)**:

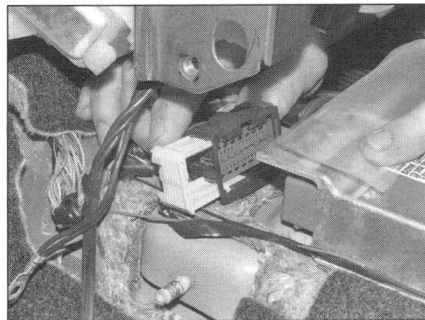
26.45 Open the locking bar and disconnect the wiring harness connector at the front of the airbag control unit

26.46a Undo the nuts and disconnect the earth lead behind the airbag control unit...

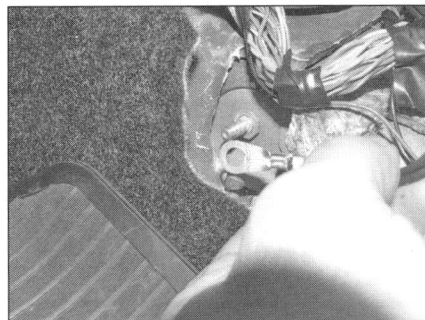
26.46b...and on the right-hand side of the passenger's footwell

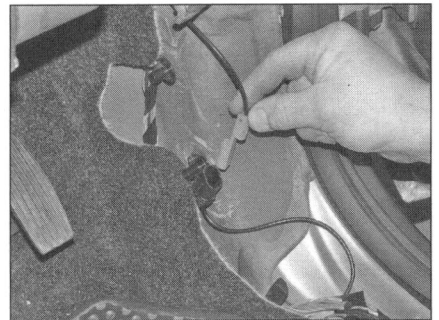
26.47 Disconnect the wiring harness connector on the side of the driver's footwell

26.48a Undo the bolt on the side of the heater blower motor housing...

26.48b...the two bolts at the top centre...

26.48c...and the lower centre bolt above the airbag control unit

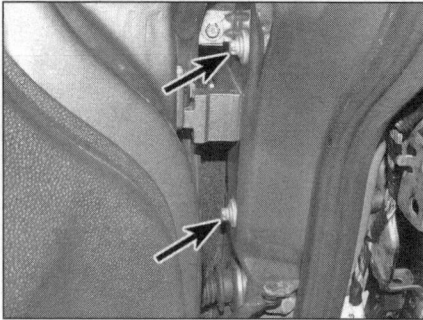

26.49 Undo the two bolts securing the crossmember to the A-pillar on each side

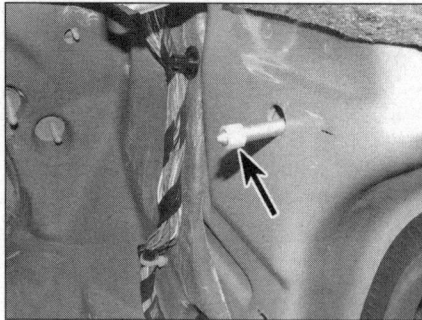

26.51a Unscrew the plastic guide sleeves from the crossmember-to-A-pillar bolts...

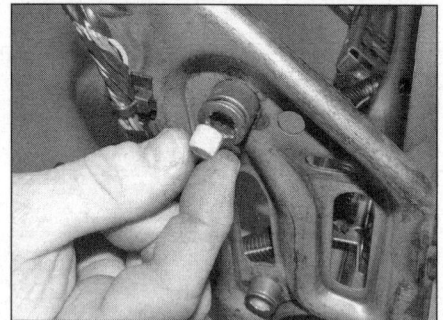

26.51b...and refit them to the captive nuts in the crossmember

a) One bolt on the side of the heater blower motor housing.
b) Two bolts at the top centre.
c) One lower centre bolt above the airbag control unit.

49 From outside the car, undo the two bolts securing the crossmember to the A-pillar on each side **(see illustration)**. Note that the bolts cannot be completely removed due to the proximity of the doors, but can be unscrewed enough to release the crossmember.

50 With the help of an assistant, check that all wiring has been disconnected, then remove the crossmember from the car.

51 Once the crossmember has been removed, unscrew the plastic guide sleeves from the crossmember-to-A-pillar bolts and refit them to the captive nuts in the crossmember **(see illustrations)**.

Refitting

52 Refitting is a reversal of removal ensuring that all wiring is correctly reconnected and all mountings securely tightened.

Chapter 12
Body electrical systems

Contents

Degrees of difficulty

Easy, suitable for novice with little experience	**Fairly easy,** suitable for beginner with some experience	**Fairly difficult,** suitable for competent DIY mechanic	**Difficult,** suitable for experienced DIY mechanic	**Very difficult,** suitable for expert DIY or professional

Specifications

System type . . . . 12 volt negative earth

Bulbs	**Wattage***
Direction indicator	21
Direction indicator side repeater	5
Foglight :	
Front	55
Rear	21
Headlight	55
Interior lights.	10
Number plate light	10
Reversing light	21
Daytime running light/sidelight.	21/5
Stop/tail light	21/5

Note: *The bulb wattage information given is for guidance only as no wattage information is provided by Vauxhall/Opel. The wattage is stamped on the base or side of the bulb.*

Torque wrench setting	**Nm**	**lbf ft**
Steering column electronics module clamp bolt	20	15

1 General information and precautions

⚠️ *Warning: Before carrying out any work on the electrical system, read through the precautions given in Safety first! and in Chapter 5A, Section 1.*

1 The electrical system is of the 12 volt negative earth type. Power for the lights and all electrical accessories is supplied by a lead-acid type battery, which is charged by the engine-driven alternator.

2 This Chapter covers repair and service procedures for the various electrical components not associated with the engine. Information on the battery, alternator and starter motor can be found in Chapter 5A.

3 It should be noted that, prior to working on any component in the electrical system, the battery negative terminal should first be disconnected, to prevent the possibility of electrical short-circuits and/or fires.

Caution: Before proceeding, refer to 'Disconnecting the battery' in Chapter 5A, Section 4 for further information.

2 Electrical fault finding – general information

Note: *Refer to the precautions given in Section 1 before starting work. The following tests relate to testing of the main electrical circuits, and should not be used to test delicate electronic circuits (such as the anti-lock braking system or fuel injection system), particularly where an electronic control unit is used.*

General

1 A typical electrical circuit consists of an electrical component, any switches, relays, motors, fuses, fusible links or circuit breakers related to that component, and the wiring and connectors which link the component to both the battery and the vehicle body. To help to pinpoint a problem in an electrical circuit, wiring diagrams are shown at the end of this Chapter.

2 Before attempting to diagnose an electrical fault, first study the appropriate wiring diagram to obtain a complete understanding of the components included in the particular circuit concerned. The possible sources of a fault can be narrowed down by noting if other components related to the circuit are operating properly. If several components or circuits fail at one time, the problem is likely to be related to a shared fuse or earth connection.

3 Electrical problems usually stem from simple causes, such as loose or corroded connections, a faulty earth connection, a blown fuse, a melted fusible link, or a faulty

relay (refer to Section 3 for details of testing relays). Inspect the condition of all fuses, wires and connections in a problem circuit before testing the components. Use the wiring diagrams to determine which terminal connections will need to be checked in order to pinpoint the trouble-spot.

4 The basic tools required for electrical fault finding include a circuit tester or voltmeter (a 12 volt bulb with a set of test leads can also be used for certain tests); a self-powered test light (sometimes known as a continuity tester); an ohmmeter (to measure resistance); a battery and set of test leads; and a jumper wire, preferably with a circuit breaker or fuse incorporated, which can be used to bypass suspect wires or electrical components. Before attempting to locate a problem with test instruments, use the wiring diagram to determine where to make the connections.

5 To find the source of an intermittent wiring fault (usually due to a poor or dirty connection, or damaged wiring insulation), a 'wiggle' test can be performed on the wiring. This involves wiggling the wiring by hand to see if the fault occurs as the wiring is moved. It should be possible to narrow down the source of the fault to a particular section of wiring. This method of testing can be used in conjunction with any of the tests described in the following sub-Sections.

6 Apart from problems due to poor connections, two basic types of fault can occur in an electrical circuit – open-circuit, or short-circuit.

7 Open-circuit faults are caused by a break somewhere in the circuit, which prevents current from flowing. An open-circuit fault will prevent a component from working, but will not cause the relevant circuit fuse to blow.

8 Short-circuit faults are caused by a 'short' somewhere in the circuit, which allows the current flowing in the circuit to 'escape' along an alternative route, usually to earth. Short-circuit faults are normally caused by a breakdown in wiring insulation, which allows a feed wire to touch either another wire, or an earthed component such as the bodyshell. A short-circuit fault will normally cause the relevant circuit fuse to blow.

Finding an open-circuit

9 To check for an open-circuit, connect one lead of a circuit tester or voltmeter to either the negative battery terminal or a known good earth.

10 Connect the other lead to a connector in the circuit being tested, preferably nearest to the battery or fuse.

11 Switch on the circuit, bearing in mind that some circuits are live only when the ignition switch is turned to a particular position.

12 If voltage is present (indicated either by the tester bulb lighting or a voltmeter reading, as applicable), this means that the section of the circuit between the relevant connector and the battery is problem-free.

13 Continue to check the remainder of the circuit in the same fashion.

14 When a point is reached at which no voltage is present, the problem must lie between that point and the previous test point with voltage. Most problems can be traced to a broken, corroded or loose connection.

Finding a short-circuit

15 To check for a short-circuit, first disconnect the load(s) from the circuit (loads are the components which draw current from a circuit, such as bulbs, motors, heating elements, etc).

16 Remove the relevant fuse from the circuit, and connect a circuit tester or voltmeter to the fuse connections.

17 Switch on the circuit, bearing in mind that some circuits are live only when the ignition switch is turned to a particular position.

18 If voltage is present (indicated either by the tester bulb lighting or a voltmeter reading, as applicable), this means that there is a short-circuit.

19 If no voltage is present, but the fuse still blows with the load(s) connected, this indicates an internal fault in the load(s).

Finding an earth fault

20 The battery negative terminal is connected to 'earth' – the metal of the engine/transmission unit and the car body – and most systems are wired so that they only receive a positive feed, the current returning via the metal of the car body. This means that the component mounting and the body form part of that circuit. Loose or corroded mountings can therefore cause a range of electrical faults, ranging from total failure of a circuit, to a puzzling partial fault. In particular, lights may shine dimly (especially when another circuit sharing the same earth point is in operation), motors (eg, wiper motors or the radiator cooling fan motor) may run slowly, and the operation of one circuit may have an apparently-unrelated effect on another. Note that on many vehicles, earth straps are used between certain components, such as the engine/transmission and the body, usually where there is no metal-to-metal contact between components, due to flexible rubber mountings, etc.

21 To check whether a component is properly earthed, disconnect the battery, and connect one lead of an ohmmeter to a known good earth point. Connect the other lead to the wire or earth connection being tested. The resistance reading should be zero; if not, check the connection as follows.

22 If an earth connection is thought to be faulty, dismantle the connection, and clean back to bare metal both the bodyshell and the wire terminal or the component earth connection mating surface. Be careful to remove all traces of dirt and corrosion, then use a knife to trim away any paint, so that a clean metal-to-metal joint is made. On reassembly, tighten the joint fasteners

3.2 Open the glovebox and remove the fusebox cover

3.3 Release the catches at each end of the fuse/relay box cover and lift off the cover

3.4 Pull the fuse out of its terminals using the plastic removal tool provided

securely; if a wire terminal is being refitted, use serrated washers between the terminal and the bodyshell, to ensure a clean and secure connection. When the connection is remade, prevent the onset of corrosion in the future by applying a coat of petroleum jelly or silicone-based grease. Alternatively, at regular intervals, spray on a proprietary ignition sealer or a water-dispersant lubricant.

3 Fuses and relays – general information

Fuses

1 The main fuses are located behind the glovebox in the facia and in the fuse/relay box on the left-hand side of the engine compartment. Additional fuses and relays on high-specification models are located in the fuse/relay box situated behind the access cover on the left-hand side of the luggage compartment.
2 To gain access to the glovebox fuses, open the glovebox and remove the fusebox cover **(see illustration)**.
3 To gain access to the engine compartment fuses, release the catches at each end of the fuse/relay box cover and lift off the cover **(see illustration)**.
4 To remove a fuse, first switch off the circuit concerned (or the ignition), then pull the fuse out of its terminals using the plastic removal tool provided **(see illustration)**. The wire within the fuse is clearly visible; if the fuse is blown, it will be broken or melted.
5 Always renew a fuse with one of an identical rating; never use a fuse with a different rating from the original, nor substitute anything else. Never renew a fuse more than once without tracing the source of the trouble. The fuse rating is stamped on top of the fuse; note that the fuses are also colour-coded for easy recognition.
6 If a new fuse blows immediately, find the cause before renewing it again; a short to earth as a result of faulty insulation is most likely. Where a fuse protects more than one circuit, try to isolate the defect by switching on each circuit in turn (if possible) until the fuse

blows again. Always carry a supply of spare fuses of each relevant rating on the vehicle, a spare of each rating should be clipped into the base of the fuse/relay box.

Relays

7 Most of the relays are located in the fuse/relay boxes in the passenger compartment and engine compartment.
8 If a circuit or system controlled by a relay develops a fault and the relay is suspect, operate the system; if the relay is functioning, it should be possible to hear it click as it is energised. If this is the case, the fault lies with the components or wiring of the system. If the relay is not being energised, then either the relay is not receiving a main supply or a switching voltage, or the relay itself is faulty. Testing is by the substitution of a known good unit, but be careful; while some relays are identical in appearance and in operation, others look similar but perform different functions.
9 To renew a relay, first ensure that the ignition switch is off. The relay can then simply be pulled out from the socket and the new relay pressed in.

4 Switches – removal and refitting

Note: *Disconnect the battery negative terminal (refer to 'Disconnecting the battery' in Chapter 5A, Section 4) before removing any switch, and reconnect the terminal after refitting.*

Ignition switch/steering column lock

1 The ignition switch is an integral part of the steering column electronics module and cannot be individually removed. Removal and refitting details for the steering column electronics module are contained in Section 16.

Steering column switches

2 The direction indicator and windscreen wiper switches are an integral part of the steering column electronics module and cannot be individually renewed. Removal and refitting details for the steering column electronics module are contained in Section 16.

Lighting switch assembly

3 Reach up under the facia and push the lighting switch out from its location **(see illustration)**.
4 Disconnect the wiring connector and remove the switch **(see illustration)**.
5 Reconnect the wiring connector and push the switch back into position.

Facia centre switches

6 The facia centre switches are contained in the switch strip assembly located in the facia centre switch/vent panel. If an individual switch is faulty the complete switch strip must be renewed. To gain access to the switch, remove the facia centre switch/vent panel as described in Chapter 11, Section 26.
7 With the switch/vent panel removed, release the retaining lugs and withdraw

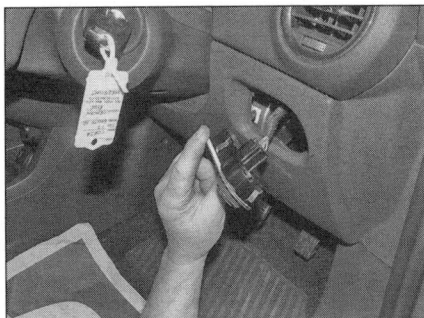
4.3 Push the lighting switch out of the facia...

4.4...then disconnect the wiring connector and remove the switch

4.7 Release the retaining lugs and withdraw the switch strip from the centre panel

4.12 Carefully prise the electric window/ mirror switch assembly out of the door inner trim panel

4.13 Open the locking bar and disconnect the wiring connector

the switch strip from the centre panel **(see illustration)**.
8 Push the switch strip back into position, then refit the facia centre panel as described in Chapter 11, Section 26.

Heated rear window and blower motor switches

9 The heated rear window and blower motor switches are an integral part of the heater control assembly. Removal and refitting procedures are contained in Chapter 3, Section 9.

Handbrake warning light switch

10 Refer to Chapter 9, Section 17.

Stop-light switch

11 Refer to Chapter 9, Section 16.

Electric window and mirror switches

12 Using a small screwdriver, carefully prise the switch assembly out of the door inner trim panel **(see illustration)**.
13 Open the locking bar, disconnect the wiring connector and remove the switch **(see illustration)**.
14 Refitting is the reverse of removal.

Air conditioning system switch

15 The air conditioning system control switch is an integral part of the heating/ventilation control unit, and cannot be removed. Should the switch become faulty, the complete control unit assembly must be renewed (see Chapter 3, Section 9).

Steering wheel switches

16 Remove the driver's airbag as described in Section 23.
17 Working through the airbag aperture in the steering wheel, depress the retaining catch on the side of the switch with a small screwdriver. Withdraw the switch from the steering wheel and disconnect the wiring connector.
18 Refitting is the reverse of removal.

5 Bulbs (exterior lights) – renewal

General

1 Whenever a bulb is renewed, note the following points:
a) Make sure the switch is in the off position, for the bulb you are working on.
b) Remember that if the light has just been in use, the bulb may be extremely hot.
c) Always check the bulb contacts and holder, ensuring that there is clean metal-to-metal contact between the bulb and its live(s) and earth. Clean off any corrosion or dirt before fitting a new bulb.

d) Wherever bayonet-type bulbs are fitted, ensure that the live contact(s) bear firmly against the bulb contact.
e) Always ensure that the new bulb is of the correct rating, and that it is completely clean before fitting it; this applies particularly to headlight/foglight bulbs.

Headlight unit

Note: If working on the right-hand headlight unit, remove the air cleaner assembly and intake duct (see Chapter 4A, Section 2 or Chapter 4B, Section 3). If working on the left-hand headlight unit, remove the fuse/relay box cover and also lift out the windscreen washer reservoir filler neck. Even with the adjacent components removed, access to the bulbs is extremely limited, if not impossible, and it is recommended that the relevant headlight unit is removed for bulb renewal (see Section 7).
Note: The outer bulb in the headlight unit is the dipped beam bulb and the inner bulb is the main beam bulb.

Dipped beam

2 Release the wire retaining clip and remove the plastic cover from the rear of the headlight unit **(see illustration)**.
3 Disconnect the bulb wiring connector **(see illustration)**.
4 Push the bulb base sideways and withdraw the bulb from the headlight unit **(see illustration)**.

5.2 Release the wire retaining clip and remove the plastic cover from the rear of the headlight unit

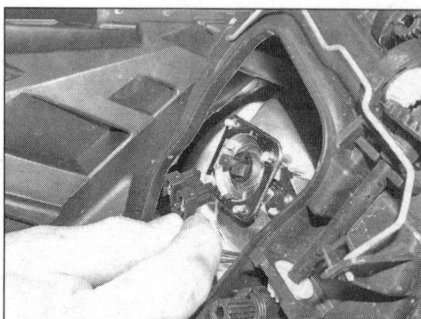

5.3 Disconnect the wiring connector from the bulb contacts

5.4 Push the dipped beam bulb base sideways and withdraw the bulb from the headlight unit

5.8 Turn the plastic cover anti-clockwise and remove it from the rear of the headlight unit

5.9 Disconnect the wiring connector from the rear of the main beam bulb

5.10a Push the legs of the retaining spring clip down and pivot the clip off the bulb...

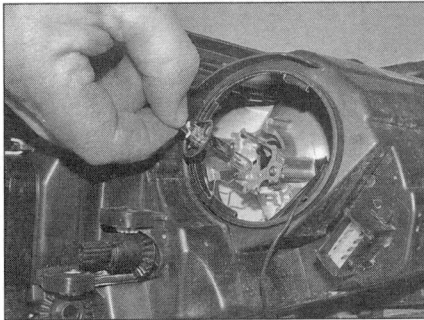
5.10b...then lift the bulb out of the light unit

5.13a Withdraw the daytime running light/ sidelight bulbholder from the rear of the headlight unit

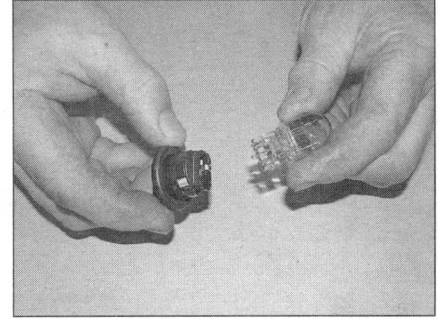
5.13b The bulb is a push-fit in the bulbholder

5 When handling the new bulb, use a tissue or clean cloth to avoid touching the glass with the fingers; moisture and grease from the skin can cause blackening and rapid failure of this type of bulb. If the glass is accidentally touched, wipe it clean using methylated spirit.
6 Fit the new bulb to the headlight unit ensuring that the tab on the bulb base engages with the slot in the headlight unit. Reconnect the wiring connector.
7 Refit the plastic cover to the rear of the headlight unit, then refit any components removed for access.

Main beam

8 Turn the plastic cover anti-clockwise and remove it from the rear of the headlight unit (see illustration).
9 Disconnect the wiring connector from the rear of the bulb (see illustration).
10 Disengage the legs of the retaining spring clip from the lugs on the bulb by pushing the clip down and swivelling it to the side. Lift the bulb out of the headlight unit (see illustrations). When handling the new bulb, use a tissue or clean cloth to avoid touching the glass with the fingers; moisture and grease from the skin can cause blackening and rapid failure of this type of bulb. If the glass is accidentally touched, wipe it clean using methylated spirit.
11 Fit the new bulb to the headlight unit and secure with the spring clip. Reconnect the wiring connector.
12 Refit the plastic cover to the rear of the

headlight unit, then refit any components removed for access.

Daytime running light/sidelight

13 Turn the daytime running light/sidelight bulbholder anticlockwise and withdraw it from the rear of the headlight unit. The bulb is of the capless (push-fit) type, and can be removed by simply pulling it out of the bulbholder (see illustrations).
14 Refitting is the reverse of the removal procedure, ensuring that the bulbholder is fully engaged. On completion, refit any components removed for access.

Indicator

15 Remove the dipped beam plastic cover from the rear of the headlight unit (see illustration 5.2).

5.16 Release and remove the indicator bulbholder from the rear of the headlight unit

16 Release the indicator bulbholder and remove it from the rear of the headlight unit (see illustration).
17 The bulb is is integral with the bulbholder.
18 Refitting is a reverse of the removal procedure. On completion, refit any components removed for access.

Indicator side repeater

19 Push the light unit toward the front of the car, and release the rear edge of the unit from the wing (see illustration). If necessary, assist removal using a suitable plastic wedge, taking great care not damage the painted finish of the wing.
20 Withdraw the light unit from the wing, and pull the bulbholder out of the light unit. The bulb is of the capless (push-fit) type, and

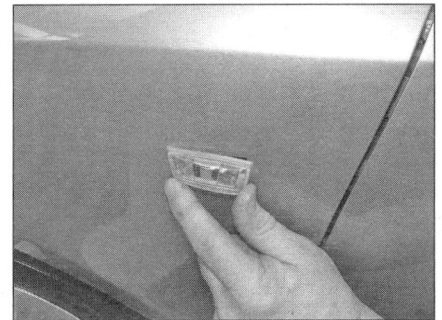
5.19 Push the indicator side repeater light unit toward the front of the car, and release the rear edge of the unit from the wing

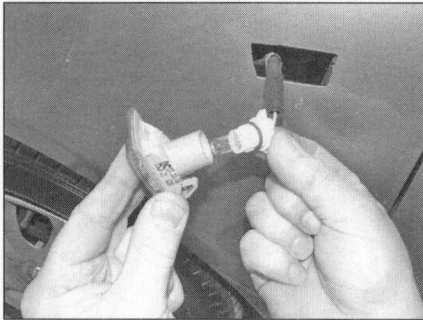
5.20a Pull the bulbholder out of the light unit

5.20b The bulb is a push-fit in the bulbholder

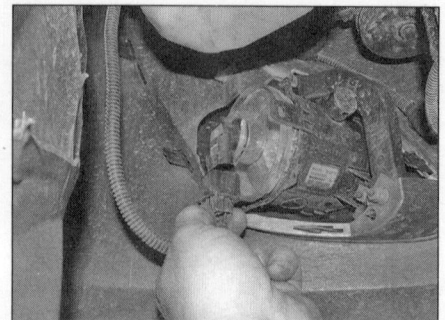
5.22 Disconnect the foglight wiring connector

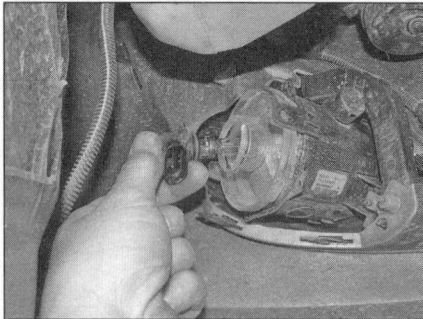
5.23 Turn the foglight bulbholder anti-clockwise and remove it from the light unit

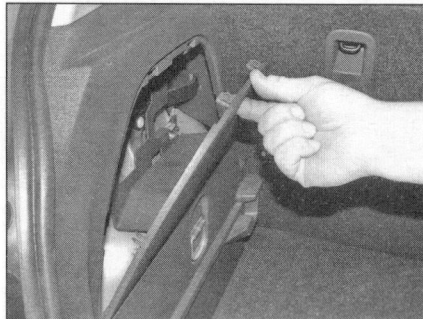
5.26 Open the access cover in the luggage compartment trim panel

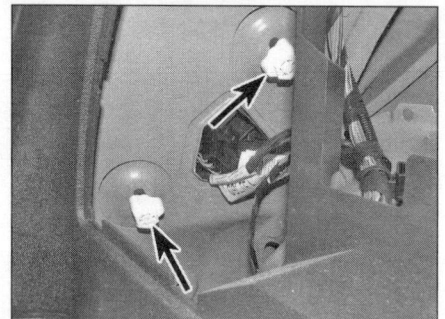
5.27 Slacken the two light cluster plastic retaining nuts and remove one of the nuts

can be removed by simply pulling it out of the bulbholder (see illustrations).

21 Refitting is a reverse of the removal procedure.

Front foglight

22 Reach up under the front bumper and disconnect the foglight wiring connector (see illustration).

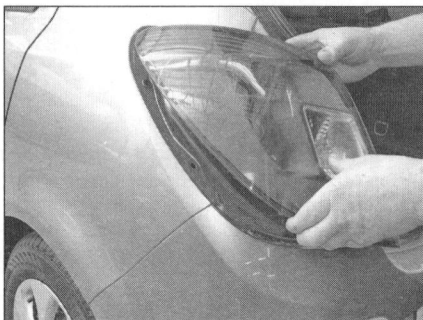
5.28 Hold the light cluster from the outside, remove the remaining nut and withdraw the cluster from the rear wing

5.29 Disconnect the wiring connector from the bulbholder, then remove the light cluster from the car

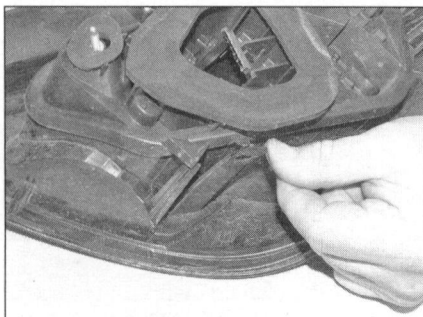
5.30a Press the three locking tabs on the outside of the bulbholder...

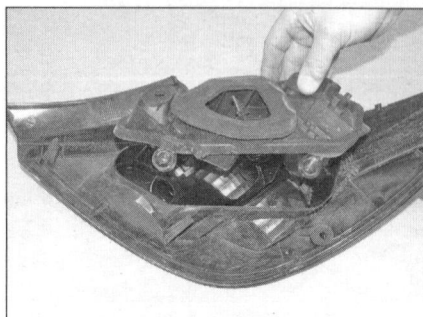
5.30b...and withdraw the bulbholder from the light cluster

23 Turn the bulbholder anticlockwise and remove it from the rear of the light unit (see illustration). The bulb is integral with the bulbholder.

24 When handling the new bulb, use a tissue or clean cloth to avoid touching the glass with the fingers; moisture and grease from the skin can cause blackening and rapid failure of this type of bulb. If the glass is accidentally touched, wipe it clean using methylated spirit.

25 Refitting is a reverse of the removal procedure.

Rear light cluster

26 Depress the catch and open the access cover in the luggage compartment trim panel (see illustration).

27 Working through the trim panel opening, slacken the two light cluster plastic retaining nuts and remove one of the nuts (see illustration).

28 Hold the light cluster from the outside and unscrew the remaining plastic nut the rest of the way. Withdraw the light cluster from the rear wing (see illustration).

29 Disconnect the wiring connector from the bulbholder, then remove the light cluster from the car (see illustration).

30 Press the three locking tabs on the outside of the bulbholder and withdraw the bulbholder from the light cluster (see illustrations).

31 The relevant bulb can then be renewed; all bulbs have a bayonet fitting (see illustration). Note that the stop/tail light bulb has offset locating pins, to prevent it being installed incorrectly.

32 Refitting is the reverse of the removal sequence, bearing in mind the following points:

a) *Ensure that the bulbholder locates securely in position on the light cluster.*

b) *Ensure that the rubber seals are in place on the bulbholder, locating pegs and retaining studs before refitting the light cluster.*

Number plate light

33 Using a small flat-bladed screwdriver, carefully prise the light unit out from its location **(see illustration)**.

34 Twist the bulbholder to remove it from the light unit, and remove the bulb **(see illustrations)**.

35 Refitting is a reverse of the removal procedure.

High-level stop-light

36 The high-level stop-light bulbs are of the LED (light emitting diode) type and cannot be individually renewed. Remove the complete light unit as described in Section 7.

6 Bulbs (interior lights) – renewal

General

1 Refer to Section 5, paragraph 1.

Front courtesy light

2 Using a suitable screwdriver, carefully prise the light unit out of position, and release the bulb from the light unit contacts **(see illustrations)**.

3 Install the new bulb, ensuring that it is securely held in position by the contacts, and clip the light unit back into position.

Front courtesy/reading light

4 Using a small screwdriver, carefully prise the light unit lens from the overhead console **(see illustration)**.

5 Pull the bulb from its socket **(see illustration)**.

6 Install the new bulb, ensuring that it is securely held in position by the contacts, and clip the light unit lens back into position.

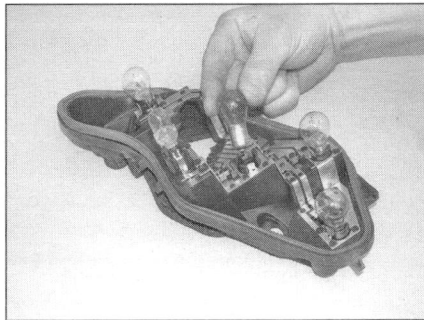
5.31 The relevant bulb can then be renewed

5.34a Twist the bulbholder to remove it from the light unit...

Rear courtesy light

7 Using a suitable screwdriver, carefully prise the light unit out of position, and withdraw the light unit **(see illustration)**.

6.2a Carefully prise the front courtesy light unit out of position...

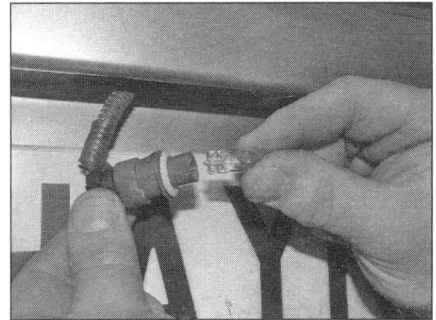
6.4 Carefully prise the light unit lens from the overhead console

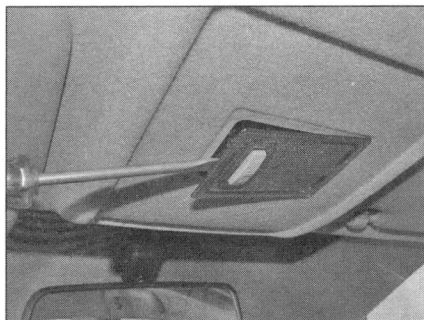
6.5 Pull the relevant bulb from its socket

5.33 Carefully prise the number plate light unit out from its location

5.34b...and remove the push-fit bulb

8 Disconnect the wiring connector and remove the light unit.

9 Unclip and remove the reflector from the base of the light unit **(see illustration)**.

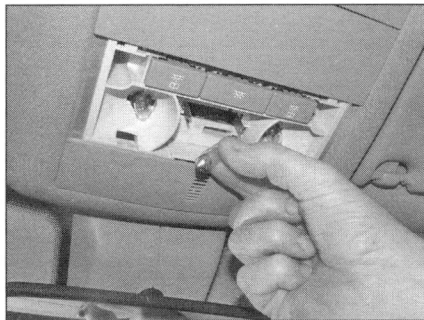
6.2b...then release the bulb from its contacts

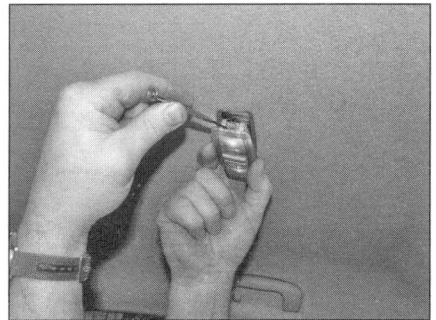
6.7 Carefully prise the rear courtesy light unit out of position, and withdraw the unit

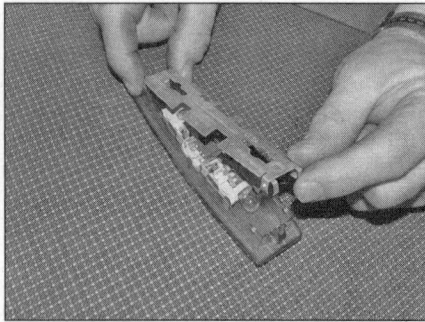

6.9 Unclip and remove the reflector from the base of the light unit

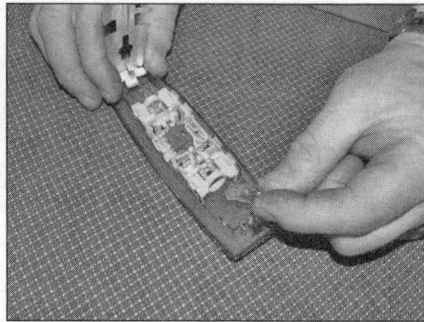

6.10 Pull the relevant bulb from its socket

6.12 Carefully prise the light unit out of position, and release the bulb from the light unit contacts

6.16 Pull the relevant heater control illumination bulb from the bulbholder

10 Pull the relevant bulb from its socket (see illustration).

11 Install the new bulb, then refit the reflector. Reconnect the wiring connector, then clip the light unit back into position.

7.3a Undo the lower outer retaining bolt...

7.3b...the upper retaining bolt...

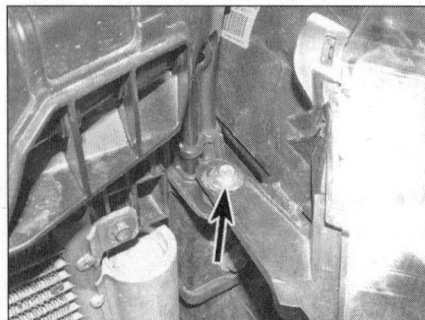

7.3c...and the lower inner retaining bolt...

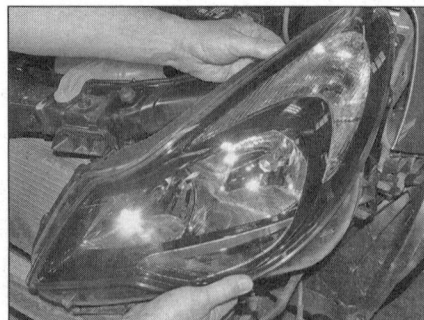

7.3d...then withdraw the headlight unit...

7.3e...and disconnect the wiring connector

Luggage compartment, glovebox and footwell lights

12 Using a suitable screwdriver, carefully prise the light unit out of position, and release the bulb from the light unit contacts (see illustration).

13 Install the new bulb, ensuring that it is securely held in position by the contacts, and clip the light unit back into position.

Switch illumination

14 All the switches are fitted with illumination bulbs; some are also fitted with a bulb to show when the circuit concerned is operating. These bulbs are an integral part of the switch assembly, and cannot be obtained separately.

Heater control illumination

15 Remove the heater control assembly as described in Chapter 3, Section 9.
16 Pull the relevant bulb from the bulbholder and fit the new bulb (see illustration).
17 Refit the heater control assembly as described in Chapter 3, Section 9.

---

7 Exterior light units –
removal and refitting

---

1 Disconnect the battery negative terminal (refer to *Disconnecting the battery* in Chapter 5A, Section 4) before removing any light unit, and reconnect the terminal after refitting.

Headlight

2 Remove the front bumper as described in Chapter 11, Section 6.
3 Undo the three retaining bolts and withdraw the headlight unit from the vehicle. When removing the retaining bolt nearest to the radiator, press down on the headlight bracket to prevent the nut under the bolt from turning. If necessary hold the nut with a spanner. The nut controls the fit tolerance of the headlight in relation to the front bumper and bonnet. Disconnect the wiring connector from rear of the headlight unit as it is withdrawn (see illustrations).
4 The headlight beam adjustment motor can be removed and refitted as follows.

7.6a Rotate the headlight adjustment motor clockwise to free the motor from the headlight unit...

7.6b...pull the motor away from the headlight unit to release the balljoint from the reflector...

7.6c...then disconnect the wiring connector

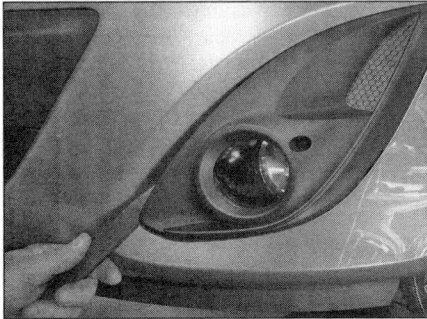

7.13a Using a plastic spatula, carefully prise out the foglight trim surround...

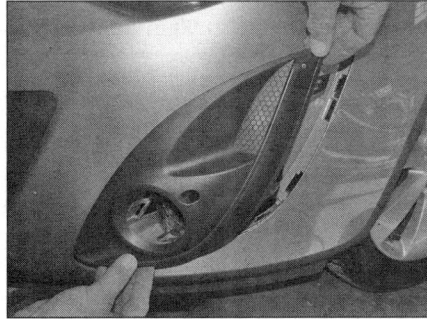

7.13b...then remove the surround from the bumper

7.14 Undo the two foglight retaining screws

5 Release the wire retaining clip and remove the plastic cover from the rear of the headlight unit (see illustration 5.2).

6 Rotate the adjustment motor clockwise to free the motor from the rear of the headlight unit. Pull the motor away from the headlight unit to release the balljoint from the rear of the light reflector, then disconnect the wiring connector (see illustrations).

7 On refitting, reconnect the wiring connector, align the motor balljoint with the light unit socket, and clip it into position. Engage the motor assembly with the light unit, and twist it clockwise to secure it in position.

8 Refitting is a reverse of the removal procedure. On completion, check the headlight beam alignment using the information given in Section 8.

Front indicator light

9 The front direction indicator lights are integral with the headlight units. Removal and refitting is as described above.

Indicator side repeater light

10 Push the light unit toward the front of the car, and release the rear edge of the unit from the wing (see illustration 5.19). If necessary, assist removal using a suitable plastic wedge, taking great care not damage the painted finish of the wing.

11 Withdraw the light unit from the wing, and pull the bulbholder out of the light unit.

12 Refitting is a reverse of the removal procedure.

Front foglight

13 Using a plastic spatula or similar tool, carefully prise out the foglight trim surround to release the eight internal retaining clips, then remove the surround from the bumper (see illustrations).

14 Undo the two screws securing the foglight to the bumper (see illustration).

15 Withdraw the light unit and disconnect the wiring connector (see illustrations).

16 Refitting is a reversal of the removal procedure.

Rear light cluster

17 Depress the catch and open the access cover in the luggage compartment trim panel (see illustration 5.26).

18 Working through the trim panel opening

slacken the two light cluster plastic retaining nuts and remove one of the nuts (see illustration 5.27).

19 Hold the light cluster from the outside and unscrew the remaining plastic nut the rest of the way. Withdraw the light cluster from the rear wing (see illustration 5.28).

20 Disconnect the wiring connector from the bulbholder, then remove the light cluster from the car (see illustration 5.29).

21 Refitting is the reverse of the removal sequence, but ensure that the rubber seals are in place on the bulbholder, locating pegs and retaining studs before refitting the light cluster.

Number plate light

22 Using a small flat-bladed screwdriver,

7.15a Withdraw the light unit from the bumper...

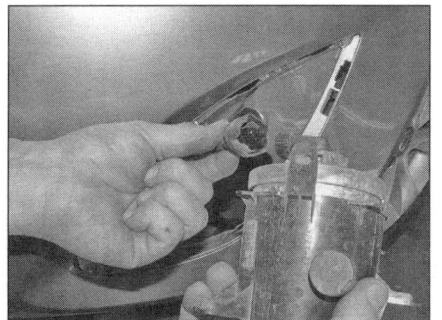

7.15b...and disconnect the wiring connector

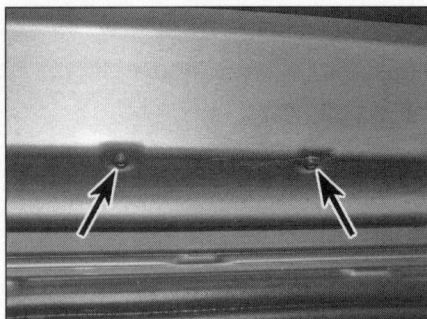

7.25 Open the tailgate and undo the two high-level stop-light retaining screws

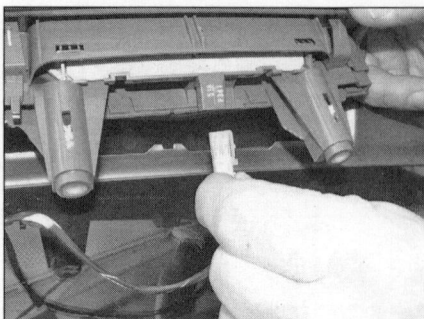

7.26a Withdraw the stop-light from the tailgate and disconnect the wiring connector...

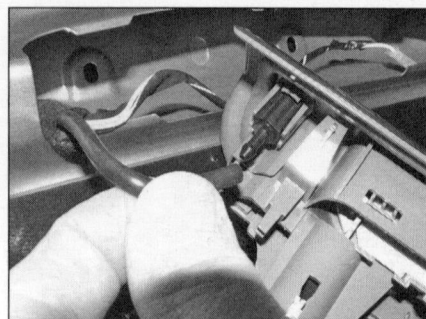

7.26b...and the tailgate washer hose

carefully prise the light unit out from its location **(see illustration 5.33)**.

23 Twist the bulbholder to remove it from the light unit.

24 Refitting is the reverse of the removal sequence.

High-level stop-light

25 Open the tailgate and undo the two high-level stop-light retaining screws **(see illustration)**.

26 Withdraw the stop-light from the tailgate and disconnect the wiring connector and the tailgate washer hose **(see illustrations)**.

27 Refitting is the reverse of the removal sequence.

8 Headlight beam alignment – general information

1 Accurate adjustment of the headlight beam is only possible using optical beam-setting equipment, and this work should therefore be carried out by a Vauxhall/Opel dealer or suitably-equipped workshop.

2 For reference, the headlights can be adjusted using the adjuster assemblies fitted to the top of each light unit. The inner adjuster alters the vertical position of the beam. The outer adjuster alters the horizontal aim of the beam.

3 Most models have an electrically-operated

headlight beam adjustment system, controlled via a switch in the facia. The recommended settings are as follows.

a) 0 Front seat(s) occupied
b) 1 All seats occupied
c) 2 All seats occupied, and load in luggage compartment
d) 3 Driver's seat occupied and load in the luggage compartment

Note: *When adjusting the headlight aim, ensure that the switch is set to position 0.*

9 Instrument panel – removal and refitting

Note: *The instrument panel is a complete sealed assembly, and no dismantling of the instrument panel is possible.*

Removal

1 Disconnect the battery negative terminal (refer to *Disconnecting the battery* in Chapter 5A, Section 4).

2 Pull the instrument panel shroud away from the facia to release the five retaining clips **(see illustration)**.

3 Undo the three retaining screws and withdraw the panel from the facia **(see illustrations)**.

4 Disconnect the wiring connector and remove the panel from the car **(see illustration)**.

Refitting

5 Refitting is a reversal of removal.

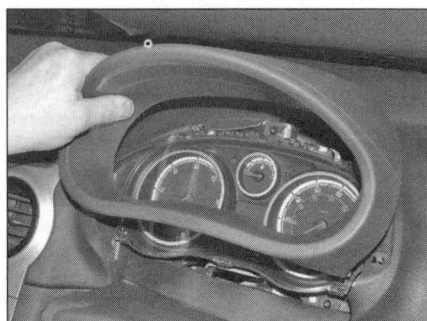

9.2 Pull the instrument panel shroud away from the facia to release the five retaining clips

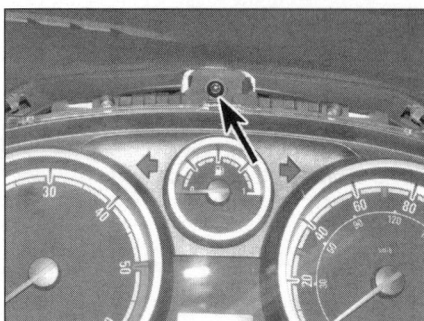

9.3a Undo the instrument panel upper retaining screw...

9.3b...lower right-hand retaining screw...

9.3c...and lower left-hand retaining screw

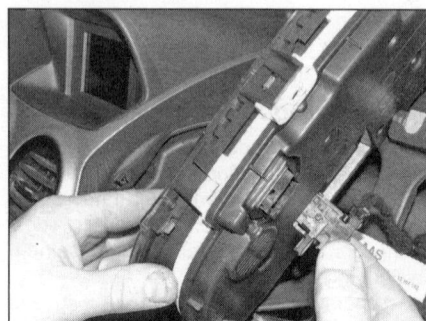

9.4 Disconnect the wiring connector and remove the panel from the car

10.2 Carefully prise free the centre speaker panel from the upper centre of the facia

10.3 Undo the retaining screw at the front of the information display cover panel

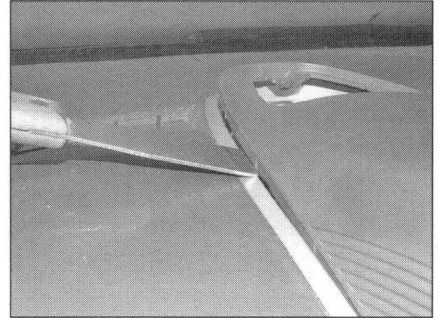
10.4a Carefully prise up the front of the information display cover panel to release the two clips each side

10.4b Once the side clips are released, move the panel forward to disengage the two lugs at the rear

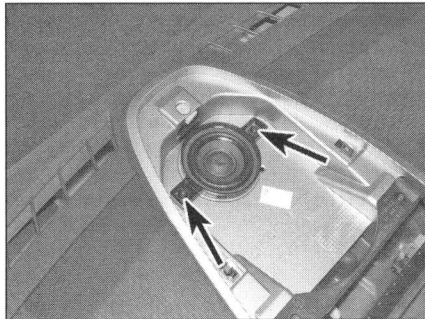
10.5a Undo the two screws securing the speaker to the centre switch/vent panel

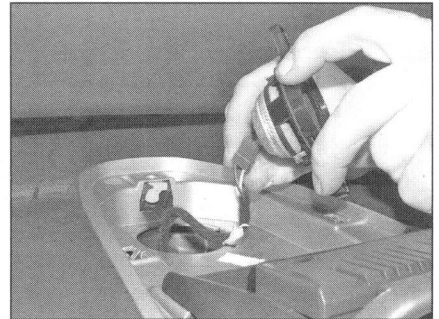
10.5b Lift out the speaker and disconnect the wiring connector

10 Information display unit – removal and refitting

Removal

1 Disconnect the battery negative terminal (refer to *Disconnecting the battery* in Chapter 5A, Section 4).
2 Using a small screwdriver, carefully prise free the centre speaker panel from the upper centre of the facia **(see illustration)**. Where applicable, disconnect the sunlight sensor wiring connector and remove the panel.
3 Undo the retaining screw at the front of the information display cover panel **(see illustration)**.

4 Using a plastic spatula or similar tool, carefully prise up the front of the information display cover panel to release the two clips each side. Once the side clips are released, move the panel forward to disengage the two lugs at the rear **(see illustrations)**.
5 Undo the two screws securing the speaker to the centre switch/vent panel. Lift out the speaker and disconnect the wiring connector **(see illustrations)**.
6 Undo the four screws securing the information display unit to the centre switch/vent panel. Lift the display unit up to release the three clips, then disconnect the wiring connector and remove the unit **(see illustrations)**.

Refitting

7 Refitting is a reversal of removal.

11 Horn – removal and refitting

Removal

1 Firmly apply the handbrake, then jack up the front of the car and support it securely on axle stands (see *Jacking and vehicle support*).
2 Working under the bumper on the left-hand side, undo the retaining nut/bolt and remove the horn(s), disconnecting the wiring connector as it becomes accessible **(see illustration)**.

Refitting

3 Refitting is the reverse of removal.

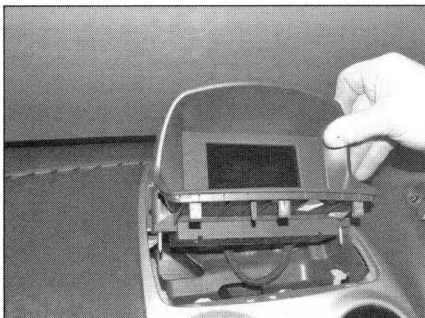
10.6a With the four screws removed, lift the information display unit up to release the three clips...

10.6b...then disconnect the wiring connector and remove the unit

11.2 The horn(s) are located under the front bumper on the left-hand side

12.2a Unclip the windscreen wiper arm spindle nut cover...

12 Wiper arm – removal and refitting

Removal

1 Operate the wiper motor, then switch it off so that the wiper arm returns to the at-rest (parked) position.

HAYNES HINT *Stick a piece of masking tape on the windscreen along the edge of the wiper blade, to use as an alignment aid on refitting.*

12.2b...then slacken and remove the spindle nut

2 Unclip the wiper arm spindle nut cover (windscreen wiper arm), or pivot the cover up (tailgate wiper arm), then slacken and remove the spindle nut and washer **(see illustrations)**.
3 Using a suitable puller, free the wiper arm from the spindle and remove the arm.
Note: *If both windscreen wiper arms are to be removed at the same time, mark them for identification. The arms are not interchangeable.*

Refitting

4 Ensure that the wiper arm and spindle splines are clean and dry, then refit the arm to the spindle, aligning the wiper blade with the tape fitted on removal. Refit the spindle nut, tightening it securely, and clip the nut cover back in position.

13 Windscreen wiper motor and linkage – removal and refitting

Removal

1 Disconnect the battery negative terminal (refer to *Disconnecting the battery* in Chapter 5A, Section 4).
2 Remove the wiper arms as described in the Section 12.
3 Remove the windscreen cowl panel as described in Chapter 11, Section 20.
4 Disconnect the wiring connector from the wiper motor **(see illustration)**.
5 Undo the two retaining bolts, and withdraw the wiper motor and linkage assembly from the scuttle **(see illustrations)**.

Refitting

6 Manoeuvre the motor assembly back into position in the vehicle. Refit the retaining bolts, and tighten them securely.
7 Reconnect the wiring connector to the wiper motor
8 Refit the windscreen cowl panel as described in Chapter 11, Section 20.
9 Install both the wiper arms as described in Section 12, and reconnect the battery negative terminal.

14 Tailgate wiper motor – removal and refitting

Removal

1 Disconnect the battery negative terminal (refer to *Disconnecting the battery* in Chapter 5A, Section 4).
2 Remove the wiper arm (see Section 12).
3 Open the tailgate, and detach the parcel shelf lifting cords from the tailgate.
4 Undo the two screws securing the tailgate inner trim panel to the tailgate **(see illustration)**. Carefully prise the trim panel from the tailgate to release the eight retaining clips.
5 Disconnect the wiring connector, then slacken and remove the three wiper motor mounting bolts and remove the wiper motor **(see illustration)**.

13.4 Disconnect the wiring connector from the wiper motor

13.5a Undo the two retaining bolts...

13.5b...and withdraw the wiper motor and linkage assembly from the scuttle

14.4 Undo the two screws securing the tailgate inner trim panel to the tailgate

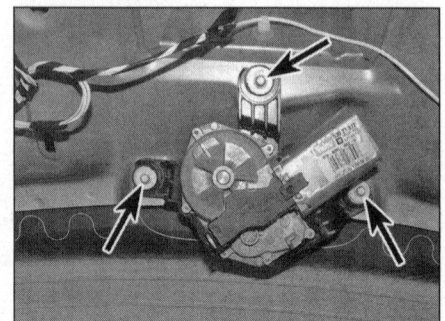

14.5 Tailgate wiper motor retaining bolts

Refitting

6 Refitting is the reverse of removal, ensuring the wiper motor retaining bolts are securely tightened.

15 Windscreen/tailgate washer system components – removal and refitting

Washer system reservoir

Removal

1 Remove the front bumper as described in Chapter 11, Section 6.
2 Disconnect the wiring connector(s) and washer hoses at the washer pump(s), then release the wiring and hoses from the side of the reservoir.
3 Drill out the two rivets securing the reservoir to the underbody **(see illustration)**.
4 Extract the upper plastic rivet and lower the reservoir out from under the car.

Refitting

5 Refitting is the reverse of removal, using new rivets to secure the reservoir. Ensure that the washer hose(s) are securely connected.

Washer pump

Removal

6 Remove the front bumper as described in Chapter 11, Section 6.
7 Disconnect the pump washer hoses, then carefully ease the pump out from the reservoir and recover its sealing grommet.

Refitting

8 Refitting is the reverse of removal, using a new sealing grommet if the original one shows signs of damage or deterioration.

Windscreen washer jets

Removal

9 Remove the windscreen cowl panel as described in Chapter 11, Section 20.
10 Depress the retaining clip, then carefully prise the nozzle from the windscreen cowl panel **(see illustration)**.
11 Disconnect the nozzle from its fluid hose(s), and remove it from the vehicle.

Refitting

12 Securely connect the nozzle to the hose, and clip it into position in the windscreen cowl panel. Refit the cowl panel, then check the operation of the jet. If necessary, adjust the nozzle using a pin, aiming the spray to a point slightly above the centre of the swept area.

Tailgate washer jet

Removal

13 Remove the high-level stop-light as described in Section 7.
14 Release the two retaining lugs and remove the washer jet from the stop-light unit **(see illustration)**.

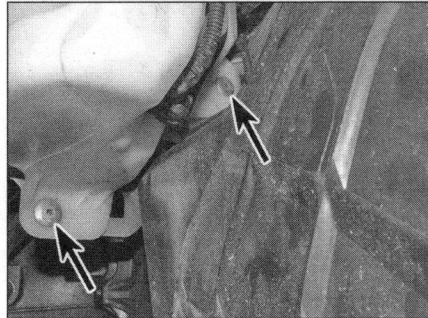

15.3 Washer reservoir securing rivets

15.14 Release the two retaining lugs and remove the washer jet from the high-level stop-light unit

Refitting

15 Ensure that the jet is clipped securely in position. Check the operation of the jet. If necessary, adjust the nozzle using a pin, aiming the spray to a point slightly above the centre of the swept area.

16 Steering column electronics module – removal and refitting

Note: *The steering column electronics module also incorporates the ignition switch, steering column lock and airbag rotary connector. These components are an integral part of the module and cannot be separated.*
Note: *Vauxhall/Opel special tool CH-48829 (or suitable alternative) will be required to unscrew the Torx-Plus tamperproof bolt securing the electronics module to the steering column.*

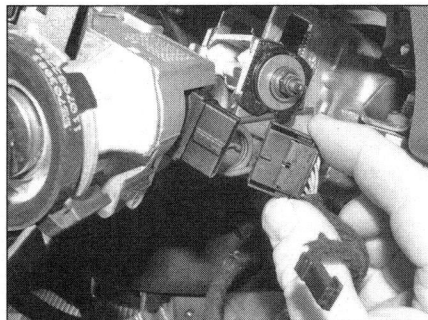

16.7a Disconnect the wiring connectors at the ignition switch...

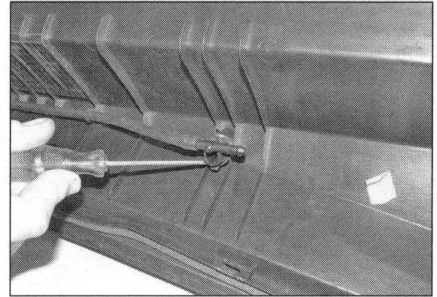

15.10 Depress the retaining clip, then carefully prise the washer jet nozzle from the windscreen cowl panel

16.6 Disconnect the main wiring harness connector at the rear of the steering column electronics module

Removal

1 Disconnect the battery negative terminal (refer to *Disconnecting the battery* in Chapter 5A, Section 4) and wait for 2 minutes.
2 Remove the driver's airbag as described in Section 23.
3 Set the roadwheels in the straight-ahead position and ensure they remain in that position during the removal and refitting procedures.
4 Remove the steering wheel as described in Chapter 10, Section 14.
5 Remove the steering column shrouds as described in Chapter 11, Section 26.
6 Open the locking bar and disconnect the main wiring harness connector at the rear of the electronics module **(see illustration)**.
7 Disconnect the wiring connectors at the ignition switch and immobiliser transponder **(see illustrations)**.
8 Using the Vauxhall/Opel special tool or

16.7b...and immobiliser transponder

16.8a Using the Vauxhall/Opel special tool or a suitable alternative...

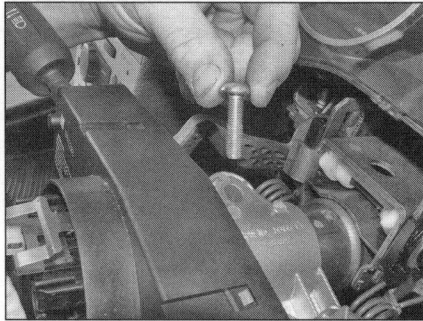
16.8b...unscrew and remove the tamperproof clamp bolt securing the module assembly to the steering column

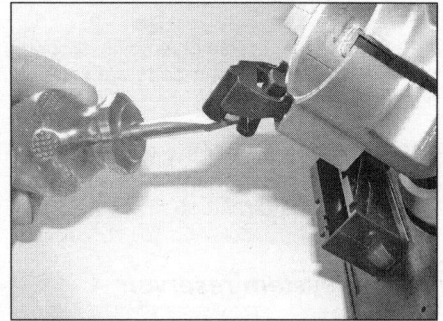
16.9a Using a screwdriver, depress the retaining catch on the underside of the module (shown removed for clarity)...

16.9b...and withdraw the module from the steering column

16.10 Use a 1.5 mm diameter rod to depress the internal retaining lug, and withdraw the switch stalk from the electronics module

17.3 Removing the radio/CD player using welding rod to compress the internal clips

a suitable alternative, unscrew and remove the tamperproof clamp bolt securing the module assembly to the steering column **(see illustrations)**.

9 Using a small screwdriver, depress the retaining catch on the underside and withdraw the module from the steering column **(see illustrations)**.

10 If required the direction indicator and wiper switch stalks can be removed from the module as follows. Insert a 1.5 mm diameter rod down the slot on the side of the stalk. Push the rod in fully, to depress the internal retaining lug, and withdraw the stalk from the module **(see illustration)**. Note that this procedure merely allows the stalks to be removed, the actual direction indicator and wiper switches themselves are an integral part of the electronics module and cannot be removed.

Refitting

11 Refitting is the reverse of removal, bearing in mind the following points:
a) *If removed, push the switch stalks back into position in the module until they lock into place.*
b) *As the module is refitted to the steering column, keep the retaining catch on the underside of the module depressed to allow the unit to fully seat on the column.*
c) *Tighten the module tamperproof clamp bolt to the specified torque.*

17 Radio/CD player – removal and refitting

Note: *The following removal and refitting procedure is for the range of units which Vauxhall/Opel fit as standard equipment. Removal and refitting procedures of non-standard units may differ slightly.*

Removal

1 All the radio/CD players fitted by Vauxhall/Opel have DIN standard fixings. Two special tools, obtainable from most car accessory shops, are required for removal. Alternatively, suitable tools can be fabricated from 3 mm diameter wire, such as welding rod.

2 Disconnect the battery negative terminal (refer to *Disconnecting the battery* in Chapter 5A, Section 4).

3 Insert the tools into the holes on the front of the unit, and push them until they snap into place. The radio/CD player can then be slid out of the facia **(see illustration)**.

4 Disconnect the wiring and aerial connections at the rear of the unit, and remove the unit from the car.

Refitting

5 To refit the radio/CD player, reconnect the aerial and wiring then simply push the unit into the facia until the retaining lugs snap into place. On completion, reconnect the battery.

18 Speakers – removal and refitting

Door small (tweeter) speaker

Removal

1 Remove the door inner trim panel as described in Chapter 11, Section 12.
2 Release the three retaining lugs and remove the speaker from the trim panel.

Refitting

3 Refitting is the reverse of removal.

Door main speaker

Removal

4 Remove the door inner trim panel as described in Chapter 11, Section 12.
5 Undo the retaining screws, then free the speaker from its location **(see illustration)**.

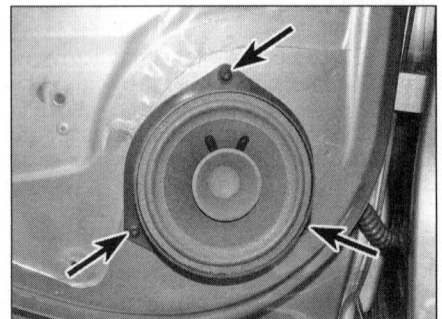
18.5 Door loudspeaker retaining screws

Disconnect the wiring connectors and remove the speaker.

Refitting

6 Refitting is the reverse of removal.

Facia centre speaker

Removal

7 Disconnect the battery negative terminal (refer to *Disconnecting the battery* in Chapter 5A, Section 4).

8 Using a small screwdriver, carefully prise free the centre speaker panel from the upper centre of the facia **(see illustration 10.2)**. Where applicable, disconnect the sunlight sensor wiring connector and remove the panel.

9 Undo the retaining screw at the front of the information display cover panel **(see illustration 10.3)**.

10 Using a plastic spatula or similar tool, carefully prise up the front of the information display cover panel to release the two clips each side. Once the side clips are released, move the panel forward to disengage the two lugs at the rear **(see illustrations 10.4a and 10.4b)**.

11 Undo the two screws securing the speaker to the centre switch/vent panel. Lift out the speaker and disconnect the wiring connector **(see illustrations 10.5a and 10.5b)**.

Refitting

12 Refitting is a reversal of removal.

19 Radio aerial –
general information

1 Where required, the aerial mast can be unscrewed from the base unit.

2 Removal of the base unit entails removal of the headlining, which is a complicated operation, considered to be outside the scope of this manual. Therefore, any problems relating to the aerial base unit or wiring should be entrusted to a Vauxhall/Opel dealer.

20 Anti-theft alarm system –
general information

Note: *This information is applicable only to the anti-theft alarm system fitted by Vauxhall/Opel as standard equipment.*

1 Most models in the range are fitted with an anti-theft alarm system as standard equipment. The alarm is automatically armed and disarmed when the deadlocks are operated using the driver's door lock or remote control key. The alarm has switches on all the doors (including the tailgate), the bonnet, and the ignition and starter circuits. If the tailgate, bonnet or any of the doors are opened whilst the alarm is set, the alarm horn will sound and the hazard warning lights will flash. The alarm also has an immobiliser function which makes the ignition and starter circuits inoperable whilst the alarm is triggered.

2 The alarm system performs a self-test every time it is switched on; this test takes approximately 10 seconds. During the self-test, the LED (light emitting diode) in the facia switch will come on. If the LED flashes rapidly, then either the tailgate, bonnet or one of the doors is open, or there is a fault in the circuit. After the initial 10 second period, the LED will flash slowly to indicate that the alarm is switched on. On unlocking the driver's door lock, the LED will illuminate for approximately 1 second, then go out, indicating that the alarm has been switched off.

3 Should the alarm system develop a fault, the vehicle should be taken to a Vauxhall/Opel dealer for examination.

21 Heated seat components –
general information

1 On models with heated seats, a heater mat is fitted to both the seat back and seat cushion. Renewal of either heater mat involves peeling back the upholstery, removing the old mat, sticking the new mat in position and then refitting the upholstery. Note that upholstery removal and refitting requires considerable skill and experience if it is to be carried out successfully, and is therefore best entrusted to your Vauxhall/Opel dealer. In practice, it will be very difficult for the home mechanic to carry out the job without ruining the upholstery.

22 Airbag system –
general information and precautions

General information

1 A driver's airbag is fitted as standard equipment on all models. The airbag is fitted in the steering wheel centre pad. Additionally, a passenger's airbag located in the facia, side airbags located in the front seats, and curtain airbags located in the headlining are optionally available.

2 The system is armed only when the ignition is switched on, however, a reserve power source maintains a power supply to the system in the event of a break in the main electrical supply. The steering wheel and facia airbags are activated by a 'g' sensor (deceleration sensor), and controlled by an electronic control unit located under the centre console. The side airbags and curtain airbags are activated by severe side impact and operate independently of the main system.

3 The airbags are inflated by a gas generator, which forces the bag out from its location in the steering wheel, facia, seat back frame, or headlining.

Precautions

⚠️ **Warning: The following precautions must be observed when working on vehicles equipped with an airbag system, to prevent the possibility of personal injury.**

General precautions

4 The following precautions must be observed when carrying out work on a vehicle equipped with an airbag:

a) Do not disconnect the battery with the engine running.

b) Before carrying out any work in the vicinity of the airbag, removal of any of the airbag components, or any welding work on the vehicle, de-activate the system as described in the following sub-Section

c) Do not attempt to test any of the airbag system circuits using test meters or any other test equipment.

d) If the airbag warning light comes on, or any fault in the system is suspected, consult a Vauxhall/Opel dealer without delay. Do not attempt to carry out fault diagnosis, or any dismantling of the components.

Precautions when handling an airbag

a) Transport the airbag by itself, bag upward

b) Do not put your arms around the airbag.

c) Carry the airbag close to the body, bag outward.

d) Do not drop the airbag or expose it to impacts.

e) Do not attempt to dismantle the airbag unit.

f) Do not connect any form of electrical equipment to any part of the airbag circuit.

Precautions when storing an airbag

a) Store the unit in a cupboard with the airbag upward.

b) Do not expose the airbag to temperatures above 80°C.

c) Do not expose the airbag to flames.

d) Do not attempt to dispose of the airbag – consult a Vauxhall/Opel dealer.

e) Never refit an airbag which is known to be faulty or damaged.

De-activation of airbag system

5 The system must be de-activated before carrying out any work on the airbag components or surrounding area:

a) Switch on the ignition and check the operation of the airbag warning light on the instrument panel. The light should illuminate when the ignition is switched on, then extinguish.

b) Switch off the ignition.

c) Remove the ignition key.

d) Switch off all electrical equipment.

e) Disconnect the battery negative terminal (refer to 'Disconnecting the battery' in Chapter 5A, Section 4).

f) Insulate the battery negative terminal and the end of the battery negative lead to prevent any possibility of contact.

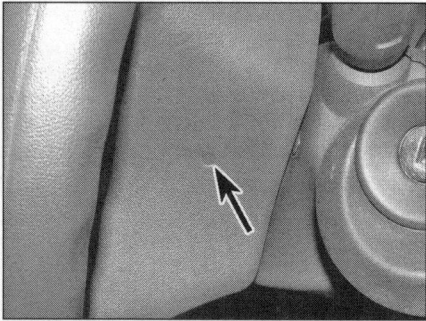

23.3a Insert a screwdriver into the holes at the rear of the steering wheel spokes...

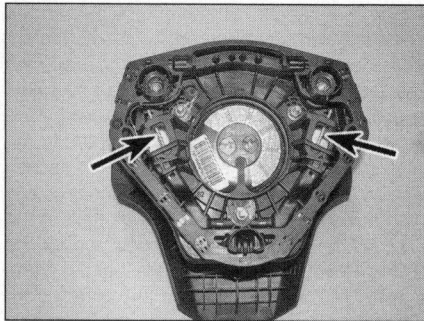

23.3b...to depress the airbag internal spring retainers (shown with airbag removed)

23.4 Release the locking clips, then disconnect the wiring connectors

23.7 Undo the bolt securing the passenger's airbag to the facia crossmember

into the holes, one at a time, to depress the internal spring retainers, and at the same time pull the airbag unit away from the steering wheel to release it **(see illustrations)**.

4 Release the locking clips, then disconnect the wiring connectors at the rear of the airbag unit **(see illustration)**. Remove the airbag unit. Note that the airbag must not be knocked or dropped, and should be stored the correct way up, with its padded surface uppermost.

5 Refitting is a reversal of the removal procedure.

Passenger's airbag

6 Remove the glovebox as described in Chapter 11, Section 26.

7 Undo the bolt securing the airbag to the facia crossmember **(see illustration)**. Withdraw the airbag and disconnect the wiring connector(s). Note that the airbag must not be knocked or dropped, and should be stored the correct way up (as mounted in the vehicle).

8 Refitting is a reversal of the removal procedure, tightening the retaining bolt securely.

Side airbags

9 The side airbags are located internally within the front seat back and no attempt should be made to remove them. Any suspected problems with the side airbag system should be referred to a Vauxhall/Opel dealer.

Curtain airbags

10 The curtain airbags are located behind the headlining above the doors on each side and no attempt should be made to remove them. Any suspected problems with the curtain airbag system should be referred to a Vauxhall/Opel dealer.

Airbag control unit

11 The airbag control unit is located beneath the centre console and no attempt should be made to remove it. Any suspected problems with the control unit should be referred to a Vauxhall/Opel dealer.

Airbag rotary connector

12 The airbag rotary connector is an integral part of the steering column electronics module. Removal and refitting procedures for the module are contained in Section 16.

g) Wait for at least two minutes before carrying out any further work. Wait at least ten minutes if the airbag warning light did not operate correctly.

Activation of airbag system

6 To activate the system on completion of any work, proceed as follows:

a) Ensure that there are no occupants in the vehicle, and that there are no loose objects around the vicinity of the steering wheel. Close the vehicle doors and windows.

b) Ensure that the ignition is switched off then reconnect the battery negative terminal.

c) Open the driver's door and switch on the ignition, without reaching in front of the steering wheel. Check that the airbag warning light illuminates briefly then extinguishes.

d) Switch off the ignition.

e) If the airbag warning light does not operate as described in paragraph c), consult a Vauxhall/Opel dealer before driving the vehicle.

23 Airbag system components – removal and refitting

1 Refer to the precautions given in Section 22 before attempting to carry out work on any of the airbag components.

2 De-activate the airbag system as described in Section 22, then proceed as described under the relevant heading.

Driver's airbag

3 Turn the steering wheel through 90° so that the two holes at the rear of the steering wheel spokes are accessible. Insert a screwdriver

FRONT DISTRIBUTION UNIT

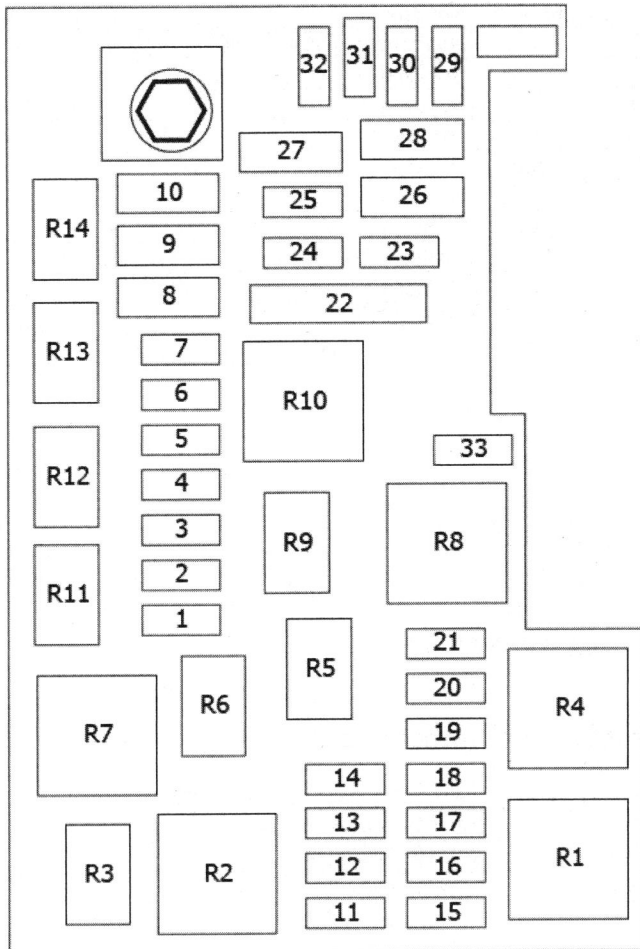

FUSE/ RELAY	VALUE	DESCRIPTION
1	30A	Starter relay
2	7.5A	Air-conditioning compressor clutch
3	30A	Heated filter
4	15A	Horn relay
5	15A	Manual transmission; Automatic transmission
6	7.5A	Engine control unit. Engine control unit relay
7	15A	Fog light relay
8	40A	Cooling fan relay
9	40A	Cooling fan relay
10	30A	Manual transmission (60A also used)
11	7.5A	Water separator sensor; Glow plug control unit; Mass airflow meter; Ignition coil Or Mass airflow meter Ignition coil (15A also used)
12	5A	Front sidelights; Additional lighting; Light switch
13	7.5A	Heating Air conditioning
14	5A	Manual transmission; Automatic transmission
15	10A	Front sidelights. Additional lighting
16	10A	Front sidelights. Additional lighting
17	10A	Injectors (cylinders 1–4). Engine control unit
18	7.5A	Engine control unit
19	10A	Airbag
20	10A	Engine control unit
21	15A	Oxygen sensor in front of the catalytic converter EGR valve; Catalytic convertor sensor; Tank vent valve; Twinport Boost pressure regulator solenoid (20A also used)
22	70A	Instrument panel
23	20A	Compressor control
24	15A	Fuel pump relay; Additional relay, fuel pump
25	30A	Anti-lock brakes
26	30A	Heated rear windscreen
27	40A	Anti-lock brakes
28	40A	Air conditioning climate control
29	20A	Cigarette lighter
30	7.5A	Air conditioning climate control
31	20A	Power windows
32	20A	Power windows
33	7.5A	Exterior mirror
R1	NULL	Cooling fan relay Or Not used
R2	NULL	Cooling fan relay
R3	NULL	Horn relay
R4	NULL	Cooling ran relay Or Not used
R5	NULL	Starter relay
R6	NULL	Engine control relay
R7	NULL	Terminal 15 relay
R8	NULL	Terminal 15 relay
R9	NULL	Fuel pump relay. Additional relay; fuel pump
R10	NULL	Heated rear windscreen relay
R11	NULL	Addional cooling fan relay
R12	NULL	Main beam relay
R13	NULL	Compressor; Air-conditioning relay
R14	NULL	Fog light relay

REAR DISTRIBUTION UNIT

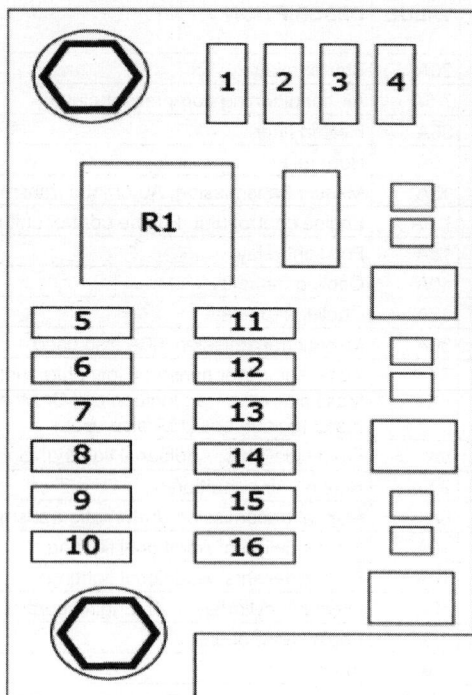

FUSE/ RELAY	VALUE	DESCRIPTION
1	20A	Seat heater
2	20A	Seat heater
3	NULL	Not used
4	20A	Front sidelights
5	NULL	Not used
6	NULL	Not used
7	NULL	No information is available
8	NULL	Not used
9	NULL	Not used
10	NULL	Not used
11	NULL	Not used
12	NULL	Not used
13	NULL	Not used
14	20A	Additional bicycle carrier
15	NULL	Not used
16	20A	Sunroof
R1	NULL	Terminal 15 relay

FUSE BOX ENGINE COMPARTMENT

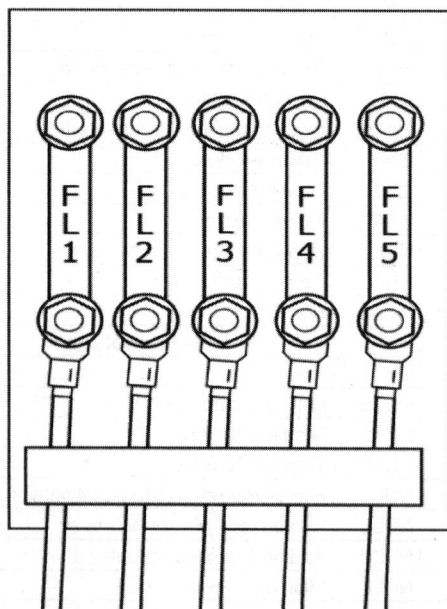

FUSE/ RELAY	VALUE	DESCRIPTION
FL1	40A	Auxiliary heating system; Additional heater
FL2	50A	Distribution control unit
FL3	60A	Additional heater
FL4	80A	Electronic power steering
FL5	80A	Glow plug control unit Or Fuel filter Or Engine control unit

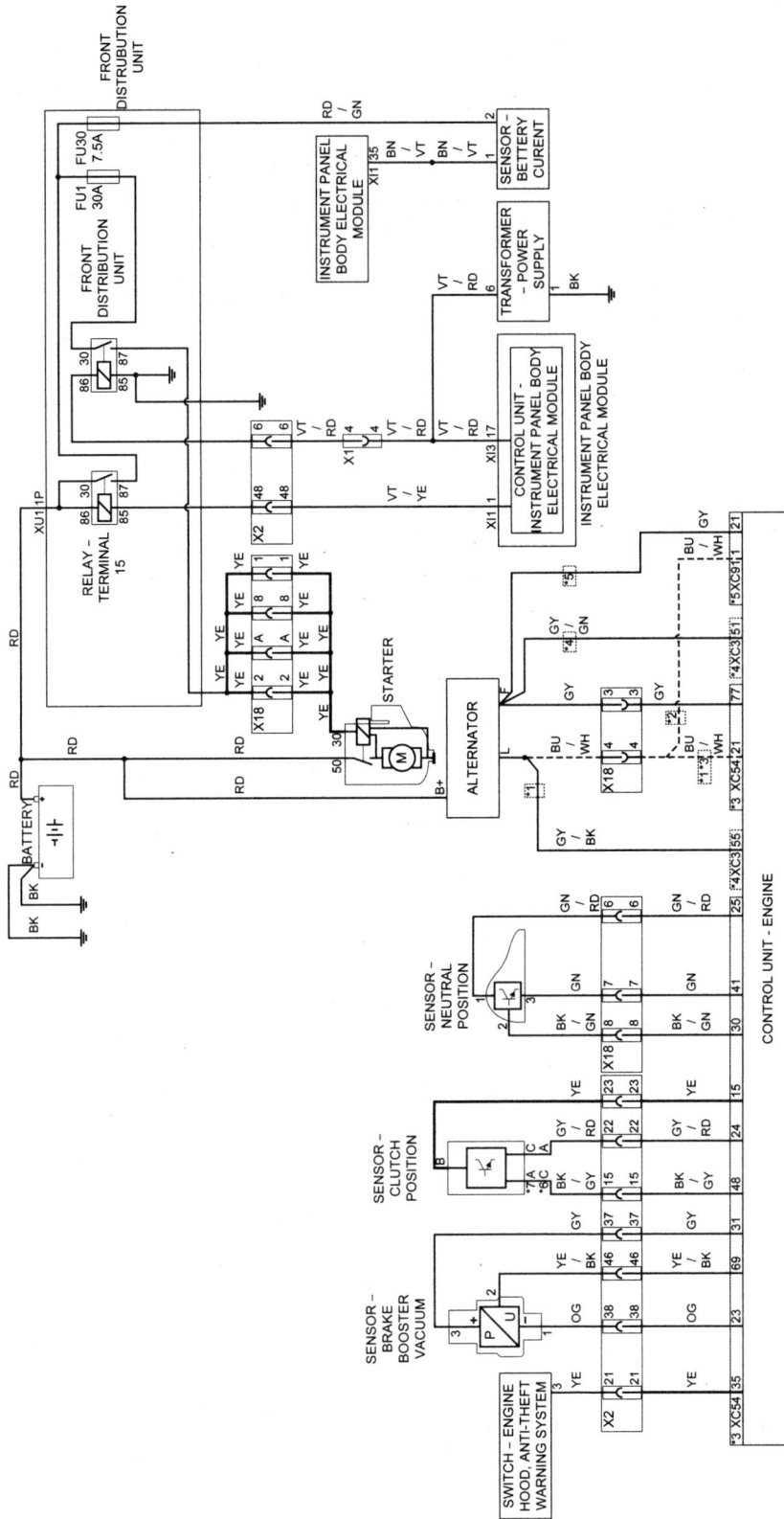

Diagram 1 – Starting and charging

FRONT DISTRIBUTION UNIT

FRONT DISTRIBUTION UNIT

FU1 30A

FU30 7.5A

FRONT DISTRIBUTION UNIT

INSTRUMENT PANEL BODY ELECTRICAL MODULE
XI11 35

SENSOR – BETTERY CURENT

TRANSFORMER – POWER SUPPLY

CONTROL UNIT – INSTRUMENT PANEL BODY ELECTRICAL MODULE

INSTRUMENT PANEL BODY ELECTRICAL MODULE

RELAY – TERMINAL 15

XU11P

BATTERY

STARTER

ALTERNATOR

SENSOR – NEUTRAL POSITION

SENSOR – CLUTCH POSITION

SENSOR – BRAKE BOOSTER VACUUM

SWITCH – ENGINE HOOD, ANTI-THEFT WARNING SYSTEM

CONTROL UNIT – ENGINE

*1 Diesel engine
*2 Petrol engine
*3 Engine code: A13DTC/A13DTE/A13DTR
*4 Engine code: Z13DTJ
*5 Engine code: A12XEL/A12XER/A10XEP/A14XEP/A14XEL/A14XER
*6 LHD
*7 RHD

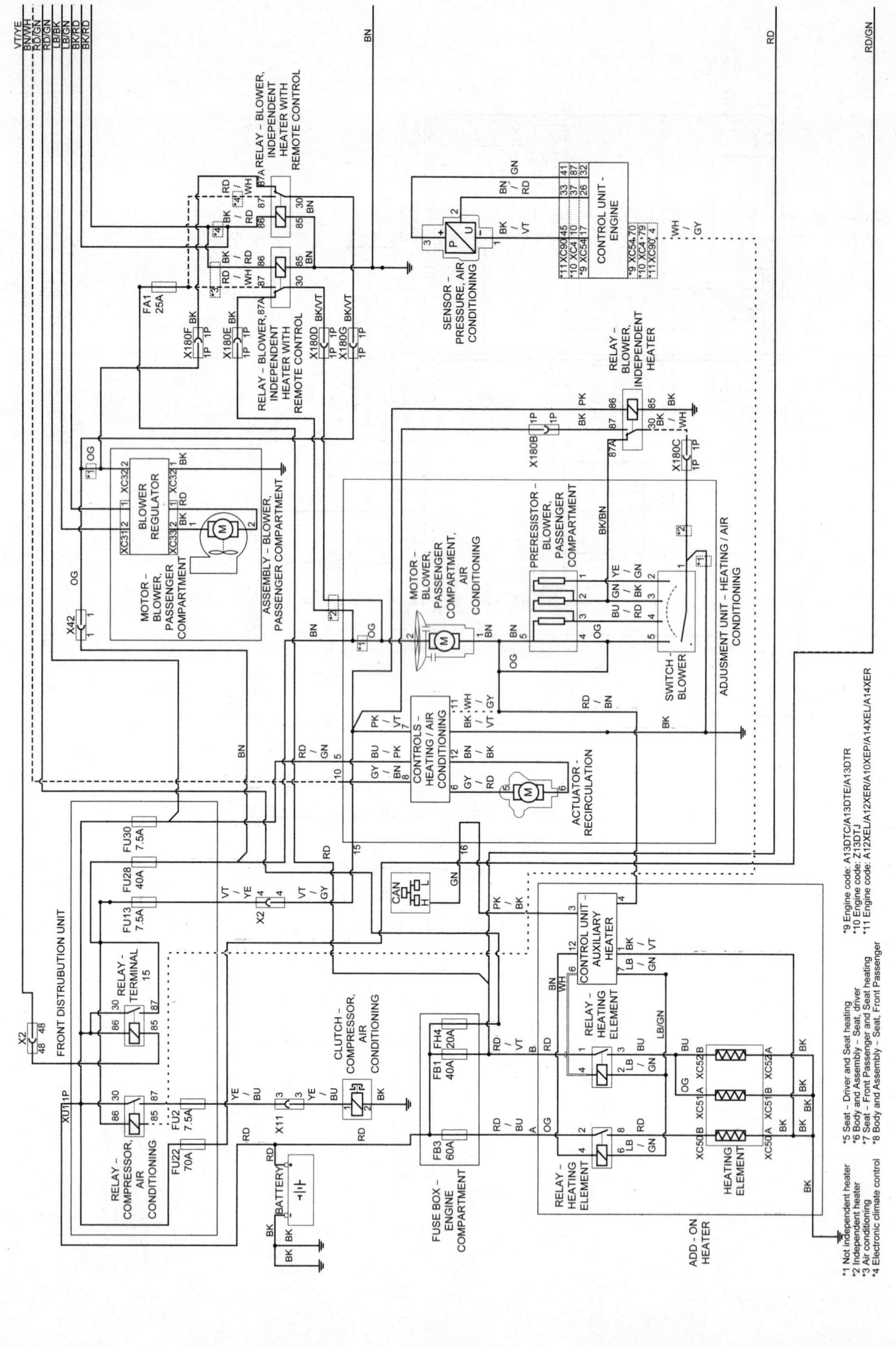
RELAY - COMPRESSOR, AIR CONDITIONING
FU22 70A
FU2 7.5A
RELAY - TERMINAL 15
FRONT DISTRUBUTION UNIT
FU13 7.5A
FU28 40A
FU30 7.5A
BATTERY
CLUTCH - COMPRESSOR, AIR CONDITIONING
FUSE BOX - ENGINE COMPARTMENT
FB3 60A
FB1 40A
FH4 20A
RELAY - HEATING ELEMENT
HEATING ELEMENT
CONTROL UNIT - AUXILIARY HEATER
ADD - ON HEATER
CAN
MOTOR - BLOWER, PASSENGER COMPARTMENT
BLOWER REGULATOR
ASSEMBLY - BLOWER, PASSENGER COMPARTMENT
CONTROLS - HEATING / AIR CONDITIONING
ACTUATOR - RECIRCULATION
MOTOR - BLOWER, PASSENGER COMPARTMENT, AIR CONDITIONING
PRERESISTOR - BLOWER, PASSENGER COMPARTMENT
SWITCH - BLOWER
ADJUSMENT UNIT - HEATING / AIR CONDITIONING
RELAY - BLOWER, INDEPENDENT HEATER
RELAY - BLOWER, INDEPENDENT HEATER WITH REMOTE CONTROL
FA1 25A
SENSOR - PRESSURE, AIR CONDITIONING
CONTROL UNIT - ENGINE
*1 Not independent heater
*2 Independent heater
*3 Air conditioning
*4 Electronic climate control
*5 Seat - Driver and Seat heating
*6 Body and Assembly - Seat, driver
*7 Seat - Front Passenger and Seat heating
*8 Body and Assembly - Seat, Front Passenger
*9 Engine code: A13DTC/A13DTE/A13DTR
*10 Engine code: Z13DTJ
*11 Engine code: A12XEL/A12XER/A10XEP/A14XEL/A14XER

Diagram 2 – Heating and air conditioning (1 of 2)

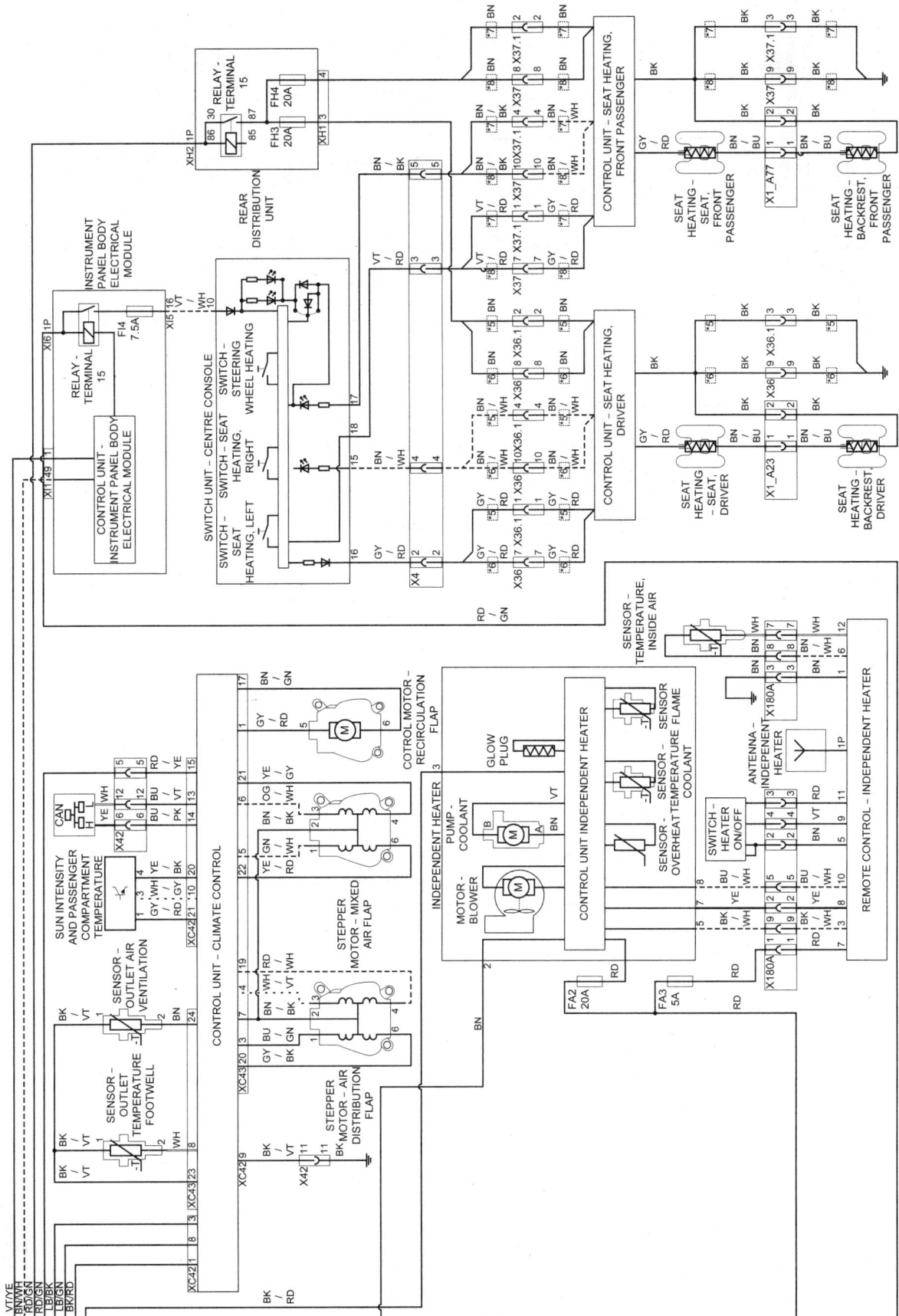

Diagram 2 – Heating and air conditioning (2 of 2)

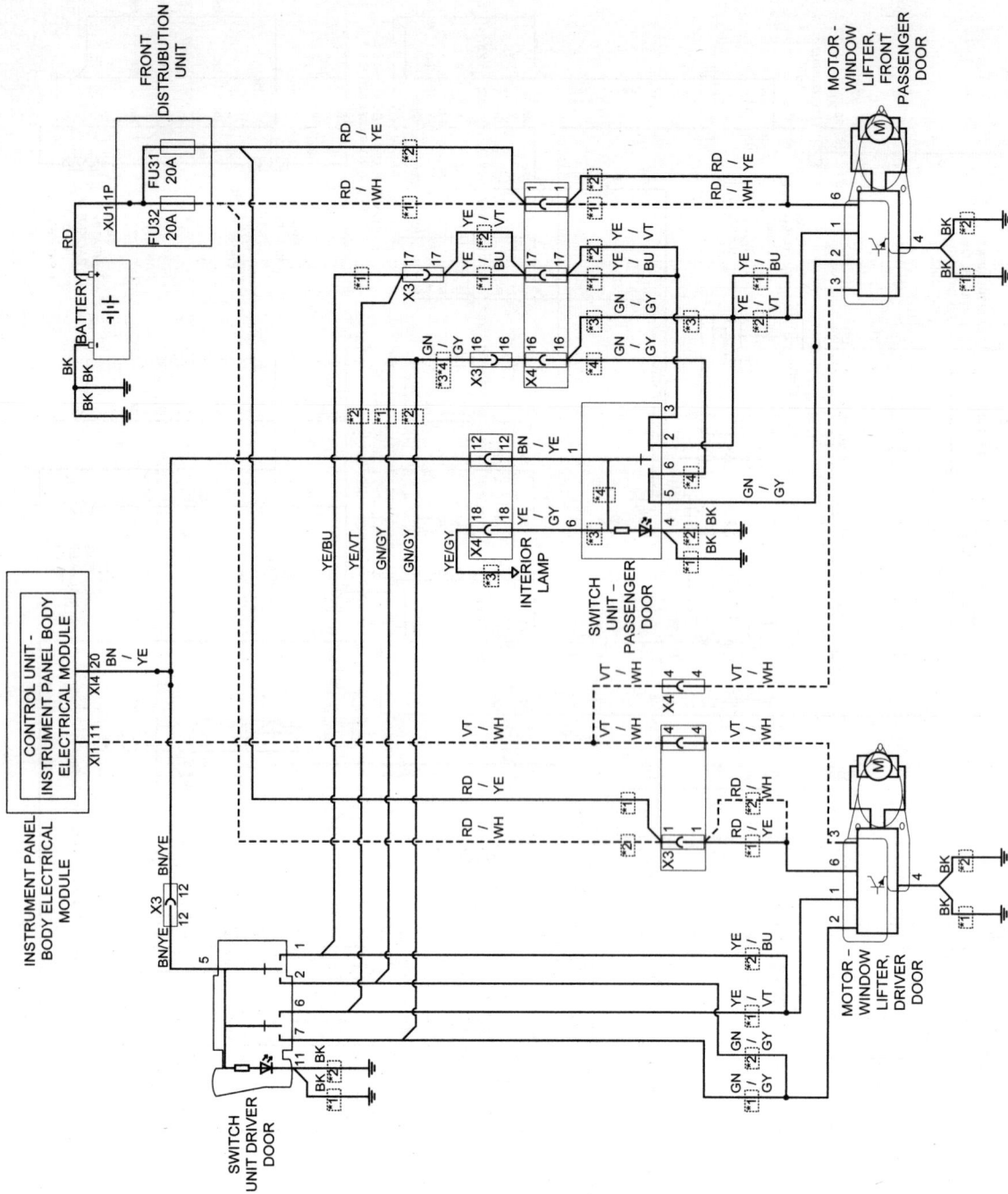

Diagram 3 – Electric windows

*1 Left-hand drive
*2 Right-hand drive
*3 With Translucent Switch
*4 Without translucent Switch

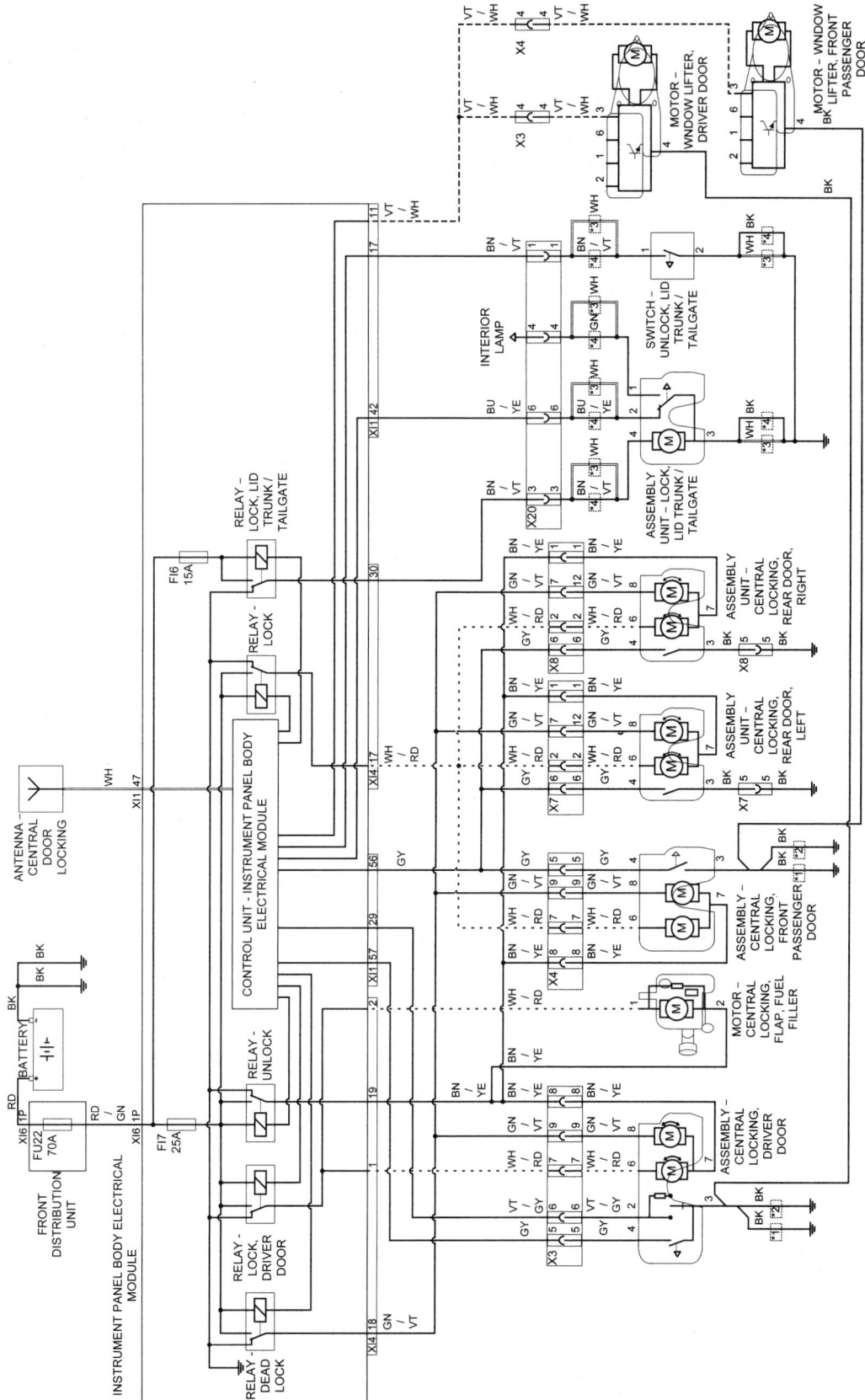

Diagram 4 – Central locking

*1 Left-hand drive
*2 Right-hand drive
*3 For Great Britain
*4 Except Great Britain

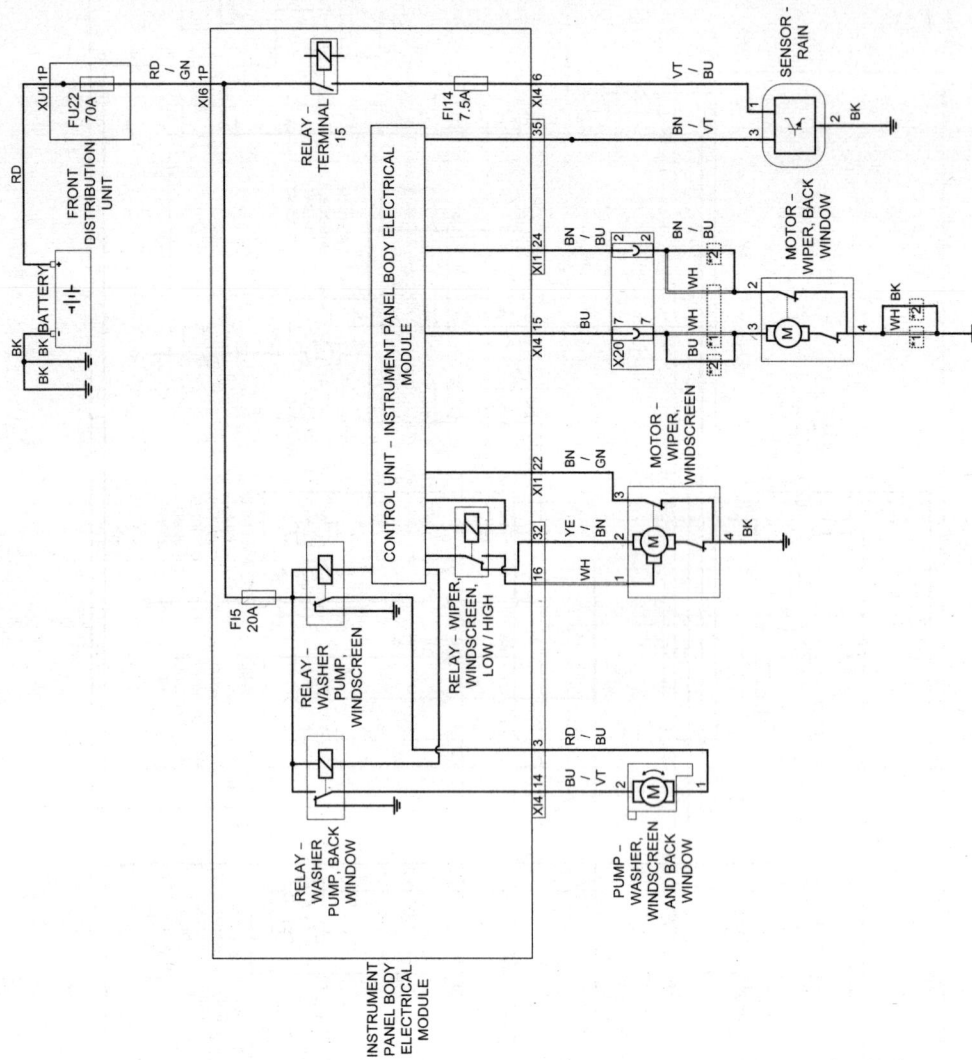

Diagram 5 – Windscreen wipers and washers

*1 For Great Britain
*2 Except Great Britain

Diagram 6a – Exterior lights

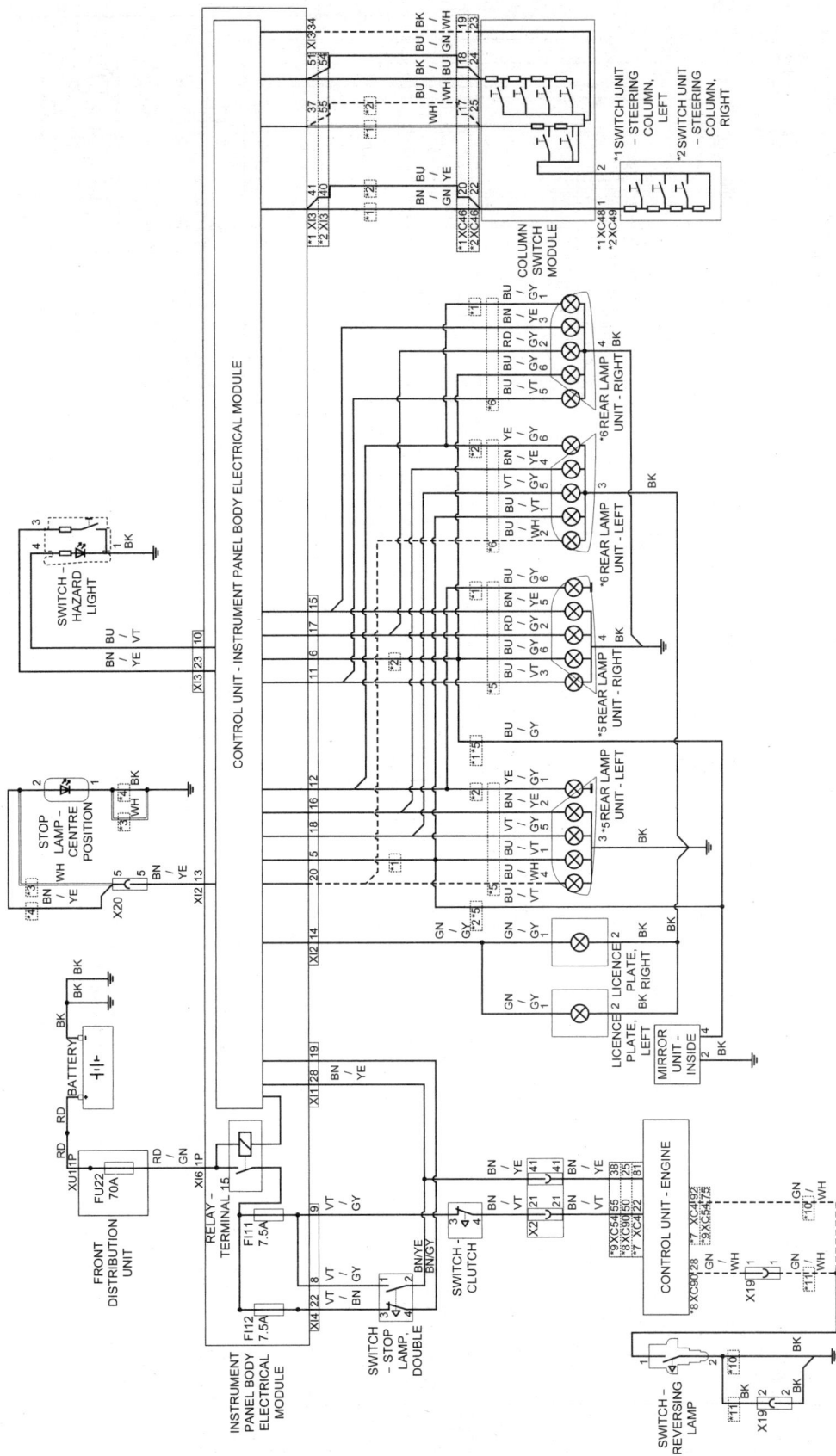

CONTROL UNIT - INSTRUMENT PANEL BODY ELECTRICAL MODULE

SWITCH - HAZARD LIGHT

STOP LAMP - CENTRE POSITION

SWITCH - STOP LAMP, DOUBLE

SWITCH - CLUTCH

SWITCH - REVERSING LAMP

CONTROL UNIT - ENGINE

INSTRUMENT PANEL BODY ELECTRICAL MODULE

RELAY - TERMINAL 15

FRONT DISTRIBUTION UNIT

BATTERY

FU22 70A

F111 7.5A

F112 7.5A

COLUMN SWITCH MODULE

*1 SWITCH UNIT - STEERING COLUMN, LEFT
*2 SWITCH UNIT - STEERING COLUMN, RIGHT

*6 REAR LAMP UNIT - RIGHT
*6 REAR LAMP UNIT - LEFT
*5 REAR LAMP UNIT - RIGHT
*5 REAR LAMP UNIT - LEFT

LICENCE 2 LICENCE 2 PLATE, PLATE, LEFT BK RIGHT

MIRROR UNIT - INSIDE

*1 For left hand traffic
*2 For right hand traffic
*3 For Great Britain
*4 Except Great Britain
*5 Hatchback 3 doors
*6 Hatchback 5 doors
*7 Engine code : Z13DTJ
*8 Engine code : A10XEP/ A12XEL/ A12XER/ A14XEL/ A14XER
*9 Engine code : A10XEP/ A13DTE/ A13DTR
*10 Petrol engines
*11 Diesel engines

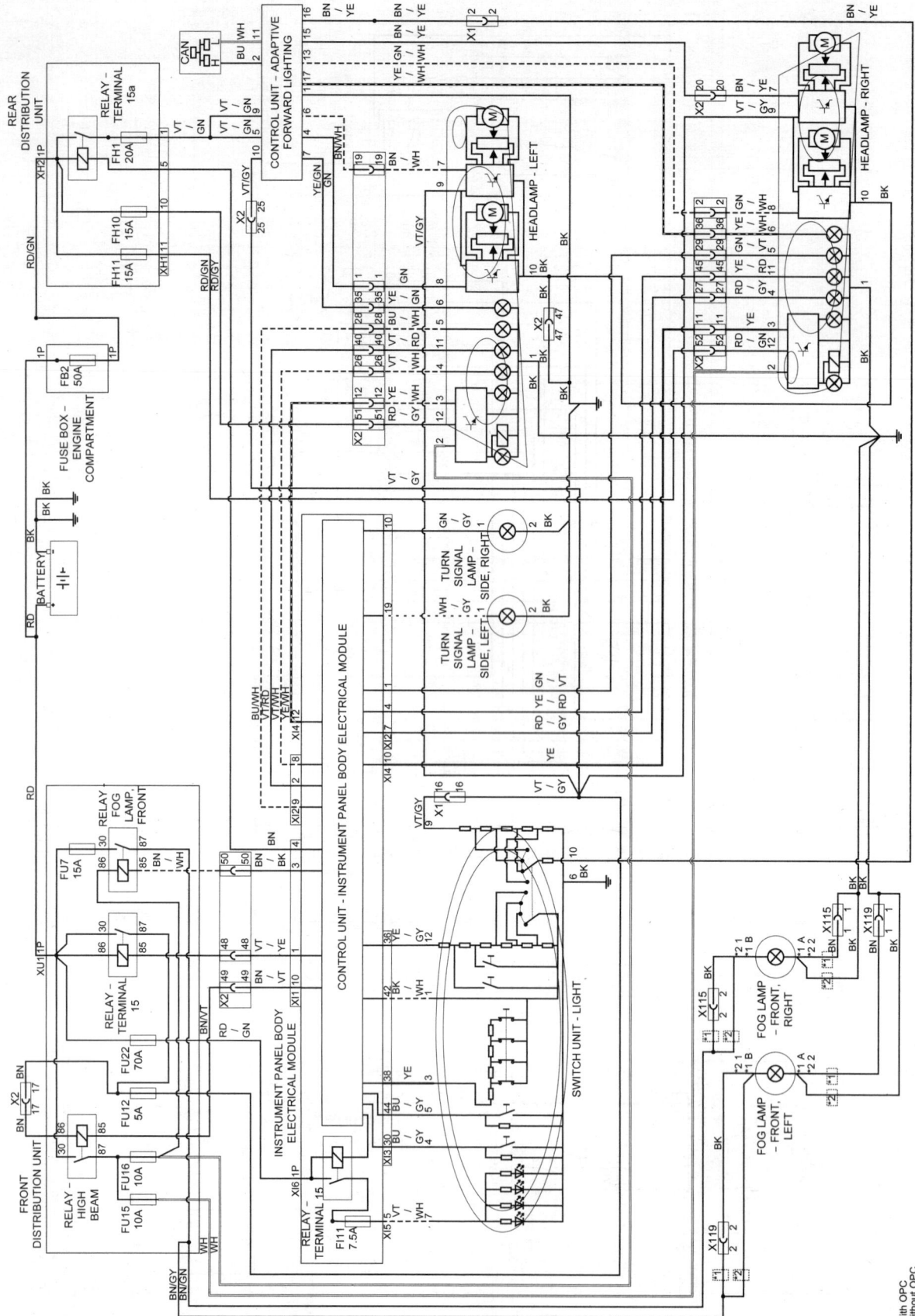

Diagram 6b – Exterior lights (with Adaptive Forward Lighting)

*1 With OPC
*2 Without OPC

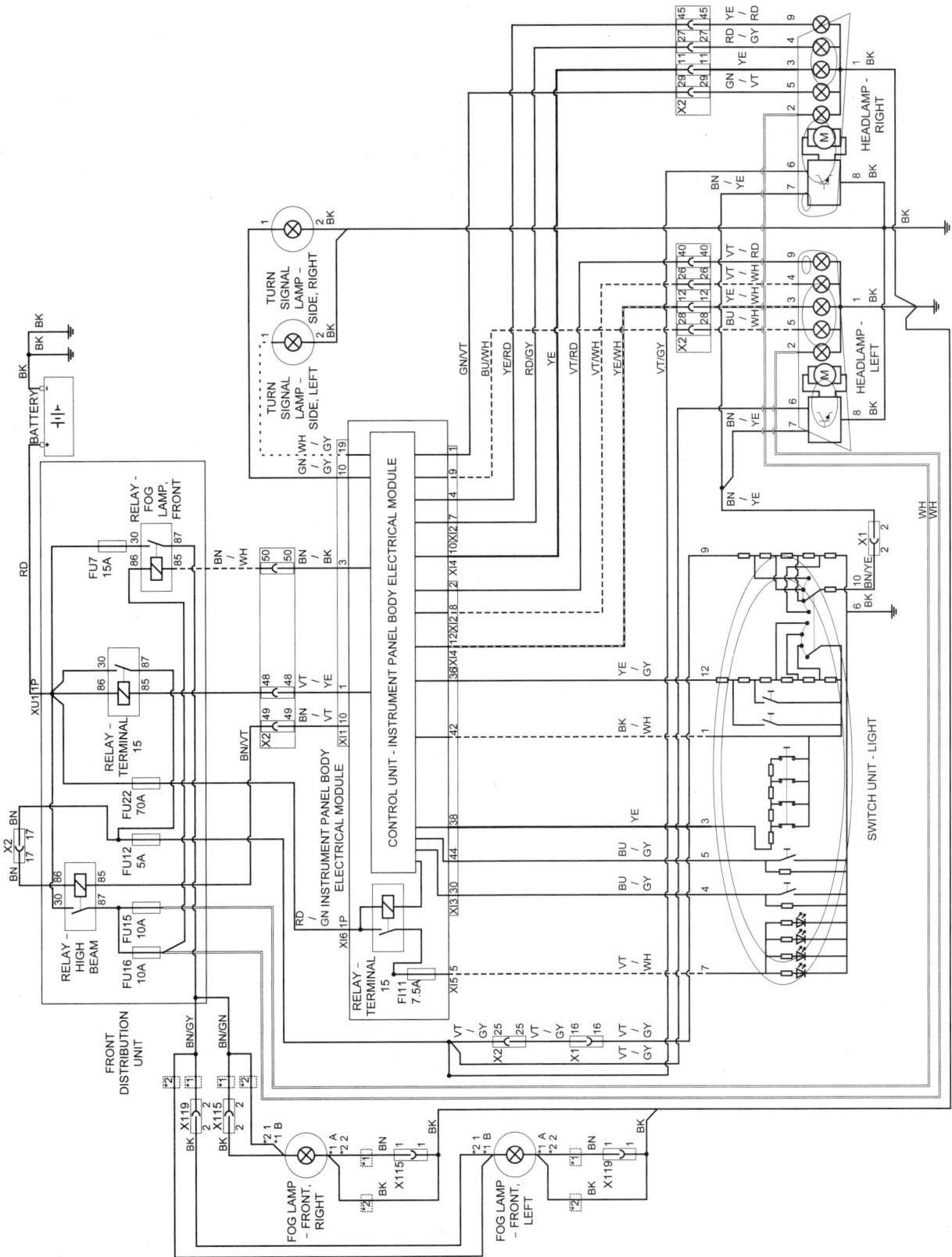

Diagram 6b – Exterior lights (without Adaptive Forward Lighting)

*1 With OPC
*2 Without OPC

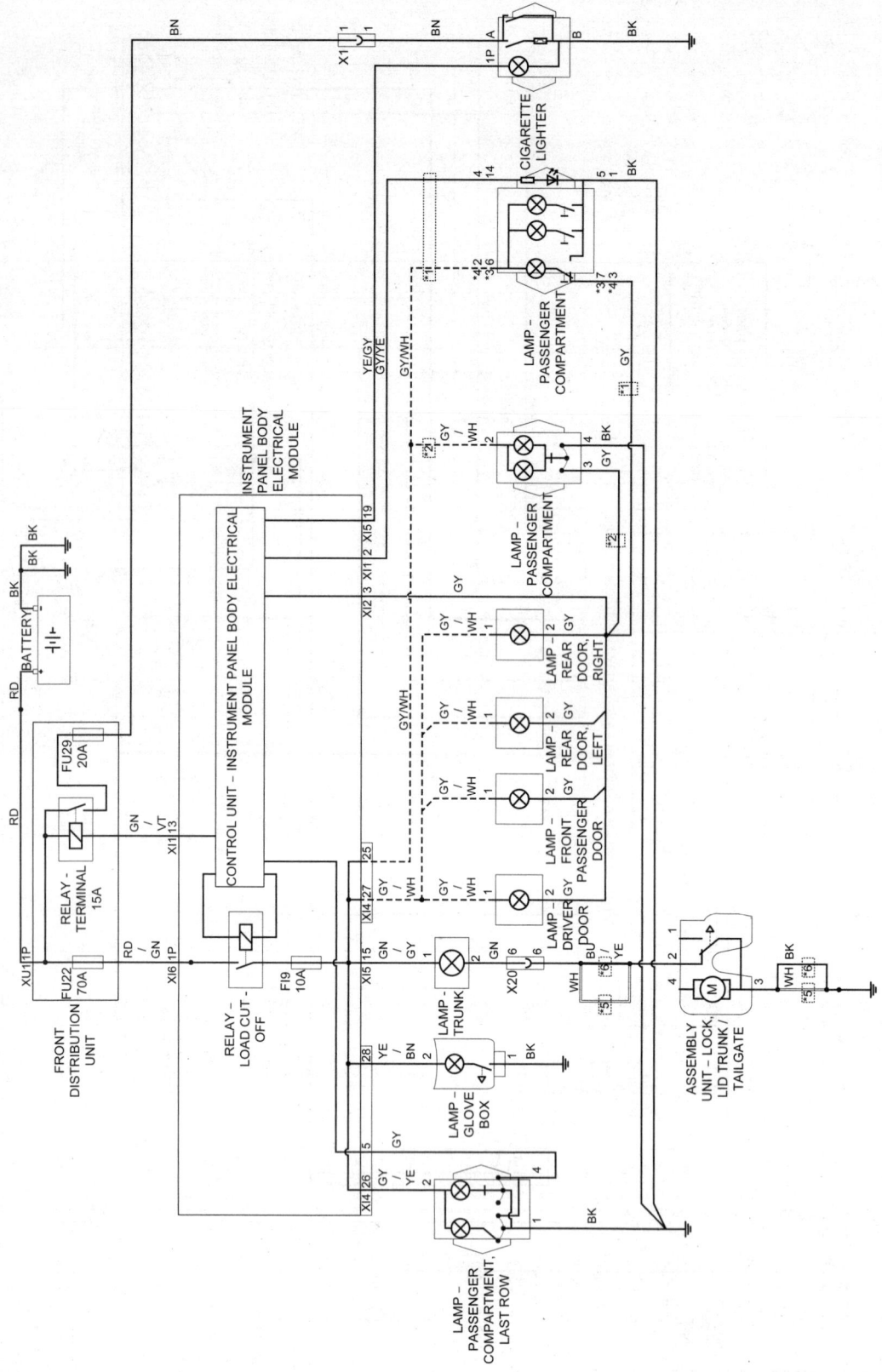

Diagram 7 – Interior lights

*1 With reading lamp, rear
*2 Without reading lamp, rear
*3 Body and assembly – lamp passenger compartment
*4 Assembly – Lamp passenger compartment and lamp, passenger compartment
*5 For Great Britain
*6 Except Great Britain

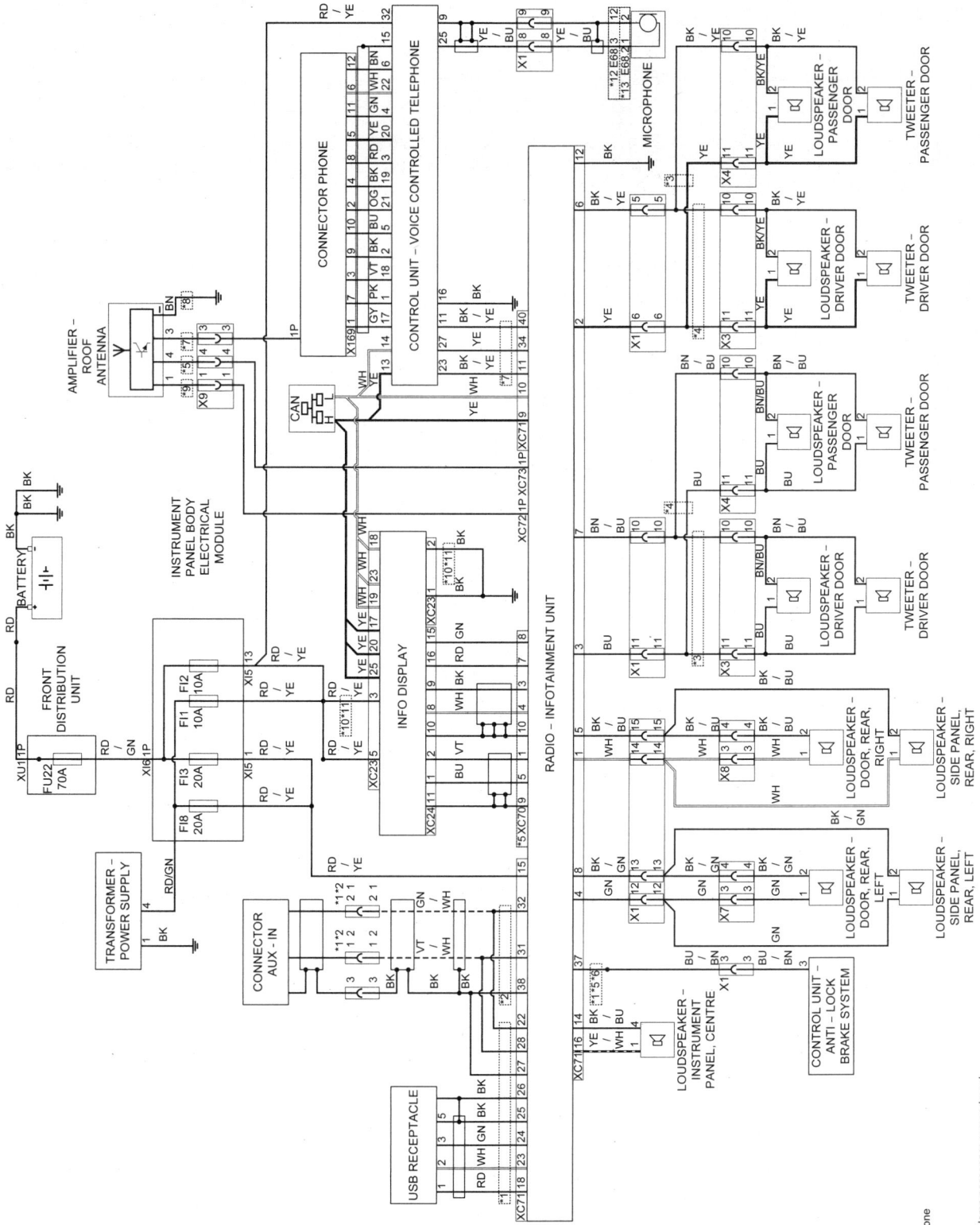

Diagram 8 – In-car entertainment

*1 UFZ Radio
*2 Not UFZ Radio
*3 Left – hand drive
*4 Right – hand drive
*5 Navigation System
*6 Carphone
*7 Voice controlled telephone
*8 Sun roof
*9 Radio
*10 Graphic info display
*11 Color info Display
*12 Body and Assembly – lamp passenger compartment
*13 Assembly – lamp passenger compartment and microphone

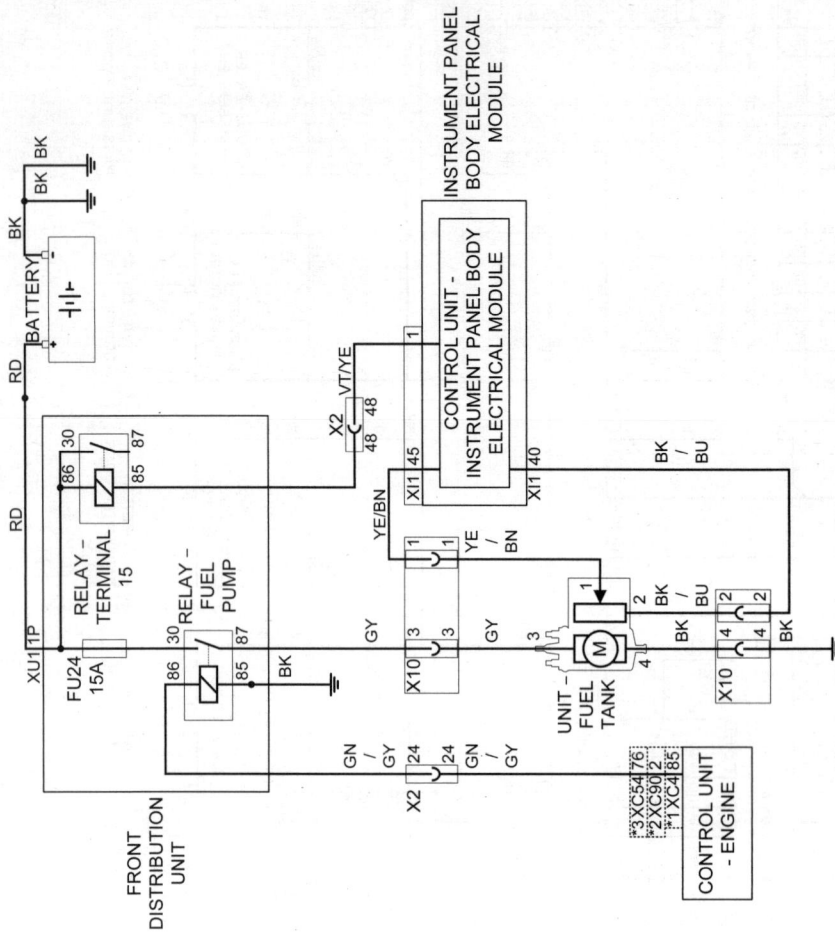

Diagram 9 – Fuel pump

*1 Engine code: Z13DTJ
*2 Engine code: A12XEL/A12XER/A10XEP/A14XELI/A14XER
*3 Engine code: A13DTC/A13DTE/A13DTR

Dimensions and weights

Note: *All figures are approximate and may vary according to model. Refer to manufacturer's data for exact figures.*

Dimensions

Overall length	3999 mm
Overall width (including door mirrors)	1944 mm
Overall height (unladen)	1488 mm
Wheelbase	2511 mm
Turning circle diameter (wall to wall)	10.1 metres

Weights

Kerb weight

Petrol models:
1.0 litre:

3-door Hatchback	1100 to 1120 kg
5-door Hatchback	1145 to 1165 kg
Van	1125 to 1145 kg

1.2 litre:

3-door Hatchback	1120 to 1135 kg
5-door Hatchback	1163 to 1178 kg
Van	1140 to 1160 kg

1.4 litre:

3-door Hatchback	1140 to 1160 kg
5-door Hatchback	1163 to 1183 kg

Diesel models:

3-door Hatchback	1163 to 1255 kg
5-door Hatchback	1199 to 1365 kg
Van	1215 to 1265 kg
Gross vehicle weight	Refer to information contained on the vehicle identification plate
Maximum roof load (including weight of rack)	75 kg

Conversion factors

Length (distance)

Inches (in)	x 25.4	= Millimetres (mm)	x 0.0394	= Inches (in)
Feet (ft)	x 0.305	= Metres (m)	x 3.281	= Feet (ft)
Miles	x 1.609	= Kilometres (km)	x 0.621	= Miles

Volume (capacity)

Cubic inches (cu in; in³)	x 16.387	= Cubic centimetres (cc; cm³)	x 0.061	= Cubic inches (cu in; in³)
Imperial pints (Imp pt)	x 0.568	= Litres (l)	x 1.76	= Imperial pints (Imp pt)
Imperial quarts (Imp qt)	x 1.137	= Litres (l)	x 0.88	= Imperial quarts (Imp qt)
Imperial quarts (Imp qt)	x 1.201	= US quarts (US qt)	x 0.833	= Imperial quarts (Imp qt)
US quarts (US qt)	x 0.946	= Litres (l)	x 1.057	= US quarts (US qt)
Imperial gallons (Imp gal)	x 4.546	= Litres (l)	x 0.22	= Imperial gallons (Imp gal)
Imperial gallons (Imp gal)	x 1.201	= US gallons (US gal)	x 0.833	= Imperial gallons (Imp gal)
US gallons (US gal)	x 3.785	= Litres (l)	x 0.264	= US gallons (US gal)

Mass (weight)

Ounces (oz)	x 28.35	= Grams (g)	x 0.035	= Ounces (oz)
Pounds (lb)	x 0.454	= Kilograms (kg)	x 2.205	= Pounds (lb)

Force

Ounces-force (ozf; oz)	x 0.278	= Newtons (N)	x 3.6	= Ounces-force (ozf; oz)
Pounds-force (lbf; lb)	x 4.448	= Newtons (N)	x 0.225	= Pounds-force (lbf; lb)
Newtons (N)	x 0.1	= Kilograms-force (kgf; kg)	x 9.81	= Newtons (N)

Pressure

Pounds-force per square inch (psi; lbf/in²; lb/in²)	x 0.070	= Kilograms-force per square centimetre (kgf/cm²; kg/cm²)	x 14.223	= Pounds-force per square inch (psi; lbf/in²; lb/in²)
Pounds-force per square inch (psi; lbf/in²; lb/in²)	x 0.068	= Atmospheres (atm)	x 14.696	= Pounds-force per square inch (psi; lbf/in²; lb/in²)
Pounds-force per square inch (psi; lbf/in²; lb/in²)	x 0.069	= Bars	x 14.5	= Pounds-force per square inch (psi; lbf/in²; lb/in²)
Pounds-force per square inch (psi; lbf/in²; lb/in²)	x 6.895	= Kilopascals (kPa)	x 0.145	= Pounds-force per square inch (psi; lbf/in²; lb/in²)
Kilopascals (kPa)	x 0.01	= Kilograms-force per square centimetre (kgf/cm²; kg/cm²)	x 98.1	= Kilopascals (kPa)
Millibar (mbar)	x 100	= Pascals (Pa)	x 0.01	= Millibar (mbar)
Millibar (mbar)	x 0.0145	= Pounds-force per square inch (psi; lbf/in²; lb/in²)	x 68.947	= Millibar (mbar)
Millibar (mbar)	x 0.75	= Millimetres of mercury (mmHg)	x 1.333	= Millibar (mbar)
Millibar (mbar)	x 0.401	= Inches of water (inH₂O)	x 2.491	= Millibar (mbar)
Millimetres of mercury (mmHg)	x 0.535	= Inches of water (inH₂O)	x 1.868	= Millimetres of mercury (mmHg)
Inches of water (inH₂O)	x 0.036	= Pounds-force per square inch (psi; lbf/in²; lb/in²)	x 27.68	= Inches of water (inH₂O)

Torque (moment of force)

Pounds-force inches (lbf in; lb in)	x 1.152	= Kilograms-force centimetre (kgf cm; kg cm)	x 0.868	= Pounds-force inches (lbf in; lb in)
Pounds-force inches (lbf in; lb in)	x 0.113	= Newton metres (Nm)	x 8.85	= Pounds-force inches (lbf in; lb in)
Pounds-force inches (lbf in; lb in)	x 0.083	= Pounds-force feet (lbf ft; lb ft)	x 12	= Pounds-force inches (lbf in; lb in)
Pounds-force feet (lbf ft; lb ft)	x 0.138	= Kilograms-force metres (kgf m; kg m)	x 7.233	= Pounds-force feet (lbf ft; lb ft)
Pounds-force feet (lbf ft; lb ft)	x 1.356	= Newton metres (Nm)	x 0.738	= Pounds-force feet (lbf ft; lb ft)
Newton metres (Nm)	x 0.102	= Kilograms-force metres (kgf m; kg m)	x 9.804	= Newton metres (Nm)

Power

Horsepower (hp)	x 745.7	= Watts (W)	x 0.0013	= Horsepower (hp)

Velocity (speed)

Miles per hour (miles/hr; mph)	x 1.609	= Kilometres per hour (km/hr; kph)	x 0.621	= Miles per hour (miles/hr; mph)

Fuel consumption*

Miles per gallon, Imperial (mpg)	x 0.354	= Kilometres per litre (km/l)	x 2.825	= Miles per gallon, Imperial (mpg)
Miles per gallon, US (mpg)	x 0.425	= Kilometres per litre (km/l)	x 2.352	= Miles per gallon, US (mpg)

Temperature

Degrees Fahrenheit = (°C x 1.8) + 32   Degrees Celsius (Degrees Centigrade; °C) = (°F - 32) x 0.56

It is common practice to convert from miles per gallon (mpg) to litres/100 kilometres (l/100km), where mpg x l/100 km = 282

Spare parts are available from many sources, including maker's appointed garages, accessory shops, and motor factors. To be sure of obtaining the correct parts, it will sometimes be necessary to quote the vehicle identification number. If possible, it can also be useful to take the old parts along for positive identification. Items such as starter motors and alternators may be available under a service exchange scheme – any parts returned should be clean.

Our advice regarding spare parts is as follows.

Officially appointed garages

This is the best source of parts which are peculiar to your car, and which are not otherwise generally available (eg, badges, interior trim, certain body panels, etc). It is also the only place at which you should buy parts if the vehicle is still under warranty.

Accessory shops

These are very good places to buy materials and components needed for the maintenance of your car (oil, air and fuel filters, light bulbs, drivebelts, greases, brake pads, touch-up paint, etc). Components of this nature sold by a reputable shop are of the same standard as those used by the car manufacturer.

Besides components, these shops also sell tools and general accessories, usually have convenient opening hours, charge lower prices, and can often be found close to home. Some accessory shops have parts counters where components needed for almost any repair job can be purchased or ordered.

Motor factors

Good factors will stock all the more important components which wear out comparatively quickly, and can sometimes supply individual components needed for the overhaul of a larger assembly (eg, brake seals and hydraulic parts, bearing shells, pistons, valves). They may also handle work such as cylinder block reboring, crankshaft regrinding, etc.

Engine reconditioners

These specialise in engine overhaul and can also supply components. It is recommended that the establishment is a member of the Federation of Engine Re-Manufacturers, or a similar society.

Tyre and exhaust specialists

These outlets may be independent, or members of a local or national chain. They frequently offer competitive prices when compared with a main dealer or local garage, but it will pay to obtain several quotes before making a decision. When researching prices, also ask what 'extras' may be added – for instance fitting a new valve, balancing the wheel and tyre disposal are all commonly charged on top of the price of a new tyre.

Other sources

Beware of parts or materials obtained from market stalls, car boot sales, on-line auctions or similar outlets. Such items are not invariably sub-standard, but there is little chance of compensation if they do prove unsatisfactory. In the case of safety-critical components such as brake pads, there is the risk not only of financial loss, but also of an accident causing injury or death.

Second-hand components or assemblies obtained from a car breaker can be a good buy in some circumstances, but his sort of purchase is best made by the experienced DIY mechanic.

Vehicle identification

Vauxhall/Opel use a 'Car pass' scheme for vehicle identification. This is a card which is issued to the customer when the car is first purchased. It contains important information, eg, VIN number, key number and radio code. It also includes a special code for diagnostic equipment, therefore it must be kept in a secure place and not in the vehicle.

Modifications are a continuing and unpublished process in vehicle manufacture, quite apart from major model changes. Spare parts manuals and lists are compiled upon a numerical basis, the individual vehicle numbers being essential to correct identification of the component required.

When ordering spare parts, always give as much information as possible. Quote the car model, year of manufacture and vehicle identification and/or engine numbers as appropriate.

The vehicle identification plate is attached to the front right-hand side door pillar (see illustration) and includes the Vehicle Identification Number (VIN), vehicle weight information and paint and trim colour codes.

The Vehicle Identification Number (VIN) is given on the vehicle identification plate and is also stamped into the body floor panel between the right-hand front seat and the door sill panel (see illustration); lift the flap in the carpet to see it.

The engine number is stamped on a horizontal flat located on the front of the cylinder block, at the transmission end. The first part of the engine number gives the engine code – eg A12XEL. Engine codes are as follows:

Petrol engines

1.0 litre	A10XEP
1.2 litre	A12XEL and A12XER
1.4 litre	A14XEL and A14XER

Diesel engines

1.3 litre	A13DTC, A13DTE, A13DTR and Z13DTJ

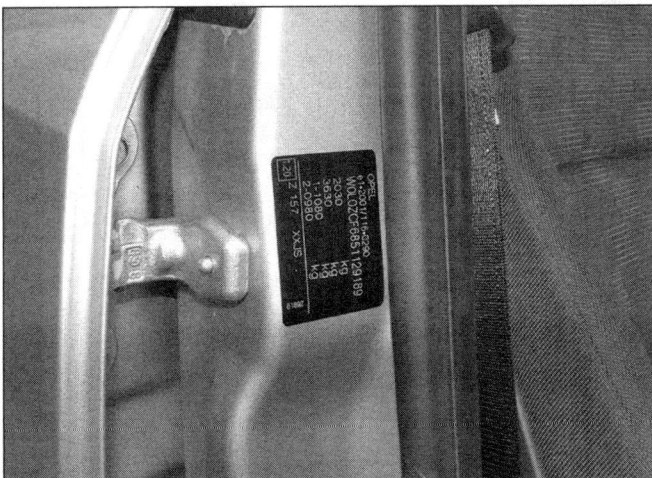

Vehicle Identification Number (VIN) plate attached to the front right-hand side door pillar

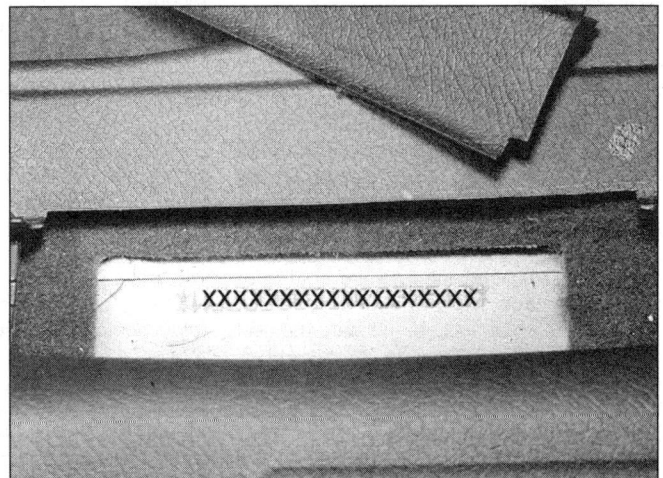

The VIN number is stamped into the body floor next to the right-hand front seat

Whenever servicing, repair or overhaul work is carried out on the car or its components, observe the following procedures and instructions. This will assist in carrying out the operation efficiently and to a professional standard of workmanship.

Joint mating faces and gaskets

When separating components at their mating faces, never insert screwdrivers or similar implements into the joint between the faces in order to prise them apart. This can cause severe damage which results in oil leaks, coolant leaks, etc upon reassembly. Separation is usually achieved by tapping along the joint with a soft-faced hammer in order to break the seal. However, note that this method may not be suitable where dowels are used for component location.

Where a gasket is used between the mating faces of two components, a new one must be fitted on reassembly; fit it dry unless otherwise stated in the repair procedure. Make sure that the mating faces are clean and dry, with all traces of old gasket removed. When cleaning a joint face, use a tool which is unlikely to score or damage the face, and remove any burrs or nicks with an oilstone or fine file.

Make sure that tapped holes are cleaned with a pipe cleaner, and keep them free of jointing compound, if this is being used, unless specifically instructed otherwise.

Ensure that all orifices, channels or pipes are clear, and blow through them, preferably using compressed air.

Oil seals

Oil seals can be removed by levering them out with a wide flat-bladed screwdriver or similar implement. Alternatively, a number of self-tapping screws may be screwed into the seal, and these used as a purchase for pliers or some similar device in order to pull the seal free.

Whenever an oil seal is removed from its working location, either individually or as part of an assembly, it should be renewed.

The very fine sealing lip of the seal is easily damaged, and will not seal if the surface it contacts is not completely clean and free from scratches, nicks or grooves. If the original sealing surface of the component cannot be restored, and the manufacturer has not made provision for slight relocation of the seal relative to the sealing surface, the component should be renewed.

Protect the lips of the seal from any surface which may damage them in the course of fitting. Use tape or a conical sleeve where possible. Where indicated, lubricate the seal lips with oil before fitting and, on dual-lipped seals, fill the space between the lips with grease.

Unless otherwise stated, oil seals must be fitted with their sealing lips toward the lubricant to be sealed.

Use a tubular drift or block of wood of the appropriate size to install the seal and, if the seal housing is shouldered, drive the seal down to the shoulder. If the seal housing is unshouldered, the seal should be fitted with its face flush with the housing top face (unless otherwise instructed).

Screw threads and fastenings

Seized nuts, bolts and screws are quite a common occurrence where corrosion has set in, and the use of penetrating oil or releasing fluid will often overcome this problem if the offending item is soaked for a while before attempting to release it. The use of an impact driver may also provide a means of releasing such stubborn fastening devices, when used in conjunction with the appropriate screwdriver bit or socket. If none of these methods works, it may be necessary to resort to the careful application of heat, or the use of a hacksaw or nut splitter device. Before resorting to extreme methods, check that you are not dealing with a left-hand thread!

Studs are usually removed by locking two nuts together on the threaded part, and then using a spanner on the lower nut to unscrew the stud. Studs or bolts which have broken off below the surface of the component in which they are mounted can sometimes be removed using a stud extractor.

Always ensure that a blind tapped hole is completely free from oil, grease, water or other fluid before installing the bolt or stud. Failure to do this could cause the housing to crack due to the hydraulic action of the bolt or stud as it is screwed in.

For some screw fastenings, notably cylinder head bolts or nuts, torque wrench settings are no longer specified for the latter stages of tightening, "angle-tightening" being called up instead. Typically, a fairly low torque wrench setting will be applied to the bolts/nuts in the correct sequence, followed by one or more stages of tightening through specified angles.

When checking or retightening a nut or bolt to a specified torque setting, slacken the nut or bolt by a quarter of a turn, and then retighten to the specified setting. However, this should not be attempted where angular tightening has been used.

Locknuts, locktabs and washers

Any fastening which will rotate against a component or housing during tightening should always have a washer between it and the relevant component or housing.

Spring or split washers should always be renewed when they are used to lock a critical component such as a big-end bearing retaining bolt or nut. Locktabs which are folded over to retain a nut or bolt should always be renewed.

Self-locking nuts can be re-used in non-critical areas, providing resistance can be felt when the locking portion passes over the bolt or stud thread. However, it should be noted that self-locking stiffnuts tend to lose their effectiveness after long periods of use, and should then be renewed as a matter of course.

Split pins must always be replaced with new ones of the correct size for the hole.

When thread-locking compound is found on the threads of a fastener which is to be re-used, it should be cleaned off with a wire brush and solvent, and fresh compound applied on reassembly.

Special tools

Some repair procedures in this manual entail the use of special tools such as a press, two or three-legged pullers, spring compressors, etc. Wherever possible, suitable readily-available alternatives to the manufacturer's special tools are described, and are shown in use. In some instances, where no alternative is possible, it has been necessary to resort to the use of a manufacturer's tool, and this has been done for reasons of safety as well as the efficient completion of the repair operation. Unless you are highly-skilled and have a thorough understanding of the procedures described, never attempt to bypass the use of any special tool when the procedure described specifies its use. Not only is there a very great risk of personal injury, but expensive damage could be caused to the components involved.

Environmental considerations

When disposing of used engine oil, brake fluid, antifreeze, etc, give due consideration to any detrimental environmental effects. Do not, for instance, pour any of the above liquids down drains into the general sewage system, or onto the ground to soak away, as this is likely to pollute your local environment. Many local council refuse tips provide a facility for waste oil disposal, as do some garages. You can find your nearest disposal point by calling the Environment Agency on 03708 506 506 or by visiting www.oilbankline.org.uk.

OIL CARE®

Note: It is illegal and anti-social to dump oil down the drain. To find the location of your local oil recycling bank, call 03708 506 506 or visit www.oilbankline.org.uk.

The jack supplied with the vehicle tool kit should only be used for changing roadwheels – see *Wheel changing* at the front of this manual. Ensure the jack head is correctly engaged before attempting to raise the vehicle. When carrying out any other kind of work, raise the vehicle using a hydraulic jack, and always supplement the jack with axle stands positioned under the vehicle jacking points.

When jacking up the vehicle with a trolley jack, position the jack head under one of the relevant jacking points (note that the jacking points for use with a hydraulic jack are different to those for use with the vehicle jack). Use a block of wood between the jack or axle stand and the sill – the block of wood should have a groove cut into it , in which the welded flange of the sill will locate. **Do not** jack the

vehicle under the sump or any of the steering or suspension components. Supplement the jack using axle stands **(see illustrations)**.

⚠ *Warning: Never work under, around, or near a raised vehicle, unless it is adequately supported in at least two places.*

Front jacking point for hydraulic jack or axle stands

Rear jacking point for hydraulic jack or axle stands

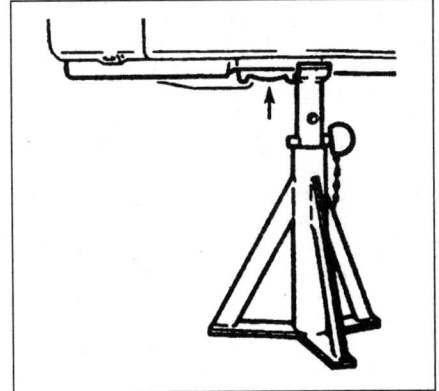

Axle stands should be placed under, or adjacent to, the jacking point (arrowed)

Introduction

A selection of good tools is a fundamental requirement for anyone contemplating the maintenance and repair of a motor vehicle. For the owner who does not possess any, their purchase will prove a considerable expense, offsetting some of the savings made by doing-it-yourself. However, provided that the tools purchased meet the relevant national safety standards and are of good quality, they will last for many years and prove an extremely worthwhile investment.

To help the average owner to decide which tools are needed to carry out the various tasks detailed in this manual, we have compiled three lists of tools under the following headings: *Maintenance and minor repair, Repair and overhaul*, and *Special*. Newcomers to practical mechanics should start off with the *Maintenance and minor repair* tool kit, and confine themselves to the simpler jobs around the vehicle. Then, as confidence and experience grow, more difficult tasks can be undertaken, with extra tools being purchased as, and when, they are needed. In this way, a *Maintenance and minor repair* tool kit can be built up into a *Repair and overhaul* tool kit over a considerable period of time, without any major cash outlays. The experienced do-it-yourselfer will have a tool kit good enough for most repair and overhaul procedures, and will add tools from the *Special* category when it is felt that the expense is justified by the amount of use to which these tools will be put.

Maintenance and minor repair tool kit

The tools given in this list should be considered as a minimum requirement if routine maintenance, servicing and minor repair operations are to be undertaken. We recommend the purchase of combination spanners (ring one end, open-ended the other); although more expensive than open-ended ones, they do give the advantages of both types of spanner.

☐ *Combination spanners:*
Metric - 8 to 19 mm inclusive
☐ *Adjustable spanner - 35 mm jaw (approx.)*
☐ *Spark plug spanner (with rubber insert) - petrol models*
☐ *Spark plug gap adjustment tool - petrol models*
☐ *Set of feeler gauges*
☐ *Brake bleed nipple spanner*
☐ *Screwdrivers:*
Flat blade - 100 mm long x 6 mm dia
Cross blade - 100 mm long x 6 mm dia
Torx - various sizes (not all vehicles)
☐ *Combination pliers*
☐ *Hacksaw (junior)*
☐ *Tyre pump*
☐ *Tyre pressure gauge*
☐ *Oil can*
☐ *Oil filter removal tool (if applicable)*
☐ *Fine emery cloth*
☐ *Wire brush (small)*
☐ *Funnel (medium size)*
☐ *Sump drain plug key (not all vehicles)*

Repair and overhaul tool kit

These tools are virtually essential for anyone undertaking any major repairs to a motor vehicle, and are additional to those given in the *Maintenance and minor repair* list. Included in this list is a comprehensive set of sockets. Although these are expensive, they will be found invaluable as they are so versatile - particularly if various drives are included in the set. We recommend the half-inch square-drive type, as this can be used with most proprietary torque wrenches.

The tools in this list will sometimes need to be supplemented by tools from the *Special* list:

☐ *Sockets to cover range in previous list (including Torx sockets)*
☐ *Reversible ratchet drive (for use with sockets)*
☐ *Extension piece, 250 mm (for use with sockets)*
☐ *Universal joint (for use with sockets)*
☐ *Flexible handle or sliding T "breaker bar" (for use with sockets)*
☐ *Torque wrench (for use with sockets)*
☐ *Self-locking grips*
☐ *Ball pein hammer*
☐ *Soft-faced mallet (plastic or rubber)*
☐ *Screwdrivers:*
Flat blade - long & sturdy, short (chubby), and narrow (electrician's) types
Cross blade – long & sturdy, and short (chubby) types
☐ *Pliers:*
Long-nosed
Side cutters (electrician's)
Circlip (internal and external)
☐ *Cold chisel - 25 mm*
☐ *Scriber*
☐ *Scraper*
☐ *Centre-punch*
☐ *Pin punch*
☐ *Hacksaw*
☐ *Brake hose clamp*
☐ *Brake/clutch bleeding kit*
☐ *Selection of twist drills*
☐ *Steel rule/straight-edge*
☐ *Allen keys (inc. splined/Torx type)*
☐ *Selection of files*
☐ *Wire brush*
☐ *Axle stands*
☐ *Jack (strong trolley or hydraulic type)*
☐ *Light with extension lead*
☐ *Universal electrical multi-meter*

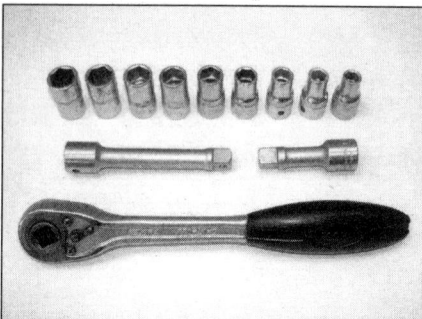

Sockets and reversible ratchet drive

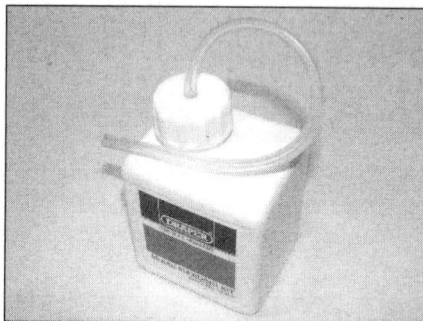

Brake bleeding kit

Torx key, socket and bit

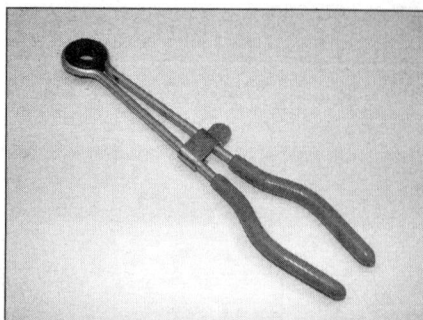

Hose clamp

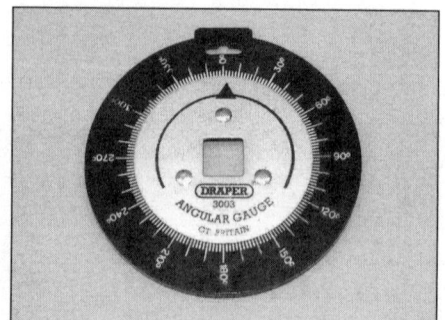

Angular-tightening gauge

Special tools

The tools in this list are those which are not used regularly, are expensive to buy, or which need to be used in accordance with their manufacturers' instructions. Unless relatively difficult mechanical jobs are undertaken frequently, it will not be economic to buy many of these tools. Where this is the case, you could consider clubbing together with friends (or joining a motorists' club) to make a joint purchase, or borrowing the tools against a deposit from a local garage or tool hire specialist.

The following list contains only those tools and instruments freely available to the public, and not those special tools produced by the vehicle manufacturer specifically for its dealer network. You will find occasional references to these manufacturers' special tools in the text of this manual. Generally, an alternative method of doing the job without the vehicle manufacturers' special tool is given. However, sometimes there is no alternative to using them. Where this is the case and the relevant tool cannot be bought or borrowed, you will have to entrust the work to a dealer.

- [ ] *Angular-tightening gauge*
- [ ] *Valve spring compressor*
- [ ] *Valve grinding tool*
- [ ] *Piston ring compressor*
- [ ] *Piston ring removal/installation tool*
- [ ] *Cylinder bore hone*
- [ ] *Balljoint separator*
- [ ] *Coil spring compressors (where applicable)*
- [ ] *Two/three-legged hub and bearing puller*
- [ ] *Impact screwdriver*
- [ ] *Micrometer and/or vernier calipers*
- [ ] *Dial gauge*
- [ ] *Tachometer*
- [ ] *Fault code reader*
- [ ] *Cylinder compression gauge*
- [ ] *Hand-operated vacuum pump and gauge*
- [ ] *Clutch plate alignment set*
- [ ] *Brake shoe steady spring cup removal tool*
- [ ] *Bush and bearing removal/installation set*
- [ ] *Stud extractors*
- [ ] *Tap and die set*
- [ ] *Lifting tackle*

Buying tools

Reputable motor accessory shops and superstores often offer excellent quality tools at discount prices, so it pays to shop around.

Remember, you don't have to buy the most expensive items on the shelf, but it is always advisable to steer clear of the very cheap tools. Beware of 'bargains' offered on market stalls, on-line or at car boot sales. There are plenty of good tools around at reasonable prices, but always aim to purchase items which meet the relevant national safety standards. If in doubt, ask the proprietor or manager of the shop for advice before making a purchase.

Care and maintenance of tools

Having purchased a reasonable tool kit, it is necessary to keep the tools in a clean and serviceable condition. After use, always wipe off any dirt, grease and metal particles using a clean, dry cloth, before putting the tools away. Never leave them lying around after they have been used. A simple tool rack on the garage or workshop wall for items such as screwdrivers and pliers is a good idea. Store all normal spanners and sockets in a metal box. Any measuring instruments, gauges, meters, etc, must be carefully stored where they cannot be damaged or become rusty.

Take a little care when tools are used. Hammer heads inevitably become marked, and screwdrivers lose the keen edge on their blades from time to time. A little timely attention with emery cloth or a file will soon restore items like this to a good finish.

Working facilities

Not to be forgotten when discussing tools is the workshop itself. If anything more than routine maintenance is to be carried out, a suitable working area becomes essential.

It is appreciated that many an owner-mechanic is forced by circumstances to remove an engine or similar item without the benefit of a garage or workshop. Having done this, any repairs should always be done under the cover of a roof.

Wherever possible, any dismantling should be done on a clean, flat workbench or table at a suitable working height.

Any workbench needs a vice; one with a jaw opening of 100 mm is suitable for most jobs. As mentioned previously, some clean dry storage space is also required for tools, as well as for any lubricants, cleaning fluids, touch-up paints etc, which become necessary.

Another item which may be required, and which has a much more general usage, is an electric drill with a chuck capacity of at least 8 mm. This, together with a good range of twist drills, is virtually essential for fitting accessories.

Last, but not least, always keep a supply of old newspapers and clean, lint-free rags available, and try to keep any working area as clean as possible.

Micrometers

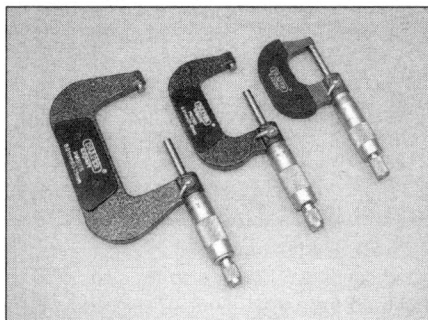
Dial test indicator ("dial gauge")

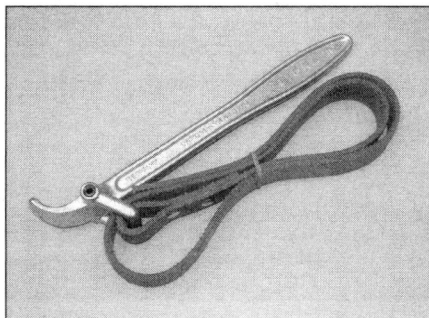
Oil filter removal tool (strap wrench type)

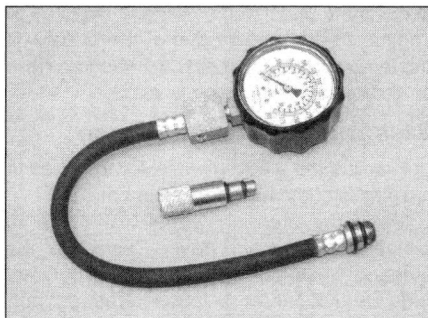
Compression tester

Bearing puller

This is a guide to getting your vehicle through the MOT test. Obviously it will not be possible to examine the vehicle to the same standard as the professional MOT tester. However, working through the following checks will enable you to identify any problem areas before submitting the vehicle for the test.

It has only been possible to summarise the test requirements here, based on the regulations in force at the time of printing. Test standards are becoming increasingly stringent, although there are some exemptions for older vehicles.

An assistant will be needed to help carry out some of these checks.

The checks have been sub-divided into four categories, as follows:

1 Checks carried out **FROM THE DRIVER'S SEAT**

2 Checks carried out **WITH THE VEHICLE ON THE GROUND**

3 Checks carried out **WITH THE VEHICLE RAISED AND THE WHEELS FREE TO TURN**

4 Checks carried out on **YOUR VEHICLE'S EXHAUST EMISSION SYSTEM**

1 Checks carried out **FROM THE DRIVER'S SEAT**

Handbrake (parking brake)

☐ Test the operation of the handbrake. Excessive travel (too many clicks) indicates incorrect brake or cable adjustment.
☐ Check that the handbrake cannot be released by tapping the lever sideways. Check the security of the lever mountings.

☐ If the parking brake is foot-operated, check that the pedal is secure and without excessive travel, and that the release mechanism operates correctly.
☐ Where applicable, test the operation of the electronic handbrake. The brake should engage and disengage without excessive delay. If the warning light does not extinguish when the brake is disengaged, this could indicate a fault which will need further investigation.

Footbrake

☐ Depress the brake pedal and check that it does not creep down to the floor, indicating a master cylinder fault. Release the pedal,

wait a few seconds, then depress it again. If the pedal travels nearly to the floor before firm resistance is felt, brake adjustment or repair is necessary. If the pedal feels spongy, there is air in the hydraulic system which must be removed by bleeding.

☐ Check that the brake pedal is secure and in good condition. Check also for signs of fluid leaks on the pedal, floor or carpets, which would indicate failed seals in the brake master cylinder.
☐ Check the servo unit (when applicable) by operating the brake pedal several times, then keeping the pedal depressed and starting the engine. As the engine starts, the pedal will move down slightly. If not, the vacuum hose or the servo itself may be faulty.

Steering wheel and column

☐ Examine the steering wheel for fractures or looseness of the hub, spokes or rim.
☐ Move the steering wheel from side to side and then up and down. Check that the steering wheel is not loose on the column, indicating wear or a loose retaining nut. Continue moving the steering wheel as before, but also turn it slightly from left to right.

☐ Check that the steering wheel is not loose on the column, and that there is no abnormal movement of the steering wheel, indicating wear in the column support bearings or couplings.
☐ Check that the ignition lock (where fitted) engages and disengages correctly.
☐ Steering column adjustment mechanisms (where fitted) must be able to lock the column securely in place with no play evident.

Windscreen, mirrors and sunvisor

☐ The windscreen must be free of cracks or other significant damage within the driver's field of view. (Small stone chips are acceptable.) Rear view mirrors must be secure, intact, and capable of being adjusted.

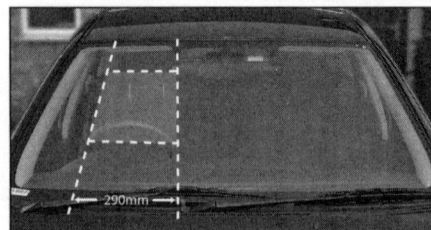

☐ The driver's sunvisor must be capable of being stored in the "up" position.

Seat belts and seats

Note: *The following checks are applicable to all seat belts, front and rear.*

☐ Examine the webbing of all the belts (including rear belts if fitted) for cuts, serious fraying or deterioration. Fasten and unfasten each belt to check the buckles. If applicable, check the retracting mechanism. Check the security of all seat belt mountings accessible from inside the vehicle, ensuring any height adjustable mountings lock securely in place.

☐ Seat belts with pre-tensioners, once activated, have a "flag" or similar showing on the seat belt stalk. This, in itself, is not a reason for test failure.

☐ The front seats themselves must be securely attached and the backrests must lock in the upright position.

Doors

☐ Both front doors must be able to be opened and closed from outside and inside, and must latch securely when closed.

Bonnet and boot/tailgate

☐ The bonnet and boot/tailgate must latch securely when closed.

2 Checks carried out WITH THE VEHICLE ON THE GROUND

Vehicle identification

☐ Number plates must be in good condition, secure and legible, with letters and numbers correctly spaced – spacing at (A) should be 33 mm and at (B) 11 mm. At the front, digits must be black on a white background and at the rear black on a yellow background. Other background designs (such as honeycomb) are not permitted.

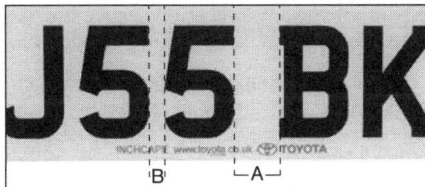

☐ The VIN plate and/or homologation plate must be permanently displayed and legible.

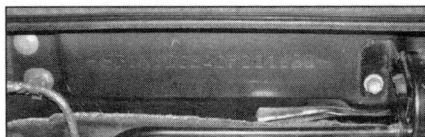

Electrical equipment

☐ Switch on the ignition and check the operation of the horn.

☐ Check the windscreen washers and wipers, examining the wiper blades; renew damaged or perished blades. Also check the operation of the stop-lights.

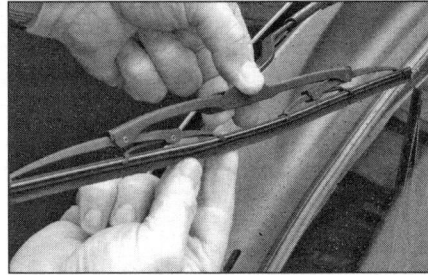

☐ Check the operation of the sidelights and number plate lights. The lenses and reflectors must be secure, clean and undamaged.

☐ Check the operation and alignment of the headlights. The headlight reflectors must not be tarnished and the lenses must be undamaged.

☐ Switch on the ignition and check the operation of the direction indicators (including the instrument panel tell-tale) and the hazard warning lights. Operation of the sidelights and stop-lights must not affect the indicators - if it does, the cause is usually a bad earth at the rear light cluster. Indicators should flash at a rate of between 60 and 120 times per minute – faster or slower than this could indicate a fault with the flasher unit or a bad earth at one of the light units.

☐ Check the operation of the rear foglight(s), including the warning light on the instrument panel or in the switch.

☐ The warning lights must illuminate in accordance with the manufacturer's design. For most vehicles, the ABS and other warning lights should illuminate when the ignition is switched on, and (if the system is operating properly) extinguish after a few seconds. Refer to the owner's handbook.

Footbrake

☐ Examine the master cylinder, brake pipes and servo unit for leaks, loose mountings, corrosion or other damage. If ABS is fitted, this unit should also be examined for signs of leaks or corrosion.

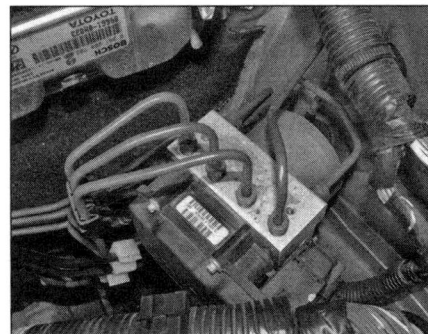

☐ The fluid reservoir must be secure and the fluid level must be between the upper (A) and lower (B) markings.

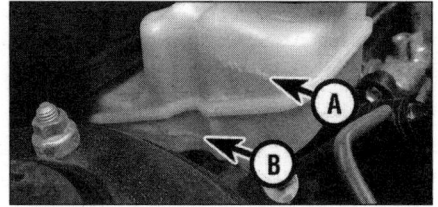

☐ Inspect both front brake flexible hoses for cracks or deterioration of the rubber. Turn the steering from lock to lock, and ensure that the hoses do not contact the wheel, tyre, or any part of the steering or suspension mechanism. With the brake pedal firmly depressed, check the hoses for bulges or leaks under pressure.

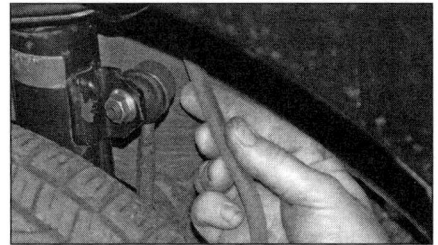

Steering and suspension

☐ Have your assistant turn the steering wheel from side to side slightly, up to the point where the steering gear just begins to transmit this movement to the roadwheels. Check for excessive free play between the steering wheel and the steering gear, indicating wear or insecurity of the steering column joints, the column-to-steering gear coupling, or the steering gear itself.

☐ Have your assistant turn the steering wheel more vigorously in each direction, so that the roadwheels just begin to turn. As this is done, examine all the steering joints, linkages, fittings and attachments. Renew any component that shows signs of wear or damage. On vehicles with power steering, check the security and condition of the steering pump, drivebelt and hoses.

☐ Check that the vehicle is standing level, and at approximately the correct ride height.

Shock absorbers

☐ Depress each corner of the vehicle in turn, then release it. The vehicle should rise and then settle in its normal position. If the vehicle continues to rise and fall, the shock absorber is defective. A shock absorber which has seized will also cause the vehicle to fail.

Exhaust system

☐ Start the engine. With your assistant holding a rag over the tailpipe, check the entire system for leaks. Repair or renew leaking sections.

3 Checks carried out **WITH THE VEHICLE RAISED AND THE WHEELS FREE TO TURN**

Jack up the front and rear of the vehicle, and securely support it on axle stands. Position the stands clear of the suspension assemblies. Ensure that the wheels are clear of the ground and that the steering can be turned from lock to lock.

Steering mechanism

☐ Have your assistant turn the steering from lock to lock. Check that the steering turns smoothly, and that no part of the steering mechanism, including a wheel or tyre, fouls any brake hose or pipe or any part of the body structure.
☐ Examine the steering rack rubber gaiters for damage or insecurity of the retaining clips. If power steering is fitted, check for signs of damage or leakage of the fluid hoses, pipes or connections. Also check for excessive stiffness or binding of the steering, a missing split pin or locking device, or severe corrosion of the body structure within 30 cm of any steering component attachment point.

Front and rear suspension and wheel bearings

☐ Starting at the front right-hand side, grasp the roadwheel at the 3 o'clock and 9 o'clock positions and rock gently but firmly. Check for free play or insecurity at the wheel bearings, suspension balljoints, or suspension mount-ings, pivots and attachments.
☐ Now grasp the wheel at the 12 o'clock and 6 o'clock positions and repeat the previous inspection. Spin the wheel, and check for roughness or tightness of the front wheel bearing.

☐ If excess free play is suspected at a component pivot point, this can be confirmed by using a large screwdriver or similar tool and levering between the mounting and the component attachment. This will confirm whether the wear is in the pivot bush, its retaining bolt, or in the mounting itself (the bolt holes can often become elongated).

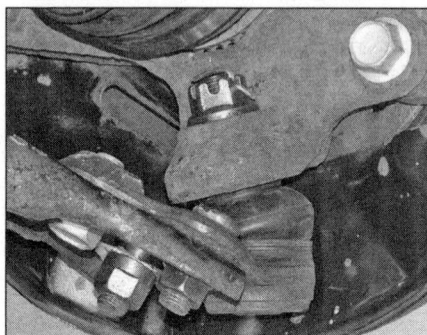

☐ Carry out all the above checks at the other front wheel, and then at both rear wheels.

Springs and shock absorbers

☐ Examine the suspension struts (when applicable) for serious fluid leakage, corrosion, or damage to the casing. Also check the security of the mounting points.
☐ If coil springs are fitted, check that the spring ends locate in their seats, and that the spring is not corroded, cracked or broken.
☐ If leaf springs are fitted, check that all leaves are intact, that the axle is securely attached to each spring, and that there is no deterioration of the spring eye mountings, bushes, and shackles.

☐ The same general checks apply to vehicles fitted with other suspension types, such as torsion bars, hydraulic displacer units, etc. Ensure that all mountings and attachments are secure, that there are no signs of excessive wear, corrosion or damage, and (on hydraulic types) that there are no fluid leaks or damaged pipes.
☐ Inspect the shock absorbers for signs of serious fluid leakage. Check for wear of the mounting bushes or attachments, or damage to the body of the unit.

Driveshafts (fwd vehicles only)

☐ Rotate each front wheel in turn and inspect the constant velocity joint gaiters for splits or damage. Also check that each driveshaft is straight and undamaged.

Braking system

☐ If possible without dismantling, check brake pad wear and disc condition. Ensure that the friction lining material has not worn excessively, (A) and that the discs are not fractured, pitted, scored or badly worn (B).

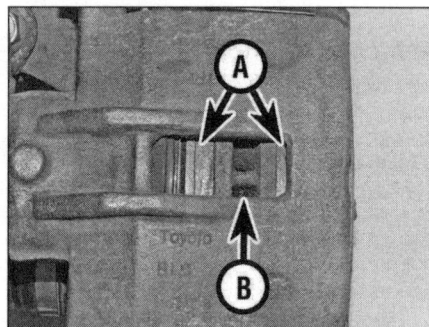

☐ Examine all the rigid brake pipes underneath the vehicle, and the flexible hose(s) at the rear. Look for corrosion, chafing or insecurity of the pipes, and for signs of bulging under pressure, chafing, splits or deterioration of the flexible hoses.
☐ Look for signs of fluid leaks at the brake calipers or on the brake backplates. Repair or renew leaking components.
☐ Slowly spin each wheel, while your assistant depresses and releases the footbrake. Ensure that each brake is operating and does not bind when the pedal is released.

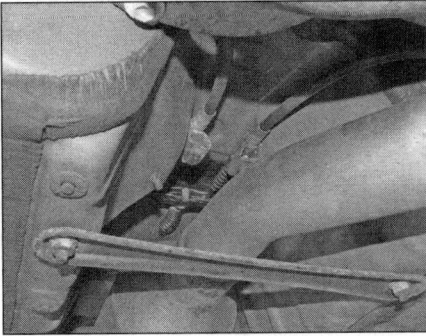

Examine the handbrake mechanism, checking for frayed or broken cables, excessive corrosion, or wear or insecurity of the linkage. Check that the mechanism works on each relevant wheel, and releases fully, without binding.

It is not possible to test brake efficiency without special equipment, but a road test can be carried out later to check that the vehicle pulls up in a straight line.

Fuel and exhaust systems

Inspect the fuel tank (including the filler cap), fuel pipes, hoses and unions. All components must be secure and free from leaks. Locking fuel caps must lock securely and the key must be provided for the MOT test.

Examine the exhaust system over its entire length, checking for any damaged, broken or missing mountings, security of the retaining clamps and rust or corrosion.

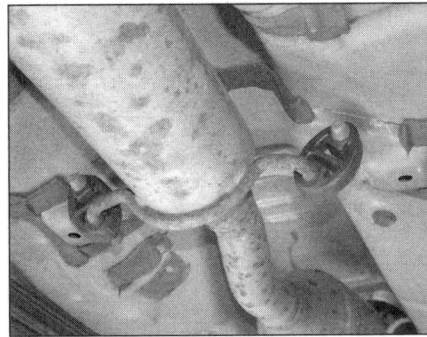

Wheels and tyres

Examine the sidewalls and tread area of each tyre in turn. Check for cuts, tears, lumps, bulges, separation of the tread, and exposure of the ply or cord due to wear or damage. Check that the tyre bead is correctly seated on the wheel rim, that the valve is sound and properly seated, and that the wheel is not distorted or damaged.

Check that the tyres are of the correct size for the vehicle, that they are of the same size and type on each axle, and that the pressures are correct.

Check the tyre tread depth. The legal minimum at the time of writing is 1.6 mm over the central three-quarters of the tread width. Abnormal tread wear may indicate incorrect front wheel alignment or wear in steering or suspension components.

If the spare wheel is fitted externally or in a separate carrier beneath the vehicle, check that mountings are secure and free of excessive corrosion.

Body corrosion

Check the condition of the entire vehicle structure for signs of corrosion in load-bearing areas. (These include chassis box sections, side sills, cross-members, pillars, and all suspension, steering, braking system and seat belt mountings and anchorages.) Any corrosion which has seriously reduced the thickness of a load-bearing area (or is within 30 cm of safety-related components such as steering or suspension) is likely to cause the vehicle to fail. In this case professional repairs are likely to be needed.

Damage or corrosion which causes sharp or otherwise dangerous edges to be exposed will also cause the vehicle to fail.

Towbars

Check the condition of mounting points (both beneath the vehicle and within boot/ hatchback areas) for signs of corrosion, ensuring that all fixings are secure and not worn or damaged. There must be no excessive play in detachable tow ball arms or quick-release mechanisms.

4 Checks carried out on **YOUR VEHICLE'S EXHAUST EMISSION SYSTEM**

Petrol models

The engine should be warmed up, and running well (ignition system in good order, air filter element clean, etc).

Before testing, run the engine at around 2500 rpm for 20 seconds. Let the engine drop to idle, and watch for smoke from the exhaust. If the idle speed is too high, or if dense blue or black smoke emerges for more than 5 seconds, the vehicle will fail. Typically, blue smoke signifies oil burning (engine wear);

black smoke means unburnt fuel (dirty air cleaner element, or other fuel system fault).

An exhaust gas analyser for measuring carbon monoxide (CO) and hydrocarbons (HC) is now needed. If one cannot be hired or borrowed, have a local garage perform the check.

CO emissions (mixture)

The MOT tester has access to the CO limits for all vehicles. The CO level is measured at idle speed, and at 'fast idle' (2500 to 3000 rpm). The following limits are given as a general guide:

At idle speed – Less than 0.5% CO
At 'fast idle' – Less than 0.3% CO
Lambda reading – 0.97 to 1.03

If the CO level is too high, this may point to poor maintenance, a fuel injection system problem, faulty lambda (oxygen) sensor or catalytic converter. Try an injector cleaning treatment, and check the vehicle's ECU for fault codes.

HC emissions

The MOT tester has access to HC limits for all vehicles. The HC level is measured at 'fast idle' (2500 to 3000 rpm). The following limits are given as a general guide:

At 'fast idle' – Less then 200 ppm

Excessive HC emissions are typically caused by oil being burnt (worn engine), or by a blocked crankcase ventilation system ('breather'). If the engine oil is old and thin, an oil change may help. If the engine is running badly, check the vehicle's ECU for fault codes.

Diesel models

The only emission test for diesel engines is measuring exhaust smoke density, using a calibrated smoke meter. The test involves accelerating the engine at least 3 times to its maximum unloaded speed.

Note: *On engines with a timing belt, it is VITAL that the belt is in good condition before the test is carried out.*

With the engine warmed up, it is first purged by running at around 2500 rpm for 20 seconds. A governor check is then carried out, by slowly accelerating the engine to its maximum speed. After this, the smoke meter is connected, and the engine is accelerated quickly to maximum speed three times. If the smoke density is less than the limits given below, the vehicle will pass:

Non-turbo vehicles: 2.5m-1
Turbocharged vehicles: 3.0m-1

If excess smoke is produced, try fitting a new air cleaner element, or using an injector cleaning treatment. If the engine is running badly, where applicable, check the vehicle's ECU for fault codes. Also check the vehicle's EGR system, where applicable. At high mileages, the injectors may require professional attention.

Engine

☐ Engine fails to rotate when attempting to start
☐ Engine rotates, but will not start
☐ Engine difficult to start when cold
☐ Engine difficult to start when hot
☐ Starter motor noisy or excessively-rough in engagement
☐ Engine starts, but stops immediately
☐ Engine idles erratically
☐ Engine misfires at idle speed
☐ Engine misfires throughout the driving speed range
☐ Engine hesitates on acceleration
☐ Engine stalls
☐ Engine lacks power
☐ Engine backfires
☐ Oil pressure warning light illuminated with engine running
☐ Engine runs-on after switching off
☐ Engine noises

Cooling system

☐ Overheating
☐ Overcooling
☐ External coolant leakage
☐ Internal coolant leakage
☐ Corrosion

Fuel and exhaust systems

☐ Excessive fuel consumption
☐ Fuel leakage and/or fuel odour
☐ Excessive noise or fumes from exhaust system

Clutch

☐ Pedal travels to floor – no pressure or very little resistance
☐ Clutch fails to disengage (unable to select gears)
☐ Clutch slips (engine speed increases, with no increase in vehicle speed)
☐ Judder as clutch is engaged
☐ Noise when depressing or releasing clutch pedal

Driveshafts

☐ Vibration when accelerating or decelerating
☐ Clicking or knocking noise on turns (at slow speed on full-lock)

Manual transmission

☐ Noisy in neutral with engine running
☐ Noisy in one particular gear
☐ Difficulty engaging gears
☐ Jumps out of gear
☐ Vibration
☐ Lubricant leaks

Automatic transmission

☐ Fluid leakage
☐ Transmission fluid brown, or has burned smell
☐ General gear selection problems
☐ Transmission will not downshift (kickdown) with accelerator pedal fully depressed
☐ Engine will not start in any gear, or starts in gears other than Park or Neutral
☐ Transmission slips, shifts roughly, is noisy, or has no drive in forward or reverse gears

Braking system

☐ Vehicle pulls to one side under braking
☐ Noise (grinding or high-pitched squeal) when brakes applied
☐ Excessive brake pedal travel
☐ Brake pedal feels spongy when depressed
☐ Excessive brake pedal effort required to stop vehicle
☐ Judder felt through brake pedal or steering wheel when braking
☐ Brakes binding
☐ Rear wheels locking under normal braking

Suspension and steering

☐ Vehicle pulls to one side
☐ Wheel wobble and vibration
☐ Excessive pitching and/or rolling around corners, or during braking
☐ Wandering or general instability
☐ Excessively-stiff steering
☐ Excessive play in steering
☐ Lack of power assistance
☐ Tyre wear excessive

Electrical system

☐ Battery will not hold a charge for more than a few days
☐ Ignition/no-charge warning light remains illuminated with engine running
☐ Ignition/no-charge warning light fails to come on
☐ Lights inoperative
☐ Instrument readings inaccurate or erratic
☐ Horn inoperative, or unsatisfactory in operation
☐ Windscreen wipers inoperative, or unsatisfactory in operation
☐ Windscreen washers inoperative, or unsatisfactory in operation
☐ Electric windows inoperative, or unsatisfactory in operation
☐ Central locking system inoperative, or unsatisfactory in operation

Introduction

The vehicle owner who does his or her own maintenance according to the recommended service schedules should not have to use this section of the manual very often. Modern component reliability is such that, provided those items subject to wear or deterioration are inspected or renewed at the specified intervals, sudden failure is comparatively rare. Faults do not usually just happen as a result of sudden failure, but develop over a period of time. Major mechanical failures in particular are usually preceded by characteristic symptoms over hundreds or even thousands of miles. Those components which do occasionally fail without warning are often small and easily carried in the vehicle.

With any fault-finding, the first step is to decide where to begin investigations. Sometimes this is obvious, but on other occasions, a little detective work will be necessary. The owner who makes half a dozen haphazard adjustments or replacements may be successful in curing a fault (or its symptoms), but will be none the wiser if the fault recurs, and ultimately may have spent more time and money than was necessary. A calm and logical approach will be found to be more satisfactory in the long run. Always take into account any warning signs or abnormalities that may have been noticed in the period preceding the fault – power loss, high or low gauge readings, unusual smells, etc – and remember that failure

of components such as fuses or spark plugs may only be pointers to some underlying fault.

The pages which follow provide an easy-reference guide to the more common problems which may occur during the operation of the vehicle. These problems and their possible causes are grouped under headings denoting various components or systems, such as Engine, Cooling system, etc. The general Chapter which deals with the problem is also shown in brackets; refer to the relevant part of that Chapter for system-specific information. Whatever the fault, certain basic principles apply. These are as follows:

Verify the fault. This is simply a matter of being sure that you know what the symptoms are before starting work. This is particularly important if you are investigating a fault for someone else, who may not have described it very accurately.

Don't overlook the obvious. For example, if the vehicle won't start, is there fuel in the tank? (Don't take anyone else's word on this particular point, and don't trust the fuel gauge either!) If an electrical fault is indicated, look for loose or broken wires before digging out the test gear.

Cure the disease, not the symptom. Substituting a flat battery with a fully-charged one will get you off the hard shoulder, but if the underlying cause is not attended to, the new battery will go the same way. Similarly, changing oil-fouled spark plugs for a new set will get you moving again, but remember that the reason for the fouling (if it wasn't simply an incorrect grade of plug) will have to be established and corrected.

Don't take anything for granted. Particularly, don't forget that a 'new' component may itself be defective (especially if it's been rattling around in the boot for months), and don't

leave components out of a fault diagnosis sequence just because they are new or recently-fitted. When you do finally diagnose a difficult fault, you'll probably realise that all the evidence was there from the start.

Consider what work, if any, has recently been carried out. Many faults arise through careless or hurried work. For instance, if any work has been performed under the bonnet, could some of the wiring have been dislodged or incorrectly routed, or a hose trapped? Have all the fasteners been properly tightened? Were new, genuine parts and new gaskets used? There is often a certain amount of detective work to be done in this case, as an apparently-unrelated task can have far-reaching consequences.

Diesel fault diagnosis

The majority of starting problems on small diesel engines are electrical in origin. The mechanic who is familiar with petrol engines but less so with diesel may be inclined to view the diesel's injectors and pump in the same light as the spark plugs and distributor, but this is generally a mistake. .

When investigating complaints of difficult

starting for someone else, make sure that the correct starting procedure is understood and is being followed. Some drivers are unaware of the significance of the preheating warning light – many modern engines are sufficiently forgiving for this not to matter in mild weather, but with the onset of winter, problems begin. Glow plugs in particular are often neglected – just one faulty plug will make cold-weather starting very difficult.

As a rule of thumb, if the engine is difficult to start but runs well when it has finally got going, the problem is electrical (battery, starter motor or preheating system). If poor performance is combined with difficult starting, the problem is likely to be in the fuel system. The low-pressure (supply) side of the fuel system should be checked before suspecting the injectors and high-pressure pump. The most common fuel supply problem is air getting into the system, and any pipe from the fuel tank forwards must be scrutinised if air leakage is suspected. Normally the pump is the last item to suspect, since unless it has been tampered with, there is no reason for it to be at fault.

Engine

Engine fails to rotate when attempting to start

- ☐ Battery terminal connections loose or corroded (see *Weekly checks*)
- ☐ Battery discharged or faulty (Chapter 5A)
- ☐ Broken, loose or disconnected wiring in the starting circuit (Chapter 5A)
- ☐ Defective starter solenoid or ignition switch (Chapter 5A or 12)
- ☐ Defective starter motor (Chapter 5A)
- ☐ Starter pinion or flywheel ring gear teeth loose or broken (Chapter 2 or 5A)
- ☐ Engine earth strap broken or disconnected (Chapter 5A)
- ☐ Engine suffering 'hydraulic lock' (eg from water drawn into the engine after traversing flooded roads, or from a serious internal coolant leak) – consult a main dealer for advice
- ☐ Automatic transmission not in position P or N (Chapter 7B)

Engine rotates, but will not start

- ☐ Fuel tank empty
- ☐ Battery discharged (engine rotates slowly) (Chapter 5A)
- ☐ Battery terminal connections loose or corroded (see *Weekly checks*)
- ☐ Ignition components damp or damaged – petrol models (Chapter 1A or 5B)
- ☐ Immobiliser fault, or 'uncoded' ignition key being used (Chapter 12 or *Roadside repairs*)
- ☐ Broken, loose or disconnected wiring in the ignition circuit – petrol models (Chapter 1A or 5B)
- ☐ Worn, faulty or incorrectly-gapped spark plugs – petrol models (Chapter 1A)
- ☐ Preheating system faulty – diesel models (Chapter 5A)
- ☐ Fuel injection/engine management system fault (Chapter 4A, 4B or 4C)
- ☐ Air in fuel system – diesel models (Chapter 4B)
- ☐ Major mechanical failure (eg timing chain snapped) (Chapter 2A, 2B or 2C)

Engine difficult to start when cold

- ☐ Battery discharged (Chapter 5A)
- ☐ Battery terminal connections loose or corroded (see *Weekly checks*)

- ☐ Worn, faulty or incorrectly-gapped spark plugs – petrol models (Chapter 1A)
- ☐ Other ignition system fault – petrol models (Chapter 1A or 5B)
- ☐ Preheating system faulty – diesel models (Chapter 5A)
- ☐ Fuel injection/engine management system fault (Chapter 4A, 4B or 4C)
- ☐ Wrong grade of engine oil used (*Weekly checks*, Chapter 1A or 1B)
- ☐ Low cylinder compression (Chapter 2A, 2B or 2C)

Engine difficult to start when hot

- ☐ Air filter element dirty or clogged (Chapter 1A or 1B)
- ☐ Fuel injection/engine management system fault (Chapter 4A, 4B or 4C)
- ☐ Low cylinder compression (Chapter 2A, 2B or 2C)

Starter motor noisy or excessively-rough in engagement

- ☐ Starter pinion or flywheel ring gear teeth loose or broken (Chapter 2A, 2B, 2C or 5A)
- ☐ Starter motor mounting bolts loose or missing (Chapter 5A)
- ☐ Starter motor internal components worn or damaged (Chapter 5A)

Engine starts, but stops immediately

- ☐ Loose or faulty electrical connections in the ignition circuit – petrol models (Chapter 1A or 5B)
- ☐ Vacuum leak at the throttle body or inlet manifold – petrol models (Chapter 4A)
- ☐ Blocked injectors/fuel injection system fault (Chapter 4A or 4B)

Engine idles erratically

- ☐ Air filter element clogged (Chapter 1A or 1B)
- ☐ Vacuum leak at the throttle housing, inlet manifold or associated hoses – petrol models (Chapter 4A)
- ☐ Worn, faulty or incorrectly-gapped spark plugs – petrol models (Chapter 1A)
- ☐ Uneven or low cylinder compression (Chapter 2A, 2B or 2C)
- ☐ Camshaft lobes worn (Chapter 2A, 2B or 2C)
- ☐ Blocked injectors/fuel injection system fault (Chapter 4A or 4B)

Engine (continued)

Engine misfires at idle speed

☐ Worn, faulty or incorrectly-gapped spark plugs – petrol models (Chapter 1A)
☐ Vacuum leak at the throttle housing, inlet manifold or associated hoses – petrol models (Chapter 4A)
☐ Blocked injectors/fuel injection system fault (Chapter 4A or 4B)
☐ Faulty injector(s) – diesel models (Chapter 4B)
☐ Uneven or low cylinder compression (Chapter 2A, 2B or 2C)
☐ Disconnected, leaking, or perished crankcase ventilation hoses (Chapter 4C)

Engine misfires throughout the driving speed range

☐ Fuel filter choked – diesel models (Chapter 1B)
☐ Fuel pump faulty, or delivery pressure low – petrol models (Chapter 4A)
☐ Fuel tank vent blocked, or fuel pipes restricted (Chapter 4A, 4B or 4C)
☐ Vacuum leak at the throttle housing, inlet manifold or associated hoses – petrol models (Chapter 4A)
☐ Worn, faulty or incorrectly-gapped spark plugs – petrol models (Chapter 1A)
☐ Faulty injector(s) – diesel models (Chapter 4B)
☐ Faulty ignition module – petrol models (Chapter 5B)
☐ Uneven or low cylinder compression (Chapter 2A, 2B or 2C)
☐ Blocked injector/fuel injection system fault (Chapter 4A or 4B)
☐ Blocked catalytic converter (Chapter 4A or 4B)

Engine hesitates on acceleration

☐ Worn, faulty or incorrectly-gapped spark plugs – petrol models (Chapter 1A)
☐ Vacuum leak at the throttle housing, inlet manifold or associated hoses – petrol models (Chapter 4A)
☐ Blocked injectors/fuel injection system fault (Chapter 4A or 4B)
☐ Faulty injector(s) – diesel models (Chapter 4B)

Engine stalls

☐ Vacuum leak at the throttle housing, inlet manifold or associated hoses – petrol models (Chapter 4A)
☐ Fuel filter choked – diesel models (Chapter 1B)
☐ Fuel pump faulty, or delivery pressure low – petrol models (Chapter 4A)
☐ Fuel tank vent blocked, or fuel pipes restricted (Chapter 4A, 4B or 4C)
☐ Blocked injectors/fuel injection system fault (Chapter 4A or 4B)
☐ Faulty injector(s) – diesel models (Chapter 4B)

Engine lacks power

☐ Air filter element blocked (Chapter 1A or 1B)
☐ Fuel filter choked – diesel models (Chapter 1B)
☐ Fuel pipes blocked or restricted (Chapter 4A, 4B or 4C)
☐ Worn, faulty or incorrectly-gapped spark plugs – petrol models (Chapter 1A)
☐ Engine overheatingAccelerator pedal position sensor faulty (Chapter 4A or 4B)
☐ Vacuum leak at the throttle housing inlet manifold or associated hoses – petrol models (Chapter 4A)
☐ Blocked injectors/fuel injection system fault (Chapter 4A or 4B)
☐ Faulty injector(s) – diesel models (Chapter 4B)
☐ Fuel pump faulty, or delivery pressure low – petrol models (Chapter 4A)
☐ Uneven or low cylinder compression (Chapter 2A, 2B or 2C)
☐ Blocked catalytic converter (Chapter 4A or 4B)
☐ Brakes binding (Chapter 1A, 1B or 9)
☐ Clutch slipping (Chapter 6)

Engine backfires

☐ Vacuum leak at the throttle housing, inlet manifold or associated hoses – petrol models (Chapter 4A)
☐ Blocked injectors/fuel injection system fault (Chapter 4A or 4B)
☐ Blocked catalytic converter (Chapter 4A or 4B)
☐ Faulty ignition module – petrol models (Chapter 5B)

Oil pressure warning light illuminated with engine running

☐ Low oil level, or incorrect oil grade (see *Weekly checks*)
☐ Faulty oil pressure sensor, or wiring damaged (Chapter 2A, 2B or 2C)
☐ Worn engine bearings and/or oil pump (Chapter 2A, 2B, 2C or 2D)
☐ High engine operating temperature (Chapter 3)
☐ Oil pump pressure relief valve defective (Chapter 2A, 2B or 2C)
☐ Oil pump pick-up strainer clogged (Chapter 2A, 2B or 2C)

Engine runs-on after switching off

☐ Excessive carbon build-up in engine (Chapter 2A, 2B or 2C)
☐ High engine operating temperature (Chapter 3)
☐ Fuel injection/engine management system fault (Chapter 4A, 4B or 4C)

Engine noises

Pre-ignition (pinking) or knocking during acceleration or under load

☐ Ignition system/engine management system fault – petrol models (Chapter 1A, 4A or 5B)
☐ Incorrect grade of spark plug – petrol models (Chapter 1A)
☐ Incorrect grade of fuel (Chapter 4A or 4B)
☐ Knock sensor faulty – petrol models (Chapter 4A or 5B)
☐ Vacuum leak at the throttle housing, inlet manifold or associated hoses – petrol models (Chapter 4A)
☐ Excessive carbon build-up in engine (Chapter 2A, 2B or 2C)
☐ Fuel injection/engine management system fault (Chapter 4A, 4B or 4C)
☐ Faulty injector(s) – diesel models (Chapter 4B)

Whistling or wheezing noises

☐ Leaking inlet manifold or throttle housing gasket – petrol models (Chapter 4A)
☐ Leaking exhaust manifold gasket or pipe-to-manifold joint (Chapter 4A or 4B)
☐ Leaking vacuum hose (Chapter 4A, 4B, 4C or 9)
☐ Blowing cylinder head gasket (Chapter 2A, 2B or 2C)
☐ Partially blocked or leaking crankcase ventilation system (Chapter 4C)

Tapping or rattling noises

☐ Worn valve gear or camshaft (Chapter 2A, 2B or 2C)
☐ Ancillary component fault (coolant pump, alternator, etc) (Chapter 3, 5A, etc)

Knocking or thumping noises

☐ Worn big-end bearings (regular heavy knocking, perhaps less under load) (Chapter 2D)
☐ Worn main bearings (rumbling and knocking, perhaps worsening under load) (Chapter 2D)
☐ Piston slap – most noticeable when cold, caused by piston/bore wear (Chapter 2D)
☐ Ancillary component fault (coolant pump, alternator, etc) (Chapter 3, 5A, etc)
☐ Engine mountings worn or defective (Chapter 2A, 2B or 2C)

Cooling system

Overheating

- [ ] Insufficient coolant in system (see *Weekly checks*)
- [ ] Thermostat faulty (Chapter 3)
- [ ] Radiator core blocked, or grille restricted (Chapter 3)
- [ ] Cooling fan or cooling module faulty (Chapter 3)
- [ ] Inaccurate coolant temperature sensor (Chapter 3)
- [ ] Airlock in cooling system (Chapter 1A, 1B or 3)
- [ ] Expansion tank pressure cap faulty (Chapter 3)
- [ ] Engine management system fault (Chapter 4A, 4B or 4C)

Overcooling

- [ ] Thermostat faulty (Chapter 3)
- [ ] Inaccurate coolant temperature sensor (Chapter 3)
- [ ] Cooling fan faulty (Chapter 3)
- [ ] Engine management system fault (Chapter 4A, 4B or 4C)

External coolant leakage

- [ ] Deteriorated or damaged hoses or hose clips (Chapter 1A or 1B)
- [ ] Radiator core or heater matrix leaking (Chapter 3)
- [ ] Expansion tank pressure cap faulty (Chapter 3)
- [ ] Coolant pump internal seal leaking (Chapter 3)
- [ ] Coolant pump gasket leaking (Chapter 3)
- [ ] Boiling due to overheating
- [ ] Cylinder block core plug leaking (Chapter 2D)

Internal coolant leakage

- [ ] Leaking cylinder head gasket (Chapter 2A, 2B or 2C)
- [ ] Cracked cylinder head or cylinder block (Chapter 2A, 2B, 2C or 2D)

Corrosion

- [ ] Infrequent draining and flushing (Chapter 1A or 1B)
- [ ] Incorrect coolant mixture or inappropriate coolant type (see *Weekly checks*)

Fuel and exhaust systems

Excessive fuel consumption

- [ ] Air filter element dirty or clogged (Chapter 1A or 1B)
- [ ] Fuel injection system fault (Chapter 4A or 4B)
- [ ] Engine management system fault (Chapter 4A, 4B or 4C)
- [ ] Crankcase ventilation system blocked (Chapter 4C)
- [ ] Tyres under-inflated (see *Weekly checks*)
- [ ] Brakes binding (Chapter 1A, 1B or 9)
- [ ] Fuel leak, causing apparent high consumption (Chapter 1A, 1B, 4A, 4B or 4C)

Fuel leakage and/or fuel odour

- [ ] Damaged or corroded fuel tank, pipes or connections (Chapter 4A or 4B)
- [ ] Evaporative emissions system fault – petrol models (Chapter 4C)

Excessive noise or fumes from exhaust system

- [ ] Leaking exhaust system or manifold joints (Chapter 1A, 1B, 4A or 4B)
- [ ] Leaking, corroded or damaged silencers or pipe (Chapter 1A, 1B, 4A or 4B)
- [ ] Broken mountings causing body or suspension contact (Chapter 1A, 1B, 4A or 4B)

Clutch

Note: *Fault finding for the Easytronic semi-automatic clutch should be entrusted to a Vauxhall dealer.*

Pedal travels to floor – no pressure or very little resistance

- [ ] Air in hydraulic system/faulty master or slave cylinder (Chapter 6)
- [ ] Faulty hydraulic release system (Chapter 6)
- [ ] Faulty clutch release cylinder (Chapter 6)
- [ ] Broken diaphragm spring in clutch pressure plate (Chapter 6)

Clutch fails to disengage (unable to select gears)

- [ ] Air in hydraulic system/faulty master or slave cylinder (Chapter 6)
- [ ] Faulty hydraulic release system (Chapter 6)
- [ ] Clutch disc sticking on transmission input shaft splines (Chapter 6)
- [ ] Clutch disc sticking to flywheel or pressure plate (Chapter 6)
- [ ] Faulty pressure plate assembly (Chapter 6)
- [ ] Clutch release mechanism worn or incorrectly assembled (Chapter 6)

Clutch slips (engine speed increases, with no increase in vehicle speed)

- [ ] Faulty hydraulic release system (Chapter 6)
- [ ] Clutch disc linings excessively worn (Chapter 6)
- [ ] Clutch disc linings contaminated with oil or grease (Chapter 6)
- [ ] Faulty pressure plate or weak diaphragm spring (Chapter 6)

Judder as clutch is engaged

- [ ] Clutch disc linings contaminated with oil or grease (Chapter 6)
- [ ] Clutch disc linings excessively worn (Chapter 6)
- [ ] Faulty or distorted pressure plate or diaphragm spring (Chapter 6)
- [ ] Worn or loose engine or transmission mountings (Chapter 2A, 2B or 2C)
- [ ] Clutch disc hub or transmission input shaft splines worn (Chapter 6)

Noise when depressing or releasing clutch pedal

- [ ] Faulty clutch release cylinder (Chapter 6)
- [ ] Worn or dry clutch pedal bushes (Chapter 6)
- [ ] Faulty pressure plate assembly (Chapter 6)
- [ ] Pressure plate diaphragm spring broken (Chapter 6)
- [ ] Broken clutch disc cushioning springs (Chapter 6)

Driveshafts

Vibration when accelerating or decelerating

- [ ] Worn inner constant velocity joint (Chapter 8)
- [ ] Bent or distorted driveshaft (Chapter 8)

Clicking or knocking noise on turns (at slow speed on full-lock)

- [ ] Worn outer constant velocity joint (Chapter 8)
- [ ] Lack of constant velocity joint lubricant, possibly due to damaged gaiter (Chapter 8)

Manual transmission

Note: *Fault finding for the Easytronic transmission should be entrusted to a Vauxhall dealer.*

Noisy in neutral with engine running

- [ ] Lack of oil (Chapter 7A or 7C)
- [ ] Input shaft bearings worn (noise apparent with clutch pedal released, but not when depressed) (Chapter 7A)*
- [ ] Clutch release cylinder faulty (noise apparent with clutch pedal depressed, possibly less when released) (Chapter 6)

Noisy in one particular gear

- [ ] Worn, damaged or chipped gear teeth (Chapter 7A)*

Difficulty engaging gears

- [ ] Clutch fault (Chapter 6)
- [ ] Worn, damaged, or poorly-adjusted gearchange (Chapter 7A)
- [ ] Lack of oil (Chapter 7A or 7C)
- [ ] Worn synchroniser units (Chapter 7A)*

Jumps out of gear

- [ ] Worn, damaged, or poorly-adjusted gearchange (Chapter 7A)
- [ ] Worn synchroniser units (Chapter 7A)*
- [ ] Worn selector forks (Chapter 7A)*

Vibration

- [ ] Lack of oil (Chapter 7A or 7C)
- [ ] Worn bearings (Chapter 7A)*

Lubricant leaks

- [ ] Leaking driveshaft or selector shaft oil seal (Chapter 7A)
- [ ] Leaking housing joint (Chapter 7A)*
- [ ] Leaking input shaft oil seal (Chapter 7A)*

* Although the corrective action necessary to remedy the symptoms described is beyond the scope of the home mechanic, the above information should be helpful in isolating the cause of the condition, so that the owner can communicate clearly with a professional mechanic.

Automatic transmission

Note: *Due to the complexity of the automatic transmission, it is difficult for the home mechanic to properly diagnose and service this unit. For problems other than the following, the vehicle should be taken to a dealer service department or automatic transmission specialist. Do not be too hasty in removing the transmission if a fault is suspected, as most of the testing is carried out with the unit still fitted. Remember that, besides the sensors specific to the transmission, many of the engine management system sensors described in Chapter 4 are essential to the correct operation of the transmission.*

Fluid leakage

- [ ] Automatic transmission fluid is usually dark red in colour. Fluid leaks should not be confused with engine oil, which can easily be blown onto the transmission by airflow.
- [ ] To determine the source of a leak, first remove all built-up dirt and grime from the transmission housing and surrounding areas using a degreasing agent, or by steam-cleaning. Drive the vehicle at low speed, so airflow will not blow the leak far from its source. Raise and support the vehicle, and determine where the leak is coming from. The following are common areas of leakage:
  a) *Fluid pan*
  b) *Dipstick tube (Chapter 1A)*
  c) *Transmission-to-fluid cooler unions (Chapter 7B)*

Transmission fluid brown, or has burned smell

- [ ] Transmission fluid level low (Chapter 7B)

General gear selection problems

- [ ] Chapter 7B deals with checking the selector cable on automatic transmissions. The following are common problems which may be caused by a faulty cable or sensor:

a) *Engine starting in gears other than Park or Neutral.*
b) *Indicator panel indicating a gear other than the one actually being used.*
c) *Vehicle moves when in Park or Neutral.*
d) *Poor gear shift quality or erratic gear changes.*

Transmission will not downshift (kickdown) with accelerator pedal fully depressed

- [ ] Low transmission fluid level (Chapter 7B)
- [ ] Engine management system fault (Chapter 4A)
- [ ] Faulty transmission sensor or wiring (Chapter 7B)
- [ ] Incorrect selector cable adjustment (Chapter 7B)

Engine will not start in any gear, or starts in gears other than Park or Neutral

- [ ] Faulty transmission sensor or wiring (Chapter 7B)
- [ ] Engine management system fault (Chapter 4)
- [ ] Incorrect selector cable adjustment (Chapter 7B)

Transmission slips, shifts roughly, is noisy, or has no drive in forward or reverse gears

- [ ] Transmission fluid level low (Chapter 7B)
- [ ] Faulty transmission sensor or wiring (Chapter 7B)
- [ ] Engine management system fault (Chapter 4)

Note: *There are many probable causes for the above problems, but diagnosing and correcting them is considered beyond the scope of this manual. Having checked the fluid level and all the wiring as far as possible, a dealer or transmission specialist should be consulted if the problem persists.*

Braking system

Note: *Before assuming that a brake problem exists, make sure that the tyres are in good condition and correctly inflated, that the front wheel alignment is correct, and that the vehicle is not loaded with weight in an unequal manner. Apart from checking the condition of all pipe and hose connections, any faults occurring on the anti-lock braking system should be referred to a Vauxhall dealer for diagnosis.*

Vehicle pulls to one side under braking

- [ ] Worn, defective, damaged or contaminated brake pads/shoes on one side (Chapter 1A, 1B or 9)
- [ ] Seized or partially-seized brake caliper piston/wheel cylinder (Chapter 1A, 1B or 9)
- [ ] A mixture of brake pad/shoe lining materials fitted between sides (Chapter 1A, 1B or 9)

- [ ] Brake caliper/backplate mounting bolts loose (Chapter 9)
- [ ] Worn or damaged steering or suspension components (Chapter 1A, 1B or 10)

Noise (grinding or high-pitched squeal) when brakes applied

- [ ] Brake pad/shoe friction lining material worn down to metal backing (Chapter 1A, 1B or 9)
- [ ] Excessive corrosion of brake disc/drum (may be apparent after the vehicle has been standing for some time (Chapter 1A, 1B or 9)
- [ ] Foreign object (stone chipping, etc) trapped between brake disc and shield (Chapter 1A, 1B or 9)

Braking system (continued)

Excessive brake pedal travel

- [ ] Faulty master cylinder (Chapter 9)
- [ ] Air in hydraulic system (Chapter 1A, 1B, or 9)
- [ ] Faulty vacuum servo unit (Chapter 9)

Brake pedal feels spongy when depressed

- [ ] Air in hydraulic system (Chapter 1A, 1B, or 9)
- [ ] Deteriorated flexible rubber brake hoses (Chapter 1A, 1B or 9)
- [ ] Master cylinder mounting nuts loose (Chapter 9)
- [ ] Faulty master cylinder (Chapter 9)

Excessive brake pedal effort required to stop vehicle

- [ ] Faulty vacuum servo unit (Chapter 9)
- [ ] Faulty vacuum pump – diesel models (Chapter 9)
- [ ] Disconnected, damaged or insecure brake servo vacuum hose (Chapter 9)
- [ ] Primary or secondary hydraulic circuit failure (Chapter 9)
- [ ] Seized brake caliper/wheel cylinder piston (Chapter 9)
- [ ] Brake pads/shoes incorrectly fitted (Chapter 9)
- [ ] Incorrect grade of brake pads/shoes fitted (Chapter 9)
- [ ] Brake pad/shoe linings contaminated (Chapter 1A, 1B or 9)

Judder felt through brake pedal or steering wheel when braking

Note: *Under heavy braking on models equipped with ABS, vibration may be felt through the brake pedal. This is a normal feature of ABS operation, and does not constitute a fault*

- [ ] Excessive run-out or distortion of discs/drums (Chapter 1A, 1B or 9)
- [ ] Brake pad/shoe linings worn (Chapter 1A, 1B or 9)
- [ ] Brake caliper mounting bolts loose (Chapter 9)
- [ ] Wear in suspension or steering components or mountings (Chapter 1A, 1B or 10)
- [ ] Front wheels out of balance (see *Weekly checks*)

Brakes binding

- [ ] Seized brake caliper/wheel cylinder piston (Chapter 9)
- [ ] Faulty master cylinder (Chapter 9)

Rear wheels locking under normal braking

- [ ] Rear brake pad/shoe linings contaminated or damaged (Chapter 1 or 9)
- [ ] Rear brake drums warped (Chapter 1A, 1B or 9)

Suspension and steering

Note: *Before diagnosing suspension or steering faults, be sure that the trouble is not due to incorrect tyre pressures, mixtures of tyre types, or binding brakes.*

Vehicle pulls to one side

- [ ] Defective tyre (see *Weekly checks*)
- [ ] Excessive wear in suspension or steering components (Chapter 1A, 1B or 10)
- [ ] Incorrect front wheel alignment (Chapter 10)
- [ ] Accident damage to steering or suspension components (Chapter 1A or 1B)

Wheel wobble and vibration

- [ ] Front wheels out of balance (vibration felt mainly through the steering wheel) (see *Weekly checks*)
- [ ] Rear wheels out of balance (vibration felt throughout the vehicle) (see *Weekly checks*)
- [ ] Roadwheels damaged or distorted (see *Weekly checks*)
- [ ] Faulty or damaged tyre (see *Weekly checks*)
- [ ] Worn steering or suspension joints, bushes or components (Chapter 1A, 1B or 10)
- [ ] Wheel bolts loose (Chapter 1A or 1B)

Excessive pitching and/or rolling around corners, or during braking

- [ ] Defective shock absorbers (Chapter 1A, 1B or 10)
- [ ] Broken or weak spring and/or suspension component (Chapter 1A, 1B or 10)
- [ ] Worn or damaged anti-roll bar or mountings (Chapter 1A, 1B or 10)

Wandering or general instability

- [ ] Incorrect front wheel alignment (Chapter 10)
- [ ] Worn steering or suspension joints, bushes or components (Chapter 1A, 1B or 10)
- [ ] Roadwheels out of balance (see *Weekly checks*)
- [ ] Faulty or damaged tyre (see *Weekly checks*)
- [ ] Wheel bolts loose (Chapter 1A or 1B)
- [ ] Defective shock absorbers (Chapter 1A, 1B or 10)
- [ ] Power steering system fault (Chapter 10)

Excessively-stiff steering

- [ ] Seized steering linkage balljoint or suspension balljoint (Chapter 1A, 1B or 10)
- [ ] Incorrect front wheel alignment (Chapter 10)
- [ ] Steering rack damaged (Chapter 10)
- [ ] Power steering system fault (Chapter 10)

Excessive play in steering

- [ ] Worn steering column/intermediate shaft joints (Chapter 10)
- [ ] Worn track rod balljoints (Chapter 1A, 1B or 10)
- [ ] Worn steering rack (Chapter 10)
- [ ] Worn steering or suspension joints, bushes or components (Chapter 1A, 1B or 10)

Lack of power assistance

- [ ] Power steering system fault (Chapter 10)
- [ ] Faulty steering rack (Chapter 10)

Tyre wear excessive

Tyres worn on inside or outside edges

- [ ] Tyres under-inflated (wear on both edges) (see *Weekly checks*)
- [ ] Incorrect camber or castor angles (wear on one edge only) (Chapter 10)
- [ ] Worn steering or suspension joints, bushes or components (Chapter 1A, 1B or 10)
- [ ] Excessively-hard cornering or braking
- [ ] Accident damage

Tyre treads exhibit feathered edges

- [ ] Incorrect toe-setting (Chapter 10)

Tyres worn in centre of tread

- [ ] Tyres over-inflated (see *Weekly checks*)

Tyres worn on inside and outside edges

- [ ] Tyres under-inflated (see *Weekly checks*)

Tyres worn unevenly

- [ ] Tyres/wheels out of balance (see *Weekly checks*)
- [ ] Excessive wheel or tyre run-out
- [ ] Worn shock absorbers (Chapter 1A, 1B or 10)
- [ ] Faulty tyre (see *Weekly checks*)

Electrical system

Note: *For problems associated with the starting system, refer to the faults listed under 'Engine' earlier in this Section.*

Battery will not hold a charge for more than a few days

- ☐ Battery defective internally (Chapter 5A)
- ☐ Battery terminal connections loose or corroded (see *Weekly checks*)
- ☐ Auxiliary drivebelt worn or faulty adjuster (Chapter 1A or 1B)
- ☐ Alternator not charging at correct output (Chapter 5A)
- ☐ Alternator or voltage regulator faulty (Chapter 5A)
- ☐ Short-circuit causing continual battery drain (Chapter 5A or 12)

Ignition/no-charge warning light remains illuminated with engine running

- ☐ Auxiliary drivebelt broken, worn, or faulty adjuster (Chapter 1A or 1B)
- ☐ Internal fault in alternator or voltage regulator (Chapter 5A)
- ☐ Broken, disconnected, or loose wiring in charging circuit (Chapter 5A or 12)

Ignition/no-charge warning light fails to come on

- ☐ Broken, disconnected, or loose wiring in warning light circuit (Chapter 5A or 12)
- ☐ Alternator faulty (Chapter 5A)

Lights inoperative

- ☐ Bulb blown (Chapter 12)
- ☐ Corrosion of bulb or bulbholder contacts (Chapter 12)
- ☐ Blown fuse (Chapter 12)
- ☐ Faulty relay (Chapter 12)
- ☐ Broken, loose, or disconnected wiring (Chapter 12)
- ☐ Faulty switch (Chapter 12)

Instrument readings inaccurate or erratic

Fuel or temperature gauges give no reading

- ☐ Faulty gauge sender unit (Chapter 3 or 4)
- ☐ Wiring open-circuit (Chapter 12)
- ☐ Faulty gauge (Chapter 12)

Fuel or temperature gauges give continuous maximum reading

- ☐ Faulty gauge sender unit (Chapter 3 or 4)
- ☐ Wiring short-circuit (Chapter 12)
- ☐ Faulty gauge (Chapter 12)

Horn inoperative, or unsatisfactory in operation

Horn operates all the time

- ☐ Horn push either earthed or stuck down (Chapter 12)
- ☐ Horn cable-to-horn push earthed (Chapter 12)

Horn fails to operate

- ☐ Blown fuse (Chapter 12)
- ☐ Cable or connections loose, broken or disconnected (Chapter 12)
- ☐ Faulty horn (Chapter 12)

Horn emits intermittent or unsatisfactory sound

- ☐ Cable connections loose (Chapter 12)
- ☐ Horn mountings loose (Chapter 12)
- ☐ Faulty horn (Chapter 12)

Windscreen wipers inoperative, or unsatisfactory in operation

Wipers fail to operate, or operate very slowly

- ☐ Wiper blades stuck to screen, or linkage seized or binding (Chapter 12)
- ☐ Blown fuse (Chapter 12)
- ☐ Battery discharged (Chapter 5A)
- ☐ Cable or connections loose, broken or disconnected (Chapter 12)
- ☐ Faulty relay (Chapter 12)
- ☐ Faulty wiper motor (Chapter 12)

Wiper blades sweep over too large or too small an area

- ☐ Wiper blades incorrectly fitted, or wrong size used (see *Weekly checks*)
- ☐ Wiper arms incorrectly positioned on spindles (Chapter 12)
- ☐ Excessive wear of wiper linkage (Chapter 12)
- ☐ Wiper motor or linkage mountings loose or insecure (Chapter 12)

Wiper blades fail to clean the glass effectively

- ☐ Wiper blade rubbers dirty, worn or perished (see *Weekly checks*)
- ☐ Wiper blades incorrectly fitted, or wrong size used (see *Weekly checks*)
- ☐ Wiper arm tension springs broken, or arm pivots seized (Chapter 12)
- ☐ Insufficient windscreen washer additive to adequately remove road film (see *Weekly checks*)

Windscreen washers inoperative, or unsatisfactory in operation

One or more washer jets inoperative

- ☐ Blocked washer jet
- ☐ Disconnected, kinked or restricted fluid hose (Chapter 12)
- ☐ Insufficient fluid in washer reservoir (see *Weekly checks*)

Washer pump fails to operate

- ☐ Broken or disconnected wiring or connections (Chapter 12)
- ☐ Blown fuse (Chapter 12)
- ☐ Faulty washer switch (Chapter 12)
- ☐ Faulty washer pump (Chapter 12)

Washer pump runs for some time before fluid is emitted

- ☐ Faulty one-way valve in fluid supply hose (Chapter 12)

Electric windows inoperative, or unsatisfactory in operation

Window glass will only move in one direction

- ☐ Faulty switch (Chapter 12)

Window glass slow to move

- ☐ Battery discharged (Chapter 5A)
- ☐ Regulator seized or damaged, or in need of lubrication (Chapter 11)
- ☐ Door internal components or trim fouling regulator (Chapter 11)
- ☐ Faulty motor (Chapter 11)

Window glass fails to move

- ☐ Blown fuse (Chapter 12)
- ☐ Faulty relay (Chapter 12)
- ☐ Broken or disconnected wiring or connections (Chapter 12)
- ☐ Faulty motor (Chapter 11)

Central locking system inoperative, or unsatisfactory in operation

Complete system failure

- ☐ Remote handset battery discharged, if applicable (Chapter 1A or 1B)
- ☐ Blown fuse (Chapter 12)
- ☐ Faulty relay (Chapter 12)
- ☐ Broken or disconnected wiring or connections (Chapter 12)
- ☐ Faulty motor (Chapter 11)

Latch locks but will not unlock, or unlocks but will not lock

- ☐ Remote handset battery discharged, if applicable (Chapter 1A or 1B)
- ☐ Faulty master switch (Chapter 12)
- ☐ Broken or disconnected latch operating rods or levers (Chapter 11)
- ☐ Faulty relay (Chapter 12)
- ☐ Faulty motor (Chapter 11)

One solenoid/motor fails to operate

- ☐ Broken or disconnected wiring or connections (Chapter 12)
- ☐ Faulty operating assembly (Chapter 11)
- ☐ Broken, binding or disconnected latch operating rods or levers (Chapter 11)
- ☐ Fault in door latch (Chapter 11)

Note: *References throughout this index are in the form* "**Chapter number**" • "**Page number**". *So, for example, 2C•15 refers to page 15 of Chapter 2C.*

Note: *References throughout this index are in the form* **"Chapter number"** • **"Page number"**. *So, for example, 2C•15 refers to page 15 of Chapter 2C.*

Note: *References throughout this index are in the form "**Chapter number**" • "**Page number**". So, for example, 2C•15 refers to page 15 of Chapter 2C.*

Preserving Our Motoring Heritage

< The Model J Duesenberg Derham Tourster. Only eight of these magnificent cars were ever built – this is the only example to be found outside the United States of America

Almost every car you've ever loved, loathed or desired is gathered under one roof at the Haynes Motor Museum. Over 300 immaculately presented cars and motorbikes represent every aspect of our motoring heritage, from elegant reminders of bygone days, such as the superb Model J Duesenberg to curiosities like the bug-eyed BMW Isetta. There are also many old friends and flames. Perhaps you remember the 1959 Ford Popular that you did your courting in? The magnificent 'Red Collection' is a spectacle of classic sports cars including AC, Alfa Romeo, Austin Healey, Ferrari, Lamborghini, Maserati, MG, Riley, Porsche and Triumph.

A Perfect Day Out

Each and every vehicle at the Haynes Motor Museum has played its part in the history and culture of Motoring. Today, they make a wonderful spectacle and a great day out for all the family. Bring the kids, bring Mum and Dad, but above all bring your camera to capture those golden memories for ever. You will also find an impressive array of motoring memorabilia, a comfortable 70 seat video cinema and one of the most extensive transport book shops in Britain. The Pit Stop Cafe serves everything from a cup of tea to wholesome, home-made meals or, if you prefer, you can enjoy the large picnic area nestled in the beautiful rural surroundings of Somerset.

> John Haynes O.B.E., Founder and Chairman of the museum at the wheel of a Haynes Light 12.

< Graham Hill's Lola Cosworth Formula 1 car next to a 1934 Riley Sports.

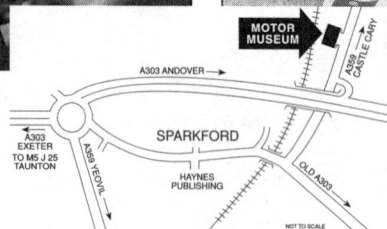

The Museum is situated on the A359 Yeovil to Frome road at Sparkford, just off the A303 in Somerset. It is about 40 miles south of Bristol, and 25 minutes drive from the M5 intersection at Taunton.
Open 9.30am - 5.30pm (10.00am - 4.00pm Winter) 7 days a week, *except Christmas Day, Boxing Day and New Years Day*
Special rates available for schools, coach parties and outings Charitable Trust No. 292048